Rich's Coaching Method Gives Your Students a Competitive Edge

Writing and Reporting News: A Coaching Method prepares students to enter the rapidly evolving world of journalism a step ahead of their peers. Author Carole Rich and new collaborator Christopher Harper emphasize the basic skills every journalist needs to know alongside thorough coverage of the latest journalistic trends—highlighting the modern convergence of print, broadcast and online media. With fresh new information about blogs, multimedia writing, and other nontraditional career paths in the media, the text guides students preparing to enter this challenging and diverse field while retaining an emphasis on writing fundamentals and ethics.

Tips and techniques from writing coaches and award-winning journalists make ***Writing and Reporting News*** accessible, and exercises and activities in each chapter make it easy for students to learn the skills of an effective reporter.

Now with News Scene 2.0—realistic reporting assignments for your students!
See pages 6 and 7 of this overview.

"Rich's textbook gets students writing right away. They become engaged quickly in the process."
—Emil Guillermo, St. Mary's College

Developing Successful Writers

Coaching Tips from top writing coaches and award-winning journalists appear at the start of every chapter.

1 **Conceive the idea:** At this stage you develop the idea for the story. If you are covering an event, such as a meeting or an accident, you need to start with the idea—the main point of what occurred. If you are writing a news story about a problem in your community, you still start with a central idea, which is the focus of your story. Once you begin reporting, you may discover some information that is more important than your original focus. Thus, you should be flexible and decide the focus for writing after you collect the material.

2 **Collect:** This is the reporting stage. Before you conduct your interview, you should look for background information: Check online sources and any available documents or clips from previous stories about your subject and your sources. Then interview sources, and gather as much information as you can about your topic. Don't rely on one source; seek several points of view. Ask more questions and take more notes than you plan to use. You should also jot down your observations and gather as many details as possible.

3 **Construct:** This is the planning and writing stage. Begin with a plan for your story developed around the focus, the main idea of your story. Then go through your notes and mark only the information related to that focus. Like a carpenter building a house, you need a blueprint. A good writer does not write a story without a plan. Jot down a few key words to indicate how you will organize your story. Then write a first draft of your story. You may revise your original draft in the next step.

4 **Correct:** After you have written your story, read it and make any necessary changes. You may decide to add or delete information or to completely reorganize the story during this stage. You should also check the spelling of all names and the accuracy of facts, and you should correct grammar, style and typing errors.

Active voice is stronger for the following example, because it emphasizes the iguana as the subject:

Rich incorporates style and writing exercises throughout the text, as well as in Chapter 6, "Grammar and Usage." An abbreviated *AP Style Guide* appears at the end of the book.

Active	Passive
A pet iguana started a fire in a split-level house in Hillsmere Shores by knocking over a heat lamp with its tail, fire officials said.	A fire in a split-level house in Hillsmere Shores was started by a pet iguana that knocked over a heat lamp with its tail, fire officials said.

In the next example, however, passive voice is preferable because it gets to the point faster:

Passive

A former employee of the University of Pennsylvania's Van Pelt Library was sentenced to seven years of psychiatric probation yesterday for the theft of $1,798,310 worth of rare books and documents.

The Philadelphia Inquirer

issues, you can go to the site of the Centers for Disease Control and Prevention at *www.cdc.gov* or a for-profit health site at *www.webmd.com*.

It is important to keep in mind that no one checks the accuracy of any site other than the individual or organization that puts it on the Web. Therefore, the reliability of a site depends on the reliability of the individual or organization. It is better to quote from sites backed by the government, which end with .gov, or reputable organizations, which end with .org or .com, and provide links to those sites so that users can determine what they think about the information.

E-mail Reporting

E-mail can be a useful reporting tool, but don't depend on it for deadline stories. You can't control when or if sources check their e-mail. Limit your questions, preferably to fewer than five. Sources may be reluctant to answer lengthy lists of questions. One or two questions are even better.

Some journalists express concern that you can't determine if the source in an e-mail interview is authentic, but if you are writing to a source you know or one affiliated with a reliable organization, that risk is minimal.

Digital Storytelling

Nora Paul, director of the Institute for New Media Studies at the University of Minnesota, has created an analysis of the various components of digital storytelling. She identifies five basic elements:

- Media
- Action

A "Web Journalism" chapter prepares students to communicate effectively over the Internet.

Creating Ethical, Unbiased Reporters

Students are encouraged to examine their own biases and identify how those biases may affect their objectivity as journalists in Chapter 15, "Multicultural Sensitivity."

Rich addresses key ethical issues throughout the text in highlighted sections spotlighting common ethical dilemmas, as well as a full chapter titled "Media Ethics."

ETHICS

The case: Your campus newspaper has received an advertisement that promotes the revisionist point of view that the Nazi Holocaust of World War II never occurred. The ad, accompanied by a $125 check, was sent by the Committee for Open Debate on the Holocaust, an organization run by Bradley R. Smith from his home in Visalia, Calif. He sent the advertisement to colleges all over the United States. In a cover letter he urges campus editors to run the ad to promote dialogue and to support the First Amendment.

You are aware that when the University of Miami campus newspaper, *The Miami Hurricane*, ran the ad, nearly 400 students demonstrated outside the newspaper. A wealthy alumnus threatened to withdraw a $2 million gift but later recanted when the school promised to offer courses on the Holocaust. Other school newspapers have refused to print the ad. You know that this ad will offend many people on your campus and in your community, but you want to uphold the First Amendment. Will you run this ad or reject it and return the check? Justify your decision.

About the Authors

Carole Rich currently teaches journalism at the University of Alaska, Anchorage. Until recently, she served as the chair of the journalism department at Hofstra University, and before that was a professor of journalism at the University of Kansas. In addition to her 16 years of experience as a journalist at three major metropolitan newspapers, Professor Rich has visited newspapers throughout the United States as a writing coach and conducted numerous writing seminars. In addition to *Writing and Reporting News,* she is the author of *Creating Online Media: A Guide to Research, Writing, and Design on the Internet.*

New collaborator **Christopher Harper** is a journalism professor at Temple University in Philadelphia, having previously taught at New York University, Ithaca College, and overseas. Prior to teaching, he was a reporter and editor for the *Associated Press*, a correspondent for *Newsweek*, a correspondent and bureau chief for *ABC News*, and a producer for *ABC News 20/20*. Professor Harper served as the editor of *What's Next in Mass Communication* and *Journalism 2001*, in addition to authoring *The New Mass Media* and *And That's The Way It Will Be: News and Information in a Digital World.*

A Greater Focus on Global and Multimedia Reporting

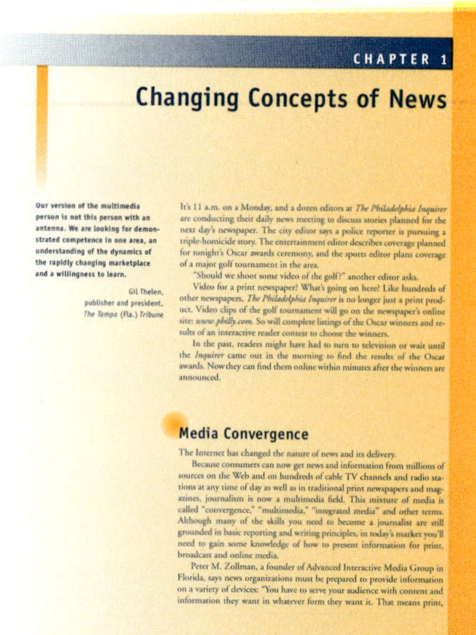

Chapter 1, "Changing Concepts of News," introduces students to the convergence of print, broadcast, and online journalism, and begins an ongoing discussion about the new ethical dilemmas and pitfalls facing reporters today.

Chapter 16, "Global Journalism," exposes students to international issues they may encounter when writing and reporting news.

Updated examples keep students informed about current issues facing journalists around the world. In the essay at left, a veteran reporter pays tribute to fellow correspondents killed while reporting in the Middle East.

Online Resources Provide the Practice Your Students Need

Each chapter includes **new breakout boxes** featuring issues and tips for multimedia reporting.

MULTIMEDIA COACH

Major stories involving disasters and tragedies are usually accompanied by sidebars that offer consumers helpful information and perspective on how this event compares to others of its kind. That type of information is now easy to get on the Web. As with all information from the Web, make sure that you are using a reliable source that is up to date. Here are some online tips:

- Check the Red Cross and other disaster-relief agencies for sidebars telling readers where to go for help and how to cope.

- Consider time lines or lists of other major disasters, available online from weather and government sites such as the National Hurricane Center at *http://www.nhc.noaa.gov*.

- Airlines often use the Web to provide information about disasters. The National Transportation Safety Board at *www.ntsb.gov* is the main investigating agency for aircraft, railroad and other major accidents.

- Use the Internet to obtain updated information from community government and other agencies on disaster conditions for your research. During some disasters, government and relief agencies provide faster updates online than by telephone or other media.

- Provide links to online information for consumers in Web, broadcast and printed media.

- Report information to editors as soon as you get it for posting on the publication's Web site. The Web is often users' first choice for breaking news during disasters.

- Check related resources on the Web site for this chapter at *http://communication.wadsworth.com/rich5e*.

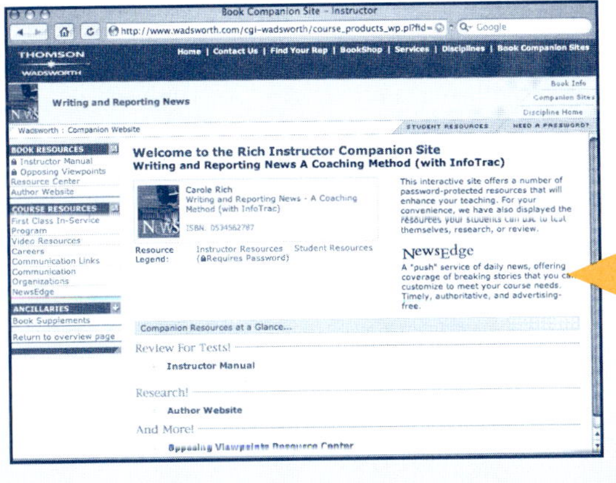

A new **Book Companion Web Site** features a wealth of updated resources, including style quizzes, writing exercises, web links, Internet exercises and access to InfoTrac® College Edition.

Plus. . . **News Scene 2.0: Online Interactive News Assignments**, an award-winning program featuring multimedia simulated assignments that allow students to practice reporting skills on their own. *See pages 6 and 7 of this preview.*

"The text is clear, authoritative, and well received by students. Many of my students have decided to keep their copies on their professional bookshelves."
–Barbara Schleppenbach, Quincy University

Award Winning!
News Scene 2.0: Online Interactive News Assignments

This innovative multimedia program lets your students participate in nine realistic reporting assignments to help hone their news writing and reporting skills in a simulated environment.

Each of the program's realistic news events is presented from multiple perspectives and accompanied by extensive source material, including video interviews, telephone messages, official documents, and database information.

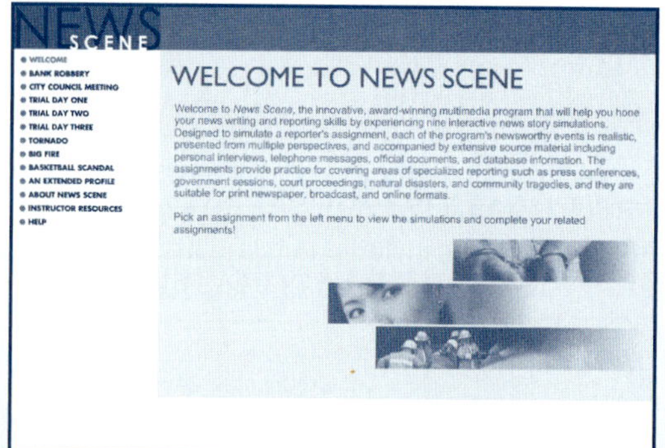

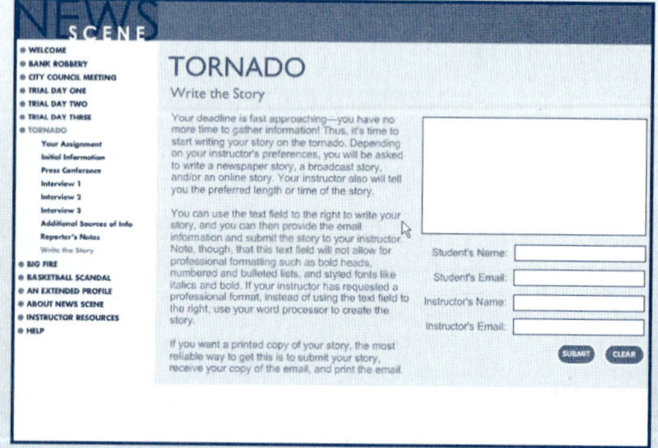

News Scene 2.0:

- **Nine simulated reporting assignments** appropriate for print, broadcast, or online story formats—including two new scenarios titled "Extended Profile" and "College Basketball Scandal."

- **Award-winning pedagogy:** "Fire Scene," the original version of "Big Fire," was awarded first place in the Teaching Category in the 2002 "Best of the Web" Design Competition sponsored by the Association for Education in Journalism and Mass Communication (AEJMC).

- **E-mail capability** for completed assignments to be sent directly to the instructor.

- **An integrated workbook** is packaged with each access code, giving students even more writing exercises linked to the progam's scenarios.

To ensure that your students have access to this outstanding online resource at no additional cost, please use ISBN: 0-495-16629-4 when placing your order.

Realistic Source Materials Help Develop Reporting Skills

The assignments provide practice for covering areas of specialized reporting such as press conferences, government sessions, court proceedings, natural disasters, and community tragedies, and are all equally suitable for print newspaper, broadcast, and online articles.

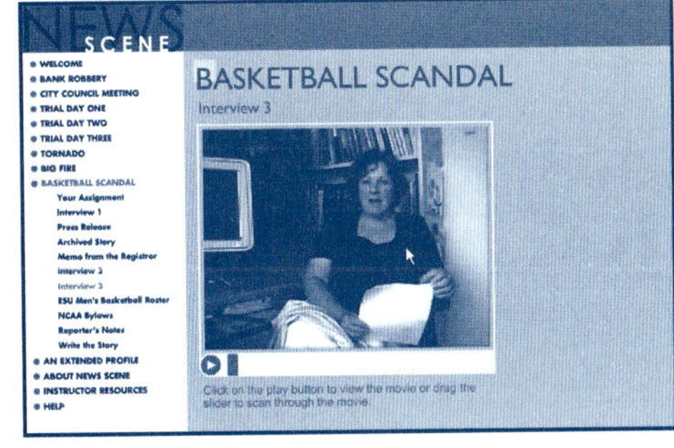

Video interviews with important sources

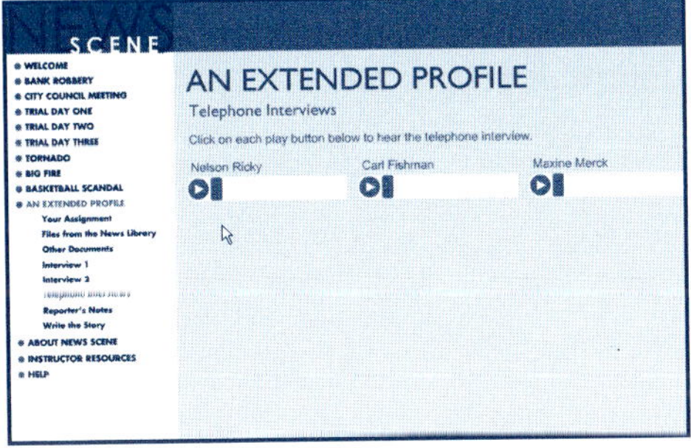

Telephone messages

Official documents

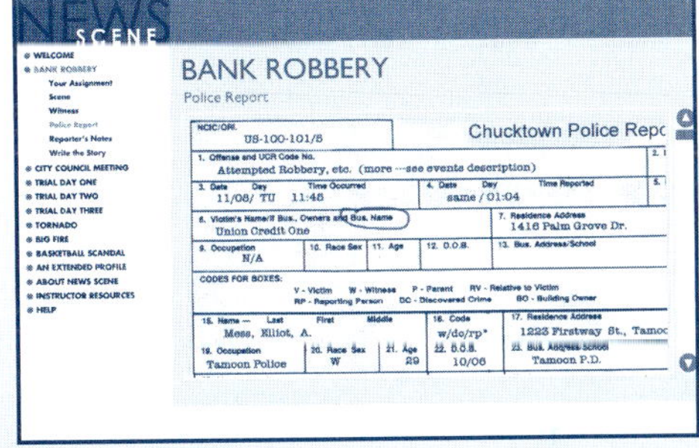

NCIC/OR. US-100-101/5		Chucktown Police Repo		
1. Offense and UCR Code No. Attempted Robbery, etc. (more —see events description)				
3. Date Day Time Occurred 11/08/ TU 11:45		4. Date Day Time Reported same / 01:04		
6. Victim's Name/if Bus., Owners and Bus. Name Union Credit One			7. Residence Address 1416 Palm Grove Dr.	
8. Occupation N/A	10. Race Sex	11. Age	12. D.O.B.	13. Bus. Address/School
CODES FOR BOXES: V - Victim W - Witness P - Parent RV - Relative to Victim RP - Reporting Person DC - Discovered Crime BO - Building Owner				
15. Name — Last First Middle Moss, Elliot, A.	16. Code w/do/rp*	17. Residence Address 1225 Firstway St., Tamoo		
18. Occupation Tamoon Police	20. Race Sex W	21. Age 29	22. D.O.B. 10/06	23. Bus. Address/School Tamoon P.D.

Database information

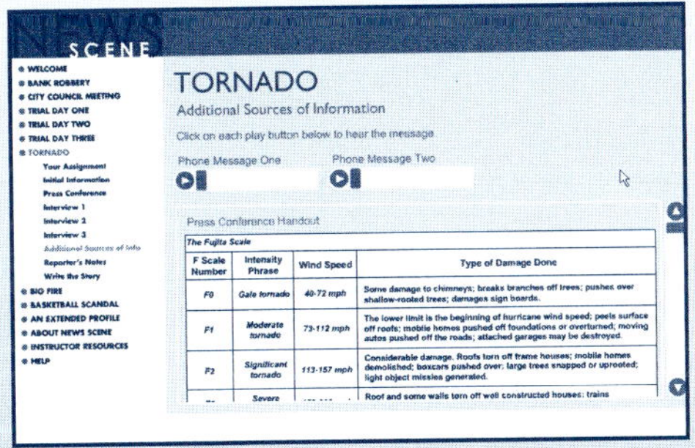

The Fujita Scale			
F Scale Number	Intensity Phrase	Wind Speed	Type of Damage Done
F0	Gale tornado	40-72 mph	Some damage to chimneys; breaks branches off trees; pushes over shallow-rooted trees; damages sign boards.
F1	Moderate tornado	73-112 mph	The lower limit is the beginning of hurricane wind speed; peels surface off roofs; mobile homes pushed off foundations or overturned; moving autos pushed off the roads; attached garages may be destroyed.
F2	Significant tornado	113-157 mph	Considerable damage. Roofs torn off frame houses; mobile homes demolished; boxcars pushed over; large trees snapped or uprooted; light object missiles generated.
	Severe		Roof and some walls torn off well constructed houses; trains

Demo News Scene 2.0! http://communication.wadsworth.com/newsscene_demo

"[News Scene] brings real-life reporting opportunities into the classroom."
— **Scoobie Ryan, University of Kentucky**

Resources for You . . .

Instructor's Resource Manual
0-495-12963-1

Created by author Carole Rich, this resource allows you to streamline your course preparation with resources such as teaching and coaching suggestions, and answers to workbook style quizzes.

. . . And Your Students!

Student Workbook
0-495-12964-X

This ideal partner to Rich's text gives your students the practice they need to become better writers. The workbook includes more than 100 writing exercises and style quizzes based on real news articles.

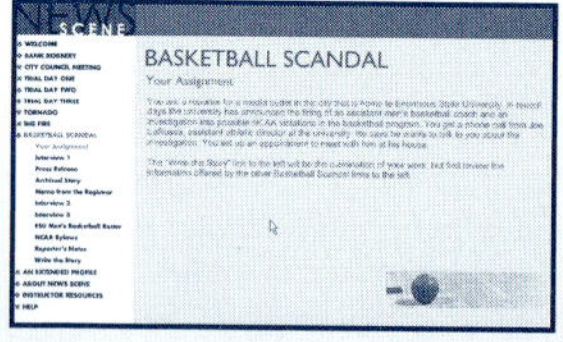

News Scene 2.0: Online Interactive News Assignments
0-495-16629-4

Give your students online access to this award-winning program at no additional cost by ordering **Writing and Reporting News** packaged with this website passcard.
See pages 6 and 7 of this preview.

InfoTrac® College Edition with InfoMarks™

By ordering a four-month subscription to **InfoTrac® College Edition** packaged with the text, you'll give your students access to this virtual library's more than 18 million reliable, full-length articles from 5,000 academic and popular periodicals and retrieve results almost instantly. They also have access to **InfoMarks™**—stable URLs that can be linked to articles, journals, and searches to save valuable time when doing research—*and to the* **InfoWrite** online resource center, where students can access grammar help, critical-thinking guidelines, guides to writing research papers, and much more.

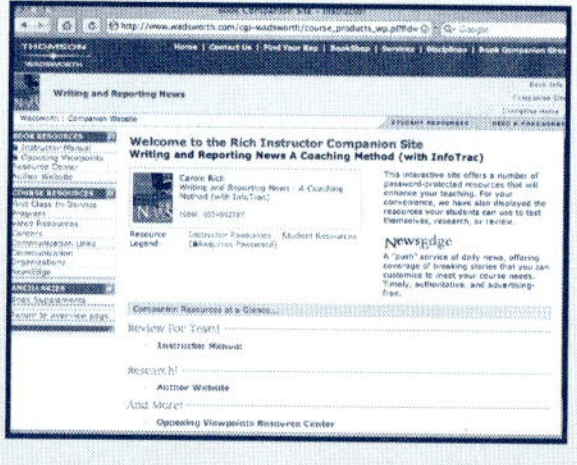

Book Companion Web Site

This online resource center gives students access to a rich array of exercises, quizzes, web links, and more!

With Thomson Custom Solutions, you can "co-author" your course materials and create your perfect journalism text!

With a wide range of personalized solutions designed to meet your course needs, Thomson Custom Solutions offers the fastest and easiest way to create unique learning materials delivered the way you want them—including the ability to:

- Choose only the chapters you use in your journalism course and create a text that you will use in its entirety
- Reorder the chapters to follow the organization of your course
- Include materials you typically photocopy and distribute in class, minimizing the risk of students' misplacing important materials

For other customization options or to learn more, please contact your local Thomson representative!

www.wadsworth.com

www.wadsworth.com is the World Wide Web site for
Wadsworth and is your direct source to dozens of
online resources.

At *www.wadsworth.com* you can find out about supplements, demonstration software, and student resources.
You can also send email to many of our authors and preview new publications and exciting new technologies.

www.wadsworth.com
Changing the way the world learns.®

Writing and Reporting News

A COACHING METHOD

FIFTH EDITION

Carole Rich
University of Alaska Anchorage

with Christopher Harper
Temple University

Australia • Brazil • Canada • Mexico • Singapore • Spain
United Kingdom • United States

Writing and Reporting News: A Coaching Method, **Fifth Edition**
Carole Rich with Christopher Harper

Publisher: Holly J. Allen
Assistant Editor: Lucinda Bingham
Editorial Assistant: Meghan Bass
Senior Technology Project Manager: Jeanette Wiseman
Senior Marketing Manager: Mark Orr
Marketing Assistant: Alexandra Tran
Senior Marketing Communications Manager:
  Shemika Britt
Project Manager, Editorial Production: Catherine Morris
Creative Director: Rob Hugel
Executive Art Director: Maria Epes
Print Buyer: Karen Hunt

Permissions Editor: Kiely Sisk
Production Service: Melanie Field, Strawberry Field
  Publishing/G&S Typesetters, Inc.
Compositor: G&S Typesetters, Inc.
Text Designer: Lisa Devenish
Photo Researcher: Annette Coolidge
Copy Editor: Donald Pharr
Cover Designer: Qin-Zhong Yu
Cover Image: Ryan McVay/Getty Images, Stockbyte/
  Getty Images
Text and Cover Printer: Quebecor World/Dubuque

Library of Congress Control Number: 2005931607

ISBN 0-495-00423-5

For more information about our products, contact us at:
Thomson Learning Academic Resource Center
1-800-423-0563

For permission to use material from this text or product, submit a request online at **http://www.thomsonrights.com** Any additional questions about permissions can be submitted by e-mail to **thomsonrights@thomson.com**

Thomson Higher Education
10 Davis Drive
Belmont, CA 94002-3098
USA

We are living in an age of rapid changes in the media, but the basic principles of good writing, accurate reporting and ethical behavior are timeless. This book is designed to teach you how to acquire the writing and reporting skills you will need to excel in your career no matter which media field you choose to enter. The book also emphasizes media ethics in every chapter so that you can gain an understanding of the problems you might encounter and learn ethical principles that will help you resolve them.

The coaching method, which is the foundation of this book, is a way of helping writers discover their problems and learn techniques to solve them. The book features tips from leading writing coaches and award-winning journalists.

This fifth edition is the first book in which author Carole Rich has collaborated with another author. Because media careers now require a convergence of print, broadcast and online skills, Rich worked with Christopher Harper, who has more than 20 years of experience in print, broadcast and international media. Harper revised the chapters on broadcast journalism and Web journalism and wrote a new chapter on global journalism.

New Material in This Edition

In addition to those chapters, this fifth edition of *Writing and Reporting News: A Coaching Method* includes the following new material:

- Multimedia Coach boxes in every chapter to help you learn the skills you will need for the convergence of print, broadcast and online media.

- Ethics boxes in every chapter to place increased emphasis on this important area of journalism, as well as a separate ethics chapter, which has been retained.

- A revised chapter on the changing nature of news, with more emphasis on convergence and blogs—the personal essays or journals on the Web that have become increasingly popular and influential.

- New material about recent controversies in the media, with an increased emphasis on the problems of plagiarism and fabrication.

- A revised chapter on disasters, weather and tragedies (Chapter 21), featuring an interview with a photographer who survived after he was buried alive in the Sept. 11, 2001, terrorist attack in New York.
- Several new examples and updated material throughout the book.

The book also includes access to *News Scene: Interactive News Assignments.* This is an award-winning interactive computer program that features news events with multimedia resources to simulate the type of stories that reporters cover in print and broadcast news organizations. The Web site for this book also contains interactive quizzes and resources: *http://communication .wadsworth.com/rich5e.*

How the Book Is Organized

If you are an instructor who has used previous editions of this textbook, you will find many changes. Although this textbook is arranged sequentially to take students through the steps from conceiving ideas to constructing stories, you do not have to use the book in the order it is written. Each chapter is self-contained so that you can design the course as you prefer.

Most of the material in the fourth edition has been retained, but several chapters have been merged so that new information could be added. Here are the changes in the order of chapters:

Part One: Understanding News

1. Changing Concepts of News (was Chapter 2)
2. The Basic News Story (merged with former Chapter 1)

Part Two: Collecting Information

3. Curiosity and Story Ideas (was Chapter 5)
4. Sources and Online Research (was Chapter 6)
5. Interviewing Techniques (was Chapter 7)

Part Three: Constructing Stories

6. Grammar and Usage (was Chapter 4)
7. Leads and Nut Graphs (was Chapter 9)
8. Story Structure (was Chapter 10 and has been merged with the former Chapter 8, "The Writing Process")
9. Storytelling and Feature Techniques (was Chapter 11)
10. Public Relations Writing (was Chapter 12)
11. Broadcast Writing and Reporting (was Chapter 13 and has been completely rewritten)
12. Web Journalism (was Chapter 14 and has been completely rewritten)

Part Four: Understanding Media Issues

13. Accuracy and Media Law (was Chapter 15)
14. Media Ethics (was Chapter 16)

Acknowledgments

I would like to thank my editor/publisher, Holly Allen; copy editor, Donald Pharr; production project manager, Catherine Morris; and production manager, Melanie Field. I am also grateful to these professors who gave their time and suggestions as reviewers of previous editions: Charles Adair, State University of New York at Buffalo; Ann C. Allen, State University of New York at Oswego; Roy Atwood, University of Idaho; Maureen Beasely, University of Maryland, College Park; Michael Berlin, Boston University; Retta Blaney, New York University; James Buckalew, San Diego State University; Ray Chavez, University of Colorado; Douglas Daniel, Kansas State University; Jack Dvorak, Indiana University; John Erickson, University of Iowa; Lynne Flocke, Syracuse University; Martha Freeman, Pennsylvania State University; Joseph Graf, George Washington University; Sandra Haarsager, University of Idaho; Bruce E. Johansen, University of Nebraska at Omaha; Lee Jolliffe, Drake University; Rachele Kanigel, San Francisco State University; Robert C. Kochersberger Jr., North Carolina State University; Susan Lampert-Smith, University of Wisconsin, Madison; Linda L. Levin, University of Rhode Island; Gary McLouth, College of St. Rose; Beverly Merrick, New Mexico State University; Susan Mountin, Marquette University; David C. Nelson, Southwest Texas State University; W. Robert Nowell III, Chico State University; JoAnn Paganetti, Marygrove College; Dean Rea, University of Oregon; Marshel Rossow, Mankato State University; Linda N. Scanlon, Norfolk State University; Ann Schierhorn, Kent State University; Norman Sims, University of Massachusetts; Jon Smith, Southern Utah University; Martin D. Sommerness, Northern Arizona University; and Carl Sessions Stepp, University of Maryland, College Park.

In addition, appreciation goes to the following people who responded to a survey for the media-enhanced fourth edition: Joan Atkins, Morehead State University; Glen Bleske, California State University, Chico; Susan L. Booker, Longwood University; Tim Boudreau, Central Michigan University, Linda Bowen, California State University, Northridge; Maureen Boyle, Stonehill College; John M. Bublic, Barton College; David W. Bulla, Iowa State University; Ben Burns, Wayne State University; John Carpenter, Bryan College; Laure Chamberlain, Southern Adventist University; Paul Chimera, Daemen College; James Crandall, Aims Community College; George L. Daniels, The University of Alabama; Sharon Dennehy, Paris Junior College; James G. Diederich, Catawba Valley Community College; John Dillon, Murray State University; Jessica Farley, Delaware Technical & Community College; Carol Fletcher, Hofstra University; William Florence, Chemeketa Community College; Kym Fox, Texas State University; Bruce P. Frassinelli, Oswego State University; Tom Gardner, Westfield State College; Gary Gately, University of Maryland; Emil Guillermo, St. Mary's College; Neal Haldane, Madonna University; Dennis F. Herrick, University of New Mexico; John Irby, Washington State University; Kirsten Johnson, Elizabethtown College; Daniel Jorgensen, Augsburg College; Joel Kaplan, Syracuse University; James W. Kershner, Cape Cod Community College; Steven Knowlton, Hofstra University; Jan LaVille, Des Moines Area Community College; Dallas Liddle, Augsburg College; Michele McKinlay, University of Dubuque/Clarke College; Jeanne Milhuff, MidAmerica Nazarene University; Kevin Miller, Huntington College; Olivia Miller, University of Memphis; Cynthia Mitchell, Central Washington University; Tracy Montgomery, College of Mount Saint Vincent; Bryan Murley, North Greenville College; Brad Owens, Baylor University; Reginald Owens, Louisiana Tech University; Jeffrey Pribble, Pensacola Christian College; Maria Raicheva, Washburn University; Bob Rawitch, California State University, Northridge; Glen Robinson, Southwestern Adventist University; Noel Robinson, County College of Morris; Stephen Ruf, Southern Adventist University; Scoobie Ryan, University of Kentucky; Louie Saenz, University of Texas at El Paso; Barbara Schleppenbach, Quincy University; John F. Schmitt, Texas State University; Gregory Selber, University of Texas–Pan American; T. M. Sell, Highline College; Ron Sereg, Louisiana State University, Shreveport; Glenn Singer, Florida Atlantic University; Debra C. Smith, University of North Carolina at Charlotte; Karon Speckman, Truman State University; Brian Steffen, Simpson College; Linda Steiner, Rutgers University; Michael Taylor, Henderson State University; Jane Tolbert, Florida Institute of Technology; Raul Tovares, Trinity College; and Peter Wollheim, Boise State University.

Carole Rich is a journalism professor at the University of Alaska Anchorage. She also served as chair of the journalism department at Hofstra University in Long Island, N.Y. Before she came to Alaska, she taught journalism at the University of Kansas for 11 years and previously worked for 16 years in the newspaper industry. She was a reporter for the former *Philadelphia Evening Bulletin,* city editor of the *Sun-Sentinel* in Fort Lauderdale, Fla., and deputy metropolitan editor of the *Hartford (Ct.) Courant.*

Rich has been a visiting writing coach at newspapers throughout the United States and has conducted many writing seminars at journalism organizations, including a seminar for professional journalists in Spain. She is also the author of *Creating Online Media: A Guide to Research, Writing and Design on the Internet,* published by McGraw-Hill.

Christopher Harper is a journalism professor at Temple University in Philadelphia. He also has taught in Poland and Russia. Before teaching, he worked for more than 20 years in journalism as a reporter and editor for the Associated Press in Chicago; a correspondent for *Newsweek* in Chicago, Washington, D.C., and Beirut, Lebanon; a correspondent and bureau chief for ABC News in Cairo and Rome; and a producer for "ABC News 20/20" in New York. He taught at New York University and held the Park Distinguished Chair of Communications at Ithaca College. Harper has edited two books, *What's Next in Mass Communication* and *Journalism 2001.* He also has written two books, *The New Mass Media* and *And That's the Way It Will Be: News and Information in a Digital World.*

Coaching Tips

Ask people in your community what
information they want from print, online
or broadcast news.

Consider different ways of presenting
your story for print, broadcast and online
media.

Compare ways that similar stories are
presented in print, online and broadcast
media.

Seek to include multicultural sources in
your stories.

Ask yourself how your story affects your
readers.

Consider whether your story needs a
photograph or a graphic.

Consider how you would update your
story for online delivery.

Changing Concepts of News

It's 11 a.m. on a Monday, and a dozen editors at *The Philadelphia Inquirer* are conducting their daily news meeting to discuss stories planned for the next day's newspaper. The city editor says a police reporter is pursuing a triple-homicide story. The entertainment editor describes coverage planned for tonight's Oscar awards ceremony, and the sports editor plans coverage of a major golf tournament in the area.

"Should we shoot some video of the golf?" another editor asks.

Video for a print newspaper? What's going on here? Like hundreds of other newspapers, *The Philadelphia Inquirer* is no longer just a print product. Video clips of the golf tournament will go on the newspaper's online site: *www.philly.com.* So will complete listings of the Oscar winners and results of an interactive reader contest to choose the winners.

In the past, readers might have had to turn to television or wait until the *Inquirer* came out in the morning to find the results of the Oscar awards. Now they can find them online within minutes after the winners are announced.

Media Convergence

The Internet has changed the nature of news and its delivery.

Because consumers can now get news and information from millions of sources on the Web and on hundreds of cable TV channels and radio stations at any time of day as well as in traditional print newspapers and magazines, journalism is now a multimedia field. This mixture of media is called "convergence," "multimedia," "integrated media" and other terms. Although many of the skills you need to become a journalist are still grounded in basic reporting and writing principles, in today's market you'll need to gain some knowledge of how to present information for print, broadcast and online media.

Peter M. Zollman, a founder of Advanced Interactive Media Group in Florida, says news organizations must be prepared to provide information on a variety of devices: "You have to serve your audience with content and information they want in whatever form they want it. That means print, audio, video on any device they want. People will want the information they want when they want it. Your deadline is whenever the heck you get it and make it available to your audiences."

Those deadlines are exactly what reporters at the *Lawrence Journal-World* in Lawrence, Kan., are expected to meet. Although the *Journal-World* is a morning newspaper, news is posted and updated throughout the day and night. When reporters get a story, they have to write it for the Web, where it will be posted shortly after the event occurred. Reporters may also appear on the company's cable television station, Sunflower Channel 6, where they might report their story or discuss it with the anchor on the nightly news. Then the reporters write a more complete or updated form of the story for the next morning's newspaper. Here is an example of updated news posted on the Web site in the "Breaking News" box:

- Nominations narrowed to three for new judge position *(Posted at 5:57 p.m.)*
- Commissioners not backing off smoking ban *(Posted at 5:12 p.m.)*
- Police searching for credit union robber *(Updated at 12:51 p.m.)*
- Temperatures in the 50s expected for weekend *(Posted at 8:57 a.m.)*

The *Journal-World* is a model of convergence. In a college town featuring the University of Kansas, the World Company publishes the newspaper and owns a cable TV station, provides an Internet service and even offers telephone service to the community. In 1991, long before convergence became a popular concept, Dolph C. Simons Jr., owner and publisher of the company, announced that his 100-year-old newspaper was no longer the only way to operate a media business.

"We believe it is important to look upon our business as an 'information business,' not merely a newspaper or a cable television operation," Simons said at an event celebrating the 100th anniversary of the *Journal-World.* "We want to stay abreast of new developments and be able to deliver news and advertising, as well as other information, however a reader or advertiser might desire."

Ten years later, Simons converted a vacant post office building into a modern convergent newsroom. A circular multimedia desk dominates the ground-floor atrium, which is surrounded by a balcony on the second floor, where the *Journal-World* and cable TV reporters work. Editors on the multimedia desk coordinate with print and broadcast reporters and editors. When a reporter airs a story on the TV station, the station promotes the story for the newspaper edition, and the newspaper edition promotes the story for the online editions.

The most vivid example of convergence is the way the reporters collaborate. Reporters who share the same beats from the newspaper and TV station sit together. The *Journal-World* city government reporter's desk is next to the reporter who covers that beat for cable 6News, and the sports reporters and editors for the newspaper, the TV station, and the Web site, *KUSports.com,* also sit next to one another.

Convergence desk at the *Lawrence* (Kan.) *Journal-World*

The award-winning Web site (*www.ljworld.com*) is the brainchild of Rob Curley, the online general manager. When Curley came to the *Journal-World* in 1998, he decided to do something daring. Because nearly 30,000 people are students and employees of the University of Kansas in Lawrence, Curley decided to create a separate Web site to appeal to the college audience. This site, *www.lawrence.com*, features content such as weekly drink specials, local bands, entertainment listings and the most popular feature—blogs, which are personal journals written by college students or members of the community.

"We really go all the way out with *Lawrence.com*," Curley says. "It's my baby. Six weeks into the site, it broke a million page views. We give a free print edition targeted to college students, but 100 percent of the content of the print edition is from the Web. We believe it is important to create separate brands. We built a really 'edgy' site. The Web site can e-mail you and remind you of items on your cell phone. The Web site will call you. It features a database of all the bands in town. The bloggers are the most visited part of *Lawrence.com*. We don't pay them. We do read all the blogs; we're looking for some stuff that could be slander or libelous. All of our bloggers have to use their real names."

The most popular blog was called "powder room confessions," which is no longer being written because the author graduated. But it was very sexually explicit. Curley says when he first read it, he feared he might lose his job, but the publisher didn't intervene. Another blog is by a gay college student who writes about his experiences.

Each blog offers readers a chance to respond. Here's an example of an excerpt from a blog on *Lawrence.com:*

> The point is I'm on a self-imposed exile from the United States of Relationships. I can't even go to Dating Land. And I'm doing this for my own good, and anyone else with the unfortunate luck of loving me.

Rob Curley, online general manager, *Lawrence (Kan.) Journal-World*

I don't (really) want to spend my days alone, with companions only when I can fit them in. There has to be some balance and I have to find it. I've never felt so selfish, yet so righteously so. How do people do it? Love, ideas, hopes, dreams, money, careers, education . . . love. How do they find the time and the headspace to make it all work?

So tell me, what's more important? Passion, comfortable friendship, or the package deal? Did you find it, did you give up, or do you still hope?

Another site Curley created, geared to the KU sports-loving community, is *www.kusports.com.* "We offer updates on game days every five minutes," Curley says. "We're trying to appeal to our audiences. We hire the smartest college kid we can find to do promotions." The site also features live chats with the coach of the KU Jayhawks and others.

The Web site has been a boon for Bill Snead, senior writer and photographer for the *Lawrence Journal-World.* Curley created a special site featuring a retrospective of 50 years of Snead's work, from his days as a White House photographer for the *Washington Post* and his photos in Vietnam to the special reports he has written for the *Journal-World.* The Web site posts far more photos than the newspaper can print. Although Snead began his career in print long before the Web existed, he has become a model of a multimedia journalist.

As the 21st century began, convergence took a different form. Media organizations weren't just merging the different technologies in the same story; they were merging with other companies that could provide the audio and video for their online sites. Consider convergence more like a marriage or partnership, in which each type of media retains a distinct identity, but instead of competing with one another, the different media cooperate and contribute to the total product.

The Taj Mahal of media convergence is the $40 million glass and concrete News Center building, home to *The Tampa Tribune,* its partner television station, WFLA-TV, and the joint Web site, *www.tbo.com,* all owned by Media General, Inc. The first floor houses a modern television station, complete with robotic cameras, and the fourth floor contains administrative offices. But the nerve centers are on the second and third floors. The heartbeat of this four-story monument is the multimedia center, a group of semicircular desks in an open atrium on the second floor. Multimedia editors can look up to the third-floor newsroom of the *Tribune,* or reporters can peer down from the balcony to the multimedia center. More often, reporters stop by the desk to pitch their stories for the Web.

Although news decisions for the TV station and the newspaper remain separate, the multimedia staff coordinates stories that both media will cover for the Web site. Kenneth Knight, multimedia coordinator of the News Center, says that despite the sophisticated computer equipment, much of the collaboration occurs by "sneakerware," running upstairs to the *Tribune* newsroom or downstairs to the TV producers' offices, which encircle the second

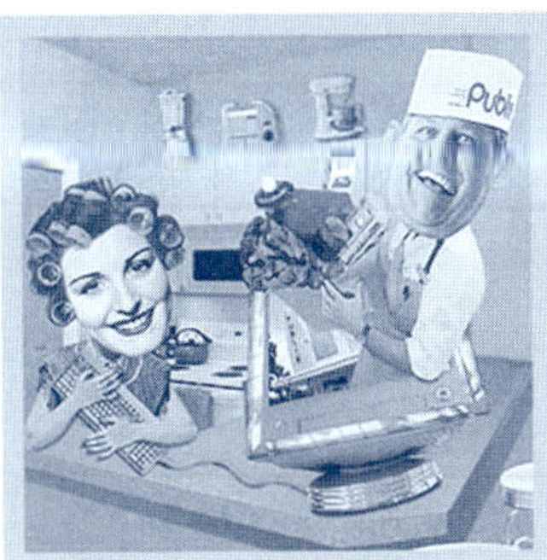

CAROL CLEERE/Tribune illustration

floor. On an almost daily basis, the multimedia desk will use video from the TV station and print stories to produce multimedia packages on the Web site.

In a report on Florida's basic skills tests for students, reporters from *The Tampa Tribune* and the TV station cooperated in live chats, and the Web site featured a bulletin board for comments, a quiz, sample test questions, and other content from print and video reports. A report about dangerous dogs was a TV multimedia production with video, and a report about online grocery shopping was a joint newspaper and Web product, which featured tips and an interactive poll.

As with the reporters at the *Journal-World,* the roles of print and broadcast journalists in Tampa are also converging. *The Tampa Tribune* newspaper reporters are being trained for broadcast because they may break their stories first on television, while WFLA-TV reporters may write their stories in print style for the newspaper or the Web.

Most editors in convergent newsrooms praise the partnerships, but the marriages are not without problems. Janet Weaver, former executive editor of the *Sarasota Herald-Tribune* in Florida, which is a partner with cable television SNN6 (Six News Now), said staff turnover was fairly high when the newspaper began its partnership with TV. The totally digital television operation is in a converted conference room off the side of the newsroom.

"There was enthusiasm among some people and resistance among others," said Weaver, currently executive editor of *The Tampa Tribune*. "One print reporter who was initially reluctant to go on TV later relented. I don't think he felt his soul was eternally damned."

The *Herald-Tribune* was one of the first newspapers to experiment with convergence. And initially there were a few disasters. Diane McFarlin, publisher of the newspaper, laughs as she recalls the first day the 24-hour news cable station went on the air. She wasn't smiling then.

Journalism students at the University of Alaska Anchorage producing multimedia video, print and webcasts of the Carrs/Great Alaska Shootout basketball tournament

"We had promoted this so aggressively. We didn't do enough rehearsal," McFarlin said. "At 6 a.m. the TV station went on the air, and the anchor began the newscast: 'Good morning and welcome to the first day of something new. Let me try that again. 5 . . . 4 . . . 3 . . . 2 . . . 1.' This was all on the air. We got a lot of razzing about that. I was sitting at home watching it and was absolutely mortified." McFarlin said she reluctantly went into work that morning, and the weather matched her mood. "It was pouring rain," she said. "It turned out that we had one of the worst floods in history." The cable station went on the air live, and the anchor helped the community get through that flood.

From that moment on, people understood the value of this new TV station, she said: "Everywhere I went people talked about that day." These days, McFarlin says the convergent operation is a great success. "This is one of the most exciting things I've ever been involved with."

Even as the media continue to converge, it's likely that all types of media will continue to survive in their distinct forms for many years.

Blogs

In 2004 the U.S. dictionary publisher Merriam-Webster reported that "blog," defined as "a Web site that contains an online personal journal with reflections, comments and often hyperlinks," was one of the 10 most looked-up words on its Web site. Also known as "weblogs," these personal journals touched off a controversial question in the media: Can blogs be considered journalism?

Reporters covering the war in Iraq were sending back blogs with their stories, and during the presidential election, reporters were also writing blogs from the national Democratic and Republican conventions. In addition, many newspapers carry blogs written by reporters about events they are covering. Many of these blogs might be considered a form of personal journalism.

But thousands of other people are also writing blogs on every conceivable subject. Another term for these blogs written by people who are not affiliated with conventional media is "citizen journalism." But can they be considered journalism? Some are simply personal reflections about people's lives and views about issues in the country; other blogs concentrate on gossip. Matt Drudge, author of the online *Drudge Report,* has made a career of reporting rumors and gossip on his blogs.

Because blogs are not edited and do not have to meet the standards of accuracy and fairness required by major news sites, their credibility is questionable.

Jonathan Dube, creator of *cyberjournalist.net,* lists more than 100 blogs written by journalists in newspapers and scores of other blogs that journalists create on personal sites. Dube has posted a "bloggers' code of ethics" on his site to encourage bloggers to practice some of the same standards that journalists espouse, chiefly to "be honest and fair in gathering, reporting and interpreting information."

Whether or not blogs can be considered journalism, they are informative and gaining popularity as a source of information. They are another factor in the changing nature of journalism.

The Impact on Journalism

The Web has changed the nature of news in other ways:

Continual deadlines: When a news story breaks, reporters at many newspaper and broadcast organizations are expected to file the story immediately for the Web and update major stories online throughout the day. Competition for readers is keen. More news sites are competing with MSNBC and CNN, which consider themselves "24/7" sites, meaning they publish news 24 hours a day, seven days a week. They are not alone.

Interactive content: One of the main distinctions of online news is the ability to interact with readers. Web news stories often feature polls, discussion groups and questions at the end of stories to prompt readers to express their views. More than ever, writers need to consider how their audience will be affected by the story, regardless of the medium.

Related links: Online news is accompanied by links to related information, so a news story may no longer be a single entity. Traditional print and broadcast news stories also refer readers and viewers to related online information. The Web has intensified research and reporting.

Nonlinear structure: Print and broadcast news stories are written in linear order—to be read or heard from beginning to end as if in a straight line. Because the Web features links, it creates a nonlinear environment, meaning that readers may access content in any order they choose. Although many online news stories are still linear, original Web content is organized in more related pieces. Instead of one story containing all the information, nonlinear news might be split into separate parts for background, profiles, timelines, databases and multimedia. Newspaper stories often feature related sidebars, but the Web may encourage more nonlinear print organization as well. We'll study more about nonlinear organization in Chapter 12, on Web writing.

Databases: Many news sites offer databases you can search to find information about health, school test scores or crime statistics in your community. For example, *The Philadelphia Inquirer* (*www.philly.com/mld/inquirer*) offers an annual report card allowing you to search a database for public and private schools in Pennsylvania and New Jersey to find out about school test scores and related facts for schools in these areas. Many other news sites also offer searchable databases for crime statistics, school test scores and other community information.

Personalized journalism: In addition to blogs as a form of personalized journalism, online news sites are reaching out to users by asking them to contribute their personal stories. Sunline (*www.sunline.net*), the Web site for the *Sun-Herald* (Charlotte, Fla.), led the way in personal journalism by allowing its users to post their own obituaries, war stories, pictures of pets and other personal sites. A more sophisticated form of personal journalism is the basis of *www.musarium.com,* a site devoted to personal narratives. The site's motto is "Discovering signs of intelligent life on earth." The stories and photo essays range from a documentary about a man seeking assisted suicide to a special section called "Interviews 50 Cents." Reporters for this section of the Web site traveled around the country with a card table and a sign offering people 50 cents for their stories, which included revelations about people's fears, hopes, dreams and love stories.

Specialized beats: Almost all news sites feature sections devoted to health, technology, money, travel and other subjects that appeal to readers' special interests. Although traditional media have always covered these subjects, sometimes limited to certain days of the week, Web news sites offer more frequent and more thorough coverage.

Public Journalism

The Web was not the only cause of change in the news industry. Years of declining newspaper circulation spurred a movement called "public journalism," also called "civic journalism," a form of reporting that involves readers in planning the news based on their concerns. It is an attempt to make readers care about their community and the news coverage. If unemployment is a concern to the community, the newspaper might ask readers to suggest problems they want the paper to address, such as job opportunities, retraining and resources. Editors and reporters then might plan a series based on those topics.

The Charlotte (N.C.) *Observer* was one newspaper that practiced public journalism extensively, especially in its election coverage. In one presidential election, the *Observer* conducted polls jointly with a local television station and asked voters what issues they wanted politicians to discuss. Reporters then interviewed candidates about those issues instead of letting candidates discuss their own agendas.

Not everyone in the media approves of this approach to news. Newspaper editors involved in public journalism call it "community leadership" because they are setting the agenda for solving local problems. Critics call it "advocacy journalism" or biased journalism, which contradicts the traditional newspaper role of remaining objective and uninvolved in the news. These days, blogs and online interactive forums are replacing the earlier forms of public journalism.

Job Skills

Whether you are seeking a job in journalism, public relations or online media, editors in all types of media stress the need for students to master basic skills of writing and reporting.

Gil Thelen, publisher and president of *The Tampa Tribune,* hopes that journalists of the future will have a better understanding of multimedia so he doesn't have to do as much cross-training of his staff. But he doesn't expect future journalists to have print, broadcast and online skills.

"Our version of the multimedia person is not this person with an antenna," Thelen says. "We are looking for demonstrated competence in one area, an understanding of the dynamics of the rapidly changing marketplace and a willingness to learn."

Morris V. Pyle, WFLA-TV's news operations manager, is a high-tech guru who helped set up the digital TV newsroom in the Tampa News Center. Despite his technical expertise, his wish list for future journalists is simple: "Writing still matters. That's what we tell students in school."

Jimmy Gentry, former dean of the School of Journalism at the University of Kansas, revamped the school's curriculum to stress convergence. He is also the consultant to the Tampa news organizations and many other convergent media operations. Despite his emphasis on multimedia skills, Gentry says the goal is to reduce the rigid thinking of students. "We're just trying to get people to think across platforms," he says.

That's fine with Diane McFarlin, publisher of the *Sarasota Herald-Tribune,* who opposes hiring a newsroom of "generic journalists." "Over time there won't have to be as much indoctrination for people who come

ETHICS

Plagiarism and Fabrication

The case: (This situation is based on the case of Jayson Blair, a former reporter for *The New York Times*.) A reporter for your campus newspaper quickly becomes a star by charming editors and professors, volunteering for stories and writing prolifically. His stories are filled with descriptive details and human-interest features that gain him a reputation as an outstanding writer. But the editor of the paper is concerned because several of his stories require corrections after they are printed, and the editor can't trace some of the sources. The editor and some staffers complain to journalism professors about this reporter's inaccuracies, but the professors dismiss the complaints as jealousy over this rising star. The reporter lands a prestigious internship with a large daily paper and later is hired full time even before he graduates from journalism school. He shows much promise and gets assigned to major national stories, but during his four years at the paper, his stories require 50 corrections, and one of his editors thinks he should be fired. However, top management at the newspaper excuses the reporter because he says that he has had several personal problems. His trail of deception, plagiarism and fabrication is uncovered after the newspaper is notified that he plagiarized a story written by one of his former campus newspaper colleagues, who was working at a newspaper in San Antonio. The story, about a Texas mother whose son died in Iraq, was only one of at least 36 articles containing plagiarized or fabricated quotes and facts. The reporter resigns, and the newspaper publishes an extensive front-page Sunday story explaining the situation and apologizing to readers.

Dilemma: What steps could have or should have been taken to prevent this situation from happening? Should a reporter be fired as soon as the first incident of plagiarism or fabrication is discovered? Should a reporter whose stories require numerous corrections be fired? What would you have done if you were the campus editor or his editor at that newspaper? What can be done to prevent plagiarism and fabrication in the media?

Ethical values: Accuracy, credibility.

Ethical guidelines: According to the code of ethics of the Society of Professional Journalists, "Seek truth and report it. Test the accuracy of information from all sources and exercise care to avoid inadvertent error. Deliberate distortion is never permissible."

from our universities because a lot of universities are changing curriculum," McFarlin says. "The most successful newsrooms will have people who are good specialists, like an outstanding education reporter. We want to get the smartest, most knowledgeable writers."

The Coaching Method

Whether you are writing for print, broadcast or online media, you still need to master the basic skills of reporting and writing. The coaching method is a way of helping writers discover their problems and learn techniques to solve them. An editor may concentrate on the results of your writing and fix the story, but a coach concentrates on the process of writing. A coach doesn't stress how you failed to write a good story; a coach stresses how you can succeed.

Like a basketball coach who trains players how to improve their techniques on the court, a writing coach trains writers how to perfect their techniques in the craft. This book aims to serve as a surrogate writing coach by anticipating the problems writers might have and offering solutions. It features tips from leading writing coaches and award-winning journalists.

The coaching method in this book has four phases:

1   **Conceive the idea:** At this stage you develop the idea for the story. If you are covering an event, such as a meeting or an accident, you need to start with the idea—the main point of what occurred. If you are writing a news story about a problem in your community, you still start with a central idea, which is the focus of your story. Once you begin reporting, you may discover some information that is more important than your original focus. Thus, you should be flexible and decide the focus for writing after you collect the material.

2   **Collect:** This is the reporting stage. Before you conduct your interview, you should look for background information: Check online sources and any available documents or clips from previous stories about your subject and your sources. Then interview sources, and gather as much information as you can about your topic. Don't rely on one source; seek several points of view. Ask more questions and take more notes than you plan to use. You should also jot down your observations and gather as many details as possible.

3   **Construct:** This is the planning and writing stage. Begin with a plan for your story developed around the focus, the main idea of your story. Then go through your notes and mark only the information related to that focus. Like a carpenter building a house, you need a blueprint. A good writer does not write a story without a plan. Jot down a few key words to indicate how you will organize your story. Then write a first draft of your story. You may revise your original draft in the next step.

4   **Correct:** After you have written your story, read it and make any necessary changes. You may decide to add or delete information or to completely reorganize the story during this stage. You should also check the spelling of all names and the accuracy of facts, and you should correct grammar, style and typing errors.

These four steps constitute the basic process for all news stories. In the coming chapters you will learn many techniques for reporting and writing news. But first you need to understand what constitutes a news story.

Qualities of News Stories

Definitions of news are changing. But these are some traditional qualities of news stories:

Timeliness: An event that happened the day of or day before publication or an event that is due to happen in the immediate future is considered timely. In broadcast and online media, timeliness is considered "immediacy" and is even more crucial. When stories are posted online immediately after they happen or broadcast several times a day, you have to consider how to update them frequently. Even print newspapers have several editions, which require updating. Some events that happened in the past may also be considered timely if they are printed on an anniversary of the event, such as one, five or 10 years after the incident. Timeliness answers this reader's question: Why are you telling me this now? The following story was timely because it was published the day after the accident:

> A bus loaded with elementary school children crashed head-on into a compact car in southwestern Jefferson County yesterday, injuring 24 students and the two drivers.
>
> The *(Louisville, Ky.)* Courier-Journal

If that story had been written for broadcast or online media, the angle would have been updated to report the current condition of the students and drivers.

Proximity: An event may be of interest to local readers because it happened in or close to the community. This story would be of particular interest to residents in the Oregon community where the man lived:

> A 71-year-old former psychologist received an eight-year prison sentence Monday for running the most sophisticated indoor marijuana growing operation ever discovered in Clackamas County.
>
> Authorities said Arvord E. Belden of Estacada may be the oldest man ever sentenced to federal prison for a drug crime in Oregon.
>
> *Dave Hogan,* The *(Portland)* Oregonian

Unusual nature: Out-of-the-ordinary events, a bizarre or rare occurrence, or people engaged in unusual activities are considered newsworthy, as in this story:

Man ticketed for walking his lizard

FORT LAUDERDALE, Fla.—Walking your dog along the beach here is illegal—and so is lounging with your lizard, Chris DeMango found out Mortimer, DeMango's 20-pound purple-tongued monitor lizard, complete with matching pink doll sweater and leash, was out for exercise Monday. DeMango said a walk makes Mortimer more docile, but police said it makes him an illegal lizard—animals are banned on the beach. DeMango was ticketed, and his lizard law violation could cost him 60 days in jail and a $500 fine.

St. Petersburg *(Fla.)* Times

Celebrities: People who are well-known for their accomplishments—primarily entertainers, athletes or people who have gained fame for achievements, good or bad—attract a lot of attention.

A California jury acquitted Michael Jackson of all counts in his trial on child molestation charges against a 13-year-old boy.

Human interest: People like stories about people who have special problems, achievements or experiences. Profiles of people who have overcome difficulties or who seek to improve society inspire readers. This example about a couple who spent $6,000 looking for their lost cat combines human interest and an unusual story:

Five-year-old Marble used to hide in the box springs of a spare bed in Bill and Carol Deckers' Denver home.

Now the Deckers' cat is hiding somewhere in the woods near Carthage, Mo.

Since Marble escaped from the couple's recreational vehicle Aug. 18, the Deckers have spent more than $6,000 trying to get her back.

"We taught her to live with us and we owe it to her," said Carol Decker, 41, a part-time accountant who gave up her job to look for Marble. . . .

Since losing Marble, the Deckers have put up posters and placed newspaper ads in Colorado, Missouri and Oklahoma, and contacted a psychic to locate her, to no avail.

The Deckers have returned to the site, often sleeping outdoors in the hope that their presence would draw Marble to them.

Tillie Fong, Rocky Mountain *(Denver)* News

Conflict: Stories involving conflicts that people have with government or other people are often newsworthy, especially when the conflict reflects local problems.

LANSING—Opponents of a new law that makes it easier to obtain a permit to carry a concealed weapon in most Michigan communities are preparing a petition drive to block the law's implementation.

Dawson Bell, Detroit Free Press

Here is an example of a story that combines conflict with human interest and unusual qualities:

The family expected to mourn Anthony Romeo, who died of heart disease in September at his Seffner home. Instead, they found a stranger in his coffin.

The Hillsborough Medical Examiner's Office had shipped the wrong body to the funeral home.

The mix-up so upset Romeo's son Joseph that he filed suit Monday against Hillsborough County, the Brandon funeral home and the private courier that delivered the body.

Rachel L. Swarns, St. Petersburg *(Fla.)* Times

Impact: Reaction stories to news events or news angles that affect readers have impact, especially when major national stories or tragedies occur in any community. Newspapers often seek local angles by writing how people in their areas are affected by the news, as in this story following a massive tsunami that killed thousands of people in 11 Southeast Asian countries:

Scientists at the West Coast and Alaska Tsunami Warning Center for years worked on a windy hilltop just outside downtown Palmer, far from the reach of potentially disastrous waves and public notice.

But with global attention on tsunami readiness galvanized by the Indian Ocean waves that killed more than 160,000 people, the center is poised for a major upgrade that could protect Alaskans as well as coastal residents around the world, a top federal administrator told staffers at the center.

Zaz Hollander, Anchorage Daily News

Some additional qualities of news to consider:

Helpfulness: Consumer, health and other how-to stories help readers cope with their lives. Online news sites abound with helpful stories.

If your head spins at the torrent of medical studies that fills newspapers, magazines and TV, join the club. It seems that each day brings another round of studies contradicting last month's hot results.

One day vitamin E is found to prevent cancer. Next, it is suspected of causing it. Margarine is good. No, it's bad.

One can almost hear a collective scream of frustration across the land.

Studies are the cornerstone of medical progress, showing doctors and patients the way to longer, healthier lives. But they can also lead us astray.

To try to help you through the hype and hustle, here's a basic outline of what studies are, how they differ, what they can tell us and where they can go wrong. Call it A User's Guide to Medical Studies. Or, How to Follow Health News Without Having a Stroke.

Phillip E. Canuto, Knight-Ridder/
Tribune News Service

Entertainment: Stories that amuse readers, make them feel good or help them enjoy their leisure time have entertainment value. In a broad sense, many of the news features in sports and lifestyle sections can be classified as entertainment. Entertainment stories often involve celebrities or have human-interest qualities. This story combines news qualities of human interest and unusual nature by entertaining readers as well as

ODESSA, Texas—When Elbert Lewis got his draft notice, he told his wife goodbye. Then he thought of his children. And his seven grandchildren. And his greatgrandchild.

The Selective Service was cracking down on potential draft dodgers, and government records showed Lewis failed to register as required by law when he turned 18 in November.

The problem: Lewis turned 18 in November 1932.

The records showed his birthdate was Nov. 11, 1976, instead of in 1914.

What's more, Lewis did register for the draft—in 1941. He served on a Navy anti-aircraft cruiser during World War II and received a Purple Heart.

When Lewis got the draft compliance notice Saturday, he broke the news to his wife, Janie.

"He came into the den and said, 'Well, I have to tell you goodbye,'" she said. "Then we called our kids. We just cut up and acted silly about it, really."

"We really got a laugh out of it, and so did all four of my kids," Lewis said.

He dashed off a copy of his birth certificate and honorable discharge to the Selective Service.

The agency removed his name from its list, spokesman Lou Brodsky said.

The idea of being 18 again was appealing, to a degree.

"I wouldn't mind it, take away the war," Lewis said.

The Associated Press

Issues or problems in the community: These stories usually include qualities such as conflict and proximity. The *St. Cloud* (Minn.) *Times* combined the trends of reader involvement with issues important to minorities in a series called "Open or Intolerant?" The newspaper sought opinions from teenagers of different races as well as from police, city leaders and residents about police treatment of young people of color.

Since moving to St. Cloud three years ago, Jacob "Cisco" Owens says he has been hassled, detained, pulled over and provoked by St. Cloud police officers more times than he can remember.

Owens, a 16-year-old Apollo High School junior, admits he's been in trouble a few times for minor things. But for every time he's done something, anything, wrong, he swears he can identify seven more times he's been confronted by police when he's done nothing at all.

"And almost all the time they ask me if I'm in a gang. It makes me angry that they just assume. It's just a given that I'm treated like that," he says. "Just because I'm young and black, I'm treated like a thug." Dozens of young people of different races in St. Cloud say it's no secret: Police here are known for targeting minority youth for bogus traffic stops, tough talk, and sometimes, rough treatment when responding to calls.

Lee Rood, St. Cloud *(Minn.)* Times

Trends: Stories may indicate patterns or shifts in issues that influence readers' lives, such as increases in crime, social issues and other forces in society.

MULTIMEDIA COACH

- Train yourself to think for multimedia. How does online news differ from traditional newspaper or broadcast journalism? Compare online news stories with those in your local newspaper. Are they the same, or do they offer links, polls, questions and other related features? If your local TV news station has a Web site, compare that site with the newspaper's Web site.

- Learn to think interactively. Analyze interactive on-line features such as polls, games, message boards and databases in your local Web news sites or others, such as CNN (*www.cnn.com*).

- Plan to update stories. Analyze how major news sites such as *msnbc.com* and *cnn.com* continually update their stories.

- Consider the role of blogs. Analyze blogs for their news or entertainment value. Check journalists' blogs at *http://www.cyberjournalist.net*. Discuss whether they are a fad or a permanent form of information.

- Consider the importance of audience. Compare the *Lawrence Journal-World* Web site, *www.ljworld,* with its companion site, *www.lawrence.com*.

- Develop your ability to conceive newsworthy story ideas. Identify qualities of news in stories on the front page of your local newspaper. Check the online site (or another online site), and study the qualities of news on the main page.

- Become a visual thinker. Compare the visuals for a news story covered in your newspaper, on TV and on-line. Consider visuals for the stories you will produce.

Many Milwaukee area public libraries no longer have strict "SH!" policies.

Libraries are shedding their image as quiet, somber places for bookworms and students only. Instead, today's libraries offer a wide variety of materials and programs in an effort to appeal to more people.

Lawrence Sussman, The Milwaukee Journal Sentinel

Hard News and Features

News falls into two basic categories: hard news and soft news. "Hard news" includes stories of a timely nature about events or conflicts that have just happened or are about to happen, such as crimes, fires, meetings, protest rallies, speeches and testimony in court cases. The hard approach is basically an account of what happened, why it happened and how readers will be affected. These stories have immediacy.

"Soft news" is defined as news that entertains or informs, with an emphasis on human interest and novelty and less immediacy than hard news. For example, a profile about a man who designs model airplanes or a story about the effectiveness of diets would be considered soft news.

Soft news can also be stories that focus on people, places or issues that affect readers' lives. These types of stories are called "feature stories." A story about the growing number of babies suffering from AIDS could be considered a soft-news story. It isn't less important than hard news, but it isn't news that happened overnight. However, a feature story can be based on a news event. Instead of being just a factual account of the event, it features or focuses on a particular angle, such as human-interest reactions.

If the action or event occurred the same day as or the day before publication of the newspaper, the event is called "breaking news." Here is an example of the lead of a breaking-news story from a Saturday edition:

Tornadoes rapped Topeka and southeast Shawnee County Friday afternoon, damaging seven homes and sending residents scurrying for cover.

No one was injured by the short, severe storm that struck unexpectedly.

Steve Fry, Topeka *(Kan.)* Capital-Journal

The preceding example of a hard-news story tells readers what happened. The newspaper also printed this feature story focusing on people affected by the storm:

Becky Clark of Topeka was told the tornado sirens that sounded Friday afternoon were a false alarm.

Then she got home from work and saw her back yard at 2411 S.E. Gemini Ave. in the Aquarian Acres neighborhood.

"I couldn't believe it," she said

A tornado had lifted up the family pontoon boat, which was parked in the back yard, and tossed it into the family swimming pool, crushing part of the boat.

"It just wanted to get in the water," said Joe Clark, Becky's husband.

"I guess it was tired of being in dry dock. . . ."

Joe Taschler, Topeka *(Kan.)* Capital-Journal

The hard-news story about the storm was the main story, called a "mainbar." Because the accompanying feature story was a different angle on the same topic, it was a "sidebar" packaged with the main story.

But many other features in a newspaper do not have a breaking-news peg. They simply focus on interesting people or topics. For example, the *Boca Raton* (Fla.) *News* printed a feature story on the growing popularity of waterbeds, a topic of interest to its readers.

The Importance of Visuals

The presentation of a story with photographs or graphics is crucial. Broadcast media depend on visuals for the majority of stories. Studies by The Poynter Institute in St. Petersburg, Fla., show an increased emphasis on graphic devices and color in print media.

In one study, called "Eyes on the News," researchers measured the movements of people's eyes as they read the newspaper. The results of this study, also known as the Eye Trac study, show that readers are drawn to color photographs first, then headlines, cutlines (captions), briefs (stories abbreviated to one to three paragraphs) and a number of other graphic devices called points of entry—points where the reader enters a story. Some of those eye-catching points include subheadlines and quotations displayed in larger type within the story.

The study also concludes that most people only scan the newspaper, looking at headlines and graphics, and that they read very few stories all the way through. The average reader skims about 25 percent of the stories in the newspaper but thoroughly reads only half of those (about 12 percent), the study concludes.

Mario Garcia, who co-authored the Poynter study and is a world-renowned consultant on newspaper design, says the majority of readers today do not remember life without television, so visual elements are crucial in a newspaper. "The marriage of visual and words has to begin early—from the first time you learn reporting," he says.

A subsequent study tracking eye movements of online readers determined that graphics were less important in online news. The study by The Poynter Institute and Stanford University found that online readers focused first on text in Web news sites rather than informational graphics. A 2004 follow-up study of online readers revealed that readers focused on banner graphics and photos but still focused more on text when they entered a Web site. Despite those findings, most online news sites make extensive use of photos. For example, *Newsday* (*www.newsday.com*) offers a regular feature called "This week in photos."

However, graphics and photos continue to be crucial in print news presentation. In fact, they are so important that some newspapers, including *The Orange County Register* and *The Dallas Morning News,* have graphics reporters. When a major story such as an airplane crash occurs, these graph-

Graphic explaining a natural disaster

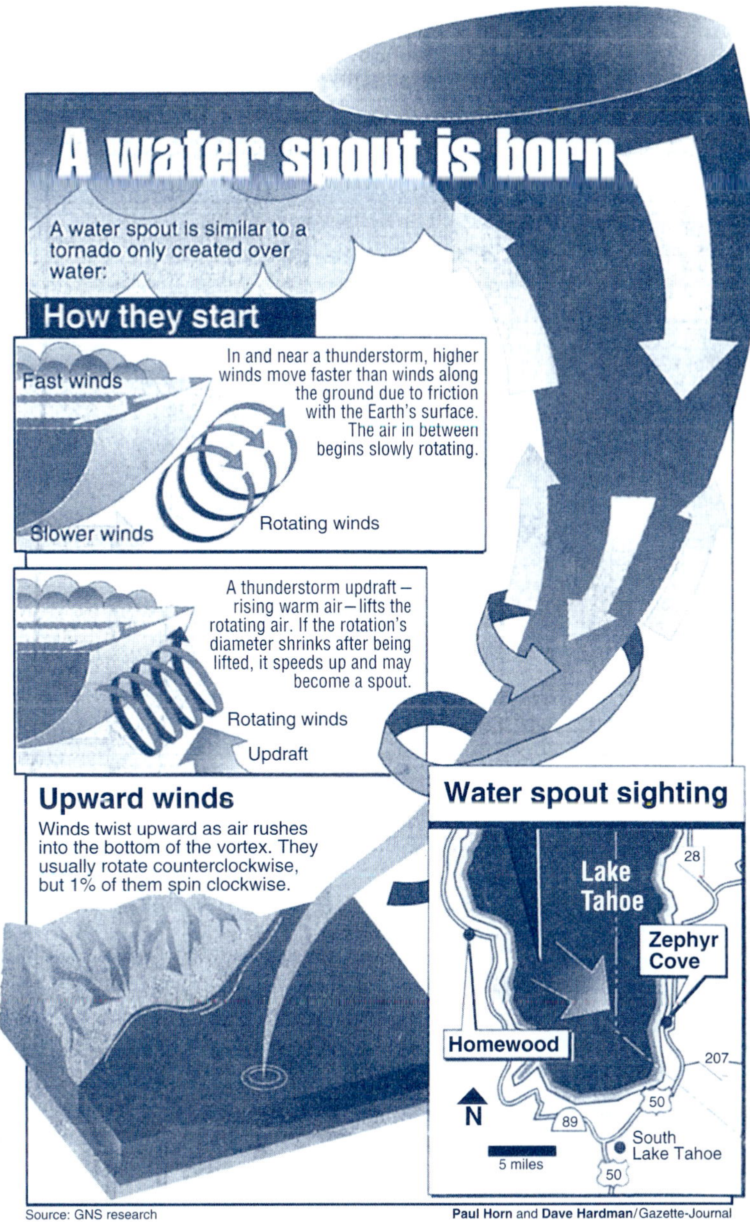

ics reporters go to the scene with other reporters to gather information for the graphics. While the regular reporters gather facts, quotes and other materials, the graphics reporters seek such details as how many feet the plane skidded, for scale drawings.

Because most newspapers do not have special reporters to gather information for graphics, those responsibilities often belong to regular reporters.

In addition, all reporters need to consider the graphic devices that may accompany the story so that information is not duplicated unless it is crucial in the story.

That is the emphasis at the *Reno (Nev.) Gazette-Journal*, a Gannett newspaper that makes extensive use of graphics. Reporters are expected to visualize their stories as a total package involving photos and graphics.

The emphasis is on using verbal and visual tools that will make information clear to readers. For example, a story about rare water spouts from Lake Tahoe was accompanied by the preceding graphic, which explained how water spouts are created. The information was not repeated in the text.

Whether stories are accompanied by graphics for print or multimedia images for online delivery, all media will incorporate visual elements.

Exercises

1 **Visual awareness:** Try this experiment to test your reading habits. Bring to class a copy of a newspaper you haven't read. Read the newspaper as you would for pleasure. Place a check on the first item you look at — a picture, graphic, headline or story. Mark the stories you read, and place an X at the point in the story where you decide to stop reading. Where did your eye go first? Why are visual elements so important? Now analyze which stories you read and how much of them you read. Where did you stop on most stories? Why? Keep in mind that because you are a journalism student, you may read more than the average reader.

2 Keep a journal of your reading or viewing habits of news for three days. Write a paragraph each day about the kinds of stories you read and didn't read, how many you read all the way through, and how many you read just through the headline or the first few paragraphs. Do the same for stories you read online. Analyze your preferences. Record the amount of time you spent reading the newspaper for pleasure, not for an assignment. Record how much you watched news on TV. Then interview three other people — students, neighbors or strangers — and ask them what kinds of stories they do and don't read in print and online. Ask where they get the majority of their news — from print, broadcast or online media. Write a summary of your findings.

3 **Blogs:** Write a blog about a personal experience or a point of view you have about some issue. You can create your own blog at *www.blogger.com* or other blog sites.

4 **Online news ideas:** Either in small groups or as a class, brainstorm topics and ideas that you would want to read in an electronic newspaper or magazine. Brainstorm at least three interactive features for an online college newspaper.

Featured Online Activity

Access the Chapter 1 resources at *http://communication.wadsworth.com/ rich5e* to link to an interactive quiz that will test your knowledge of convergence and qualities of news.

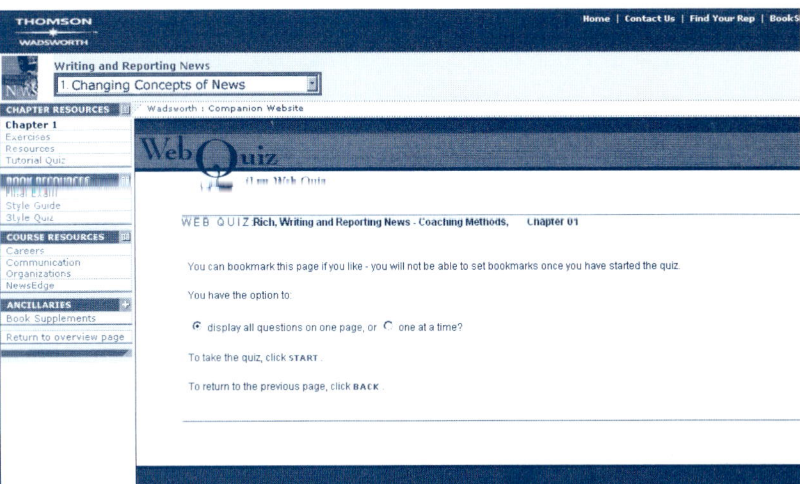

State the focus, the main idea, of your story in one sentence.

To find your lead, ask yourself: What is most important or most interesting?

Write the story as though you were telling a friend.

Consider how your story will affect readers.

Visualize your story with text and graphics or photographs.

Make sure your quotes don't repeat your transitions.

Test the quality of your quotes: Are they good enough to be used as pull quotes?

What is the main impression you want to leave with your readers? Write a discussion or poll question for online readers.

CHAPTER 2

The Basic News Story

Too many stories fail to answer the reader's most challenging question: So what?

Roy Peter Clark,
writing coach and author

The basic news story is told upside down. It usually is called a hard-news story. That doesn't mean it should be hard to read. Quite the contrary. It really should be called an easy news story because the facts are presented in a direct form that makes it easy for the reader to get the most important information quickly.

A hard-news story often presents the result of a news event first so that the key facts are in the first few paragraphs. If a news story were a mystery story, you would solve the mystery in the beginning and then devote the rest of the story to telling the reader how and why it happened.

Dan Henderson, the late assistant managing editor of *The Commercial Appeal* in Memphis, Tenn., described it this way: "A basic news story is similar to a formula for writing a novel about the Old West: Shoot the sheriff in the first paragraph."

For example, if the state officials who regulate higher education—often called the Board of Regents—had met yesterday to discuss an increase in tuition at universities in your state, you wouldn't write that the Board of Regents met to consider a tuition increase. You would give the results. What did the regents decide? This is a direct approach: "The Board of Regents voted yesterday to raise undergraduate tuition next fall at state universities by $100 to $4,700." Or you might say, "Tuition will increase next fall by $100 for undergraduate students at the state's universities." Then you could explain that the decision was made yesterday by the Board of Regents and give details about the tuition increase and its impact. Here is an example:

GRAND RAPIDS, Mich.—Tuition for a full-time student at Grand Valley State University will go up by $285 a semester despite the pleas of student representatives.

The GVSU Board of Control unanimously approved the tuition increase Wednesday, saying the lack of support from the state and enrollment increase of 1,000 students left them no choice.

The vote raises tuition for a full-time student from $1,681 for the current semester to $1,966 starting in January—a 17 percent increase.

The Holland *(Mich.)* Sentinel

Determining Your Focus

Not all basic news stories have to start with such a direct approach. Some stories start with a storytelling approach, such as an anecdote about a person or place. Regardless of how you start or structure your story, all news stories are developed around one main point—a focus. The rest of the story should contain quotes, facts and information to support that main focus. Because readers are bombarded with so much information these days, they are impatient to know why they are reading or hearing this story, so you need to tell them the focus in the first sentence or within the first few paragraphs of the story.

Selecting Information

Once you get your focus, you should select only the information that supports that basic idea. It is the key to organizing your story. The coaching method for determining your focus involves two simple steps: deciding what the story is about and how you would tell the story to a friend. These steps will also help you find a lead and a structure for the story.

What's the story about? This is the first question to ask yourself. You should be able to write the answer in one sentence, preferably in fewer than 35 words. That is your focus statement. Put this sentence at the top of your story as a guide to remind you of the focus, although it will not be published with the story. You could use this focus statement as your lead if you decide you want the first sentence to get directly to the point of your story. If you prefer a more creative lead, this statement will become your focus paragraph—also called a "nut graph." Think of the nut graph as the kernel or core idea of the story. Here's an example in a story about the "freshman 15." The main idea is in the third paragraph, which is the nut graph.

Lead

When freshmen begin college, they often feel like the world is their oyster.

Unfortunately, many 18- and 19-year-olds are swallowing that big oyster in one gulp—and bellying up for seconds.

Nut graph

There's a name for this behavior—it's called the "freshman 15," and it has been a part of college life for about as long as young people have been heading off in pursuit of higher education. That term is used to describe the typical weight gain many freshman experience their first year away from home.

Jim Baker, Lawrence *(Kan.)* Journal-World

How would you tell the story to a friend? Another way to determine your focus is to use the "tell-a-friend" technique. This is a natural conversational method, particularly important in broadcast writing.

Imagine that your friend asks what the story is about and what happened. Chances are that you might talk about the most interesting information first. Thinking in these terms will give you a clue for your lead and your organization.

If you mention something that isn't clear, your friend will probably ask you to explain. That's another clue for organizing your story. When you write one paragraph that raises a question in a reader's or viewer's mind, follow it immediately with information that answers the question or substantiates the point, either with quotes or facts.

Here is how Leslie Barewin used the coaching method to write her first news story when she was in journalism school at the University of Kansas. Barewin got the idea for the story when she went to the university health center because she had been feeling ill. The nurse stuck a thermometer in her ear. Barewin was surprised. She had never seen a thermometer like that. She decided that other students might be unaware of that type of thermometer and so it would make a good news story.

She started by asking herself what the story was about and wrote this focus statement, which was not printed with the story but helped her identify the main point:

> Temperature probes are being used to take patients' temperature through the ear at Watkins Memorial Health Center.

Then she used the tell-a-friend technique to write her story. Although you might tell your friend this story in a different order, the style is basically a conversational storytelling method. Barewin's original lead on her first draft was as follows.

> You might not have to waste three minutes of your time at Watkins Memorial Health Center.

After she wrote her story, during the correcting/revising process her professor asked her this coaching question to brighten the lead: What struck you as most interesting about this story? Barewin said it was the fact that the probes were used in the ear, the concept she had written in her focus statement. That was what gave her the idea for her revised lead on the story, followed by the focus written in a nut graph.

New lead
> Don't be surprised if a nurse at Watkins Memorial Health Center tells you to stick it in your ear.
>
> It's the current method of taking your temperature at the center.

Watkins is using the latest in thermometer technology. For more than a year, temperature probes have been used to take a patient's temperature through the ear instead of through the mouth or rectum.

Basic questions All news stories answer some basic questions: who, what, when, where, why and how?

As newspaper readership declines and competition increases because of all-day coverage in broadcast and online media, editors increasingly want the answer to another question: so what? What is the significance to readers? How can you make readers see and care about the story?

Eugene Roberts, a former editor at *The New York Times* and *The Philadelphia Inquirer,* tells this story about how his editor influenced him to write vividly enough to make the reader see. Roberts was a reporter at the *Goldsboro News-Argus* in North Carolina. His editor, Henry Belk, was blind. Many days Belk would call in Roberts to read his stories to him, and Belk would yell: "Make me see. You aren't making me see."

Advice from Roberts: "The best reporters, whatever their backgrounds or their personalities, share that consummate drive to get to the center of a story and then put the reader on the scene."

Much has changed in the media since Roberts was a reporter many years ago. But his advice is just as relevant today. Identify the center of the story, which is the focus, gather information to make the reader see, and write a compelling story to make the reader care.

Elements of the Basic News Story

News stories in all media share some common elements. The basic news story has a headline and three general parts: a beginning, called the "lead," a middle, called the "body," and an ending. Other elements are backup (support) for the lead, nut graph (which is the paragraph explaining the focus), impact, attribution, background and elaboration.

Headline

The headline is the line on top of the story that tells the reader what the story is about. It usually is written by a copy editor or editor, except at very small newspapers where the editor also may be the reporter/writer. For a basic news story, the copy editor bases the headline on the main points of the story, which the reporter is expected to write in the first few paragraphs.

Online news sites and many newspapers today are using secondary headlines—called "deck heads," "summary lines" or "summary blurbs"—under the main headline. The two headlines together give the reader a quick overview of the story's content. Here is an example from a newspaper that uses summary lines on most of its major stories:

Headline

Salmon spawn a new crisis

*Deck head, summary line
or summary blurb*

Dwindling numbers and fading strength threaten to add the fish to the list of endangered species. But some question if the Northwest will pay the price to save the animals.

Los Angeles Times

Even though you won't write the headlines for your own stories, you can use the concept as a writing tool. If you are having trouble identifying the main point of a story, think of a headline for it.

Lead

At the beginning of the story, the hook that tells the reader what the story is about is called the "lead." A good lead entices the reader to continue reading. In a hard-news story, the lead is usually written in one sentence—the first sentence of the story—and gives the most important information about the event. But even a basic story can have a creative lead, called a "soft lead" or "feature lead."

The most common type of lead on a hard-news story is called a "summary lead" because it summarizes the main points about what happened. It answers the questions of who, what, when, where, why and how. The rest of the story elaborates about what, why and how. Hard-news leads do not have to answer all those questions in the first sentence if doing so would make the lead too long and difficult to read.

Shorter leads of fewer than 35 words are preferable, but that number is only a guideline.

The writer has to decide which elements are most important to stress in the first sentence. The summary lead in the following example stresses who, what, where and when; the rest of the story gives more details, such as the names of the professor and the suspect:

A Northwestern University professor of hearing sciences was shot and seriously wounded in a university parking lot Thursday.

Backup for the Lead

The lead should be backed up, or supported, with facts, quotes and statements that substantiate information in the lead. Here is an example:

GAINESVILLE, Fla.—A University of Florida law student suffering from amnesia after mysteriously disappearing in July has recalled her abduction under hypnosis, authorities said.

Elizabeth "Libby" Morris, 32, slowly has regained memory of her life before her disappearance from the Oaks

> Mall parking lot but has never con-sciously remembered what occurred during the five days she was missing, said Lt. Spencer Mann, a spokesman with the Alachua County Sheriff's Office.
>
> *The Associated Press*

Nut Graph

The "nut graph" is a sentence or paragraph that states the focus—the main point—of the story. It should tell in a nutshell what the story is about and why it is newsworthy. A news story may contain many comments and points, but it should be developed around one major theme or concept, and all other information should relate to that focus.

In a hard-news story with a direct summary lead, the lead contains the focus, so you don't need a separate nut graph. When the lead takes a softer, more creative approach and does not immediately explain the main point of the story, the nut graph is a separate paragraph. The nut graph is even more crucial when a story starts with a feature lead because the reader has to wait for a few paragraphs to find out the reason for the story.

The nut graph should be placed high in the story, generally by the third to fifth paragraph. But if the lead is very compelling, the nut graph could come later. Rigid rules can ruin good writing.

Here's an example of a story with a creative lead and nut graph:

Lead

RAVENNA, Ohio—There's no room at the Portage County Jail for Matthew P. Dukes—and he's trying hard to get in.

Backup

The Newton Falls resident has tried six times in 15 months to serve a 30-day sentence for driving while intoxicated. But each time, deputies have turned him away.

The jail is full, they say. Come again.

Nut graph

But Dukes has gone to court, filing a federal suit against the county sheriff and alleging that he is suffering cruel and unusual punishment by being prevented from going to jail.

Several area lawyers say it may be one of the first cases of its kind—a test of civil liberties that may pave the way for others who are idling away the hours while they wait to serve sentences in filled-to-capacity facilities for crimes such as shoplifting, theft or drunken driving.

For Dukes, 26, the unserved sentence is a constant source of frustration and embarrassment, a situation that he said has helped to turn him away from a hard-drinking lifestyle.

He said that he had not had a drink in a year and that he wanted to put the sentence behind him.

Carol Biliczky, Knight-Ridder/Tribune News Service

Lead Quote

The first quote that backs up the lead is called the "lead quote" or the "augmenting quote." It is usually the strongest quote you have, and it supports the concept in the lead without repeating the same information or wording. A lead quote isn't required in all stories, but a strong quote placed within a paragraph or two after the lead helps make the story interesting.

PENSACOLA, Fla. (AP)—Soon-to-be graduate student Michael Kearney hasn't chosen a major yet—but give him time, he's only 11.

Michael will begin tackling graduate studies at the University of West Florida in Pensacola this summer.

"We don't push him," said his mother, Cassidy Kearney. "He pushes us. We just try and keep up with him."

The Associated Press

Impact

Whenever possible, the writer should explain how the news affects readers. The "impact" sentence or paragraph should answer these questions: What is the significance of this story? What in the story makes the reader care? Sometimes the impact is explained in the lead or in the nut graph; sometimes it is lower in the story, in an explanatory paragraph.

Not all stories can show direct impact on readers, but they should all have a clear paragraph explaining the reason for the story. In some stories, such as police stories, the impact is that the news happened in the community and should be of interest to local residents.

Lead

When Oregon's mandatory automobile seat belt law goes into effect Dec. 7, police won't have any trouble enforcing it—all they have to see is a shoulder harness or a lap belt dangling unused.

Backup

"Police officers routinely tell us that safety belt laws are easy to enforce," said Geri Parker, safety belt program coordinator for the Oregon Traffic Safety Commission.

Oregon voters approved a ballot measure Nov. 6 to extend mandatory seat belt use to people age 16 and older. Seat belts or safety seats already are required for everyone under 16.

Impact

Beginning Dec. 7, everyone in the front and back seats of a car will need to buckle up—if belts are available—or face a fine of up to $50.

Phil Manzano, The *(Portland)* Oregonian

Online news sites provide impact in several interactive ways. Databases let readers search statistics about education, crime or property values in their communities; interactive calculators give readers a chance to figure what a tax increase might cost them; and feedback questions or polls ask readers to comment on issues.

Attribution

Where did you get the information? Who told you these facts? How can the reader be sure what you say is true? The "attribution" provides those answers. You need to attribute all quotes—exact wording of statements that people made—and much information that you did not witness. If the information is common knowledge or indisputable, you do not have to attribute it. You also need to attribute any statements that express opinions. (A more complete discussion of how to use quotes and attribution comes later in this chapter.)

The attribution should be in the lead for controversial or accusatory information, but in many other cases it can be delayed so it doesn't clutter the lead. Police stories often have attribution in the lead, especially if you get the information by telephone or if the information is accusatory:

Lead with attribution

ST. PETERSBURG, Fla.—A 15-year-old boy was stabbed twice in the chest Thursday afternoon when he apparently tried to break up a fight in a crowded parking lot at Northeast High School, authorities said.

Backup

Police and school officials said the stabbing, believed to have occurred after one student took another's hat, was the first they could recall at Pinellas County schools.

St. Petersburg *(Fla.)* Times

In the next example, general attribution is in the lead, but the specific attribution is in the third paragraph. The sources for the study are too cumbersome to use in the lead.

Lead with general attribution

A smoky bar may be more harmful to your health than a city street filled with diesel truck fumes, according to a new study.

Smoky bars and casinos have up to 50 times more cancer-causing particles than air in highways and city streets clogged with diesel trucks, the study says.

Backup with specific attribution

Indoor air pollution virtually disappears when smoking is banned, according to the study published in the Journal of Occupational and Environmental Medicine and partially funded by the

Robert Wood Johnson Foundation of New Jersey, a philanthropic organization devoted to health care.

Background

Is there any history or background the reader needs in order to understand how a problem or action occurred? Most stories need some background to explain the action, as in this example:

Lead

Lock your doors.

Nut graph

That's the advice of University of Iowa security chief Dan Hogan in light of recent reports of a prowler slipping into unlocked dormitory rooms at night.

Backup with lead quote

"I can't stress that enough," he said. "It's a very serious situation."

Background

Since Aug. 24, there have been six reports of a man entering women's rooms between 3 a.m. and 5:30 a.m. Five incidents were in Burge Hall and one was in Currier Hall.

Two times the man touched the sleeping women, Hogan said. But there was no force or violence. In each instance the man ran when the woman discovered him.

More recently, a woman in Burge Hall heard someone at her door. She opened it and saw a man running down the hall, Hogan said.

Valoree Armstrong, Iowa City Press-Citizen

Elaboration

Supporting points related to the main issue constitute "elaboration." These can be statements, quotes or more detail to explain what happened, how and why the problem or action occurred, and reactions to the event.

In this part of the story, seek other points of view to make sure you have balance and fairness. A story based on one source can be too biased. The preceding story about the University of Iowa continued with more explanation:

George Droll, director of residence services, said main doors to the halls were locked from midnight to 6 a.m. But each resident has a key. Some floors have 24-hour visitation.

Often students feel more secure than they should because the buildings are large and are home to many of their friends, he said.

MULTIMEDIA COACH

Focus is crucial in broadcast and online news. Competition for viewers and readers is keen in both media. If the focus of the story is unclear to broadcast viewers, they will turn to another channel. If the focus in an online story is not clear in the headline or summary blurb under the headline, readers may not even click into your online story. Ask yourself these questions:

- What is the most important idea that will entice viewers to listen to your story?

- What is the most important idea that will entice online readers to click into your story?

- Before you write your story for any medium, write a focus sentence in fewer than 35 words. This also can

be the lead of your story for an online site or a broadcast story. Now convert the focus into a headline of no more than six words for an online site. Here's an example from an Associated Press story:
  - Headline: Campus booze arrests jump 24 percent
  - Summary blurb under the headline: Sex, drug, weapons violations also increase.

- Online stories often have questions or polls seeking readers' feedback. If you were seeking feedback on the main idea of your story, what question would you ask? The question may give you a clue for finding your focus.

Ending

The most common type of ending includes one of these elements: future action, a statement or quote that summarizes but does not repeat the previous information, or more elaboration. If the future action is a key factor in the issue, it should be placed higher in the story. Avoid summary endings that repeat what you have already said. In a basic news story, end when you have no more new information to reveal.

The ending on the Iowa story follows the residence director's comments about why students feel secure in large buildings where they have friends:

Summary quote ending

"That's a strength, but it can also be a weakness in terms of people securing their rooms," Droll said.

Here is the ending from the story about the prospective inmate who wants to go to jail to serve his sentence for drunken driving:

Future action pending

Although a new, 184-bed facility costing about $15 million is planned, that does nothing to stem the tide of today's inmates, who Howe said are coming in record numbers.

Visuals

Visual elements such as photographs, charts and other graphic illustrations are crucial to news presentation. Research shows that 98 percent of readers are drawn first to a photograph on a newspaper page. Photographs and other graphic illustrations not only help make your story look good; they can also make it easier to read.

Here are some other visual elements used to enhance news stories:

Summary blurb A paragraph or sentence summarizing the story is called a "summary blurb." It is placed below the headline. When you ask yourself what the story is about, you are really envisioning a summary blurb. Even though copy editors actually write the summary blurb, you should use the concept to write your focus statement.

Summary blurbs are used extensively in online news stories. Here is an example of a summary blurb on a story about a term paper scandal at the University of South Florida:

<table>
<tr><td>Headline</td><td>

Papers a lesson in criminology</td></tr>
<tr><td>Summary blurb</td><td>

A USF professor follows a paper trail to a former student wanted on charges he sold term papers to criminology majors.</td></tr>
</table>

In online news the summary and lead of the story may be the same because the blurb may be on an index page linking to stories inside the site. The repetition can help readers know they have accessed the correct story. But in print stories when the blurb is published directly over the story, the lead does not have to repeat the summary. It can be more creative, as in this example on the term paper story:

> A. Engler Anderson's term papers weren't just bad. They were a crime, said one professor.
>
> Anderson, 31, is wanted on charges that he sold term papers to two University of South Florida students.
>
> Their major?
>
> Criminology.
>
> The charge—selling a term paper or dissertation to another person—is only a second-degree misdemeanor, but if he is caught, Anderson will be held without bail because he failed to appear for a court hearing this week.
>
> St. Petersburg *(Fla.)* Times

The story then explains how William Blount, chairman of the USF Criminology Department, received two papers that he thought were "awful" and then discovered they were written by Anderson, a former student.

Pull quote A good quote might be broken out of the story, placed in larger type and used as a point of entry to entice the reader. Although a copy editor will decide which quotes to pull for graphic display, when you write your story, consider which quotes could be used to entice readers. Then use your best quotes high in your story. In a story explaining sexual harassment, this "pull quote" from an employment lawyer was used for emphasis:

> *I think what the law says is that if you hit on me, and I say, 'No way, Buster,' I'm entitled to have you accept my rejection of you, and it shouldn't interfere with my work."*

> —Judith Vladeck, employment lawyer

Facts box Information from a story is sometimes set off in a "facts box," also called a "highlights box," for reading at a glance or providing key points in the story. A facts or highlights box can include the dates in a chronology or the main points of a proposal or meeting. It is especially useful for breaking statistics out of a story. Although some information from a facts box may be crucial to include in the story, the writer should guard against too much repetition.

Here is an example of a facts box that accompanied a story from *The Kansas City Star* about the dangers of lightning. These statistics were not repeated in the story:

Lightning deaths and injuries

Figures below were compiled from 35 years of U.S. lightning statistics.

Location of incident
- Open fields, recreation areas: 27%
- Under trees (not golf): 14%
- Water-related (boating, fishing, swimming, etc.): 8%
- Golf/golf under trees: 5%

Months of most incidents
- July 30%

Deaths by state, top five
- Florida, Michigan, Texas, New York, Tennessee

Source: National Oceanic and Atmospheric Administration

Infographic A chart, map, graph or other illustration meant to provide information is an "infographic." Examples of infographics are diagrams of plane crashes or major accidents and illustrations explaining how something works. The most common type of infographic, called a "location map," pinpoints the location of an accident, a crime or any other major news event.

Infographic from *The University Daily Kansan*
Reprinted with permission

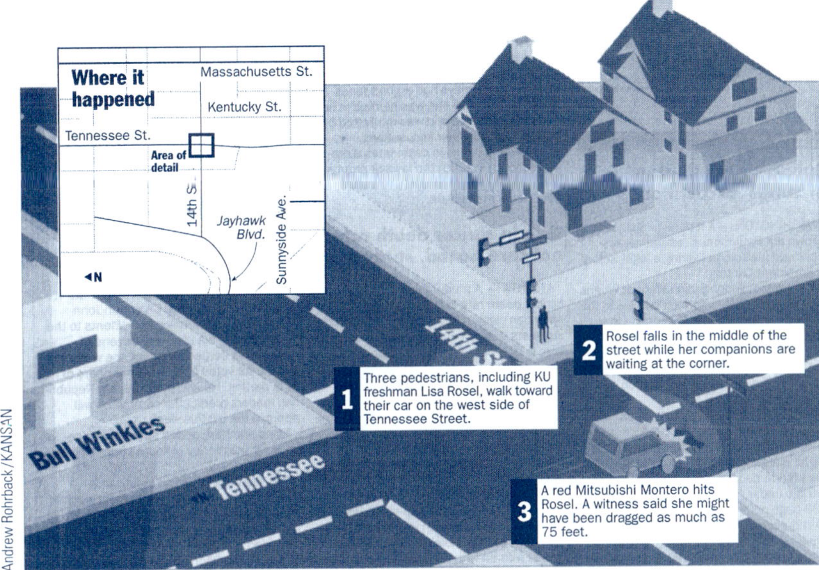

It is the reporter's responsibility to supply the information for those maps. So when you report a story that may need a map, make sure you gather information about the exact location of the event by noting the streets, the number of feet or yards from a spot where an explosion or major crime occurred, or any other crucial information that would help readers visualize the location.

The University Daily Kansan, the campus newspaper of the University of Kansas, used the location map and graphic shown here to accompany a story about a traffic accident in which a student was killed.

Many of the visual elements—such as headlines, boxes of information and summary sentences—are written by copy editors, and decisions about display are made by these editors or by page designers. However, reporters are expected to plan photos for their stories and to provide information for some of the graphics.

When a chart, a graphic or a facts box will accompany your story, you need to consider whether the story needlessly duplicates information that could be presented visually. So in the writing process, don't just think about information to put into your story; think also about information to pull out for visual devices.

Examples of Basic News Stories

The following examples will show you how elements of the basic news story fit together. The first example is a standard news story with a summary lead. The story is organized in inverted pyramid form, giving the most important information first and the rest in descending order of importance. This story contains most of the basic news elements described in this chapter:

Thousands gather on Capitol steps for animal rights

By Joan Mower

The Associated Press

Summary lead: who, what, when, where, why

WASHINGTON—Thousands of animal rights activists rallied in the nation's capital yesterday, seeking to promote the humane treatment of animals in the wild, on farms and in research laboratories.

Backup for lead, with differing opinions about crowd size

U.S. Capitol Police said an estimated 24,000 people attended a rally on the steps of the Capitol after a one-mile march down Pennsylvania Avenue under sunny skies. Organizers said more than 50,000 people from around the country showed up.

Elaboration

Marchers chanted, "Animal rights—now." Many carried banners and placards with pictures and slogans saying things such as "Fur Is Dead" and "Animals Have Rights, Too." Some brought their dogs.

Background

Organizers said "March for Animals"—the first event of its kind—was a milestone in a movement they said was once viewed as outside the mainstream.

Among the groups participating were the American Society for the Prevention of Cruelty to Animals, People for Ethical Treatment of Animals, the U.S. Humane Society and the Doris Day Animal League.

Peter Linck, coordinator of the march, said the ultimate goal of the animal rights activists was to stop the use of animals in scientific research. However, he conceded it was unlikely the public would adopt that stance.

Impact

"In the meantime," he said, "we want to improve the condition of animals and promote alternatives to reform society."

Elaboration

The event attracted a wide variety of animal supporters, Linck said. They ranged from those who want protection of species, such as elephants, to those seeking to end medical testing on animals. Many were seeking changes in the way animals are raised for slaughter, as well as a ban on fur clothes.

Reaction: balance from different points of view

Health officials are particularly sensitive about efforts to end animal testing, a move they say could be disastrous for science.

Health and Human Services Secretary Louis W. Sullivan has criticized the animal-rights advocates who use violence and intimidation to block testing of animals.

"They are on the wrong side of morality," he said last week.

Sullivan said some of the greatest advances in medicine, such as the cure for polio, never would have been achieved had animals not been used in tests.

Ending: future action

Participants in yesterday's march planned to lobby Congress today in support of bills that deal with animal issues.

The next example is a basic news story with a softer lead that stresses the impact of the story. The nut graph gives the crucial information. It states the problem, the "so what" of this story. Attribution is limited in the beginning because the backup for the lead is factual: a law that has been enacted. However, note that quotes and opinions are attributed.

ETHICS

Ethical dilemma: What do you do if a source tells you not to quote him or her at the end of or after an interview but before you go to press or on the air?

Ethical values: Decency, fairness, accuracy, responsibility to readers and sources, credibility.

Ethical guidelines: The decision is more difficult when sources want to withdraw their quotes after you conduct an interview. Try to avoid this situation by making it clear at the start of your interview that you want your source to go "on the record." If you still encounter a source who wants to retract a quote, you can negotiate with the source, or you can insist that you have a right to use the information because you identified your purpose clearly. But that may not help you. Here are some questions to consider when asked to withdraw a quote:

- Are you being fair to your source?
- Are you being fair to your readers?
- Are you jeopardizing your credibility if you print the quotes against the source's will?
- Are the quotes essential to your story?

These are tough decisions. You can read more about what constitutes "on the record" and "off the record" or "not for attribution" in Chapter 5, "Interviewing Techniques."

Throw the book at them

Deck head
Law could lead to arrests for overdue library books

Soft lead
BOSTON—Drop the novel. Step away from the car. You're under arrest for having an overdue library book.

Nut graph: what, why, when, so what, impact and background
Starting Thursday, overdue books could land you in police custody. A new law would allow the arrest of library scofflaws if they had received notice that their books were 30 days overdue.

The law also raises the maximum fine for an overdue book from $50 to $500.

Elaboration
Although the law makes no provision for an overdue book, it allows for up to five years in prison and a fine of $25,000 for the theft of library property worth more than $250.

Reaction
Gregor Trinkaus-Randall, a collection management consultant for the Massachusetts Board of Library Commissioners, said librarians needed tough enforcement tools.

Attribution for quote
"Any library book that is not returned therefore has to be replaced by the library, and that is money out of the town's pocket that could be spent on other materials," he said.

David Linsky, a defense lawyer in Cambridge, criticized the measure.

More reaction
"I think the police are having enough trouble chasing down murderers and rapists without having to keep up with people who have overdue library books," he said.

Linsky said that the law allowed the arrest of library scofflaws without a warrant, something that could not be done with an offense such as assault and battery. He said the measure was unenforceable.

Ending: reaction quote
"If the police are told by an employee of the library that you have an overdue library book, then the police can arrest you in any public place and put the handcuffs on you," he said. "That's the real horror show of this thing."

The Associated Press

Quotes and Attribution

Good quotes can back up your lead and substantiate information in your story. In addition, good quotes let the reader hear the speaker. In a broadcast story, sound bites take the place of quotes. They add drama and interest to your story in both media. But boring quotes can bog down stories. If they repeat what you have already said, it's better to paraphrase or eliminate them.

Susan Ager, a columnist and writing coach for the *Detroit Free Press,* said reporters should consider quotes as the spice of the story, not the meat and potatoes. "Readers come to the newspaper the way they come to a party," she said. "They want to talk to interesting people. Long quotes usually are not very interesting."

When to Use Direct Quotes

Here are some guidelines for deciding when to use quotes:

- Is the quote interesting and informative?
- Can the quote back up the lead, the nut graph or a supporting point in your story?
- Ask yourself: Is the quote memorable without referring to your notes? If so, it's probably a good quote.
- Do your quotes repeat your transitions? Could the quote or the transition be eliminated?
- Can you state the information better in your own words? If so, paraphrase.
- Does the quote advance the story by adding emotion, interest or new information?
- Are you including the quote for your source or for your readers? That is the most important question of all. The readers' interests always take priority.

Here are some types of quotes to avoid:

- Avoid direct quotes when the source is boring or the information is factual and indisputable. For example, a city official who says, "We are going to have our regular monthly meeting Tuesday night" is not worth quoting directly.
- Avoid any direct quote that isn't clearly worded. If a government official says something in bureaucratic language that you don't fully understand, ask for clarification and then paraphrase.
- Avoid accusatory quotes from politicians or witnesses of a crime. If you intend to include any accusations, get a response from the person accused. A direct quote does not save you from libel. If police or other criminal justice officials make accusations in an official capacity, you may use direct or indirect quotes, providing that you attribute them carefully.

- Avoid quotes that don't relate directly to the focus and supporting points in your story. Some of the best quotes a source says may have nothing to do with your focus. It's better to lose them than to use them poorly.

How to Write Quotes

On the surface, writing quotes may seem easy: You just write down what somebody else has said. But in reality, you must observe the following guidelines if you want to use quotes correctly and effectively:

- Always put commas and periods inside the quotation marks: "There are no exceptions to that rule," the professor said.
- A question mark and other punctuation marks go within the quotation marks if the punctuation refers to the quoted material; otherwise, they go outside the quotation marks: He asked, "When does the semester end?" Who said, "I hope it ends soon"?
- Each new speaker must be quoted in a separate paragraph:

"Never place quotes from two speakers in the same paragraph," Professor Les Polk said.

"Even if it's short?" Janet Rojas asked.

"Yes," Polk answered.

- Don't attribute a single quote more than once. If you have two quoted sentences from the same speaker in the same paragraph, you need only one attribution:

"You must study your Associated Press Stylebook," the professor said. "You will have a test Tuesday on material in the first 30 pages."

- "When the quote is two or more sentences in the same paragraph, attribute it after the first sentence," Carol English said. "Don't make the reader wait until the end of the paragraph to discover who is speaking."
- Attribution in the middle of a quote is acceptable but not preferable if it interrupts the thought:

"It isn't the best way," he said, "to use a direct quote. But it is all right if the quote is very long. However, it's better to put it at the end of a complete sentence."

- Don't tack on long explanations for the quote. If the quote isn't clear by itself, paraphrase. For example, avoid the following:

When asked how he learned about the fire at his apartment complex, he said, "I heard the news on the television."

Just as bad:

"I heard the news on the television," he said when asked how he learned about the fire at his apartment complex.

Instead, introduce the quote with a transition:

> He was at a friend's house when the fire broke out at his apartment. "I heard the news on television," he said.

- Limit the use of partial quotes. They are acceptable when the whole quote would be cumbersome, but too many partial quotes make a story choppy. And the reader wonders what was left out. If you follow a partial quote with a full one, you must close the partial quote:

> McDonald says he sees the government as "weak and inept" and fraught with "major-league problems."
>
> "There's a crisis in our leadership," McDonald says.

- Limit the use of ellipses, which are sets of dots that indicate part of the quote is missing. Use three dots for the middle of a sentence, four (one of which is the period) for an ellipsis at the end of the sentence. Use the ellipsis when you are condensing whole quotes or long passages from which you delete several sentences. It's useful for stories about speeches or excerpts from court rulings. Be careful not to leave out material that would change the speaker's meaning.

When to Use Attribution

All quotes must be attributed to a speaker. In addition, you need to attribute information you paraphrase.

Plagiarism Copying the words of other writers is plagiarism, a cardinal sin in journalism. Even if you paraphrase information you receive from other publications, you are plagiarizing if you don't attribute it. Plagiarism is grounds for dismissal at most news organizations. If you take information from written or online resources, make sure you attribute it. Here are some guidelines for material you need and don't need to attribute:

- You don't need to attribute facts that are on record or are general knowledge:

> The trial will resume tomorrow.

> A suspect has been arrested in connection with the slaying of a 16-year-old girl in Hometown last week.

- You don't need to attribute information that you observed directly:

> The protesters, carrying signs and chanting songs, gathered in the park.

- You don't need to attribute background information established in previous stories about the same subject:

> The defendant is accused of killing the three Overland Park women whose bodies have never been found.

- You do need to attribute information you receive from sources if it is accusatory, opinionated and not substantiated and if you did not witness it—especially in crime and accident stories. However, you don't always have to attribute everything in the lead. The following statement is factual, so no attribution is needed:

  A 2-year-old girl escaped injury when a mattress she was sitting on caught fire and engulfed the studio apartment in flames at Wheatshocker Apartments.

- Attribution is needed here, however, because the cause of fire is accusatory and the amount of damage is speculative:

A 2-year-old girl playing with a lighter started the fire at the Wheatshocker Apartments near Wichita State University that caused about $400,000 in damages, fire authorities said Thursday.

"She was just kind of flicking it, and she caught the bedding on fire," said fire Capt. Ed. Bricknell.

The Wichita *(Kan.)* Eagle

Wording of attributions For most hard-news stories, the word *said* is preferable. Although there are many synonyms for *said,* they make the reader pause. *Said* does not. Don't worry about overusing the word.

- Strictly speaking, *said,* the past tense, should be used if someone said something once. If someone always says the same thing, use *says,* the present tense. However, that rule is very restrictive. You could also just use *said* for most hard-news stories and use *says* for feature stories (if *says* seems appropriate to the context). In either case, keep the tense you choose throughout the story; if you start with *says,* continue using it for the rest of the story.

- Avoid substitutions for *said,* such as *giggled, laughed* or *choked.* It's almost impossible to giggle, laugh or choke at the same time you are speaking. If you want to convey the emotion, write it this way: "I'm going to try out for the circus," she said, laughing.

- Use *according to* when you are referring to inanimate objects: "*according to* a study." It is acceptable to say "*according to* police" but not preferable. People talk. Use *said* or *says* when you attribute to people; *according to* is vague.

- Normal speaking order is preferable. You should place *said* after the name or pronoun. If the person has a long title, *said* can be placed before the name and title.

  Awkward: "Normal speaking order is preferred," said the professor.

  Preferable: "Normal speaking order is preferred," the professor said.

Overview attribution This is a technique that allows you to attribute information to one speaker for several paragraphs without attributing each statement or each paragraph. It is useful when you are giving a chronology of events, as in a police story. But if you change speakers, you need to use attribution for the new speaker. Overview attribution is a brief statement followed by a colon.

> Police described the incident this way:

> Witnesses said this is what happened:

> Police gave this account:

Second references The second time you refer to a source in your story, use the last name only. If you have several sources—or two sources with the same last name, such as a husband and wife—use the full name again or an identifying phrase:

> James Jones, the director of public safety, was injured in a three-car crash yesterday. Jones was taken to Memorial Hospital, where he was treated for bruises and released.

If you have mentioned several other people and want to get back to Jones later in the story, remind the reader who Jones is by using his title:

> Public Safety Director Jones said he would return to work Monday.

Titles When a person's title is used before the name, capitalize it, as in the preceding example. When it is used after the name, use lowercase letters:

> Police Chief Ron Olin said the crime rate has gone down.

> Olin, police chief of Lawrence, said the crime rate has gone down.

Courtesy titles Most newspapers and TV scripts no longer use courtesy titles—Mr., Miss, Mrs. or Ms.—before people's names. There are exceptions. *The New York Times* and *The Wall Street Journal* still use courtesy titles. Other newspapers use them in obituaries. For general purposes in this book, courtesy titles will be eliminated unless they are contained in examples from newspapers that still use them.

Exercises

1   **Basic news story:** Write a story based on the following information. Write a focus sentence before you start your story. For this story, your focus sentence should be the results of the study. If you want a lead that gets directly to the point, your focus sentence could also be your lead. Once you've written a focus sentence, add a suggestion for visual presentation—a photograph, chart, facts box or other graphic illustration. Decide what facts, if any, should be duplicated in the story and the graphic. Then use the tell-a-friend technique to relate what

you thought was the most interesting information. The following material is based on a story from *The* (San Bernardino, Calif.) *Sun*.

> **Who/what:** A study comparing the death and accident rates of left- and right-handed people.
>
> **When:** Study was conducted last year and was reported in today's edition of the *New England Journal of Medicine*.
>
> **Where:** Study was conducted by Diane Halpern, a psychology professor at California State University at San Bernardino, and Stanley Coren, a researcher at the University of British Columbia.
>
> **Why:** To determine why fewer left-handed people are among the elderly population.
>
> **How:** Researchers studied death certificates of 987 people in two Southern California counties. Relatives were queried by mail about the subjects' dominant hands.
>
> **Backup information:** The following points are not necessarily in the order they should be used in your story.

The researchers found that the average age at death for right-handed people was 75, for left-handed people 66; left-handed people represent 10 percent of the U.S. population; right-handed females tend to live six years longer than left-handed females, and right-handed males live 11 years longer than left-handed males; left-handed people were four times more likely to die from injuries while driving than right-handers and six times more likely to die from accidents of all kinds.

Halpern said, "The results are striking in their magnitude." Halpern is right-handed. She said her study should be interpreted cautiously. "It should not, of course, be used to predict the life span of any one individual. It does not take into account the fitness of any individual." Left-handed women die around age 72; right-handed women die around age 78. Left-handed men die about age 62; right-handed men die about age 73.

"Some of my best friends are left-handed," Halpern said. "It's important that mothers of left-handed children not be alarmed and not try to change which hand a child uses," she said. "There are many, many old left-handed people." "We knew for years that there weren't as many old left-handers," Halpern said. "Researchers thought that was because in the early years of the century, most people born left-handed were forced to change to their right hands. So we thought we were looking at old people who used to be left-handed, but we weren't. The truth was, there simply weren't many left-handers left alive, compared to right-handers."

"Almost all engineering is geared to the right hand and right foot," Halpern said. "There are many more car and other accidents among left-handers because of their environment."

2   **Reaction story:** Interview at least three students on campus who are left-handed. Ask them what problems they encounter because they are left-handed. Using the study in Exercise 1 as a focus for your story, write a reaction story with the students' comments. Make sure you get the full names of the students, their majors and year of study (freshman, sophomore and so on) so you can identify them properly in the story.

3   **Find the focus:** Using your local newspaper, find the focus paragraph (the nut graph) in news stories on the front page and local-news pages.

4   **Online focus exercise:** Access an online news site for your community or for a national source, such as *www.cnn.com* or *www.msnbc.com,* and discuss the following points:

- Do the headlines and/or summary blurbs clearly identify the main point of the story?

- Compare the online headlines of major news stories in two online sites.

- Which headlines entice you to click into the story? Why?

- How long are the average online headlines?

- Do summary blurbs add or detract from your interest in reading the full story? How much information should the summary blurb reveal about the story? What type of summary blurbs do you prefer: a single sentence, a paragraph or a few paragraphs?

5   **Quotes and attribution exercise:** Check the appropriate column to indicate whether attribution is or is not needed:

	Not		
Needed	*Needed*		
☐	☐	**a**	Two leading figures in the growing national debate about political correctness on American college campuses will be at the University of South Florida in Tampa tonight.
☐	☐	**b**	Dieting doesn't work for the vast majority of people.
☐	☐	**c**	A 40-year-old woman went berserk in her ex-boyfriend's apartment early Monday, shooting him to death with seven shots from two guns.
☐	☐	**d**	Members of a local gay rights group protested Thursday in support of a gay University of Tampa student's efforts to take an Army ROTC class.
☐	☐	**e**	City council members voted unanimously Thursday to increase city fines for prostitution.
☐	☐	**f**	A York College sophomore died early yesterday after drinking at a dormitory party.
☐	☐	**g**	Alumni members of Skull and Bones, an all-male secret society at Yale University, have voted to admit women.

6   **Enterprise:** Attend an event on your campus, and write a basic news story about it. (Look in your campus newspaper or your university's online site for a list of activities that will take place during the week, or check bulletin boards for notices of activities.) Talk to friends about other story possibilities. Here are some other possible topics for a news story at the start of the semester: a new course, problems that students are having enrolling in certain courses, a new club or organization on campus, a student support group.

7   **Class reunion feature:** This exercise will give you practice gathering and writing quotes. The scenario: Imagine you are attending a class reunion of your

department 25 years from now. Interview your classmates in small groups, and rotate among the groups so you get comments from at least five different students.

Ask them their age and occupations, and make sure you spell their names correctly. For female students who may be using a married name, include their maiden names if they were unmarried when they graduated. Even though you should never make up quotes, for this exercise students can use their imaginations about their future careers, but they must give the same information to everyone who interviews them.

Write the story as though you were a reporter for a local newspaper. Do not use first-person (*I* or *we*); pretend you were an observer, not part of the reunion. Give the time and place— somewhere in your school— and the number of students attending the reunion. Try a creative lead focusing on one interesting person.

Then use a nut graph: She (or he) was one of _____ students attending a class reunion of (your school). Try to get as many complete quotes as you can.

8   **Online textbook quiz:** How well did you understand this chapter? Access the Web site for this chapter and take the online multiple-choice quiz.

<table>
<tr>
<td>

Featured *News Scene* Assignment

Access *News Scene* at *http:// communication.wadsworth.com/ newsscene2* to view the news simulation titled "Bank Robbery," and write a basic news story based on the information provided.

</td>
<td>

</td>
</tr>
</table>

Coaching Tips

Imagine yourself as an eyewitness at the scene of the story you are covering. How would you describe the situation if you were being interviewed?

Using all your senses, record the sights, sounds, smells and other details you can observe when you are reporting. Use concrete nouns; avoid adjectives.

When you are gathering information, ask yourself what vivid action verbs could describe your observations.

Does your idea have a strong news element so that you can answer the question "What's new?"

Does your story pass the "so what" test?

Have you searched the Internet for story ideas about your topic?

CHAPTER 3

Curiosity and Story Ideas

Martha Miller, magazine writer and editor

The blood spots made the difference.

A woman shot her boyfriend. He fled to a nearby store to seek help, and he died two hours later in a hospital.

It was just a basic news story for Martha Miller, then a police reporter. But when she went to the scene, she saw the blood spots.

First Miller measured the spots with a dime. But they were larger than that. So she tried a nickel. That fit. Then she counted the spots. She wrote a hard-news lead stating that the woman had shot and killed her boyfriend, and in the middle of the story she wrote this:

> Brown, who was shot several times, staggered out of the apartment and down two houses to the Waystation convenience store on Virginia Street— his path easily traceable by 41 nickel-size blood splotches that dotted the sidewalk.
>
> *Martha Miller,* Reno *(Nev.)* Gazette-Journal

Why bother measuring and counting the blood spots? "I was curious," says Miller, now a magazine writer and editor for *Better Homes & Gardens.* "I saw them and I wanted to follow where they led. I wanted to show how he fled and that he was dripping blood. I wanted the reader to picture that."

The technique is one you learned in kindergarten: Show and tell.

Curiosity

A good reporter also possesses a trait you had in kindergarten—curiosity.

You probably badgered your parents with questions: What's that? Why?

Those are still good questions for gathering news. Just add a few more: Who, when, where, how and so what?

Most writing teachers tell you, "Show, don't tell." But you need to do both. To show, you need to observe. To show and tell, you need to be curious. You need to ask questions the reader will want answered in the story.

How do you know what questions to ask, what to observe and report? Start with the basics:

Who: Get the full names of people involved, complete with middle initials, and always check the spelling. A person named "John" might spell it Jon or other ways. If your source is known by a nickname, write the full name on the first reference and put the nickname in quotes after the first name. Ask your source how he or she prefers to be addressed. Use the last name on second reference except for children.

What: Get an account of what happened. In some stories, especially police stories, you may want to recount the sequence of events. You don't have to write the story chronologically, but you need to understand the sequence.

When: Note the day and time of the event. If you are writing a story for the Web, consider writing a time line as a sidebar, which might be linked to the story or placed in a box on the same page.

Where: Get the location. Describe the scene. You may have to provide details to a graphic artist for a location map, so gather specific details about the location.

Why: Understand what caused the event. What was the conflict, and what is the resolution, if any?

How: Seek more information about what happened. How did it occur? In what order did events unfold?

So what: What impact did this event have on the participants? What impact could it have on readers? What makes this story newsworthy or significant?

Now for the harder questions: What does the reader need to know to understand and care about your story? You can't explain the event unless you understand it yourself, and you can't understand it unless you dig for answers. The key is to unleash your curiosity. Here are some techniques for developing your curiosity:

Role-playing: Put yourself in the role of the reader. What makes the story important and interesting? If you were affected by this story, what would you want and need to know?

Imagine that you are a reporter for your campus newspaper. The phone rings. The caller tells you there is a fire and then hangs up. You call the fire department. A dispatcher gives you the address of the fire. It's your address. What are the first questions that come to your mind? If you have a roommate, chances are you would want to know if he or she was injured. Was anyone else in the building killed or injured? Is your cat OK? Was your apartment or room destroyed? What was the extent of the damage? What caused the fire? When did it start? How long did the building burn? Where will residents of the building live if their apartments were destroyed or heavily damaged?

Then you might be concerned about other questions: How long did it take to put the fire out? Were there eyewitnesses? Who called the fire department? How quickly did the department respond? Is this the first time this building has been struck by a fire? Did the building have sprinklers? If so, did they work?

The list could go on. That's the basic concept of role-playing, and it can generate dozens of questions for you in many stories.

Using time lines. Another method of using curiosity to generate questions is pinning down the sequence of events. Start with the present; then go to the past and then to the future. What is happening now? How did this action develop? In what order did the event evolve? What is the next step?

Questions involving time sequence will give you answers for background and chronology in your stories.

Being a detective: Imagine that you are a detective at the scene of a crime, a protest rally or any other event that involves a mystery or conflict. What questions would you ask to solve the crime or the problem? These questions will center on what happened, the motives, the consequences and the clues to uncovering the truth.

Observation

Good writers must be good reporters first. And good reporters observe and gather details with all their senses: sight, sound, smell, and less often, taste and touch. You can use your observation powers in any story—from a fire scene to a county fair.

Mary Ann Lickteig turned an ordinary story about the Iowa state fair into a fun one by observing these details:

Off in an exhibit room, Nancy Pelley, a home economist from Tone Brothers spice company, looked over five cakes. One of them looked back. It had teeth and a tongue hanging out between the layers. "Isn't that something," Pelley mused.

"What category is that?"

It was the Ugliest Cake category.

A green one with gummy worms on top won first place. Eight year old Jonathan Eddy of Des Moines named his entry "Green Mean Wormy Machine."

To satisfy the requirement to include his recipe, Jonathan penciled on an attached card: "I made a cake. I frosted my cake. I made it ugly."

Mary Ann Lickteig, The Des Moines *(Iowa)* Register

The Show-in-action Technique

If you want the reader to visualize your source or the scene, one of the best techniques is to show the person in action. This technique is more commonly used in feature stories with descriptive writing. But it can also be used in hard-news stories or for a soft lead on a news story. Regardless of the type of story, you need good observation skills. Here is an example of the show-in-action technique:

> ST. PETERSBURG, Fla.— On a palm tree at the University of South Florida's St. Petersburg campus, a squirrel munches on an acorn. A few feet below, three students quietly assemble their equipment.
>
> One keeps an eye on the squirrel. One sets up a video camera. Another prepares the bait, a fake, Caddyshack-esque squirrel with a robotic tail.
>
> If the tail is convincing enough, the squirrel in the tree may try to communicate with the robot on the ground. That could provide new clues about what it means when a squirrel bats its tail.
>
> This research, conducted entirely by undergraduates, is part of a new philosophy at USF and in universities across the nation.
>
> *The Associated Press*

Hard News vs. Soft News

You need good observation for both hard-news and feature stories. Although descriptive detail based on observation is more common in feature stories, you can use the same observation techniques in gathering information for hard-news stories. Stories about weather disasters, fires and other events where the scene is crucial lend themselves to descriptive detail based on observation. At a protest, use observation to report what signs the protesters carried and what they were chanting. At a trial, use observation to help the reader see how the defendant and other people in the courtroom reacted.

Here is an example of descriptive detail based on observation by reporters in a hard-news story about a train wreck. SEPTA stands for Southeastern Pennsylvania Transportation Authority, well known to Philadelphians, so this acronym is not defined in this story.

> A SEPTA train crowded with morning rush-hour passengers derailed beneath Market Street yesterday, killing three people and injuring more than 100 others in the underground wreckage.
>
> In what sounded like scenes from a mine disaster, witnesses described flashlights playing in the darkness over knots of terrified victims, a rail car disemboweled by tunnel girders and passengers' cries for help in the damp cold just on the west side of the Schuylkill River.
>
> Amid the subterranean chaos of the deadliest SEPTA disaster ever, doctors wearing green scrubs and firefighters in yellow helmets used knives and power tools to cut flesh and metal in order to free trapped victims, while a policeman asked surviving passengers to pray. . . .
>
> Physicians and paramedics wriggled through the jagged wreckage to inject victims they could barely reach with pain-killing morphine and saline solutions.
>
> *Michael E. Ruane,* The Philadelphia Inquirer

Fact vs. Opinion

You need to use observation to gather facts and details about an incident, but you should not express your opinions about what you saw. In news stories, all opinions, judgments and accusations must be attributed to a source. The only places for reporters' opinions or interpretations are in columns, stories labeled "analysis" or first-person stories, which are usually labeled or preceded by an editor's note.

A few newspapers have been allowing reporters to insert first-person references (*I* or *me*) in feature stories, but that is a technique usually reserved for magazines or weblogs, also known as "blogs," which are personal journals written for the Web. Most newspaper editors insist that the reporter stay out of the story. Although broadcast news can be more personal, reporters do not usually refer to themselves in news stories unless they are responding to questions from the news anchor.

In the previous examples, the writers reported the sights, sounds and smells they observed. Those observations were factual—evidence of conditions that anyone on the scene could have observed. The writers let the readers form their own opinions.

In the following excerpt, the example labeled "Appropriate" is a description from a story about a plane crash. Most of this story is detail based on observation. The second paragraph contains a vivid description of the crash site. Note that an opinion is expressed in the last paragraph, although it is attributed to someone on the scene, not to the reporter. In contrast, the example labeled "Inappropriate" shows how not to write the story. Note the improper use of the first person (inserting the reporter in the story). Opinion that is not attributed to someone else is printed in italics.

Appropriate	**Inappropriate**
A US Air jetliner landing at Los Angeles International Airport collided on the ground with a SkyWest commuter plane Friday night, creating a fiery tangle of wreckage. At least 12 people were killed, 24 were injured and 21 were missing, officials said.	A US Air jetliner landing at Los Angeles International Airport collided on the ground with a SkyWest commuter plane Friday night, creating a fiery tangle of wreckage *that was horrifying to behold.*
Orange flames boiled up from the fuselage, and a huge column of smoke towered over the airport. Spotlights and the lights from police, fire and other rescue vehicles silhouetted the smoldering wreckage against the darkened sky.	*I saw* orange flames that boiled up from the fuselage, and a huge column of smoke towered over the airport. *It was eerie to see* the spotlights from police and other rescue vehicles silhouetting the smoldering wreckage against the darkened sky. *It was a frightening sight*
"It was a sight beyond belief," said Brett Lyles, 23, of San Francisco.	
Los Angeles Times	

Observation to Find Questions

Use observation as a reporting tool, not just as a writing tool. When you observe action or details at a scene, what questions occur to you?

When Martha Miller observed the blood spots, she wondered not only how big they were but also how many there were and how long it took the

ETHICS

Ethical dilemma: You belong to a campus organization that is sponsoring a charity event that you think will make a good story. Should you write the story? Is it a conflict of interest to report and write a story about an organization to which you belong?

Ethical guidelines: The Society of Professional Journalists Code of Ethics says journalists should be free of obligation to any interest other than the public's right to know. Journalists should avoid conflicts of interest, real or perceived, and should disclose unavoidable conflicts.

man to get to the convenience store after he was shot. Details make a difference in your reporting and writing.

Observation for Visual Presentation

When you are at the scene of an accident or an event, many of the basic reporting questions are likely to come to mind. Just as important are ideas for a good photograph or graphic illustration. Does the story need a graphic to explain how something works? Would a photo, graphic or chart eliminate the need for lengthy explanation in your story? What do you see that you would want the reader to see as well? Don't forget to observe locations and pinpoint them by proximity to major streets or specific distances from a site that the artist can interpret and the reader can understand. When you collect information, you need to see your story as well as hear it.

Ways to Find Story Ideas

The basic concepts for news—local interest, human interest, timeliness, unusual events, conflict, celebrity, impact of news events—can generate story ideas. A major national or local news event might be worth a local reaction story. If you are on a college campus, you are surrounded by experts in many fields. Professors can be good sources for national stories that need a local angle or interpretation.

The primary way to get story ideas, especially if you are assigned to a beat, is to contact your sources regularly and ask them what is going on in their workplace. Another way of getting story ideas is to examine records related to your beat, such as government documents.

Many good stories result from curiosity and observation. Have you noticed anything unusual or different on campus or in your community? Photo journalists usually excel at observing people and places for good pictures. An idea for a good photograph might also be an idea for a good story.

The visual concepts are as much a part of the story idea as the verbal concept. Does the story need a photograph, graphic illustration (such as a chart or map) or highlights box? Think about those elements when you devise your story idea.

Here are some other suggestions for ways to find stories:

Brainstorm: Discuss ideas for stories with other students and with people in your community. What topics on campus or in your community are of interest to people? Does anyone have an unusual course, a professor worth a profile or an interest in an organization that is newsworthy? Think of consumer stories—how to get the best buys on books, tips for winter or spring break, and health tips for students, especially during exam periods.

Check databases: Check computer databases of other stories. When you begin a beat or a major story, check for sources and angles in previous articles about the subject in your own publication and in other newspapers, magazines, databases and the Web. Be careful not to copy information or quotes—that's plagiarism—but use these stories for ideas.

Map the topic: "Mapping" is a form of brainstorming suggested by researchers who have studied the functions of the left side of the brain (the logical reasoning part) and the right side (the creative part). It is a process of word association that helps you explore different facets of a topic of interest to your readers. Draw a circle or a trunk of a tree for the main topic, and list the related ideas as spokes or branches—or just write a list.

For example, you might want to explore whether tuition is increasing. Tuition is the topic in the center of the circle or on the trunk of the tree. The related topics might be the effects on out-of-state students, where the money goes, a comparison to other colleges and so on. Once you have generated several ideas related to the main focus, you can eliminate the ideas that don't seem worthy of a separate news story.

Another topic for possible mapping is a holiday. How many ideas can you devise for stories related to Thanksgiving, spring break or Valentine's Day?

Try this technique with the weather. If your area has had floods, hurricanes, tornados, earthquakes or an extended drought, think of all the people, businesses and other groups affected by the weather. The diagram on page 54 shows how the topic of floods could be mapped.

Assume other points of view: This technique is similar to mapping. Take an issue and role-play to discover how other people might think about it. Does that process give you an idea for a feature or a profile about someone who is affected by the issue? If the state cuts funding to your university, how are students, programs, departments and related campus activities affected?

Another potential source of ideas is special interest groups. What groups of people don't get much coverage in your newspaper? Do minorities on your campus have concerns that could generate news stories?

What problems do elderly residents in your city have? Do women's groups in your school or town have special problems and interests that would make good ideas for news? What are the needs of people with disabilities? Do veterans in your community have special needs that are newsworthy? Do you have an active gay rights group on campus? Contacts with members of these groups can generate dozens of story ideas.

Observe: Look at bulletin boards on campus or in local government offices. Look around your city. Are there new stores or buildings that are worth

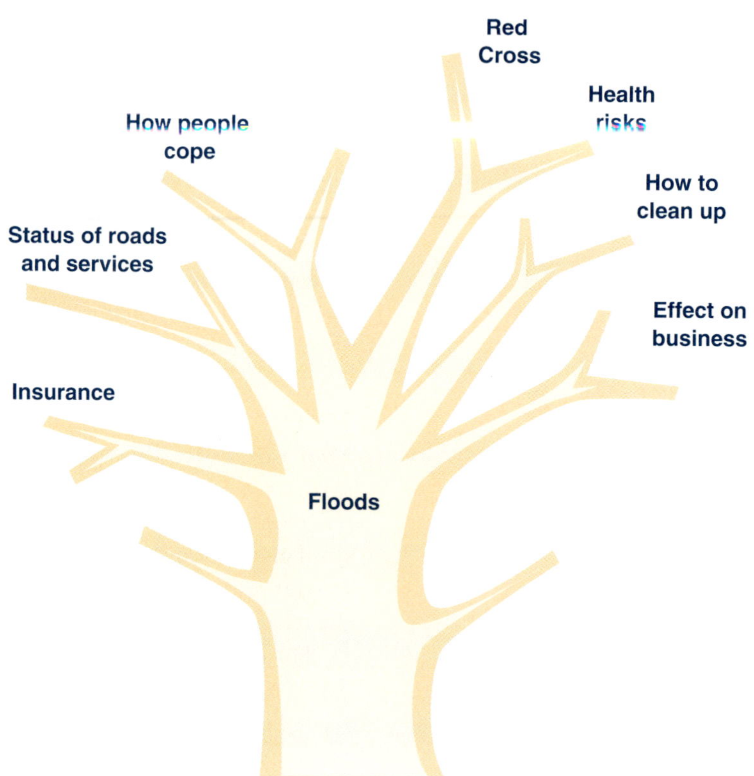

telling the reader about? Are there old buildings, landmarks or stores that are closing, such as a famous hangout? Does anything make you curious? Do you notice something new on campus or in the community? Is there a program or event that might be newsworthy?

Talk to people: Ask your friends what interests them. Eavesdrop at lunch to find out what people are talking about. When you are out in the community, ask people what they read in newspapers or view on television or the Web and what they would like to read.

Check directories: Universities and many government agencies have directories listing departments and personnel. Do any people, places or programs seem newsworthy? Does your school directory list organizations or departments that sound unusual or worthy of a feature?

You could also check the yellow pages of your telephone book for ideas about interesting services and places. For example, how many escort services are advertised in your city? In Fort Lauderdale, Fla., the yellow pages list more than 20 escort services. Dan Lovely, a Florida newspaper editor, wrote an investigative story about escort services when he was a reporter at the *Sun-Sentinel* in Fort Lauderdale. He began by checking out the escort services in the phone book, and through interviews and documents, he found that some of the escort services were fronts for a prostitution ring.

Read local newspapers and watch local TV news stations: Does a news story suggest angles that could be developed into a separate story? Does it name people who could be profiled? Sometimes the best feature stories are offshoots of a breaking news story.

Is there a larger story to be developed from a news event? If an apartment building in your community or a campus building is cited for fire safety violations, is there a larger story about fire inspections or problems with apartments, especially in areas that rent to students?

When a big story breaks in your community, are there experts or other people affected by the problem who would be worth a separate story? For example, if the teachers in your town are on strike, consider all the different people who are affected. Is there an expert on campus or in your city who is worth a feature because of his or her views on the issue?

Almost all major stories affecting your community—such as disasters, strikes, crimes and court rulings—need follow-up stories to explain the next step or action resulting from the issue.

Read classified advertisements: Look for unusual items. An advertisement in a campus newspaper about services to provide term papers could make a good investigative story. Other ads about adoption, unusual research offers or new services could generate news stories. Also look in the lost and found column. Is there a human interest story behind a lost pet or other item?

Patricia Rojas, a former reporter for *The Des Moines* (Iowa) *Register,* was scanning the classified section of her newspaper when this ad caught her attention:

> LOST WARRIOR, blue tick Coonhound, male, stupid but friendly.

"When I saw 'stupid but friendly,' I had a feeling there was a good story behind this ad," Rojas said. There was. The dog had wandered two blocks from home and couldn't find his way back. It turned out that the dog had led a difficult life. One time he was stolen from his owner, Lisa Volrath of Des Moines, and he nearly starved after his captor abandoned him. This time he was luckier. Someone found him and took him to an animal shelter. Rojas ended her story with this quote from Volrath after she had recovered her dog:

> "I could tell from his stupid expression that he was my dog," Volrath said.

It was just a little story, but people enjoy reading about dogs, cats and other pets. And Rojas said her editors appreciated her initiative in finding the story.

An advertisement for a lost pet cobra turned into a fun story for another reporter. This story could be broadened into a feature about unusual pets.

Localize national news: Is there a national story that you can apply to your area? What are the local angles? What are the reactions of people in your community? National elections, tragedies, terrorism, war and other national events can all be localized by focusing on people in your area who are affected. In many cases when a natural disaster occurs in another state, people from your community might volunteer to help, so check churches and local agencies to find out if there is a local angle.

Seek profiles: Is there a person who is in the news or someone who should be in the news because of his or her accomplishments? Is an expert mentioned in a story worthy of a separate profile?

Can you find stories about people who have accomplished something special, triumphed over adversity, or experienced pain or joy in relation to a news event? Or can you find stories about people who represent a particular aspect of a news event? Such stories often make good human-interest features.

If you are writing for a campus newspaper, you can find many people to profile, including new professors, retiring professors or campus employees and staff members who provide important functions behind the scenes.

Read letters to the editor and feedback on Web sites: You can get many story ideas from the problems and reactions that people express in letters to the editor in print or online forums.

Track programs and events: Check your campus Web site for upcoming events, speakers and scheduled entertainment. Is there a campus or government program that would be of interest to your readers? Is it a new program? Is an old program approaching an anniversary? Has it been effective or ineffective? Is there a program that a private citizen or group is trying to establish? Is the program related to the season or to an event in the news? For example, does your university have a program affected by budget cuts?

Holidays, news events and anniversaries of major news events also make good features. Plan ahead and think of stories related to these topics.

Good editors and reporters in all media keep tickler files, which are organized by weeks or months to remind them about stories that should be followed. When you are reporting, especially on a beat, you should start your own tickler file so you can remind yourself about stories you should follow. You could start a computerized tickler file listing the months and story ideas that need updates during those months.

Rewrite news releases: Government agencies, organizations in your community and campus organizations issue news releases about events. These news releases often contain ideas for features. If you are assigned to cover a specific beat, ask the key sources to send you any news releases they issue.

When you use a news release, remember that it is not a balanced news story. It is written by an advocate for the organization. Even though you may copy information in the release without plagiarizing, you should always check the information. You also should try to contact sources listed in the release and seek other sources to confirm, deny or give other points of view.

If the news release contains quotes, you may use them, but it is better to get the comments directly from the source. If you can't, you should attribute the comments to the release—for example, "the chancellor said in a prepared statement" or "according to a news release."

Follow issues and trends: Are there problems on campus or in your community that reflect national problems? Do any local news events reflect a larger problem? For example, if four women have been attacked on campus in separate incidents, is there a larger story about rape on campus or lack of security?

When you write issue stories, make sure that you have a narrow focus. A topic such as AIDS or homeless people is too broad. Focus the story on one aspect of the problem. You might do a story about the growing number of AIDS cases on your campus or a story about how your city is or isn't handling the problem of caring for AIDS patients. Or you might do a story about an aspect of the homeless problem in your city, such as an increase in the number of homeless women with children.

Be curious and concerned: These qualities, above all, will lead you to good stories.

The Internet

The Internet has exerted a profound influence on the way reporters and editors in all media are gathering story ideas. Almost all online media sites post feedback questions or polls attached to stories or major issues. These responses can generate ideas for follow-up stories.

Discussion groups on the Internet are another venue for gathering story ideas. Reporters join various discussion groups to read messages that online users post. Some of those messages may spark ideas for news stories. In other cases, reporters may post questions to a discussion group to gain ideas about topics. Before using responses from these discussion groups in a story, however, the ethical approach is to contact the people who posted the messages to seek permission to use their comments for publication and to check the accuracy of the messages.

Weblogs: Also known as "blogs," these are personal essays or journals that have proliferated on the Web in recent years. Some blogs are written by reporters who give their "behind-the-scenes" or personal views of an event, while other blogs are posted by people who just want to express their thoughts. Blogs may generate story ideas because they express problems or thoughts about which people are concerned.

Be careful about quoting or using information from blogs in a news story. Although some blogs may contain factual information, they are unedited journals or essays that do not have to adhere to principles of journalistic credibility. Because they are not checked for accuracy even if they are written by journalists, blogs have spawned a controversy in the media over whether they can be considered journalism. Regardless, they are a popular form of expression on the Web. Jonathan Dube, a journalist who authors a comprehensive site called *Cyberjournlist.net,* lists more than 150 blogs by journalists and

MULTIMEDIA COACH

- Use the Internet for ideas, but do not copy information from a Web site without attributing it to the source. That's plagiarism. Ideas are not copyrighted, but the information on the site is protected by copyright laws even if the site does not have a copyright symbol or notice.

- If you refer to an online source, The Associated Press Stylebook recommends that you cite the URL (the Internet address) at the end of your story.

- Use a search engine to find ideas. Type in the topic and surf. The most popular search engine is *www.google.com.*

dozens more by news freelance writers. You can also use a blog search engine such as *http://www.blogsearchengine.com,* where you will find blogs grouped by topics such as politics, health and travel.

Search engines: The ability to search the Internet by topic provides an incomparable way of gaining story ideas. Suppose you are writing a story about Halloween or another holiday. Click on your search button and type in "Halloween," and from the Google search engine alone, you will retrieve more than 8 million Web pages containing information and ideas about this holiday. Other search engines will generate more ideas, angles and background for stories. The Internet also provides access to thousands of online news sites. By surfing through such news sites, you can gain story ideas about issues that you can tailor to your community.

Idea Budgets

Some story ideas are assigned by editors, but most editors expect reporters to provide their own story ideas, especially if the reporter covers a beat. The daily "story budget" contains a brief description of each story planned for the next day's newspaper, TV news show or online news site. Each budget item, or "budget line," begins with a "slug" (a one-word title) and is followed by a few sentences describing the story. Many news organizations also use a planning story budget, describing story ideas for the week and long-range stories.

The budget line is also a tool to help you focus your ideas. As you write your budget lines, you should be keeping the focus—the "so what" factor—in mind. Your budget line is your way of selling the story idea to your editor, so you need to make it sound like an essential news story or a compelling idea.

To write a budget line, give your story a slug, and describe the idea in a paragraph or two. Include potential sources and possibilities for photos or graphics. Here's an example of a budget line by Buddy Nevins, a reporter who covered the transportation beat for the *Sun-Sentinel* in Fort Lauderdale, Fla.

Pedestrians: Broward has one of the highest rates of pedestrian deaths in the nation. One problem is that the roads haven't been designed for pedestrians, and many don't have sidewalks or crosswalks because of a lack of money. What is being done to solve the problem?

Graphics: Charts, maps of worst roads

A good budget line should summarize the main point of your story. It will also give you a head start in writing your lead or nut graph.

Exercises

1   **The dart method:** This idea comes from Alison Plessinger, Ph.D., an assistant professor at Slippery Rock University. It's like playing a game of darts except that wherever the dart lands on a map, you write a story about that place. Here's how it works: Take a large campus or community map pasted to a corkboard, and throw a dart at the map. Using that area of town or campus, write a story about someone or something in that area. For example, Plessinger says, you could go to the room or apartment where you lived as a freshman and interview the current occupant. Or you could use the campus or local phone directory and select a name at random to write a profile about the person. The concept, she says, is that everyone has a story to tell. Plan a backup of a few names in case the first person you contact is not available or willing to talk to you.

2   **Role-playing for curiosity training:** You have lent your car to a friend. You find out that your friend has had an accident with your car. Write a list of questions that come to your mind. Now add any questions you might need to answer to make the incident a news story. Write a list of the sources you would contact.

3   **Description for observation training:** Describe in detail some statue, painting or special landmark at your school.

4   **More description for observation training:** Without looking at the person next to you, write a brief paragraph describing what he or she is wearing and everything else you can remember about the person's appearance.

5   **Show-in-action technique for observation training:** Write a descriptive paragraph about a professor, a relative or a good friend. Use the show-in-action technique to describe the person's mannerisms, characteristic expressions and other details.

6   **Observation:** Describe the office of a source you have interviewed or of a professor you confer with frequently. List at least 10 items that are memorable. Do not include such standard items as desk and bookcase.

7   **Graphic exercise for observation training:** Imagine that a rare painting was stolen from a museum on your campus or in your city but was discovered the next day in a recycling bin or large trash receptacle on your campus. Go to that

site (choose any area containing a large bin), and collect all the information you can for a location map or graphic illustration describing exactly where the painting was found. Write a list of information that you would give to an artist so he or she could draw a location map. Make sure that you include nearby streets, the number of feet or yards from a recognizable spot, dimensions of the garbage bin and other details you think would be helpful to the artist. Then, using your own directions, draw a location map to test whether you have gathered good information.

8   **Create a mood piece or scene:** Go to some favorite or interesting place on campus or in your community (a park bench, for example), and observe the surroundings and people. Use all your senses. Write a few paragraphs or a brief essay creating mood as though you were describing the scene for a feature news story or a short story. Include dialogue if you overhear people speaking or any other details that might help create the mood. If you use a demonstration or rally for your observation exercise, write a feature story about the event.

9   **Field trips:** Talk to people on your campus and in your community about what they read or don't read in the campus or local newspaper and what kinds of stories they would like to see in their newspaper.

10   Look in your local newspaper for ideas for profiles. People used as sources might be interesting subjects for a separate story. Pick at least three names of people who might be newsworthy to interview.

11   Read the classified advertising section of your newspaper, and look for items that could generate stories of human interest, new businesses, trends or unusual news.

12   Write a story budget with three ideas for stories you would like to cover. Identify some sources you would interview, and consider photo or graphic possibilities. Use the story budget format in this chapter, or modify it as you or your instructor wishes.

13   Take a walking tour of your campus or your community (individually, in small groups or as a class). Write as many story ideas as you can based on your observations.

14   Localize a news story based on a national issue. For example, localize a story about the problems and legal issues of gay marriages or gays in the military. How would you localize your story, and whom would you contact?

15   **Enterprise:** Write a news story from one of your story ideas. If you are still having trouble, consider a story about an upcoming holiday. You might get some other ideas if you check the office of institutional research at your college or university for any studies the office has done, check some club sports that don't regularly get covered in your campus newspaper or check clubs and support groups on your campus or in your community. Who are some of the people behind the scenes who perform valuable services in your community? You could do profiles such as a day in the life of a postal carrier, the city clerk, a sanitation worker or other people in service jobs. You might also check news releases on your school's Web site to gain story ideas of interest to your community.

Featured Online Activity

Access the Chapter 3 resources at *http://communication.wadsworth.com/rich5e* to link to "Curiosity and Story Ideas: A to Z."

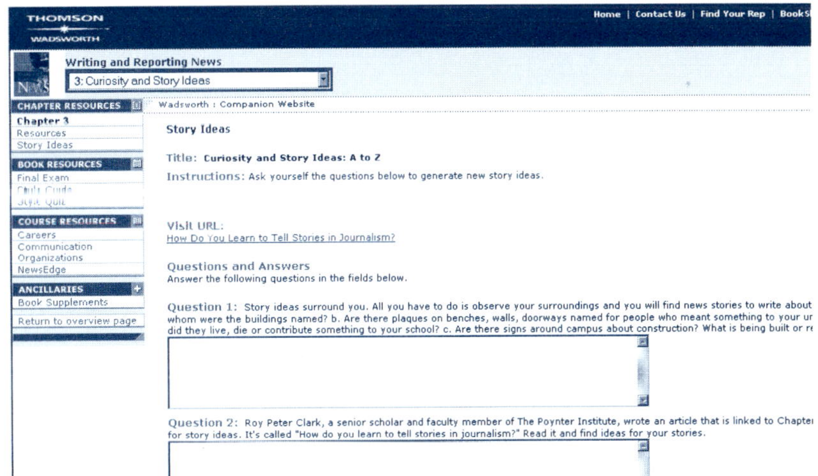

Coaching Tips

Use the matchmaking technique: Ask one source to recommend another one who is knowledgeable about the subject you are researching.

Check newspaper clips or databases before you begin your reporting.

Check any records or documents related to your story.

Check the Internet for information about your sources or topic.

Check the credibility of Web sites before you use information from them. Does the site date its information, attribute sources, list authors, and provide e-mail and/or telephone contacts?

Sources and Online Research

Mark Potter calls his source book his "bible." He takes it with him everywhere. It is a 7-by-9-inch address book, so worn that it is held together by sturdy strips of packing tape. Potter, a reporter for NBC, says he couldn't function without his source book. It is so crucial to his job that he keeps a duplicate in his home.

Potter cross-indexes his source book three ways: by the source's name, occupation and location. If he wants to contact an FBI agent he once interviewed in Detroit but whose name he may have forgotten, Potter looks up the agent's name under *FBI* or *Detroit.* Under each listing, Potter records the source's addresses and telephone numbers for work and home.

Getting the home phone numbers is not always easy, especially for police officers, who keep their numbers unlisted. So Potter asks for the information this way: "How can I reach you in the off hours?" That way, if the source does not want to reveal a home number, he or she can give an option of another way to be contacted, Potter says. It avoids placing a negative tone on the interview.

Potter and many other reporters also note in their source books some personal information, such as sources' birthdays, favorite pastimes or anything else that would be helpful to remember.

It's not too early in your career for you to start a source book. The people you interview in college, such as professors who are experts on foreign policy or the economy, may be good sources for stories later in your career. If you are creating your source book in your computer or personal digital assistant, be sure to back it up on a CD-ROM or other storage device. And although it may seem old-fashioned in these days of digital devices, it's a good idea to have a printed copy of your source book.

A good reporter needs people to interview and written sources, such as public records. But how do you get sources, and how do you know which ones to use for a given story?

CBS News made the mistake of using documents it could not verify when it aired a story on "60 Minutes Wednesday" about President George W. Bush's military record. The incident created a huge credibility problem and embarrassment for the network. During Bush's 2004 re-election campaign, Dan Rather reported that Bush received preferential treatment when he was in the Texas Air National Guard in 1968 to 1972, based on

Mark Potter, NBC reporter (third from left)

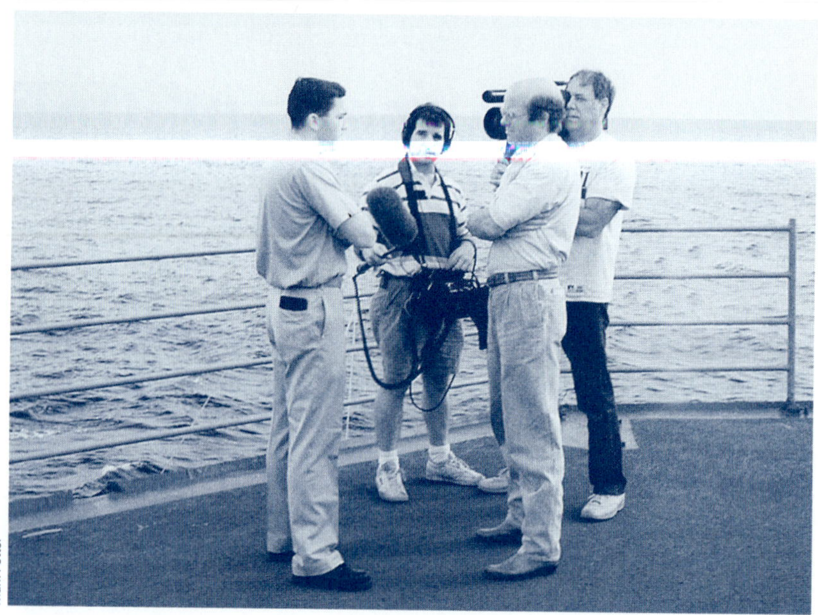

documents CBS had obtained. But the documents—photocopies of four memos allegedly written by Bush's squadron commander, who had died in 1984—could not be authenticated. Shortly after the segment aired, blogs were posted claiming that documents had to be forged because the typography (font and character spacing) were created on a word processor that did not exist on typewriters used in the 1970s, when the documents were supposedly written.

CBS originally backed the story, but after much press coverage about the controversy, Dan Rather apologized and admitted there were problems with the documents. An independent panel appointed by CBS to investigate the story concluded that the documents could not be verified and that the story had been rushed onto air without adequate checking and without enough interviews of people who might have corroborated the allegations in the memos. CBS fired the segment's producer and three executives, and Rather resigned as anchor of CBS News a few months later, although he did not tie his resignation to the scandal. This case is discussed more thoroughly in Chapter 13, "Accuracy and Media Law." So even when you get written sources and public documents, you need to check their accuracy and conduct interviews with several sources.

Human Sources

Newswriting needs human sources to make the story credible and readable. Information from eyewitnesses and participants lends immediacy to a story, and direct quotes make a story interesting. You can find human sources in a number of ways.

Newspaper files: Before you begin reporting for any assignment, your first step is to check the clips and do online research. There you can find the names of people cited in previous stories about the subject. All newspapers have reference libraries, which used to be called "morgues," where clips of stories that have been published in the paper are stored. Most print and broadcast newsrooms these days store names of articles or video in online databases so that it is easier to search for previous stories. You can also find human sources on the Internet in news groups and discussion forums or simply by using a search engine. If you are searching for a source by name, check to make sure that the source is the person you want; many people have the same name, and the information you retrieve may not be for the correct source.

When you are assigned to a breaking-news event, such as a fire or accident, you may not have time to check previous stories before you leave the office. But you should check them before you begin writing. The building that burned may have had problems with sprinkler systems or previous fires in the past.

The same recommendation applies to crime stories. A suspect arrested on charges may have been arrested previously for the same or other charges. If you find a story about a suspect's previous arrest, make sure that you find out if the charges were dropped or what happened in the case.

Use caution: Newsroom files may not be up-to-date, and follow-up stories may not have been written about crime suspects. Even more problematic is the Web, which can archive everything, but if the document is not dated, you may not be getting the most accurate information. (More about checking the credibility of Web information appears later in this chapter.)

Use caution as well to avoid plagiarism, claiming information from published sources as your own work. Because the Web makes so much material accessible, plagiarism has become rampant in the media industry. You must attribute information you take from any sources—traditional media or online. If you attribute to an online source, give the name of the site and consider including a link (online) or the site address at the bottom or side of your story.

Sponsorship: Suppose you find a source who is reluctant to talk to you, such as a police official. You can use a technique that Mark Potter calls "sponsorship," getting someone who knows and trusts you to recommend you to the new source.

For example, when Potter was working on a story about the problems of Haitians in Miami, the Haitian refugees were reluctant to talk to him. Many of them were illegal aliens. Potter said they thought he was an immigration official who was seeking to deport them. So he asked a community social worker who had gained the trust of several Haitians to recommend him to one of them. The social worker introduced him to a Haitian named Pierre, but Pierre didn't have the information Potter wanted. However, Pierre said his brother-in-law might help, and Pierre introduced Potter to him. After establishing trust with the brother-in-law, Potter asked him to get other Haitians to talk to him. And that's how he got the sources he needed for his story.

The Gannetteer, Gannett Co., Inc.

You also can use sponsorship as a self-introduction technique when you set up an interview. Give your name and say, "Chief Joe Smith suggested I call you" or "Chief Joe Smith gave me your name." Then explain the purpose for your call.

Self-sponsorship: Nancy Tracy, a former reporter for *The Hartford* (Conn.) *Courant,* was in trouble. She was working on a follow-up story about three people who survived when the Mianus River Bridge collapsed and their vehicles plunged into the river. But a key source, Eileen Weldon, wouldn't talk to her or anyone else in the media. Weldon had severe injuries and was tired of press coverage.

So Tracy tried self-sponsorship, a way of recommending herself. "I'm going to send you some clips of other stories I have done to show you that I am a very sensitive reporter," she told Weldon. "Please read them. I'll call you in a few days. If you don't think I can be fair, I won't ever bother you again." Tracy got the interview. Her clips "sponsored" her.

Matchmaking: You have found a source, and you are interviewing her or him. But you want the names of other sources for the story. Try "matchmaking," a form of sponsorship. Ask the source who else might know something about the subject or have an opposing point of view. Who else is involved in the issue? Ask how you can reach those people.

Primary and secondary sources: When you are conducting an interview, if your source says something about another person, particularly if it is derogatory or controversial, make sure that you check with that other person. The first source's statements not only could be wrong; they could also be libelous. You should even check out written information about sources to make sure that it is accurate.

In most cases, except when your secondary sources are famous people, such as the president or celebrities who cannot be contacted, do not use someone's name in a story without making an attempt to check with that person.

The up/down principle: If you want to learn how to sweep floors, talk to a janitor, not to the corporation president. The same principle is involved in reporting a story. If you want to get the most accurate and vivid information about a story, talk to the people who were directly involved. Go down the organizational ladder. Contact the police officer who wrote the report (the name is listed on a police report), the researcher who conducted the study or the source closest to an incident.

Another version of the down-the-ladder principle is to be kind to secretaries, often called administrative assistants. Remember their names, and be genuinely friendly. A good secretary can be like a pit bull guarding the boss. If you want to interview an official, your first source is the person who schedules that official's time.

After you have interviewed people down the ladder, go up the ladder of the organization. Who is the next supervisor with responsibility? Who is the official with ultimate responsibility for the department or organization?

You can proceed either way. You can start with a top official and then go to the primary people, or the reverse. In many cases, police officers and people in corporations, government and other bureaucratic organizations will refuse to talk to you until they have authorization from their supervisors. As a result, you may have no choice but to start with the top officials.

Anonymous Sources

Many people will be willing to talk to you if you promise not to use their names. An anonymous source is one who remains unnamed. (The terms "anonymous source" and "confidential source" are used interchangeably by most people.) But should you make this promise? Most editors today would say no, unless there is no other way to get the information. And even then, many editors would refuse to grant that immunity from identification. The more you rely on unnamed sources, the less credibility your story has.

In the past, reporters who promised their sources anonymity had a good chance that they could honor their promise even if they were subpoenaed to reveal their sources. Most news organizations fought any court attempts to reveal sources and often won. But in the last few years, judges in several courts penalized reporters by sentencing them to jail for refusing to reveal their sources. In 2004 *New York Times* investigative reporter Judith Miller and *Time* magazine reporter Matt Cooper were both found in contempt of court for refusing to testify before a grand jury about confidential sources who leaked the name of Valerie Plame, a CIA operative whose identity was jeopardized when her name was first revealed in a column by Robert Novak. Although Novak revealed in his column that the leak came from "senior administration officials," he has refused to say whether he had been questioned about his sources. Cooper wrote a story in *Time* that government officials leaked Plame's name, but Miller never even wrote a story about it.

ETHICS

Ethical dilemma: Should you show your story to a source before publication?

Discussion: Most journalists are opposed to prepublication review by a source because of fears that the source may recant his or her statements or may wish to change the copy. Steve Weinberg, an author of several books and former director of the Investiga-tive Reporters and Editors organization, strongly favors checking the story with a source because, he says, it will ensure accuracy. Other journalists have always favored reading parts of a story, especially technical or sensitive information, back to a source. In most cases, deadline pressure prevents journalists from waiting for sources to review the whole story. But if such review is possible, should it be allowed? What do you think?

Ethical guidelines: Fairness, credibility, accuracy. The Society of Professional Journalists Code of Ethics says journalists should "test the accuracy of information from all sources and exercise care to avoid inadvertent error."

Both reporters' organizations appealed the case to the U.S. Supreme Court, which refused to hear arguments, meaning the case was remanded to the U.S. District Court judge who had ordered the reporters to be jailed if they did not testify to the grand jury. In a complicated turn of events, Cooper's boss at Time Inc. subsequently required him to obey the court order to turn over his notes and e-mails to the grand jury. Cooper then testified to the grand jury after his source, presidential adviser Karl Rove, granted him a waiver from his pledge of anonymity. As a result, Cooper was spared from going to jail.

However, Miller refused to turn in her notes or testify, and she was sent to jail until she would agree to testify or until the federal grand jury term expired, a four-month period. Miller served 85 days of her sentence. She was released and testified to the grand jury after her source released her from her promise of confidentiality.

The case has prompted support for a federal shield law that would prohibit federal courts from forcing reporters to reveal their confidential sources. In 1972 the U.S. Supreme Court ruled that journalists have a duty to provide grand juries information relevant to criminal trials. Since then, all states except Wyoming offer some protection of journalist–source privileges either by shield laws or precedents from case law, but these state statutes do not apply to federal courts.

In another case, WJAR television reporter Jim Taricani of Providence, R.I., was convicted of contempt of court for refusing to reveal his source for a confidential videotape he received about an undercover FBI investigation even though the source identified himself. Taricani was sentenced to six months of home confinement; he decided not to appeal the sentence. He served four months of the sentence, and the judge then released him.

Despite the problems with anonymous sources, it's unlikely that news organizations will eliminate them altogether. If you must use anonymous sources because you have no other alternative, you should check the information with other sources, preferably ones who will allow use of their names, and check documents. Many sources, named or unnamed, have their own agenda and want to manipulate reporters so the sources can promote their cause. For fairness and balance, it is crucial for reporters to check with other sources to confirm, deny or provide other points of view.

When using unnamed sources, you may identify the person with a vague reference, such as "according to one official." Or you might give the person a pseudonym, a false name. Although most editors discourage pseudonyms, they are sometimes allowed in feature stories about sensitive subjects such as rape. But they are rarely used in hard-news stories. It is preferable to use no name or a first name only. If you use a full-name pseudonym, which is not preferred, you should check your local telephone directories to make sure that you aren't using the name of someone in your community. And in all cases, to protect the identity of the source you must tell the reader that this is a false name.

Janet Cooke didn't do that. And she touched off a furor in the newspaper industry that persists years after the incident. Cooke, then a reporter for *The Washington Post,* won the Pulitzer Prize in 1981 for a story called "Jimmy's World," about an 8-year-old heroin addict. There was only one problem: Jimmy didn't exist. When she first discussed the story with her editors, she said she had located the child's mother, who was reluctant to talk. Her editors said she could grant the mother anonymity. Cooke turned in a compelling story about the child and his mother. But when Cooke won the Pulitzer and was profiled in newspapers, some discrepancies in her résumé were discovered. That led to questions about her story. She ultimately admitted that she had made up the story about Jimmy and his mother. The *Post* returned the Pulitzer, and Cooke resigned in disgrace.

Cooke's story wasn't based on an anonymous source; it was a fabricated source. The impact was a crisis of credibility for the press. Newspapers throughout the country began developing policies against using pseudonyms, and many editors banned the use of anonymous sources altogether.

Fabrication of sources and other information in news stories surfaced as a problem again in the late 1990s and beyond in several high-profile scandals. Most notorious was the case of Jayson Blair, a reporter for *The New York Times,* who made up quotes, fictionalized scenes and plagiarized material in dozens of the stories he wrote during his four years at the newspaper. His deception was discovered after he plagiarized material from a story written by a Texas newspaper reporter with whom Blair had worked when he was a reporter on the student newspaper at The University of Maryland. Blair never graduated from the school and was hired by the *Times* after his internship there because he showed so much promise. After the discovery of this and other stories that were fabricated or plagiarized, Blair resigned in disgrace, and the *Times* published an extensive Sunday story about his deception.

Blair's trail of fabrication and plagiarism mirrored the pattern of Stephen Glass, a rising star at *The New Republic,* who was fired after his editor discovered that he had fabricated sources in many of his stories. His deception was discovered when a reporter for an online site questioned a story Glass had written about a convention of hackers. The convention didn't exist, nor did the software company cited in the story. Glass even created a phony Web site for the nonexistent software company. A complaint from an online magazine spurred the investigation, which revealed that the article was a hoax, and several others Glass had written were also fiction. A few years later, Glass published an autobiographical novel called *The Fabulist* about a reporter who fabricates stories. The Glass story also became the subject of a movie called *Shattered Glass.*

Both Blair and Glass were reporters in their 20s with limited experience but great promise that landed them these prestigious jobs. On the other hand, Jack Kelley was a veteran reporter with 21 years of experience at *USA Today* when he resigned at age 43, after evidence surfaced that he had fabricated sources. His work was questioned after he submitted a story about a woman who died fleeing from Cuba by boat. The woman whose photo Kelley submitted with the story was a Cuban hotel worker who had neither fled from Cuba nor died. Further investigation by the newspaper revealed problems with numerous stories, including one for which he had been a Pulitzer Prize finalist.

Patricia Smith, a former columnist for *The Boston Globe,* had also been nominated for a Pulitzer Prize. She resigned after the *Globe* discovered that she had fabricated sources and quotes in her columns. In her last column she apologized and explained why she had attributed quotes to people who didn't exist.

"I could give them names, even occupations, but I couldn't give them what they needed most—a heartbeat," she wrote. "As anyone who's ever touched a newspaper knows, that's one of the cardinal sins of journalism: Thou shall not fabricate. No exceptions. No excuses." A few months later, Mike Barnicle, a famous Boston *Globe* columnist, was also fired after editors checked some of his columns and concluded that he had fabricated sources in a column. They also accused him of plagiarizing material from entertainer George Carlin in another column. He denied the accusations and has since been hired as a columnist for another Boston newspaper.

Promises Dan Cohen made the issue of anonymous sources even more complicated. He was a public relations executive. In 1982 he gave reporters from the Minneapolis *Star Tribune* and the *St. Paul* (Minn.) *Pioneer Press* damaging information about a candidate for lieutenant governor in Minnesota on the condition that they would not reveal him as the source. The reporters agreed to grant Cohen anonymity. But editors of the two newspapers overruled the reporters and insisted on printing Cohen's name in the story. The editors decided that since Cohen was working for the opposing political party, the readers had a right to know the source of the information.

Cohen sued on the grounds of breach of contract. He claimed that the newspapers had violated an oral contract of confidentiality and that, as a result, he had suffered harm by losing his job. A jury at the first trial level agreed that a reporter's promise of confidentiality is as legally binding as an oral contract. The newspaper appealed and lost. The case went all the way to the U.S. Supreme Court, which ruled in 1991 that the First Amendment does not protect journalists from being sued if they break promises of confidentiality. The high court sent the case back to the Minnesota Supreme Court for a ruling on damages, and Cohen was awarded $200,000.

Before you agree to grant a source anonymity, you should check with your editors to determine the policies of your organization.

Even when sources agree to be identified, they often ask for anonymity for portions of the interview. They'll say, "This is off the record." Sometimes they aren't even aware of what the term means.

On and off the record Here are some definitions of the terms used most often to establish ground rules in an interview:

On the record: The source agrees that all information can be used in a news story and that he or she can be identified as the source of it. The easiest way to establish this understanding is to identify yourself as a reporter immediately and state your purpose for the interview. If you are interviewing people who are not accustomed to dealing with the media, you may need to remind the source during the interview that you are quoting him or her about the material, especially if you are writing about controversial issues. Such a reminder may jeopardize your chances of using some of the material, but it is better to take that chance during the interview than later in a courtroom after you have been sued.

Off the record: The information from this source may not be used at all. If you can get the same information from another source, you may use it, but you may not attribute it to the source who told it to you off the record.

Not for attribution: You may use the information as background, but you may not identify the source.

Background: This is similar to the term "not for attribution." Generally, it means that you may use the information but can't attribute it. Some reporters define background as the ability to use the information with a general attribution, such as "a city official said." If you are in doubt during the interview, ask the source how you can identify her or him, and give the specific wording you intend to use.

Deep background: This term is rarely used or understood by most sources except for officials in Washington, D.C. It means you may use the material for your information only but may not attribute it at all, not even with a general term, such as "government official."

Multicultural Sources

How you deal with sources is one problem. Which sources you choose is another important factor in gathering news. For example, can you imagine a modern newsroom without women? Do women have different views from men about how news should be covered? Perhaps not, in some cases. But you and your readers will never know if you don't seek women's views.

The same is true for minority groups. The overwhelming amount of news about minorities is negative and promotes stereotypes, according to a series of articles on the subject by David Shaw, media critic for the *Los Angeles Times:* "If all one knew about real-life blacks and Latinos in particular was what one read in the newspaper or saw on television news . . . one would scarcely be aware that there is a large and growing middle class in both cultures, going to work, getting married, having children, paying taxes, going on vacation, and buying books and VCRs and microwave ovens."

And that's the problem. If a racial disturbance were to occur in your community, you would seek the opinions of community leaders representing the groups involved. But would you seek the opinions of African-Americans (the term preferred by many blacks), Latinos and Asian-Americans who are experts in various fields for other stories?

Reporters from *USA Today* do. The newspaper urges reporters to make an effort to get views in all news stories from people of both sexes and various ethnic and racial groups.

"It comes up in every story conference or in every photo/graphic assignment," says J. Taylor Buckley Jr., senior editor at *USA Today.* "If you are doing a story on the new techniques of orthodontia, it's just as easy to find a black kid with braces as a white kid. It's not only the right thing from a standpoint of fairness and equality, it's smart. The opportunities are there, and anyone who fails to exploit them is stupid.

"In the early days of the newspaper, in our effort to just get gender diversity, the editor would tear up pages if they didn't feature women," Buckley says. "If you are looking for authoritative sources on anything, there are people of all nationalities."

A related issue is the identification of people in newspaper stories by race or ethnicity. Almost all newspapers have policies against mentioning a person's race or ethnic background unless it is relevant to the story. To show that it uses multicultural sources, *USA Today* prints pictures, especially in columns containing readers' points of view.

Written Sources

You can find many additional clues for human sources and other information from a variety of written sources.

Telephone directories: The white and yellow pages of telephone books are primary places to locate sources. Most local telephone books also contain information about city and county government agencies, utilities, and other frequently used services. Even though you can find information online, don't forget about some of these standard sources.

Reverse directories: These directories, also called "city directories" or "cross-directories," list residents of a community three ways: by name, address and telephone number. Imagine that you are on deadline and have the address of a woman whose house is on fire and that you want to reach her neighbors for comments. How can you do this if you don't know the neighbors' names? You can look in the cross-directory under the address you have. The adjacent homes will be listed first by address, with names and telephone numbers of the occupants beside the address (unless they have unlisted telephone numbers). If you have a phone number but not the name, check the section for phone numbers.

The reverse directory is one of the most useful ways of locating people for comment when you can't go to the scene. These directories are published by real estate firms in most major communities and are kept in most newsrooms and libraries. Some online search engines, such as *www.reversephonedirectory .com,* will provide the same information.

Libraries: Your local public library and your college library contain a wealth of source material to help you find background about a story. Some of the most useful reference works are The Reader's Guide to Periodical Literature, encyclopedias, almanacs and other books of facts, population data and financial records of major corporations. Many of these resources are also online.

Most college and university libraries also have a section devoted to federal and state documents and publications. In this section you can find transcripts of congressional hearings, publications from federal and state agencies, and reports from all sorts of government offices.

Online Sources

You are writing a story about sexually transmitted diseases among college students. You check the Web for background by typing "sexually transmitted diseases" in a search engine such as *www.google.com.* You will get more than 3 million listings.

The World Wide Web is an essential tool for finding background information. How do you know what information is credible? How can you keep from being overwhelmed? Stephen C. Miller, assistant to the technology editor at *The New York Times,* offers his "trust-o-meter," a technique he uses to determine credibility of Web information. Miller says his first choice is government sources because the information is official and public. For background in the story about sexually transmitted diseases, the National Institutes of Health or the Centers for Disease Control would be considered reliable government sources. Information from national health organizations might also be credible in this case.

Next, Miller likes university studies because they are peer-reviewed, but he says they should be linked to university sites or research journals. He finds personal sites the least trustworthy.

You might still check personal sites for ideas or contacts, but be wary of citing them without checking the information. Even if the information is

MULTIMEDIA COACH

Here is a checklist to help you determine credibility of Web sites and search more effectively:

- **Who:** Is an author, site owner or name of sponsoring organization listed on the site? Avoid unnamed sites.

- **What:** Is the site affiliated with a government agency, an educational institution or a nationally credible organization? Check the site index for an "about us" page for further information.

- **When:** Is the site dated? This is crucial. Use the most current information you can find.

- **Where:** Does the site have any contact information— a phone number, address or names of individuals, not just "Webmaster"?

- **Why:** Does the site have a bias or promotional agenda? If so, either avoid it or get other points of view, and check the accuracy.

- **How:** Narrow your search by typing specific key words instead of a broad topic.

- **Attribution:** Print the information you plan to use so you can document it; sites frequently disappear. Copy the site name and URL (address) for a link or citation. Don't copy anything from a site without attributing it.

---

trustworthy, you can still spend needless hours wading through it if you don't search effectively.

Effective Searching

Narrow your search: Try to be as specific as possible when you type a request in a search engine. For example, if you just want definitions of sexually transmitted diseases, typing those last three words will give you general sites. But if you are seeking rates of these diseases among college students, add rates and college to your search request.

Understand domains: You can guess the address of many sites by using their domain extension. The domain is part of the address that identifies the type of site: *.gov* for government, *.edu* for education, *.com* for commercial, *.org* for organization and *.net* for network. If you were looking for the U.S. Census Bureau, you could guess *www.census.gov,* and you would be correct.

In 2000 additional domain names were added—*.biz* and *.info* for general purpose sites, *.name* for personal sites, and *.museum, .aero, .coop* and *.pro* for community sites—but the primary endings are still the most common.

Find site contacts: If the site doesn't list contact information, you can find who owns or operates the Web site by using "whois" databases. These databases are not inclusive, but they will list owners and addresses of sites registered with a domain server if you type the site name and domain. For nongovernmental sites, check *www.networksolutions.com/cgi-bin/whois/whois.* An even easier way is to use the Whois search engine (*www.betterwhois.com*).

Check state sites: State government sites are good places to seek background information for state-related news. All states with Web sites have a similar address formula: the word *state* followed by the postal abbreviation and *us* for

United States. For example, the state government address for California is *www.state.ca.us.*

If you are writing a crime story or you just want to check a source's background to make sure that the person is not a sexual offender, nearly 40 states have sex offender registries. An easy way to find these registries is to start with your state site. In one case a student in doing a background check on a candidate for the campus student senate found the person on a local sex offender register.

Understand search engines and directories: Search engines will locate sites with the specific words you seek, while directories such as Yahoo! group documents by categories such as news and travel. If you have no idea what kind of information exists in a topic you are researching, you might try a directory.

Use metasearch engines: If you want to save time and find out the responses to your request from several search engines simultaneously, use a metasearch engine. This type of multisearch engine queries several search engines and lists the relevant returns. For information on how search engines work and which ones are the most comprehensive, check *www.searchenginewatch.com.*

Use journalism directories: Several journalists have created Web sites with links to all sorts of valuable resources for the media. From government agencies to businesses and public records, you can find useful sources without scouring the Web yourself. For example, the Investigative Reporters and Editors organization has a Web site with links to topics for numerous beats in its resource center: *www.ire.org.* One of the most complete sites is "A Journalist's Guide to the Internet," *http://reporter.umd.edu,* created by Christopher Callahan, former associate dean of journalism at the University of Maryland and now dean of the journalism school at Arizona State University.

Find experts: From anger management to zoo animals, an expert on almost every topic is willing to provide information to journalists. You can find these experts easily in *www.yearbook.com,* a site created to provide journalists with expert sources. Profnet (*www.profnet.com*) is another site devoted to serving journalists with expert sources throughout the world. Designed for professional journalists by PRNewswire, this resource should be used for publications, not for term papers.

Find a map: If you are seeking directions to a location for an assignment or for personal use, use a mapfinder such as *www.mapsonus.com, www.mapquest.com* or any other maps linked to most search engines. They will pinpoint the location and even provide you with driving directions.

Find press releases and wire services: Check *www.prnewswire.com, www.prweb.com, www.uwire.com* (for college wire stories) or *www.businesswire.com* (for business news).

Build an online source book: When you find sites that you plan to use frequently, bookmark them. But computers can crash, and you may lose your bookmarks. You should also build a source book with the names and URLs of your most helpful sites just as you would create an address book for your favorite sources. When you interview people, make sure that you ask for their phone numbers and e-mail addresses, and add them to your source book.

Find media jobs and internships: Job sites abound, but if you are seeking a job or internship in the media, you will find opportunities faster by checking media organizations such as PRSSA (Public Relations Student Society of America), RTNDA (Radio-Television News Directors Association), ASNE (American Society of Newspaper Editors) and minority media groups.

Find people: Almost all search engines have yellow and white pages where you can search for people's phone numbers, addresses and e-mail addresses. However, many of these are inaccurate. Although it's still worth a try if you are trying to locate a source, it's best to ask sources for their e-mail addresses and phone numbers when you interview them.

Use e-mail and discussion groups: Several media discussion groups that send messages to your e-mail are good ways to find sources in your field. You have to subscribe to these groups, but most are free. It's best to "lurk" for a while and read the messages before you post your own so that you can understand the nature of the discussions. Most media discussion groups involve professionals, so you should take care not to post questions about research you could have done yourself. You'll find links to media discussion groups for American and Canadian groups at *www.journalismnet.com.* Julian Sher, a Canadian investigative journalist who created the site, gives tips on how to search for sources and even how to spy on people in news groups or chat groups. He suggests going to Google's news groups, selecting a topic and clicking on the name of the person who sent the message. Other sources for media news groups are listed on Christopher Callahan's Web page under list-servs (*http://reporter.umd.edu/listserv.htm*).

Usenet is a group of more than 30,000 public discussion forums to which anyone may post a message. In many cases, people don't use their real names on these groups. They are not as credible for sources, but you can find topics and people in *www.google.com* under "groups."

Databases

A database is a collection of information. The term now generally refers to massive collections of information stored in computers. Many newspapers subscribe to databases containing newspaper and magazine stories compiled by a commercial company.

For daily news stories such as meetings, local events and other breaking news, checking a database is too time-consuming. But when you are seeking background for an in-depth story or feature, databases are worth checking. For instance, if you are working on an in-depth story about date rape on college campuses, a database check would be helpful. By reading other stories, you can get ideas for an angle on your story or find expert sources to contact.

The best way to learn how to use a database is to go to the library and ask for assistance. Each database has a different set of instructions; many include charges for use. One of the most popular databases for newspaper and magazine writers is NEXIS, a collection of newspaper, business and trade sources. It is available in some libraries but often with restrictions for users. LEXIS, the other part of this service, contains the text of court decisions, legislative records and legal resources. It is available in most law libraries. It is also available online for a fee.

Many other databases contain only an abstract (a summary) of the article in a journal, newspaper or magazine. You still have to look up the paper or microfilm version to see the entire article.

Public Records

Many government records, such as data from state and local agencies, may be obtained from databases consisting of public records. Access to such records has spurred a type of reporting called "computer-assisted journalism." Using software programs that have sophisticated mathematical tools, reporters have been able to do complicated searches and analyses of huge banks of data that they would not be able to do with paper records. For example, if you want to find out who earns the highest salaries in each department at your university or college, you could spend days sifting through a printed version of the budget and trying to compare salaries. But if the budget is available on a database, you can use a computer program to analyze this information for you in minutes. However, a large database can still be time-consuming to interpret, which is a deterrent to computer-assisted reporting at some publications.

The hardest part of using such databases may be convincing public officials to release the computerized records. You may have to file a request under the Freedom of Information Act (which is explained later in the chapter). That is what Mike McGraw and Jeff Taylor did to receive 8.2 million records about farm programs from the U.S. Department of Agriculture. With the help of their newspaper's database expert, Gregory Reeves, they spent 16 months analyzing those records and conducting hundreds of interviews, which resulted in a seven-part series about abuses in the USDA. They won the Pulitzer Prize for their efforts.

Although the statistical results were dramatic, McGraw stresses that computer-assisted reporting is only one tool in gathering information for a good story. He says it is crucial for reporters to do old-fashioned, face-to-face interviewing as well. For his series, he traveled to meat plants for on-site observation and personally interviewed scores of inspectors and other officials.

Other Public Records

An official at your university tells you that there are no serious fire safety violations on campus. But you want to be sure, so you decide to check the state fire marshal's report on the last fire safety inspection of campus buildings. The report may list many violations that the official might not have deemed serious. Records on paper or in computer form are valuable information sources.

Not only do such records as fire and police reports provide detail about investigations; they also give names of people to contact. When police officers investigate an accident or a crime, they fill out reports with details of the scene and crucial information about the people involved, including names, addresses, birth dates, physical descriptions and other material. Most of the records are public.

The following list mentions just a few of the public records that should be available to you locally. In addition, government offices in your state capital contain records from all state agencies, including your college if it is state-owned. Federal offices in a state capital contain many records of federal agencies and of federally funded programs in your locale. The location of these records varies from city to city, and access may also vary.

Political contributions: To check campaign contributions to candidates for state offices, you can access a searchable database for each state at *http://www.followthemoney.org.*

Real estate records: Mortgages, deeds (which record the property owners, purchase date and sale price in some states), the legal property description, indexes listing previous property owners, and commercial property inventories (lists of everything the commercial property owner has, such as trucks, supplies and equipment) are available in the Register of Deeds office. This office also has maps showing all the property in the county and individual maps called "plats," which show the zoning of each piece of property. Records for tax rates and the assessed value of the property are located in the county assessor's office. If you don't have a property description or know what property your subject owns, the county clerk's office has a listing of who owns what. Some states post property records online.

Voter registration records: These records, located in the county clerk's office, list the person's political party if he or she is a registered voter, as well as the person's address and date of birth. They also list telephone numbers. In some cases, people who have unlisted telephone numbers may have listed their numbers on these records.

Fish and game licenses: These are also recorded in the county clerk's office.

Salaries of county employees: The salaries are listed by position only (usually not by employees' names) in the county clerk's office. In some counties or cities, names may be included.

County government expenses: These can also be found in the county clerk's office.

Corporate records: Articles of incorporation, which list the officers of the corporation and the date the company registered with the state, are very useful if you are trying to find out who the company officers are. Articles of incorporation are located in the Register of Deeds office or in the state office that regulates corporations.

Court records: Filings in all civil and criminal court cases, except juvenile cases, are open to the public. They are located in your county courthouse.

Military records: You can find out the details of individuals' military service in the Register of Deeds office in some municipalities, but only for people who registered for military service in that county. Otherwise, you have to file a request under the Freedom of Information Act to the individual branch of the service.

Personal property loans: If a person has taken out a loan of more than $1,000 or has used credit to buy something worth more than $1,000, such as a stereo, the information could be on file under the Uniform Commercial Code listings kept in your county courthouse. Some states also have these listings online.

Tax payments or delinquent tax records: These records are kept in the county treasurer's office.

Motor vehicle registrations: These records and the personal property tax are on file in the county treasurer's office.

Building inspection records and housing permits: These are available in the city's building inspection and housing department. Also available are all the complaints that have been filed against a property owner, which are useful for stories on substandard housing. This office also has records on all permits issued for construction or building improvements.

City commission meeting records, local ordinances and resolutions: The city clerk's office keeps these records.

City expenses: Information about purchase orders, accounts payable, the inventory of city agencies, budgets, expenditures and the like are available in the city's finance department. Records of purchase orders and accounts payable are extremely useful if you are investigating the expenditures of any city department or the actions involving any contract the city has with a vendor or builder.

Public works records: Plans for public works projects—such as sewers, traffic signals and traffic counts—should be available in the public works department of your municipality.

Fire department records: These include records of all fire alarms, calls (including response times), fire inspections, and firearms owners and registration (which may be in a different location in some cities). Also on file, but not available to the public, are personnel records, including pension records and other items of a personal nature. However, salaries are public record. These are in the fire department or in your city or county clerk's office.

Police records: Criminal offense reports, statistics of crime, accident reports and driving records are in the local police department and the sheriff's department. Records of ongoing investigations are generally not available to the public.

Utility records: Water records—such as bacterial counts, water production, chemical usage and other items pertaining to the city's water and sewage operations—are available in the city utilities department.

School district records: Almost all information pertaining to the expenditure of public school funds—including purchase orders, payroll records, audits, bids and contracts—is available from the school district. Personnel records of employees are also available in limited form. Names, addresses, home phone numbers, locations of employment, birth dates, dates hired and work records are available, but information about employee work performance and other personal information is not public. Information about students, other than confirmation that they are enrolled, is not public.

The Freedom of Information Act

The Freedom of Information Act was established by Congress in 1966 to make federal records available to the public. It applies only to federal documents. In addition, the act allows for several exemptions that prohibit the release of documents. Records classified by the government because their release would endanger national defense or foreign policy are exempted. So are certain internal policies and personnel matters in federal agencies, as well as a number of records involving law enforcement investigations. If an agency refuses to release documents you have requested through the FOIA, you may appeal the decision.

In many cases, the document you request comes with information blacked out or cut out. Some documents look like paper doll cutouts by the time they are released. Another drawback to using the FOIA is that it is time-consuming. Although an agency is required by law to respond to your request within 10 working days, delays are common.

However, many reporters have found the FOIA invaluable. The documents they have received have led to major investigative stories, such as the series by Mike McGraw and Jeff Taylor discussed earlier.

Before you file an FOIA request, try the direct approach: Ask the agency for the records. You might get them. If you must file a formal FOIA request, it is a good idea to check first and make sure that you are contacting the appropriate agency for your request. You can access an interactive sample FOIA letter generated by the Reporters Committee for Freedom of the Press at *http://www.rcfp.org/foi_letter/generate.php*. See page 81 for a print version.

For questions or more advice, you can call the libel and FOI hotline, 24 hours a day, seven days a week: 800-F-FOI-AID. You can also access a complete online guide to the FOIA through the Internet:

Freedom of Information Center: *http://web.missouri.edu/~foiwww*
FOI Resource Center: *http://spj.org/foia.asp*

Sample Freedom of Information Act request

[Date]

[Agency head or Freedom of Information Officer]
[Agency]
[City, State, Zip Code]

Freedom of Information Act Request

Dear [FOI Officer]:

This is a request under the federal Freedom of Information Act.

I request that a copy of the following documents [or documents containing the following information] be provided to me. [Identify the documents or information as specifically as possible.]

In order to help determine my status to assess fees, you should know that I am [suitable description of the requester and the purpose of the request, such as

• A representative of the news media affiliated with the newspaper (magazine, television station, etc.), and this request is made as part of news gathering and not for a commercial use

• Affiliated with an educational or noncommercial scientific institution, and this request is made for a scholarly or scientific purpose and not for a commercial use

• An individual seeking information for personal use and not for a commercial use

• Affiliated with a private corporation and seeking information for use in the company's business]

[Optional] I am willing to pay fees for this request up to a maximum of [dollar amount]. If you estimate that the fees will exceed this limit, please inform me first.

[Recommended] I request a waiver of all fees for this request. Disclosure of the requested information is in the public interest because it is likely to contribute significantly to public understanding of the operations or activities of government and is not primarily in my commercial interest. [Include a specific explanation.]

Thank you for your consideration of this request.

Sincerely,

[Signature]
[Your name]
[Address]
[Telephone number]
[Fax number]
[E-mail address]

When you file your request, be sure to write "Freedom of Information Request" on the envelope and on the letter. You do not have to explain your reason for the request. The agency may charge copying and processing fees, but if you are not using the material for commercial purposes and the material is likely to contribute to an understanding of government operations, you may be entitled to a fee waiver.

You can use a form letter for your request. The sample shown here is recommended by the Society of Professional Journalists. If you prefer to be contacted by mail, omit your telephone number.

Exercises

1 **Reverse directory:** Imagine that the mayor of your town or another city official has disappeared. You want to talk to members of his or her family and to the neighbors. Find the missing person's telephone number in the cross-directory or an online search engine such as *http://www.reversephonedirectory.com.* Now find three neighbors you could interview by using the street address searches.

2 **Databases:** Select a topic for a feature story about an issue on your campus, such as date rape, racial tensions on college campuses, alcohol bans, political activism or such health issues as sexually transmitted diseases among college students. Now check the Internet or go to your library and use a database to find stories about your topic. Make note of any national experts on the subject and any statistical material or reports you would find helpful in your story.

3 Get copies of a police report, a university study, or any other report that has been released at your school or in your community. Make note of the primary sources (officers, investigators or researchers) you would contact.

4 Conduct a record search of a person, preferably a politician or other person in your community who owns property. Your task is to construct a paper-trail profile. Try to find out all you can about the person without ever talking to him or her. However, you may drive by the person's home to observe the property and include that information in your report. Write the profile based only on records and observation. You may be surprised how much you can write. Here are some suggestions for records that should be available to you:

- Land records, which should include a complete description of the person's house
- Court records of criminal and civil suits, possible marriage or divorce, or even birth records
- Delinquent tax records
- Corporation records for ownership of personal property or corporation papers (if applicable)
- Records of voter registration, auto registration and tax liens
- Educational background, including curriculum vitae for university employees
- Financial disclosure (for politicians)

Check the Internet by conducting a search for your source.

5   Write a Freedom of Information Act request for some information from a federal agency that funds a program in your school or community.

6   **Enterprise:** Write a story about the people for whom buildings or landmarks on your campus are named. Using your campus library, check the archives to find the background of these people. Then conduct interviews with students who use these buildings, or who live in them if they are residence halls, and find out how much or how little the students know about these people. In the clips, try to find interesting anecdotes about the namesakes and reasons for naming the buildings for them.

Featured Online Activity

Access the Chapter 4 resources at *http://communication.wadsworth.com/ rich5e* to link to interactive online scavenger hunts.

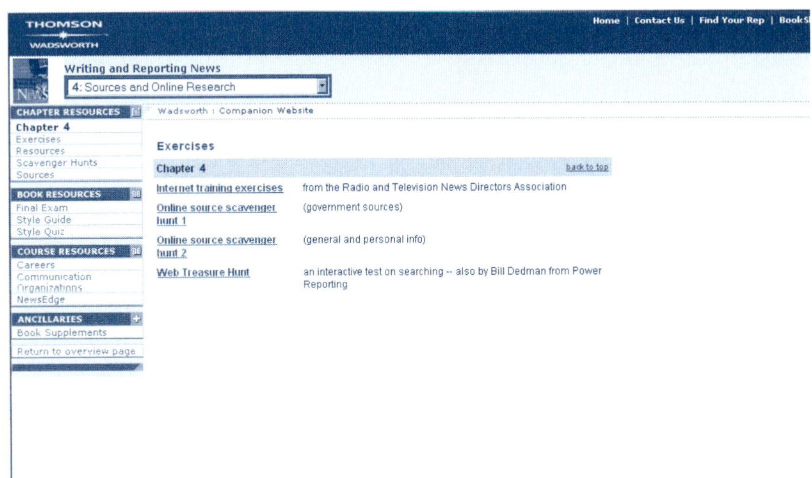

Coaching Tips

Write your observations in your notes; include specific details.

Mark the information in your notes, such as quotes and facts that you plan to use when you write the story.

When interviewing athletes or people who have been interviewed frequently, try to find a new angle or a question they haven't been asked.

Always check the spelling of the source's name and the wording of job titles.

Ask the follow-up questions "why" and "how," and ask sources to give you an example.

Gather details for graphics.

Get information an artist would need to draw a map or other illustration. Details will make your writing more vivid as well.

Interviewing Techniques

Barbara Walsh, reporter

Barbara Walsh says one of the "stupidest" things she ever did almost ruined the interview that led to a Pulitzer Prize. Walsh had tried for months to get an interview with convicted murderer William R. Horton Jr. Finally, his lawyer gave her permission. She walked into the jail, met Horton and learned a painful lesson.

Horton was serving two life sentences plus 85 years in a Massachusetts prison for the murder of a gas station attendant and a subsequent crime he committed while out of prison on a furlough (a brief stay in the community). He broke into the home of a Maryland man, slashed him repeatedly and raped his fiancee twice.

Walsh, then a reporter for the *Lawrence* (Mass.) *Eagle-Tribune*, faced Horton through the window that separated them. "The first question I asked was 'How the heck did you get out on furlough?' It was the stupidest thing I've ever done," she says.

Horton wanted to terminate the interview. Walsh salvaged the interview with Horton by switching to something he wanted to discuss.

"I asked him, 'What do you want to tell me?' And he said, 'I'm not a monster. You people (the press) have made me out to be a monster,'" Walsh says.

The interview then went on for two hours, and eventually Walsh returned to the tough questions she wanted to ask Horton.

The story was one of a series about the Massachusetts furlough program that earned Walsh the Pulitzer Prize. Walsh, who later worked at newspapers in Fort Lauderdale, Fla., and now is a reporter in Maine, says she was lucky that Horton talked to her, but she learned a valuable lesson about interviewing techniques: "Save your tough questions for last."

She still asks tough questions—but at the end of the interview. "I've learned to be real slow and real patient," she says. "I'm more inclined to let people talk longer. You may not use all the information, but you can offend them if you rush." Walsh says the key to good interviewing is good listening. "In interviewing, if you are sincere and the sources know that you have compassion, they're going to talk. A lot of the skill is just being open to what they have to say."

But when sources are reluctant to answer her questions, she rephrases the questions and asks them again—sometimes three or four times—as in the following story about women in a Florida prison. "I asked one of the female inmates on death row, 'What's it like to sit there and know the state wants to electrocute you?' She skirted the question the first time. I asked it three times during the interview." Eventually Walsh got the answer. "If you ask—not in a cold way, but sincerely ask what was it like for you—they'll answer." The result was this revealing portrait (also notice how Walsh weaves in her own observations):

Kaysie Dudley spent two years on Death Row meditating and learning more about how the state was going to kill her.

"I did a lot of research on what they were going to do to me," Dudley says. "It was very morbid, but I wanted to know." Dudley, 28, was sent to Death Row at Broward Correctional Institution in 1987 after she was convicted with her boyfriend of strangling and slicing the throat of an elderly Clearwater woman.

"My boyfriend killed her," Dudley says. "I held the woman in my arms as she took her last breath. It was a terrible experience." As she talks, Dudley sits in the cafeteria of the women's prison, nervously rubbing her fingers together, her nails raw and bitten to the quick.

From her neck hangs a small silver cross.

It is cool, and Dudley wears a black sweater over her state-issued aqua dress.

"I wasn't afraid of dying," Dudley says. "But I didn't like to think about electricity running through my body. . . ." After spending two years on Death Row, Dudley says, she feels she has suffered more than enough.

"I was 22 when they locked me up in there," she says. "I feel like in a way they've already killed me. It took me almost a year to get my facial expressions back, my emotions, my ability to laugh.

"I was a zombie when I came out of there," she says, absently twisting her hair with her constantly moving fingers.

Barbara Walsh, (Fort Lauderdale, Fla.) Sun-Sentinel

Although Walsh usually takes notes, she says a notebook can be threatening. She waits until she has established rapport with her source before she opens her notebook. And she rarely uses a tape recorder—too unreliable and threatening, she says.

Her advice to student reporters? Don't overlook anyone as a source. "When I go to the courthouse, I consider anybody who talks as a source—from the janitor to the people who sell coffee. These are real people who may not be high-priced attorneys, but they know what is going on. Reporters narrow their sources too much."

Walsh certainly didn't narrow her sources for a recent series she wrote. She interviewed more than 700 families, doctors, police officers, and social workers and reviewed more than 4,000 pages of state, federal documents and databases for a five-part series in the *Portland Press Herald/Maine Sunday Telegram* about the effects of poverty on children in Maine's rural towns. Despite those thousands of statistics, Walsh humanized the plight of the children by her intensive reporting and use of details as in this story about a 16-year-old girl who was abandoned by her mother:

It was the dolls that she wanted. The porcelain dolls her mother kept in the china closet. Delicate faces, their eyes painted black, lashes long and lacy, their dresses, puffy, purple and pink, tiny princesses.

It was the dolls that Jillian Higgins remembers most in the trailer where she lived. The dolls and their beauty stark against the inside of a trailer filled with trash, dog feces, floors covered with everything "you can imagine."

"My mom had these dolls she got for every birthday from the time she was like 5 till she was 17," she says. "They were so cool and I wanted them, I always wanted them. I'm not sure why."

Barbara Walsh, Portland Press Herald / Maine Sunday Telegram

Gathering Details

Like Barbara Walsh, Edna Buchanan won a Pulitzer Prize—in her case, as a police reporter for *The Miami Herald.* Buchanan recounts one of her mistakes when she didn't ask the right question. Now an author, Buchanan offers this advice in her book *The Corpse Had a Familiar Face:*

> What a reporter needs is detail, detail, detail.
>
> If a man is shot for playing the same song on the jukebox too many times, I've got to name that tune. Questions unimportant to police add the color and detail that make a story human. What movie did they see? What color was their car? What did they have in their pockets? What were they doing the precise moment the bomb exploded or the tornado touched down?
>
> Miami Homicide Lieutenant Mike Gonzalez, who has spent some thirty years solving murders, tells me that he now asks those questions and suggests to rookies that they do the same. The answers may not be relevant to an investigation, but he tells them, "Edna Buchanan will ask you, and you'll feel stupid if you don't know."
>
> A question I always ask is "What was everybody wearing?" It has little to do with style. It has everything to do with the time I failed to ask. A man was shot and dumped into the street by a killer in a pickup truck. The case seemed somewhat routine—if one can ever call murder routine. But later, I learned that at the time the victim was shot, he was wearing a black taffeta cocktail dress and red high heels. I tracked down the detectives and asked, "Why didn't you tell me?"
>
> "You didn't ask," they chorused. Now I always ask.

Sensitivity

The way you deal with sources can differ, depending on whether they are public or private individuals. Because public officials are accustomed to dealing with the media, you have a right to expect them to talk to you. Private individuals do not have to deal with the media, and you need to operate with more sensitivity when interviewing them. If a public official utters an outrageous quote, it's fair game. When a private individual does, you could remind the person that it will be published and make sure that the source will stand by the comment. Although many reporters believe that once they have identified themselves as members of the media, anything in an interview is fair game, reporters who display extra sensitivity usually end up with more information.

All sources, public and private, want to be portrayed well in the media. Many sources, especially public officials, will manipulate reporters by revealing only information that furthers their cause. As a result, reporters need to be aware of the source's bias and ask probing questions that go beyond what the source wants to reveal. It is also crucial to check the information and seek alternative points of view.

Listening and Note-taking Skills

Truman Capote knew how to be a good listener. He didn't take notes during his interviews for his book *In Cold Blood.* Nor did he use a tape recorder. He was convinced that a notebook or a tape recorder would inhibit his sources. "People would reveal themselves, he maintained, only in seemingly casual conversations," wrote his biographer, Gerald Clark.

With his childhood friend Nelle Harper Lee, Capote conducted scores of in-depth interviews for the book, a nonfiction story recounting how two men murdered a family in rural Kansas. Each night Capote and Lee would return to their hotel and write notes about the interviews they had conducted that day. "Each wrote a separate version of the day's interviews; then they compared notes over drinks and dinner. . . . When their combined memory failed, as it sometimes did, they went back and asked their questions in a slightly different way. On occasion they talked to the same person three times in one day," Clark wrote in his book *Capote: A Biography.*

That technique is impractical for a reporter on a daily newspaper. And these days, when the credibility of newspapers is under attack, trying to reconstruct interviews and direct quotes from memory is downright dangerous. When freelance writer Janet Malcolm reconstructed quotes, she got sued for libel. Even though the U.S. Supreme Court ruled that it's acceptable to reconstruct quotes as long as the meaning isn't changed, if you don't have Capote's memory, it's better to take good notes.

Capote said he trained himself to be a good listener. "I have a fantastic memory to begin with," he said in an interview with Charles Ruas, author of *Conversations With American Writers.* "I can repeat almost verbatim any conversation up to as long as eight hours. I could never have written *In Cold Blood* if I had ever produced a pencil, much less a tape recorder."

The Pros and Cons of Tape Recorders

Capote's objections to using tape recorders are well founded. A tape recorder is not a substitute for good notes. Tapes can break, and machines can fail you when you need them most. They can inhibit a source. They can also prevent you from taking good notes if you rely on them too much. And tape recorders can't pick up observations—a smile, a nervous tic, a source's appearance or mannerisms. But they can be useful.

As more online news organizations add audio and video to their Web sites, reporters will need to tape interviews, meetings, speeches and other events to provide sound bites. With the growth of media Web sites, reporters will be expected to provide information for many forms of delivery.

In addition, if you want to get the exact wording of quotes, or if you are interviewing a source about a controversial subject, a tape recorder is beneficial. But you shouldn't play back the entire tape and transcribe it before you write your story. That is too time-consuming. If you use a tape recorder, scan the tape until you get to the quotes you need.

Before you begin taping your interview, follow some etiquette. Start your interview with basic introductions—who you are and why you are there— and some opening conversation. To put the source at ease, you might even ask a question or two before you ask the source if he or she would object to the recorder. Then, if the source agrees to allow the recorder, don't place the machine directly in her or his face. Put it off to the side of the desk or table, where it is not so intrusive.

If you want to record a telephone interview, be aware of the laws in your state. Ten states prohibit tape-recorded conversations without the consent of the person being taped: California, Florida, Illinois, Maryland, Massachusetts, Montana, New Hampshire, Oregon, Pennsylvania and Washington. Other states mandate that only one person must be aware of the taping, either the reporter or the person being interviewed. For a list of laws regarding taping in each state, check the Reporters Committee for the Freedom of the Press at *http://www.rcfp.org/taping.*

You can't secretly tape any conversation between two other people when you are not a part of the discourse. For example, if you are on an extension phone and neither party knows you are taping the conversation, you are violating a federal law against wiretapping. The Federal Wiretap Statute provides for penalties of up to $10,000 in fines and up to five years in prison.

The most ethical approach is to let your source know you are taping the interview, except in a very few situations. For example, if you are conducting an undercover investigation in a state where the one-party rule applies, you could tape a conversation without the source's knowledge. However, most editors consider the use of deception or other undercover techniques a last resort.

Listening Tips

Before you write notes or record conversations, you should follow Capote's example and develop good listening skills. Here are some tips:

Focus on the "hear" and now: Concentrate on what the source is saying now, not on what you will ask next. One of the major obstacles to good listening is poor concentration caused by worrying about what you will say instead of focusing on what the source is saying. Your next question will be better if you have heard the answer to your last one.

Practice conversational listening: Base your next question on the last sentence or thought the source expressed, as though you were having a conversation with your friend. If you want to move to another topic, you can do so either with a transition—"On another subject"—or by just asking the question. But if you are really paying attention, the order of your questions will be more compatible with the source's trend of thought.

Practice critical listening: Evaluate what the source is saying as you hear it. Listen on one level for facts, on another for good quotes, and on a third level for elaboration and substantiation. Is the source making a point clearly and supporting it? Do you understand the point? If not, ask the source to repeat, elaborate or define the meaning. If you listen for meaning, you can direct the interview instead of letting the source control it.

Be quiet: Whose interview is this anyway? Do not try to impress the source with what you know. You can't quote yourself. Let the source explain a point, even if you understand it, so you can get information in the source's words.

Be responsive: Make eye contact frequently so your source knows you are listening. Let the source know you are paying attention. If you don't understand something, say so. "Why?" "How?" "I don't understand" and "Please explain" are good follow-up reporting questions based on good listening.

Listen for what isn't said: Is the source avoiding a topic? Who or what isn't the source talking about—a family member (in a personal profile), a close official, a crucial part of his or her background? Sometimes, what is omitted from a conversation is more revealing than what is included.

Listen with your eyes: What kind of body language is the source displaying? Is the source fidgeting or showing signs of nervousness at some point in the interview? Is the source smiling, frowning or exhibiting discomfort when you ask certain questions? Are these telltale signs that the source may be lying or withholding information? Observation can be a good listening tool.

Be polite: If the source starts to ramble or give you irrelevant information, don't interrupt. Wait for the source to pause briefly, and then you can change the subject.

Block out personal intrusions: You've had a bad day, your car broke down, you failed a test or you have some emotional concerns. Make a determined effort to block out these personal thoughts. They intrude on your concentration while you are trying to listen. Your problems will still be there when the interview is over. The source will not.

Develop listening curiosity: Don't go to your interview with a rigid agenda of questions. Although you may start with prepared questions, allow yourself to be surprised when the interview goes in another direction, and follow that course if it is interesting. Listen for what you want to know and what you didn't expect to know.

Note-taking Tips

When the late Foster Davis was a writing coach at *The Charlotte* (N.C.) *Observer,* he checked reporters' notes to determine if problems in the stories originated in the reporting process. "The quality of stories has something to do with the quality of notes," Davis said in an interview a few years ago. "Writing is the least important part of it; everything that leads up to it is what matters."

Davis said he looked at notes to see if they were legible and if they included names and dates as well as reporters' observations. "When the notes said 'trees,' were they specific trees? Were the notebooks dated? Were exact titles spelled out? Detail is what makes the difference between good and bad notes," he said.

Detailed notes give you this advantage: When you begin writing your story, you may need more information than you anticipated during the reporting process. When you take notes can be as important as how you take them. Note taking can make some sources nervous. If you are dealing with people who are not accustomed to being interviewed, start your interview slowly by asking a few nonthreatening questions. After you have established some rapport with the source, take out your notebook.

Here are some tips to help you take good notes:

Be prepared: Bring extra pens or pencils. You may run out of ink, or your pencils may break. In addition, take *both* pens and pencils. If you do an interview in the rain, you'll want to have pencils handy.

Concentrate: When you hear a good quote or the start of one, write rapidly. Concentrate on what you are hearing and block out everything else until you have written the quote. Even if you are concentrating on a previous thought, you will still hear what is being said. So if the person says something better than the last quote, you can switch your concentration to the new information. Thinking of your next question while you are trying to write down a complete quote will interfere with your concentration.

Use key words: When you are not trying to get a direct quote, jot down key words to remind you of facts and statements. The better your memory, the fewer full sentences you will need in your notes.

Develop a shorthand: Abbreviate as many words as possible. The word *government* might become *gov,* and *you* could be abbreviated as *u.* Some type of shorthand is especially important when you are trying to write complete quotes.

Slow the pace: When you are taking notes for a quote, slow the pace of the interview by pausing before your next question until you write the quote. If you think you are pausing too long, ask a question that will not require a crucial answer. You could ask the source to elaborate about the last statement. If your source is speaking too fast, politely ask him or her to slow down.

Request repetition: Don't be afraid to ask your source to repeat a quote or fact you missed. Although the quote may not be worded exactly as before, it will be close enough. In fact, the repeated statement may be even better. When people have had a chance to think, they often state things more clearly.

Make eye contact: Don't glue your eyes to your notes. Make sure that you look at your source during the questioning and while you are taking notes. Practice taking notes without looking at your notebook.

Mark your margins or notebook covers: When you hear something that prompts another question in your mind—a fact you want to check or the name of another source you want to contact—jot it in the margin as soon as you think of it. Don't depend on your memory to think of it later. Some reporters use the covers of their notebooks to write questions that come to mind during the interview so that they can find them easily without flipping through notebook pages. And don't forget to take notes on your observations, either in the margins or elsewhere.

Verify vital information: Make sure that you get the exact spelling of your source's name and his or her title during or at the end of the interview. Don't go by a nameplate on a door or desk. That could be a nickname. Ask the source the name he or she prefers to use, and ask for the spelling even if you are sure of it. A simple name such as "John Smith" could be spelled *Jon Smythe.* If you get this information at the end of your interview, you also could ask for a home telephone number and an e-mail address at this time.

Double-check: If your source says he or she has three main points or reasons for running for office, make sure that you get all three. Write "3 reasons" in the margin, number them as you hear them and check before you conclude the interview.

Be open-minded: You may have one idea for the story when you begin taking notes. But don't limit your notes to one concept. Your story angle could change at any time during the interview. You can't always envision how you will write the story. When you do, you may be sorry you didn't take better notes, especially if you decide to change the focus during the writing process.

Use a symbol system: To save time writing your story, while you are taking notes, put a star or some symbol next to the information or quotes you think will be important. Develop your own system.

Stand and deliver: Practice taking notes while you are standing. You will not have the luxury of sit-down reporting, especially at the scene of fires, accidents, disasters and most other breaking-news stories.

Save your notes: You should save your notes before and after the story is published. How long you should save them is debatable. Lawyers disagree whether notes are helpful or harmful in court cases if you are sued for libel or any other reasons. But most editors advise saving the notes at least for a few weeks after the story in case any questions about it arise. For this reason, it is helpful to date your notebooks.

Transcribe notes only for major stories: Should you transcribe your notes in your computer before you write a story? Definitely not if you are on deadline. Some reporters find it helpful to rewrite their notes before they write a major story because it refreshes their memory, especially if a story will involve many sources and be written over a period of days. If you haven't mastered the art of writing clear notes, it may also help you to transcribe your notes immediately after your interviews.

Tips for Interviewers

The following sections present some tips to help you become a good interviewer. But before you even start, consider your mission. You are a reporter, not a stenographer who just receives information and transcribes it. A reporter evaluates information for its accuracy, fairness, newsworthiness and potential to make a readable story. During the reporting process, you will look for facts, good quotes, substantiation and answers to the five W's— who, what, when, where, why—and also "how" and "so what." One question should lead to another until you have the information you need.

An interview with one source is just the beginning of reporting for most stories. For credibility and fairness, you need other sources—human and written—for differing points of view and accuracy checks.

Planning the Interview

If you are sent to cover a breaking-news story, you should get to the scene quickly and find sources there or start calling sources on the telephone. The planning stages described here apply only to interviews that you need to set up in advance. Most of the other reporting techniques apply to both kinds of stories.

Research the background: Check news clippings and available documents—court records, campaign records or other relevant written and online sources—to familiarize yourself with the topic and the source. Check with secondary sources—friends and opponents—before or after you interview the subject of a story. Ask the source's friends, secretaries or co-workers to give you anecdotes and tell you about the person's idiosyncrasies.

Plan an interesting question to start your interview. Try to find a question or approach that would interest the source, especially if the person is a celebrity, an athlete or an official who has been interviewed often. These people often give standard answers to questions they consider boring because they have been asked the same questions so many times. If you research well, you will find some tidbit or angle to a story that might lead to an unusual question—and an interesting answer.

Identify your goals: What kind of information are you hoping to get from this source? Is it primarily factual, as in an interview with a police officer for a story about an accident? Or do you want reaction from the source to an issue or to something someone else said? Is the source going to be the central focus of the story, as in a profile, or just one of several people cited in the story? Get a general idea of why you need this source so you can explain briefly when you call for an interview.

Plan your questions: This step may seem premature, considering that you haven't even been granted an interview. However, if the person refuses to see you when you call for an interview, you might be able to ask a few questions while you have the source on the phone. If you are a good interviewer, you can prolong the conversation and wind up with a good interview.

Prepare your list of questions in two ways: Write all the questions you want to ask, preferably in an abbreviated form. Then mark the questions you must ask to get the most crucial information for your story. If your source refuses to grant you the time you need, you can switch to the crucial list during your interview.

Request the interview: Now you are ready to call for an appointment. The most important point is to plan ahead. Officials, educators and many other sources are busy people. They may not be able to see you on brief notice.

When you make the call, first state your name and purpose. Or try the sponsorship technique: "I'm working on a story about date rape on campus, and Officer John Brown suggested that I call you. I understand that you have some information about a survey the university conducted on this subject." Then ask what time would be convenient. If you want an hour but the source can't spare the time, settle for a half-hour.

If you are calling an official, you probably will have to negotiate through an administrative assistant. Be courteous and persuasive. First, ask to speak to the source. If that's not possible, tell the assistant that you would like to interview his or her boss about a story you are writing. You don't need to elaborate unless you are asked to do so.

You can also try contacting a source by e-mail to set up an appointment. Often, it is easier to reach busy people by e-mail than by telephone. State your name, affiliation and purpose. Save your questions until you find out if you can get a telephone or face-to-face interview. (Interviewing by e-mail is discussed later in the chapter.)

Dress appropriately: If you are interviewing a source on a farm, don't wear a business suit. On the other hand, show your source respect by dressing neatly. However, if you are interviewing corporate officials or people in more formal business settings, you should dress as though you worked there.

Arrive on time: You could arrive 10 to 15 minutes early, but don't arrive too early because you could inconvenience people who are busy. And never come late.

Conducting the Interview

Interview questions can be classified as two types: closed-ended and open-ended. You need both types.

Closed-ended questions are designed to elicit brief, specific answers that are factual. They are good for getting basic information, such as name and title, yes or no answers, and answers to some of the who, where, when questions. For example, these are closed-ended questions: How long have you worked here? Who was at the meeting? How many people were at the rally? When did the accident occur?

Open-ended questions are designed to elicit quotes, elaboration or longer responses. Avoid being judgmental in the way you frame your questions or respond with follow-up questions. The more neutral you are, the more responsive your source is likely to be. Keep your questions brief and simple; don't ask a double question or precede a question with a long explanation.

The questions that will elicit the most quotes and anecdotes start with *what, why* and *how:*

- What (What happened? What is your reaction? What do you mean by that? Can you elaborate?)

- Why (Why did you do that . . . ? Why do you believe . . . ?)

- How (How did something happen? How did you accomplish that?)

- Give me an example (a follow-up question to explain how the source felt, thought, acted in a specific situation)

Keep your questions brief. A long lead-in to a question can confuse the source. Slow the pace between questions so you can take notes. Ask unimportant questions or ask for elaboration while you are writing down quotes.

Remember to be responsive by making eye contact frequently during the interview.

Beginning reporters often worry that they will appear dumb to sources. Don't worry about what you don't know. You are there to listen and learn, not to be the expert. The whole point is to get information from the source. In fact, acting dumb can give you an advantage. Even if you know the answer to a question, you should ask it anyway so that you can get the information in the source's words. If you think a question is too simple, you might apologize for not knowing more about the subject. You might say, "I'm sorry I don't understand this. Could you explain so I can write it clearly for my readers?" Most sources enjoy taking the teaching role or showing off what they know.

Acting dumb does not mean forgetting about preliminary background work. It is dumb if you can't tell your readers something because you were afraid to ask. It's better to feel dumb during the interview than afterward, when you turn your story in to an editor or when you read it in the newspaper or hear it on a broadcast.

Here are some ways to conduct the interview and some types of questions to ask. Not all of these techniques and questions apply to every story.

Start out by using icebreakers: Introduce yourself and briefly state your purpose. Be friendly. Establish rapport with some general conversation. Don't pull out your notebook immediately. Try to sit at an angle to your source so you are not staring directly at her or him in a confrontational manner. A desk might serve as a barrier and provide enough distance so you don't appear threatening.

Observe the surroundings. Do you notice something you can mention as an icebreaker, a way to establish rapport? Don't be artificial. If an official has a picture on his desk of his family, don't get overly familiar. Use good judgment. Then explain a little more about what you are seeking in your story.

Put your questions in nonthreatening order: In most cases you will want to follow Barbara Walsh's advice and start with nonthreatening questions. However, if you have only five minutes with a source, you may have to ask your toughest question first or whichever one will yield you the most crucial information for your story.

Ask the basic questions: Who, what, when, where, why and how are the most basic. Then add the "so what" factor: Ask the significance. Who will be affected and how? This question will give you information for your impact paragraph.

Ask follow-up questions: These are the questions that will give you quotes and anecdotes. Use a conversational technique. Let the interview flow naturally. When a source answers one question, follow the trend of thought by asking why and how and asking the source to explain or give examples. Frame your next question on the information you have just heard by focusing on key words in the last answer. When you want to change the subject, ask an unrelated question or use a transition: "On another topic . . ." or "I'd like to go back to something you said earlier. Could you explain why you were at the scene where the murder occurred?" Use follow-up questions to go from the general to the specific. If the source makes a vague statement, ask for specific examples.

You may have a long list of questions, but don't let your source see them. A long list can make the source watch the clock. One student reporter took out a press release during the interview. When the source saw it, he told the student to use the comments in the release and terminated the interview. It would be better to write your questions on the front or back of your notebook so you can refer to them easily without turning pages frequently.

Control the interview: If your source rambles or prolongs an answer and you want to move the interview in another direction, don't interrupt. Wait for a natural pause and ask your next question, using follow-up question techniques.

Repeat questions: You've asked an important or sensitive question, and the source has given you an evasive or incomplete answer. Even a request to elaborate does not produce a satisfactory response. What should you do? The best tactic is to drop the question and continue the interview. After you have discussed a few other points, repeat the question you want answered, but state it in a slightly different way. Sometimes a source will recall more the second time the question is raised.

Ask background questions: Get the history of the issue, if applicable. How and when did the problem or program start? Why?

Ask about developments: Go from the present to the past and to the future. What are the current concerns and developments? How did the issue evolve? What is likely to happen in the future? The answer to the future developments question may provide you with a good ending for your story. In some cases, it may give you a lead and a new focus for your story. The next step is often the most newsworthy angle. Many newspapers, broadcasters and online producers prefer this approach, which is called "advancing the story."

Construct a chronology: This tip is somewhat related to the previous point. When appropriate, ask questions to establish a sequence of events. You don't need to write the story in chronological order, but you need to understand the order in which events occurred.

Role-play: If you were in the reader's place, how would you use the information? For example, if you needed to apply for a loan, what steps would you have to take, and where would you go? What does the reader need and want to know?

Ask about pros and cons: Ask your source to discuss both sides of an issue, when relevant. Who agrees and disagrees with her or his point of view? What are her or his responses to the opposition?

Ask for definitions: Your job is to translate jargon for readers. So always get your source to define any bureaucratic or technical terms in language that you and your readers will understand. Don't accept or write any information that you can't explain. To clarify, you might restate the information in your own words and ask the source if you have the correct interpretation. For example, you might ask, "Do you mean that . . . ?" or "Are you saying that . . . ?"

Verify: Ask questions even if you know the answers. You need to quote or attribute information to your source, not yourself. Always check the spelling of your source's name—first and last names and middle initial. Check the person's title and the dates of crucial events. Check the accuracy of information on a résumé or news release. You don't have to repeat everything, but you should ask the source if the information released is correct. Then ask some questions that expand on the basic information. For example, if you are interviewing the president of MADD (Mothers Against Drunk Driving), you might ask, "Have you ever been involved in an accident involving a drunken driver, or were you ever arrested for drunken driving?" Such a question may not be as insensitive as it seems because many people get involved with causes after they have had a personal experience with the problem.

Also, remember that if the source tells you something about another person, you must check it out with that person.

Use the silent treatment: Pause for a few seconds between questions to let the source elaborate. If the pause seems uncomfortable, the source may break the silence first. One reporter was writing a profile of a nun. He asked her if she missed having a sex life and how she coped without one. She gave a brief, expected answer that she had made a conscious choice of abstinence when she took vows of celibacy. The reporter was disappointed with the answer. He said nothing. She said nothing. For several seconds they just sat in silence. Both were slightly uncomfortable. Then she broke the silence and began elaborating about how difficult celibacy was for her at times. Sometimes the best follow-up question is no question.

Use the "blame others" technique: When you have to ask tough questions, blame someone else: "Your opponent says you cheated on your income taxes. How would you respond to that?" Reporters and editors have mixed feelings about warning the source that a tough question is coming. Don't do it, they say, in confrontational interviews when you are trying to get a source to reveal information that could be damaging. It puts the source on notice and gives him or her a few seconds to become defensive and evasive. But do warn the source or apologize if it's going to be a tough, emotional question, especially if you are interviewing grieving people, says Jacqui Banaszynski, who won a Pulitzer Prize for a series about a man with AIDS. She tells sources that she will ask tough questions, but they don't have to answer them. "But I'll try to convince them to do so," she says.

Handle emotional questions with tact: Emotional questions can be difficult. Ask your source to recall how he or she was thinking or feeling at the time of an incident. "Were you frightened when the train lost power? What were you thinking at the time?" Avoid insensitive questions. There's a saying in journalism that there are no stupid questions, only stupid answers. That's not exactly true. "How do you feel about the death of your three children?" is not only a stupid question; it's insensitive as well. Instead of asking such an emotionally loaded question, ask the person to recall specific memories about his or her children, or ask how the person is coping with the tragedy.

Ask summary questions: Restate information, or ask the source to clarify the key points he or she is making—for example, "Of all the goals you have expressed, which would you say are the most important to you? What do you think are the three major issues you face?"

Use the "matchmaker" technique: Ask if anyone else is involved in the issue or if there are other people the source would suggest you contact. Remember that you will want more than one source for your story so that you can strive for fairness and balance.

Ask free-choice questions: Ask the source if there is anything he or she would like to add.

End on a positive note: When you have finished the interview, thank your source. Ask if you can call back if you have any further questions. At this point, you also could ask for a home telephone number or another way to reach the source, such as an e-mail address or cell phone number.

Reporting for Visuals

Whenever you go on an assignment—especially a breaking-news story involving an accident, a disaster such as a flood or explosion, or a crime—gather information for the graphic artist. Even if you don't use all these details for a graphic, you can use many of them to make your writing more vivid. Get maps, brochures or any other written materials that might be available to help the graphics department pinpoint the location of the crime or disaster scene.

And ask questions as though you had to describe the scene to a blind person. How many feet or yards away from the landfill is the nearest house? What buildings are in the area? When the gas pipe exploded, how many feet from the gas line was the nearest building? Detail, detail, detail!

Locations: Get the names of streets and major intersections nearest to the site of the incident. Ask details about specific measurements: yards, feet, number of city blocks or whatever else would help pinpoint locations.

Chronology of events: Get specific times or dates and other information to recount the sequence of events. For example, suppose that a terrorist takes a hostage. When did the incident occur? At what time did each development occur before the hostage was released or killed?

Statistics: Think of charts. If your city council has raised taxes, what have taxes been during the past five years? How much has tuition increased during the past several years? How does this year's enrollment compare with enrollments in previous years? Statistics like these can be boring to read. But they are easy to understand in chart form.

Highlights: Gather information for a facts box, such as important dates or highlights of someone's career. Suppose that you are doing a profile. Instead of listing key dates and incidents in your story, could you place them more effectively in a box? Ask about interesting hobbies, favorite books, favorite movies, marital status or other personal information that might help the graphic artist—and the reader. In the past, when a reporter turned in a story that was reported and written well, editors used to say, "Your story looks good." It's up to you to make sure that it does—both verbally and visually.

E-mail Interviews

Although e-mail is an effective tool for contacting sources, it is not an effective method for interviewing people. But in some cases, it may be the only way you can get comments from a source. Use it as a last resort if you can't interview a source in person or by telephone.

Advantages: E-mail gives the source some time to think about his or her responses to your questions. It also saves you from taking notes, and you can get accurate quotes when the source responds in writing.

Disadvantages: E-mail interviews prohibit spontaneity and good follow-up questions. You also can't observe the source's reactions and body language, nor can you gather descriptive detail.

Tips:

- **Limit the number of questions:** Sources will respond better to one or two questions than to a long list. Strive for a maximum of five questions.
- **Clarify your purpose:** Make it clear that you intend to use the e-mail message in a news story. Personal e-mail messages are not intended for publication.

MULTIMEDIA COACH

Broadcast Interviews

Although it is possible to do a telephone interview for broadcast news, you usually have to conduct an interview in person.

Preparation: Do your research before you sit down for an interview. Write down your questions, and put them into a logical order. Have an idea of how the interview subject may answer each question.

Type of questions: Ask questions that begin with "how," "describe," "why" or "tell me about." It is rare to ask a question for which the immediate answer is "yes" or "no." The answers may often be difficult to edit. Ask one question at a time. If you ask more than one question, the interviewee is likely to answer only the last one.

Listen: Good interviewers are generally good listeners. Let the interview subject speak. You can follow up on a question if it was not on your original list of questions.

Time: Broadcast interviews take more time than print or e-mail interviews because it takes time to set up recording devices for radio and television and even more time for television lighting. Explain to the interview subject that the extra time will make everyone look better.

Important question: Make certain that you get an answer to your most important question. Also, make sure that you ask that important question no matter how difficult it may be for you and the interview subject.

- **Verify the source's full name and title:** E-mail addresses do not always include the source's proper name.

- **Limit your follow-up e-mails:** You may have to reply to the source's e-mail with another question or a request for more information. But don't badger the source with several e-mail messages.

- **Attribute to e-mail:** Although not required, it is preferable to explain in your news story that the source made the comments in an e-mail interview.

The GOAL Method of Interviewing

The "GOAL method" is a concept to help you frame questions for a variety of stories, especially profiles, features, and stories about programs and issues. It is a variation of a technique devised by LaRue W. Gilleland, a former journalism educator. It does not work with all stories, nor should you limit your questions to these concepts. But it is a starting framework. Here's what the letters stand for:

G = goals

O = obstacles

A = achievements

L = logistics

Many interviews can be designed around the GOAL concept, especially for profiles and features about new programs. If you structure your questions

ETHICS

Ethical dilemma: Should you accept gifts from sources? Does the value of the gift make a difference?

The case: You are working on a feature story about a new music store in your community. After you finish the interview, the store owner offers you some gifts, such as a CD case, a baseball cap and a T-shirt with the store logo, and a few CDs featuring your favorite musical artists. You do not plan to write reviews of the CDs. The total worth of the gifts is about $35. Should you accept some, all or none of these gifts? If you plan to review the CDs, should you keep them after you review them?

Ethical values: Credibility, conflict of interest.

Ethical guidelines: The Society of Professional Journalists Code of Ethics says journalists "should refuse gifts, favors, fees, free travel and special treatment and shun secondary employment, political involvement, public office and service in community organizations if they compromise journalistic integrity." Several newspapers, such as the *Detroit Free Press* and *The Philadelphia Inquirer,* prohibit reporters from accepting any gifts, books, records or other items of value from news sources who will be included in a news story.

around these ideas, you will get answers to the questions of why, how and what. Here are some ideas for specific questions using this method:

Goals: "What are or were some of your goals in this program (or in your career)? What are you trying to accomplish? Why do you want to do this?" Try to discern the person's motivation for his or her actions.

Obstacles: "What were some of the obstacles you faced (or are facing)?" Get specific examples or anecdotes. "What is one example of a difficult problem you experienced?" Try not to qualify your question by asking for the most difficult problem or the funniest or happiest moment. People have difficulty deciding what is best, worst, hardest, easiest, happiest or saddest. They need clues, such as a specific period during their life.

Achievements: "How did you overcome these obstacles? How did you achieve your goal (or how do you plan to achieve it)?" Again, get specifics.

Logistics: "How did you or the program get to this point?" This is the background: past, present and future. "How did your background affect your goals, obstacles and achievements? What factors in your background relate to the focus of the story? Is there a chronology of events that will help the reader understand the story?" Weave in the background where it will be interesting and relevant.

Telephone Interviewing

Edna Buchanan was persistent. The former *Miami Herald* police reporter spent much of her life making difficult phone calls to people who were grieving. If a source hung up on her, Buchanan waited a minute or two. Then she called back. The second time she identified herself again and said, "We were cut off." Sometimes her sources changed their minds, or someone else who was willing to talk answered the phone. But if they hung up again, she didn't call a third time.

More often than not, people are willing to talk to reporters, especially on the telephone. For many sources, talking about a loved one who died is cathartic.

Not all telephone interviews involve difficult situations. Reporters on a daily newspaper get many of their stories by telephone—from daily checks with police about crime stories to interviews with politicians, government officials and community leaders for reaction stories, issue stories and a wide range of features.

Nancy Tracy, a former *Hartford* (Conn.) *Courant* reporter, had a way of almost seeing through the telephone. She would ask her sources for details. She asked what they were wearing, what they were doing, what they were thinking, how they were coping and reacting. She was always empathetic. Sometimes she would apologize for asking difficult questions; sometimes she would sympathize. Then she would ask more questions. And rarely did anyone refuse to answer her.

Here is an excerpt from a story Tracy did about a Georgia couple who survived when their truck plunged into the Mianus River in Connecticut when the bridge collapsed. In her telephone interview with David Pace, Tracy asked such questions as "Where are you sitting now? What is your daily routine? What do you think about and dream about?" and even "What is the weather today?"

Some days when the pain isn't too bad, he stands by the front door, watching trucks roll by on Highway 41 on their way to Macon. Then the memories come flooding back, the crash, the pain.

Inside the small mobile home, his wife also remembers the day their world fell apart, when a metal and concrete span that was the Mianus Bridge split, sending them and four others tumbling 70 feet to the Mianus River in Greenwich.

It is a year today since the bridge collapsed, but for David and Helen Pace of Perry, Ga., it's as if it happened yesterday. It still figures in their nightmares, still limits their days.

A living hell, 27-year-old David Pace calls the past year.

It is raining. Helen Pace has taken to her bed. On damp or rainy days, her back hurts more than usual. On the days she is up, she wears dark stockings to cover the scars on her legs. She used to be proud of those legs, her husband says.

They had been married six months, and he'd gotten into the habit of bringing her with him on the long-distance runs. The night the bridge fell down, they were on their way to New Hampshire with 26,000 pounds of empty beer bottles in their semi-trailer.

He loved trucking—the good money it brought, the chance to see the country. Now, David Pace says, his and his wife's injuries are so severe that his parents are afraid to leave them alone.

"I've had to turn to my mother-in-law, my father-in-law, my mom and dad," he says. "It kind of takes a part of my manhood away from me. It hurts. It hurts bad."

Nancy Tracy, The Hartford *(Conn.)* Courant

Tracy got all that information by telephone.

Although interviewing people in person is preferable, it is often not practical, especially if you are on deadline. You won't be able to observe facial reactions, gestures and surroundings when you conduct telephone interviews, but you still can gather information accurately and thoroughly.

The techniques of telephone interviewing are very similar to the methods of interviewing in person. The major difference is that you need to work harder at keeping the source's attention and focusing your questions. Researchers suggest that the average telephone interview should be limited to 20 minutes. After that, the attention span of the person responding wanes. If you call a source at home, he or she may be further distracted by children or other family concerns.

Here are some guidelines for telephone interviewing:

Identification: Immediately state your name and affiliation and the purpose for the call.

Icebreakers: These may not be necessary. Get to the point quickly. If you use any icebreaker to establish rapport, keep it very brief.

Length of questions: Keep questions very short. Phrase each question clearly and simply. Limit questions to no more than two sentences; one is better.

Clarification: Make sure that you understand the information you receive. It may be harder to understand information in a telephone interview, so clarify anything that is confusing. Repeat any confusing terms or information in your own words, and ask your source to verify your interpretation.

Specifics: Ask for details and examples. If you want to describe the scene, ask your source to give you the descriptive details.

Chronology: A chronology is especially important in police and fire stories you receive by telephone. If you do not understand how an event occurred, try restating the chronology: "Let me understand—is this how it happened?" Or after a source tells you the high points of what happened, you could ask him or her to explain the order in which events unfolded.

Limits: Because your time may be limited by many events beyond your control, limit the number of questions in a telephone interview. Plan two lists: all the questions you want to ask and crucial questions. If you have time for only a few questions, switch to the crucial list. You may also want to ask your questions in a different order. Don't wait too long to ask the crucial ones. You never can tell when the source will be interrupted and will terminate the interview.

Control: Changing the subject to get to the questions you need to have answered is even more crucial in a telephone interview than in person. You can't spare too much time for establishing rapport or engaging in nonproductive conversation. Be mindful of the information you must get for your story.

Verification: Double-check the spelling of the name, title and other basic information. If you haven't heard it clearly, spell it back to the source. This basic information is crucial when dealing with police officers. They usually do not identify themselves by their full names when they answer the phone on duty, so make sure that you get first and last names and the proper rank, such as lieutenant, sergeant or captain.

At the end of the interview, thank the source and ask if you may call back if you have more questions. Use judgment here. Don't ask this of police or reluctant sources; just call back if you must have more information.

Exercises

1   Interview a reporter from your local newspaper, radio station or television station about his or her reporting techniques. Or choose a reporter whose stories you like, and interview him or her about techniques.

2   Make a list of questions you would use as icebreakers to interview a professor or a source whose office you have visited.

3   **Reporting scenarios:** Develop questions for the following situations:

   • You learn that there is a fire in a residence hall on your campus. List at least 10 questions you would ask. List five sources you would contact. What kind of background information do you need?

   • A professor on campus has received a $1 million grant to study plagiarism among college students. List at least five questions you would ask if you were interviewing the professor. What other sources will you use to make this a good story?

   • A study at another university says college students are sleep-deprived. Women students get less than six and a half hours of sleep, and men get seven to eight hours of sleep. You are writing this story for your campus newspaper. How will you localize this story? What sources (other than students) do you need to make this a credible story for your university audience? Where will you find them?

4   **Note taking:** The object of this exercise is to see how accurately you can quote sources. Tape an interview from any television news show. Use a VCR or a voice recorder. As you are watching the show, write down some direct quotes. If you use videotape, watch the screen periodically as though you were making eye contact with a source. Then play the tape to test your accuracy. If you do this in a classroom, you can compare your notes with classmates' notes. Analyze what caused you to be inaccurate—if you were—and how you can improve your note taking.

5   **Notes:** Submit your notes for the last story you wrote. Share your notes with another student, and critique each other's notes on the points Foster Davis recommends. Are your notes legible? Do they have names, dates, titles and details? Compare your rating of your notes with another student's evaluation of them. Discuss improvements in your note taking that might have helped your story.

6   Interview a local police officer about a crime or accident. In addition to getting basic information, ask questions to establish the chronology of events. If possible, get a copy of the police report. If the class is not doing this exercise as a

group, check to make sure that several people will not be interviewing the same officer.

7   **Technical clarity:** This exercise was suggested by Jacqui Banaszynski, senior editor at *The Seattle Times*. Interview a source about some technical information you don't understand. The source could be anyone from an auto mechanic to a scientist. Work on clarifying jargon and other information you don't understand. Then write the results of your interview in a brief story or several paragraphs explaining the technical information clearly.

8   **Graphics:** Check your local newspaper or another newspaper that uses graphic illustrations. Study a graphic, and write a list of questions you would have asked to gather the information that the artist used to design it.

9   **Enterprise:** Conduct an interview in order to write a news story about an issue on your campus or in your community. Here are some suggestions:

- Write a reaction story based on interviews with students or local residents about any controversial topic in the news.

- Attend a demonstration, rally, meeting or other public event on your campus or in your community.

- Check your campus and local newspapers for clubs and support groups in your community.

- Write a story about the economic or psychological impact that any unusual weather in your area may have had on businesses, agriculture or people.

Featured *News Scene* Assignment

Access *News Scene* at *http:// communication.wadsworth.com/ newsscene2* to view the news simulation titled "Big Fire." Take notes on the press conferences conducted by the fire chief and the captain, and then check your note-taking skills by listening to clips again. Finally, write at least five more questions you would ask if you were interviewing these members of the fire department.

Coaching Tips

When in doubt, check it out.

Don't depend on computer spellers and grammar checkers.

Don't turn in copy without checking it for grammar, spelling and style.

Keep a dictionary and stylebook on your desk as you write. Use them.

Grammar and Usage

Test your knowledge:

Whom or *who* should you contact for jobs and internships?

Will grammar have an *effect* or *affect* on your career?

Do you expect to go *further* or *farther* in your career if you get a good journalism background?

Do you know how the media *is* or *are* changing the way news is covered?

Does this sentence look *alright* to you? If it does, you need to study this chapter well.

The correct usage is in this paragraph: *Whom* should you contact for an internship? Check directories in your field. A good grasp of grammar will have a beneficial *effect* on your career, but poor grammar will *affect* your chances of getting a good job. You will go *further* in your career if you understand how the media *are* changing the way news is covered. It is never *all right* for you to write *alright*.

Many news organizations require you to take a grammar and style test if you are applying for a job as a reporter or copy editor. Public relations practitioners also need good writing skills. If you don't have a good grasp of grammar and usage, you won't be considered a good writer. And you can't rely on an editor or your computer to catch all your errors.

Now that you understand how to write a news story, make sure that you avoid these common errors in grammar and usage:

Affect, effect: *Affect* is an active verb, and *effect* is a noun. Think of *affect* with an *a* for action and *effect* with an *e* for the end result. *Effect* can be used as a verb with *to,* as in "to effect change," but that is not a common use.

Failing your style tests will *affect* your grade. But the *effect* on your writing will be more serious.

A lot, alot: Two words, please. Always. If you can't remember, use *many* instead of *a lot.*

Alright: *Alright* is listed in the dictionary as all right in informal dialogue, but it is not all right, according to the Associated Press Stylebook, which says *never* use that spelling. Use two words, *all right,* to mean OK.

It is not *all right* to use *alright.*

Among, between: *Among* is used with more than two items; *between* is used with two items.

> The conflict was *between* two students. The pay increases were divided *among* 10 employees.

Ampersand: Do not use the ampersand (&) as a substitute for *and.* This symbol should be used only when it is part of a company's name, such as Dun & Bradstreet.

Anxious, eager: *Anxious* means you are worried; *eager* means you are excited or looking forward to something.

> In your cover letter, don't say you are *anxious* to work for a company.

> If you are worried about the job, you are probably *eager* to get it.

As, like, as if, as though: Use *as, as if* or *as though* to introduce a sentence or clause with a verb. *Like* means "similar to" and should be used only to compare nouns or pronouns. Whenever you are confused, just see if *similar to* would fit in the sentence. If the sentence or clause contains some action, use *as.* Think *a* for *as* for action.

> *As I said* (not *like I said*), she plays basketball *like* a professional.

> It looks *as if* she will become a professional basketball player.

Bad, badly: *Bad* is an adjective that modifies a noun, as in "You wrote a *bad* paper." *Badly* is an adverb that modifies a verb, as in "You played *badly* in the game." These words are used *badly* most of the time when used with the linking verb *feel.* "You *feel bad*" means that your health, emotional or mental state is bad. "You *feel badly*" means that your sense of touch is poor. (See *Linking verbs* for more explanation.)

> Don't *feel bad* if you have made this common mistake, but don't write *badly* anymore in this context.

Before, prior to: *Before* is appropriate and less formal for most uses. *Prior to* is appropriate when the connection between the two events makes it clear that one event must precede the other.

> Every passenger must show identification *before* a ticket will be issued.

> Every passenger must show identification *prior to* boarding the plane. (*Before* would also be acceptable here.)

Between, among: See *among.*

Between you and I* or *you and me: Never use *I* in this case. *Between* is a preposition that must be followed by a pronoun in the objective case: *me, her, him, them, us.* Every time you are tempted to use *I,* mentally substitute *he* or *we.* You're not as likely to say "between you and he" or "between they and we."

Board* with *of: A reference to a board of directors or a board of education or any other board followed by an *of* phrase describing it takes a singular verb,

MULTIMEDIA COACH

Online sites with poor grammar and spelling errors lack credibility. Online news stories use Associated Press style. TV "crawls," the print that scrolls across the bottom of a screen, must also adhere to good grammar and usage even though these headlines are brief.

- Proofread your copy carefully before you post anything online.

- Most people's e-mail messages are notoriously sloppy. Check spelling and grammar before you send your e-mail messages, particularly if you are sending an e-mail for an interview, an online résumé or other career-related activities.

- Although broadcast journalists also use Associated Press style, the medium features the spoken word. Therefore, you may want to use a phonetic spelling of a name that is difficult to pronounce. But anything that is shown on the screen, such as a name or a title, should be checked for accurate spelling and grammar.

such as *is, was* or *votes.* The board is considered a singular entity; it's still one board even if it has 30 members. Ignore the modifying phrase.

> The *Board of Education is* meeting tonight. The *Board of Regents votes* on the issue tomorrow. (If that sounds awkward, you might say "*Members of the Board of Education are meeting* tonight.")

Can, may: *Can* means you are capable of doing something; *may* means permission or the chance to do something.

> You *may* get a promotion if you *can* create Web pages.

Clause, phrase: A clause is a group of words containing a subject and a verb. An independent clause forms a complete sentence; a dependent one depends on the rest of the sentence to make sense. Use a comma after an introductory clause. A phrase is a group of words without a subject or a verb. If you want to write well (that's a dependent clause), don't interrupt your subject and verb with a long clause.

> *Poor:* The student, who was fond of writing long, complicated sentences with clauses between his subject and verb, was an English major.

> *Better:* The student, who was an English major, was fond of writing long, complicated sentences.

> *Phrase: After the game,* the fans celebrated at a local pub.

Comma: Use a comma between two independent clauses joined by a conjunction—*and, but, for, or, no, so, yet*—unless the clauses are short. Use a comma after an introductory clause unless it is short. Always put commas inside the quotation marks in a direct quote. Check The Associated Press Stylebook for a more complete discussion.

> "When a sentence includes a direct quote (that's an introductory clause), the comma always goes inside the quotation marks," the professor said. "So does the period."

Comma splice: Never join two sentences with a comma. That's called a comma splice. Learn to love the period, especially in newswriting. If the sentences are closely related, you might use a semicolon.

> People who use commas to join sentences are making a dreadful mistake; comma splices indicate bad writing.

Compared to/compared with: Use *compared to* when you liken one thing to another. Use *compared with* when you examine the similarities and differences of two or more items.

> She is very smart *compared to* her sister. *Compared with* all the other students in her class, she is the best writer.

Complement, compliment: *Complement,* with *e,* means "to complete," also with *e. Compliment,* with *i,* means to flatter or praise.

> "If you can't get a *compliment* any other way, pay one to yourself," Mark Twain said.

> If you want a scarf to *complement* your outfit, buy one.

Consensus: This word means an agreement of opinion, so do not say "*consensus of opinion.*" That's redundant.

> After six hours of debate, the board of commissioners reached a *consensus* about building a new parking garage.

Criteria, criterion: *Criteria,* referring to the factors that will be used to judge something, is plural. If only one factor is involved, it is a *criterion.*

> The *criteria* to get an A in this class are good writing, spelling, grammar and punctuation. The *criterion* for expulsion from the journalism school is plagiarism.

Currently, presently, now: *Currently* means now; *presently* means soon, although it can mean now; and if you are confused, just use *now.*

Dangling modifier: A phrase or a participle (an adjective made from a verb ending in *ing*) is said to dangle if it is not placed directly before the noun or pronoun it modifies.

> *Dangling participle:* After *studying* for three hours, the *test* was canceled. (The test did not study for three hours. The student did.)

> *Correct:* After *studying* for three hours, the *student* learned that the test was canceled.

Desert, dessert: A desert is a barren place; a dessert is something to eat.

> You probably won't find a delicious *dessert* in a *desert.*

Either, neither: Each of these words requires a singular verb and a singular pronoun. Think of *either one* or *neither one.* But if *either* joins a singular word and a plural word, the verb agrees with the closer subject.

> *Either* student *is* qualified for the position.

> *Neither* the president nor the vice president *is* available for comment.

Neither of the students *plans* to present *her* project tomorrow.

Either the president or several members *are going* to attend *their* fraternity's philanthropic event.

Embarrassment, harassment: These words are often spelled incorrectly. *Embarrassment* has two *r*'s and two *s*'s; *harassment* has just one *r*. You are probably embarrassed more than you are harassed, so give it the extra *r* for being a regular occurrence.

Etc.: This is an abbreviation for the Latin word *et cetera,* meaning "and other things." You can substitute *and so on* or *and so forth,* but it is best to avoid this term. It leaves the reader wondering what else should follow. As the late John B. Bremner, a renowned authority on usage, wrote, "Above all, don't use *etc.* as a cover for ignorance when you have run out of ideas."

Everyone, everybody, every one, each: Each of these words takes a singular verb and a singular pronoun. If the previous sentence sounds strange to you, mentally eliminate the prepositional phrase (*of these words*). The phrases that intervene between *everyone, each* and *everybody* and the verb or pronoun are what cause the confusion. If you really get confused, substitute *all* or another plural word for *everyone, each* or *everybody.*

> *Every one* of the students *is* seeking a good job in *his* or *her* field. (Stress the *one* in this sentence. You wouldn't say *everyone are* or *everybody are seeking.*)

Farther, further: *Farther* is distance; *further* involves length of time, quantity or intensity.

> How much *farther* do we have to drive?

> I'll give this *further* thought.

Feel: This word indicates a state of being or a sense of touch. Don't use it to mean "think" or "believe."

> You will *feel* bad if you don't get an A on the quizzes at the end of the chapter.

> You *think* or *believe* you are doing well (not you *feel* you are doing well) in the course.

Fewer, less: Use *fewer* to refer to a specific number of items that you can count; use *less* to refer to a collection of items, a period of time or a quantity. *Less* is often used with a sum of money.

> *Fewer* than 10 graduates took jobs in which they made *less* than $15,000.

Fragment: An incomplete sentence, sometimes just a word or phrase. (That is a fragment.) Fragments can be effective as a writing technique for emphasis but should be used cautiously and rarely.

Goes without saying: If it does *go without saying,* then why say it? This is a stupid expression often used in corporate memos.

Half-mast, half-staff: On naval ships and at naval stations, flags are flown at *half-mast.* Other flags are flown at *half-staff,* usually to commemorate a person or tragic event.

Hyphenate compound modifiers: When two or more adjectives are used together to modify a noun that follows them, use a hyphen. Don't use a hyphen for *very* or adverbs ending in *ly*. Do not use a hyphen if a compound adjective follows an action verb.

> The *3-year-old* child had a chronic ear infection. But: The child is 3 years old.

> She was an *honor-roll student* in high school (compound adjective modifying *student*). But: The student was on the honor roll in high school (no modifier).

> The *part-time job* pays well (compound adjective modifying *job*). But: I work part time in the office (compound adjective after an action verb).

> The student had a *poorly furnished apartment* (no hyphen after *ly* adverb).

> A *very strong wind* blew off the roof (no hyphen after *very*). Limit the use of *very* in your writing; it's a weak modifier.

I, me: *I* does the action; *me* receives it. The same rule applies to the pronouns *he, she* and *we*. Don't use these words after the prepositions *to* or *with*. *I, he, she* and *we* are in the nominative case, meaning they should be used as subjects. *Me, her, him, us* and *them* are in the objective case and should be used as objects in sentences.

> Whenever the newspaper needs someone to work overtime, Julie and *I* always get picked.

> The chancellor gave the report to several journalism students and *me* to review before he made a decision.

If I were: Do not use *if I was. If* is a word used in the subjunctive mood, meaning it expresses a condition; it should always be used with *were*.

> *If I were you,* I'd learn to use *were* with *if* when I mean it in a conditional sense. *If I were he,* I'd probably reword the sentence, because it is correct but sounds weird. *If she were* in my reporting class, she wouldn't use *was* in a sentence starting with *if*.

Irregardless: There is no such word, *regardless* of what you may believe and *regardless of the fact that it is listed in the dictionary as nonstandard usage.* Don't use it.

It's, its: Wordsmith John B. Bremner calls the misuse of *it's* and *its* "possibly the most sickening example of literary ignorance." *It's* is a contraction for *it is; its* is a possessive word meaning "belonging to it."

> *It's* going to cost more to attend college next year because the university raised *its* tuition.

Join,* not *join together: *Join* means to connect. Can you *join* something apart? *Together* is superfluous.

Judgment: No *e*. There is no judge in *judgment*.

Lay, lie, laid, lain: *Lay* means to place or put something somewhere; it always takes an object when used in this sense. If you can substitute the verb *place,* use *lay. Laid* is the past tense. *Lie* means to recline. Its past tense is *lay,* and therein lies the confusion. It might help you to mentally use *down* with *lie* or to substitute *recline. Lain* is the perfect tense of *lie.*

> Please *lay* the book on the desk. She *laid* the book on the desk yesterday.

> *Lie* down and take a nap for a few hours. She *lay* on the beach for three hours yesterday and was badly sunburned. (This still sounds awkward, and it might be preferable to say, "She *was lying* on the beach" or "She *had lain* on the beach for three hours. . . .")

> He *had lain* on the sofa for three hours.

Less than/under: When you are using a collection of items rather than a specific number of items, *less than* or *under* is acceptable. For a comparison of a specific number, use *fewer than* (see *fewer*).

> She makes *less than* $20,000 per year.

> She makes *under* $20,000 per year.

> He weighs *less than* 200 pounds.

> He weighs *under* 200 pounds.

Like, as: See *as, like.*

Linking verbs: The *to be* verbs are linking verbs: *am, is, are, was, were, have been.* Verbs expressing the senses are also considered linking verbs: *appear, feel, smell, sound, taste, look.* Linking verbs join the subject with a predicate nominative, meaning a noun or pronoun in the same case as the subject. The pronoun that follows a linking verb could be used as a subject. The adjective after a linking verb modifies the subject and is called a predicate adjective.

> It *is* she. She *is* it. (You wouldn't say "Her *is* it.") The food *tastes good* and the music *sounds good,* but I still *feel bad.* (*Good,* a predicate adjective, modifies *food* and *music,* not the verb. You wouldn't say "The food *tastes well* and the music *sounds well,* but I still *feel badly.*")

Lose, loose: If you *lose* your assignment, you're in trouble. If your pants fall down because they are too *loose,* you'll be embarrassed. You might also be in trouble. You'll certainly be in trouble if you mix up the spelling of these two words.

Media: This word is plural and takes a plural verb for agreement. Television is one *medium,* but newspapers, magazines and television are the *media.*

> The *media are planning* major coverage of the election. The *media are changing* the way *they* cover news.

More than, over: *More than* is better when referring to numbers; *over* is better when referring to spatial relationships, as the opposite of *under.* In

ETHICS

Ethical Dilemma: Should you clean up quotes? If a speaker uses poor grammar, should you fix the grammar?

Ethical values: Accuracy, fairness, sensitivity.

Ethical Guidelines: The Associated Press Stylebook says, "Never alter quotations even to correct minor grammatical errors or word usage. . . . Do not routinely use abnormal spellings such as *gonna* in attempts to convey regional dialects or mispronunciations."

The guidelines reinforce the concept that a quote must be someone's exact words. However, what is stylistically correct may not be ethically sensitive. If you are trying to convey that a politician uses poor grammar and that concept is relevant to a profile or to the person's way of speaking, you may want to use the ungrammatical language. However, if you are interviewing someone who may be an immigrant and does not speak English well, it could be insensitive to quote exactly. Instead of using the exact quote, consider paraphrasing or using a partial quote. Avoid using too many partial quotes because they disrupt the flow of a sentence and cause the reader to wonder what was left out.

some cases, *over* can be used with numbers, such as ages or amounts of money.

> *More than* 300 people attended the hearing.

> The car went *over* the bridge. He is *over* 20. She earns *over* $400 per week. (This last sentence is acceptable, but so is *more than* $400 per week.)

Needless to say: If it's *needless to say,* don't say it. This is another stupid expression.

None: When you use *none* as in *not one,* use a singular verb. Use a plural verb when you mean *no two or more* or *not any* in a collective sense.

> *None* (*not one*) of these students *is* going to graduate school.

> *None* (*not any*) of the student fees *are* being used for health care.

Off of: *Off* is enough. *Off of* is unnecessary and ugly usage.

> The manager took 10 percent *off* the regular price.

Passive voice, active voice: Avoid passive voice whenever possible. You are using passive voice when you indicate that something has happened to you or the subject. You are using the active voice when you indicate that you or the subject is doing the action. The action verbs that characterize the active voice have more impact than passive verbs. But sometimes you need the passive voice. Place the most important information first in the sentence, and that will determine if you need active or passive voice. Active voice is preferable for print media and essential for broadcast media.

> *Active voice:* Three students *received* scholarships.

> *Passive voice:* Scholarships *were received* by three students.

Appropriate use of passive: The serial killer *was sentenced* to death by the judge. (That's probably better than saying "The judge *sentenced* a serial killer to death today" because the emphasis should be on the killer, not the judge.)

Pleaded, pled: *Pled* as the past tense of *plead* is considered acceptable in English usage, but the Associated Press Stylebook considers it colloquial and prefers *pleaded.*

> The defendant *pleaded* guilty, but if he *pled* guilty, he would still go to jail regardless of whether the Associated Press style gurus approved of the term he used.

Restaurateur: No *n* as in restaurant. Think of a *restaurateur* as the person who manages the place where you ate, not a place for an ant.

Should have, not should of: *Of* should never be used as a verb. Also wrong: *could of* and *would of* in place of *could have* and *would have.*

> By the time you are in college, you *should have* learned never to write *should of.*

Stationary, stationery: *Stationary* means something stays the same (note the *a*'s); *stationery* is the paper you use for letters (note the *e*'s).

Subject/verb agreement: The verb must agree with the subject. If the subject is singular, the verb must be singular as well. Plural subjects take plural verbs. Here's why that is not as easy as it seems:

> The number of students who drop classes *is* increasing. The subject is *number,* not *students.* When you have a noun, *number,* followed by a prepositional phrase with a plural word such as *students,* identify the subject. Don't be misled by the phrase. When *number* is the subject, it always takes a singular verb.

> The rate of dropouts *is* increasing. The subject is *rate,* not *dropouts.*

> There *are* fewer students enrolled in the print journalism program. The subject is *students,* not the expletive *there.* Avoid starting sentences with *There* because you are forced to use a weak verb. Better: Fewer students are enrolled in the print journalism program.

> A singular subject, followed by the phrase *as well as,* takes a singular verb. The city budget, as well as the tax proposal, *was* approved. Better to say: The city budget *and* the tax proposal *were* approved.

> *Everyone, each, either, neither, every* take singular verbs. Imagine the word *one* as the subject when you use those words. *Each* (one) of the students *is* creating a Web page. If that sounds awkward, use *All* of the students *are* creating a Web page.

> When a compound subject (two or more subjects) is joined by *and,* it takes a plural verb. The *professor and the students were* sick.

> Singular or plural: When a compound subject is joined by *or, nor, but, either, neither,* the verb agrees with the subject closer to it. *Neither* the

mayor *nor* the council members *have* proposed a solution. The desk *or* the computers *have* to be sold to raise the money.

Collective nouns such as *audience, jury, board* take singular verbs. The *Board of Commissioners is* scheduled to meet after the holidays. If that sounds awkward, just say The *commissioners are* scheduled to meet after the holidays. The audience *was* enthusiastic about the performance.

See other entries for *none, board, everyone.*

Than, then: *Than* is used for comparison; *then* is used for time. Think of *then* and *when.*

That, which: When a clause is essential (or restrictive), meaning the sentence won't make sense without it, use *that.* If the sentence can stand alone without the clause (if the clause is nonessential or nonrestrictive), use *which.* Use a comma before a clause with *which;* don't use a comma to precede a clause with *that.* And don't use either word to refer to people. Use *who.*

> The committee *that* banned reporters from the hearing was fined. (What committee was fined? The clause is essential to the meaning of the sentence.)

> The Lawrence School Board, *which* meets regularly on Tuesdays, will discuss changing school boundaries this week. (The sentence is clear without the clause telling when the board meets.)

> The school board members, *who* will vote next week, were elected to two-year terms. (Use *who* when referring to people.)

Their, there, they're: *Their* means "belonging to them"; *there* means "where" or is sometimes used to begin a sentence; *they're* is a contraction for *they are.*

> Students who did not qualify for *their* loans this year said *they're* going to file new applications while *there* is still time.

There is or **there are:** Avoid starting sentences with these words. They always force you to use the weak *to be* verbs. Turn the sentence around and insert an active verb.

> *Poor:* There are no internships being offered at that newspaper.

> *Better:* That newspaper is not offering any internships.

Toward, towards: Use *toward* without the *s.*

Unique: *Unique* means "one of a kind, incomparable." You cannot have something that is more unique or most unique. If it's unique, it is beyond comparison or qualification.

Who, whom: *Who* is the subject; *who* does the action. *Whom* is the object and receives the action. These words are confusing in clauses. Try to reverse the sentence or clause and see if *who* can be the subject. Deciding on the right word is even trickier when *who* or *whom* is the subject of a clause.

> Are you the person *who* called me about the job? (*Who* is the subject of this clause; *who* does the action; *who* called.)

Are you the student *who* is seeking the job? (*Who* is the subject of the clause *is seeking.*)

Are you the student *whom* I hired last week? (*Whom* is the object of *I hired; whom* received the action.)

Whom do you wish to see about the job opening? (*You*—the subject— wish to see *whom*—the object, the person who receives the action of your wish.)

The personnel director will choose *whoever* she thinks is the most qualified. (She thinks *whoever* is qualified; *whoever* is the subject of the clause *whoever is most qualified.*)

Who's, whose: *Who's* is a contraction for *who is; whose* is a possessive meaning "belonging to whom."

Whose team project was late, and *who's* responsible?

Your, you're: *Your* is possessive, meaning "belonging to you," and *you're* is a contraction for *you are.*

Now *you're* ready to test *your* skill by doing the following exercises.

For more tips on usage, see "Appendix: Style Guide."

Exercises

1   **Grammar A–K:** Study the grammar and usage tips from A to K, and correct the errors in the following sentences. Not all sentences contain errors; some may contain more than one error. Type the errors and the corrections, or type the entire sentence in correct form if your instructor prefers.

   a   She felt bad about missing the school board meeting, but her editor fired her irregardless of her excuse.

   b   We will all join together in prayer for the students who died in the shooting, and we will fly the flags at half-mast.

   c   It's alright if you miss class for a job interview, you can make up the test tomorrow.

   d   We'll divide the workload between three students.

   e   The St. Joseph Board of Commissioners are planning to submit a proposal for a bond issue to pay for road improvements, and they are hoping the election committee will reach a consensus of opinion to put the issue on the ballot.

   f   I know you are anxious to get this job, but each of the applicants will have a chance to discuss their strengths and weaknesses with the personnel director.

   g   Based on your writing skills, it looks like you could be a good journalist.

h   Each of the students is going to receive a plaque with their diplomas at graduation.

i   She was embarrassed that she had less than five answers correct on the quiz.

j   After the boss read the report, he gave it to Jim and I to rewrite and said its due back by Monday.

2   **Grammar L–Y:** Study the grammar and usage tips from L to Y, and correct the errors in the following sentences. Not all sentences contain errors; some may contain more than one error. Some of the errors in these sentences are also discussed in A through K. Type the errors and the corrections, or type the entire sentence in correct form if your instructor prefers.

a   The people that attended the gay rights rally said it was one of the most unique events the school had sponsored.

b   However, the participants in the rally said the media was annoying when they converged on the speakers with cameras and microphones.

c   Some of the speakers felt badly that the crowd became unruly and the organizer said he was embarassed when some of the participants complained.

d   Needless to say, next year the rally will be planned better.

e   None of the five students involved in the fracas is going to be punished.

f   The first-place award, that was an engraved silver bowl, was received by the class valedictorian.

g   The three top restauranteurs in the city provided food for the banquet, but over 200 people got sick after the event.

h   The City Board of Health, that investigates such cases, said the food smelled and tasted well, but they are withholding judgement on the cause of the illness until the food can be tested.

i   Irregardless, alot of people were laying on the ground, holding their stomachs in pain.

j   The city health inspector wanted to know who he should blame, and he said he was moving towards a solution to the mystery of revealing whose responsible for the food poisoning outbreak.

3   **Edit a story:** The following poorly written story would never be accepted for publication. Ignore the wordiness, and edit it only for grammar and usage errors. When you retype the story, underline, circle or use boldface to identify the errors, and type in the corrections.

In 1918 William Strunk Jr. produced a little book for his English course at Cornell University, it had a great affect on his students. E. B. White, one of the students who the professor taught, published the book in 1957. Today, the book, that was originally known as "The Little Book," is still having a great effect on writers. Its called *The Elements of Style.* Like I said, it's still popular, and every writer should have their own copy. It's presently available on the World Wide Web.

Strunk never thought it was alright to use alot of unnecessary words. One of his famous sayings are "Omit needless words". Between you and I, that advice is still good today, and I feel badly that this story is filled with errors that would of made Strunk cringe. It goes without saying that Strunk would have been embarrased if I was in his class. None of these sentences are perfect, and if this was the way a student wrote, Strunk would have issued stern judgement. Poor grades were received by students who wrote this badly.

Their is no excuse for writing badly, Strunk might have said. "Vigorous writing is concise", Strunk wrote. The media does not always follow Strunk's advice. He was the most unique teacher of his time. If your anxious to be a good writer, you'll check out his book online.

Featured Online Activity

Access the Chapter 6 resources at *http://communication.wadsworth.com/ rich5e* to link to the online guide to grammar and sentence skills called "Grammar Bytes." The site includes tips and rules as well as exercises.

TERMS

Find detailed definitions of common grammar terms--everything from *abstract nouns* to *verbs*!

Coaching Tips

Keep leads short—preferably fewer than 35 words.

Points of emphasis: Place the key words at the beginning or the end of the sentence for emphasis.

Write a focus sentence at the top of your story.

Avoid suffering: If you can't devise your lead, start with your nut graph and write your lead later, or write several leads and choose one later.

Don't invent your lead. Base it on the backup in your notes.

Leads and Nut Graphs

Don Fry, writing coach

The lead is the beginning of the story that entices the reader, so why does renowned writing coach Don Fry write his leads last? Most writers agonize over their leads, but Fry almost never worries about what he is going to say first.

Fry says he begins the writing process long before he sits down at his computer. "I'm imagining the story while I'm reporting it," he says. Fry concentrates on what he calls the "point statement," also known as a focus graph or nut graph. He asks himself what the story is about and what the point of the story is. Any information that doesn't relate to the point statement doesn't get included in the story.

And then he starts writing. Not at the beginning, but at the paragraph containing the point statement. He continues writing until he gets to his ending, which he calls the "kicker." Then he writes his lead. After that, he revises.

The point statement, which we've discussed throughout the book as a focus statement, may end up being the lead, or it will give you the idea for the lead. You may still prefer to write your stories by starting with the lead, as most writers do. But thinking about your story before you write it will give you a better chance of writing a good lead.

Mervin Block, a leading writing coach for broadcast journalism, has similar advice. "Think. Don't write yet. Just think," he says in his book *Writing Broadcast News*. "Think about what you want to say and how best to say it: clearly, concisely, conversationally. . . . Start strong. Well begun is half done."

The lead is crucial in any medium, especially these days, when readers and viewers are bombarded with so much information from print, broadcast and online sources. If you access any online news site, you may get a choice of 20 or more stories with headlines and leads on the main page. Studies show that most newspaper and online readers are scanners, who just read headlines. How can your leads entice the readers, listeners or viewers to continue? Think, plan, write and rewrite until you have written a lead to a story you would want to read.

Peanuts reprinted by permission of United Feature Syndicate, Inc.

Hard-news Leads, Soft Leads and Nut Graphs

The lead (originally spelled *lede* to differentiate it from "lead" type) tells the reader what the story is about. Think of the lead as a teaser or foreshadowing of what will come in the story. No matter what type of lead you write, you must back it up with information that substantiates it. If you haven't got material to support your lead, you have the wrong lead.

If you have been writing focus statements above your stories, you have a head start on writing leads. To write a focus statement, you asked yourself: What is the story about? What is the most important information? What is the point of this story? Those are the same questions you need to ask yourself to write a lead or a nut graph.

Sometimes nut graphs and leads are the same; sometimes they aren't. Here's how to tell the difference:

Hard-news leads: Also called a "summary lead," a hard-news lead summarizes in the first sentence what the story is about. A hard-news lead is usually only one sentence or two at most. It gets directly to the point. In this example, the first sentence is a summary lead. It tells who, what, when, where and why.

> HUDSON, Fla.—A 13-year-old girl shot and slightly wounded her stepfather with a BB gun after he hit her mother on the head with a frying pan Saturday afternoon, according to the Pasco County Sheriff's Office.
>
> *Larry Dougherty,* St. Petersburg *(Fla.)* Times

Nut graphs: Also called the "focus graph," the nut graph is a paragraph that explains the point of the story—what the story is about. A summary lead often tells that information and takes the place of a nut graph.

Soft leads: Also called a "feature lead" or a "delayed lead," a soft lead can be several paragraphs long and can take a little longer to get to the main point of the story. It delays telling the reader what the story is about by teasing the reader with description or a storytelling approach. With a soft lead, you must tell the reader the point of the story in the nut graph. In these days of impatient readers, the nut graph should be early in the story—usually by the third to fifth paragraph. Here is an example combining a soft lead and a nut graph:

Soft lead: who, what	SAN JOSE, Calif.—A nervous flight attendant was having trouble taking a urine drug test. So she drank a glass of water—and another—and another.	The unidentified San Mateo County resident is the first drug-test taker known to suffer from "water intoxication," doctors reported yesterday in the *Journal of the American Medical Association.* There have been only seven other reported cases of healthy people with the dangerous condition, which causes waterlogged brain cells and a dilution of body minerals. One died.	***Nut graph: The focus tells "so what." The story is about the dangers of water intoxication in connection with drug testing.***
More what	After guzzling three liters in three hours, she still couldn't urinate. But hours later, the 40-year-old woman staggered into a Burlingame, Calif., hospital, her speech slurred, her thinking fuzzy.		
Where	The diagnosis: She was drunk—on water.	*Knight-Ridder/Tribune News Service*	

How do you decide whether to use a hard or soft lead? The choice depends on several factors: the significance of the news, the timing, proximity (interest to your local readers or viewers), subject matter, and in many cases, your editor's preference. If the subject is serious—death, disaster, a major change in the law—consider a hard-news approach. Breaking news that happened yesterday or today also lends itself to a hard-news lead.

The next two examples are about the same subject. Consider why one was written with a soft lead and the other with a hard lead. (Note that these examples begin with a location in capital letters, called a "dateline." It indicates that the news occurred in a location outside the newspaper's circulation area. Newspapers have their own guidelines about when to use datelines.)

Soft lead

SAN MATEO, Calif.—The dog in her arms was shaking, its rheumy eyes wide with fear.

"Just relax, sweetheart, it's OK," crooned Chris Powell, the manager of the Peninsula Humane Society animal shelter, where 10,000 unwanted pets are put to death each year.

The dog settled into Ms. Powell's embrace, making it easier for a veterinarian to inject a lethal dose of sodium pentobarbital.

In seconds, the dog was dead, carried to a can, atop a mound of puppies and kittens, all awaiting pickup by a rendering company that would turn the animals into fertilizer.

"There's not a day when you don't think about walking away from this misery," Ms. Powell said.

Nut graph

Tired of carrying out the daily killings, officials at the Humane Society in San Mateo, on San Francisco Bay, have proposed a novel solution to the pet overpopulation problem: a moratorium on breeding cats and dogs that will be considered by the San Mateo County Board of Supervisors on Nov. 13.

The ordinance, thought to be the first of its kind in the nation and opposed by professional breeders, would fine animal owners who allow their pets to reproduce and would prohibit transporting cats and dogs outside the county for that purpose.

Jane Gross, The New York Times

Hard-news lead and nut graph

REDWOOD CITY, Calif.—In an effort to reduce the number of unwanted pets put to death each year, the San Mateo County Board of Supervisors on Tuesday passed the nation's first law requiring owners of dogs and cats to buy a breeding license or get their pets sterilized.

The action, which affects pet owners in the unincorporated area of San Mateo County, culminates a heated and emotional two-month effort by local humane society officials to educate the public about the problems of pet overpopulation.

Fed up with putting more than 10,000 unwanted cats and dogs to death each year, the Peninsula Humane Society launched a grisly campaign to generate support for the ordinance. First, the group bought advertising inserts in local newspapers and subjected readers throughout the Bay Area to pictures of trash barrels full of dead cats.

Then the society held a public pet execution at a press conference, injecting five cats and three dogs with poison from a bottle marked "Fatal Plus" as cameras whirred and reporters jotted notes.

Miles Corwin, Los Angeles Times

Timing and proximity were factors in the choice of lead. The story in *The New York Times* was written before the law passed and was intended for a national audience not directly affected by the law. The hard-news version in the *Los Angeles Times* was written immediately after the law passed, and it affected people in the newspaper's circulation area.

There is no set rule to determine whether you should use a hard-news lead or a soft lead. The choice is really a matter of judgment. If the subject is very important, sensational, or involves a major event or breaking news, chances are you will want to get directly to the point and use a hard-news lead, also known as a summary lead.

Hard-news Leads

Summary Leads

A summary lead should answer several, but not all, of the basic questions: who, what, when, where and why, plus how and so what. If you cram all of them into the lead, it could be cumbersome.

Choose the most important factors for the lead. Save the others for the second or third paragraph. This example stresses who and what, the most common type of summary lead:

Who, what, when, why

TALLAHASSEE, Fla.—A Florida law student was held Tuesday on a charge she hired a hit man to kill a secretary who found out the student had stolen an exam, police said.

This example stresses who, what and why:

WASHINGTON (AP)—The Federal Aviation Administration said Tuesday it would hire 12,500 new air traffic controllers over the next decade to offset a wave of looming retirements.

In the next example, who, what, where, when, why and how are stressed, but by the time you breathlessly get through this lead, you may not want to know any more. This lead is an example of cramming; the lead has 68 words! Try reading it aloud:

Who, what, when, where

NEW YORK—Police scuba divers inspecting the hull of an oil tanker in New York Harbor made an unusual discovery Thursday, and it was not only 366 pounds of cocaine hidden under water in the rudder compartments, but also the people who were guarding it: two shivering and louse-infested Colombians who had survived five stormy days in a 10-foot square compartment, virtual prisoners of the sea, authorities said.

The New York Times

Subject–verb–object order: Summary leads are most effective when they follow subject–verb–object order (who did what). This order is also favored for broadcast writing. The following lead starts with who, what, why and when:

> BUFFALO, N.Y.—A radio station programmer has been fired for breaking the station's rules against taking gifts from business contacts, a station executive said Wednesday.
>
> The firing of Dave Universal from Entercom Communication Corp.-owned WKSE-FM comes amid increasing scrutiny of the relationship between the recording industry and the broadcasters who play their songs.
>
> *The Associated Press*

Avoid writing long summary leads that begin with clauses, as in this example:

> Declaring that property owners must be protected from an arrogant government, House Republicans are nearing approval of legislation that would weaken federal efforts to protect wetlands and endangered species.
>
> *The Associated Press*

This lead would have been clearer if it had begun by explaining who is doing what: "House Republicans are nearing approval. . . ."

Order of information When you write a summary lead, how do you decide which basics to include and in what order? The points of emphasis should be the first or last words in the lead. Decide which elements are the most important—who, what, where, when, why, how or so what. Usually it is safe to use a subject–verb–object format: who did the action, what happened, to whom. But sometimes the how or why is most important.

Here are some facts presented in a story:

Who: Three boaters

What happened: Two killed, the third injured when the boat capsized

When: Sunday

Where: Lake Harney, near the Volusia-Seminole county line in Florida

Why: High winds and waves

How: Explained later in the story

The lead that appeared in the newspaper stresses who first, followed by what:

> Two boaters were killed and a third was injured Sunday when their small boat capsized in high winds and waves on Lake Harney near the Volusia-Seminole county line.
>
> The Orlando *(Fla.)* Sentinel

Now look at the way the lead would read with different elements placed first:

What

A small boat that capsized in high winds and waves on Lake Harney near the Volusia-Seminole county line caused the death of two boaters and injuries to a third Sunday.

Where

On Lake Harney near the Volusia-Seminole county line, a small boat capsized Sunday in high winds and waves, causing the death of two boaters and injuries to a third.

When

On Sunday two boaters were killed and a third was injured when their small boat capsized in high winds and waves on Lake Harney near the Volusia-Seminole county line.

Why

High winds and waves on Lake Harney near the Volusia-Seminole county line caused a small boat to capsize Sunday, killing two boaters and injuring a third.

The actual lead from the newspaper seems the most logical because the point of emphasis—the important news (boaters died)—is first. The last lead, focusing on why, is the next best option; the point of emphasis (boaters died) is at the end.

Most of the time when you write a hard-news lead, you will put the most important information first. Or you might want the point of emphasis at the end of the sentence, as in this example:

> A consumer group said Thursday that some sunscreens and cosmetics contain an ingredient that can promote cancerous skin tumors, and it called on the government to <u>halt their sale</u>.
>
> *The Associated Press*

Active vs. passive voice Active voice is generally preferable to passive in print and always preferred in broadcast writing. Active voice stresses who is doing the action; passive voice stresses those to whom the action is done. But you may need to use passive voice when the emphasis is on what happened instead of who caused it to happen, especially in police or court stories.

Active voice is stronger for the following example, because it emphasizes the iguana as the subject:

Active

A pet iguana started a fire in a split-level house in Hillsmere Shores by knocking over a heat lamp with its tail, fire officials said.

Passive

A fire in a split-level house in Hillsmere Shores was started by a pet iguana that knocked over a heat lamp with its tail, fire officials said.

In the next example, however, passive voice is preferable because it gets to the point faster:

Passive

A former employee of the University of Pennsylvania's Van Pelt Library was sentenced to seven years of psychiatric probation yesterday for the theft of $1,798,310 worth of rare books and documents.

The Philadelphia Inquirer

The sentence was imposed by Philadelphia Common Pleas Court Judge Russell M. Nigro, as the story later explains. The emphasis in the lead is on the employee who was sentenced. Here is how the lead would sound in active voice:

Active

Philadelphia Common Pleas Court Judge Russell M. Nigro yesterday sentenced a former employee of the University of Pennsylvania's Van Pelt Library to seven years of psychiatric probation for the theft of $1,798,310 worth of rare books and documents.

In the active version, it takes longer to get to the point of the story, and the emphasis is on the judge, not the employee.

Where to say when The time element can be confusing in a lead. In breaking news, when something happened yesterday, the time element usually does not come first in the sentence. But you need to place it where it is accurate, even if it sounds awkward.

Here is an example of a confusing time element:

University officials agreed to raise tuition by $100 Monday.

As written, the lead indicates the tuition will increase on Monday. Wrong. Tuition won't go up until next fall. Here's what really happened:

University officials agreed Monday to raise tuition by $100.

Delayed identification When the who in your lead is not a well-known person in your community or in the nation, you can identify the person by age, location, occupation or another modifier in the first paragraph. Then identify the person by name in the second paragraph. When you use delayed identification, even if your story involves several people, the first name you use should be the one you referred to in your lead.

All states have laws restricting the release of juvenile offenders' names, and several states prohibit the release of names of rape victims. In addition, many newspapers have policies to withhold names of criminal suspects until they are formally charged with crimes. Therefore, you need to use alternative forms of identification in these situations as well.

The following examples show how to say who in the lead and delay identification:

Age

An 18-year-old Tampa man was shot and killed Wednesday after he and two friends confronted a gunman who had beaten a friend of theirs, Tampa police said.

Warren Smith III, of 3524 E. 26th Ave., was shot behind his right ear at 6:40 p.m. and was pronounced dead shortly after arriving at Tampa General Hospital, police said.

St. Petersburg *(Fla.)* Times

Occupation

Two Minneapolis meter monitors have been charged with stealing an estimated $35,000 worth of nickels, dimes and quarters from parking meters.

Dale Timinskis, 42, and Leroy Siner, 40, both of Minneapolis, were arrested Tuesday after police watched their activities.

Minneapolis Star Tribune

Location

An Anchorage woman who embezzled more than $450,000 pleaded guilty Friday in U.S. District Court in Spokane, Wash., to charges of identity theft and filing a false tax return.

Jana J. Josey, 44, who now lives in Wenatchee, Wash., used various schemes to embezzle money while working as an accounts payable clerk for Quality Asphalt Paving, an Alaska construction company.

The Associated Press

Other identifier

A former Duke University student who posed as a wealthy French baron was a con artist with lavish desires, said a judge who sentenced the imposter to three years in prison for fraud.

Maurice Jeffrey Locke Rothschild, 38, who changed his name from Mauro Cortex Jr., was sentenced in Greensboro, N.C. for bilking two banks by posing as a nobleman from France's wealthy Rothschild family. The charges involved $12,000 Rothschild received after submitting false information on credit card applications.

Newsday

If you are writing a story about a person who has been in the news frequently, such as a suspect in a trial, you may use the name, but add a phrase or clause to identify the person, as in this example:

Lisa Fox, the Ames (Ia.) woman convicted of shooting an Iowa State University professor, has asked for a new trial, saying her daughter, who wasn't allowed to testify, can prove she is innocent.

Fox, 34, was found guilty March 15 of attempted murder for shooting poultry science professor Robert Hasiak a year ago in the home they shared. Her daughter, Sonya, 17, also charged with the shooting, pleaded guilty the week before.

The Des Moines *(Iowa)* Register

Updated Leads

The summary lead usually stresses basic facts about the news in the immediate past, and it is usually written in past tense. This type of breaking-news lead is often referred to as a "first-day lead," as if readers were hearing the news for the first time.

Because television and online news sites require immediacy, leads are often updated by advancing the story to the next step, a process called "forward spin" or "advancing the lead." Newspapers also refer to updated leads as "second-day leads." *USA Today* uses this approach regularly.

The first example is a standard summary lead that appeared in a morning paper. It stresses what happened yesterday in the search for a missing University of Arizona professor.

Rescue workers combed a rugged area in the Tucson Mountains yesterday evening in search of a UA music professor who has been missing since Tuesday night.

The *(Tucson)* Arizona Daily Star

The second example appeared in a competing afternoon newspaper. It gives the story a forward spin, stressing what will happen today even though there is no new information.

Deputies planned to resume a search this morning in rocky terrain in the Gates Pass area for missing University of Arizona music Professor Roy Andres Johnson, 58, who they fear was killed.

Tucson *(Ariz.)* Citizen

A few days later the professor's body was found; he had been murdered.

Here is an example of how you might update a lead, especially for broadcast:

Original Version

Princeton University officials have placed a cap on the number of A's that professors can award in an effort to crack down on grade inflation.

Updated Version

Students at Princeton University won't be receiving as many A's this year. School officials are cracking down on grade inflation by placing a cap on the number of A's professors can award.

Adapted from an Associated Press story

Impact Leads

The "impact lead" explains how the readers and viewers will be affected by an issue. This type of lead is also good for broadcast stories. It is an excellent tool to make a story seem fresh and relevant. The impact lead is especially helpful on bureaucratic stories. It answers the questions "So what? What does this news mean to a reader?"

Impact leads can be written in a hard-news summary form or in a more creative form, such as a soft lead. The information you give must be factual, not your interpretation. And if you use an indirect lead, you must write a clear nut graph early in the story.

The previous updated lead is also an example of an impact lead because it starts with how students at Princeton University will be affected by the new grade restrictions.

This impact lead uses a direct summary approach:

Summary lead with impact

Southwest Missouri State University must release its campus crime reports to the public, a federal judge ruled Wednesday in a case that could affect colleges across the nation.

U.S. District Judge Russell G. Clark called the withholding of those reports unconstitutional and ordered university officials to provide the public and media access to them.

The ruling, thought to be the first of its kind in the nation, has prompted the U.S. Department of Education to begin re-evaluating its stand on the release of campus reports.

Backup with more impact

The Kansas City *(Mo.)* Star

Here is an impact lead that directly addresses readers and viewers; this is a broadcast lead that would work equally well in print or on the Web:

Are you avoiding the bathroom scale? Is it a struggle to pull on last year's clothes? If the answer is "yes," you probably need to take off some extra pounds. But what you might not know is that a little extra sleep could be the answer.

Studies show that people who sleep too little are actually more likely to raid the refrigerator.

Fairbanks *(Alaska)* Daily News Miner Webcast

Here is another broadcast impact lead that would work as well in print:

Anchorage homeowners will soon be seeing green. On Friday the city sent out the annual green cards with estimates of how much property is worth. And this year, as valuations rise again, city leaders predict that your tax bill will not. Those little green cards tell you how much the city assessor thinks your property is worth.

KTUU-TV, Anchorage, Alaska

Attribution in Leads

Attribution tells the reader where you got your information. Too much attribution can clutter a lead. Too little can get you in trouble. So when should you use it?

- If you know the information is factual and you witnessed it or have first-hand knowledge that it is true, you may eliminate the attribution. If you received the information by telephone, as in police or fire stories, attribute it to your source.

- Whenever you are saying anything accusatory, as in police or political stories, you must attribute the information.

- You also must attribute the quotes or partial quotes you use in a lead.

To keep attribution clutter to a minimum, you may give a general reference to some sources—such as "police said" or "experts say"—if their titles are long. Then, as in delayed identification, give the specific name and title in the second reference.

Fact vs. opinion Here are some examples that demonstrate when to use attribution:

Fact: No attribution is needed.

An 88-year-old man died Monday afternoon when fire spread through his second-floor apartment at the Wellington Arms Apartments in north St. Louis County.

Opinion: Speculation about the cause needs to be attributed.

An 88-year-old man died in north St. Louis County Monday afternoon, apparently after he started a fire while smoking in bed, authorities said.

Attributed fact: Attribution for fact is needed because the reporter got the information secondhand (by telephone).

The body of a man who had been fatally stabbed was discovered Monday morning in a city trash bin in the Lewis Place neighborhood, police said.

Accusations A person is innocent until proved guilty in court. In crime stories, attribute any accusatory statements to police or other authorities, especially when you are using a suspect's name. If the person has been charged with a crime, you may state that fact without attribution. The word *allegedly* can be used when the charges have not been proved, but direct attribution to the police is preferable. Here are some examples:

No attribution is needed.	A University of North Florida chemistry major has been charged with building a 35-pound "megabomb" powerful enough to destroy everything within a radius of 150 yards. *The Associated Press*
Attribution is needed for an accusatory statement.	David Roger Flint killed 16-month-old Brittany K. Boyer on Monday by dangling her by the arms, swinging her side to side and beating her head against the floor and wooden furniture, police say. The 23-year-old Flint was arrested about 10:30 p.m. Tuesday and accused of murder. *Jane Meinhardt,* St. Petersburg *(Fla.)* Times
*The word **allegedly** is used because it has not yet been proved that the kidnap and rape occurred.*	A 38-year-old paroled murderer has been arrested in St. Croix County, Wis., for allegedly kidnapping and raping two 16-year-old girls in Minneapolis last month. . . .
Later, the lead is backed up this way.	He was charged with two counts of first-degree criminal sexual conduct and two counts of kidnapping. St. Paul *(Minn.)* Pioneer Press
This lead would be a safer alternative.	A 38-year-old paroled murderer has been charged with kidnapping and raping two 16-year-old girls in Minneapolis last month.

Quotes Whenever you quote someone directly, indirectly or partially, you need to attribute the statement.

Full quotes are difficult in leads and can be awkward. Reading a story that starts with a full quote is like coming into the middle of a conversation; it's hard to tell the context and meaning of the quote. Full quotes are also ineffective for broadcast writing.

A more effective technique is the use of partial quotes, especially when the speaker says something controversial or dramatic. Leads may also contain reference quotes, a few words referring to something controversial. Both partial and reference quotes should be backed up later in the story with the full quote or with the context in which the statement was made.

A full quote is used in this lead because it is dramatic, but it is still confusing.

"I've done everything out there," 31-year-old Gilbert Franco told his wife Thursday. "All that's left to do is learn the Bible and to die."

The next day, San Jose police say, Franco entered the C&S Market at East Julian and 26th streets and shot to death Katherine Young Suk Choe, 40, whose family owns the store.

Seconds later, 50 yards away, Franco fatally shot himself in the head.

San Jose *(Calif.)* Mercury News

In this example a partial quote is used and backed up later with the full quote, a technique used more often in stories about speeches, politics and court stories:

A reference quote is used in the lead.

The University of Pennsylvania announced yesterday that it was penalizing a senior scientist for "lapses of judgment" in an experiment last April in which more than 120 people may have been exposed to a virus that can cause a fatal form of leukemia. . . .

The committee concluded that the professor was not guilty of research misconduct as defined in a school policy. However, the committee concluded that there were "lapses of judgment and failures of communication" in the experiment.

The Philadelphia Inquirer

The backup puts the partial quote in context.

Attribution first or last The rule of thumb in the lead is to put the most important information first. If the attribution is cumbersome and will slow the lead, put it at the end. If it is brief, you can put it first. In broadcast writing, however, you need to put the attribution first. If the attribution is cumbersome, refer to the source broadly as in "a new study" or "a state official," and state the full attribution in the next paragraph.

Attribution last

Casual drug use has dropped sharply during the last five years, but the number of addicts using cocaine daily has not changed significantly, the federal government reported yesterday.

The Philadelphia Inquirer

Attribution first (acceptable, and preferable for broadcast writing)	The federal government reports that casual drug use has dropped sharply during the last five years, but the number of addicts using cocaine daily has not changed significantly.
Attribution last (because name is cumbersome and not as important as conclusions)	In a typical week, about 85 percent of the adult U.S. population uses a newspaper, according to a landmark study of daily newspaper readership released today. The Impact Study of Newspaper Readership is part of a project to help the country's nearly 1,500 daily newspapers gain readers. The study was conducted by the Readership Institute of the Media Management Center at Northwestern University, Evanston, Ill.

Cluttered attribution In the example that follows, note how a long attribution at the start of the sentence clutters the lead:

Cluttered	**Uncluttered**
Karen Davisson, child protection worker with the Kansas Department of Social Rehabilitation Services district office in Emporia, said Tuesday that only rarely are neglected or abused children removed from their parents' care and placed in foster homes or put up for adoption.	Neglected or abused children are rarely removed from their parents' care and placed in foster homes or put up for adoption, a state social worker said Tuesday. Karen Davisson is a child protection worker with the Kansas Department of Social Rehabilitation Services district office in Emporia.

One of the most common causes of clutter in leads is too much information about where and when something was said. Put some of this material in the second paragraph. Put the location of the meeting much farther down in the story, or eliminate it altogether unless it is important to the reader.

Cluttered	**Uncluttered**
Fort Riley is being considered as a possible host for the proposed joint landfill for Geary and Riley counties, Riley County Director of Public Works Dan Harden said during an informational meeting Tuesday night at the Geary County 4-H Senior Citizens Center.	Fort Riley is being considered as a possible site for a landfill, a Riley County official said Tuesday. Dan Harden, director of public works, said. . . .

MULTIMEDIA COACH

The techniques for writing broadcast leads are similar to those for print. However, remember that the writing style for broadcast is conversational.

Three types of leads are used most often in broadcasting: summary, descriptive and anecdotal. A crime story, a fire, an accident or a political story often starts with a summary lead. But don't discard a descriptive or anecdotal lead for a hard-news story.

People want to hear about people. A tightly focused lead on an individual in a hard-news story can often entice a listener or viewer to stay with the story. Keep in mind that radio listeners and television viewers cannot go back to repeat the broadcast if they don't understand some part of the story.

Online writing is similar to print, but summary leads are often preferred because readers are impatient to discover the main point of the story. If the headline and blurb are in summary form, the lead might be descriptive or anecdotal. But make sure that the nut graph is high in the story if you use a soft lead. With millions of Web sites competing for readers' attention, readers will click to another story or site if the lead or nut graph is not clear. Because the content on most online news sites mirrors print versions, you need to consider how your lead and nut graph will work both in print and online. Descriptive and anecdotal leads work well for feature stories, trends and profiles in broadcast writing and on the Web.

Here are some guidelines for broadcast and online writing:

- Use active voice, with an emphasis on short, uncomplicated sentences. State who is doing the action rather than to whom the action was done. Clarity and simplicity are even more critical in broadcast than in print.

- Use simple sentences, preferably structured in subject–verb–object order (who did what). Avoid long sentences that begin with clauses.

- Put the most important information first in the sentence.

- Use a conversational tone. Addressing the reader as "you" works well in broadcast and on the Web.

- For broadcast, place attribution first, not at the end of the sentence; either order works for the Web. If the attribution is cumbersome, put it in another paragraph, as in this example:

New research indicates that eating lots of red meat may create about as much of a certain cancer-promoting chemical in the colon as smoking does.

The findings, presented Saturday in Lyon at the European Conference on Nutrition and Cancer, were part of a study that also appears to revive the theory that fiber wards off colon cancer, the second most deadly cancer worldwide.

The Associated Press

- Most important, get to the main point quickly. This story begins with a soft lead sentence, but the main point is still in the lead:

Never mind what the label says. The new brands of energy drinks are aimed more at marathon partiers than serious athletes. And that has health officials worried.

The drinks come in flashy cans and bottles with names like Red Bull, Adrenaline Rush and Jones Whoop-Ass Energy Drink. They don't taste great by almost universal consensus, but they're the fastest-growing segment of the beverage market because they deliver a quick punch of energy.

The Associated Press

Soft Leads

Coaching Tips

Try writing many different leads instead of struggling to find the perfect one. Don't wait for a creative muse.

Make sure that your lead is related to your focus and can be backed up in your story.

Do not strain to "create" a lead from your head. Pull from the story, not from your head, for inspiration.

Soft leads can be fun to write and fun to read. They can also be painful. If you don't get to the point quickly, they can also be tedious. They can be as effective in broadcast writing as in print.

Although soft leads are also called "delayed leads," the lead is still first. Only the nut graph is delayed. Remember that all leads, especially soft leads, must be backed up in the story and must lead to a nut graph. It is preferable to place the nut graph high in the story, by the third to fifth paragraph.

Most breaking-news stories contain summary leads, but in 2005 the Associated Press announced that it would begin offering two types of leads—hard and soft—on many of its stories, especially spot-news stories that happen early in the day. "One will be the traditional 'straight lead' that leads with the main facts of what took place. The other will be the 'optional lead,' an alternative approach that attempts to draw in the reader through imagery, narrative devices, perspective or other creative means," according to an article in *Editor & Publisher*.

That's a major change for the 156-year-old news wire service, which primarily offers the summary lead. It's a recognition that readers need different approaches to stories.

There are many types of soft leads. They can be used on both news and feature stories. Most of them follow a simple concept: specific to general. Use a specific example at the beginning to illustrate the main point of the story.

People like to read about other people. As a result, many soft leads start with something about a person who is one of many people sharing the same problem. The idea behind these soft leads—called "anecdotal leads"—is that readers can relate better to one person's problem than to a general statement of a problem.

Other common types of soft leads are descriptive and narrative. "Descriptive leads" describe a person or a scene. "Narrative leads" are storytelling leads that recount the event in a dramatic way to put the reader on the scene as the action occurs.

And then there are leads that are just clever or catchy.

It's not what you call soft leads that matters; it's how you write them. The important point is to tell a good story. When writers struggle with soft leads, it is often because they think they must create something clever. All too often, the result is a cliche. It is best to look at your notes and build a lead based on something interesting in the story, instead of waiting for the creative muse.

The sections that follow show a variety of ways to structure a soft lead. The basic techniques are descriptive, anecdotal and narrative.

Descriptive Leads

This type of lead describes a person, place or event. It is like the descriptive focus-on-a-person lead, but it doesn't have to focus on a person who is one of many. It can be used for news or feature stories.

ETHICS

Ethical dilemma: You want to write an anecdotal lead focusing on a person for your story, but you don't have a real source. Should you use a hypothetical person without telling the reader? Should you use a hypothetical situation at all?

Ethical values: Credibility, accuracy, truthfulness.

Ethical guidelines: The Society of Professional Journalists' code of ethics says, "Seek the truth and report it. Avoid misleading re-enactments or staged news events."

In this example, the story focuses on the man who is causing the problem:

Skippack farmer John W. Hasson stood ankle-deep in mud, pumping milk into a wooden trough as his pigs, squealing and grunting, snouts quivering, climbed over each other to get to their feed.

Hasson inhaled deeply.

"Does that smell sour to you? That's what they call noxious fumes," he said with a sniff toward his new neighbors, Ironbridge Estates, a subdivision of two-story colonial houses costing $200,000 plus.

Ironbridge's developers say Hasson's farm smells.

And his 250 pigs squeal too much.

So they have filed suit in Montgomery County to force him to clean up his act. The case is scheduled to be heard May 8.   *Nut graph*

Erin Kennedy, The Philadelphia Inquirer

Anecdotal Leads

This type of lead starts with a story about a person or an event. In a sense, all soft leads are anecdotal because they are all storytelling approaches. Many combine descriptive and anecdotal techniques.

This lead is an anecdote—the story behind a woman's court case:

Late one spring night, after drinks at a bar and a bit of protest, Elaine Hollis agreed to her boyfriend's desire to capture their passion on videotape.

Inside Edward Bayliss' apartment, the video camera rolled at the foot of his bed.

He promised to erase the tape.

Seven years later, Hollis, who has a son with Bayliss, was in Delaware County Court accusing him of contriving to bring her into disrepute by exhibiting the tape.

Bayliss, president of Philadelphia Suburban Electrical Service in Upper Darby, admitted showing the tape to one of his friends.

Hollis contended he showed and distributed the tape in Delaware County and surrounding areas, as well as gave copies of it to two bar owners in Darby, who played it for customers.

Last week, after three years of litigation, a county judge upheld an Oct. 15 Common Pleas Court order that mandated Bayliss pay Hollis $125,000 to settle her lawsuit.   *Nut graph*

Patrick Scott, The Philadelphia Inquirer

The next example contains another anecdotal lead that tells a story but incorporates the news in the first sentence. It is a good example of how to update the news about a minor earthquake that occurred the previous day by using a storytelling approach. (If the earthquake had been greater and had caused death or injuries, a summary lead would have been more appropriate.)

When the shock wave from a magnitude 4.7 earthquake rolled through Anchorage Wednesday morning, dentist Kendall Skinner had just inserted a 3-inch needle into the mouth of a patient and begun an injection.

"It was jarring," Skinner said. "It's such a sharp object in the back of somebody's mouth."

With a somewhat unsteady hand, Skinner finished the injection as fast and safely as he could, then pulled out. His patient, a 20-something woman who needed a filling, told him she was fine. The numbing started before the shaking, so she didn't feel a thing.

Nut graph — People all over Anchorage and the Matanuska-Susitna Valley were shaken but not stirred from their regular workday routine Wednesday when a quake struck beneath the Point MacKenzie area a few miles north of downtown — then triggered an afternoon of minor aftershocks.

Doug O'Harra, Megan Holland and Zaz Hollander, Anchorage *(Alaska)* Daily News

This lead uses both anecdotal and descriptive techniques:

Dawn Clark's cat walked carefully across the lawn, then stopped suddenly, looking bewildered.

The cat sniffed tentatively, then bolted off the grass and spent the next few minutes licking its paws — trying to clean the paint flecks from them.

The lawn had recently been mowed and was green as a billiard table, because it had just been painted with a vegetable dye.

Nut graph — Santa Barbara residents have devised innovative ways to keep their yards green since the city, faced with an expected water shortfall of nearly 50 percent for the year, declared a "drought emergency" in late February and banned lawn watering.

Extension of nut graph — Clark's cat had just experienced one: Several landscape companies now offer painting and local nurseries are stocking their shelves with green paint and pump sprayers.

Miles Corwin, Los Angeles Times

Narrative Leads

Like an anecdotal lead, a narrative lead tells a story with enough dramatic action so readers can feel as if they are witnessing the event. Narrative writing uses all the techniques of fiction, including dialogue, scene setting and foreshadowing — giving the reader clues to what will happen. It takes longer to set up the nut graph for this kind of lead, but if the story is dramatic enough, the narrative approach may work.

Police Officer Juan Cabrera felt the barrel of the gun press against his head.

"I'm gonna kill you," a voice from behind said.

"I didn't see who it was. I didn't know what was happening," Cabrera said. "I just thought someone was going to kill me."

Cabrera instinctively knocked the gun away, wrestled the suspect to the ground and handcuffed him.

The suspect was a 12-year-old boy. The gun was a toy.

"It looked like a .38-caliber short-barrel revolver," said Cabrera, a five-year veteran of the force. "It was a cap gun."

The incident was no joke for the boy. He was arrested on a charge of battery on a law enforcement officer.

Kevin Davis, The *(Fort Lauderdale, Fla.)* Sun-Sentinel

Other Soft Leads

Soft leads can be written in many other ways. The following techniques are variations on the three main types of soft leads, combining features of descriptive, anecdotal and narrative leads.

Focus-on-a-person leads You can focus on a person in two ways: Use an anecdotal approach, telling a little story about the person, or use a descriptive approach that describes the person or shows the person in action. This type of lead can be used in profile stories about the person or in news stories about issues, where the person is one of many affected by the point of your story. This approach, used by many newspapers and broadcast stations, is also called the *Wall Street Journal* format because that newspaper uses this format daily on its front-page features and originated the term "nut graph."

This example uses the descriptive approach:

Nita walked slowly down the narrow hall, deftly guiding her tottering 11-month-old son around the abandoned baby walkers, strollers and toys.

Inside her tiny bedroom, the 17-year-old mother pointed to photographs of her son's father and some of her friends. Cards congratulating her on her recent high school graduation were nearby. The baby's crib was crammed into an area near the door.

Nita, one of 85 residents at Florence Crittenton Services in Fullerton, is one of a growing number of teenagers having babies in Orange County—a figure that has increased 36 percent in five years.

Janine Anderson, The Orange County *(Calif.)* Register

Nut graph: points out that person is one of many

Here is another example of this popular *Wall Street Journal* lead format because it starts by focusing on a person who is used to illustrate a problem that affects many others like her:

SEATTLE—Natasha Khachatourians has so much student debt that she's working two jobs. Eight hours a day, she staffs the front window at Seattle University's financial-aid office. Three nights a week she's at her second job, working at Lovers Package until 10:30. Saturdays she pulls another eight-hour shift at the adult-entertainment store.

She's barely staying afloat. Khachatourians, 23, graduated from Seattle University last year, and her debt tally is $60,000 in education loans, plus $4,500 on four credit cards. After consolidating her federal loans, her education payments are $300 a month.

"I eat a lot of bread," she said. "It's cheap."

Nut graph | Her predicament reflects that of many college graduates: Students are leaving college owing more and more, and that swelling debt is out-pacing the rise in other higher-education costs.
Sharon Pian Chan, The Seattle Times

Contrast leads This type of lead can be used to set up stories about conflicts or unusual circumstances. The two most common ways to write contrast leads emphasize circumstances and time:

But-guess-what contrast: Contrast leads that revolve around circumstances can be used to explain something unusual:

William Pearce, known to his patients as Dr. William J. Rick, was charming and slick, say his former associates and police detectives.

He came to town with medical degrees, numerous national board certificates and myriad other qualifications.

But the real Dr. Rick died in 1986, police say.

And now William John Pearce, 57, is in jail on charges of impersonating a doctor. — *Nut graph*
Sharon McBreen, The Orlando *(Fla.)* Sentinel

Here is a descriptive lead setting up contrast without the "but":

DENVER—Above a pond labeled "Industrial Waste," two bald eagles perch on a tree limb. Down the road from workers in white protective suits, scores of prairie dogs scurry across a field. Around the corner from hundreds of barrels containing remnants of mustard gas, a dozen mule deer stand in a thicket.

It's a paradox that some view as almost poetic: The Army's Rocky Mountain Arsenal—a shut-down war factory, a boarded-up lesson in how not to treat the environment, one of the most poisoned pieces of land in the United States—has become a haven for wildlife. — *Nut graph*
John Woestendiek,
The Philadelphia Inquirer

Then-and-now contrast: Time contrasts—then and now—are useful ways to show change. This type of lead can also be used when the background is interesting or important and is relevant to the focus.

It was March 1964 when Lewis "Hackie" Wilson, the 7-year-old son of a St. Petersburg firefighter, disappeared after stopping to pick up flowers on his way home from school.

His case received national attention a month later when a sheriff's posse on horseback, flushing out rattlesnakes ahead of a line of 80 searchers, found the child's bones in a field south of Venice.

Now the case may be revived. Prosecutors in Sarasota County have realized that Joseph Francis Bryan, a convicted child kidnapper indicted for Hackie's murder in 1965, has never been brought to trial. — *Nut graph*
Karen Datko, St. Petersburg *(Fla.)* Times

Teaser leads These leads use the element of surprise to tease the reader into the story. The nut graph may also be a contrast, but the first sentence sets it up as a tease into something unusual.

BURLINGTON, Vt.—This is no ordinary public library.

For one thing, there are only four books on the shelves. For another, you won't find any of these works, or the many that are expected to join them soon, at other libraries or bookstores.

You probably never will.

That's because the Brautigan Library, which opened here last weekend, has a unique policy—it only accepts books that have never been published.   *Nut graph*

Steve Stecklow, The Philadelphia Inquirer

Mystery leads Like teasers, these leads promise the reader a surprise or a treat for reading on. They set up the story like a mystery novel. They're fun to write and fun to read, but they won't work unless the subject matter lends itself to this approach.

One technique for writing mystery leads is to start with a vague pronoun, *it* or *they,* and to delay naming the noun to which the pronoun refers: "It began at midnight." Later you specify what "it" was. Here is an example of a mystery lead:

They know who you are, what you eat, how you procreate—and where to find you.

Do you like ice cream? The U.S. government has used that information to track down draft-dodging 18-year-olds who signed up for ice cream parlor "birthday clubs." . . .

Been turned down for a MasterCard or Visa? List Brokerage and Management, a New York list marketer, may have your name. It rents a list of 1.6 million people rejected for bank cards—obtained, the company says, from the very banks that turned you down. . . .

Computer companies are hooking up with credit bureaus and massive data banks to allow people with only a desktop computer to single you out by income, age, neighborhood, car model or waist size.   *Nut graph*

Stephen Koff, St. Petersburg *(Fla.)* Times

This next lead uses not only the mystery approach but also the format of the novel as part of the lead:

The case has all the elements of a 1950s film noir mystery.

The characters: the scheming husband, the trusting wife, the other woman.

The story: The husband, Ray Valois, buys a lottery ticket, scratches it and finds three "Spin, Spin, Spin" symbols. That makes him eligible to win up to $2 million in the California "Big Spin" lottery, but he does not want to tell his wife, Monica, according to his statement in San Luis Obispo County Superior Court records. So he gives the ticket to another woman, waitress Stephanie Martin. She agrees to cash in the ticket, according to court records, and secretly give him half.

The inevitable plot twist: Valois and Martin turn on each other. He claims that he owns the ticket. She claims that she owns the ticket.

The conclusion: Martin spins and wins $100,000. But the wife finds out and sues both of them for fraud.

Now neither Martin nor Valois has the $100,000. His wife's attorney, Gary Dunlap, obtained a temporary restraining order, restricting lottery officials from awarding the winnings until a court hearing today.

Nut graph

Miles Corwin, Los Angeles Times

Build-on-a-quote leads If you have a great quote, build your lead around the quote that will back up your first sentence. But be careful not to repeat too much of the quote in your lead; that's boring and repetitious. Building on a quote is an easy and effective way to find a lead, provided that the quote is related to the focus of the story. This technique works equally well for hard-news leads.

ANDOVER, Kan.—Melinda Easterbrook knows exactly how long it took for a tornado to blast apart her comfortable home while she and her husband huddled in the basement.

"It lasted five Hail Marys and two Our Fathers, but you have to say them quickly," she said yesterday.

While she was praying, the concrete basement rumbled and shook. When she and her husband, Bryan, came upstairs, they were hardly prepared for the scope of the destruction that had swept through this small town about five miles east of Wichita.

Nut graph

Larry Fish, The Philadelphia Inquirer

The next example is the kind of build-on-a-quote lead to avoid. The backup quote says the same thing as the lead, and it's right after the lead, so it's boring. In broadcast writing this is called "parroting," with the reporter introducing a sound bite that repeats what the source says on tape. It should be avoided as well.

A commitment to high-tech learning and small classes taught by professors has made Fort Hays State University the fastest-growing university in the state Board of Regents system, FHSU's president said today.

FHSU had the largest spring semester enrollment increase among the six regents' universities—2.4 percent compared with the previous spring.

"We've been the fastest growing of the regents' institutions over the last five years," FHSU President Edward Hammond said.

List leads If you have a few brief examples to lead into your focus, you may list them in parallel sentences—making sure that your sentences have the same construction, such as subject–verb–object order. Three seems to be a magic number; more than three can be awkward and tedious.

Boston College has an assistant dean for alcohol and drug education. Rutgers University sets aside dorm rooms for recovering student alcoholics. The University of Nevada bars students from leaving school sports events to make alcohol runs.

Increasingly, colleges are confronting problem drinking by providing education and rehabilitation programs, alternatives to the campus bar scene and stricter regulation of on-campus parties.

The Associated Press

Nut graph

Question leads These can be effective if the reader is interested in finding the answer to the question you pose. If not, you could lose the reader. One way to test question leads is to determine if the answer would be yes or no. Those are the dangerous ones. A question that raises a more thoughtful, and more interesting, answer is preferable.

What are the odds of finding your true love by placing an ad with a telephone dating service?

About one in 40, according to Terry Ehlbert.

On April 13, Ehlbert is planning to marry Scott Anderson, who was the last of 40 guys she agreed to meet after plac-

ing a voice-mail ad with the 1-976-DATE service she saw advertised on TV. . . .

The phone services work in much the same way published personal ads do.

Rick Shefchik, St. Paul *(Minn.)* Pioneer Press

Nut graph

The next example is a little dangerous. What if you don't want to buy cigarettes at all? Will you read on?

Want to buy cigarettes while at the gas station? Or while sipping a cocktail at your favorite bar?

Not in Lower Merion, if township officials have their way.

Nut graph　Officials there, concerned about the availability of cigarettes to minors, have

proposed a municipal law prohibiting cigarette vending machines in the township. The law would be the first of its kind in Pennsylvania.

The Philadelphia Inquirer

Cliche leads In general, avoid cliches. But occasionally, a play on words will work as a clever lead. Consider this:

Nick Agid's workshop is just a stone's throw from the Torrance post office. Good thing, too. When Agid drops a post card into the mail, it lands with a five-pound thud.

Nut graph　Agid is a sculptor who carves messages on leftover chunks of marble and

granite. They become postcards when he adds scratched-on addresses and slaps stamps on the slabs.

Bob Pool, Los Angeles Times

Leads to Avoid

The leads described in this section are strained, obtuse, rambling or just plain awful. They don't work for a variety of reasons.

Good news/bad news leads: The bad news is this type of lead. They're cliches, and they're used so often that they're boring. They're also judgmental.

> Some good news for city workers: The county administration has been giving signals that it might not have to give out any pink slips, at least for now.
>
> Some bad news for city taxpayers: The county administration has shown no signs of scaling back its proposal to raise taxes for the next several years.
>
> *Newsday*

Crystal ball leads: These are dream-sequence leads that foretell the future. If you were writing about psychics, perhaps you could write this kind of lead. But most people can't predict the future. "John Jones never imagined when he boarded the plane that it was going to crash." Would he have been stupid enough to board it if he had known? Leads that emphasize "if only they had known" are far-fetched. Consider the following. It's unlikely that a child who is choking is thinking about the future—much less about what he can do for someone else.

> When 10-year-old Jason Finser of Clermont was saved from choking to death at a family dinner two years ago, he never dreamed he would be able to return the favor.
>
> *Nut graph*   But luckily for his classmate, 9-year-old Abby Muick, Jason knew exactly what to do when she choked on a chocolate-and-Rice Krispies treat in the lunchroom at Minneola Elementary School.
>
> *The Orlando (Fla.) Sentinel*

Nightmare leads: These are also dream leads, usually relating to a past experience. The nightmare analogy is overused: "The past three days were like a nightmare for John Jones." For the reader, too. Every bad experience someone has does not have to be compared to a nightmare.

> The nightmare became reality for local police yesterday when a Niagara Falls drug dealer was arrested at the Greater Buffalo International Airport. Hidden in his baggage were $50,000 worth of heroin, some PCP, and a sampling of a new drug he referred to as "smokable cocaine."
>
> Niagara *(N.Y.)* Gazette

Plop-a-person leads: This type of lead is a misuse of the focus-on-a-person lead. When the writer just tops the story with a sketch of a person and does not back it up in the text, that's plopping. It's also misleading. The reader starts the story thinking that the person has something to say or do in the story. But after the lead, the person disappears.

Tuesday was a good day for psychology professor Carnot Nelson.

He spent most of it helping an honors student work on her thesis. He read another student's doctoral dissertation and two master's thesis proposals. Then he went to a meeting, which he left after an hour and a half so he could do some reading of his own.

This is the last time we hear about Nelson, despite his being a good example.

Nelson, a senior professor at the University of South Florida, who also teaches large undergraduate classes and small graduate seminars, is a good example of the range of activity involved in teaching Florida university students.

"Education is a one-at-a-time, hand-made business," said state university spokesman Pat Riordan. "You can't mechanize it, you can't computerize it and you can't put it on an assembly line."

But college professors in Florida are under increasing pressure to do exactly that. Recurring state budget cuts have made some classes larger and eliminated many others. And a political climate that says there can be no new taxes until a state government becomes "more productive" has fueled a drive to force professors to spend more time in the classroom.

Nut graph

St. Petersburg *(Fla.)* Times

Weather-report leads: These leads set the scene by describing the weather: "It was a dark and stormy night." Avoid using the weather as a lead when it isn't related to the story.

It was hot and humid the day the city council decided to ban smoking from all public buildings.

The ordinance, passed unanimously, will go into effect immediately.

Stereotype leads: These are most common in features about older people, women and groups with special interests. The writer tries hard to be complimentary but instead only reinforces stereotypes.

This is the lead for a story about Senior Olympics, games for people over age 60:

At the age when most of their contemporaries are in rocking chairs, these athletes will be competing in swimming, archery, badminton, bicycle racing—just about every imaginable sport, through the long jump and shot put.

The Baltimore Sun

If you look around your college campus, you're likely to see many professors in their 60s, and most of them don't spend much time in rocking chairs.

Soft leads can be enticing and creative, but they must be accurate.

How to Find Your Lead

To find a lead that will work for you in your story, first find your nut graph. Ask yourself what the main point of the story is. Then ask some of these questions to find your lead:

Reader interest: What did you or would the reader find most interesting about this subject?

Memorable item: What was the most memorable impression or fact?

Focus on a person: Is there someone who exemplifies the problem or issue? If you tell a story about this person or show the person in action, will it lead to the point in the nut graph?

Descriptive approach: Will a description of the scene relate to the focus?

Mystery approach: Can you tease the reader with a surprise that leads to the nut graph?

Build on a quote: Is there a great quote to back up the lead? Then write the lead so it refers to the quote without repeating it.

Contrast: Would a then-and-now approach work?

Problem/solution: Can you set up a problem so the reader wants to discover the solution?

Narrative storytelling: If you were just telling a good story, how would you start? Can you reconstruct the events to put the reader on the scene?

Exercises

1   **Hard-news leads:** Write summary leads from the following information. For the time element, use the day of the week instead of *yesterday* or *today*.

    a   A study was released yesterday by the University of Colorado. The study was funded by the Alfred P. Sloan Foundation. The study said that 60 percent of college students who begin studying science, mathematics or engineering switch to another major. The study cited poor teaching and an aloof faculty as the cause.

    b   There was a fire yesterday at a pizza restaurant. It is located at 2035 Main St. Two firefighters were injured when the roof fell in. They were treated at

St. Luke's Medical Center for minor injuries. The fire started in the basement of the building. The cause is under investigation. The roof collapsed, and the inside of the restaurant was destroyed. Damages are estimated at $100,000. The information comes from fire officials in your community.

c   The Centers for Disease Control today released the results of a survey of nutritional supplements. Nutritional supplements include vitamins, protein supplements and products promising muscle growth. Only supplements in powder, capsule or tablet form were surveyed. "It turned out that at least half of the ingredients have no documented medical effect," said Rossane Philen, a medical epidemiologist at the National Center for Environmental Health and Injury Control. She was part of the surveying team. The survey said many nutritional supplements have no medical support for their advertised claims.

2   **Active/passive voice:** Change this lead to active voice:

> A 29-year-old Phoenix man was killed Tuesday when his motorcycle was struck by a car on East Ina Road.

Write a lead in passive voice from this information:

Jones County Circuit Court Judge Billy Landrum yesterday sentenced a 17-year-old high school sophomore to two consecutive life terms for the murder of two men in a convenience store.

3   **Delayed identification:** From the following information, write a lead using delayed identification.

Background provided by the police: Michael Stephens, who lives in the 3700 block of North Camino Street in Tucson, was driving a flatbed truck in central Tucson early yesterday morning. He lost control of his truck, and it overturned on East 15th Street near South Kino Parkway. He died of head injuries at the scene of the accident at 2:30 a.m. He was 44 years old.

4   **Updated lead:** From this information, give the lead a forward spin for the next day's paper or update it for the next edition of TV news.

Background: Vandals broke into the Midtown Magnet Middle School at 300 Fifth Ave. just before 7 p.m. on Sunday. They broke windows and damaged 11 classrooms and an office area. They damaged computers and other equipment. The cost of the damages has not yet been estimated. Classes are scheduled to resume today. School was closed Monday while school district employees spent the day cleaning up damage to the school.

5   **Impact leads:** Write impact leads from this information:

a   The Board of Regents (or the governing body of universities in your state) has approved an increase in rates for campus housing at your university. The biggest increase will be in residence halls, where rates will increase 14.8 percent for double-room occupancy. The current rate is $2,684, and it will increase to $3,080 next fall.

b   The Rockville City Council will meet at 7 p.m. Tuesday. The council will consider adopting an ordinance that would impose penalties for false alarms that are sent to the police department from faulty or improperly operated electronic security systems. Under the proposed ordinance, an alarm system owner would be allowed six free false alarms. The owner would have to pay a $30 penalty for each additional false alarm.

6   **Attribution:** Write a summary lead from the following information. Decide whether you need to include attribution.

Capt. J. Randall Ogden, a spokesman for the Tucson Fire Department (or use your local fire department spokesperson): A fire destroyed a home on East 17th Street. It was started by a cigarette that was discarded in a sofa. The fire left the husband, his wife and their four children homeless. The fire started at 1 a.m. and caused $30,000 in damages.

7   **Anecdotal, focus-on-a-person lead:** Write an anecdotal lead with a person focus from the following information; include a nut graph. Your focus is about the frustrations that students experience trying to park on campus because the parking department has sold too many permits.

Background: Nancy Pauw is a graduate student. One morning, she circled the parking lot east of the computer center three times before she found a parking space. Last year, there were 7,565 student parking permits sold for 3,930 spaces. "I have to get here an hour early so I can get to class on time," Pauw says. She is one of many students (on your campus) who experience the daily frustration of not finding a parking space even though they have purchased $30 and $50 permits.

8   Write a soft lead, including a nut graph, that uses the specific-to-general technique to convey the following information:

Background: The General Accounting Office, the investigative arm for Congress, issued a report yesterday that said record keeping at the National Park Service is defective. The report said information in the Park Service's financial statements is inaccurate and filled with accounting errors. Property owned by the Park Service is overstated by more than $90 million, the report stated. Examples of inaccurate data in the Park Service records include a vacuum cleaner that is really worth $150 but is listed in records as worth $800,000, a dishwasher worth $350 but valued at over $700,000, and a fire truck worth $133,000 but undervalued at 1 cent.

9   Write a descriptive lead for a story about apartments that violate city codes and are considered hazardous but that are often rented to students anyway.

Background: You interviewed a student who lives in an attic apartment. His story is similar to the stories of many other students in this neighborhood, known as the Oread neighborhood. As you climbed the steps to his apartment, you noticed that duct tape keeps the banister in place on the stairs. You saw that the kitchen is infested with mice and roaches. The student, Ted Flis, took you to the bathroom and said it has no electricity. "It's a dump," said Flis, a senior majoring in architecture. "But it was the cheapest thing I could find." This apartment is located at 1032 Main St.

10 Change this lead into a narrative lead:

A man threatening suicide kept police at bay for more than nine hours Sunday before he was pulled back from the ledge of a parking garage rooftop.

The man, a 36-year-old Topeka State Hospital patient and Wichita resident whose name wasn't released, threatened to jump from the south ledge of St. Francis Hospital and Medical Center's three-story parking garage at S.W. 6th St. and Mulvane.

Louis Cortez, St. Francis public safety officer, spotted the patient walking toward the ledge on the roof of the garage about 8:40 a.m. Sunday. Cortez stopped his vehicle and told the man to move away from the ledge.

The patient shook his head, "No."

"I stepped out and asked him, 'Can I help you, sir?' and he said, 'I'm going to jump,'" Cortez said.

Shortly before 6 p.m., several teenagers in front of St. Francis House, 701 S. W. Mulvane, began shouting, "Don't jump!" and "It's not worth it." The patient shouted back, "You want to see me jump?"

But the teens distracted the patient just long enough for Cortez to grab him around his waist and pull him from the ledge.

11 Leads analysis: Use two or three different newspapers so you can see if they have different writing styles. Find leads as directed, and attach copies of the leads to your report.

    a Find an example of a descriptive lead, an anecdotal lead and a narrative lead. Label each type. Analyze whether your examples are effective, and explain why or why not.

    b Find three feature news leads you like. Explain what techniques the writers used and why you like them.

    c Find three feature leads you do not like, and explain why.

12 Using your local or campus newspaper, change the leads on three newspaper stories to broadcast form.

Featured *News Scene* Assignment

Access *News Scene* at *http://communication.wadsworth.com/newsscenes* to view the news simulation titled "Big Fire." Assume that you are writing a follow-up story to the fire. Write three hard-news leads for a second-day story and two feature leads, focusing on the interviews with the tenants.

Coaching Tips

Write a first draft; mark "fix later" if you get stuck. Don't perfect every line during the drafting process.

Read your story aloud when you finish. You will hear the pacing and also catch errors.

Use lists to move the reader quickly through the story.

Test your endings to see if you have overwritten or strained your last paragraph. Put your hand over your last paragraph and see if the previous paragraph or the one before that is a better ending.

Lead reversal: Would your ending work as well as a lead? Sometimes the lead and ending can be reversed.

Envision your story order as a blueprint for designing a building. What shape will the story take?

Story Structure

Ken Fuson

When Ken Fuson was in high school, he played the drums. He still hears the beat of the drums when he writes his stories for *The Des Moines* (Iowa) *Register*. "I think a lot about rhythm," he says.

"I work at getting the tap, tap, tap. I want to make sure every paragraph doesn't sound the same." To achieve that musical quality, Fuson reads all his stories out loud.

Rhythm, also called pacing, helps readers move through the middle of a story. And Fuson wants to make sure that they read to the end. "I probably spend as much time on the ending as I do on the beginning," he says. He thinks a good ending makes a story memorable. "If readers remember a story I wrote, that's better than money." One time, after he won a prestigious award from the Gannett Co., which owns the *Register,* he told company executives that editors who cut the ending of a story should be executed.

Getting from the beginning to the end of a story isn't a haphazard process for Fuson. He carefully plans the parts of his stories. First, he thinks: "I look for ways to show conflict and to describe the mood. I think a lot about what is the right tone and the personality of the story." Then he starts organizing his material: "I type up all my notes. I select what I want to use. Then I put that information in an order. I need to know where I'm going and what the ending will be. Once you know what you're going to say and the way you're going to say it, then you can worry about what goes first."

And worry he does. "The first paragraph has to be perfect," he says. "And the second paragraph has to be perfect. I wish I had learned a better way of writing instead of worrying about what I'm going to say first." It may not be the best writing process, but it works well for Fuson, who consistently wins awards.

The Writing Process

Writers work in many different ways. Some writers pace around the newsroom before they write. Others outline their stories or write a rough draft first. And many writers just stare at their computer waiting for a muse to inspire them to create the perfect lead. They insist that they can't write the rest of the story until they find their lead. Deadline approaches, and the rest of the story gets short shrift because the writer is almost out of time. But the writing process doesn't have to be that painful; you can use several techniques to develop a writing process that works for you.

The FORK Method

In this chapter, you will study several ways of organizing stories. But before you get to those specific methods, try the following writing process—called the FORK method of organization—to help you organize stories before and while you write:

F = focus

O = order

R = repetition of key words

K = "kiss off"

Focus This is the main point of your story. In a hard-news story, the focal point could be in your lead. In a soft-news story, it is your nut graph. But the focus is also a crucial organizing tool; once you find it, you have to keep it. Your lead should lead to the focal point, and all other information should relate to it. Information in your notes that does not relate to this focus should not go in the story. If you don't know the focus of your story, your story will ramble.

Here are a couple of tips for finding your focus:

Headline technique: Try writing a headline for your story. If you had only a few words to express the main point, what would they be?

Tell-a-friend technique: If you were telling someone about your story, how would you describe it? How would you answer the question "What's it about?" Explain your story in one or two sentences.

Even Pulitzer Prize–winning writers and editors use the tell-a-friend technique to find their focus. For example, Laura Sessions Stepp, a writer at *The Washington Post*, tells a story about when she was the editor of a Pulitzer Prize–winning series at *The Charlotte* (N.C.) *Observer*. For nearly a year, she had worked on a series about brown lung disease, which cotton pickers were getting from inhaling the dust of the cotton.

After all the editing was completed, she sat down to write a brief introduction explaining what the series was about. And she sat. And she sat. The city editor, noticing her agony, came over and asked what the problem was. "I'm stuck. I can't write a lead for this," she said.

"What's it about?" he said.

"Cotton dust is killing people, and farmers are . . ."

"Stop!" he said, as she was about to drone on.

Cotton dust is killing people. That was the lead. And the focus of the series.

Jacqui Banaszynski, winner of a Pulitzer Prize for feature writing, uses a slightly different version of the tell-a-friend technique, which she calls the "stoplight technique." Imagine that you are at a stoplight and have 30 seconds to tell your story before the light changes. Chances are in 30 seconds you'll express the focus—or the lead. This technique is the supercharged version of "What's it about?"

Order Look through your notes, and mark information you want to use. On a separate piece of paper or in your computer, write key words or phrases to remind you of the items you want to use. Then put them in the order that you will use them in your story. You can change the order when you start writing if you don't like your initial plan.

Some writers need a very complete outline; others need only a few words to plan their stories. Decide what works for you.

Susan Ager, a columnist for the *Detroit Free Press*, calls the "order" step a road map. Envision a story as though you were planning a trip. You need a map to tell you where you are going, she says.

Graphics also affect your story content and order. Consider whether some statistics or other material to be presented in a graphic would be redundant in the text. However, if the information is crucial to understanding the story, leave it in both places.

Here are some suggestions to help you decide an order:

Topics: List all the main points you want to cover. Decide which are the most important and which point naturally follows another. Then put them in that order. Arrange information from the most important to the least important. Then group together all the information—quotes, supporting facts—related to a specific point or topic.

Graphics: If you were writing a highlights box, what would your main points be? Use the highlights as a guide for organization, giving clues about what to include and in what order.

Question/answer: Jot down an idea for your lead (you don't need the exact wording at this point). What questions does it raise that need to be answered and backed up in the story?

Ending: Decide how you want to end the story. Do you have a quote that summarizes the main point or refers back to the lead? Is there a future angle? After you have a lead and an ending, figure out what kind of information you need to get from the beginning to the end.

Time sequence: Does the story have distinct time elements? Consider arranging the story in some chronology. You could start with what is happening now, go to background (the past action), then return to the present and end with the future. Or you may decide that only a part of your story should be in chronological order.

Quotes: Mark the quotes that are most important, and design your story by sources, starting with the ones who have the most important points to make and proceeding to the lesser quotes. Vary the pace. Mix quotations with paraphrased information, facts and anecdotes. If you have a very good quote, you might base your lead on the concept and use the quote for backup to the lead.

Free-writing: If you are stuck, put away your notes and just write what you remember. Then review what you have written, and arrange it in an order that seems logical. Plug in quotes and facts later.

Tell-a-friend technique: The method of telling a friend may also give you an order.

Repetition of key words This is a technique that provides smooth transitions during the writing process or serves as a thought bridge to get you from one concept to the next. The technique is also known as "stitching" because it helps stitch one paragraph to the other.

As you write, look at the last sentence in each paragraph and find a key word that will lead you to the next paragraph. That key word can trigger a question you can answer in the next paragraph, or it can serve as a bridge for the next thought. You may either repeat the word in the next sentence as a transitional device or just use the concept of the word as a bridge to the idea in your next paragraph. Don't overuse the exact repetition of key words for transitions because your writing may become boring.

In the following example, the underlined key words serve as transitions to the next thought. In some cases the writer repeats the key word, and in others he uses it as a thought bridge.

What we need are some mandatory classes that you would attend before you attempted to move your household. These would be much more useful than those classes you go to before you have a <u>baby</u>.

When you have a <u>baby</u>, you are surrounded by skilled professionals, who, if things get really bad, give you <u>drugs</u>, whereas nobody performs any such service when you move. This is wrong.

*Key word **drugs** serves as a bridge to the next thought.*

The first thing the burly men should do when they get off the moving van is seize you and forcibly inject you with a <u>two-week supply of sedatives</u>, because moving, to judge from its effect on my wife, is far more stressful than <u>childbirth</u>.

Even in the worst throes of <u>labor</u>, even when she had become totally irrational and was making voices like the ones Linda Blair made in "The Exorcist," only without the aid of special effects, my wife never once suggested that we should put wet, filthy scum-encrusted rags, which I had been cleaning toilets with, into a box and have paid professionals to transport them 1,200 miles so we could have them in our new home.

*Key word **childbirth** serves as a bridge to elaborate the idea.*

Dave Barry, syndicated columnist

The kiss off Do you get annoyed when a person's last name is mentioned in a story on a second reference but you have forgotten who the person is? The kiss-off technique helps eliminate such confusion. It is a way of organizing information by using sources in blocks instead of sporadically throughout a story. After a person is identified by full name once, newspapers use only the last name if the person is mentioned again in the story. If only one or two people are mentioned in a story, this device isn't confusing. But the reader will have trouble remembering sources by their last names if the story refers to several of them.

The problem is even more confusing for online readers when a story spans several screens or Web pages.

Here is how the kiss-off technique works to avoid this problem: When you have three or more sources in a story, use each source once or in consecutive paragraphs, blocking all his or her comments in one place, and then kiss off that source. Do not weave back and forth with sources unless you have fewer than three. If you must use a source again in another part of the story, reintroduce the person by title or some reference to remind the reader of the person's identity. The exception is a well-known source, such as the mayor, the governor, the president, a celebrity or the central character in a story. The name of such a source may be placed anywhere in the story without confusing the reader.

The kiss-off concept may also be used for a story that has several different supporting concepts. After you have determined your main focus, plan an order for each supporting point. Block all the backup material related to that point, and then kiss it off. If you have several people discussing several ideas, as in a meeting, you will have to be selective about which comments to include. Even in a story arranged by topics, you still should try to block information from each source—if you have more than three—in one place so that you don't confuse the reader by weaving too many people throughout the story.

In this example of the kiss-off technique, notice how the sources are organized in blocks:

Beginning next spring, smokers at Lansing Community College will have to take their habit outside.

Focus

The LCC Board of Trustees has approved a smoke-free campus at the end of the next spring term. It is expected to make LCC the first campus with totally smoke-free facilities in the state.

1 (first speaker)

"It gives a year for the thing to settle in and for people to accept it and adjust to it," said Erik Furseth, chairman of the board.

Under its current policy, smoking is permitted only in designated areas, such as portions of cafeterias. When the new policy takes effect, smoking will be banned in all parts of all buildings.

***Key word* buildings leads to next thought.**

"We do have a smoking area. It's outside the building," said Trustee Judith Hollister.

2 (second speaker)

Karen Krzanowski, assistant executive director of the American Lung Association of Michigan, said she believes that LCC is the first community college in the state to adopt a smoke-free policy.

3 (third speaker)

"We're delighted," she said. "I think they are taking the lead and others will follow."

3
***Key word* others leads to next thought.**

A growing number of employers statewide are banning smoking, Krzanowski said. Those include Michigan Bell, Comerica and the state Public Health Department.

LCC trustees adopted the policy after holding hearings and developing a comprehensive report on smoking. The one-year delay in implementation is designed to give employees and students a chance to prepare.

4 (fourth speaker)

The college will offer assistance to people trying to quit, perhaps by offering smoking cessation sessions, said Jacqueline Taylor, vice president for college and community relations.

LCC also will develop an education program to explain the policy and encourage people not to smoke.

5 (fifth speaker)

"I think it's great," said Elizabeth Saettler, a non-smoker from Owosso. "I certainly think it benefits the majority of people."

6 (sixth speaker)

Sherry Brettin of East Lansing said she could accept the new policy. "I smoke, but I'll go outside. It doesn't bother me," she said.

7 (seventh speaker)

"I plan to stop smoking anyway," said Geoff Waun of East Lansing. "I still think there should be a place for people to smoke."

Chris Andrews, Lansing *(Mich.)* State-Journal

The kiss-off technique is only a guideline and should not be strictly adhered to when the story order would be more logical if sources were repeated in different places throughout the story. Plan your story first by topics and the natural order of one concept following another; then decide if the kiss-off technique for sources will be effective.

How to Revise Stories

Revising your story doesn't mean just going back and cleaning up the grammar and style. Do what a writing coach does when working with a reporter to discover the problems in a story: Ask questions to reveal where the problems originated. They could be at any point in the process, from conception to collection to construction. A coach would ask questions like these: What did you like about the story? Where did you struggle? What were you trying to say? When you revise your story, ask yourself some of these coaching questions as well:

Conceive: Is the idea well focused? Should the story be developed around another angle?

Collect: Have you checked online and other resources to make sure that your material is accurate and that you have enough information for background? Does the story need more information or sources?

Construct: Does the order work? Is it logical and interesting? Is the focus clear?

Correct: Did any problems occur in the earlier stages? Can anything be added to or cut from your story? Have you checked accuracy of names, grammar and spelling?

Although you may need additional information, more often you will need to cut the story. *USA Today,* which is known for brevity, offers these guidelines to its writers for focusing, tightening and revising stories:

Squeeze a fact on every line: Allow one idea per sentence.

Focus tightly: Think about what the real story is, and choose a slice of it. Emphasize what's new, what's coming and what it means to readers. Tell them the impact, how they can act on or use this information.

Use impact leads: Don't ignore the news just to be different, but avoid rehashing what readers already know. Think forward spin. Instead of writing "A jet crashed Tuesday, killing 534 people," write "Airline takeoff procedures might be overhauled after Tuesday's crash that killed 534 people."

Make the story move: Make your point early. Use only the information that helps make the point.

Keep it tight: Propel the story with punctuation. Colons, semicolons and bullets can replace some words and help the reader move faster.

Use specific details instead of adjectives: Instead of writing "the ancient windmill," refer to "the 100-year-old windmill."

Don't over-attribute: You don't need a "he said" after every sentence, although it should be clear where the information came from.

Use strong, lively verbs: Instead of writing "There were hundreds of people in the streets to see the pope," write "Hundreds of people lined the streets to see the pope" (or *jammed, crowded* or *thronged* the streets). Sentences that start with *there* force you to use a weak *to be* verb.

Avoid weak transitions: A well-organized story needs only a few transitions.

Choose quotes that advance the story: Avoid quotes that merely illustrate the last point made. And don't paraphrase if you have a good quote. Be selective. Don't repeat.

Writing Process Tips

Here are some other tips to help you during the writing process:

Remember your focus: Put your focus graph (the "so what" paragraph) at the top of your story as a reminder to choose only material related to the focus for the body of the story. Then remember to place the focus within your story.

Write many leads: Instead of struggling to get the perfect lead, try writing several leads. Then write the rest of the story. Choose one lead when you've finished.

Fix later: As you are writing, when you get to a sentence or paragraph that doesn't sound right, write "fix" next to it or follow it with question marks to indicate that you want to return and polish it. Don't get slowed down by perfectionism as you draft your story.

Use the question/answer technique: As you are writing, does one paragraph raise a question or point that should be answered or explained in the next? Try to anticipate the reader's questions and answer them.

Read aloud: If you are struggling with a sentence that doesn't sound right, read it aloud. Also read your story aloud after you finish writing it,

You'll hear the cumbersome parts that your eye didn't catch. Find them and fix them.

Check accuracy: Go back and check names, titles and quotes. Make sure that you have the right person's name attached to the quote you have used. Check for typos and spelling.

Use active voice whenever possible: Here's an example of active voice:

She will always remember her first story.

Here is the same sentence in passive voice:

Her first story will always be remembered by her.

The active voice has more impact.

Write short sentences: On average, your sentences should have fewer than 25 words.

Write simple sentences: Keep the subject and verb close together. This example shows what happens when you don't. It is from a story about school board approval of remodeling and construction projects at the city's two schools.

> Those two projects—calling for construction of classrooms, office area and media center at Wakefield and construction of a new district-wide kitchen and computer lab plus remodeling projects at the high school—will be paid for by using approximately $800,000 of the district's special capital outlay fund.

Whew! That's a long sentence. The subject is *projects,* and the verb is *will be paid.* They are separated by too many words. Split it into three sentences:

> One project will involve construction of classrooms, an office area and a media center at Wakefield. The other includes building a new district-wide kitchen, a computer lab and remodeling projects at the high school. The $800,000 approximate cost of the projects will be paid from the district's special capital outlay fund.

Vary the pace: Follow long sentences with short ones. If you use complex sentences, follow them with short, punchy ones:

Pamela Lewiston thought she was leading a normal life as the daughter of Dr. Normal Lewiston, a respected Stanford University physician, and his wife, Diana.

She thought wrong.

Her father had been married to—and lived with—two women besides her mother, all at the same time. His carefully managed deception ended in a cascading series of revelations after his death from a heart attack in August.

S. L. Wykes, San Jose *(Calif.)* Mercury News

Avoid jargon: Translate bureaucratic terms into simple ones; define technical terms. Here's advice from writer George Orwell:

> Never use a metaphor, simile or other figure of speech which you are used to seeing in print. Never use a long word when a short one will do. If it is possible to cut a word out, always cut it out. Never use the passive when you can use the active. Never use a foreign phrase, a scientific word or a jargon word if you can think of an everyday English equivalent. Break any of these rules sooner than say anything outright barbarous.

Here's an example of garbled writing from the U.S. federal budget:

> Funds obligated for military assistance as of September 30 may, if de-obligated, be reobligated.

Write the way you speak: Unless you speak like the bureaucrat who wrote that budget item.

Middles of Stories

In the previous chapter we studied several types of leads. The lead is a crucial part of your story, but it's only the window to the rest of it. If you want people to read your stories all the way through, you have to keep the middle moving and provide a good ending.

Transition Techniques

Getting smoothly from one paragraph to the next may require a transition. But the best transition is no transition—a story so well organized that one thought flows naturally into the other. The information in one paragraph should raise a question that needs to be answered in the next. Or it can present information that can be backed up with a supporting quote or facts in the next paragraph. If it does that, you don't need any special transitions. But when you do, you can try some of these techniques to pave the way for the next paragraph:

- *Use cause and effect.* If one paragraph raises a question, answer it in the next paragraph or elaborate with an example or quote. Try to anticipate questions the reader might have.

- To introduce a new speaker after a previous speaker, use a statement about or from the new person. Then lead into the quote or paraphrased material. For example:

A controversial proposal that would require all Temple University undergraduates to take a course related to racism drew strong support yesterday from a racially mixed group of students and faculty members who testified at a campus hearing.

Anika Trahan, a junior, said the proposed requirement would encourage more dialogue among students who come to the university from largely segregated neighborhoods. "They (white students) come from communities where they are never able to interact with black people," she said.

But opinion was sharply divided on whether the course should focus on black-white relations in America or include racism against Asian Americans and other groups.

Molefi K. Asante, chairman of Temple's African American studies department, contended that the requirement should focus on the white racism toward African Americans because that has been "the fundamental pattern of racism" in the United States. *(Transition to new speaker)*

A white student, sophomore Amy Dixon, agreed. "Our predominant problem on campus is black-white relations," she said. *(Transition to new speaker)*

Huntly Collins, The Philadelphia Inquirer

- To insert background, you can use words and phrases, such as *Previously* or *In the past,* or specific time elements, such as *Two months ago.* If you are going to recount part of the story chronologically, you can set it up with a phrase like *The incident began this way.*

- To get from one point to another, especially in stories about meetings where several issues are discussed, you can use transitional phrases: *In another matter, On a related issue, Other items discussed included.*

- A word or phrase from one paragraph can be repeated in the next. Here is an example that uses repetition of key words:

With a relentless sun beating on him as he cut through fields, swamps and shaggy forests, Earl Davis always looked ahead to the next leg of the project.

The legs were long and stretched interminably. The crews made slow progress. Mosquitoes whined about their heads, and snakes thrashed away when the right-of-way crews stumbled across them. . . .

Davis, who had lived in Pinellas County for almost 50 years, sympathized and suffered with them (the road builders).

The suffering wouldn't be over for a long time.

Mark Davis, The Tampa *(Fla.)* Tribune

Techniques for Maintaining Interest

There are many other ways a writer can keep the middle moving. Here are some of them.

Parallelism Parallel sentences help the reader move quickly through the story. Parallel construction means the sentences are worded in the same grammatical order. Some of the words can be repeated for effect, especially those at the beginning of sentences. In this example, the writer uses parallelism at the beginning of the story, but you can use it anywhere:

> Rudolph Almaraz kept his battle with AIDS his personal business, even though his professional business was surgery.
>
> He didn't tell his patients. He didn't tell officials at Baltimore Johns Hopkins Hospital, where he was a cancer surgeon. He didn't tell the doctor who bought his medical practice earlier this year.
>
> But now the case of Dr. Almaraz, who died of AIDS on Nov. 16 at the age of 41, has frightened his patients.
>
> *Matthew Purdy,* The Philadelphia Inquirer

Pacing Vary the length of sentences. Follow long ones with short, punchy ones.

> On New Year's Eve Lisa Botzum visited the emergency room of the Hospital of the University of Pennsylvania, complaining of nausea and vomiting. She was given a pregnancy test. She was elated by the result.
>
> Few others were.
>
> *Loretta Tofani,* The Philadelphia Inquirer

Dialogue When possible and appropriate, use dialogue in your story. It works well in feature stories, news stories about council meetings and especially stories about court cases. In this feature story, "13: Life at the Edge of Everything," *St. Petersburg Times* reporters spent several months reporting about the lives of middle school students. Then they wrote a series in dramatic storytelling form, making extensive use of dialogue to put the reader on the scene. In this section, Joanne, the mother of a teenage girl, Danielle, is worried about her daughter, who is starting to date:

A few months ago, when Danielle started to show more interest in boys, Joanne cornered her.

"You're not doing anything, are you?"

Danielle looked at her. "What do you mean?"

"You're not doing anything with that boy that calls up?"

Meaning Nelson.

"No," said Danielle. "We're just friends."

Thomas French, Monique Fields, Dong-Phuong Nguyen, St. Petersburg *(Fla.)* Times

BBI: Boring but important stuff Many stories, especially government stories, need explanation or background that could be boring. Don't put all the boring information in a long block. Break it into small paragraphs and place it where it will fit, but not in one long, continuous section. Also consider graphics as a way to present statistics and other information that could clog a story.

In their Pulitzer Prize–winning series about the U.S. Department of Agriculture, reporters Mike McGraw and Jeff Taylor used charts for many of their statistics. But in the body of the following story, called "Deadly Meat," they broke up much of the potentially boring but important factual material with quotes, anecdotes and lists. (They also used shorter sentences for complex material, as suggested in the next section.)

Each year tainted food kills up to 9,000 Americans. And it makes anywhere from 24 million to 81 million people sick, according to estimates gathered by the Centers for Disease Control. At least a third of the cases, according to congressional research, can be traced to meat and poultry.

Why is this happening? Agriculture Department officials typically blame consumers for the outbreaks. Families undercook their dinner, they say, or food service workers don't wash their hands. . . .

For consumers, one of the most crucial breakdowns may be in the warning system designed to keep those problems from ending up in the meat drawers of their refrigerators.

In its simplest form, it's supposed to work this way: In about 7,000 federally checked meat plants across the country, 7,000 USDA meat inspectors ensure that only wholesome meat comes off the assembly line. Slaughter plants must always have an inspector on duty, but processing plants operate under a system in which one inspector can check several plants each day.

If those inspections fail, and hazardous meat gets to consumers, the Washington-based "emergency programs staff" is supposed to recall it and issue a public warning.

Sometimes both systems fail. Indeed, sometimes even the watchdogs don't feel safe.

Earlier this year, after a day of classes at the USDA's training center in College Station, Texas, six veterinarians told a reporter they don't order rare beef for dinner. Too big a chance of getting sick, they say.

Halfway across the country in suburban Virginia, Carl Telleen serves reporters a vegetarian dinner. After working 30 years for the inspection service—including several years on an inspection review team—the retired veterinarian won't eat poultry and eats little red meat. He doesn't trust the process.

Mike McGraw and Jeff Taylor, The Kansas City *(Mo.)* Star

Simple sentences for complex information The more difficult the information is, the simpler your sentences should be. Use short sentences with simple construction, especially for bureaucratic information that would be hard for the reader to comprehend. This excerpt is from a story explaining how the judiciary committee of the Connecticut legislature works:

The judiciary is one of the legislature's busiest. By the end of the five-month session in June, the committee will have drafted, amended, approved, or killed about 500 bills—about 14 percent of the 3,649 bills filed with the Senate and House clerks.

Judiciary's 14 percent will touch nearly everyone. The committee considers matters of life and death, marriage and divorce, freedom and imprisonment.

This year's issues include surrogate parenting, birth certificates, and adoption. The death penalty and letting the terminally ill die. Longer prison sentences and home release. Committing the mentally ill to hospitals.

Mark Pazniokas, The Hartford *(Conn.)* Courant

Lists Itemizing information, especially results of studies or the main points in government actions, is an excellent way to keep the flow going through the middle of your story. You can use lists in a couple of ways:

- To itemize a group of statistics or any other cumbersome information
- To highlight key points within a story

Lists are usually preceded by a dot called a "bullet" or by some other graphic device.

Finally, some facts to justify cursing at people with car phones.

A recent study of car phoning showed that drivers involved in car-phone conversations were 30 percent more likely to overlook potential hazards, such as your rear bumper.

"They were so engrossed in the phone call that they were oblivious to what was going on," said James McKnight, whose experiments with 51 drivers were the basis for the findings.

What McKnight found through controlled tests on driving simulators was this:

- Even casual chitchat or just dialing a car phone distracted drivers enough so that they failed to respond to hazards nearly 7 percent more often.
- When talk turned to solving simple math problems—designed to simulate business conversations—drivers failed to respond to hazards nearly 30 percent more often.

- When engaged in casual or businesslike conversations, drivers 50 or older failed to respond to hazards 38 percent more often than younger drivers.
- Drivers who had experience with car phones were as easily distracted as drivers who were using the phones for the first time.

Mark Vosburgh, The Orlando *(Fla.)* Sentinel

Endings

Call them lasting impressions. To many writers, the ending is as important as the beginning of the story. Unfortunately, many readers don't get that far. But if they do, you should reward them with a memorable ending.

The ending also is called the "kicker." Think of it as a clincher. It should give a summary feeling to your story without repeating any information you have stated previously.

For columnists, the ending is more important than the beginning. The twist or main point the writer is trying to make is at the end of the column. Roger Simon, a writer for *U.S. News & World Report* and former newspaper columnist, once said he sometimes switches his leads and endings. He uses whichever is strongest. In many cases the lead could be an ending. And returning to your lead as a way to find your ending is an excellent technique.

The following sections describe some ways to form your endings.

Circle Kickers

Circle kicker, which ties together the lead and the ending

When you return to your lead for an idea to end your story in a full circle, you are using a circle kicker. Ken Fuson frequently uses this technique to devise his endings. In this example from a story about how families cope with Alzheimer's disease, Fuson repeats phrases from the lead—but ends with a twist:

"Mother, mother, mother, other, other, other. . . ."

The sound comes in short, grating bursts, like a children's record played at too high a speed.

Every day, relentlessly, another small slice of the person that once was Betty Jennings disappears. The brand of hell called Alzheimer's disease has reduced the 58-year-old woman to a stoop-shouldered, hand-wringing blabber of meaningless words and phrases.

She must be fed, bathed and diapered. Some mornings, after a particularly brutal night, Gordon Hanchett will look in the living room and see that his sister has attacked her plastic diaper, ripping it apart with her fingers and leaving small pieces littering the floor.

"It looks like a miniature snowstorm," he says.

The limits of devotion are stretched thinnest in the homes of Alzheimer's victims. Often operating on little or no sleep and frequently ruining their own physical health, family members witness the disintegration of a loved one's mind with the understanding that no matter what they do today, tomorrow will be worse.

The story continues with more about the family in particular and the disease in general. Here's how it ends:

"Mother, this mother, this other . . . Daddy, daddy, daddy."

The chatter is loud, constant and haunting. His sister's voice fills the house.

"Oh that," says Hanchett, waving his hand. "I don't even hear that anymore."

Ken Fuson, The Des Moines *(Iowa)* Register

Quote Kickers

The most common type of ending for features and hard-news stories is the quote kicker. Look for a quote that sums up the mood or main idea of the story. When you end with a quote, put the attribution before the quote or, in a two-quote ending, after the first sentence. Do not let the last words the reader remembers be "he said."

Last three paragraphs and quote kicker

Hotmail, the free e-mail service from Microsoft, is divulging subscribers' e-mail addresses, cities and states to a public Internet directory site that combines the information with telephone numbers and home addresses.

Hotmail customers are automatically added to Infospace's Internet White Pages directory unless they remove the check from a box in their registration form and "opt out," company officials said. . . .

John Mozena, spokesman for Coalition Against Unsolicited Commercial E-mail, said the public lists are a problem. "Spammers never do anything one-by-one," he said.

Hotmail user Chris Livermore of Redmond, Wash., said he keeps one Hotmail address private, given out only to friends. But now he gets almost 20 unwanted e-mails a week. His address is on the White Pages lists.

"Within a couple months, the account will be unusable," Livermore said. "To try to wade through about 20 spam messages to get to your own messages, it's horrible."

The Associated Press

Future-action Kickers

Many stories end with the next step in the development of an issue. But this technique works only if the story lends itself to a future element. If the next step is crucial to the story, it should be higher in the body. But if it works as a natural conclusion, then it can be the ending. It can be in the form of a statement or a quote.

HERRING BAY, Alaska—World attention focused Friday on the attempt to rescue birds and animals from the oil spilled in Prince William Sound. Cameras in Valdez focused on the few animals saved—fewer than 20 birds and four sea otters by evening Friday. The birds on the evening news were expensive symbols for Exxon, costing more than $1,000 apiece to rescue.

But on the water, the rescue efforts getting all the attention stumbled along with the air of a Sunday outing. In this bay at the north end of Knight Island, a diverse and committed group of people tried to learn to perform a futile task.

The story continues with detail about the rescue operation. Here is the ending:

By Friday afternoon, about two miles of the shore of Herring Bay had been thoroughly searched.

Only a few thousand left to go.

Charles Wohlforth, Anchorage *(Alaska)* Daily News

Climaxes

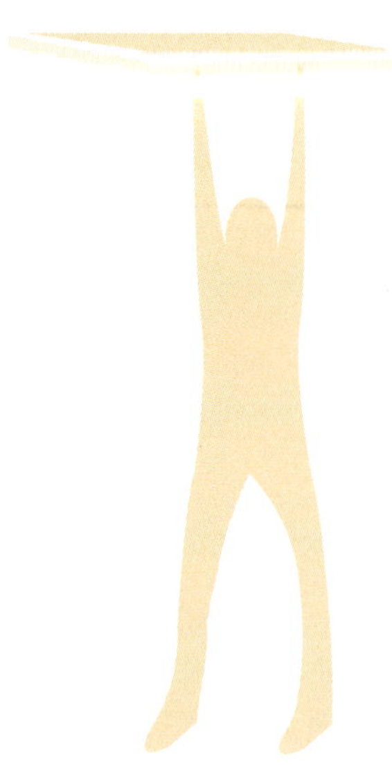

Cliffhanger, or suspense ending

This type of ending works on stories written like fiction, where the reader is kept in suspense until the end. It is more suited to features in narrative style or short news stories that tease the reader in the beginning and compel the reader to find out what happens.

Scott T. Grabowski sat Tuesday in the courtroom where a federal judge would determine his future, hoping that when the words were pronounced he would hear probation and not prison.

But Grabowski, 27, of Greenfield, is an admitted drug dealer. Early last summer, he pleaded guilty to a charge of possessing 3 ounces of cocaine that he intended to sell on behalf of an international drug network.

The story continues with the arguments from Grabowski's defense lawyer and the prosecutor. But what sentence did he receive? The reader doesn't find out until the end.

Finally, after a 2½ hour hearing, Curran (the judge) sentenced Grabowski to 30 months in prison, to be followed by three years of parole.

And with a nod to the parents, Curran told Grabowski: "I'm sure their hearts are aching as they sit here today."
Jill Zuckman, The Milwaukee Journal

Cliffhangers

Every day millions of people watch soap operas. The concept is a simple one: Give the readers or viewers a mystery, and make them want to find out what happens next. In writing, this kind of suspense ending is called a "cliffhanger." It is usually reserved for the endings of stories arranged in sections or series that will continue on another day. But it also can be used in the middle of stories to compel the reader to continue.

Cliffhangers are excellent devices for stories on the Web. At the end of a cliffhanger in the middle of a story, you could place a hyperlink to entice readers to click to the next section.

Not all stories lend themselves to cliffhangers. But many could be structured that way by putting the key points of the story on the front page and stopping with a question or suspenseful point in the last sentence before the story continues or "jumps" to another page.

This method is much more conducive to narrative storytelling, especially in a long feature, but it can be applied to hard news if the story stops at a crucial point.

This is only the beginning of a story that uses cliffhangers. Would you want to turn the page to continue reading?

In Fort Myers: Money, mercy and murder

Patricia Rosier's death was supposed to be peaceful and dignified.

She had made all the arrangements. Ordered food for the wake. Said a final goodbye to friends and family. Put the children to sleep.

On the nightstand rested a bottle of Seconals, powerful sedatives prescribed by her husband, Dr. Peter Rosier. Suicide would finally free Pat, 43, from the pain of invading cancer.

When the time came, she downed Seconals like "jellybeans," one witness recalled.

Cliffhanger

But something went wrong in the Rosiers' stylish Fort Myers home that January night in 1985.

Pat wouldn't die.

Peter frantically began injecting doses of morphine to finish the job. Pat's breathing slowed to a rasp.

But after 12 hours of the grim ritual, Pat would not die.

Finally, Pat's stepfather, Vincent Delman, decided something had to be done. Pat, he would later tell prosecutors, was suffering too much.

He took Pat's two half brothers into the bedroom and closed the door.

Twenty minutes later, the door opened. The Delmans walked out, their faces sullen. Peter was waiting in the living room, calming his ravaged nerves with a beer.

"Patty is dead," Vincent said.

Another cliffhanger

After the funeral, the Delmans left Fort Myers. They carried with them the dark secret of what happened behind the bedroom door.

On Monday, Peter Rosier, 47, is scheduled to go on trial for the first-degree murder of his wife of 22 years.

And another cliffhanger

The Rosier story has it all—sex, love, wealth, murder and a major mystery: Who really killed Pat Rosier?

Mark Stephens and William Sabo, Fort Myers *(Fla.)* News-Press

On the jump page you would find out why Peter is on trial and what kind of evidence exists to try him. You also would find out why this is an unusual case: There's no body and no autopsy report. Pat's body was cremated. There are no morphine syringes; they were thrown away when she died. And there is one other unusual twist: Peter wasn't even in the room when Pat was killed.

Court stories lend themselves to this kind of dramatic structure. But so do many others.

Factual Kickers

These are strong factual statements that could sometimes substitute as leads. They are statements that summarize the mood, tone or general character of the story. They are harder to write than quote kickers, but if done well, they give the reader a powerful punch. They are truly kickers.

Strive for a very short, simple sentence that states a fact. But choose a meaningful fact that will leave a lasting impression.

Julie Sullivan is a master of the factual kicker. In the following example, she is writing about a man who lives in a run-down hotel in Spokane. This ending is a simple statement that is circular in its reference to the lead.

Here is the lead:

Joe Peak's smile has no teeth.

His dentures were stolen at the Norman Hotel, the last place he lived in downtown Spokane before moving to the Merlin two years ago.

Gumming food and fighting diabetes have shrunk the 54-year-old man's frame by 80 pounds. He is thin and weak and his mouth is sore.

But that doesn't stop him from frying hamburgers and onions for a friend at midnight or keeping an extra bed made up permanently in his two-room place.

"I try to make a little nest here for myself," he says.

The story continues with detail about the difficulties that Peak encounters living in the Merlin. It ends with factual statements. Here are the last few paragraphs:

When conditions at the Merlin began worsening three months ago, junkies and gray mice the size of baby rats moved in next door. He hated to see it, but he isn't worried about being homeless.

He's worried about his diabetes. He's frightened by blood in his stool and sores on his gums. He wonders whether the white-staffed hospitals on the hill above him will treat a poor black man with no teeth.

Julie Sullivan, The *(Spokane, Wash.)* Spokesman-Review

Out-of-gas Endings

You can always just end when you have no more to say. This method is appropriate for hard-news stories, particularly those structured with a summary lead and arranged with supporting points in descending order of importance. You can end on a quote, future action or another fact in the story.

Here is a story with a factual out-of-gas ending:

TAMPA, Fla.—For the first time, a shrimper has been imprisoned for failing to use a federally mandated turtle protection device on his boat, the National Marine Fisheries Service said.

The story continues with the basic who, what, why, when and where and ends with this fact:

The government estimates more than 11,000 sea turtles drown in shrimp nets in U.S. waters each year.

The Associated Press

Body Building From Start to Finish

Here is a short story that could have been written as a routine police story. The writer makes it interesting by using many of the techniques described in this chapter. Note how the writer uses good pacing, parallelism and a circle kicker:

Mystery call has police barking up wrong tree

Mystery lead

The following nail-biting police drama probably won't find its way onto the "Rescue: 911" TV show, but it's had some folks around Eldridge talking about it since it happened at the end of last week:

Short sentences

A call comes to the Eldridge police dispatcher over the 911 emergency line. The dispatcher answers and asks what the problem is.

Fragments for emphasis and drama

No response. Silence. The dispatcher can hear very heavy breathing. That's all. Pretty obvious somebody's in trouble.

Pacing: long sentence followed by short ones

Police Chief Martin Stolmeier, on patrol in the area, takes 20 seconds to get to the Frank and Paula Griggs residence, where the dispatcher's computer says the call is originating.

Key word still for parallelism

The caller is still on the line. Still breathing heavily. Still needing help.

Short, choppy sentences to build drama

Stolmeier arrives. Announces loudly that the police are there, begins a room-by-room search. Stolmeier knows somebody needs help. He enters the situation assuming someone may have broken into the house. Maybe some sort of struggle.

Foreshadowing

Stolmeier nears a downstairs bedroom. The dispatcher hears him over the phone getting closer. On the other side of the door is the situation—the burglar, killer or heart attack victim.

Cliffhanger

Right about now, if this were a movie, the camera would zoom in very close on Stolmeier's perspiring face and the music would be building to a crescendo of tension and you would be going crazy as Stolmeier at last comes face to face with . . . with . . .

Paragraph could also work as a climax kicker

Blaze. A 6-month-old black Labrador who seemed very energetic and very happy to see Stolmeier. In a fit of rambunctious puppyness, Blaze had knocked the phone off the wall and somehow dialed 911.

Circle kicker (returns to concept in lead)

No word on whether Blaze's phone privileges have been restricted since the incident. But they'd better not tell him about 900 numbers or the Home Shopping Network.

Patrick Beach, The Des Moines *(Iowa)* Register

Here are some guidelines for writing middles:

- Read aloud to check your pacing. Do short sentences follow long ones? Do your paragraphs start in different ways? Do you have too many sentences with clauses?

- Would lists of short sentences itemizing findings or material substitute for lengthy paragraphs?

- Could you eliminate any transitions? Would some quotes naturally follow the previous point without needing a transition?

Here are some guidelines for endings:

- Have you overwritten or strained the ending? Try the hand test. Put your hand over the last paragraph and see if the previous one or two paragraphs would make a better ending. Does your ending repeat previous points?

- Have you avoided ending with the attribution?

- Is your ending memorable? Could it even be a lead?

- Is your ending too repetitious? Does it summarize the story like a term paper? If you are repeating information, cut the story to the last important point or last good quote.

Story Forms

Jack Hart tells writers to think logically when they organize their stories. He calls the process "sequencing." Hart, managing editor and writing coach at *The* (Portland) *Oregonian,* says writers should organize the information in a sequence that helps readers understand how one item leads to another.

Hart also says sequencing helps writers visualize a shape for their story. When he coaches writers, he uses models of organization and gives the models names so writers will remember them.

"I think we are lexicon impoverished," Hart says. "We haven't had many names for story structures. I am a firm believer that if you walk through the woods and you know the names of all the plants, you'll see a lot more. A lot of writers get halfway through a story and don't realize that they are writing in a particular structure."

Although many other writing coaches don't stress names and shapes of stories as much as Hart does, almost all coaches talk about order and logic and storytelling. They ask writers to envision what the reader needs to know and in what order. And they often tell writers to let the story flow naturally, as though they were telling it to a friend.

All stories should help readers understand the focus, the conflict, the background and solutions to the central topic. Most stories can be arranged by a topical order, points of view or chronological order for all or part of the story. Models of story structures can help you plan the organization. Your choice of structure depends on the type of material you have. Although there are many structures, the following are the most common:

Inverted pyramid: This is one of the most basic story forms. It is used most often for hard-news stories. The structure is a summary lead that gives the focus, followed by supporting points in descending order of importance.

***Wall Street Journal* formula:** This structure is based on the principle of specific to general. The formula is to start with an anecdotal lead, usually

Jack Hart

Jack Hart, writing coach

focusing on a person or event that exemplifies the main issue, which is expressed in a nut graph. The body of the story is arranged topically, with one point leading to another. The ending usually comes full circle, referring back to the lead. This structure is useful for stories about trends, major issues, features, news sidebars and news events that lend themselves to a feature approach. Although it is used in newspapers throughout the country for many news and feature stories, it is named after *The Wall Street Journal* because that newspaper originated the term "nut graph" and recommended this format to its reporters many years ago in a memo discussing ways to humanize business stories and make them readable for all types of readers.

Hourglass: The hourglass form starts with the hard news and then proceeds in chronological order for part or the rest of the story. It ends with comments or the outcome of the news. It is useful for police and court stories and other stories that lend themselves to some storytelling. It is also a good technique for avoiding attribution in every sentence because the writer can use an overview attribution before the chronological portion—for example, "Police gave this account," or "Neighbors describe the incident this way."

List: This structure starts with a lead and a few paragraphs of backup information and then includes lists of supporting points. The list items are usually presented in brief form with a large dot, square, check or other graphic item to set each one off. This technique is useful when you want to give many facts in short form. Lists can be used anywhere in the story.

Sections: This is a technique of dividing a story into sections, like book chapters, and separating them by a graphic device such as a large dot or a large capital letter. Each section can present a different point of view or a different time element (present, past and future). It works best for in-depth stories such as investigations or long features. The most effective section stories have good leads and good endings for each section. This form lends itself to cliffhanger endings for each section or for each day's installment if the story is presented as a series. Think of the sections as separate chapters, complete in themselves but tied together by the overall focus and story plot.

Nonlinear: Linear stories are structured from beginning to end as though they were in a straight line. Nonlinear stories on the Web are structured with hyperlinks that allow readers to choose the order in which they want to access the information. A nonlinear story might be organized like the sections format, with a part of the story on one Web page and links to other parts or elements on other Web pages. Other elements might be links to audio or video, graphics, time lines, additional stories and related Web sites. Envision a nonlinear story as a tree with hyperlinks as branches or as a circle with spokes leading to other elements of the package.

Understanding these basic structures will help you plan the lead and the order of your story. Regardless of the structure you use, you still can organize your information by topics, points of view, chronology or a combination of these factors.

Inverted Pyramid

The inverted pyramid structure organizes the story from the most important information to the least important. It usually starts with a summary lead that gives some of the basics: who, what, when, where, why. The elements that can't fit in the lead are in the backup. This is one of the most common forms for hard-news stories.

How do you decide what is most important and what should follow in descending order of importance? Use your judgment. Some questions to ask: What will affect the reader most? What questions does the lead raise that need to be answered immediately? What supporting quotes are strongest?

The advantage of this form is that the reader gets the crucial information quickly. The disadvantage is that the reader may not read past the crucial information.

This form is the primary structure for breaking news, and it is an important form for online journalism, where readers have unlimited choices and more control over their story selections. Because of the volume of material available online, the inverted pyramid is a useful way to let readers determine immediately whether they are interested in the story.

Regardless of the medium, stories still must be well-written to entice readers. Adding an impact paragraph—explaining how the story affects readers—is one way to strengthen the inverted pyramid. Here is an example of a basic inverted pyramid story:

Summary lead

Backup (quotes or facts)

Supporting points

Ending

Inverted pyramid structure

Headline

Teen sentenced to read book about Holocaust

Summary headline

He must write report on "Diary of Anne Frank" for his role in cross burning on black family's lawn

Summary lead: who (delayed identification), what, why

SEATTLE—Instead of being sent to jail, a teen-ager was sent to the library to read the grim Holocaust tale, *The Diary of Anne Frank,* for his part in a cross burning on a black family's lawn.

Backup: who, when

Matthew Ryan Tole, 18, was sentenced Friday to read the famous story by a young Jewish girl of her family's failed attempt to escape Nazi persecution during World War II.

Supporting facts: why

King County Superior Court Judge Anthony Wartnik said Tole received a light sentence because he was not one of the leaders in the April 16 cross burning in Bothell, a suburb north of Seattle.

Supporting quote

"The Anne Frank book is great for someone to get a picture of the most extreme thing that can happen if people aren't willing to step forward and say this is wrong," Wartnik said. "I'm hoping it will make him more sensitive."

More explanation

Wartnik told him to write a book report on *The Diary of Anne Frank* within three months.

Background

Tole pleaded guilty to rendering criminal assistance in the cross burning, which involved at least a dozen Bothell High School students. The cross was built during a party at Tole's home.

Factual ending

Tole did not help build or light the cross, but some of the materials belonged to him.

The Associated Press

MULTIMEDIA COACH

Story Structures for Broadcast and the Web

The summary lead with the main idea in the beginning is the most popular story form for broadcasting and the Web because listeners and online readers want information quickly. But almost any story structure can work for broadcast and the Web.

Before you decide how to construct your story, you need to determine what elements you have— sound bites and video for broadcast and the Web, hyperlinks, interactive questions and perhaps a discussion forum for the Web.

A broadcast story is almost always going to be shorter than a print story or an online story. Therefore, you need to make your points quickly but with precision. Don't try to make too many points. Still, don't discard the *Wall Street Journal* approach simply because it takes longer to get to the nut graph of the story.

Alternatives to the inverted pyramid may be preferable for broadcast, according to Annie Lang and Deborah Potter in their article "The Seven Habits of Highly Effective Storytellers," written for Newslab, a training center for broadcasters. As they explain, "To engage your viewers, tell stories on television the way you tell them in person. Use strong, chronological narratives whenever possible. Studies have found that narrative stories are remembered substantially better than stories told in the old 'inverted pyramid' style. Whatever structure you choose, don't make viewers search their memories in order to understand your story. Give them the information they need when they need it, so they can follow each part of the story. Use words which connect the pieces of the story to each other, and which make the chronology of events clear."

Here are some other tips for adapting story structures to the Web:

- **List technique:** Lists help online readers scan through text quickly. Use lists in any story structure when appropriate.

- ***Wall Street Journal* formula:** This popular form works well on the Web, but you need to insert the nut graph high in the story, preferably by the third paragraph. The same is true of any story with a feature-type lead.

- **Sections technique:** This form is ideal for long stories on the Web. Limit each section to three or four screens, and break on a compelling point that makes readers want to click to the next part. Try cliffhanger endings for each section.

The *Wall Street Journal* Formula

The *Wall Street Journal* format starts with a soft lead, focusing on a person, scene or event. The idea is to go from the specific to the general, starting with a person, place or event that illustrates the main point of the story. The concept, whether stated or implied, is that this person or scene is one of many affected by the issue in the nut graph. The lead can be anecdotal, descriptive or narrative. It is followed by a focus graph—nut graph—that gives the main point of the story. This paragraph should explain what the story is about and why it is important (the "so what" factor).

The story then presents backup for the lead and supporting points. The body of the story may be organized by different points of view or by developments related to the focus.

The ending is often a circle kicker, using a quote or anecdote from the person in the lead or a future development of something mentioned in the beginning of the story.

This is a very versatile formula that can be applied to many news and feature stories. It is useful for brightening bureaucratic stories. While you are reporting, seek out a person who is one of many exemplifying your point, or try to find an anecdote that illustrates the main point of your story.

The following story uses the *Wall Street Journal* formula. It is a trend story about casino gambling among college students. Note that the story starts with an anecdotal lead, that the sources are blocked, and that the ending is circular, returning to the person in the lead.

Soft lead

Nut graph

Backup for lead and nut graph

Supporting points: quotes, facts, anecdotes

Developments: cause/effect, explanations, points of view

Circle kicker: anecdote, description, future action related to lead

Wall Street Journal formula

Soft lead: focus on a person who illustrates the main point of the story

Backup quote

Nut graph

Supporting information

More supporting information

Casinos sinking college dreams

College students who live close to casinos may be more prone to gambling addiction. Numbers have been increasing in recent years.

By Kia Shanté Breaux

Associated Press Writer

KANSAS CITY, Mo.—Michael Hudspeth started gambling when he was in junior high, shooting craps for lunch money on the cafeteria floor. When he went off to college, he played dice aboard Missouri's riverboat casinos.

His losses grew from the $2 a day his mother gave him for lunch to $2,000 he once borrowed as a student loan—and he lost that in one night.

"I would go to the boat every day," said Hudspeth, 24, who often skipped his classes at Missouri Western College in St. Joseph to gamble five minutes away at the St. Jo Frontier Casino. "I don't know; it's just something about all the people and excitement that keeps me going back."

The spread of casinos around the country may be contributing to problem gambling among college students.

Students who live close to casinos are more prone to gambling addiction, said Michael Frank, a professor of psychology at Richard Stockton College in New Jersey, which has a dozen casinos in Atlantic City. "It seems to be increasing in recent years."

According to a study by Harvard Medical School's Division on Addictions, about half of the college students surveyed in the United States and Canada said they had gambled at a casino during the previous year.

At Louisiana State University in Baton Rouge, with two riverboats less than two miles from campus, a student was accused recently of bilking the school out of about $3,000 in a payroll scheme to support his gambling.

In New Jersey, "gambling is festering in every high school and college in New Jersey," said Edward Looney, director of the New Jersey Council on Compulsive Gambling. "It's absolutely epidemic. Just about any college in the country has students who gamble at racetracks and casinos."

At Kansas University, which is within an hour's drive of six casinos, students formed a Gamblers Anonymous chapter last year.

"Given that statistics show there's a tendency for younger people to develop gambling problems, it is of particular concern having casinos so close to college campuses," said Steve Taylor, spokesman for the Missouri-based Casino Watch, an anti-gambling organization.

The legal age to gamble is 21 in most states, and casino operators can face big fines if a minor is caught gambling. But underage students have found ways to get in, just as they've managed to buy alcohol or get into bars.

Many use fake or borrowed ID or get through the door without being asked for proof of age. Many college students have easy access to cash either from a parent or from a student loan. Students are also flooded with credit card offers, and a parent usually is not required to co-sign.

All 11 of Missouri's riverboat casinos have adopted a program called Project 21 to remind minors that it is illegal for them to gamble and to teach staff members how to spot underage gamblers.

Jeff Hook, director of marketing at Harrah's North Kansas City Casino & Hotel, said Harrah's staff checks identification before a patron gets on the boat and again afterward if there are questions about the person's age.

Hudspeth was raised in Kansas City, Mo., and gambling had been around him all his life. He would borrow a driver's license from his best friend to get into the casinos, and also bet on sports, sometimes with money his mother sent him for rent. He maxed out his credit cards and took out student loans to support his addiction. He did not finish college, and instead went to work full time to pay off his debts. *Circular ending*

Hourglass Structure

The hourglass form can start like the inverted pyramid, giving the most important hard-news information in the top of the story. Then it contains chronological storytelling for a part or for the rest of the story.

Use the hourglass structure when the story has dramatic action that lends itself to chronological order for part of the story. The technique is useful in crime or disaster stories to recount the event.

To set up the chronological narrative, an overview attribution is often used, such as "Police gave the following account" or "Witnesses described the accident this way," and then followed by a colon. However, this type of attribution should be used only for a few paragraphs so the reader does not forget who is speaking. All quotes still need attribution. If the speaker changes, the new source must also be attributed.

Advantage: The narrative storytelling in the chronological portion adds drama to the story.

Disadvantage: The chronological portion of the story may repeat some of the key information in the top of the story, making it longer than a basic inverted pyramid.

Hourglass structure

Boy, 3, shoots 16-month-old

Summary lead TAMPA, Fla.—A 3-year-old boy shot and seriously wounded his 16-month-old half brother Thursday after he found a .32-caliber pistol under a chair cushion in the family's apartment, Hillsborough sheriff's deputies said. *Attribution*

Melvin Hamilton, shot once in the chest about 9:30 a.m., was flown by helicopter to Tampa General Hospital, where he was in serious but stable *Backup for lead*

Attribution

Basic inverted pyramid structure with attribution for each point

Observation: no attribution needed

Facts

Overview attribution: chronological narrative begins and continues to the end

condition late Thursday after surgery, hospital officials said.

Otis Neal, who pulled the trigger, did it accidentally, authorities said.

Sheriff's officials said they did not know who owned the handgun but were still investigating. Under state law, the gun's owner could be criminally liable for leaving the gun in a place where a child could get it. . . .

Hours after the accident, Otis sat bewildered on a curb outside his family's apartment as television camera crews and reporters jockeyed around him.

"He is saying very little. I don't think he really knows what is going on," sheriff's spokeswoman Debbie Carter said.

Otis and Melvin live with their mother, Dina Varnes, in the Terrace Oaks Apartment complex at 6611 50th St.

Relatives and sheriff's officials gave this account:

The two youngsters were downstairs in the living room playing Thursday morning, while a 15-year-old friend of the family slept on the couch. Ms. Varnes was upstairs.

Melvin was walking around the living room when Otis found the gun under the seat cushion. He pulled the gun out and fired one shot.

Arabell Ricks, Ms. Varnes' aunt and neighbor, said she was walking to the store when her niece ran out of the apartment screaming.

"She said, 'Melvin is shot.' She said the oldest shot Melvin," Ms. Ricks said. "I went in and looked at him, and then I just ran out of the house and started praying."

She said she flagged down a sheriff's deputy who was patrolling the area.

"I said, 'Lord, please don't let him die,'" Ms. Ricks said.

Ending reaction quote

Heddy Murphy, St. Petersburg *(Fla.)* Times

Summary lead and backup

Key points

-
-
-

Summary lead and backup

Key points

-
-
-

Elaboration

Ending

List technique

List Technique

Lists can be useful in stories when you have several important points to stress. Think of a list as a highlights box within the story or at the end of the story. This technique works well for stories about studies, government stories such as meetings, and even features about people or programs if there are several key points to list.

When using a list for the body and ending of a story, you can start with a summary lead or a soft lead followed by a nut graph. Give some backup for the lead with quotes, facts or both. Then itemize the main points until the ending. Investigative reporters often use the list high in the story to itemize the findings of their investigation.

Limit lists in the beginnings and middles of stories to five items or fewer; lists at the end can be longer. Parallel sentence structure is most effective, but not essential, for lists. Each item should be in a separate paragraph. Lists are often used in stories about meetings to itemize actions not related to the

ETHICS

Dilemma: Would you use information for a news story that you got from messages posted by discussion groups (special interest e-mail lists) without contacting the people who posted the messages?

The case: You are working on a story for your campus newspaper and its on-line edition about a sexual harassment complaint filed by a female student against a male professor. The affirmative action office at your school confirms that the complaint has been filed but will not release the name of the student or the professor's name and his department.

You check a discussion group, open to the public, sponsored by the women's center at your school. You find messages posted by three women who also claim they were sexually harassed by this professor. They claim that he requested sex from them and implied that their grades would suffer if they refused.

Two of the women named the professor in their messages. You have tried unsuccessfully to reach these students by e-mail and phone. The professor refuses to respond to you by e-mail, by phone or in person.

Will you use quotes from the discussion group messages in your story, and will you name the professor and the women who wrote the messages? You are aware that messages to

Internet discussion groups may not bear real names and may not be true. But you are on deadline, and this is a competitive story. What will you do?

Ethical values: Accuracy, truth, fairness, privacy.

Ethical guidelines: The Society of Professional Journalists Code of Ethics makes these recommendations:

- Journalists should test the accuracy of information from all sources and exercise care to avoid inadvertent error.

- Journalists should diligently seek out subjects of news stories to give them the opportunity to respond to allegations of wrongdoing.

---

lead. The list is preceded by "In other business" or a similar transition. The following example uses two sets of lists:

Summary lead	Campus crime records must be open to the public, a judge in Springfield, Mo., ruled Wednesday in a case with far-reaching implications.
Backup: reaction quote	"The gentlemen who wrote the Constitution would be proud," says Traci Bauer, 22, editor of the Southwest Missouri State University newspaper.
Background	Bauer sued the school, saying it concealed crime reports to protect its image. Federal Judge Russell Clark ruled:

- Withholding crime investigation and incident reports is unconstitutional.
- Campus crime records aren't exempt from Missouri's open-records law or protected as educational records.

Media-law experts say the ruling could set a precedent.

Testimony showed:

- A rape allegedly committed by a star athlete was not disclosed and no charges were filed.
- Springfield police were not told of several crimes.
- Drugs were seized and destroyed without disclosure.

University spokesman Paul Kincaid says regents will meet Friday to consider an appeal.   *Future action kicker*

Claude Burgett, USA Today

Sections Technique

The technique of separating the story into sections is very useful for in-depth stories. It can be used with many kinds of feature and news stories. The key to the sections technique is to treat each section like a separate chapter, with a lead and an ending that will compel readers to continue.

One common way to organize section stories is by points of view. For example, in a story about a controversial government issue, such as a new landfill, you could arrange the story to have a section for each group affected by the proposal.

The other way frequently used to organize section stories is by time frames—starting with the present, then moving to the past for background and back to present developments, and ending with the future. Although the order can be flexible, the opening section must contain a nut graph explaining why you are telling the reader this story now. This technique is very effective for stories written in narrative style.

To determine whether your story is suitable for sections, envision subheads for it. Then decide if you have enough information in each subhead group to warrant a separate section.

The following story uses a combination of points of view and time sequences to organize the sections. This is written in dramatic narrative form, using storytelling that reconstructs the event. Notice how the sections are structured as separate chapters with kicker endings.

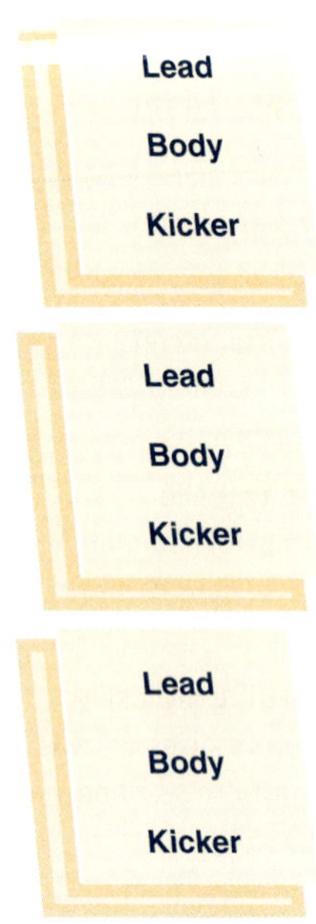

Sections technique

They got out alive, but no one was spared

BOULDER, Colo.—For weeks after the crash, David Hooker found the love notes his fiancee had hidden around the house.

In the medicine cabinet: "David, I love you this much."

In the sock drawer: "Poo—Here's a hug for you! Susan."

In the silverware tray: "I'll miss you! Take care."

This paragraph tells why you are reading this story now.

Five months have passed since Susan Fyler boarded United Airlines Flight 282. Hooker carefully stacks the yellow slips of paper into a neat pile on the corner of his dresser, next to the framed photographs of Fyler and the mahogany box that holds her ashes.

Less than a half-hour away in Denver, Garry Priest can't sleep.

He watched a movie—he doesn't even remember what it was about—and one scene stuck. A woman is thrown from a car and the pavement scrapes her skin raw.

Suddenly it was July 19 again and Priest was back in Sioux City, Ia., escaping from the plane, racing along the runway, seeing the debris, the charred metal, the boy's body.

Then he thinks of Christmas.

And his eyes will not close.

Five months ago, they were strangers, bound only by an airplane flight.

Susan Fyler was headed to Ohio to surprise her parents with news of her engagement. Garry Priest was going to Chicago on business.

Both boarded Flight 232 in Denver. She sat in seat 31K, he in seat 15G. Fyler was one of 112 people killed in

This section gives the crucial information that ties the story together.

the crash. She was 32. Priest was one of 184 survivors. He is 23.

For those most directly affected—the family and friends of the victims, the survivors and their families—the holidays are proving that time has not healed all wounds. . . .

Five months later, they are strangers, but David Hooker and Garry Priest share a common grief.

■

Every night, David Hooker walks into his bedroom, lights a candle and shares his day with Susan Fyler. Shortly after the crash, a friend admonished Hooker to stop feeling sorry for himself and to ask Fyler for guidance.

"I asked Susan to come live with me inside my body and to stay alive inside my body," he says, "and right after I did that, I felt a very dramatic change going on in me. I just felt all this energy coming over me."

After he lights the candle, Hooker may read the Lord's Prayer or flip through the love notes Fyler left him or look at the five photographs on his dresser.

■

It didn't make sense.

Why, Garry Priest wondered, were people acting this way? He had survived one of the worst airplane disasters in U.S. history. He had seen horrible things, scenes that made his legs shake, pictures he will remember the rest of his life.

So why was everyone calling him lucky?

"People want to pinch you," he says. "They say, 'Let's play bingo,' or 'Let's buy a lottery ticket.' They pat your head.

"I don't feel lucky at all. If I was lucky, I wouldn't have been on that plane. Nobody would have been on the plane."

■

They are strangers, but Garry Priest would like David Hooker to know that he, too, mourns Susan Fyler.

"Could you do me a favor?" Priest asks. "Could you tell all the people who lost loved ones and all the people who survived that I wish them a merry Christmas and that my thoughts and prayers and love are with them?"

Ken Fuson, The Des Moines *(Iowa)* Register

Exercises

1   **Inverted pyramid exercise:** Organize the information for this story in the inverted pyramid order. Here are your notes, based on a story from The Associated Press:

Who: Connecticut State Police

What: Ordered ban of hand-held radar guns

When: Yesterday

Where: Meriden, Conn.

Why: Because of concerns that troopers could develop cancer from long-term exposure to the radiation waves emitted by the devices. The ban was ordered as a precaution while researchers study the possible links between cancer and use of the devices.

How: The ban affects 70 radar guns, which will be withdrawn from service. State troopers will continue to use radar units with transmitters mounted on the outside of their cruisers.

Source: Adam Berluti, a state police spokesman

Backup information: "The feeling here is to err on the side of caution until more is known about the issue," Berluti said. "The whole situation is under review." The move is considered to be the first of its kind by a state police agency. It comes two months after three municipal police officers in Connecticut filed workers' compensation claims, saying they developed cancer from using hand-held radar guns.

2   *Wall Street Journal* **formula exercise:** Here are some excerpts from a story that was originally written according to the *Wall Street Journal* formula by Matt Gowen of the *Lawrence* (Kan.) *Journal-World*. Rearrange the paragraphs to conform to the *Wall Street Journal* style. Use an anecdotal lead followed by a nut graph and a circular ending.

College students are most susceptible to online obsession, experts say

Jonathan Kandell, assistant director of the counseling center at the University of Maryland, has found that college students— especially those in the 18 to 22 age range— are quite susceptible to an Internet obsession. Kandell, an assistant professor of psychology at Maryland, recently published his theories in the journal "CyberPsychology and Behavior."

A few years ago, Stacie Kawaguchi started tinkering with the Internet. She clicked her mouse, surfed around and delved into an international pen-pal site. At the time a Kansas University graduate student in botany, Kawaguchi "met" folks from Canada, France, Japan and Brazil. Through the Internet, she even met her eventual fiance, a Ph.D. candidate in engineering at Virginia Tech University.

"When you first start, you get really into it," said Kawaguchi, 26. "You get stuck on it for long periods of time."

The search for identity, the need for intimate relationships and the need for control often play a significant role in this potentially unhealthy behavior, Kandell said. Logging on, whether in chat rooms or through Web sites, can help students ranging academically from the inept to the astute cope with life's hardships. "If it's fulfilling a need, it's hard to give it up," Kandell said.

Simply put, Kawaguchi was online and overwhelmed. "You stay up late instead of going to sleep," she said. "It sucked up a lot of time." In a few months, the novelty began to wear off. "After a while, it was like, geez, this is enough," she said, adding that many of her chatmates were there night after night, even when she was gone for weeks at a time. "Basically, their whole world revolved around being there."

Studies on college campuses have shown between 6 percent and 12 percent of students may be spending too much time online, thanks in part to the ease of campus Internet access.

Kawaguchi saw the obsessive side of the Internet and managed to escape it. Others aren't as lucky.

Kandell was quick to note, however, that "addiction" was probably not the most accurate term in these cases. He compared overuse of the Internet to compulsive behaviors such as pathological gambling.

"I do see it as a psychological dependency," Kandell said. Kandell's evidence is mostly anecdotal, culled from student clients and classrooms filled with students who say they're downloading to the point of distraction.

In one class he visited, between 70 percent and 80 percent of the students raised their hands when asked whether the Internet was their chief obstacle to concentrating on projects and papers. "People are staying up all night, not going to class, not doing their homework— ultimately flunking out of school," Kandell said. "It's more pervasive than people think. There's something inherently tempting about the Internet."

For example, administrators at New York's Alfred University have found a correlation between high Internet use and a dropout rate that more than doubled. And the University of Washington has limited the amount of Internet time available to students to cut down on overuse. Several other colleges have set up support groups for Internet addiction.

Kawaguchi sees both good and bad in the Internet. The native of Oahu, Hawaii, considers it an effective communication tool but not a surrogate for human relationships. She calls it "luck" that she met her Iowa-born husband-to-be online. They traded photos and talked on the phone for a long time before taking the big step of meeting in person. The couple plan to wed in June in Lawrence. "Personally, I wouldn't recommend someone going out to look for someone on the Internet," she said. "I completely lucked out."

In addition to academic problems, jobs and relationships can be affected as social isolation grows. The Internet can provide an arena for people to simulate personal contact without actually having to meet face to face.

The underlying problem may be that the Internet's many facets are still new and somewhat unfamiliar. "I think we're just kind of scratching the surface," Kandell said. "I think it'll be a good five or 10 years before people have a good understanding of everything that's going on right now."

3   **Hourglass structure exercise:** Arrange these facts in hourglass order, placing attribution where it is needed. (This story is taken from the *St. Louis Post-Dispatch* of Missouri.) Attribute information to Capt. Ed Kemp of the Jefferson County Sheriff's Department unless otherwise noted.

Who: Two bank couriers

What: Helped police capture three suspects in a robbery

When: Last night

Where: At the Boatman's Bank of Pevely, Mo.

How: One courier, Dennis Boushie, who lives near Festus, chased a suspect on foot. The other courier, Willie Moore of St. Louis, drove a bank van, chasing a getaway car.

Police have booked three people on suspicion of drug possession. The three, who were found in the getaway car, are being held in the jail at Pevely.

Backup information: "This is beyond the call of duty. They acted more like police officers than private citizens or bank couriers," said Capt. Ed Kemp.

Boushie said he had asked the teller who was robbed if the robber had a weapon, and she said he did not. He said his pursuit of the robber had been "just common sense."

A man entered the bank shortly after it opened Tuesday morning and shouted, "Give me the money or else!" The teller gave the man an envelope containing the money, and the man ran out the front door.

Boushie chased the man on foot, and when the suspect jumped into a car, Boushie pointed the car out to Moore, who pursued it in a bank van. A few minutes later, Boushie got in a police patrol car and helped police track the getaway car.

Police broadcast a description of the getaway car, which had continued north on I-55 carrying two men and a woman. Police spotted the car, stopped it and arrested three suspects.

Police said they had found several thousand dollars in the car. The female suspect had stuffed money down her pants, police said.

Police were seeking federal warrants for bank robbery.

4   **List technique exercise:** Write a news story based on this information from the National Science Foundation.

Who: Jeffrey Cole, director of the Center for Communication Policy at the University of California. The center organized the World Internet Project, and the National Science Foundation is the sponsor.

What and why: A report, "Surveying the Digital Future," part of the World Internet Project, based at UCLA. The report is part of a multiyear study of how the Internet is affecting Americans' behavior and attitudes.

When: The first results of the report were released today.

How: The study evaluates what users do online, how they use— and whether they trust— the media, how consumers behave, how the Internet affects communication patterns, and what social and psychological effects ensue. The 2,096 respondents in the study, both Internet users and nonusers, will be contacted each year to explore how Internet technology evolves for continuing users, those who remain nonusers, and those who move from being nonusers to users.

Elaboration: The findings of the report show that Americans use the Internet exclusively without sacrificing their personal and social lives. It also revealed that users and nonusers have strong concerns about privacy.

"Our findings refute many preconceived notions that persist about how the Internet affects our lives," said Cole, founder of the World Internet Project. "Yet deeply rooted problems still exist that have long-range implications for this powerful technology."

The study found that more than two-thirds of Americans have some type of access to the Internet. More than half use e-mail (54.6 percent), and 51.7 percent of Internet users make purchases online. Nearly two-thirds of users (66 percent) and nearly half of nonusers (49.3 percent) believe that new communication technologies, including the Internet, have made the world a better place.

"Historically, Americans have been quite concerned about their privacy," Cole said, "but those concerns focused on government intrusion in their lives. Today, the concerns about privacy are quite different and focus directly on perceptions of private companies collecting information and tracking our movements on the Internet."

5   **Sections technique exercise:** Find a long story or project in a newspaper, and organize it in section form. Mark where it could be divided into sections, and rewrite the kickers if needed.

6   **Nonlinear Web story:** Using the sections story in this chapter or another sections story from your newspaper, plan it as a Web story. Organize the story in chunks, with links to other parts and other elements.

Featured *News Scene* Assignment

Access *News Scene* at *http://communication.wadsworth.com/newsscene2* to view the news simulation titled "Basketball Scandal." Plan how you would write the story using three different story structures: inverted pyramid, hourglass and *Wall Street Journal* formula. Then choose one structure you prefer, and write the story in that form.

Coaching Tips

Gather as many specific details as possible while you are reporting. Take notes of your observations as well as information from sources.

Use show-in-action techniques. Describe what people are doing.

Use vivid action verbs.

For narrative writing, try to envision yourself at the scene.

Gather details and chronology to reconstruct events as they occurred.

Think of your story as a plot with a beginning, middle and climax. Envision your sources as characters in a book; make your reader see, hear and care about them.

To write well, read well. Read as much fiction and nonfiction as you can, and study the writing styles.

Storytelling and Feature Techniques

Tom French was fascinated by Karen Gregory's case. He wrote a 10-part series about her murder and the man on trial for it. It was called "A Cry in the Night."

Something very unusual happened when the series began. Readers ran out to greet the newspaper delivery trucks each day to get the next chapter in the series. Why were they so eager to read these stories? You decide.

> The victim wasn't rich. She wasn't the daughter of anyone powerful. She was simply a 36-year-old woman trying to make a life for herself. Her name was Karen Gregory. The night she died, Karen became part of a numbing statistic. . . . It was what people sometimes casually refer to as "a little murder."
>
> *Tom French*, St. Petersburg *(Fla.)* Times

This passage was the introduction to the series. The first story began with a description of the trial of George Lewis, a firefighter who lived across the street from Karen Gregory and the person who was charged with her murder:

His lawyer called out his name. He stood up, put his hand on a Bible and swore to tell the truth and nothing but. He sat down in the witness box and looked toward the jurors so they could see his face and study it and decide for themselves what kind of man he was.

"Did you rape Karen Gregory?" asked his lawyer.

"No sir, I did not."

"Did you murder Karen Gregory?"

"No sir."

He heard a scream that night, he said. He heard it, and he went out to the street to look around. He saw a man he did not know, standing over in Karen's yard. The man said to go away, to not tell anyone what he'd seen. He waited for the man to leave—watched him walk away into the darkness—and then he went up to Karen's house. There was broken glass on the front walk. He knocked on the front door. There was no answer. He found an open window. He called out to ask whether anyone needed help. There was still no answer. He looked through the window and saw someone lying on the floor. He decided he had to go in. He climbed inside, and there was Karen. Blood was everywhere.

He was afraid. He ran to the bathroom and threw up. He knew no one would believe how he had ended up standing inside that house with her body. He had to get out of there. He was running toward the window to climb out when he saw something moving in the dark. He thought someone was jumping toward him. Then he realized he was looking at a mirror, and the only person moving was him. It was his own reflection that had startled him. It was George.

Tom French, St. Petersburg *(Fla.)* Times

Todd Richardson

Tom French

The entire series was written like a mystery novel. But it was all true, based on interviews with more than 50 people and 6,000 pages of court documents. The writing style, called narrative writing, is a form of dramatic storytelling that reconstructs the events as though the reader were witnessing them as they happened. French later turned the series into a book called *Unanswered Cries*.

French says he never believed his series would be so popular. "The way the readers responded was so gratifying," he says.

French relied heavily on dialogue throughout the series, even from the dead woman. Although most of the dialogue and description were based on interviews and his own observations, Karen's dialogue was second-hand information, based on recollections about her.

"After I wrote it, I spent three weeks checking everything with all the participants," French says. "I read it to them word for word to make sure it was accurate."

In 1998 French won the Pulitzer Prize for another narrative series about murder. This time he researched 4,000 pages of police reports and court documents and conducted scores of interviews to reconstruct the chilling story of an Ohio woman and her two daughters. They were on vacation in Florida when they were raped, killed and dumped into Tampa Bay. Once again, French wrote a gripping account of their murders, the three-year search for their killer and his trial. The killer was convicted and sentenced to death.

Narrative Writing

"Narrative writing" is a dramatic account of a fiction or nonfiction story. Newswriting in this style requires thorough reporting and descriptive detail. Dialogue also enhances the storytelling. Narrative writing is more like a novel or a play than a hard-news story, and the sources are like characters who relive the events in their lives. The story still must include the basic factual elements of news, but the presentation differs.

Jeff Klinkenberg, a *St. Petersburg* (Fla.) *Times* writer, views the five W's this way: *Who* is character, *what* is plot, *when* is chronology, *why* is motive and *where* is place.

French uses all these elements in his stories by weaving facts with description and dramatic tension. In this section from his Pulitzer Prize-winning series, "Angels and Demons," French uses descriptive detail to reveal how the bodies of the women were found.

It was a female, floating face down, with her hands tied behind her back and her feet bound and a thin yellow rope around her neck. She was naked from the waist down.

A man from the *Amber Waves* (sailboat) radioed the Coast Guard, and a rescue boat was dispatched from the station at Bayboro Harbor in St. Petersburg. The Coast Guard crew quickly found the body, but recovering it from the water was difficult. The rope around the neck was attached to something heavy below the surface that could not be lifted. Noting the coordinates where the body had been found, the Coast Guard crew cut the line, placed the female in a body bag, pulled the bag onto the boat and headed back toward the station. The crew members had not yet reached the shore when they received another radio message: A second female body had just been sighted by two people on a sailboat.

This one was floating to the north of where the first body had been sighted. It was 2 miles off The Pier in St. Petersburg. Like the first, this body was face down, bound, with a rope around the neck and naked below the waist. The same Coast Guard crew was sent to recover it, and while the crew was doing so, a call came in of yet a third female, seen floating only a couple of hundred yards to the east.

Tom French, St. Petersburg *(Fla.)* Times

In the following section, French uses dialogue to reconstruct the scene when Hal Rogers, the husband and father of the dead women, tells the boyfriend of his daughter Michelle that his wife and daughters won't be coming home:

That day, Jeff Feasby phoned the Rogers house again, hoping Michelle would be back.

Hal picked up. His voice was strange. He sounded furious.

"Who is this?" he demanded.

Jeff told him who it was and asked if he'd heard anything. With that, Hal broke down.

"They're not coming home," he said, his voice trembling.

Jeff paused for a second. He didn't understand.

So Hal told him. They were gone, he said. All of them.

Tom French, St. Petersburg *(Fla.)* Times

Reading to Write

French did not become a compelling storyteller without effort. Good writers are good readers, and French said he was inspired to do narrative writing after he read a book by the great Latin American writer Gabriel García Márquez. *The Story of a Shipwrecked Sailor* is a riveting story about a man who survived 10 days at sea without food and water.

French was also influenced by the literary journalists, a group of writers who, in the 1960s and 1970s, used the storytelling techniques of fiction for nonfiction newspaper and magazine stories. These journalists— Joan Didion, John McPhee, Tracy Kidder and Tom Wolfe—were influenced by Truman Capote's nonfiction book *In Cold Blood.* The literary journalists immersed themselves in a subject and wrote their stories with characters, scene, dialogue and plot. These were factual stories written like fiction.

Journalists often think storytelling techniques are limited to feature stories, but as you will see, you can apply this kind of writing to news about crime and courts and many other daily news stories.

Reporting Tools

Mary Ann Lickteig has a storyteller's instincts. A former feature writer for *The Des Moines* (Iowa) *Register,* she knows how to find extraordinary angles in ordinary events.

It is summer, and Lickteig is covering the annual Iowa State Fair. She is strolling from one booth to another in search of a good feature story. A pitchman is hawking a Robo-Cut slicing machine. Space-age plastic, he bellows. Lickteig laughs. Great angle for a story, she thinks.

Backstage at the pageant to choose the state fair queen, 77 girls are primping and practicing to compete for the crown. Lickteig decides that will be a good angle for another story.

Now it is midnight. The fairgoers have gone home. Lickteig has not. In the center of the midway, a Catholic priest is baptizing four children. Lickteig listens. She can hear pool balls cracking in the background, where carnival workers may be playing.

The next day *Des Moines Register* readers will hear them, too, when Lickteig writes about the baptism and describes the empty paths in the midway—quiet "except for the hum of a giant generator and the occasional crack of pool balls." Or when she describes the sights and smells of the fair in this excerpt:

> The day before the fair opened to the public, hot dogs spit as they turned on roasters; tattooed midway workers smeared with grease hauled pieces of steel out of the back of trucks and turned them into carnival rides; brand new pig feeders stood waiting to be admired under a sign that pronounced them non-rusting, non-caking and non-corrosive.
>
> Odors emanating from the horse barn indicated the exhibits had arrived.
>
> *Mary Ann Lickteig,* The Des Moines *(Iowa)* Register

Lickteig, now a freelance writer in Vermont, always looks for a good angle or theme for her stories. The focus is the reason for the story, which should be stated in a nut graph, but the theme is a literary device of an angle or unifying approach.

Mary Ann Lickteig, feature writer

"You hope the theme will present itself," Lickteig says. "Usually, if you see something that fascinates you, it probably will fascinate the readers."

That's one way to find either the theme or just an idea for a story, she says. "I don't think about covering the whole Iowa State Fair. You need to break it down—show the fair through one family, one idea, one theme." The key to good feature writing is gathering good details and then selecting the ones that will work in your story.

"You want people to be able to see your story," Lickteig says. "Choose the details that stick out in your mind, the ones you remember when you run back to the office and tell somebody what you've found."

Like the last 83 steps of a man's life. Lickteig was writing a story about a man who had murdered three women and had spent 17 years on death row. He was scheduled to be executed. Lickteig wanted to convey what steps were involved in execution—figuratively and literally. So she walked from the inmate's cell to the electric chair, in 83 steps.

These kinds of observation techniques are crucial tools for a storyteller.

William Ruehlmann, author of *Stalking the Feature Story,* says writers must concentrate when they observe and then analyze what they observe. He gives this example: "Flies take off backward. So in order to swat one, you must strike slightly behind him. An interesting detail, and certainly one a writer would be able to pick up on. Other people see flies; a writer sees how they move."

During the reporting process, you don't always know what details you will need when you write your story. So gather all the details you can—from how many steps to the electric chair to what the inmate had for his last meal. Ask what were people thinking, saying, hearing, smelling, wearing and feeling. Be precise.

To help you gather specific details, envision a ladder with rungs leading from general to specific. Start with the broadest noun, and take it to the most specific level, as in the adjacent diagram. Then use those details to write. For example:

A tan and white Lhasa apso named Joe ran onto the baseball field and interrupted the game when he stole the ball. It was only natural. After all, his namesake was Joe DiMaggio.

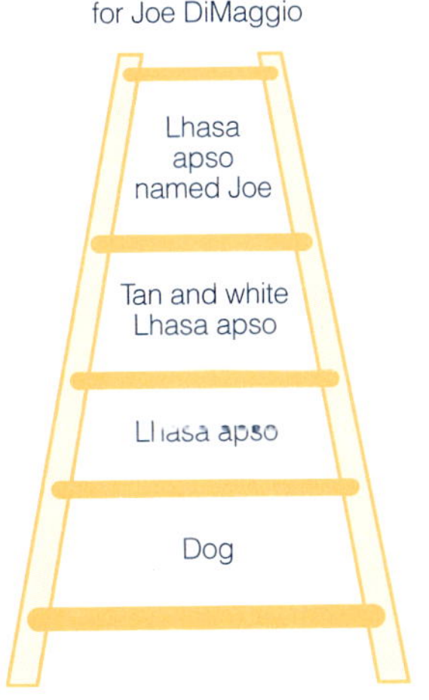

Ladder of details

Writing Tools

Once you've gathered all those details, what do you do with them? The better you are as a reporter, the more you will struggle as a writer deciding what information to use. The three basic tools of storytelling are theme, descriptive writing techniques and narrative writing techniques.

Theme

Before you begin writing a feature story, develop a theme—a concept that gives the story meaning.

David Maraniss, a *Washington Post* writer who won a Pulitzer Prize, describes it this way:

> The theme is why readers want to read the story, not the nut graph required by many editors. To write something universal . . . death, life, fear, joy . . . that every person can connect to in some way is what I look for in every story.

Descriptive Techniques

Too much description will clutter a story. Too little will leave the reader blank. How much is enough? First decide if the story lends itself to description of the scene or person. Then take the advice of Bruce DeSilva, a writing coach and news/features editor of The Associated Press:

> Description, like every element in either fiction or nonfiction, should advance the meaning of your story. It would be a good idea to describe the brown house in more detail only if those details are important. Description never should be there for decoration. It never should be there because you are showing off. And when you do describe, you should never use more words than you need to trigger that mental image readers already have in their minds.

Techniques for good descriptive writing include the following:

Avoid adjectives Write specific detail with vivid nouns and verbs, but avoid modifiers. When you use adjectives, you run the risk of inserting your opinions into the story. Author Norman Mailer put it this way:

> The adjective is the author's opinion of what is going on, no more. If I write, "A strong man came into the room," that only means he is strong in relation to me. Unless I've established myself for the reader, I might be the only fellow in the bar who is impressed by the guy who just came in. It is better to say: "A man entered. He was holding a walking stick, and for some reason, he now broke it in two like a twig." Of course, this takes more time to narrate. So adjectives bring on quick tell-you-how-to-live writing. Advertising thrives on it. "A super-efficient, silent, sensuous, five-speed shift." Put 20 adjectives before a noun and no one will know you are describing a turd.

Use analogies A good analogy compares a vague concept to something familiar to readers. For example, what is a "fat" man? David Finkel leaves no doubt in his story about a circus performer. How do you visualize the "World's Biggest Man" at 891 pounds? Finkel uses familiar items to help the reader see.

> Now: 891 and climbing. That's more than twice as much as Sears' best refrigerator-freezer—a 26-cubic-footer

with automatic ice and water dispensers on side-by-side doors. That's almost as much as a Steinway grand piano.

David Finkel, St. Petersburg *(Fla.)* Times

Limit physical descriptions Use physical descriptions only when they are relevant to the content. They work well in profiles; in stories about crime, courts, and disasters; and whenever they fit with the context. They don't work when they are tacked onto impersonal quotes.

Avoid stage directions—descriptions of people's gestures, facial expressions and physical characteristics inserted artificially as though you were directing a play. You don't need to describe what city commissioners are wearing at a meeting or how they gesture unless their clothing and movements enhance what they are saying and doing.

Effective	**Ineffective**
The 50-year-old airline pilot—who prosecutors say killed his wife by unknown means, cut up her body with a chain saw, and disposed of it with a wood chipper—testified with a voice and manner that was so calm it bordered at times on nonchalance. *Lynne Tuohy,* The Hartford *(Conn.)* Courant	The study shows college students are becoming more conservative, the researcher said, blinking her blue eyes and clasping her carefully manicured hands.

The color of the researcher's eyes and her hand motions have nothing to do with her comments about the study.

Avoid sexist/racist descriptions When you decide to include descriptions of people, beware of sexism, racism or other biased writing. Writers often describe men with action verbs showing what they are doing and women with adjectives showing what they are wearing and how they look. One way to avoid bias is to ask yourself if you would use a similar description for both men and women or equal treatment for all racial and ethnic groups.

Consider this example:

Ineffective

Even Chandra Smith, busy being adorable in her perky non-runner's running outfit, actually looked at the track. A minute later, she was jumping around and yelling, along with most of the other 41,600 people on the old wooden benches at Franklin Field.

The Philadelphia Inquirer

The story about the Penn Relay Carnival, a track meet in Philadelphia, also mentions a few men among those 41,600 people, including some volunteers who wear gray trousers and red caps. But they aren't adorable or perky.

Show people in action One of the most effective ways to describe people or places is to show action. For example, Tom French doesn't write only about murder. In a series about life in a Florida high school, he used the show-in-action technique extensively, as in this passage about a history teacher's first day on the job. The teacher, Mr. Samsel, has given his home-room students some forms to fill out:

The future leaders of America sit silently, some of them slumped forward, staring into space through half-closed eyes. Over to the side sits a boy. He is wearing a crucifix, blue jeans and a T-shirt. On the front of the shirt is a big smiley face. In the center of the face's forehead is a bullet hole, dripping blood. . . .

Around the room, students begin writing.

"Isn't this great?" says Samsel. "Just like real life—forms and everything."

Smiley Face looks at one of the sheets in front of him. He reads aloud as he fills it out.

"Please list medical problems."

He stops.

"Brain dead," he says.

Tom French, St. Petersburg *(Fla.)* Times

Use lively verbs News is action, says Jack Hart, *The Oregonian's* writing coach and senior editor for writing and staff development. But writers often "squeeze the life out of an action-filled world," he says. "We write that thousands of bullet holes were in the hotel, instead of noting that the holes pocked the hotel. We report that a jumper died Monday when his parachute failed, instead of turning to action verbs such as *plummeted* or *plunged* or *streamed.*"

Mitch Albom, a sportswriter and author of two best-selling books, knows the value of action verbs. Notice the ones he uses in this story about the day Detroit Tigers baseball player Cecil Fielder hit his 50th home run. Also notice the analogies and the show-in-action description.

He swung the bat and he heard that smack! and the ball screamed into the dark blue sky, higher, higher, until it threatened to bring a few stars down with it. His teammates knew; they leaped off the bench. The fans knew; they roared like animals. And finally, the man who all year refused to watch his home runs, the man who said this 50 thing was "no big deal"—finally even he couldn't help himself. He stopped halfway to first base and watched the ball bang into the facing of the upper deck in Yankee Stadium, waking up the ghosts of Maris and Ruth and Gehrig.

And then, for the first time in this miraculous season, Cecil Fielder

> jumped. He jumped like a man sprung from prison, he jumped like a kid on the last day of school, he jumped, all 250 pounds of Detroit Bambino, his arms over his head, his huge smile a beacon of celebration and relief.
>
> The Big Five-O.
>
> *Mitch Albom,* Detroit Free Press

Set the scene You need to set the scene by establishing where and when. Although it is common to establish the time and weather, often in a lead, beware of using that technique unless time and weather factors are relevant to your story. "It was 2 a.m. and the wind was blowing" is akin to the cliche "It was a dark and stormy night." In this story from a California State University student newspaper, the time and weather conditions are relevant to the story:

> TIJUANA, Mexico—Shivering in the mud under a 2-foot high chaparral, Jose carefully lifts his head into the cold night mist to monitor the movements of the U.S. Border Patrol.
>
> On a ridge above a small ravine, patrol trucks scurry back and forth while a helicopter above provides the only light, turning spots of the nighttime terrain into day.
>
> In the distance, guard dogs growl, bark and yelp.
>
> At one point a patrol truck speeds toward Jose and his group of six Mexican farm laborers. Squatting in the brush, they quickly slide flat into the mud like reptiles seeking shelter.
>
> Within seconds the helicopter hovers above them as its searchlight passes nearby, then at once directly over them. All their faces are turned downward to avoid detection by the brightness of the light that illuminates every detail of the soil, roots and insects that lie inches under them.
>
> Soon, the truck and helicopter make a slow retreat. Jose and his group, safe for the moment, will remain motionless in that same muddy spot for the next three hours as the mist turns to rain and the rain turns back to mist.
>
> To those who have never passed this way before, the sights and sounds are of another world. But to the expert scouts called "coyotes," this alien land between Mexico and the United States is home.
>
> Every weekday evening, approximately 2,000 people attempt to illegally cross the border from Mexico to the United States. On weekends the numbers can climb to between 5,000 and 10,000, said Victor Clark, director of the Binational Center for Human Rights in Tijuana, Mexico.
>
> *Brett C. Sporich, (Long Beach, Calif.)* Daily Forty Niner

Nut graphs

In the next example, the story is about a reading program. Although the lead about the weather is backed up by a quote, the weather has nothing to do with the focus or the rest of the story.

> It was a beautiful spring-like Sunday, and the heat on the first floor of the Kansas City Public Library Downtown was on full blast. But that didn't stop about 400 people from crowding inside to read and hear their favorite selections from African-American authors.
>
> The crowd, people of all ages and races, was there to take part in the national Read-In sponsored by the Black

Caucus of the National Teachers of English.

"That is true commitment," said Mamie Isler, program director for Genesis School, which helped coordinate the event in Kansas City.

The second annual Kansas City Read-In opened with a performance by 30 students from the Genesis School choir.

The Kansas City *(Mo.)* Star

Narrative Techniques

Narrative writing combines show-in-action description, dialogue, plot and reconstruction of an event as it occurred. This type of writing requires a bond of faith with the reader because attribution is limited. You need to make it clear where you got the information, but you don't need to attribute repeatedly. You can also use an overview attribution for portions of the story and then attribute periodically, especially when you are quoting sources.

Before you can do narrative writing, you need to do thorough reporting. It takes a different kind of questioning to gather the information you will need to reconstruct a scene with dialogue and detail. Narrative writing is not fiction. You must stick to the facts even though the story may read like a novel. You need to ask questions like these: What were you thinking at the time? What were you feeling? What did you say? What were you wearing? What were you doing? You need to get details about colors, sounds, sights, smells, sizes, shapes, times, places.

If you were witnessing the event, you would see, hear, smell and feel—perhaps even taste—the experiences of your subject. Because you are reconstructing the event, you need to ask the questions that will evoke all those images.

Those are the kinds of questions Jane Schorer asked when she wrote this Pulitzer Prize–winning story about a woman who had been raped. The woman had agreed to use her name. In this opening part of her series, Schorer sets the scene (with relevant weather and time references) and reconstructs the woman's experience so the reader is a witness to the event:

She would have to allow extra driving time because of the fog.

A heavy gray veil had enveloped Grinnell overnight, and Nancy Ziegenmeyer—always methodical, always in control—decided to leave home early for her 7:30 a.m. appointment at Grand View College in Des Moines.

It was Nov. 19, a day Ziegenmeyer had awaited eagerly, because she knew that whatever happened during those morning hours in Des Moines would determine her future. If she passed the state real-estate licensing exam that Saturday morning, she would begin a new career. If she failed the test, she would continue the child-care service she provided in her home.

At 6 a.m. Ziegenmeyer unlocked the door of her Pontiac Grand Am and tossed her long denim jacket in the back seat. The weather was mild for mid-November, and her Gloria Vanderbilt denim jumper, red turtleneck sweater and red wool tights would keep her warm enough without a coat.

The fog lifted as Ziegenmeyer drove west on Interstate Highway 80 and she made good time after all. The digital clock on the dashboard read 7:05 as she pulled into a parking lot near Grand View's Science Building. She had 25 minutes to sit in the car and review her notes before test time.

Suddenly the driver's door opened. She turned to see a man, probably in his late 20s, wearing a navy pin-striped suit. He smelled of alcohol.

"Move over," the man ordered, grabbing her neck. She instinctively reached up to scratch him, but he was stronger than she was. He pushed a white dish towel into her face and shoved her into the front passenger seat, reclining it to a nearly horizontal position. Then he took her denim jacket from the back seat and covered her head.

He wasn't going to hurt her, the man said; he wanted money. She reached toward the console for the only cash she had with her—$3 or $4—and gave it to him. He slid the driver's seat back to make room for his long legs, started the car and drove out of the parking lot.

"Is this guy going to kill me?" Ziegenmeyer wondered. "Is he going to rape me? Does he just want my money? Does he want my car!" She thought about her three children—ages 4, 5, and 7—and realized she might never see them again.

Jane Schorer, The Des Moines *(Iowa)* Register

Use foreshadowing When you give a clue about something that will happen later in the story, you are using foreshadowing. It is a way of providing mystery and teasing the reader to continue. In this example, the writer teases the reader by indicating that more ghostly experiences are coming:

SULLIVAN HARBOR, Maine—Gail Stamp was doing the dishes when she heard a noise in the hall stairway. Her husband was away, and she thought she was alone in the living quarters over the store here.

Stamp doesn't scare easily, so she went to investigate. She entered the hallway, and there, at the top of the stairs, she saw the gray form of a man.

"I stopped dead in my tracks," she said. "We both kind of froze for a second." Then the form turned and went down the stairs.

"It shook me up a little bit," she said. "But I knew right away who he was."

It was the ghost of Cling Clang, she said, a man whose life, marred by tragedy, ended about 130 years ago, next to the building the Stamps now own.

That was the first encounter she had with a ghost.

But it wouldn't be the last.

Now she and Jim, her husband, are convinced they are not alone. They believe the ghost of Cling Clang inhabits their home with them.

And therein begins this story of spirits of the dead.

Foreshadowing

Tom Shields, Bangor *(Maine)* Daily News

Create tone Hard-news stories often have an objective, factual tone, mostly an absence of mood. But in storytelling, you should create a "tone," or "mood," such as happiness, sadness, mystery, excitement or some other emotion.

You don't need to tell the reader that the mood of the place was festive or mournful. You can show it by the images you select for your story.

Another way of creating tone is by your writing style. Mary Ann Lickteig creates a lighthearted tone by writing this profile of a hypnotist as though the reader were undergoing hypnosis:

You will read this story.

You will hang on its every word, and you will not get sleepy.

As you proceed, you will learn about hypnosis and a Clive hypnotherapist whose work has led her to the International Hypnosis Hall of Fame.

You are ready to begin. Shari Patton is sitting on the couch in her home telling you that she first went for hypnosis "like a doubting Thomas." She was a student at the University of Minnesota when a friend was going to be hypnotized and wanted Patton to come along. Listen, now, to what she has to say:

"My friend had said, 'Go with me.' And I had said no, and after several requests begging me, I said 'All right. I'll go.' And I went to stop smoking, not believing that it would work, but very much wanting to stop smoking, and I was so amazed and delighted that it worked for me that I went back and started using hypnosis for weight control and lost 90 pounds."

That's how she got started.

Mary Ann Lickteig, The Des Moines *(Iowa)* Register

In contrast, Saul Pett wanted to create a somber tone to reflect the mood of the nation when President Kennedy was killed. Pett chose vivid details that showed what people were feeling, and he did something else that was quite unusual. He established the reverent tone of his story by emulating biblical style.

Another way Pett created the mournful tone of his story was through the length of his sentences. Short, choppy sentences can reflect fear, excitement, anxiety or stabbing pain. Long sentences can project suffering, thoughtfulness or a quiet mood.

Pett broke many traditional journalistic rules in his article describing the four days after Kennedy was shot: His sentences were long, he used the first-person *we* and he made no attempt to write objectively. Yet his story is one of the great feature articles of the 20th century. Here is an excerpt:

And the word went out from that time and place and cut the heart of a nation. In streets and offices and homes and stores, in lunchrooms and showrooms and schoolrooms and board rooms, on highways and prairies and beaches and mountaintops, in endless places crowded and sparse, near and far, white and black, Republican and Democrat, management and labor, the word went out and cut the heart of a nation.

And husbands called wives and wives called friends and teachers told students and motorists stopped to listen on car radios and stranger told stranger. Oh, no! we cried from hearts stopped by shock, from minds fighting the word, but the word came roaring back, true, true, true, and disbelief dissolved in tears.

Incredibly, in a time of great numbers, in a time of repeated reminders that millions would die in a nuclear war, in a time when experts feared we were being numbed by numbers and immunized against tragedy, the death of a single man crowded into our souls and flooded our hearts and filled all the paths of our lives.

A great shadow fell on the land and the farmer summoned to the house did not find the will to return to the field, nor the secretary to the typewriter, nor the machinist to the lathe.

There was a great slowing down and a great stopping and the big bronze gong sounded as a man shouted the market is closed and the New York Stock Exchange stopped, just stopped. The Boston Symphony Orchestra stopped a Handel concerto and started a Beethoven funeral march and the Canadian House of Commons stopped and a dramatic play in Berlin stopped and the United Nations in New York stopped and Congress and courts and schools and race tracks stopped, just stopped. And football games were canceled and theaters were closed and in Dallas a nightclub called the Carousel was closed by a mourner named Jack Ruby.

In Washington, along Pennsylvania Avenue, they had waited all that Friday night outside the iron picket fence, their eyes scarcely leaving the lovely old house. Early in the morning the guards had kept them moving and so they walked slowly down the street, eyes right, and at the corner they turned and came back on the street side of the sidewalk, eyes left. They looked like a strange silent group of mournful pickets demonstrating love, not protest.

In the chill darkness before dawn they were still there, now motionless, standing, staring across the broad lawn and through the bare elms at the house, at the softly lighted windows in the family quarters, at the black crepe lately hung over the door under the north portico.

They saw the blinking red lights of the police cars up Pennsylvania Avenue and they knew this was the moment.

The president was coming home. No sirens, no police whistles, no barking of orders that usually accompanied his return. At 4:22 a.m., Saturday, Nov. 23, 1963, there seemed to be no sound on the street or in the land.

The gray Navy ambulance and the six black cars behind it paused at the northwest gate and turned in. And along the fence, men removed their hats and teen-agers removed their hands from the pockets of their jeans and women tightened their fingers around the pickets of the fence. Tears stained their faces, their young and their old faces, their white and their black faces.

At the gate the procession was met by a squad of Marines and led in along the gracefully curving drive between the elms. In days to come there would be larger and more majestic processions, but none so slow, none so geared to the rhythm of tears, as the cadence of the Marines this Saturday morning. In two straight lines, glistening bayoneted rifles held across their chests at port arms, they marched oh so slowly up the drive and all that could be heard was the sound of their shoes sliding on the macadam.

Under the portico, under the handsome hanging lantern, they stopped and divided and lined up with the soldiers and sailors and airmen on the sides of the steps, at the stiffest, straightest attention of their lives. Jacqueline Kennedy emerged first from the ambulance, still wearing the same pink suit stained through eternity the afternoon before.

With her husband's brother, the attorney general of the United States, with his other brother, the youngest member of the United States Senate, with his sisters and his friends and aides whom he had led to this house, this far and now no farther, Jacqueline Kennedy waited in motionless silence while the flag-covered casket was removed from the ambulance. Then she and they turned in behind it and walked up the steps and through the glass doors and into the lobby and down the long corridor lined with stiff, silent men in uniform and finally came to a stop in the East Room.

There the casket was laid gently onto the black catafalque that held Mr. Lincoln on another dark incredible night almost 100 years ago. There, the kneeling priests began praying as they and others would through the long day and night by the flickering light of the candles, which silhouetted the honor guard riveted to the floor.

It was now 10 o'clock in the morning of a Saturday and Jacqueline Kennedy, still sleepless, returned to the silent East Room. She kissed her husband for the last time and the casket was sealed. A few moments later, she returned with her children and spoke to them quietly, trying to tell them something of the fact and the meaning of death. A fact and a meaning for which millions groped that day.

Saul Pett, The Associated Press

Storytelling Structure

Up to this point in the book, even though you have had many story structures from which to choose, you probably have been organizing your stories by focus and supporting topics or in chronological order. Even with a storytelling approach, you still need to get the focus first. A narrative story can then be arranged topically or chronologically, or it can follow a literary plot form—with a beginning, a middle and an ending called a "climax."

"Most news stories are endings without beginnings attached," says Jon Franklin, a Pulitzer Prize–winning writer and author of *Writing for Story*. Reporters miss the dramatic point of view when they concentrate only on the result instead of on the actions leading up to the event. Franklin says stories should be built around a complication and a resolution. In the middle is the development, how the central character gets from the problem to the solution.

If you have a story that lends itself to this kind of plot, your focus would be the complication that the main character has to overcome. The organization could be chronological, starting with the inception of the problem.

MULTIMEDIA COACH

Charles Kuralt was a consummate storyteller who wrote human-interest features for "On the Road," a series for CBS-TV's "Sunday Morning" show. Long before convergence became a buzzword for a type of journalism merging print, broadcast and the Web, Kuralt epitomized a multimedia journalist. He began his career as a print reporter for the *Charlotte News* in North Carolina, where he won the Ernie Pyle Memorial Award in 1956 for his offbeat human-interest columns. When he joined CBS in 1957, he continued producing human-interest features and later wrote several books about his adventures on the road and the people he met. He loved storytelling about people in newspapers, television and books, but he was a bit baffled by the Web.

"For most of my career I didn't do stories about things that go wrong," he once said. "I did stories about unexpected encounters, back roads, small towns and ordinary folk, sometimes doing something a little extraordinary. I would not argue that it was important to society at large; it was just fun," according to the Web site *Annenberg/CPB learner.org* (*http://www.learner.org/catalog/extras/interviews/ckuralt/ck02.html*).

Kuralt always found something extraordinary in the people and places he visited. "I don't know what makes a good feature story," he said. "I've always assumed that if it was a story that interested or amused me, that it would have the same impact on other people."

Kuralt learned early in his career at CBS that a good feature story for television was dependent on visuals. He said a CBS writer told him that "you must never write a sentence that fights the picture."

"If you're conveying some information that is not in tune with the picture that's on the screen, the viewer's going to be watching the picture and miss entirely what you're saying," Kuralt said. "It's always possible to fashion a sentence, it seems to me, so that it complements rather than struggles with the picture."

Whether you are writing feature stories for print, broadcast or the Web, take Kuralt's advice and find a story that interests you. Seek universal qualities of human interest such as people's hopes, fears, dreams, love, hate, the ability to triumph over adversity or the ability to achieve something special— like a story Kuralt did about the fellow in Indiana who could hold more eggs in his hand than anybody else.

Then, if you want to become a good feature writer for print or broadcast, take some tips from Kuralt, as he related in an interview with the Web site of Academy of Achievement: "I think good writing comes from good reading. And I think that writers, when they sit down to write, hear in their heads the rhythms of good writers they have read. Sometimes I could even tell you which writer's rhythms I am imitating. It's not exactly plagiarism, but it's just experience. It's falling in love with good language and trying to imitate it."

(To read the entire interview with Kuralt, access the Academy of Achievement Web site at *http://www.achievement.org/autodoc/page/kur0int-1.*)

The middle would be how the character wrestles with the problem, and the climax would be the resolution of the problem.

Or you can start in the middle of the action, as long as you explain to the reader why you are telling this story now (the "so what" factor). This approach is somewhat like using the time frame organization—starting with the present, going to the past, back to the present and on to the future. The technique of developing the story in sections, perhaps arranged by points of view, can also work in a narrative story.

Regardless of the technique you choose, you should plan your order before you write.

William Blundell, who spent years writing features and profiles for *The Wall Street Journal,* suggests in his book *The Art and Craft of Feature Writing* that features should be organized around "The Laws of Progressive Reader Involvement":

Stage one: Tease me, you devil. (Give the reader a reason to continue reading.)

Stage two: Tell me what you're up to. What is the story really about?

Stage three: Oh yeah? Prove what you said. (Include the evidence to support your theme.)

Stage four: Help me remember it. (Make it clear and forceful, and give it a memorable ending.)

Blundell says features should include the following elements, but not necessarily in this order:

Focus: What is the central theme?

Lead and nut graph: What is the point of the story? (Often, it is introduced anecdotally or descriptively.)

History: How did the problem develop?

Scope: How widespread is the development?

Reasons: Why is this problem or conflict happening now?

Impacts: Who is affected and how?

Moves and countermoves: Who is acting to promote or oppose the development, and what are they doing?

Future: What could happen as a result of the situation and developments?

Blundell also suggests blocking material from any one source in one place in the story, especially if the story has many sources—which is basically the kiss-off technique. The organization is not as rigid as the list implies. If the material lends itself to narrative storytelling, it can be told in chronological order or natural story order: beginning, middle, climax, ending.

Here are some reminders of good storytelling techniques:

- Use concrete details rather than vague adjectives.
- Use dialogue when possible and appropriate.
- Set a scene.
- Use action verbs.
- Observe or ask questions involving all your senses.
- Use show-in-action description.
- Tell a story like a plot, with a beginning, middle and climax. Get a chronology or sequence of events. You may want to use the chronology in all or part of your story. Even if you don't use chronological order, you need to understand the sequence of events.
- Follow Mark Twain's advice: "Don't say the old lady screamed—bring her on and let her scream."

Human-interest Profile

This next example is the type of human interest story that Charles Kuralt would have enjoyed reporting. If you work in a small community for a newspaper or TV station, chances are you will seek stories about people who are doing interesting or unusual things in your community. Consider how this story would work for broadcast and the Web.

- Does it have good visual possibilities?
- Is there a clear focus/nut graph?
- Are there relevant links?
- Could you add an interactive element such as a poll question or a blog?

Cooper Landing man revels in clover collection

KENAI—Some people believe the Kenai Peninsula is the luckiest place on Earth. Cooper Landing resident Ed Martin Sr. said he believes it is time somebody proved it.

Martin has been finding four-leaf clovers since his childhood and started to save them only two years ago. Since then he has rounded up more than 76,000 clovers.

Some people likely would ask why a person would be so concentrated on how many mutated clovers they found, especially a collection well into five figures. The answer is it has to do with a little competition, and a little bit of pride.

Martin has surpassed the previously largest known four-leaf clover collection held by George J. Kaminski, who collected 72,927 clovers within prison grounds in Pennsylvania (Guinness World Records). Kaminski has held the record since April of 1995.

Although Martin's world record-breaking application still is being completed, he is confident it will stand officially. The city of Soldotna, where many of the clovers were found, is handling the paperwork.

Kathy Dawson, assistant to Mayor David Carey, is making sure the project stays within the Guinness office record guidelines. This includes clear documentation in multiple forms.

"This is just amazing. I've got file cabinets full of clovers," Dawson said. "The mayor had kids from the schools counting all these clovers, and there are still more to be counted."

Actually finding 76,000 clovers, let alone a handful, is a difficult task, so Martin shared his secret:

"I look for mutated clovers, ones with four clovers and above. Now, you're not going to believe this, but once I found 880 in one day. I found 90 percent in the Soldotna-Kenai Borough area."

It's a knack, Martin said. "People just don't see what I see," he said.

Martin expects to break a world record, but he says the accomplishment goes beyond that.

"I'm interested in the good that will come out of this," he said. "We have a wonderful country, a wonderful state and community. We are all lucky to be living here. It's just a fact of life. I really think this is the luckiest place in the world, and this will prove it. Maybe this is why the fishing is so good here."

Martin, a former member of the Matanuska-Susitna Borough Assembly, said he hasn't been as involved as he used to be—although competing for a world record in the name of your homeland seems to be a good contribution.

"When you're meeting a challenge, when you do your best in anything, there is a feeling of pride that goes with it," Martin said. "I'm going to keep looking for clovers."

Layton Ehmke, The Peninsula Clarion

Narrative Storytelling

Martha Miller interviewed Vietnam veteran Dan Vickroy several times before she wrote this story about his injuries in the war. Each time he remembered more. She asked him to recall what he was thinking, feeling, saying and experiencing when he was injured, 25 years earlier.

Miller also reconstructed dialogue, based on Vickroy's recollections as he related them to her. The technique is acceptable if you are basing your information on documents and sources, but it is not preferable. If you can't confirm the dialogue with the original source, you can attribute it to the

ETHICS

Ethical dilemma: Is it OK to make up quotes? Is it OK to reconstruct scenes in feature stories?

Tom French reconstructed scenes, quotes and dialogue in his story about the murdered woman in one story and the other women in "Angels and Demons" based on court documents and interviews with sources who knew the women. How does that differ from the cases of Jayson Blair, a reporter for *The New York Times*, and Stephen Glass, a reporter for *The New Republic*, who were both fired in disgrace for fabricating information in their stories?

Ethical values: Credibility, truth, accuracy, fairness.

---

source who related it. If it is not controversial and you are sure it is accurate, you can reconstruct it as Miller has done.

After she finished all her interviews and filled several notebooks, Miller sat down to write the story. She was overwhelmed. She planned the story and organized it by different periods of Vickroy's life. Then she tried free-writing, just writing what she remembered to get it out of her head. After that she began refining the story, and before she revised her final draft, she read the story aloud.

The part of the story included here, the second section, contains almost no direct attribution. It is all based on Vickroy's recollections. Do you as the reader need attribution? Is the story believable without it?

A soldier's story

By Martha Miller

Iowa City Press-Citizen

Descriptive beginning for section: sets scene

Two hands lifted the sheet that covered what was left of Dan Vickroy's body.

"You're one tough son of a bitch," the surgeon said from behind a green mask.

Reconstructed dialogue

"I'm a Vickroy," Dan said. "Take me in and sew me up."

They did.

Narrative chronological storytelling through Vickroy

Vickroy regained consciousness. He figured he was in the base hospital at Cam Ranh Bay. He could see nothing through the bandages over his eyes, but he could hear the squeaks of rubber soles in the hallway and hushed conversations between doctors as they hurried from bed to bed. It sounded like a busy place.

He was scared, scared to death he was blind.

His ears wanted to believe what he heard, but his eyes would believe what they saw.

The nurses told him they were bandages and that he was strapped down. They told him he had been in bed for almost two weeks. And they told him he had a 104-degree temperature. He knew that. He couldn't stop shivering.

Clues of attribution without direct attribution (he remembered)

As he lay there, his memory returned. He knew the mine had exploded and that he was badly hurt. He remembered waking up twice in surgery. The last time, he felt a surge of pain. He saw a surgeon cutting off his leg with a bone saw.

The days and nights came and went. All the same. Dark.

Scene

This time, it was night. Someone shut off all the lights in his hospital room. The doctors were back. Slowly, they unraveled the gauze around his eyes.

Vickroy held his breath. He opened his eyes and saw a faint light. It burned, but this time it was a good sign. Doctors had worked through the night cleaning his eyes. What he saw made him want to put the bandages back on.

There were wire stitches in his stomach and his right hip. There were tubes in his nose and left arm. Instead of legs, he saw blood-soaked gauze wrapped around two stumps.

The doctors told him what happened: His right leg was blown away by the explosion and his left leg was amputated in surgery; his right arm was amputated below the elbow; and he had lost part of his stomach. Being so close to the mine saved his life; the blast threw him up and out of the way.

His face was intact, saved by that last glance back to camp.

Vickroy took the news better than most.

Direct quote with no attribution: speaker understood

"Psychologically, I was pretty positive."

He had no legs, but he did have a wife and new baby. He had married Sharon Kay in 1968 in Tulsa. She was 8½ months pregnant when he left for Vietnam. Danny Ray was born March 28, 1969.

Baby pictures were taped, one under the other, on the side of his bed so Vickroy could look at Danny Ray while lying on his back.

Those pictures and thoughts of heading back to the United States kept Vickroy's hopes up. But back home, his family wasn't so positive.

Short sentences and pacing

Dan's mother, Louise, was waiting tables in a Cedar Rapids restaurant when an Army officer handed her a telegram. She cried.

Louise had never wanted her youngest to join the service. She wouldn't sign his enlistment papers and couldn't see him off.

Vickroy had started to believe he could live without legs until the day a nurse read him a letter. It had arrived at Cam Ranh Bay several days earlier, but nobody wanted to read it to him.

It was from his wife. She wanted a divorce.

Punch ending to this section: short sentences

"She told me she didn't want half a man."

Here are some of the techniques used by Miller:

Reporting techniques: Establishing chronology, gathering detail, asking questions to get source to reconstruct specific events using all senses.

Writing techniques: Organized by sections technique in time sequences; although most of the story takes place in the past, each section deals with a different part of the character's life. Primarily follows chronological order, with cliffhanger endings for each section. Other techniques: short sentences, pacing, dialogue, definitions, description, narration.

Serial Narratives

Stories written like novels in chapter form are called "serial narratives." The form is related to the sections technique, but each part is a separate story in a continuing saga. Tom French has been writing his stories in this form for many years.

This style of storytelling has become very popular for long stories presented in a series, with each part published on a separate day. If the story is compelling enough, readers will come back for the next part. The format is well suited for the Web, where each chapter can be presented on separate Web pages.

A serial narrative needs a compelling plot with these elements:

- A character coping with a problem
- Development of the situation
- Resolution

Narrative writing puts the reader on the scene by recreating the events. The story often includes dialogue, suspense and chronological order of the plot rising to a climax just as in a fiction story. But all the information must be true, based on interviews and documents. Cliffhangers at the end of each chapter entice the reader to seek the next part of the serial.

Roy Peter Clark, a senior scholar at The Poynter Institute, experimented with a short form of the serial narrative called "Three Little Words." Each chapter of this story about a woman coping with her husband's death from AIDS was limited to about 1,000 words, approximately three screens on the Web. He likened it to a "breakfast serial," where readers could read each part while having their morning coffee.

To write a story in this form, you need to start with a good plot. Organize the story by dividing it into parts with logical breaks, just as in the sections technique. One organization technique is time frames:

- Past and present—what led to the situation and the current status to explain why you are telling the reader this story now
- Past—development of the situation
- Present—return to present
- Future—what lies ahead

Web Storytelling

The Web is an ideal medium for storytelling in many forms. Short segments are preferable to long stories that span several screens. But the Web is a perfect place to experiment with new forms of storytelling, especially nonlinear treatment with links to elements of the story.

No single form is right for all stories on the Web or in any other medium. However, one form of storytelling gaining popularity on the Web is personal journalism. Consider the Web a people's platform where readers relate more to writers than in impersonal journalism. Consumer journalism with helpful tips is another storytelling form that works well on the Web.

But innovative story forms abound on the Web. Storytelling on the Web can be in multimedia format, photo essays, short chunks or serial narratives. Most of all, storytelling can be interactive on the Web. Stories can involve readers by asking them to participate in polls, answer questions, write their own endings or opinions, or submit their own experiences. For an example of innovative storytelling and personal journalism, access *Musarium* (*www.musarium.com*), a site that offers stories in several creative forms.

Exercises

1   **Scene:** Go to a busy place on campus or to the cafeteria and listen to people talking. Gather information about the scene. Then write a few paragraphs setting the scene and weaving in dialogue.

2   **Analogies:** Study some objects on your campus. Write similes and metaphors to describe the objects.

3   **Narrative writing exercise:** Interview a classmate about any experience he or she has had, preferably a traumatic or emotional one. If your subject can't think of one, ask him or her to describe the morning routine from today or yesterday. Imagine that the nut graph is "And then (your subject) disappeared and hasn't been seen since." You will need to ask specific questions, such as what was the person wearing, what color and kind of car was he or she driving (if a car is involved), what time of day did the events occur, what was he or she thinking, feeling, doing, saying. Get the person to reconstruct the event exactly as it happened by asking questions about the sequence of events and details. Then write the information in narrative style in a few paragraphs or a brief story.

4   **Multimedia storytelling:** Adapt the story about the four-leaf clover for broadcast and/or the Web. Rewrite it as a script with sound bites, and indicate visuals.

5   **Web storytelling:** Write a story about a personal experience in narrative form. Divide the story into parts, with each part ending on a cliffhanger.

6   **Timed free-writing:** This exercise, borrowed from Lucille deView, former writing coach for *The Orange County* (Calif.) *Register,* requires you to write very quickly— in 10 to 15 minutes. Write a story about a personal experience and let your mind ramble, or write your thoughts about a topic. Remember that you are just getting your thoughts on paper. You can take any words that trigger thoughts—*soup, pizza, cars*— or a topic the instructor gives the class. Some topic suggestions from deView:

The happiest day of my childhood

My favorite assignment

My worst assignment

The most interesting person I interviewed (or know)

A turning point in my life

7   **Read well to write well:** Copy the leads or some excerpts from three news stories you read this week, or copy excerpts from other fiction or nonfiction stories that you consider great writing. Try to find examples of the kind of writing you wish you could write.

Access the Chapter 9 resources at *http://communication.wadsworth.com/ rich5e* to link to "How to Tell Stories in Journalism," an article with exercises by Roy Peter Clark of The Poynter Institute.

Poynter online
Posted, Jan. 1, 1998
Updated, Jan. 1, 1998

How Do You Learn To Tell Stories in Journalism?

By Roy Peter Clark (more by author)
Senior Scholar, Poynter Institute

Reprinted from Workbench: The Bulletin of the National Writers' Workshop, Vol. 4

Here are some exercises:

Go to a busy public place with a notebook in hand. Develop
your ear for dialogue. Write down snatches of overheard

Coaching Tips

Study your audience. Find out if the editors you want to reach prefer hard-news or soft-news style, short or in-depth releases, and single releases or media kits.

Find your focus. Use the focus statement as a headline or guideline for your lead.

Consider visuals—charts, illustrations, photographs, diagrams—to make your package more appealing.

Write a fact sheet. Even if you don't include a separate fact sheet with your release or media kit, use it as a writing tool to make sure that you have provided crucial facts about the organization in your story.

Always include the name, telephone number and e-mail address of a person to contact, the date information can be released, an address and the date the release was written.

CHAPTER 10

Public Relations Writing

You have to write as professionally in public relations as if you were writing in a newspaper. Avoid hype and be realistic about what you are selling.

Evie Lazzarino, director of public affairs, Claremont McKenna College

Evie Lazzarino, director of public affairs, Claremont McKenna College

When Evie Lazzarino studied journalism in college, she didn't think it would lead to an all-expense-paid trip to China. But just a few years after she graduated, she wound up in front of the Great Wall of China with a bunch of dolls called Cabbage Patch Kids. She was coordinating part of a world tour featuring children from America who went to seven foreign countries as "ambassadors" for the dolls, then among the most popular toys in the United States.

"The Chinese people had never seen a Cabbage Patch doll. It was fun to see people's first reaction to them," says Lazzarino, who was then working for a Los Angeles public relations agency that handled the Cabbage Patch Kids account. "My job was like an advance job for a politician. I went to China to set up a party, places we could visit, and I met with all the Western press, such as bureaus of *The New York Times* and *Los Angeles Times*. I tried to get them to cover what we were doing. We did a photo shoot on the Great Wall, and the photo moved worldwide."

The trip to China was one of the high points in a varied public relations career. Lazzarino began her career as a reporter for her local newspaper in Kansas after graduating from the University of Kansas with a journalism degree. She is now director of public affairs and communications for Claremont McKenna College in California. But along the way she has worked as an information specialist at Hallmark Cards in Kansas City, manager of community affairs for the *Los Angeles Times,* and communications director for the Richard Nixon Library and Birthplace in Yorba Linda, Calif.

Lazzarino's experience reflects the wide range of jobs in the public relations field. In addition to working with the media, she has been responsible for developing products, writing speeches for corporate officials, coordinating trade shows, and promoting plans for several major accounts, including Polaroid and Mercedes-Benz of North America.

Whether you work for one client or an agency that serves many, in public relations you are serving several masters at once, Lazzarino says. If you are writing a press release, you are not only trying to please your client; you also have to please an editor at a newspaper, magazine or television station. So in a sense, you are working for several people.

Cabbage Patch doll at the Great Wall of China

She says her journalism background helped her understand the kind of writing the media wanted. "You have to write as professionally in public relations as if you were writing in a newspaper. Avoid hype and be realistic about what you are selling."

Students going into public relations may think deadlines in public relations are not as strenuous as they are in newspapers. But you have many deadlines because you may have five or 10 clients you are trying to serve at one time, Lazzarino says. "People are paying a lot of money for your services. When it's someone else's money, there's a real sense of risk that you could lose clients." One of her main suggestions is to know your audience: "You have to know different styles. Some magazines may prefer something clever, but if you are pitching something to *The Wall Street Journal,* you should have a great news story. You have to study your market. Go out and meet editors, and find out what they want."

The Media's Needs

Many news releases are not read all the way through. But most editors at least skim the releases to find out if there is some newsworthy information. Community newspapers and local television stations rely heavily on news releases about events in their area.

Newsworthiness

Judith Brower, president of the Brower, Miller & Cole public relations and strategic marketing firm in Newport Beach, Calif., says the test of newsworthiness is the same for a public relations release as it is for a newspaper, magazine or television station. The basic principles of timeliness, local interest and unusual nature apply. With magazines, especially trade magazines, information that imparts new knowledge or something that will help readers is especially helpful, she says.

"If you are looking to place something in the media, take your subject and envision the headline the newspaper might print. Use that as an angle to force yourself to determine what is newsworthy about your information," says Brower, whose company specializes in public relations for real estate markets.

She also stresses the importance of visuals—charts, graphs and photos. "Magazines and newspapers have become much more graphic," she says. "Although many of the larger newspapers prefer to use their own photographers, the weeklies and small community newspapers prefer something they can just grab."

Good Writing

There is no substitute for good writing. "The more we can write the way journalists want the information to come out, the more chance it has of being published," Brower says. "You must have the basic skills for news writing." She has even implemented a writing test for people she wants to hire.

Despite the similarities between public relations and newspaper writing, there is a major difference in approach, Brower says. Public relations practitioners are advocates for their clients.

Writing Skills for News Releases

Mark O'Brien, a former media communications representative for Binney & Smith, makers of Crayola products, favors a brief approach to news releases. He targets newspaper editors as his first audience.

"You have to listen to the editors out there," O'Brien says. "They get a lot of material across their desks each day. If you have to read a page before you get to the meat of the subject, that's too much. Very few newspapers are going to print your story exactly. The release is just to pique their curiosity."

O'Brien, who now operates his own public relations agency, began work in public relations for General Foods after graduating from the University of South Florida. He says he studied what worked by comparing releases and newsletters that got published and those that didn't. Now his news releases rarely exceed two double-spaced, typewritten pages; most are just a few paragraphs on one page. (Double-spacing is another requirement for press releases because it is easier to read.) But he also includes fact sheets in a media kit with product samples, all enclosed in a folder with a bold graphic.

And his releases get results. In one year *USA Today* printed six front-page stories based on his releases. O'Brien included these essential elements:

- The company address
- A contact (himself, in this case), with telephone number
- The date of the release
- The date when the release can be published (for immediate release, in this case)

These days, you might also add a cell phone number and e-mail address.

O'Brien sent the following release out a week earlier than the date on it so editors could publish it the day the news was supposedly announced. That's another quality of a good publicist. Editors want timely information. Unless special arrangements are made to hold the news, they usually will print it as soon as possible. As a result, "for immediate release" is a good way to write the release date.

Compare O'Brien's release and the story, which also included information (underlined) from fact sheets in the media kit and a phone call to the company. (Note that because Crayola is a trademark, it should be capitalized in all news stories.) Although the AP Stylebook prefers the term "news release," publicists continue to use the term "press release."

Illustration from media kit

Press release

Binney & Smith Inc.
1100 Church Lane
P.O. Box 431
Easton, Pennsylvania 18044-0431
[company telephone number]

For Immediate Release

Contact: Mark J. O'Brien
Media Communications
[telephone number plus direct extension]
[e-mail address]
[date]

CRAYOLA INTRODUCES NEW CRAYONS THAT ARE LITERALLY "OFF THE WALL"

EASTON, Pa.—Parents can put away the scrub brushes and stain remover thanks to Binney & Smith. The maker of Crayola products has introduced a totally off-the-wall product—washable crayons.

Unlike the billions of crayons produced before them, Crayola washable crayons are made from a patented formula that washes from most surfaces, including walls and fabric.

Front-page story

Crayola cleans up kids' act

Parents can now offer junior artists a crayon that won't leave permanent impressions of childhood—on walls, draperies and floors.

Binney & Smith, maker of Crayola brand, is introducing a crayon made from a formula that can be cleaned with soap and water.

"Washable crayons address our number-one consumer complaint," says company official Mark O'Brien.

That's good news for parents: According to Binney & Smith, <u>the USA's kids spend almost 6.3 billion hours a year with crayons in hand.</u>

Unlike traditional crayons, washable ones aren't made of the waxy substance paraffin. The substitutes are water-soluble compounds found in cosmetics.

<u>Grown men and women colored on walls coated with a variety of paints and wallpapers to test formulas.</u>

Press release (continued)

"Washable crayons address our number one consumer complaint—getting crayon marks off different surfaces," says Mark O'Brien, Binney & Smith spokesperson. "Each year we receive thousands of calls and letters regarding crayon stains, mainly from parents of preschool children. With the introduction of washable crayons, parents can breathe a little easier when it comes to crayon mishaps."

The difference between traditional and washable crayons is in their formulas. Washable crayons contain special water soluble polymers found in many health and beauty aids. This allows them to be removed from most surfaces by simply using soap and water. Tests have shown washable crayon marks can even be removed from walls and fabric one to two months after being stained. However, crayon marks are easiest to remove if washed soon after they happen.

Crayola washable crayons are nontoxic and available in two sizes. The So Big size, for younger children, comes six to a box and has a suggested retail price of $2.99. Boxes of eight, large size washable crayons will sell for approximately $2.59.

\# # #

Front-page story (continued)

"They are truly Mom-friendly," says Binney & Smith's Brad Drexler.

So your toddler's wayward works of art can be cleaned off most walls and other surfaces up to two months after they're made.

One rub: Washable crayons are being marketed for preschoolers only in Crayola's large and "So Big" sizes.

<u>But they come in the same eight colors—red, green, orange, blue, black, brown and violet—as the first Crayolas in 1903.</u>

USA Today

Although print and broadcast news organizations depend on news releases, they receive scores of them every day. Most of them end up in the trash. If you want your news event to be covered, you need to consider that you are competing with many other events and stories that these media will cover. How do you get the attention of the assignment editors? Here are some tips for writing your releases:

- Find a newsworthy angle for your target audience. If you are targeting a local newspaper or TV station, localize the angle.
- Identify the news element in the headline and lead. Don't make your intended reader wade through several paragraphs to determine if the event or news you are touting should be covered.
- Consider a visual element. If you are targeting a television station, the visual impact is crucial. You should list photo opportunities for print and video possibilities for television.
- Relate your information to your audience—how will readers or viewers in this target area be affected? Why is your information or event important to them?

ETHICS

Ethical dilemma: How truthful should you be when you are faced with a conflict between protecting your client and dealing with the media?

The case: You are the public relations director for a company that manufactures portable baby cribs. The chief executive officer of your company informs you that two babies died when their cribs collapsed. However, he is reluctant to issue a recall because more than 100,000 cribs of this particular model were sold, and it would cost the company a fortune.

He says the product development team warned him a few years ago that the sides of the crib were not secure but that to replace the design would have been too costly. He wants you to reassure the media that the cribs are safe and that there is no proof the deaths of these children were a direct result of any faulty crib parts. If the media asks, he wants you to deny that the company ever had any indication the cribs might be defective.

Will you lie or withhold information to protect your employer? What steps will you propose to the CEO?

Ethical values: Truth, credibility, fairness, loyalty to your client.

Ethical guidelines: The Public Relations Society of America offers these guidelines in its code of ethics:

- A member shall adhere to truth and accuracy and to generally accepted standards of good taste.

- A member shall safeguard the confidences of present and former clients.

- A member shall not engage in any practice that tends to corrupt the integrity of channels of communication or the processes of government.

- Keep your information factual. Avoid adjectives, superlatives and promotional language.
- Provide diverse sources and consider how to include multicultural segments of the community in your projects, visuals and materials. The Public Relations Society of America has launched a campaign to promote diversity in the organization and to foster "ideology that promotes the co-existence of different cultures in America." For more information, access the society at *www.prsa.org*.

The Structure of News Releases

News releases differ very little from basic news stories. Some have a feature approach; others are organized the same as a hard-news story, with a summary lead. As with any news story, you need to get to the point quickly in a press release. If you have a soft lead, put the nut graph high in the release, preferably by the second paragraph.

Here are some basics:

Target your audience: Make sure that your information is newsworthy for the publication. Check the name and spelling of the person who should receive the release. Don't use nicknames (unless you are very familiar with the source), and make sure that you have the correct gender. Don't send duplicate releases to several editors. You might also send a copy to a reporter assigned to the beat covered in your news release. Ask if the publication prefers a faxed release or an e-mail release.

Allow lead time: Send your releases in advance of the publication's deadlines. A magazine might have a lead time of several months. Some TV stations might prefer only a few days of lead time. Check with the publication for preferred advance notice. Include the release date, preferably for immediate release, unless there is some important reason for an "embargoed until" date.

Style: Use one side of the paper. Double-space the body copy (or use 1.5 line spacing). Keep the release short, preferably one page and no more than two. If the release continues to a second page, write "more" at the bottom of the first page.

Check spelling and style: Use AP style for releases to newspapers and most magazines.

Major elements in this order:

> **Company name** or logo at the top.
>
> **FOR IMMEDIATE RELEASE** (preferably in caps and boldface).
>
> **Date of release** (This could be placed under the previous item or attached to the dateline.)
>
> **Contact information:** Write "CONTACT:" followed by the name, title, phone numbers and e-mail address of the person to contact. This information can be placed on the left or right side; it can be single-spaced.
>
> **Headline:** Skip two lines after your contact information. The headline can be in uppercase or upper- and lowercase. Boldface is optional but suggested.
>
> **Dateline:** This is the city of origin for your press release, followed by the state abbreviation if not a major city. You may put the date here, preceded by a hyphen.
>
> **Lead:** A direct lead is preferable, including who, what, when, where, but a feature lead immediately followed by the key information is acceptable.
>
> **Body:** Briefly summarize the key points. Include a quote or comment from a company official if possible. Keep paragraphs short. Use lists if you have key points.
>
> **Ending:** End with a brief paragraph about the company—if relevant. Repeat a contact or other relevant source for further information. Include a Web site if available. Skip a space and type a symbol for the ending: three # # # or —30—.

Your format should look like this:

Organization Name on Letterhead
[Heading information can be single-spaced]

For Immediate Release	Contact: Name, title
Date of release	Phone number
Story by [optional]	Fax number
	E-mail address

[Leave about 2 inches before headline]

HEADLINE

[Double-space body copy]

DATELINE—[Location for the origin of the release (in capital letters) plus a dash, followed by the first line of the lead]

Lead: Preferably start with some hard-news lead, especially on releases for news events or announcements.

Body: Write tightly. Limit copy to one page if possible, no more than two. If you have two pages, write "more" at the end of the first page and number the pages.

Ending: As part of the ending, you could tell where more information is available, such as graphics and Web sites.

−30−   or   # # #

Public Service Announcements

Public service announcements, commonly called "PSAs," are messages that TV or radio stations will air without charge, provided that the messages have noncommercial and nonpolitical content. PSAs generally run from 15 seconds to one minute. You should check with the stations for their format requirements and submission dates.

- Read your copy aloud because the message will be heard by the audience.
- Keep it brief and include only the most crucial information.
- Include the dates and times of any event you are promoting.
- Use broadcast style of all capital letters and double-spacing for video.

Here is a 15-second PSA from the Federal Trade Commission:

THE FEDERAL TRADE COMMISSION SAYS ANYONE WITH A PHONE COULD BE A VICTIM OF A SCHEMING TELEMARKETER. DON'T GIVE AWAY YOUR CREDIT CARD OR BANK ACCOUNT NUMBERS ON THE PHONE. IF YOU HAVE ANY DOUBT ABOUT AN OFFER YOU HEAR ON THE PHONE, CHECK IT OUT AND GET IT IN WRITING. A MESSAGE FROM THE FEDERAL TRADE COMMISSION AND THIS STATION.

Media Kits

Public relations practitioners often use media kits to promote corporate products. These kits are usually decorative folders containing a variety of news releases, fact sheets about the company and its products, and samples of the company's products.

Planning a media kit can be a very creative experience. You should design a striking cover or package for your media kit and include information that will be useful for different kinds of stories. A brief sheet of facts about the

MULTIMEDIA COACH

E-mail News Releases

Online news releases must be shorter than print so the information can be seen on the first screen. Limit the release to one or two screens, about 400 words at most. Use single-spaced copy with a space between paragraphs.

- Target your audience. Ask sources if they prefer to receive releases by e-mail. Don't send unsolicited e-mail. Personalize the release if possible.

- Write a brief summary of the topic in the e-mail subject line.

- Headings: Insert company name and contact information at the top, FOR IMMEDIATE RELEASE and date of release. Insert a space before the headline.

- Write a clear summary headline. Insert another space.

- Write a summary lead with basic information: who, what, where, when. Make sure that it is visible in the first screen.

- Use lists to itemize information when relevant.

- Avoid adjectives and superlatives. Keep the writing simple and newsworthy.

- Repeat the contact information (phone, fax, e-mail and any related Web site) at the bottom of the release.

- Proofread. E-mail is notoriously filled with typos, spelling and style errors. Sloppy work is a poor reflection on you and your client.

- Don't send attachments. Your users may not be able to open your documents.

company is usually helpful. If you have a product sample that is suitable for enclosure, consider it part of your media kit.

The cover letter for your media kit should briefly state what is included. Here is a cover letter for a media kit from Hallmark Cards Inc.

Dear Editor:

The latest in Easter card and gift-giving trends from Hallmark Cards is tucked inside. We hope you find this information helpful as you prepare your springtime holiday stories.

Hallmark offers about 250 gift and party items. The Easter gift line includes wicker baskets, stuffed animals, activity products for children (such as washable markers, stickers and coloring books), decorations, and partyware.

In addition to Hallmark's regular line of Easter products, selected Hallmark Crown stores will be offering exclusive Easter items, such as Hallmark Keepsake Easter ornaments and fresh-cut flower bouquets.

A good media kit should contain these items:

Attractive cover: The kit is usually contained in a folder with the company name and logo.

Brief letter or note: A very brief explanation of the purpose of the kit should be provided for the editor. It could be on the inside of the cover.

News release: The first item after the editor's note should be a news release.

Fact sheet: Present information about the organization in simple list form. You might use headings such as *Who, What, Where, When, Why* and *How.*

Backgrounder: You might include a feature story, such as a profile of a person or the organization. Don't include information in the backgrounder that should be in the news release. This is additional material, not a substitute for news.

Story ideas: The story idea sheet is optional, but if you include it, try to offer suggestions for localizing the information. This sheet should be written in list form or short paragraphs. You might also include suggestions for photos, video opportunities or graphics.

Corporate Publications

When you are writing news releases for the media, use newspaper style. If you are writing a company magazine with news and features about people and events in the organization, newspaper style still applies. But when you are writing a memo or proposal to the company president or other corporate officials, you need to state your position in an analytical way.

That's where many business writers have difficulty, says Anne Baber, a writing coach who conducts seminars in corporations to improve communication techniques. She has also conducted seminars for the International Association of Business Communicators and has written books and many articles about career topics.

The key factor is to know the audience, she says: "There are some psychological problems people have when they write for folks up the ladder in management. One of my theories is that power warps communication. When people are writing for a boss, it's like a teenager talking to a parent. The parent says, 'Where are you going?' The teenager answers, 'Out.' The teen isn't saying everything he or she knows because of the power structure. In corporations, the power structure also affects communication. The writing becomes very formal, very passive. The writers don't want to put themselves forward as being initiators of action. They hide behind the third person. They write *the employee* rather than the word *you.*"

Baber bases her theories on many years of experience in corporate communications. A former director of communications for United Telecom (now called Sprint), she now heads her own consulting firm, Baber and Associates, in Kansas City, Mo.

Many of the coaching techniques she uses are similar to those described earlier in this book. But the outcome is different. "News writing operates on the idea that if you give the public enough information, they will inform themselves," she says. "We're not doing that in an organization. We want to create attitudes or actions. It's much more like advertising." Here are Baber's tips for writing proposals and company plans:

Reporting Steps

Make a list: Ask what the audience — in this case, management — really wants to know. Then itemize all the points you can. (This is the same as brainstorming for a news story.)

Envision the result: Ask yourself: What kind of action is the reader expected to take as a result of this information?

Make a checklist of what and why: Write a sentence beginning "I want to tell you that . . . ," and then answer why. Then add this teaser to support the why factor: "This is necessary because. . . ." (This teaser is similar to the focus—"so what"—sentence at the top of your news stories.)

Writing Steps

Draw a "mind spill": Get all the research together. Draw a circle in the center of a large piece of paper. Put the main topic in the center circle. Then draw more circles, filling each one with an idea. With a colored pencil or highlighter, mark the key links between these ideas. Draw a line to connect one related idea to another so that all like information is grouped together. Then number the points, preferably in the order you will write them in the proposal. (This is the same technique as mapping for ideas or reporting.)

Organize the order: Write a topic sentence (the same as a focus sentence) that completes this thought: "I believe that. . . ." For example, "I believe that we should market Mother's Day cards a different way." Then write the word *because* followed by point one, point two, point three—like the list technique. The most persuasive structure is three in parallel style.

Use inverted pyramid style: Put the strongest point of the proposal in the lead, and then plan your proposal with supporting points.

Put information in perspective: Ask yourself: What does the reader know already, and what is new? If this is one of a series of proposals, you may need just a summary sentence referring to past information the reader already knows. The reader is going to read this proposal quickly and will get irritated if he or she has to wade through previously known material.

Write a strong conclusion: Summarize, but do not repeat, your lead. If you have written a proposal about marketing Mother's Day cards and you have given the supporting points that answer why you should change the method, the ending could be a strong statement such as "We should start marketing these new cards in six months." If that time frame is part of your proposal, you could just end with a statement telling why it is a good idea.

Check your verbs: After you have written your draft, go back and circle the verbs and see if they are strong action words. If not, revise.

Corporate Web Sites

Jakob Nielsen, the leading expert in how people use the Web, says "corporate Web sites get a 'D' in PR." A study he conducted of how journalists use these online corporate sites showed that they found the information they were seeking only 60 percent of the time. "That percentage equals a 'D' grade," Nielsen says.

According to his study, here are the top five reasons journalists visit a company Web site:

- To find a PR contact (name and telephone number)
- To check basic facts about the company, including the spelling of executives' names, location of the company and so on
- To discover the company's "spin" on events
- To check financial information
- To download images for use as illustrations in stories

If you are writing information to be posted on a corporate Web site, keep that information in mind and follow these guidelines:

- Avoid promotional language and adjectives. Keep the writing simple and straightforward.
- Include a person's contact information, the company address and phone number. Do not have as the only contact an e-mail address to an anonymous webmaster.

Exercises

1 Gather information from an organization for an event on your campus or in your city. Write a news release announcing the event.

2 Study a company in your community. Devise a media kit to promote some product or aspect of the company. This activity may require some coordination so that many students do not bother the same firm. If a team of students or the whole class is studying a large company, divide the responsibilities so students are studying different aspects of the company.

3 **Write a news release:** As the contact, use your name, phone number and e-mail address. The company is Excaliber Entertainment Inc., 1955 Larkspur, San Antonio, Texas 78213. This information is adapted from a press release for a former

online contest site owned by Excaliber. You may use a direct or creative lead. Assume that the Web site still exists for your news release, which should be limited to one page.

Who: *www.vaultcracker.com*, a contest Web site.

What: Sponsoring a contest, "Junkiest Dorm Room in America."

When: Use now through the next two months.

Where: *www.vaultcracker.com*.

Why: To promote the new Web site.

How: The contest will award $300 to a college student whose pictures of his or her dorm room are judged the junkiest. Second prize is $100. The contest is open to all students who are enrolled full time at a college or university in the United States.

Comments: From Richard McNairy, founder and president of *www.vaultcracker .com:* "We know how busy college students are and we wanted to turn a negative into a positive. I'm sure students with messy rooms get criticism from others. Now two students with junky rooms will be able to brag about the fact that they earned cash because of their junky rooms."

More information: Visit *www.vaultcracker.com*.

4 **E-mail news release:** Write a one-page e-mail news release (about 150 words) based on the following information; use your name, phone number and e-mail for contact information:

The U.S. Department of Commerce's census bureau released a report today about the value of various college degrees. The report is called "What's It Worth? Field of Training and Economic Status." The data are from a panel of the Survey of Income and Program Participation. College graduates who work full time and have a bachelor's degree in engineering earn the highest average monthly pay ($4,680), while those with education degrees earn the lowest ($2,802), according to the report. "Majoring in a technical field does pay off even if you don't finish a four-year degree," said Kurt Bauman, co-author with Camille Ryan of the report. "The average person with a vocational certificate earns around $200 more per month than the average high school graduate; but if the certificate is in an engineering-related field, the boost in earnings is close to $800." At the top of the earnings scale were those with professional degrees, such as doctors and lawyers ($7,224 per month), followed by full-time workers with master's degrees ($4,635), bachelor's degrees ($3,767), high school graduates ($2,279) and those without a diploma ($1,699).

Business was the most popular field of training beyond high school; 7.5 million people had bachelor's degrees in business and earned a monthly average of $3,962. An additional 1.9 million had master's degrees in business administration or other advanced degrees in business. The average monthly earnings of people with master's degrees in business was $5,579. Of people with managerial jobs, 46 percent had bachelor's or higher degrees. Of people in professional occupations, 71 percent held bachelor's or higher degrees. By comparison, no more than 8 percent of those in craft, service, farm and production occupations had completed this much education. Associate degrees generally require a two-year course of study, but people took an average of more than four years to complete them. Bachelor's and higher degrees took an average of five or more years to complete.

5   **Public service announcement:** Write a 15-second public service announcement (about 65 words) based on this information:

This message is from the Federal Emergency Management Agency. It's about tornadoes. They can be deadly. Tornadoes strike nearly every year with the most powerful winds on Earth. Remember these three tornado danger signs: One—Before a tornado hits, the wind may die down and the air may become very still. Two—Tornadoes can be nearly invisible, marked only by swirling debris at the base of the funnel. An approaching cloud of dust or debris can mark the location of a deadly tornado. Seek shelter immediately. Three—Tornadoes generally occur near the trailing edge of a thunderstorm. When a thunderstorm moves through your area, be alert for tornadoes. For more information on tornado preparedness, visit the FEMA Web site at w-w-w-dot-f-e-m-a-dot-gov, or contact the Red Cross. Plan ahead to survive the next tornado, and listen to this station for more emergency preparedness information from FEMA.

6   **Promote a product:** Working in small groups, create a new product and a company name and address. Use your name and contact information. Each person in the group should then write a press release promoting this product.

Featured Online Activity

Conduct your own informal usability study by visiting the Web sites of three to five corporations that interest you. On each site, search for basic PR information described in this chapter, and note your findings. Do the sites contain the basic contact information that you would need, such as phone numbers, addresses and key corporate officers? Do the sites contain a good description of the company's purpose? What other information do you think these Web sites should contain?

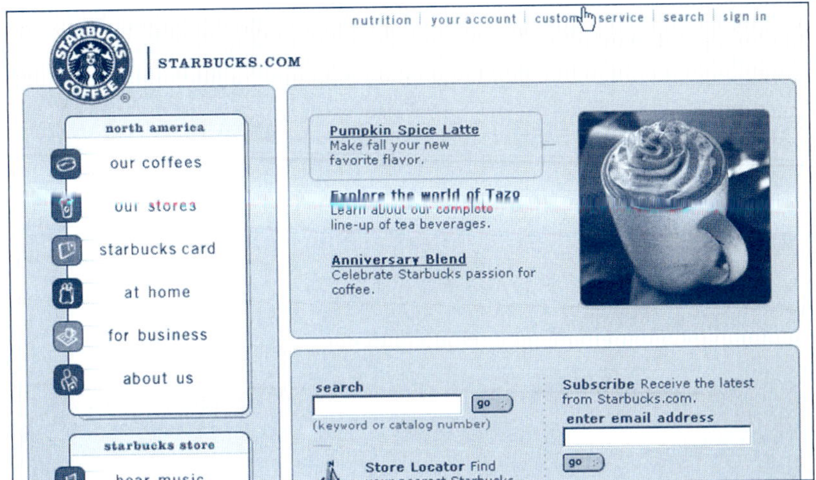

Coaching Tips

Plan your questions to get good sound bites.

Don't leave the location of a story until you have everything you need.

Write in a conversational style.

Read your copy aloud before recording it.

Use short sentences, one idea per sentence.

Use active voice.

Use present tense when possible and appropriate.

Give attribution first—tell who said what before telling what was said.

Use subject–verb–object order: who did what.

Broadcast Writing and Reporting

It is a cold, wintry day in Elmira, N.Y., a city of 30,000 where Mark Twain spent his final days. It is 9 a.m., and Shelby Stafford is a long way from her hometown of San Diego and a long way from her alma mater of the University of Southern California, where she studied journalism.

After a brief stint in Coos Bay, Ore., Stafford became a reporter two years ago for WETM-TV in Elmira, one of the smallest markets in the United States. But WETM is a station where young reporters get a chance to work after graduating from college and then move on to bigger markets in Syracuse, Buffalo, Rochester, Boston and sometimes New York City.

Today, as the health reporter for the station, she is finishing a story about a new herbal treatment to combat colds and flu. She also anchors the noon news.

"The good thing about local news is that you know who your audience is," she says. "You write your stories; you design your stories around the viewers. It's all about figuring out how it pertains to them and how they live their lives."

Unlike many television reporters, Stafford has no desire to work for the networks. She plans to spend her career at local stations because she thinks they have a better understanding of what the viewers want than the networks: "I want to stay in local news. That is where my heart is."

Stafford is part of a new generation of broadcast journalists who must work for a variety of news outlets. She writes a health column—based on her WETM reports—for the local newspaper, the *Elmira Star-Gazette*, and posts additional material about health issues to the WETM Web site.

"When I am writing for television, I have video," she explains. "When I am writing for the newspaper, I am lucky if I have one photograph. You have to be able to adjust. On the Web site, it is more like writing for print. You really have to realize how to manage your time when you are writing for all of these outlets."

Stafford is convinced that more media companies will require journalists to report a story once and publish it in a variety of ways: TV packages, newspaper stories and Web contributions. After she polishes her story about the cold treatment, she has to prepare for the noon news, a broadcast that includes news, weather and features. Today she also helps Chef Fred cook an Italian dish. It turns out that the pasta is her lunch.

Shelby Stafford with meteorologist Joe
Pasquarelli of WETM-TV, Elmira, N.Y.

Shelby Stafford

Then she hurries back to the newsroom to make certain that the health story is edited. She plans to do an interview for an upcoming segment, but there's a fire at a local convenience store. Stafford and a photographer hurry out to the scene, but the fire is already out. No story. It has been a busy day: anchoring the noon news, preparing the health story for the evening report and filing additional material about the remedy to the Web site.

News Director Scott Nichols followed a different route to WETM and WTTX, the UPN affiliate staffed by the same news team. After he graduated from college, Nichols started at the station in 1991 as a photographer and then became a producer and anchor. He switched to WBNG in Binghamton, N.Y., as the assistant news director. He returned in 2002 as news director at WETM, which is owned by Clear Channel, a huge broadcasting company with radio and television outlets throughout the country.

"There are some people who love being on the air. I love production and managing. It was a perfect fit because this is my town. I was a reporter here, and nobody is going to beat me in my hometown," he says.

Nichols oversees a staff of 27—a mixture of young reporters and photographers who may stay only two years or so and long-time anchors such as Carl Proper, who has worked for WETM for more than 40 years. The coverage area, which runs through southern New York and northern Pennsylvania, is mostly rural and has many older viewers. The news director supervises four-and-one-half news shows Monday through Friday: two hours in the morning, 30 minutes at noon, one hour in the evening and one hour at night.

Nichols says he looks for people who can cover breaking news, know how to incorporate people into a story and show interest in a broadcast package

Scott Nichols, news director of WETM-TV,
Elmira, N.Y. with anchor Leigh Kjekstad

Scott Nichols

rather than simply narrating it. "My last opening I got more than 100 tapes. I look for that raw talent: Do people want to watch them? Do they know the basics? Do they know how to write?"

Working in the Field

Good broadcast journalism depends on finding a solid story, doing research, obtaining information and interviews, and writing the story clearly and in an interesting way. Radio reporters often work alone like print journalists, using a tape recorder as a notebook.

Covering a television story is more complicated, mainly because of the need to work with a team, which sometimes includes a photographer, a video editor, a director and many others who help put a broadcast together.

Getting Good Pictures

Pictures play a crucial role in television. Various types of pictures make a story move more smoothly—a process called sequencing. A sequence uses a series of pictures—usually three to five—to tell part of a story. These include three basic shots: the close-up, the medium shot and the wide shot. These shots have variations, such as the extreme close-up and the extreme

Example of sequence wide shot

Example of a sequence medium shot

wide shot, or panorama. You can add motion to these shots. These motions include a pan, or moving the focus of the shot from left to right or vice versa; a zoom, or moving from a wide or medium shot to a close-up; and a pullback or reveal, or moving from a close-up to a medium or wide shot.

A sequence is built upon these shots. For example, imagine that you are covering a building fire. The sequence could include a wide shot of the burning building and the firefighters working to put out the flames. The next shot in the sequence might be a medium shot of a firefighter moving up a ladder with a hose. The next shot might focus on a tight shot of the firefighter's hands as he or she tries to put out the flames. This opening sequence allows the reporter to describe where the building is located and how many firefighters arrived on the scene. The sequence also enables the reporter to describe more details about the extent of the fire.

It is important to keep in mind that there is no precise way to create a sequence. A sequence generally includes a variety of shots, but the order depends upon the story and the quality of the visuals.

The next sequence would probably turn to an eyewitness or the head of the fire unit at the scene to describe what happened. Interviews also require sequencing. The opening shot of the interview sequence would often be a medium shot of the interview subject to allow the reporter to introduce the speaker. The second shot may be a tighter shot when the interview subject starts to speak. It is advisable for the reporter and photographer to shoot a medium shot of the reporter listening to the speaker, or a cutaway. The cutaway allows the reporter to go from one part of the interviewee's comments to another part—similar to placing attribution in the middle of a quote to eliminate unnecessary words in a print story.

Interviews

In broadcast interviews, the reporter must ask questions that elicit sound bites, which are crucial to an effective broadcast story. Therefore, it is important for the broadcast journalist to ask questions that start with "how," "what," "describe" or "tell me about what happened."

For example, what happens if you ask, "Was it a big fire?" The eyewitness may simply answer, "Yes." A better question would be "Can you describe what the fire looked like?" What happens if you ask, "Were you afraid?" The answer again may be "Yes." A better question would be "Describe how you felt."

If the interview subject is the head of the fire unit, the reporter often wants to ask about the cause. What happens if you ask, "Can you tell me how the fire started?" The answer may be "No." A better question would be "What do you think caused the fire?" The fire chief will usually say what is known at that point of the investigation.

A broadcast journalist still needs to obtain the same information as a print reporter, including the proper spelling of the names of the interview subjects. That way, the information can be used to introduce and identify the people interviewed.

The Stand-up

In most cases, the reporter will want to do a piece on camera, commonly called a "stand-up." This subject will be covered later in the chapter, but a stand-up creates an on-air presence and provides credibility to the story by showing that the television team traveled to the scene. Three basic types of stand-ups are a live opening to introduce a taped report, a bridge that provides a transition between one aspect of the story and another, and a stand-up close.

Reporters rarely use a taped stand-up at the beginning of a taped report, mainly because television is a visual medium. However, it is common for a reporter who is on the scene of a story to do a stand-up to introduce a taped package. The stand-up also allows for reporter involvement in the story—perhaps by showing the journalist with firefighters in the background. A stand-up close or a live satellite close at the end of a package provides a final thought for the story or recasts information that may not have visuals to support the information.

Writing the Story

After you have reported the story, you need to write and edit it for broadcast. Talk to your photographer about the best shots that will match the information you have. You also need to look at the visual material and sound bites

ETHICS

Ethical dilemma: When, if ever, should you do undercover reporting? Can deception be justified?

The case: You have received complaints from African-American students on your campus that apartment managers engage in discrimination. The students claim that when they asked to look at apartments, especially in "white neighborhoods," the agents told them the apartments they were interested in had just been rented. A white reporter on your staff and an African-American reporter decide to go undercover by seeking apartments separately and finding out if rental agents or apartment managers give different responses to their requests to see available apartments. The reporters plan to use hidden cameras. Is deception the best or only way you can get this story?

Ethical values: Truth, public interest, fairness.

Ethical guidelines:

- The code of ethics for the Radio-Television News Directors Association advises to "guard against using audio or video material in any way that deceives the audience."

- The Society of Professional Journalists Code of Ethics says to "avoid undercover or other surreptitious methods of gathering information except when traditional open methods will not yield information vital to the public."

you have before writing—a process known as "logging." A log should include a description of the image and the exact time of the picture on the tape. That way, you can write more precisely to the material you have and provide specific information about the image and the time on the tape for the editor. Sometimes the editor will do the logging, although the reporter should view the important parts of the audio and video images before writing. It is often better to use an audiotape recorder in addition to the camera so that you can isolate the sound bites you intend to use.

Keep in mind that you have only one chance to interest the audience and only one chance to make your story understandable. Unlike a newspaper or magazine reader, who may stop reading and resume later, a listener or viewer must be interested and must be paying attention to what's on the air.

A broadcast journalist writes in a conversational tone, often with simple and direct sentences, rather than the more formal structure of print reports. Many broadcast stories run only about 250 words, and each of those words can be precious when it comes to reaching the listener or viewer.

Story Structure

A broadcast story needs a clear focus, a lead, body and ending. Broadcast writing should be geared to audio and video.

Bob Dotson, an NBC correspondent who has received numerous awards for his writing, calls the focus sentence a commitment statement. It is still a one-sentence summary of the story, but it is concentrated more on visual impact—what you want the audience to take away from the report. Provide the commitment visually.

In speeches he makes to journalism groups, Dotson offers these tips:

Beginning: Write to your pictures first. Build your lead around a visual that foreshadows the story to come.

Middle: Usually no more than three to five points, which you prove visually.

Use strong natural sound to let the viewer experience what happened.
Use people engaged in compelling action that is visual.
Use surprises to keep viewers involved and lure uninterested viewers.
Use short sound bites.

Ending: Build to a strong ending throughout the story, and make it visual.

Make your viewers care about the story and the people.

That's the overall structure. Here are some ways to structure each part:

Lead Every story needs its own lead. However, remember that the anchor in the studio will introduce your story. The package, which is the story that includes narration, sound bites and images, starts after the anchor introduction. In most cases, it is worthwhile to make suggestions to the anchor or the show producer about what should be included in the studio lead-in.

Shelby Stafford's story about Airborne, the herbal treatment, had this anchor lead-in:

ANCHOR VO (voice over— the anchor's voice over video images)	It's an herbal remedy that's taken the world by storm. One Elmira chef says he's used Airborne several times to relieve his cold symptoms. As WETM-18 Health Reporter Shelby Stafford explains, Airborne is so popular, pharmacies have a hard time keeping it in stock.

That lead-in makes it easier for the reporter to decide where to start. Whether the story needs a hard or soft lead depends on the content of your story. Feature stories may take softer leads; a breaking-news story calls for a direct approach. In all cases, you must get to the nut graph—the main reason for the story—quickly, generally by the second or third sentence.

Regardless of the type of lead, most of the basic news elements—who, what, when, where, why, how, so what—must be included in the story. But you can't include all of them in a simple, coherent sentence for the lead. So select the ones that are most important to your story.

In broadcast writing, the placement of points of emphasis for these elements often differs from print journalism. The most common elements to stress in a broadcast lead are where, when and who; why and how can take too long to explain in a simple sentence. Here are some ways to use these elements in hard-news leads:

Where: Because most radio and television stations reach such a broad audience, the location of a story is even more important in broadcast than in print. Newspapers can use datelines to indicate location. Broadcast reports can superimpose the name of the location on the screen, but you also need to say it in the story. If the story follows a series of other stories from different regions, you might start it this way:

> In Pawtucket, Rhode Island, police are looking into the suspicious death of a 15-month-old baby.

When: Almost all broadcast stories, except features, have a "today" element. Avoid using *a.m.* or *p.m.* If the specific time element is important, say something like "An earthquake struck Southern California at 7:15 this morning." In most cases, a general reference, such as "this morning" or "earlier today," is sufficient. Place your time element after the verb, which is a more natural, conversational order:

> *Awkward:* At least five people today were arrested in an anti-abortion protest outside a Milwaukee clinic.

> *Preferred:* At least five people were arrested today in an anti-abortion protest outside a Milwaukee clinic.

Who: Identify a speaker by title before the name:

> *Say:* Broward County Sheriff John Law said today he would not seek re-election when his term ends next year.

> *Do not say:* John Law, sheriff of Broward County, said today. . . .

Avoid using unfamiliar names in a lead and too many names in a story. When you have video sound bites, you may not even need the name in the story. The person can be identified by a superimposed title under his or her image in the taped segment. For a delayed identification, follow the same guidelines as for print journalism. Identify the person by an age, a location, an occupation or some other generic identifier. Then follow with the person's name:

One of two suspects in the fatal kidnapping of Exxon executive Sidney Reso (Ree-Soh) has pleaded guilty.

Irene Seale entered the plea to charges of extortion and conspiracy to commit extortion. She appeared in court in Newark, New Jersey.

The Associated Press

Put a human face on the story whenever possible: Try to find someone personally affected by the issue. You can start with the specific example, using a person first and then going to the nut graph. Shelby Stafford does exactly that in her story about the cold and flu treatment:

STAFFORD VO (voice over)	Chef Fred Ball spends most of his time in the kitchen. If he's not cooking up something on WETM-TV, he's busy cooking up a feast at the Lindenwald Haus Bed and Breakfast in Elmira.
	The worst thing that can happen to a chef is to catch a cold or get sick during the height of your busy season. The last thing

you want is a runny nose, sniffles and watery eyes when you're trying to prepare food for folks.

So when he starts feeling sick, Chef Fred takes this. It's called Airborne and helps relieve cold and flu symptoms.

Using *you:* Not all stories directly affect people's lives. But when possible, try to stress the impact within the first few sentences. Use an element that will make viewers care or make them understand why this story is important, unusual or interesting. Use *you*, especially in consumer stories, to heighten impact. Try this approach:

You're about to pay more for your music. That's because a judge ruled today that online music companies must pay higher royalties to musicians.

When you can, advance the lead, stressing the next step:

Immediacy: Two people remain in serious condition from a car accident this afternoon.

No immediacy: Two people were injured in a car accident today.

The focus-on-a-person lead works as well in broadcast as in print, especially for a feature or a news story that the anchor introduces with a hard-news lead-in. Like the *Wall Street Journal* formula, this type of lead goes from the specific to the general. The person is one of many affected by the problem.

Judy and Joe Westbrook spent the morning cleaning up the furniture in their front yard. The Blue River had overflowed its banks and forced its way into their Independence home.

More than 25 families share their predicament. Late this afternoon all of those families were awaiting word about their flood insurance claims.

The mystery-teaser lead is another effective soft-lead technique, as long as you don't keep the viewer wondering what the story is about for too long. You must get to the point within the first few sentences.

In some ways it looks like an ordinary camp. It has hiking trails, a swimming pool and tennis courts.

But you don't have to worry about what clothes to wear. In fact, this is one of the few places where you'll feel out of place wearing clothes.

At this camp near Denver, men and women of all ages frolic in the nude.

SOUND BITE: Nudism is about the only recreation that anybody can do whether they're rich or poor. We all share in the same satisfaction, so it's a very great equalizer.

Adapted from NBC News

Body After you identify your lead or focus, you need to determine the order of your supporting points—facts or quotes from sources in sound bites. A chronological format usually works after the lead or nut graph. One point should follow another one naturally.

In the story about the herbal treatment Airborne, the reporter follows the personal story with background about the product:

STAFFORD VO	Airborne was created by a California schoolteacher who was tired of catching colds from her students.

The reporter then relates the story to the local community, including a sound bite from a local pharmacist:

STAFFORD VO	Pharmacies, like Gerould's, have a hard time keeping Airborne in stock.
SOT (sound on tape—a sound bite)	
FRANK STEED/PHARMACIST	Right now, it's going very quickly. In the last month to two months, we've had a lot of use for it. We've got a lot of people who have used it traveling and people using it as a preventative product.

When you need a transition from one point to another, you can use the key-word technique, picking up on a word in the last sentence and repeating it in the next to bridge the thought from one concept to the next.

Reporter	The harsh reality for millions of American women is that they will probably never be able to retire. In order to survive, they will have to work until they die.
SOT	I know people who are working into their late seventies and up into their eighties. Now a lot of them have cut down, but retirement the way we dream of it and think of it doesn't happen to a lot of people.
Reporter	It has not happened for Beverly Lange. At 74 she works 20 hours a week as a sales clerk to supplement the $800 a month she collects in Social Security.

ABC News

Ending The most common endings for a broadcast story include the reporter's name and broadcast outlet, known as the "sign-off," and one of the following:

Summary: A close that reinforces the main idea without repeating previous points.

Future: The next step that happens in the story.

Consumer: Helpful items, such as where to call or go for additional information.

In the Airborne story, the reporter relies on a summary:

| STAFFORD VO | Chef Fred says he's making room in his kitchen for Airborne. Not to cook with, but to grab the next time he starts feeling sick. |

In Elmira, I'm WETM-18 Health Reporter Shelby Stafford.
The Airborne story also represents an example that uses "bookends." The report starts with an individual, the chef, as one bookend and returns to the chef at the end for the other bookend.

Step-by-step Storytelling

Many stories lend themselves to step-by-step storytelling. One of these forms is called the "summary lead," in which the most important information comes first. For example, look at this weather story from NBC News. The anchor begins in a summary news lead:

| ANCHOR VO | Weather is making news in the southeastern United States tonight. Snow, sleet, freezing rain have all brought travel to a standstill from Arkansas through the Carolinas. And more rough weather could be on the way for lots of people. |

Another step-by-step storytelling technique is the "hourglass." The reporter begins with a summary lead and proceeds to tell the rest of the story in a step-by-step fashion, moving from specifics to more general information. The following report from NBC News uses the hourglass technique:

| REPORTER VO | In Atlanta, the worst ice storm in years threatened to halt a city that's always on the move. The airport, which normally operates four runways, was down to just one by midday with hundreds of flights canceled. |

The reporter then supports his first narration with a sound bite:

| SOT | Unidentified Man #1: I lost my flight. I am still here. |

The reporter then moves to another fact: roadways.

| REPORTER VO | Roadways were worse than runways. Central to north Georgia woke up to streets and highways coated with ice a quarter to a half-inch thick. |

The reporter then uses another step in the process by supporting his narration with a sound bite:

| SOT | Unidentified Woman: I lived in Austria. I know how to drive in this stuff. I just don't like it. |

The reporter expands on the specific incidents throughout the area:

REPORTER VO	At one time or another today, portions of every Interstate in metro Atlanta were shut down. At least two traffic deaths are blamed on the storm. The ice brought down tree limbs, which dragged down power lines. Tens of thousands of customers across the state are without electricity, a number that could grow into hundreds of thousands.

Again, the reporter supports the story with another sound bite:

SOT	Unidentified Man #2: Hey! Customer said there's another tree on the line about a block away!

The reporter then looks toward the future:

REPORTER VO	That same system is moving north, spreading misery as it goes.

The story is supported with another sound bite:

SOT	
BILL KARINS, NBC METEOROLOGIST	The worst locations are going to be from Raleigh to Washington, D.C. We could expect two to three inches of a mixture of everything, sleet, freezing rain and snow.

The story ends with an added fact about kids who had some fun:

REPORTER VO	The slippery storm did have a silver lining. For many kids, the only thing that would have made it better was if it had been a weekday.
SOT	
UNIDENTIFIED VOICE	Ready, go. Push!

A "chronology" is another step-by-step storytelling technique. For example, a crime happened at a particular time. That was followed by the arrival of the police. The police caught a suspect. The suspect was taken in for questioning. The suspect was charged with a crime.

Writing Tips

Some information contained in print stories simply doesn't make it into a broadcast story—often because broadcast journalists must emphasize a conversational tone or have less time and fewer words for a story. For example, a typical newspaper story about the day after a 160-point decline at the New York Stock Exchange might include the following:

> "It's very tense. I'm waiting to see what happens. I'm very nervous," said Arthur S. Simon, a stockbroker, as he waited for today's market opening to see if stocks would plunge further.

The broadcast journalist has to treat the story in a different way: The identifying title of stockbroker goes first. The verb becomes present tense, not past tense. The middle initial is eliminated.

Stockbroker Arthur Simon says he's nervous about what the market may do today after a 160-point fall.

The quotation, or sound on tape, gets shortened:

SOT	It's very tense. I'm waiting to see what happens.

The broadcast approach is closer to the way you would speak. The broadcast approach also eliminates less important information because broadcasters have less time to tell a story.

Active voice vs. passive voice: Broadcasters generally should write in active voice, although there are times when it may be important to write in the passive voice because that may be the best way to sequence pictures.

Active voice: Police say they have arrested the subject, a 27-year-old man from Syracuse, in connection with the burglary. (Active voice works if you start with pictures of police.)

Passive voice: A 27-year-old man from Syracuse was arrested by police in connection with the burglary. (Passive voice works if you start with pictures of the suspect.)

Use present tense whenever possible: Present tense gives the story a sense of immediacy.

Present tense: Rescuers in California <u>are digging</u> through a mountain of mud and debris to find survivors from yesterday's mudslide. So far, at least three people <u>are known</u> to be dead.

Past tense: Rescuers in California <u>have dug</u> through a mountain of mud and debris to find survivors from yesterday's mudslide. So far, three people <u>died</u>.

But don't strain to convert a sentence to present tense. Use the tense that fits the story naturally. In the next example (note the underlined verbs), the present tense becomes awkward because it is mixed with the past tense:

72 people <u>go</u> to jail after a protest in Milwaukee <u>turned</u> disorderly.

It's better to use the past tense (or present tense) consistently:

72 people <u>went</u> to jail after a protest in Milwaukee <u>turned</u> disorderly.

Put attribution first: Tell who said something before telling what was said. Don't make the reader wait to find out who made the statement.

Write: Investigators say they believe someone could have started a fire that left two children dead.

Do not write: Someone could have started a fire that left two children dead, investigators say.

Use action verbs: Avoid the various tenses of the verb *to be*, such as *am, are, was* and *were*.

Weak verb: There is a new study that shows that coffee may help to prevent liver cancer.

Stronger verb: Coffee may help to prevent liver cancer.

Names and titles: Spell difficult pronunciations of names and locations phonetically. Some anchors prefer only the phonetic spelling instead of the actual name.

Syrian President bah-SHAR AW-sod (the phonetic spelling of Bashar Assad)

The city of KAY-row, Illinois (the phonetic spelling of Cairo in that state; not the KY-row in Egypt)

Who: Identify a speaker by title before the name:

Write: Attorney General Peter Harvey says he plans to file a lawsuit against Blockbuster.

Do not write: Peter Harvey, the attorney general, says he plans to file a lawsuit against Blockbuster.

Identify a person by an age, a location, an occupation or some other generic identifier. Then follow with the person's name:

<u>Former director</u> Robert Stern says Disney made a wise decision when it fired <u>former president</u> Michael Ovitz.

When you have sound bites in a television story, you may not need to identify the individual in the narration. The person can be identified by a superimposed title under his or her image in the taped segment.

Numbers: Write out *hundred, thousand, million, billion* and *trillion.* Round off numbers when possible. Write numbers to be read, as follows: "15-hundred, 14-thousand, 23-million." More complicated numbers would be written this way: "373-thousand," not "373,000"; "14-million-250-thousand," not "14,250,000."

Spell out fractions: one-half, three-quarters.

For decimals, write out the word *point:* "It comes to 17-point-2 million dollars." Write out the word *dollars* at the end rather than using the dollar symbol at the beginning.

There are some exceptions. Addresses, telephone numbers and time of day are written in numerals: "She lives at 5 Westbrooke Avenue."

Avoid a.m. and p.m. in times. "The accident occurred at 10:30 this morning."

Separate numerals with hyphens so that they can be read more easily: "The telephone number to call for information is 5-5-5-1-2-3-4."

Writing for Radio

Radio news follows many of the same writing principles as television news. But you don't have any images to show. You have to create pictures with words and sounds. The amount of time for a radio report depends on the type of newscast. Some radio stations have three-minute newsbreaks at the top of each hour, so the stories must be short. National Public Radio (NPR) and its affiliates offer news stories that run several minutes or longer. Take a look at this NPR story and its studio introduction, which focuses on the hard-news angle of the story:

ANCHOR VO	The federal government has released a new report on alcohol and drug use. . . . Colorado was near the top of that list on both drug and alcohol use, and excessive drinking was already an issue in that state after at least four students died from alcohol poisoning since the start of the school year.

During the course of the segment, the reporter uses a variety of techniques, including the focus-on-a-person approach:

REPORTER VO	No one called 9-1-1 for Samantha Spady last fall. The college freshman was partying after a Colorado State University football game and passed out. Friends let her sleep it off, not knowing that what she really needed was immediate medical attention. Sam died of alcohol poisoning.

The reporter also uses an expert to walk through the streets, establishing setting by identifying the various bars:

SOT STEVEN WALSH	And on the corner we have The Sink. Moving up the street, we've got Mamacita's, the Players Club, the Fox Theater, Tulagi.
REPORTER VO	Steven Walsh is with the University Hill Neighborhood Association in Boulder. He counts more than a dozen places to buy booze just a few hundred feet from the University of Colorado campus, and he says students walk by these places advertising cheap drinks every day.

The close emphasizes the future:

<table>
<tr><td>REPORTER VO</td><td>It'll take time. . . . After all, it was decades from the first surgeon general's report before smoking became less acceptable. Lawmakers say they know it'll take time, but, they counter, legislation could help that change come about faster.

Jeff Brady, NPR News, Denver</td></tr>
</table>

Preparing Copy for Broadcast

The preparation of broadcast copy differs considerably from the preparation of newspaper copy. When you are writing copy to be read aloud, punctuation changes. Everything should be written so that the anchors, reporters, editors and directors can read it easily.

Even though an Associated Press Stylebook exists for broadcasting, it is not as widely used as the print edition. The rules for copy preparation differ from station to station. For example, although many stations use capital letters for both text and directions, others use uppercase letters for story text and lowercase text for sound bites. You will have to adapt to the station's preferences.

Television scripts are written in two columns. Information for the director and editor is on the left, and the narration is on the right. Set each column for a width of two inches.

Radio scripts do not need to be set in columns. But the line length should be slightly less than the default margins—about four inches or 70 characters wide.

Most radio and television stations use a computer that will automatically put your story into the broadcast system, although most producers, directors and anchors still want a printed copy of all of the stories in case technical glitches occur.

Here are some general guidelines:

- Give the story a "slug" (a one- or two-word title), and write it at the top left-hand corner of each page. Follow it with the date and the name or initials of the writer. Make certain that you identify the broadcast for which the story is intended. Put a slug on every page. If the same story continues for several pages, use that title. When the story changes, use a new slug for that story.

- Double-space all copy. Write on only one side of the paper.

- Number every page. If a story continues to another page, you may want to number it 1A, 1B and so on until the next story, which would start with the number 2.

- Use a separate page for each story.

- End each page with a complete sentence.
- Type instructions for directors, producers and editors on the left side of the page.
- Type the story on the right side of the page in a column approximately two inches wide.
- Do not split or hyphenate words at the end of a sentence. Let the broad cast team see the whole word.

The following is an example of a script for television:

Airborne
01/15
Stafford
CG: (character generator to insert graphic)

AMAZED BY AIRBORNE	<<Nat sound of Chef Fred cooking>> <<VO>> Chef Fred Ball spends most of his time in the kitchen. <<Nat sound of cooking on WETM>> <<VO>> If he's not cooking up something on WETM-TV, he's busy cooking up a feast at the Lindenwald Haus Bed and Breakfast in Elmira.
SOT FULL CG: FRED BALL/CHEF	<<SOT>> The worst thing that can happen to a chef is to catch a cold or get sick during the height of your busy season. The last thing you want is a runny nose, sniffles and watery eyes when you're trying to prepare food for folks.
Length: 0:10	<<VO>> So when he starts feeling sick, Chef Fred takes this. <<Nat sound of dropping Airborne in water>> <<VO>> It's called Airborne and helps relieve cold and flu symptoms.
SOT FULL	<<SOT>> This particular product works. I don't know that it cures the cold, but it relieves the symptoms to a point where you are not miserable whatsoever.
Length 0:06	Airborne was created by a California schoolteacher who was tired of catching colds from her students.
SOT FULL	<<SOT>>

CG: SHELBY STAFFORD (This is a stand-up.)	The directions say adults can take one tablet once every three hours. Drinking Airborne <<takes a sip>> tastes a little bit like orange, but it does have a little bit of an aftertaste.
Length 0:12	<<VO>> Pharmacies, like Gerould's, have a hard time keeping Airborne in stock.
SOT FULL CG: FRANK STEED/PHARMACIST	<<SOT>> Right now, it's going very quickly. In the last month to 2 months, we've had a lot of use for it. We've got a lot of people that have used it traveling and people using it as a preventative product.
Length: 0:12	<<VO>> Chef Fred says he's making room in his kitchen for Airborne. Not to cook with, but to grab the next time he starts feeling sick. In Elmira, I'm WETM-18 Health Reporter Shelby Stafford.

Narrating the Story

Now that you have written the story, you need to narrate it so it can be edited for broadcast.

You need to determine how to pace the narration and what to emphasize. You should vary each sentence. Sometimes the material is important and may be read slowly. Other information that is less important may be light and lively.

A narrator often emphasizes verbs, comparisons and numbers and does not emphasize adjectives, adverbs and prepositions. You can literally take a pen to mark up your copy to determine what you should emphasize.

People get nervous doing narrations. It is important to relax and take a few deep breaths. Tension tends to constrict the vocal chords and to limit proper breathing, making almost everyone's voice move up an octave or so.

You should always check the audio levels with your editor. You should count down from three. If you make a mistake, you should say what take you are doing. Don't worry about making mistakes; worry about getting the best take possible. Don't rush!

Editing for Broadcast

The digital revolution has made camera and editing equipment less expensive and easier to use. Many television stations continue to use nonlinear or analog cameras and editing equipment, but more and more outlets are moving to

MULTIMEDIA COACH

Using audio on the Web works relatively well. Audio files do not take up a great deal of space, and they sound fairly good. Placing video on the Web is not difficult. However, video takes up a lot of digital space, so many people with dial-up connections simply cannot download the material. Even high-speed lines take a while to download video.

Here are some tips to make online video better to watch and faster to download:

- Limit movement of the camera. Zooms and pans take up more space.

- Stay away from dark places and multicolored backgrounds.

- Limit identification of individuals with what are called cgs, Chyrons or lower thirds. Graphical identifications do not show up well online.

- Video on the Web must be compressed, which means that the picture quality will not be as good as in traditional broadcasting. A TV segment will have 30 frames per second; a Web package may have 10 to 15 frames per second, or less visual information.

digital equipment. If you had not had sufficient training on analog equipment, it is best to let photographers and editors take care of these parts of broadcast journalism.

You also need training on digital, or nonlinear equipment, but such equipment is far easier to use. The most popular editing program today is Final Cut Pro, or FCP. Avid and Adobe Premiere are other digital-editing programs.

The digital camera captures the material on a tape, which can then be transferred to a computer. You can also use standard analog video. It is important to know that FCP is an editing program designed *only* for Macintosh computers.

Final Cut Pro has three basic components: clips, sequences and projects. A clip is a specific section of a video, audio or graphics file. A clip may be a single shot or an entire program, depending on how you capture the material. A sequence, as outlined earlier in this chapter, contains a series of clips edited together. A project includes clips, sequences and files for a particular segment.

Four steps occur during the editing process: acquisition, editorial, effects and distribution. Acquisition involves the capturing of all the types of media you intend to use in your program. You will need to log your materials by noting the type of shot or audio clip and the time code, or the specific time on the tape generated electronically by the camera. The logging process will allow you and the editor to find the material much more quickly.

The editorial process involves taking the material you have logged and importing it into the computer program, creating the edited package and augmenting the material with narration and visual transitions. It is important to note that you should always edit the narration first in this process. The effects stage allows you to add titles to identify speakers in sound bites or to identify other visual information, such as the location of the story. The distribution stage enables you to record the material back to videotape (the most common choice for news), a QuickTime movie for the Web, or a compact disc.

To set up Final Cut Pro, you will need the FCP program, a Macintosh computer, a digital video camcorder or tape deck, a FireWire cable (a specific cable that allows the high-speed transfer of video), and audio speakers. Note that using an external FireWire drive will allow you to download your material and not overload your computer's hard drive.

After selecting the relevant preferences for the program, you will see four editing and project elements: the browser, the viewer, the canvas and the time line.

The browser is a collection of files that correspond to actual files on your hard disk. The viewer acts as your monitor for material from your video, audio or graphical sources. You can choose specific in and out points for editing an individual clip. You use the log-and-capture function to select the material you want to use. The log-and-capture feature places the selected information into the browser as a file.

The canvas is a window that functions as the record monitor and shows what you have edited. In the canvas, you can select a clip from the browser window to insert material, overwrite, replace, superimpose or create a transition, such as a dissolve. A dissolve changes a specific cut by softening one image into another. You make your selections based on beginning and ending time codes. Each edit you make will appear in the time line with a video input and an audio input. You usually want at least two video inputs and two audio inputs for news, but you can select many more if you want to do so.

A control bar allows you to replay, pause, play and fast-forward. You can also use computer shortcuts to perform the same functions.

You can make changes in your edited package by simply choosing a clip from the browser and placing it either on the canvas or directly into the time line. You can also screen the clip and revise it before putting it into the canvas or the time line. Unlike analog, or nonlinear editing, the computer will automatically make the changes. You do not have to replace the video or audio in real time by re-recording the material.

Once you have completed your edited package, you need to render the material. You can do this step as you edit the package. The rendering process takes the clips from the hard drive and places the actual audio and video into your edited time line.

You select the render control tab under "user preferences." You then select the material you need to render. The process may take several minutes, depending upon the amount of material you have edited.

The final step involves selecting your output to video, QuickTime or CD. Video is the usual medium for news. If you plan to use the material on the Web, however, you will have to adjust the amount of information in the final edited package by reducing the quality of the audio and video and determining the precise size of the image to be shown on the computer. This step is necessary because the package you have created contains a large amount of computer information. The higher the quality, the slower the package will download to a user's computer. For more information about Final Cut Pro, you should access *www.apple.com/finalcutpro.*

Avid and Adobe Premier, which work for IBM-compatible computers, function in a similar fashion, although the specific input selections vary. Information about Avid editing can be found at *www.avid.com/training/index.html,* and information about Adobe Premiere is available at *www.adobe.com/products/premiere/training.html.*

Putting the Broadcast Together

One of the final steps in putting the broadcast together involves writing the material before and after the reporters' segments. A lead-in is the anchor's introduction to a story that a reporter will present. Lead-ins immediately precede the story package by a reporter. They are written more like a lead to a story, but they should not repeat the reporter's beginning. The lead-in gives the essence of the story, like a focus line, and ends with a statement that the reporter, usually cited by name, has more.

In the case of the Airborne story, the lead-in went like this:

ANCHOR VO	It's a herbal remedy that has taken the country by storm. As WETM-18 Health Reporter Shelby Stafford explains, Airborne is so popular pharmacies have a hard time keeping it in stock.

A tease uses a few words or a sentence to entice a listener to stay tuned for the story that will come in the next newscast or after the commercial. The concept behind these promotional briefs is "Stay tuned; you'll want to hear this." Use the tell-a-friend technique, as though you were saying "Guess what?" or "You won't believe what happened."

In the case of Shelby Stafford's story, the anchor's tease occurred before the commercial:

ANCHOR VO	It works so well local pharmacies can't keep it stocked on their shelves.
	Coming up next on WETM-18 News, we'll tell you whether the herbal cold remedy Airborne lives up to the hype.

Although lead-ins and teases precede the story, they are written by the producer or anchor after the reporter turns in the story.

The anchors will also do small packages, known as "readers" or "voice overs," for short segments in the broadcast. Another frequent video package is called a "donut," during which the anchor will do a brief narration before a sound bite and then follow with additional voice over after the sound.

Putting the Broadcast on the Air

The final step in the broadcast day is putting the stories on the air. A show producer has compiled a computer-generated rundown: the chronological order and running time of each element of the broadcast, including specific instructions about who is doing what on the air.

WETM has a news program at 5:30 p.m. and another that starts at 6 p.m. Therefore, the producer has generated rundown for both shows. She gives a copy of this rundown to the director. The director operates the technical side of the broadcast, arranging robotic cameras and lighting, overseeing graphics, and making certain that the tapes roll into the broadcast properly. The director coordinates the program with the technical director, who oversees the actual inclusion of tapes into the broadcast and other technical aspects of the broadcast, such as sound quality.

5:30/6PM NEWS COMBO   Producer Rundown

Date: Tuesday, January 11, 2005   Time: 5:28:30 PM   Out Time: 6:30:00 PM

Page	Story/Slug	Type	OnCam	Edit #	Graphic	Length	Back
A01	OPEN1/FLU	SS/VO	Matt	1	SS: COMING UP/GENERI 5:30	00:10	5:30:00 PM
A02	OPEN2/PAROA	W/VO	Matt	2		00:05	5:30:05 PM
A03	OPEN3/WEATH	LIVE	Jonathan			00:10	5:30:15 PM
A04	OPEN4/TO BREAK	SS	Matt		SS: COMING UP/GENERI 530	00:05	5:30:20 PM
A05	****BREAK 1 ****	ROLL	*************	OPEN	SHOW OPEN	01:10	5:31:30 PM
A06	5:30COLD/FLU:	W/VO	Matt	3		00:05	5:31:35 PM
A07	FLU SHOTS	SS/VO	Matt	4	SS: TOP STORY/GEN 5:30	00:25	5:32:00 PM
A08	FLU SHOT SOT	SOT	Matt	5		00:10	5:32:10 PM
A09	FLU SHOT GFX	W/GFX	Matt		d/GFX (1)	00:10	5:32:20 PM
A10	DOCTOR SHOTS	SS/VO	Matt	6	d/SS: DOCTORS' DOSES/flu shot	00:30	5:32:50 PM
A11	DOCTOR SOT	SOT/VO	Matt	7		00:35	5:33:25 PM
A12	PA FLU SHOTS	W/VO/GFX	Matt	8	d/GFX (1)	00:40	5:34:05 PM
A13	PA STORM	SS/VO	Matt	9	d/SS: SLIPPERY ROADS/trac trailer on road	00:25	5:34:30 PM
A14	CA WEATHER	SS	Matt		d/SS: DEADLY MUDSLIDE/ taken away by mud	00:10	5:34:40 PM
A15	CA PKG	PKG		10		01:26	5:36:06 PM
A16	CA TAG	SS	Matt			00:15	5:36:21 PM
A17	STORM OPEN	SOT		11		00:05	5:36:26 PM
A18	FIRST WEATHER	LIVE/GFX	Jonathan			00:45	5:37:11 PM
A19	FIRST TAG	LIVE	Jonathan			00:05	5:37:16 PM

Beginning of WETM 5:30 p.m. broadcast rundown

The WETM broadcast opens with a story about flu shots in the A block, which includes the most topical news stories. The stories number A01 to A29. The type of story includes VO, or voice over; PKG, a designation for a reporter's story; or LIVE, a designation that the anchor is talking on camera.

OnCam designates who is talking.

Edit# refers to the numbered tape that has the prepared material, which must be physically put into an edit machine.

Graphic designates what, if any, computer-generated material will appear on the screen and must be inserted by the technical director.

Length designates the time of the story, and Back shows the running time of the complete show.

The B Block includes more news from B01 to B07, including stories about cancer and asthma.

The C Block focuses on weather.

The D and E blocks return to news.

The 5:30 p.m. broadcast does not have a separate block for sports, whereas the 6 p.m. and 11 p.m. newscasts do.

Using Broadcast Terms

Before you start a broadcast career, you need to understand some basic terms. Some of these have already been mentioned.

Actuality: Recorded comments from a news source. Same as a sound bite, but this is the term used in radio.

Anchor: The person who reads the news from the studio.

Backtiming: Exact time in the newscast that a segment will air. The timing of each segment is determined by counting back from the end of the broadcast. As an example, for a story that will air 10 minutes before the end of a 30-minute newscast, the backtiming will be listed at 20:00, alerting the anchor and technicians that the segment must start at precisely that time or it will have to be cut.

Brief: Short news story, from 10 to 20 seconds long.

B-roll: Video without the sound bite. It originates from a time when video with sound was on one tape (such as A-roll) and video without the sound was on another tape; the tapes would have to be switched from one to another. Today, computers can merge both on the same tape.

Character generator: A computer that produces the letters, numbers or words superimposed on the screen to label a visual image, such as a person or place.

Chyron: The name of a character generator machine, but some stations write "Chyron" or "Chiron" in the script instead of "CG" opposite the source's name.

Donut: In the studio, a brief anchor segment that includes narration followed by a sound bite, which is followed by more narration.

IN: Indicates the beginning of the source's quote to start a sound bite. The entire sound bite should be used in a script so that the editor can find the precise quote and so that closed captioning for the hearing impaired can be produced.

Lower third: A computer-generated graphic that identifies an individual by name and title.

News director: The person who oversees news operations at the station.

OUT: Indicates the last words of the source's quote, ending the sound bite. Again, the entire sound bite should be included in the script.

Package: Reporter's story, including narration, visual images and interviews with sources.

Producer: Oversees the broadcast or the individual package in the field. The broadcast producer may write the copy that anchors read for the newscast.

Reader: Story that the anchor reads without visuals or sound bites.

Rip-and-read: Copy from the wire services that is read exactly as it was written instead of being rewritten.

ROSR: Pronounced roser, as in rose-er, the acronym stands for radio on-scene report.

Seg time: Length of time for a news segment. A brief may be :10, or 10 seconds; a reporter's package, including the lead-in by an anchor, may be 1:45.

SOC (standard out cue): Reporter's sign-off comments at the end of the story. For example, "This is Shelby Stafford for WETM-18 in Elmira."

SOT (sound on tape): A sound bite indicated in copy along with the amount of time the taped comments will take.

Sound bite: Video segment showing a source speaking.

Super: Letters, numbers or words produced by the character generator and superimposed over visual images—often used to identify the person appearing on the tape. At some stations, the letters *CG*—for character generator— are used to indicate the super. A lower third is another way to designate a super that identifies an individual by name and title.

Tease: A brief reader to promote a story on the newscast, to tease viewers to tune in.

Teleprompter: Video terminal that displays the script for the anchor to read.

Video on demand (VOD): Digital video that is available for downloading. Broadcast networks will often supply video on demand to their affiliates.

VO (voice over): Voice over video images.

Voicer: Radio news story narrated by a reporter live or on tape; it is the same as a reader, but the reporter, not the anchor, reads it.

Web Sites for Broadcast

Broadcast news Web sites allow journalists to include much more information than a television newscast would allow. Many broadcast sites offer line-ups of programs and provide multimedia and additional information about specific stories. In the case of the report on Airborne, the cold remedy, the reporter included additional information about the remedy. During the broadcast, the anchor told viewers to go to *www.wetmtv.com* to learn more about the medicine.

Other Web sites, such as *www.cnn.com,* include archives of previous video stories, audio reports or streaming video, the actual program on the air.

Exercises

1   Record a television broadcast from a local station. Compare the content of the broadcast to the next day's local newspaper. What stories were the same? What stories were different? Evaluate whether the television broadcast or the newspaper provided better coverage of the same stories. Why do you think the broadcast or the newspaper did a better job?

2   Write a broadcast brief of about 15 seconds based on this information from a CNN News story:

Who: Mark Thomas, 21, of Salt Lake City, Utah.

What: He was hiking and fell 1,000 feet down the side of Mount Nebo near Mona, Utah, just ahead of an avalanche.

When: Today.

Backup information: He suffered only a minor back injury and minor frostbite in his feet after being covered in snow. County Sheriff described Thomas as "extremely lucky."

3   Write a one-minute, 30-second broadcast package based on the following information from ABC News:

An estimated 25 million children under the age of 13 are overweight. People in government and education have begun to believe that the problem cannot be left to parents alone. Legislation has been proposed in Texas that would create an obesity report card. The legislation would require all children attending Texas public schools to be weighed. The results would then be sent to parents along with each report card.

Tamatha Hamblen's daughter Amber, 12, weighs 200 pounds, or 100 pounds overweight, and is on the verge of getting diabetes

Texas is not the first state to consider school obesity reports. Arkansas began weighing all students in 2003. And nearly 500,000 students were classified as overweight. Texas cities lead the list of fattest cities in America. Possible sound bites:

SOT

TAMATHA HAMBLEN, MOTHER	She probably wouldn't have gained so much weight if I had known how to take care of it.

SOT

DR. SARAH BLONSTEIN, PEDIATRIC OBESITY SPECIALIST	It's one other way to get the message out to parents about it so they can act on that information and start to make some changes.

SOT

STATE SEN. LETICIA VAN DE PUTTE, TEXAS	While it seems tough, we're trying to save kids' lives. The data show us that this generation of students will pre-decease their parents because of their health status.

SOT

GOV. MIKE HUCKABEE, R-ARK.	I don't want the government being the grease police. But what we have to do is to create an atmosphere in which healthier choices of life are rewarded.

SOT

ERIC ALLEN, ASSN OF TEXAS PROFESSIONAL EDUCATORS	How many times have you taken a report card when you were a student and walked down the hallway and compared it with your friends? Now, it's not just your grades. It's "Are you skinny or not?"

Featured *News Scene* Assignment

Access *News Scene* at *http://communication.wadsworth.com/newsscene* to view the news simulation titled "Bank Robbery." Write a one-minute, 15-second story for broadcast, including narration, sound bites and a stand-up.

Coaching Tips

Determine what will be on your home page.

Be concise with headlines and stories.

Consider what multimedia elements, such as graphics, photos, audio and video, you want to include.

Make it easy for your users to find what they want.

Determine how often you want to update the page.

CHAPTER 12

Web Journalism

I want news judgment. I want people to write sharp headlines. I want people to know AP style. I do like people if they are users of the Internet. I like a little geekiness.

Mike Walker, editor, *syracuse.com*,
Syracuse, N.Y.

Mike Walker sends an instant message to his senior editor, Jamie Clewis, to change a headline. Clewis responds with an instant message that he's fixed the headline, but he says Walker needs to check a hyperlink that doesn't work. Walker and Clewis move methodically through the Web pages of *syracuse.com,* making sure that everything looks right for the update at 9 a.m. Walker, the editor of the Web site, can't make the site active, or live, until he receives a graphic from the company's headquarters in New Jersey. Once he gets it, he tells Clewis to put up the new home (opening) page.

It isn't exactly the equivalent of watching the presses roll at a daily newspaper or the television countdown to air at a broadcast station, but Walker and his seven-person team have made deadline—going live with the morning update that contains an interesting mix of news.

Today the weather in Syracuse, N.Y., is cold. So are the Syracuse Orangemen, the college basketball team that has recently lost four games. Several important crime stories, including the third part in a series on teenagers drinking and driving, provide hard news. Railroad crossings have not been repaired in certain parts of Syracuse, a city of 150,000 in upstate New York. A real-estate developer owes thousands of dollars in taxes.

"This is one of the best news days we have had in a while, so it makes it easy," says Walker, a 1994 Boston University graduate who has worked for several Internet operations and newspapers in Pennsylvania, New Jersey and New York.

Syracuse.com is a joint Web site for the *Syracuse Post-Standard;* WTBH-TV, a CBS affiliate; and several radio stations. The site depends primarily on these outlets for its news, but *syracuse.com* also has an eclectic mixture of discussion groups and homegrown bloggers whose combined efforts reached nearly 500,000 viewers a month with 25 million individual page views. That's a increase of 30 percent over the previous year.

"More people are just going on line for news," Walker says. "We try to make the site inviting so people will come back. But we clearly are riding the tide of people moving to the Internet to get their news."

Mike Walker, editor of *syracuse.com*

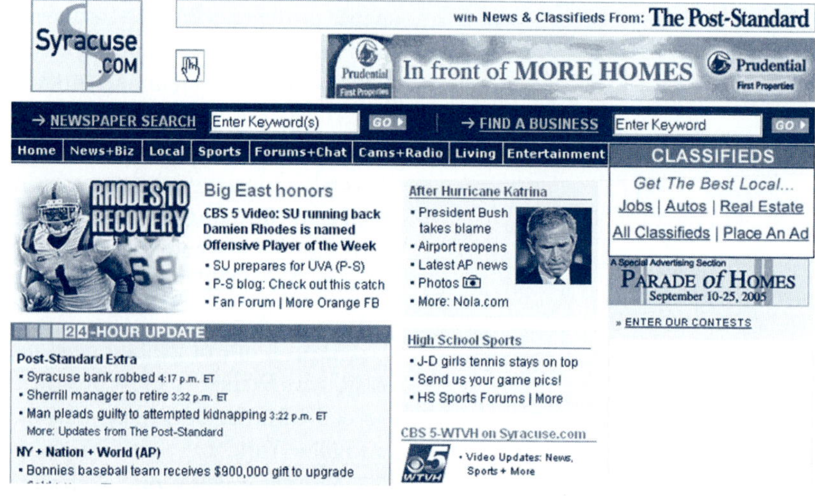

When Walker studied at Boston University in the early 1990s, the Internet did not play an important role in people's daily routine. He says he got involved in the Internet because he saw it as a growing part of providing information to people. Walker says he doesn't necessarily need people who have all of the technical skills to operate computer software programs—although such knowledge helps. He focuses on good journalistic skills. "I want news judgment. I want people to write sharp headlines. I want people to know AP style," he says. "I do like people if they are users of the Internet. I like a little geekiness."

Immediacy

Availability and immediacy are key elements in the growth of *syracuse.com,* Walker says. "The Internet audience is not as patient as the newspaper audience. On the Web things need to be shorter, more direct and more concise."

Walker views the site's role as providing news in the easiest way possible, with major updates in the morning and two in the afternoon, mainly for people at work: "The majority of our users say their main interest is sports. So we will make it easier for them to find sports."

Walker says the news organizations see the Web site as simply another way to deliver content. The newspaper is the primary source of that content. The Web editor sees some similarities and differences between the *Syracuse Post-Standard* and the site. The front page of the newspaper and the home page of the Web site basically have the same stories: weather, crime and some sports. But the prominence given these stories is often different. For example, the story on dangerous railroad crossings makes the home page of the Web site with less prominence than the newspaper. A story about whether the point guard of the Syracuse University basketball team will play in the NCAA tournament gets prominent play on the Web site.

Interactivity

Interactivity sets the Web apart from other media. Web readers at *syracuse.com* can actively search, read and click on links that include news, entertainment, business, sports, discussion forums and blogs. Interactivity can be as simple as providing a discussion question at the end of a story or as complex as creating searchable databases for school test scores or crime statistics.

Syracuse.com has developed a series of discussion boards, including many about college and high school sports. One of the most popular sites is "Yada, Yada, Yada," where people can post on just about everything that's on their minds. "It's like a whole society going on there," Walker says. You can even listen to police and fire calls via a link to a scanner on the Syracuse site.

The Web site has added Web logs, or "blogs"—a topic discussed later in this chapter—about entertainment and travel in the region, and several blogs about sports. "It's great for us. It gives us great content," Walker says. "We can use something from a blog later in the day and put it up for more discussion." Some bloggers post news about suburban communities, including local events that ordinarily wouldn't be covered in the paper.

Reporting for the Web

The Project for Excellence in Journalism determined that more than 150 million people in the United States use the Web, including many who go there for news. Even though print and television news remain the primary information choices for many people, the Web has grown significantly as a source for news. Moreover, people have started to trust the accuracy of Web sites.

The Web differs from other media in many ways. It is a combination of other media—print, radio, television and graphics—that places much more control in the hands of the user. Simply put, the Web allows users to go where they want to go, or in a nonlinear order, meaning that users can access information in any order they choose. Print and broadcast stories are usually written in linear order from beginning to end, as in a straight line, offering people no other choice except to stop reading or to stop listening.

Even though many stories may be written in linear order, the Web offers readers nonlinear choices of accessing related elements linked to the story or the site. A Web package created in nonlinear order might be divided into smaller chunks spanning several pages or might contain links to time lines, related stories, polls and other elements.

Reporting for the Web does not differ significantly from reporting for other media except that you have to gather material in a variety of media. You still need to have a good story idea, coupled with good research. The difference is that you may also have to worry about getting information on an audiotape recorder or providing video and photographs.

Keep in mind that broadcast interviews require more attention to the proper phrasing of questions. Ask someone to describe and explain what happened. Make certain to start questions with "what," "how" and "why" rather than "do" or "is." Using this approach will encourage the interview subject to provide a more expansive answer, which usually means a better sound bite. If you start a question with "do" or "is," you are likely to get an answer that begins and possibly ends with "yes" or "no." That makes the sound bite difficult to edit and possibly useless. Even though these techniques remain important for print, they are the best way to gather good sound bites for broadcast and the Web.

Finding Information

Governments, corporations, public interest groups, trade organizations and many other outlets have created Web sites to provide information and commentary. These sites can be extremely useful for any reporting. If you are covering a story about crime, for example, you can access your area's statistics from the FBI at *www.fbi.gov/ucr/ucr.htm.* If you are writing about health

Nora Paul's Digital Storytelling Web site

issues, you can go to the site of the Centers for Disease Control and Prevention at *www.cdc.gov* or a for-profit health site at *www.webmd.com*.

It is important to keep in mind that no one checks the accuracy of any site other than the individual or organization that puts it on the Web. Therefore, the reliability of a site depends on the reliability of the individual or organization. It is better to quote from sites backed by the government, which end with .gov, or reputable organizations, which end with .org or .com, and provide links to those sites so that users can determine what they think about the information.

E-mail Reporting

E-mail can be a useful reporting tool, but don't depend on it for deadline stories. You can't control when or if sources check their e-mail. Limit your questions, preferably to fewer than five. Sources may be reluctant to answer lengthy lists of questions. One or two questions are even better.

Some journalists express concern that you can't determine if the source in an e-mail interview is authentic, but if you are writing to a source you know or one affiliated with a reliable organization, that risk is minimal.

Digital Storytelling

Nora Paul, director of the Institute for New Media Studies at the University of Minnesota, has created an analysis of the various components of digital storytelling. She identifies five basic elements:

- Media
- Action

- Relationship
- Context
- Communication

Paul defines "media" as the material used to create the story package. Four elements of media are "configuration," or whether a Web site focuses primarily on using a single medium or more than one medium to tell a story. "Type" identifies exactly what media are used to tell a story. "Currentness" depends on whether the information arrives immediately to a user, such as a live news conference. "Time and space" focus on whether the material is edited or not.

A wide variety of Web sites exist. Some focus on delivering content in only one medium, such as text or broadcast, whereas others combine a variety of media sources. Paul outlines these sources, which include text, graphics, animation, photographs, audio and video. She also defines a Web site by whether it delivers asynchronously, or delayed by editing, or synchronously, which is content delivered as it happens, such as live webcasts or streaming video. Paul further defines digital storytelling by whether it is a complete speech, for example, or an edited version.

SignonSanDiego.com, the Web site for the *San Diego Union-Tribune*, provides an excellent example of such elements in its award-winning report, "The Week of Fire." The project chronicled the wildfires that killed 16 people, destroyed 2,500 houses and burned 400,000 acres.

The opening (index) page used text to provide a brief overview of what happened. The bottom of the page used graphics to display a daily time line. A dramatic photograph demonstrated the extent of the fire. The site provides linear and nonlinear choices for the user to read text stories, listen to audio or watch video.

Paul's second focus, action, depends on whether the developer controls the content, the user does, or a combination of the developer and the user controls the information. Her third element depends on the relationship between the user and the content. This relationship depends on whether users can create their own reading pattern for stories through a custom version of the content, such as a personal news source that provides specific information. That information could include the weather in a particular city or sports scores from a favorite team. This factor includes what Paul describes as "calculation," or mathematical input, such as a poll.

Under the category of relationship Paul also includes manipulation—the ability of the user to change the content—and appendage—the ability of the user to add information through an outlet such as a forum.

The fourth element of Web sites analyzes context. Context in newspapers, for example, can be provided by sidebar stories. Even though Web sites can provide sidebars, links to other stories or sites often serve as the main element of context for the digital story.

The fifth element of Web sites depends on the type of communication between the digital storyteller and the user. Certain variations exist, but Paul basically defines sites that encourage communication, known as two-way communication sites, and those that do not encourage interaction, which are

signonsandiego.com Web site

known as one-way communication sites. (For further information about Paul's work on digital storytelling, go to *www.inms.umn.edu/elements/index.php.*)

Planning a Web Site

Web designers plan sites by creating a storyboard, which is similar to an organizational chart, to show the main parts and related pieces. A storyboard can be used for news stories as well. You could also draft a simple outline to plan elements of the story:

- First, decide what type or types of media you intend to use. An online story can include audio, video, photographs or graphics.

- Second, decide who will control the action of the movement through the story: you, the user or a combination of the two.

- Third, determine how little or how much you want the user to participate in the process. A story could feature a discussion question, a forum or a poll.

- Fourth, decide how much and what type of context will exist for a story. A story could lend itself to background created as a time line, a searchable database or short biographies of the sources. Hyperlinks, or the Web addresses of other sites, often accompany online stories. The links can be provided in the body of your story or at the end.

- Fifth, decide if you want to have communication with your users. Not all news sites include e-mails of reporters and editors, but it's a good idea to add your e-mail address to your byline. Interactivity between readers and reporters will most likely increase in the future.

Once you have thought about the various elements for the story, you can outline the elements or create a rough sketch of a storyboard to guide you. For example, CNN provided a historical guide of the network's 25 years in broadcasting. The Web team made the following decisions:

- Media: The site included text, photos, graphics, audio and video.
- Action: CNN provided most of the information, but the network also asked people to provide examples of specific news stories that affected them.
- Relationship: Users participated in a poll to select individuals who made important contributions over the 25 years, including the most influential woman scientist and the most influential African-American.
- Context: The Web site provided mainly internal links to other CNN stories, ensuring that users were not sent off to other organizations.
- Communication: CNN asked users if they wanted to have special news alerts on technology or politics.

Story Planning

A Web story often includes various layers or individual pages. A way to plan for Web stories might include a checklist to determine what elements should be used:

- Headline
- Summary, known as blurbs and briefs
- Main story—one scrolling text page or
- Main story—divided into chunks of several Web pages
- Breaking news brief or updates
- Links to related stories and sources
- Time lines
- Short biographies of main sources
- Full text of speeches, reports, budgets or lists of winners
- Photos and/or graphics
- Audio and/or video
- Searchable databases
- Interactive elements
- Polls
- Games or quizzes
- Discussion questions or a forum
- E-mail link to reporter

MULTIMEDIA COACH

The Web is an ideal medium for storytelling in many forms. Short segments are preferable to long stories that span several screens. But the Web is a perfect place to experiment with new forms of storytelling, especially a nonlinear treatment with links to elements of the story. No single form is right for all stories on the Web or in any other medium.

One form of storytelling gaining popularity on the Web is personal journalism, known as "Web logs" or "blogs." Consider the Web a people's platform where readers relate more to writers than in impersonal journalism.

Consumer journalism with helpful tips is another storytelling form that works well on the Web.

But innovative story forms abound on the Web. Storytelling on the Web can be in multimedia format, photo essays, short chunks or serial narratives. Most of all, storytelling can be interactive on the Web. Stories can involve readers by asking them to participate in polls, questions, writing their own endings or opinions or submitting their own experiences. Consider storytelling on the Web as including the best of traditional media and inventing new ways to tell stories.

Reaching the Audience

It is not entirely clear how online readers acquire and use information on the Web. Some studies show that online readers scan text rather than read every word. That's why many news sites offer a printer-friendly version for people who want to print out an entire copy of an article to read it thoroughly.

Other studies confirm that Web readers skim text but that they will read thoroughly if they find information they want. The Poynter Institute and Stanford University tested how readers viewed online news by tracking their eye movements with special glasses that look like binoculars. The Poynter Institute had conducted a similar study several years earlier by tracking the eye movements of newspaper readers. The significant difference between the two studies was that online readers focused first on text while newspaper readers focused first on graphics or headlines.

The Poynter and Stanford researchers found that online users read about 75 percent of online news stories. The results should be viewed cautiously because the participants were regular online readers, who may not reflect the general public.

Jakob Nielsen, a well known specialist on Web design, recommends employing the following techniques to make sites easier to use:

Jakob Nielsen

Jakob Nielsen, Web usability expert

- Write short, simple sentences. Reading on computer monitors is more difficult than reading print. Avoid sentences with long clauses and complex sentences. Be concise.

- Use bulleted lists to help readers scan text.

- Limit each paragraph to one idea.
- Use boldface subheads placed periodically throughout a text story to help readers scan. Write meaningful subheads—not clever ones—that tell the reader what the section is about.

Writing for the Web

Good writing matters in any medium. Choose the form that best suits the story. It could be a summary lead. It could be a chronological approach. It could be an anecdotal lead or a narrative story form. Whatever the approach, place the nut graph early in the story, preferably by the third or fourth paragraph.

As with all other writing discussed in this textbook, start with the focus. The focus sentence could be your lead, or it could be a summary blurb under the headline. Starting with a headline and summary blurb is a good way to identify your focus.

Headlines, Blurbs and Briefs

Headlines, summary blurbs and briefs represent some of the most important factors in determining whether someone will choose to read a story. Clarity is crucial. The headline and a summary blurb of one or two sentences should accurately provide a summary of the story. Readers often want to know exactly what they're getting when they select a story. Unlike a newspaper, which offers only a handful of stories on each page, a Web page offers dozens of headlines and links competing for attention.

Although headlines are often written *after* the story is submitted, one of the best ways to focus your story is to write a headline and summary blurb *before* you write the full story.

Because most major news organizations also require reporters to submit briefs for the Web before publication in a newspaper or on a broadcast newscast, writing your brief first is another good way to identify the essential information for a fuller story.

Here are some guidelines for Web headlines that link to the main story:

Write brief headlines: Fewer than six to 10 words create better links than headlines that span two or three lines:

Help test Einstein's theories @ home

Use strong verbs:

Crime sleuths cope with "CSI" effect

Put the most important words first:

Garden of Eden slowly returns to life

Avoid articles (*the, a, an*) at the start of a headline:

Sexy scent lures roaches to doom

Not: The sexy scent lures roaches to doom

Use question headlines if the subject is interesting enough to entice readers:

Looking for fear? It's in the eyes.

MSNBC.com

Blurbs

Many news sites simply repeat the story lead for the blurb under the headline. That's fine if it's a summary lead. But if the lead doesn't give the main point of the story, write a clear summary or use the nut graph as the blurb.

For example, this headline from the Web site of *The Tampa* (Fla.) *Tribune* is vague standing by itself. It needs the summary blurb that accompanies it:

Checking it out for themselves

LAKELAND—With a customer and brand base on its side, Publix is going after an online home-delivery market in a venture where others who tried it have seen their businesses marked down or shelved.

The next headline is somewhat catchy, but it depends on the summary blurb for clarification:

Woman seeks divorce over mynah indiscretions

A Chinese woman launches divorce proceedings after the family's pet mynah bird blabs about husband's affairs. The bird began repeating the words, "I love you" and "divorce" from the husband's phone calls to his lover.

Blurb Tips

Write a clear summary: If the lead is creative, choose the nut graph as the summary blurb. The headline mentioned earlier about fear may provoke curiosity, but it could use a blurb for clarification:

Headline   ## Looking for fear? It's in the eyes.

Blurb   If you look into the eyes of someone who is frightened, your brain will pick up on the fear in a split second, well before you can consciously put a name to the emotion, scientists say.

Avoid writing summaries that repeat the headline: The first sentence in this blurb is redundant:

Headline   ## Is work a pain in the neck . . . or hands?

Blurb   Has work become a real pain? If so, the problem might not be your job but your workstation. Judy Gibson, manager of the Physical Therapy department at Fairbanks Memorial Hospital, says proper ergonomics is essential to preventing problems.

Address the reader when appropriate: Use the "you" voice:

Headline   ## Get free cash for college

Blurb   You can collect thousands of dollars in scholarship money just by filling out a form.

Briefs

Blurbs are usually a few sentences, but a brief can be a few paragraphs. A brief can stand alone in place of a story, whereas a blurb intends to entice readers to read more. Sometimes, little difference exists between a blurb and a brief. In the majority of cases, the blurb and the brief repeat the lead or the first few paragraphs of the full text. The main reason to use blurbs and briefs is to offer readers a choice of layers. Some Web readers want to read only the headline, others want a brief summary and others want the complete story. Here is an example:

Headline   ## Toxic Treats

Blurb   Regulators have found unsafe lead levels in 112 brands of candy—most made in Mexico—but test results almost always are kept from parents and health officials.

Brief   The state Department of Health Services has found high levels of lead in 112 distinct brands of candies. Of those, 84 brands were made in Mexico, eight were made in other countries and 20 were of unknown origin.

The state has issued seven public-health advisories, affecting 11 candy brands after high lead tests. Advisories are sent to the media and local health officials and posted on the state health department's Web site.

The complete story—part of a series in both English and Spanish in the *Orange County* (Calif.) *Register*—described the threat of the candies to children.

Story Structure

Get to the point of the story quickly—within the first 50 words. If you consider that a news site on the Web usually has a title image, a banner advertisement and a story headline, this doesn't leave you much room. To complicate matters, readers may use small portable devices to get their news. In addition, text on most news sites is enclosed in tables about four inches wide to aid readers. That translates to about 100 to 150 words per screen.

Many traditional news organizations favor the inverted pyramid for Web stories because the main idea happens in the lead or first few paragraphs. This form is fine for basic news stories, but it is too restrictive for features and other types of storytelling. As long as the nut graph expressing the main point is high in the story, writers may have as much flexibility for Web stories as for print.

The headline, blurb and lead may be repetitious, but this doesn't harm readability because it helps readers know they have accessed the correct story from among the dozens of others that may be linked to the site.

Here is an example of the inverted pyramid with a summary lead:

Headline	**Police find millions in idling big rig**
Blurb	Tractor-trailer was unattended for two days; driver found nearby
Lead	Trenton, N.J.—New Jersey state police seized more than $5 million in cash Thursday from a tractor-trailer found idling unattended for two days on the shoulder of a roadway, authorities said.
	The driver, Salvadore Delarosa, 46, of San Bernardino, Calif., was arrested on a money laundering charge.
	The Associated Press

ETHICS

The case: You are the Web editor for your campus newspaper or broadcast station. In either situation, when you print or air a story, you usually post related links on the Web site. Your newspaper or broadcast station reports a story about plagiarism, in this case involving term papers that are for sale on the Internet. The story mentions several sites that sell these term papers. When you transfer this story to the Web, should you provide links to these sites where students can buy term papers? Ethically, you know that plagiarism is wrong, and that is the point of the story. If you post links to these sites, are you encouraging students to use them?

This example also uses an inverted pyramid form with a creative lead, but the nut graph is in the third paragraph:

Headline | **Officials seize hurt animals**

Blurb | Animal control authorities haul away more than 150 injured and neglected animals—some close to death

Lead | The sign on the stable welcomes visitors to the "Heaven and Earth" animal sanctuary.

But authorities say the so-called animal shelter was a living hell.

Animal Control officials spent Friday seizing more than 150 animals from the 20-acre property where they say pets and livestock were neglected, some of them almost to the point of death.

Jamie Malernee, St. Petersburg *(Fla.)* Times

List Format

Lists within stories break up the text and help readers scan Web stories quickly.

Headline | **Something unspoken**

Blurb | What not to say in an interview

Lead | If you're a smart job candidate, you've thought about the points you want to make to sell yourself in an interview. Maybe you've even practiced your spiel. That's good, but know too that career experts caution that saying too much in an interview can hurt your prospects.

You already know to avoid mentioning the office-supplies pilfering complaint filed against you in your last job—and that reprimand for arriving late on 18 days in one month. But here are some less obvious things you should avoid saying at a job interview.

- Don't address your interviewer by his or her first name, unless and until it's clearly established that the session is on a first-name basis. Here, the rule is to let the interviewer speak first.

- Don't use the wrong name. First or last.

- Don't say anything that conveys you're desperate for the job. Even if you are.

Larry Keller, CNN.com

Question/answer Format

A question/answer format is a good alternative form for Web writing. The story still needs an introduction. This CNN example includes an interactive poll, an ideal feature for online stories. It also has a question lead, which works better online than in print stories. Note the conversational "you" voice, also good for online writing.

Headline

Selling yourself again: The job interview revisited

Lead

"If you were a squirrel, which commodity would you inventory first—the nuts or the berries?"

May you never encounter that question in a job interview.

But the knee-knocking trial of it all, the sleepless nights leading up to it, the 18 cups of coffee before you get there, the sudden feeling that your resume belongs to someone else and your clothes do, too, for that matter . . . it's all here again for a lot of people. Some may have thought they wouldn't be facing this particular ordeal again soon, if ever.

It's a job interview. And with the wake of layoffs widening—nearly 300,000 in the United States in the first quarter of this year, according to data from Randstad North America and Roper Starch Worldwide—a lot of people are finding themselves back in that very hot seat.

CNN: So we applied ourselves to ETICON'S Ann Humphries, asking her to tell us what's important to know from the business etiquette standpoint, what to do when it's time to grip 'n' grin. And before we give you Ann, any squirrel knows the answer is berries, inventory them first—nuts have longer shelf life.

The story continues with the question/answer format from professional management consultant Ann Humphries and is accompanied by an interactive poll.

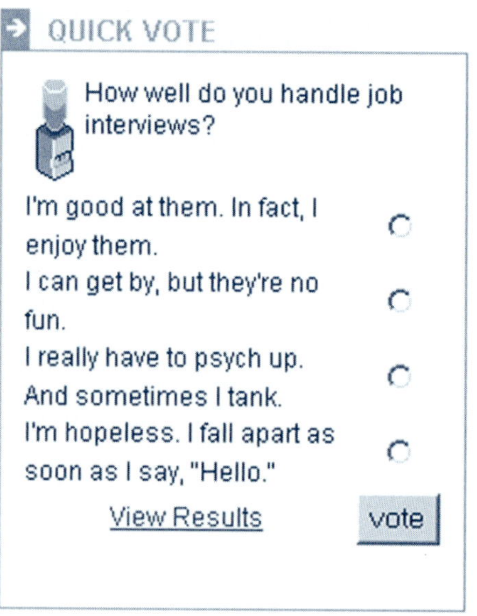

Time Line Format

Time lines help readers scan Web stories quickly.

Headline   **80 days that changed the world**

CNN, in cooperation with *Time*, created a visual time line of the most important stories of the past 80 years, coinciding with the magazine's 80th anniversary. The graphic allowed users to select specific decades and years, including the ability to see what stories were chosen. The reader could then open up a specific story.

Writing Tips

Every medium has its peculiarities. Here are some other important writing tips for the Web:

- Use conversational style. Write as though you were talking to a single reader. Borrow the techniques for broadcast writing outlined in Chapter 11.
- Write in active voice: Who did what rather than what was done to whom.

  Write: The student won an award.

  Don't write: An award was won by the student.

- Keep paragraphs short and insert a space between them.
- The "you" voice works well online. Try to let readers know what the story means for them.
- Avoid using only a person's last name on second reference in subsequent screens or Web pages. Don't use the source elsewhere in the story unless the person is the main source or is well known enough to be placed anywhere in the story without confusing the reader. If you must reuse a source in another section for context, re-introduce the person with some reference.

Narrative Storytelling

Narrative writing can also be compelling on the Web, especially if it is split into several pages with cliffhanger endings that entice readers to continue. The Web specials on the *St. Petersburg* (Fla.) *Times* site offer several examples, including this narrative story, "The last full measure of devotion," about the death of Sgt. Paul Smith in Iraq. The multipart Web package was organized in chunks and featured this enticing one-screen introduction:

> The men who served under Sgt. Paul Smith didn't much like him. He trained them too long, they said, and too hard.

> On April 4, outside of Baghdad, these men suddenly found themselves confronted by a much larger force of Iraqi troops. In the deadly classroom of combat, they suddenly understood the lessons Smith had tried to teach them—even as Smith fulfilled his vow to give "all that I am to ensure that all my boys make it home."
>
> *Alex Leary,* St. Petersburg *(Fla.)* Times

The rest of the story continues in dramatic storytelling with a description of Smith, his unit, the battle in which he died and the recommendation that he receive the Medal of Honor, the nation's highest military decoration.

Personal Storytelling

People want to hear, read and *share* stories. And that's how the Web can exceed any other medium in history. Personal storytelling thrives on the Web, and it is increasing on news sites. Some of the best personal storytelling sites are not traditional broadcast or newspaper sites. *Musarium* (*www .musarium.com*), a site that describes itself as devoted to "the power of human storytelling," is an example. It features innovative multimedia packages with personal stories in several formats. Some of the storytelling is told in photo essays.

"The Boys of Bundy Cottage," for example, chronicles the lives of 13 boys in an orphanage in Oxford, N.C. The author, Joe Weiss, describes the project as a constant struggle for the boys, "who share a common bond of a broken home life and hope together to be part of a family in their new environment."

Another section of the site includes the Web stories of Alex Chadwick, a National Public Radio reporter, who traveled around America with producer Ray Farkas carrying a card table and a handmade sign: "Interviews 50 cents." "There are so many people with stories and willing to tell them if you ask," Chadwick wrote on the Web site. In different places, from Key West to the Indiana State Fair, people tell their stories about failed marriages, spiritual healing and, in one man's case, about "being too scared to move" when two boys threatened to shoot him.

For other examples of innovative storytelling and Web design, try Derek Powazek's *www.fray.com.* Both of these sites encourage readers to share their stories.

Blogs and Podcasts

Blogs have become an interesting and powerful force in journalism. An estimated eight million blogs exist, including an estimated 50,000 that are updated daily. Blogs exist for almost every intellectual and personal experience, from golfing to religion.

In many cases, blogs serve as the equivalent of the editorial page of a newspaper, with opinion and commentary as the content. The traditional notions of objectively, fairness and balance often play almost no role in blogs, where individuals can express their viewpoints.

Podcasts are the audio equivalent of blogs, which can be uploaded to a Web site for listeners. Andrew Sullivan, one of the most popular bloggers, worked as the editor for *The New Republic* and still freelances for a variety of publications. But his main calling is his "Daily Dish" at *www.andrewsullivan .com.* He told the *Washington Post* that he sees the site as "a way you can throw ideas around without having to fully back them up, just to see what response you get." Although some bloggers might quibble with Sullivan's definition, his description would fit many blogs.

Blogging has become increasingly important as a watchdog of politicians and the media. In recent years, blogs have been responsible for forcing the resignation of Sen. Trent Lott as majority leader of the U.S. Senate for racist remarks he made, causing the resignation of CNN President Eason Jordan for comments he made, and battering both presidential candidates in the 2004 election campaign. The Web site *www.powerlineblog.com* is generally credited with forcing CBS to admit that Dan Rather and "60 Minutes" had relied on bad reporting when they broadcast accusations about President Bush's National Guard service record.

Publishing to the Web

Once you have assembled the various parts of your story and the media that go with it, you need to publish the material to the Web. If you are working for a news organization, it has probably already established a specific protocol for publishing the material. If you are publishing to your own site, you need to know a little bit more about publishing to the Web.

The creation of basic Web publishing programs, such as Dreamweaver and Front Page, has made creating and publishing much easier. If you are creating your own Web site, the first step is to determine what content you expect to use: text, graphics, photographs, audio, video or anything else. Before you turn on the computer, use a blank sheet of paper to determine where the content will exist and how you expect the user to go from one page to another, known as "navigation."

Many Web publishing programs are available. If you intend to use photographs, it is better to use a program such as Adobe Photoshop, but it is not absolutely essential.

You must have a file transfer protocol (FTP) program to take your material from the computer to the Web. Again, you have many choices. Winsock works on IBM-compatibles; Fetch works on Apple computers. If you plan to add audio and video to your site, you will need specific tools to create these media for moving, or uploading, to the Web. Several audio and video programs are available and work in essentially similar ways. See Chapter 11 for an overview of Final Cut Pro, a video program that can also be used for audio-only editing.

Your files must be ready to move to the Web. First, you need an address, or uniform resource locator (URL), to place the material on. Your news organization, academic institution or Internet service provider can give you this address. Second, select the FTP program. Provide the proper URL, user name and password. Third, select the file you want to upload to the Web.

Give each file a specific name. It is best to use only lowercase letters without spaces or underscores. For example, your first page, or index, should be www.companyname.com/index.htm or index.html. A tag of .htm generally means that an IBM-compatible program created the material, while .html usually comes from a Macintosh computer.

If you have photographs on any page, these usually must be uploaded separately with an ending of .jpg or .jpeg. Audio and video files also have separate file endings, which should be generated by the Web program. Audio files are generally .aiff or .wav, while video files are generally .mov. Make sure that your users can download the appropriate software to listen to or watch the material by including links to Real Audio, Windows Media Player and/or QuickTime.

Once you have uploaded your material, check that the files uploaded properly. This troubleshooting process may take some time. Perhaps you have not entered the proper URL, or you may have made a mistake in a hyperlink in the text of your pages. You can delete or overwrite these mistakes with the FTP program.

If possible, check the pages in Internet Explorer, Netscape and Safari. What looks good on your computer may not look so good on someone else's computer. Make sure that you refresh the browser when you change anything. Often, the browser will go back to the last page it has read, which means you will be seeing what you uploaded the first time rather than succeeding tries. Here are some other tips:

- Make sure that users can navigate where they want to go. That means that every page should have a link back to the index page or to any opening page.

- Color backgrounds make it difficult for users to print the pages. For stories, use white backgrounds with black type.

- You can create "anchors," which are simple commands that allow the user to go back to the top of the page. Select an anchor in the Web design program, and place the anchor where you want it.

- You generally want to select a size for the pages, usually as a percentage of a full page, so that the material stays inside the limits of the user's browser.

- A target is a useful option that allows you to have a linked page emerge from your index page. Your index page can remain in the background. You simply select "target" and insert "blank" in the design program.

- Place a date on the page to show when the material was updated.

- Put your e-mail address on the index page by using the mailto: command in the Web design program. This selection will automatically create an e-mail message box for someone to send you comments or questions.

- Your Web page can be as simple or as complicated as you want it to be. You can find more information at *www.dreamweaver.com* and *www .microsoft.com/frontpage*.

Exercises

1 **Headlines and blurbs:** Using your local or campus newspaper, write Web headlines and summary blurbs for news and feature stories that you find.

2 **Converting a story for the Web:** Using any news or feature story you have written for this course, convert it to Web style as suggested in this chapter. Add a discussion question.

3 **Web story:** Write a story for the Web based on the following information. Include a headline and summary blurb. To simulate Web width, set your margins to a width of 4 inches. Use a bulleted list, add a discussion question to the end of your story and consider creating a poll. Use Web style— a space between each paragraph.

New data on marriage, divorce, and remarriage in the United States show that 43 percent of first marriages end in separation or divorce within 15 years, according to a report released today by the Centers for Disease Control and Prevention (CDC). The report, "First Marriage Dissolution, Divorce, and Remarriage: United States," also shows that one in three first marriages end within 10 years and one in five end within five years.

The findings are based on data from the National Survey of Family Growth, a study of 10,847 women 15–44 years of age.

"Separation and divorce can have adverse effects on the health and well-being of children and adults," said CDC Director Jeffrey Koplan. "Past research has shown that divorce is associated with higher rates of mortality, more health problems, and more risky behaviors such as increased alcohol use."

The study also showed that duration of marriage is linked to a woman's age at first marriage; the older a woman is at first marriage, the longer that marriage is likely to last. For example, 59 percent of marriages to brides under 18 end in separation or divorce within 15 years, compared with 36 percent of those married at age 20 or over. About 97 percent of separated non-Hispanic white women are divorced within five years of separation, compared with 77 percent of separated Hispanic women and only 67 percent of non-Hispanic black women. Younger women who divorce are more likely to remarry: 81 percent of those divorced before age 25 remarry within 10 years, compared with 68 percent of those divorced at age 25 or over. Non-Hispanic black women are less likely than other women to remain in a first marriage, to make the transition from separation to divorce, to remarry, and to remain in a remarriage.

"These data offer an important glimpse into the social fabric of this country," said Dr. Edward Sondik, director of CDC's National Center for Health Statistics, which conducted the study. "The implications of divorce cut across a number of societal issues—socioeconomics, health, and the welfare of our children."

Featured Online Activity

Using the example of personal journalism at *musarium.com,* write your own Web log or online story about a personal experience. You can create your own blog at *www.blogger.com.*

Coaching Tips

Seek documents to substantiate sources' claims.

Check résumés and other materials from sources.

Seek other sources with alternate points of view.

Role-play: If you were the source or the source's attorney, what would you find libelous or objectionable in the story?

If you are writing about a police or court case, check for the latest charges or disposition in the case.

Don't use online information you can't verify, especially if it includes accusations about a person.

Accuracy and Media Law

His last word was "courage." And with that word Dan Rather signed off his final broadcast as anchor for CBS News, after 24 years in that position and 43 years at the network. His word was directed to soldiers in dangerous places, to disaster victims and "to my fellow journalists in places where reporting the truth means risking all. And to each of you: 'Courage.'"

Reporting the truth—or failing to do so—was at the heart of a scandal that rocked CBS and led to the firing of four top news employees. Rather, who was 73 at the time, didn't tie his resignation as anchor to the story aired on "60 Minutes Wednesday," which was based on documents that claimed President Bush had received favored treatment when he was in the Texas Air National Guard in the early 1970s during the Vietnam War. Rather said he had planned to retire anyway, but his announcement came just six weeks before an independent review of the incident was due to be released. Rather planned to continue as a correspondent for "60 Minutes."

The documents cited in the show were allegedly memos from the late Lt. Col. Jerry Killian, Bush's commander at Ellington Air Force Base in Houston. Aired in the middle of Bush's campaign for re-election to a second term, the documents claimed that Killian ordered Bush to be suspended from flight status for failing to meet training certification and failure to take a flight physical examination as ordered. Killian died in 1984, and CBS officials said the documents were from an anonymous source.

Less than four hours after the broadcast, a blogger identifying himself as "Buckhead" questioned the validity of the documents and claimed they could not have been typed in 1972 because typewriters in those days did not have the Times New Roman or Palatino font style and a proportionally spaced superscript "th."

It was the end of an era and the beginning of a new one—an era when the watchdogs weren't just the press anymore. They were an army of "citizen journalists" who were watching the watchdogs.

CBS originally stood by the story but convened an independent panel to investigate whether the documents were forged. At the end of a three-month investigation and a 224 page report, the panel members could only conclude that they didn't know. The investigators, Louis Boccardi, former chief executive of the Associated Press, and Dick Thornburgh, a former

U.S. attorney general, said they weren't going to fall into the same trap of saying something that they couldn't know for sure. However, they were sure that the report had violated the network's standards of accuracy and fairness. They also said the report was rushed onto air, "driven in part by competitive pressures," without adequate checking, called "vetting."

Following the investigation, CBS chairman Leslie Moonves issued an apology: "As far as the question of reporting is concerned, the bottom line is that much of the September 8 broadcast was wrong, incomplete or unfair. We deeply regret the disservice this flawed '60 Minutes Wednesday' report did to the American public." In addition, he created a new position of vice president of standards and special projects to review the authenticity of sources, use of confidential sources and use of hidden cameras.

As for the blogger who wrote the first message questioning the documents, he was suspected of having an agenda of his own. A *Los Angeles Times* investigation revealed that "Buckhead" was Harry MacDougald, an Atlanta lawyer and Republican who was affiliated with two prominent conservative legal groups. Bloggers accused Republicans of orchestrating the incident to help Bush, while other bloggers claimed Democrats had set up this "Rathergate" incident to help Bush's opponent, John Kerry, but neither position was ever proved.

The incident may soon be forgotten, just a footnote in history books about the 2004 election—one of many scandals in political campaigns. But the message was clear: Accuracy is paramount, and without it, credibility will plummet.

How do you know when a story is inaccurate? You don't unless you check it out. Make one more phone call. Check one more document. And when you can't reach someone for comment, try and try again.

Deadline pressure, especially for breaking news, may force you to run the story when some key source can't be reached for comment. You should say that in the story so the reader knows you tried. But one try isn't enough. The rush to break stories online because of increased competition has added constant deadline pressure and, in some cases, has led to inaccuracy as well. The CBS incident should serve as a model of the kind of damage that can occur when a story is questionable, especially in these days when bloggers may catch what news editors miss.

The Importance of Accuracy

Accuracy is paramount for a good journalist. Every mistake you make jeopardizes the newspaper's or broadcast station's credibility with readers and viewers. Because of that credibility factor, newspapers throughout the country print corrections every day, many for the incorrect spelling of names. That's another reason why you should always double-check the names in your stories.

Checking Information

NBC television reporter Mark Potter found out the hard way how important it is to check not only names but also information on résumés. When he worked for the ABC network, he was reporting a story about a drug rehabilitation counselor in Detroit who said he was an All-American football player in college. Potter and his camera crew completed the interviewing and taping for the story. Then Potter returned to his home base in Miami and called the university to get some tape of the former football star in college. The university had never heard of the man. Potter killed the story. He said he could have kicked himself for not checking the man's résumé before he and the camera crew went to Detroit.

You don't have to suspect everyone of lying. However, you should make an effort to check documents and seek balance in your stories. And you should realize that many sources, especially politicians, try to use the media to promote their own agendas. However, most problems with inaccuracy result not from sources but from carelessness.

Showing Copy to Sources

Should you show your story to sources or read it to them before you print it? Many of your sources will ask you to do that. And many editors will say you shouldn't. They claim the risks are too great that sources will recant what they have told you or ask you to delete any information that puts them in a bad light.

Steve Weinberg, former director of Investigative Reporters and Editors and a leading authority on researching records, says it's time to change that traditional way of thinking. "I am convinced that my practice of pre-publication read-backs and manuscript submission has led to more accurate, fair and thorough newspaper pieces, magazine articles, and books," he wrote in *Quill* magazine. "There is no such thing as a minor mistake, not even just one or two little errors in a lengthy manuscript."

Weinberg makes it clear that the source who is checking the story has the right only to check for accuracy, not to make any changes.

If you don't show the entire story to your source, it is considered acceptable — even wise — to ask a source about any technical information you may not fully understand. You can read what you have written and, like Weinberg, ask the source to check its accuracy.

If you are sure that your information is accurate and you don't want to read the information to sources before publication, you could try this suggestion from Bill Marimow, two-time winner of the Pulitzer Prize. Marimow, former editor of *The Baltimore Sun* and currently managing editor of NPR News, suggests calling a source the day after the story is published and asking if the story was accurate and fair. He claims that call will deepen the source's respect for you, and the source may even give you information for a follow-up story.

Several newspapers also check reporters' accuracy by contacting sources after the stories have been published. But that system usually antagonizes reporters.

Libel

Accuracy is critical because truth is a defense in libel suits. The First Amendment to the U.S. Constitution provides the media with protection against censorship, and this amendment is often referred to during the defense of libel suits:

> Congress shall make no law respecting an establishment of religion or prohibiting the free exercise thereof; or abridging the freedom of speech, or of the press; or the right of people peaceably to assemble, and to petition the Government for a redress of grievances.

Libel is publication of a falsity that causes injury to someone's reputation. Anyone can sue or threaten to sue for libel, claiming injury to his or her reputation. The real concern is whether the person has grounds enough to win.

"Libel is essentially a false and defamatory attack in written form on a person's reputation or character. Broadcast defamation is libel because there is usually a written script. Oral or spoken defamation is slander," according to Donald Gillmor and his co-authors in *Mass Communication Law: Cases and Comment.* The "script" is not limited to a news story, the authors explain; it can take the form of headlines, photos, cartoons, film, tape, records, signs, bumper stickers and advertisements.

Several libel suits have also resulted from messages that people posted to online discussion groups. If the defamatory statements are published—whether online or in print—they can still be considered libelous.

The key factors to consider are whether you published untrue information that hurt the reputation of an identifiable person and whether you were either negligent or reckless in failing to check the information:

- Are you publishing something you aren't sure is truthful?
- Are you carelessly publishing something that is inaccurate?
- Are you publishing something accusatory that you haven't checked out?
- Are you publishing something that clearly identifies a person and harms that person's reputation?

If your answer is yes to any of those questions, you could be in trouble for libel.

Times v. Sullivan

Those standards were the ones the U.S. Supreme Court applied in 1964 in a landmark libel case, *New York Times Co. v. Sullivan,* and the standards have been applied since then to public officials.

The *New York Times* case stemmed from an advertisement the newspaper accepted in 1960 from a group of people in the civil rights movement.

The group was trying to raise money for the Committee to Defend Martin Luther King. The ad claimed that King had been arrested seven times and that his home had been bombed. It also claimed that black students who had staged a nonviolent civil rights demonstration at Alabama State University had been the target of police brutality. The advertisement accused the Montgomery, Ala., police department of being armed with shotguns and using tear gas to subdue students.

Even though the police commissioner, L.B. Sullivan, had not been named in the advertisement, he sued for libel. He claimed that the ad contained factual errors concerning the police and damaged his reputation. He claimed that the police did not ring the college campus or padlock the college dining hall, as the ad had claimed. Furthermore, Dr. King had been arrested four times, not seven, and three of the four arrests had occurred before Sullivan was commissioner.

Sullivan won in the lower courts and the Alabama Supreme Court. But the U.S. Supreme Court reversed the decision in its landmark ruling about "actual malice." Malice, in this context, does not mean intent to harm someone; it means that you published something knowing it was false or not bothering to check its truth or falsity. As the justices wrote,

> The constitutional guarantees require, we think, a federal rule that prohibits a public official from recovering damages for defamatory falsehood relating to his official conduct unless he proves that the statement was made with "actual malice"—that is knowledge that it was false or with reckless disregard of whether it was false or not.

The court placed the burden of proving libel on the plaintiff, the person who is suing. The justices made this a constitutional issue, applying the First Amendment right of a free press to publish matters of public concern. In the ruling, Justice William Brennan wrote the following:

> Thus we consider this case against the background of a profound national commitment to the principle that debate on public issues should be uninhibited, robust, and wide-open, and that it may well include vehement, caustic, and sometimes unpleasantly sharp attacks on government and public officials.

The *Times v. Sullivan* ruling applied only to people who are public officials. The application was later broadened to include "public figures."

Public Officials

For purposes of libel law, who is a public official? Elected officials and candidates for office are definitely considered public officials. Appointed officials may or may not be. Here are the criteria: Do they have authority to set policy in the government, and are they under enough public scrutiny to have easy access to the media?

The Supreme Court defined public officials this way in *Rosenblatt v. Baer,* a case about the status of appointed officials:

> It is clear, therefore, that the "public official" designation applies at the very least to those among the hierarchy of government employees who have, or appear to the public to have, substantial responsibility for or control over the conduct of government affairs.

Is a police officer a public official? Courts in Pennsylvania are split on that decision, but most courts have ruled that law enforcement officers are public officials because they have the power to make arrests, a form of control in government. However, teachers, professors and other employees in a public education system are not usually defined as public officials because they are carrying out policies set by other officials of the school district or university. But if they achieve fame or notoriety, they may become public figures.

Public Figures

Who is a public figure, and why is the distinction between public officials and public figures important? People may be considered public figures if their achievements or notoriety places them in the public eye or if they seek attention by voluntarily thrusting themselves into a public controversy. But if they are brought into the public spotlight involuntarily, they may not be public figures. A court will usually determine whether the person qualifies as a public figure.

Like public officials, public figures also bear the burden of proving that the information in contention was libelous. The person or organization being sued does not have to disprove libel.

The courts identify three types of public figures: pervasive, vortex and involuntary.

A "pervasive" public figure is a person who has gained prominence in society or great power and influence. Well-known entertainers and athletes and people who voluntarily seek public attention are in this category.

A "vortex" or "limited" public figure is a person who has voluntarily thrust himself or herself into a public controversy to influence the outcome. The Supreme Court has stated that people in this category are not public figures for all aspects of their lives but only for the aspects that relate to their role in a particular public controversy. A key point is the "voluntary" concept. An individual does not automatically become a public figure if he or she is thrust into a newsworthy situation; the involvement in the controversy must be the person's choice. Access to the media is another factor in determining whether someone is a public figure. The person must have enough regular and continuing access to the media to counter criticism and expose falsehoods.

Consider the case of *Hutchinson v. Proxmire.* In 1975, when former Sen. William Proxmire issued his annual "Golden Fleece" awards, which satirized some government-funded research projects as wasteful, he issued a press release targeting a researcher who was using monkeys to study stress. The scientist, Ronald Hutchinson, sued Proxmire for damaging his reputation and subjecting him to public ridicule by falsely claiming Hutchinson's research was wasteful. Key to the case was determining whether Hutchinson was a public figure.

Proxmire claimed the scientist was a public figure because he had received federal grants and had access to the media when they contacted him about receiving the Golden Fleece award. A federal district court agreed with Proxmire and dismissed the suit. But Hutchinson appealed.

The U.S. Supreme Court ruled that Hutchinson was not a public figure because he was not willingly involved in a public controversy until Proxmire caused it. The court said Hutchinson did not automatically become a public figure by being thrust into a newsworthy situation. Also, the court determined that Hutchinson did not have regular and continuing access to the media. He was sought out by reporters only to respond to Proxmire's criticism. Hutchinson ultimately received $10,000 from Proxmire.

The third type of public figure, "involuntary," is someone who does nothing voluntary to garner attention or to get involved in a public issue but finds himself or herself in the middle of a public controversy anyway. Courts have found that this category rarely fits an individual in a libel suit.

Private Figures

The difference between being a public or private figure is crucial because the standards for proving libel can differ. Many states have made it easier for private persons to prove libel than for public figures. The Supreme Court has left it up to the states to determine their own standards of liability for private figures:

> We hold that, so long as they do not impose liability without fault, the States may define for themselves the appropriate standard of liability for a publisher or a broadcaster of defamatory falsehood injurious to a private individual.

The court made this ruling in a 1974 case, *Gertz v. Welch.* Elmer Gertz was a Chicago lawyer who claimed he had been libeled when a John Birch Society magazine, *American Opinion,* published an article labeling him a Communist. He sued the publisher, Robert Welch. Even though Gertz was a prominent lawyer, the Supreme Court ruled that he was a private person under the circumstances of this case. The court also declared that because private people don't have the same access to the media to defend themselves as public officials, they shouldn't be held to the same strict standards in proving libel.

In *Gertz v. Welch,* the court decided that a private individual needs to show only that the material was published with carelessness or negligence instead of proving actual malice, which means publishing with knowledge or reckless disregard of falsity. But all libel plaintiffs, public and private, have to prove the material is false and damaging to their reputation.

Even though the Supreme Court left it up to states to determine their own libel standards in cases involving private figures, the *Gertz* case paved the way for allowing private people to abide by less rigid standards than public officials and figures. Many states have followed the "simple negligence" standard in the *Gertz* case. Others require private individuals to abide by the same "actual malice" standard as public individuals. "Negligence" in this context means you failed to exercise reasonable care in doing your job as a journalist. That type of care might include talking to all sides of a controversial issue, using relevant documents, taking accurate notes and checking your information for accuracy before publishing it.

Corrections

The most common cause of lawsuits is carelessness. Most news media don't publish material that they know or suspect is false.

Although newspapers get sued by people targeted in major investigative projects, the majority of libel suits stem from much less important stories. Incorrect captions, defamatory headlines, an inaccuracy in a police story or a feature can result in a libel suit.

Printed corrections don't prevent libel suits. They may assuage an angered source enough to forestall a lawsuit, or they may be evidence of the newspaper's good faith, but corrections do not undo the harm of inaccurate published material. It's up to a jury to decide if you were negligent, careless or reckless in your disregard for the truth.

A printed correction by the *National Enquirer* didn't stop entertainer Carol Burnett from suing the tabloid in 1976 for insinuating that she was drunk. The article said that she had an argument with Henry Kissinger at a Washington restaurant and then "accidentally knocked a glass of wine over on one diner—and started giggling." Burnett denied the incident occurred, and even though the *Enquirer* apologized in a retraction, Burnett pressed her lawsuit. She was awarded a total of $1.6 million by a Los Angeles jury and ultimately settled for an undisclosed amount.

Even when you use the word *alleged,* meaning that the accusation is a charge without proof, you are on dangerous ground. This word, although widely used by reporters in police cases, does not save you from libel. It is better to attribute the information to official sources or records.

If you don't name the person against whom the accusation is made, you still can be sued for libel. A person who can claim he or she was identified—either by enough information to describe the person physically or by position—can then sue.

Nor does attribution save you. Say that a candidate for mayor tells you his or her opponent is a crook. You print the statement and attribute it to the candidate. The opponent could sue you and your newspaper. Just because you named the source of the statement, you cannot avoid responsibility for it. And if it isn't true and you haven't documented it as true, you could be considered guilty of reckless disregard for the truth.

If you are going to print any accusations that could be defamatory, you should always check with the person being accused and ask for a response. Cross-checking may not save you from libel, but it at least gives you a chance to prove you were not reckless.

There are times when you can print accusatory or damaging information, especially when you are writing about crime. You have certain privileges as a member of the press, and so do some of the officials who deal with you.

Privilege

Privilege—in a legal sense—comes in two forms: absolute and qualified.

"Absolute privilege" means that public officials, including law enforcement officials, can make statements in the course of their official duties without fear of being sued for libel. This form of privilege extends to court proceedings, legislative proceedings, public and official meetings, and contents of public records. For example, if Senator Proxmire had announced his Golden Fleece awards on the floor of the Senate instead of in a news release, he would have had absolute privilege and could not have been sued by Hutchinson, the researcher who claimed he was libeled.

As a member of the media, you have "qualified privilege." You may print defamatory statements made by people who are absolutely privileged as long as you are being fair and accurate and the information is from a public proceeding or public record. But if your report contains errors, you could lose that qualified protection.

If during a public meeting a city council member calls another member a crook, you may print the accusation. If the same city official makes the same comment to you during a telephone interview or after the meeting, you can't print it without risking libel. The key is that the defamatory statement must be made in an official capacity during an official proceeding. Or you may use, with attribution, something stated in court records. But you must make it clear that the accusations were made by other people in records or meetings and are not proven fact.

Suppose that a police officer tells you something about a suspect. You may print this information if the officer is acting in an official capacity and if the information is documented in a public record, such as a police report or court files. However, you still should be careful about how you word accusations in crime stories. The police officer may say the man stabbed his wife, but you may not say the same thing without attribution. If the information is not stated in a public record, such as a police report or court record, it can be libelous. Generally, statements made outside of the court by police are not privileged, but some states may extend privilege to these comments.

Never call anyone a murderer unless he or she has been convicted of murder in court. Don't call suspects robbers or use any other accusatory term before they are convicted. Use terms such as "the suspect," "the man accused of murder," "the woman charged with the robbery." Suppose that a man has been murdered and you go to the neighborhood for reaction. A neighbor says the man's wife killed him. The neighbor isn't an official acting in an official capacity, and the wife hasn't been convicted. The neighbor's comments could be libelous, and you could be sued for printing them.

ETHICS

The case: You are attending a school board meeting as a reporter. During the public comment portion of the meeting, a woman accuses a male guidance counselor in the high school of having had sex with students. This is a small town, with only one high school and two guidance counselors, both male. The school board says it will conduct an investigation. You are on deadline and must get the story in right after the meeting. You can't reach either guidance counselor for their reactions. The comment was made at a public meeting, and it is part of the public record. Even if you have the legal right to publish this information, what are your ethical concerns? Will you include this information in your story?

Neutral Reportage

Another type of privilege, called "neutral reportage," has been recognized in about 10 states. It gives the news media First Amendment protection in writing accusations about a public official or figure in a public controversy as long as the reporter states them accurately and neutrally. If one official or person considered responsible and newsworthy accuses another public figure of wrongdoing, you may print the information as long as you get reactions of the accused or other participants.

Under neutral reportage you aren't responsible for determining whether the accusations are true. However, many states don't extend this type of privilege to the media, so it's always safer to beware of printing unsubstantiated accusations.

The best defense for a reporter is the "truth" defense, proving that what you wrote is true. What you can do and what you ought to do may differ. You may have the right to print statements from court records or meetings, but if you think they could be untrue or unfair, should you print them? Those are the kinds of ethical decisions journalists must make. Most editors advise this: When in doubt, leave it out.

Fair Comment and Criticism

Suppose you are writing a review of a play, concert or book, and your review is very negative. Can you be sued? Yes. You can always be sued. But you are protected under the right of fair comment.

Writers of editorials, analysis stories, reviews and other criticism may express opinions, but they may not state inaccurate facts. A factual error can be grounds for libel; an opinion is protected.

To qualify as fair comment, a comment must generally be on a matter of public interest, it must be based on facts known or believed to be true, and it may not be malicious or made with reckless disregard for the truth. In this case also, truth is considered a good defense.

Invasion of Privacy

Issues of privacy involve ethical decisions, not matters of accuracy. However, with the proliferation of invasion of privacy lawsuits, a journalist should understand the legal issues. Privacy is not a right guaranteed by the Constitution. In privacy cases, damage is usually considered the mental anguish that results from wrongfully revealing to the public some part of the plaintiff's life. Truth may not be enough of a defense in privacy cases.

Suppose that a child drowns and a mother stands on the dock as her son's body is dragged from the river. She is hysterical. A photographer takes her picture without her consent. Has the photographer invaded her privacy? Perhaps, if the photographer was on private property. The photographer could be considered an intruder. However, it is not an invasion of privacy if the photographer was on public property. Even if a scene on private property is visible from public property, the photographer would be within his or her rights to take pictures.

The courts have acknowledged four grounds for invasion of privacy lawsuits: intrusion, public disclosure of private and embarrassing facts, false light, and misappropriation of a person's name or image without permission.

Intrusion Into a Person's Solitude

Eavesdropping, harassing someone and trespassing on private property can be considered intrusion. So can going onto private property and using a telephoto lens, listening behind doors and using any device to enhance what the unaided eye can see or the unaided ear can hear. In other words, a journalist who uses subterfuge to obtain and publish confidential material could be risking a suit for invasion of privacy. The intrusion can be either physical or mental.

In *Dietemann v. Time Inc.*, two *Life* magazine reporters were sued for going undercover as husband and wife to do a story on a plumber, A.S. Dietemann. The plumber was believed to be practicing medicine with herbs. The so-called healer told the female reporter she had cancer and prescribed an herbal cure. The female reporter taped Dietemann's comments, and her partner took pictures with a concealed camera. Even though the plumber later pleaded no contest to a charge of practicing medicine without a license, he sued the magazine company for invasion of privacy. A California court awarded him $1,000. An appeals court upheld the award and said that the undercover methods, used without Dietemann's consent, were an invasion of his privacy. "The First Amendment is not a license to trespass, to steal, or to intrude by electronic means into the precincts of another's home or office," the court opinion said.

Unlike libel suits, publication isn't required for someone to claim invasion of privacy in this type of case. Truth isn't a defense either. After ABC-TV reporters on "Prime Time Live" used undercover techniques and hidden cameras to expose unsanitary conditions at Food Lion grocery stores, the supermarket chain sued for trespass and fraud. Reporters who had falsified employment applications to obtain jobs at Food Lion reported that the supermarket chain sold spoiled meat, fish dipped in bleach and rat-gnawed cheese. Food Lion didn't challenge the television show's findings—only the methods reporters used. In 1997 a jury awarded Food Lion $5.5 million, which was reduced to just $2 on appeal. The rationale was the same as it was 25 years earlier in the Dietemann case: Even if the news report is true, reporters don't have license to trespass.

Public Disclosure of Private Facts

Publishing such facts as information about a person's sex life or medical history that the public considers offensive could be considered invasion of privacy, even if it's true. But if the facts are taken from the public record, such as court documents, they will probably be considered fair to publish.

In 1975 the Supreme Court ruled in *Cox Broadcasting Co. v. Cohn* that a television station in Atlanta was within its First Amendment rights to publish the name of a rape victim even though state law prohibited doing so. The victim's family had sued for invasion of privacy, claiming a private fact had been disclosed. The family had won, but Cox appealed the decision to the U.S. Supreme Court. The court said the news media had the right to report matters on the public record.

Information not on the public record is more susceptible to lawsuits. The courts have ruled that the media may be invading privacy if the private facts in question would be offensive and objectionable to a reasonable person and would not be of legitimate public concern. Community standards of what is "offensive" may vary from one place to another. That's why these are difficult cases for courts to decide.

Regarding the public concern standard, the case often cited is *Sidis v. F-R Publishing Corp.*, which involved a profile in *The New Yorker* magazine of James Sidis, a genius who had graduated from Harvard at age 16. Twenty years later the magazine wrote a profile about his life as a recluse. Sidis sued for invasion of privacy, but the courts ruled that he was a public figure who had lost his right to privacy and that his life was, therefore, newsworthy or of legitimate public concern.

Publicity That Puts a Person in a False Light

If a published story or picture gives the wrong impression and is embarrassing to the person, the possibility exists that the court will consider a "false light" verdict. For example, in one case a television station doing a story about teenage pregnancy took pictures of a young woman walking down the street. The television station did not say she was pregnant, nor did the station identify her. However, she claimed the picture put her in a false light—indicating that she was a pregnant teenager—and she won her lawsuit against the station.

False light is related to defamation, but the story or picture does not have to defame a person to be considered false light. It does have to portray the person inaccurately. Truth is a defense in these cases. Generally, the plaintiff has to prove that the media showed actual malice by knowingly publishing false information.

The case often cited here is *Time Inc. v. Hill,* because it was the first false-light case to reach the Supreme Court. James Hill, his wife and five children were held hostage in their suburban Philadelphia home by three escaped convicts in 1952. After the incident, the Hills moved to Connecticut. A few years later, *Life* magazine was planning to publish a review of a play partially based on the incident. The magazine took the cast of the play to the Hills' old home and photographed the actors in some scenes from the play. James Hill sued, saying the pictures in *Life* gave readers the impression that the scenes portrayed the family's real experiences. Hill initially won his suit. But it eventually went to the Supreme Court, which ruled that Hill would have to prove actual malice on the part of *Life* magazine. The court sent the case back for retrial to a lower court, but Hill dropped the suit.

Another Supreme Court decision (*Cantrell v. Forest City Publishing Co.*) also upheld the standard of proving actual malice in a false-light case. In this case, Margaret Cantrell sued for false light and invasion of privacy, claiming that *The* (Cleveland) *Plain Dealer* had inaccurately portrayed her as living in poverty several months after her husband died in a bridge collapse. In a follow-up story to the bridge disaster, the reporter described Cantrell as wearing the same "mask of non-expression" she wore at her husband's funeral and living in abject poverty. But the reporter talked only to Cantrell's children; he never talked to her. She won the case because she proved that some information was untrue and that it was damaging to her reputation.

Use of a Person's Name or Picture Without Permission

This doctrine applies when the picture is used for commercial purposes, such as advertising or promotion. For example, use of an athlete's photograph to promote a product without her or his consent could be grounds for a lawsuit. The easiest way to avoid this kind of lawsuit is to have the person sign a consent form.

Television personality Vanna White sued Samsung Electronics when an advertisement the firm used featured a robot that resembled White as she appeared on the game show "Wheel of Fortune." White claimed her image was appropriated without her permission, and a court agreed.

Online Legal Issues

The Internet is spawning many new legal issues and laws regarding pornography, libel, copyright and privacy.

Communications Decency Act: The first major test of free speech on the Internet to reach the U.S. Supreme Court was the Communications Decency Act (CDA) of 1996, a federal law that restricted distribution of indecent material on the Internet to people under age 18. The American Civil Liberties Union challenged the law, which was ruled unconstitutional by a federal three-judge panel in Philadelphia, but the government appealed the ruling in *Reno v. ACLU.* In 1997 the U.S. Supreme Court struck down portions of the act that censored online material. In the ruling, Associate Justice John Paul Stevens wrote that the CDA's "use of undefined terms 'indecent and patently offensive' raises special First Amendment concerns because of its obvious chilling effect on free speech." Since then, however, more than 25 states have enacted laws to limit children's access to sexually explicit online information.

Children's Online Privacy Protection Act: Efforts to protect children from various abuses on the Internet resurfaced in 1998 when the Children's Online Privacy Protection Act (COPPA) was signed into law and then modified in 2000. This act makes it a federal crime—with penalties of $10,000 per violation—for collecting information from children under 13 and using it for commercial purposes considered harmful to minors. The law requires operators of commercial Web sites or online services and general-audience sites to obtain verifiable parental consent before collecting information from pre-teens and to post notices on the site of how any information would be used. The law covers such information as the child's full name, home and/or e-mail address, telephone number, and any other information that would allow someone to identify or contact the child. It further restricts access by minors to sites that contain information considered harmful.

The Federal Trade Commission, which is responsible for enforcing COPPA, recently settled two major cases against UMG Recordings, which paid a civil penalty of $400,000, and Bonzi Software, which paid $75,000. UMG is a music recording company that operates Web sites promoting its music and offers e-mail newsletters, bulletin boards and other activities requiring registration. Bonzi markets software such as BonziBuddy, a purple cartoon gorilla, but to download the joke-telling gorilla, registration was required. Mrs. Fields Cookies and Hershey Foods were also fined for collecting information from children without parental consent.

Another law aimed at protecting children is the Children's Internet Protection Act, passed in 2000, which requires public schools and libraries that receive federal funds to install software to block online material considered "harmful to minors," basically pornography and obscenity. The American Library Association and the ACLU challenged this law as a violation of First Amendment free speech rights, but the Supreme Court upheld the law in a narrow margin even though two justices dissented on the grounds that some of the blocking software would deny access to constitutionally protected speech.

These types of legal issues are certain to continue as the government attempts to regulate the Internet.

Libel: If someone posts a libelous message to an online discussion group, is the service that provides the forum responsible? The standards for determining libel are the same for online materials as for print or broadcast. In 1998 the U.S. Supreme Court upheld a lower court ruling that protected Internet

MULTIMEDIA COACH

Broadcasters and Web journalists face the same legal dilemmas as print publications do. But there are other considerations for broadcast and online publications. Remember that you— as the journalist— are responsible for what goes on the air or on the Web even if your source is wrong. Broadcasters face many laws— mainly because the government grants licenses for radio and television stations to operate. Here are a few tips on how to prevent legal problems in broadcasting:

- Find out about consent laws. These laws govern the ability to record conversations, and each state has its own law. A one-party consent law means that you can covertly record a conversation. A two-party consent state means you cannot. You need to check with your legal adviser or the local chapter of the Society of Professional Journalists.

- Be aware of fair use, which allows you to use up to one minute of copyrighted material. For example, a movie star dies. You broadcast an obituary. You may use up to one minute of audio or video about that movie star without paying copyright fees.

Legal issues involving the Internet are constantly emerging. Few attempts to regulate the Internet have been successful because it is a global medium, and laws in one country may not apply to those in another. But laws continue to be passed, and court cases continue to evolve. Here are a few tips on how you can prevent online legal problems:

- Don't copy material from the Internet (including images) without permission. Many images are offered free for personal use, but check the site notices to be sure.

- Don't write any defamatory messages to a discussion group.

- Avoid writing defamatory or derogatory comments in personal e-mail messages. E-mail is often passed to other users without permission or knowledge of the source.

- Consider the accuracy of material you find on the Internet. Check the site owner and organization to make sure that you are using a responsible site. You should also verify the accuracy of any information from the Internet.

- Check the posting dates of online material to determine whether the information is still accurate. Much online information may be outdated.

service providers from liability for information posted by subscribers. The ruling ended much confusion that was created by two earlier cases.

Cubby v. CompuServ was one of the first cases questioning the liability of Internet service providers for information posted on their services. Cubby Inc., which planned to publish a newsletter about the broadcast industry, claimed that a competing organization posted libelous messages to a CompuServ discussion group. In 1991 a New York State court ruled that CompuServ wasn't responsible because the Internet service provider hadn't exercised any editorial control over messages posted to its service.

In 1995 another New York State court gave the opposite ruling in *Stratton Oakmont v. Prodigy*. It decided that Prodigy was responsible for libelous messages in one of its discussion groups because the Internet service provider had exercised editorial control. Prodigy marketed its service as one that prohibited users from posting offensive messages. Stratton Oakmont, a securities investment firm, claimed that an anonymous user had posted defamatory statements about a stock offering the company planned to offer.

The first online libel case to reach the U.S. Supreme Court was *Zeran v. America Online Inc.* Kenneth Zeran, a Seattle man, sued AOL for negligence in failing to promptly remove defamatory messages about him. Zeran began receiving death threats after someone posted his telephone number on an AOL message board and said he was selling T-shirts and key chains with offensive slogans about the bombing of the federal building in Oklahoma City, where 168 people died. Zeran's case was dismissed in 1997 by a U.S. District Court, which ruled that portions of the Communications Decency Act of 1996, which had not been struck down, protected online service providers from liability for subscribers' material. In 1998 the U.S. Supreme Court upheld that decision.

Copyright: If you take pictures or documents from the Internet without permission, are you violating copyright laws? Absolutely. U.S. copyright laws passed in 1976 protect everything that you or others write the minute the information is offered in "a fixed form," which includes online or print information.

Although many unresolved issues remain about intellectual property rights for online materials, additional laws to protect software and online materials were enacted in the late 1990s. The No Electronic Theft Act, signed into law in 1997, provides penalties of up to five years in jail and fines of up to $250,000 for individuals and up to $500,000 for organizations for copying software or online materials even if you don't make a profit. The Digital Millennium Copyright Act of 1998 provides further penalties of up to $1 million for copying online materials for profit. More cases continue to come before the courts regarding peer-to-peer file sharing of music, such as the controversy involving Napster, which has since transformed itself into a fee-based site for downloading files. Rulings are pending on other cases involving companies that furnish the software for file sharing, and these issues are likely to continue.

However, copyright laws allow you to copy portions of materials under a doctrine known as "fair use." The law favors academic use or use of portions of works if the copied material does not deprive the creator of profits.

Privacy: If you want to buy something on the Internet with a credit card, you probably want the site to contain "encryption" codes that scramble the data so only authorized people on that site can receive it. The U.S. government wants agencies such as the FBI to have access to encryption codes of software companies for security purposes. Legal issues to protect users' online privacy continue to be debated.

Exercises

1   **Actual malice:** Write a paragraph explaining "actual malice" and "reckless disregard for the truth" as defined by the U.S. Supreme Court in *Times v. Sullivan.*

2   Discuss this scenario for libel potential: You are the editor of your local newspaper. A U.S. senator has decided to seek re-election. Five women who worked for him several years ago say he sexually harassed and abused them while they

were in his office. The women refuse to be named. Their allegations range from stories that he plied them with drugs and alcohol and then sexually abused them to accusations of rape. All the women are reputable, including a political lobbyist and a former secretary to the senator, but none have gone to the police. As a result, you have no record of formal complaints about their allegations. However, three years ago a formal complaint by a former employee charged him with sexual molestation, but the charges were dropped. Will you print these women's allegations and use his name? If you do, will the senator have grounds for a libel lawsuit?

3   **Privacy issue 1:** A candidate for city council in your community had a nervous breakdown 10 years ago. The candidate's opponent has slipped you a hospital document confirming this fact. Should you print the story? Why or why not? If you do, does the candidate have any grounds to sue you for invasion of privacy?

4   **Privacy issue 2:** You are a photographer who went on assignment to the county fair. You snapped a picture of a woman whose skirt blew up to her shoulders, exposing her underwear, as she emerged from the fun house. Your editor decided that this picture captured the fun mood of the fair and used it. The woman is now furious and is suing the paper for invasion of privacy— disclosure of a private fact. Discuss whether she has grounds for a lawsuit and whether you think you should have taken the picture.

Featured Online Activity

Access the Chapter 13 resources at *http://communication.wadsworth.com/ rich5e* to link to a self-graded tutorial that will test your understanding of libel.

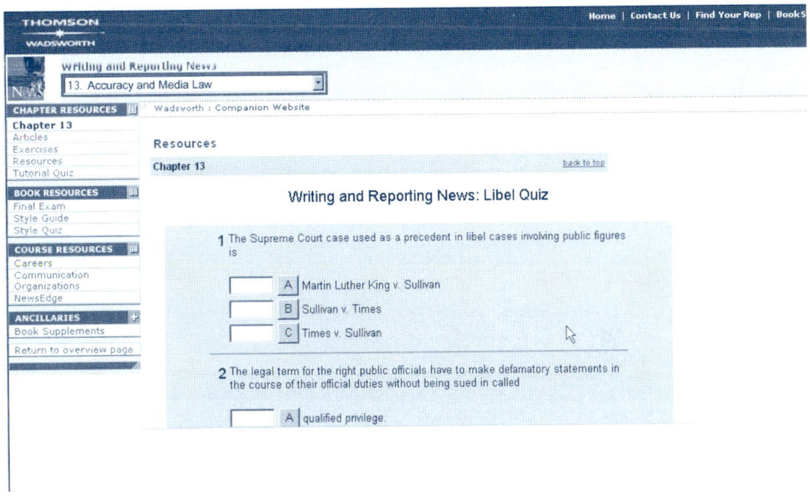

Coaching Tips

Examine all your alternatives.

Consider all the parties who will be affected. Do you need other points of view?

Weigh the benefits and harms of your decision.

Justify why you are making this decision.

Media Ethics

Imagine that you are a reporter for your local newspaper. A drunken driver almost kills a young girl in an accident in your town. You call the hospital for information about her condition, but officials will not release it except to family members. So you ask a fellow reporter to call the hospital and identify himself as the girl's uncle. He gets the information.

Would you do that? Is it ethical?

This was one of 30 cases presented to 819 journalists in a survey conducted by Louisiana State University journalism professor Ralph S. Izard for the Society of Professional Journalists several years ago. Eighty-two percent of the journalists who responded said they would not ask their colleague to lie to gain information. Do you think their responses would be the same today? Journalism codes of ethics say deception should be a last resort, but undercover journalism and deceptive practices still abound.

Ethical dilemmas, with guidelines from various codes of ethics, have been included in chapters throughout the book. In this chapter we'll examine some major cases and causes of ethical problems and then study some approaches that can be used to make ethical decisions.

Deception

A case of deception that generated considerable media discussion in the 1990s was the Food Lion/ABC-TV case. ABC television network reporters lied on job applications to get hired by the Food Lion supermarket chain and then used cameras hidden in their hair. The reporters for "PrimeTime Live" then produced a story accusing Food Lion of selling rotten meat, fish and cheese. Food Lion didn't challenge the facts but instead sued for trespass and won a $5 million judgment, but the trial judge said that was too much and cut the award to $315,000. ABC appealed, and a federal court reduced the award to just $2—a dollar for trespassing and another dollar for breaching employees' legal duty of loyalty to an employer.

Could the reporters have gained the story any other way? ABC doesn't think so, but many other journalists have questioned the use of deception in this and other situations.

A classic case of deception occurred in 1978, when investigative reporters at the *Chicago Sun Times* set up a bar called The Mirage and posed as bartenders and waiters. With hidden cameras and tape recorders, they provided evidence that building inspectors, police officers and other city officials were soliciting bribes to allow them to operate the bar. Although the series won several awards, the Pulitzer Prize board ruled that the reporting methods were unethical and rejected it for the media's highest award. The case renewed debate about deception, and today this type of reporting is considered a last resort by many editors.

Although print and broadcast media have used hidden cameras for many years, they proliferated in television news magazine shows during the 1990s. One reason was the improved technology of cameras, which could be small enough to be hidden in tie clips. But media critics charged that a more common reason for using hidden cameras was sensationalism.

Before using any form of deception, ask yourself if there is any other way to get the story. Louis Hodges, professor emeritus of ethics at Washington and Lee University, suggests that you apply three tests: importance, accuracy and safety. Ask yourself this: Is the information of such overriding public importance that it can help people avoid harm? Is there any way you could obtain the information through conventional reporting methods, such as standard interviews or public records? Are you placing innocent people at risk? For example, you should not pose as a nurse, law enforcement officer or employee in a job for which you are not trained.

Deceptive reporting techniques are fraught with risks, such as lawsuits for invasion of privacy. On the other hand, deception may be the only way to reveal matters of great public concern. Even with such reasoning, using deception may still be unethical.

Plagiarism

The subjects of plagiarism and fabrication have been discussed in several other chapters in this book. Why so much attention to something you surely wouldn't do? Even though technology has made it easier to plagiarize because accessibility to thousands of news sources is so easy, stealing words from someone else without attribution is not a new phenomenon. Nor is fabrication, which is making up quotes, adding false description and basically passing fictional material off as news.

Despite considerable publicity about Jayson Blair, a *New York Times* reporter who made up sources and scenes in at least half of the national stories he wrote for the newspaper and fabricated as many as 600 other articles he wrote earlier, journalism students and veteran journalists are apparently not getting the message that plagiarism and fabrication are serious infractions that can lead to firing and ruined careers. Since the Jayson Blair affair in 2003, which led to his dismissal and the resignation of two top editors at the *Times,* numerous cases of plagiarism have occurred.

Size doesn't seem to matter when it comes to plagiarism. From college newspapers and small newspapers to large newspapers, journalists have been fired for plagiarism. Here are just a few examples of such ethical infractions that occurred in the last few years:

- *The University Daily Kansan* at the University of Kansas suspended a reporter who was copying material for its "Weekly Choice" calendar items from the local newspaper's Web site, *Lawrence.com*.

- *The Cavalier Daily* at the University of Virginia fired two student reporters after discovering they had written movie and music reviews lifted from other publications.

- An entertainment editor for the *Macon* (Ga.) *Telegraph* resigned after editors discovered that he had copied material about a Ringling Bros. and Barnum and Bailey circus from the Ringling Bros. Web site. A few months earlier, another *Telegraph* reporter had been fired for plagiarizing material in several stories from other stories in newspapers or on Web sites.

- A sports editor for the *Bozeman* (Mont.) *Chronicle* was suspended without pay for plagiarizing a column taken from another columnist in North Dakota.

- A reporter from the *Sedalia* (Mo.) *Democrat* was fired after a reader called to complain about similarities in a movie review to a review by syndicated movie reviewer Roger Ebert.

- *USA Today* veteran reporter Jack Kelley, a foreign correspondent who was nominated for a Pulitzer Prize, resigned after being told he would be fired for fabrication in numerous stories over a 10-year-period, and three top editors at the paper subsequently resigned for failure to catch the problems. *USA Today* hired an independent panel to research stories Kelley had written. The panel concluded that "Jack Kelley's dishonest reporting dates back at least as far as 1991. . . . Policies, rules and guidelines in place at the newspaper, and beyond that, routine editing procedures, should have raised dark shadows of doubt about Kelley's work, had his editors been vigilant and diligent. They were not."

  Despite a *USA Today* policy prohibiting use of anonymous sources, Kelley routinely used them, according to the report. In one story he wrote about a woman and her child who drowned while trying to flee Cuba. The independent investigators concluded it was "a story he had concocted in every detail." The report says, "In Kelley's case, he acted duplicitously for years in the way he handled unnamed sources—and his editors let him get away with it."

The list of cases involving fabrication and plagiarism could go on—at least 13 newspapers have reported incidents in which they fired or suspended reporters for these problems in the few years following the Jayson Blair case. Prior to this case (between 1991 and 2001), at least 20 reporters were fired for plagiarism or fabrication. Why is this happening at such alarming rates?

Lori Robertson, author of the article "Ethically Challenged," in *American Journalism Review*, concluded from a dozen interviews that the Internet was the main culprit. "It used to be to plagiarize from another publication, you'd have to type the information letter by letter, staring at your source," she wrote. "It took a little more effort than what you can do now: cut and paste."

Using someone else's idea for a story is usually not considered plagiarism. U.S. copyright laws don't protect ideas. In the news business, it's considered good practice to localize a national story idea or use an idea from another newspaper and do original reporting. The key is "original reporting." If you use all the same sources and the same anecdotes from another publication or broadcast, it may not constitute plagiarism, but it raises ethical questions.

Privacy Issues

Some of the most wrenching ethical dilemmas the media face involve people's privacy. You may have the legal right to publish certain information, but do you have the ethical right?

To understand the ethical concerns, it may help to define "ethics." Ethics is the study of choices about what we should or should not do. So ethics can be considered the process of making decisions about the way a person behaves.

Some of the thorniest ethical dilemmas facing journalists concern public officials, celebrities, rape victims and photo subjects.

Public Officials

Would you print information about the sex life of a politician? When is the private life of a public figure relevant? When does it serve the public interest to publish such details?

In the summer of 1987, reporters and editors at *The Miami Herald* decided that the private life of a politician was relevant. Former Sen. Gary Hart was seeking the Democratic nomination for the presidency. Rumors of Hart's infidelity to his wife had circulated for months, and during the campaign the rumors called into question his character and credibility. When asked about the rumors, Hart challenged reporters to "follow me around. . . . They'd be very bored." Acting on a tip that Hart had a relationship with a Florida model, *Herald* reporters staked out his townhouse. They revealed that Hart spent the night with the woman, Donna Rice. Hart never admitted that the relationship with Rice was sexual. Nevertheless, he withdrew his candidacy the day before *The Washington Post* was set to reveal evidence about his involvement in another affair.

At the time of this incident, although previous presidents and presidential candidates had engaged in extramarital affairs, their private lives had not been dissected in public. The sexual affairs of President Kennedy were not revealed until long after his assassination. But the Gary Hart case changed the nature of political reporting.

Four and a half years later, when Bill Clinton was campaigning for his first term as president, rumors of his infidelity surfaced. But the circumstances differed from the Hart coverage. The *Star,* a tabloid newspaper, broke the story. It printed allegations by former television reporter Gennifer Flowers that she had had a long-term affair with Clinton; the *Star* paid Flowers for her story. The mainstream press, which had not been able to verify the allegations, then picked up the story.

Their justification was that it had become news, especially after Clinton appeared on the CBS show "60 Minutes" to respond to the allegations. He admitted that he and his wife had had marital problems over the years but denied Flowers' claim of a 12-year affair with him. The American public didn't decry his behavior; the public blasted the press instead.

But during Clinton's second term in office, a media frenzy erupted when former White House intern Monica Lewinsky testified to a grand jury that she had engaged in a sexual relationship with the president during her internship. Clinton denied the allegations when he testified in a court case brought against him by an Arkansas woman, Paula Jones, who claimed sexual harassment against Clinton when he was Arkansas governor. Then the day after his testimony, in a dramatic reversal of his previous denials, he admitted on national television that he had engaged in an "inappropriate relationship" with Monica Lewinsky.

The media followed Lewinsky day and night. Competition for any tidbit of information was keen. The media published unsubstantiated rumors, including sexual details, and relied heavily on anonymous sources and other media for news.

Thus far, media references to sex were tame compared to what was about to happen. Kenneth Starr, a special prosecutor investigating Clinton for obstruction of justice and perjury, released a grand jury report that contained graphic sexual details, the likes of which had never before been printed in mainstream media. The majority of newspapers in the United States either printed the entire report in a special section or posted it on their Web sites. Many newspapers offered a disclaimer that the content might be considered offensive. This report laid the groundwork for impeachment hearings on the charges that the president had committed perjury under oath when he originally denied having an affair with Lewinsky.

In November 1998, almost four years after the case began, Clinton agreed to pay Jones $850,000 to drop the case. But it didn't prevent him from being impeached.

Despite the serious turn the case took, media critics and the public still questioned whether the media had acted responsibly in relying heavily on anonymous sources and publishing rumors in the early stages of the saga. And the debate raged about whether a politician's private life should be dissected in public. The ethical dilemmas these stories posed will continue to be debated for years.

Although the sex lives of politicians dominated the headlines in the 1990s, reporters also face other ethical dilemmas when covering politicians. For example, is it in the public interest to reveal the criminal background of a candidate if he or she withdraws from the race before you can print the story?

Editors at the campus newspaper of the University of Kansas faced this dilemma after they found out that a candidate for student government had been convicted of indecent solicitation of a child six years earlier. When the candidate learned that the newspaper was planning to print the information, he held a press conference to resign his candidacy. He claimed it was because he had just learned he was HIV-positive. At the same time, he resigned as director of the organization representing gays and lesbians on campus.

University of Kansas students dumping
the campus newspaper to protest a story

He never referred to his criminal record, nor would he answer reporters' questions.

Was his criminal record relevant to the public now that he was no longer a candidate for office or leader of the gay rights group? What harm would the publication of his record cause him? The student's friends pressured the editor not to run the story, saying it would cause their friend immense personal suffering when he was already suffering from the HIV-positive news. In addition, they said, he had already paid his debt to society by serving time in prison.

Stephen Martino, editor of *The University Daily Kansan* at the time, said the decision was the most difficult one he ever had to make as an editor. He said he decided to run the information because it was relevant; it was why the candidate resigned. Martino said the candidate had learned about his HIV-positive status three weeks earlier and had made no attempt to resign then. "To my way of thinking, omitting the truth is the same thing as lying. Had the *Kansan* not reported the full story as it knew it, it would have been accused of a cover-up, and its credibility would have been destroyed," Martino wrote in an editorial page column the day the story ran on the front page.

Angry students protested the next day by dumping copies of the *Kansan* on the lawn in front of the newspaper offices in the journalism school.

Celebrities

A privacy case that caused even more media backlash was the disclosure a year before he died that tennis star Arthur Ashe had AIDS. And it posed even greater ethical hand-wringing because Ashe was not running for public office and was no longer playing on the professional circuit. Is the private life of a public figure always fair game for disclosure in the media?

Ashe didn't think so. When *USA Today* received an anonymous tip that Ashe had acquired the disease from a blood transfusion many years earlier, a sportswriter from the newspaper interviewed Ashe to check it out. Ashe didn't confirm or deny anything. But he called the paper's managing editor for sports to find out the status of the story. The editor, Gene Policinski, said that the newspaper would not print the story without confirmation from a credible, named source but that the paper would pursue it. Ashe still did not confirm the story. Instead, he called a press conference the next day and reluctantly told the world. He said he was sure that some newspaper eventually would publish the story, and he wanted to be able to tell the story on his terms. Although he acknowledged that he was a public figure and that the story was newsworthy, he said his privacy had been invaded.

Public opinion polls seemed to agree. The day the story was published in *USA Today*, the newspaper received 481 phone calls. Most calls were from readers critical of the coverage, even though the newspaper published the story only after Ashe announced he was going to have a press conference. Policinski, in a sidebar to the press conference story, explained his reason for pursuing the story: "There was no question that this was a significant news story. A great U.S. athlete could be critically ill. If he had cancer or a heart attack—as he did in 1979—it was and is news."

Privacy issues like these are among the most difficult ethical dilemmas for the media. Is the story fair? Is it in the public interest to know? What harm or benefit will result? Those are questions reporters and editors often ask before they publish such stories. And rarely is there unanimous agreement on the decision.

Consider another case that has given the media an ethical black eye. A pipe bomb had exploded in a park on the site of the Olympic games in Atlanta on July 27, 1996. One person was killed, and 111 others were injured. Initially, a security guard at the site, Richard Jewell, was declared a hero for alerting police to the bombing. Three days later, Jewell became a suspect when law enforcement officials leaked his name to the press.

Most newspapers withhold the name of a suspect until formal charges are filed. But this was a case of great national interest. Would you have published his name? The *Atlanta Journal-Constitution* did, stating that Jewell was a "target" of the investigation. That was just the beginning.

For the next 88 days, Jewell was profiled and followed by the media, and his past, present and future were the subject of news stories. Only one factor was missing: He was never charged in the crime. On Oct. 26, 1996, the FBI apologized and publicly admitted that Jewell was no longer a suspect.

In an emotional press conference, Jewell said his life had been ruined. "For 88 days, I lived a nightmare. . . . Now I must face the other part of my nightmare," he said. "While the government can tell you that I am an innocent man, the government's letter cannot give me back my good name or my reputation.

"In its rush to show the world how quickly it could get its man, the FBI trampled on my rights as a citizen," Jewell said. "In its rush for the headline that the hero was the bomber, the media cared nothing for my feelings as a human being." Jewell sued the *Atlanta Constitution-Journal* and NBC for publishing defamatory statements indicating he was the bomber, not merely the suspect. He settled with NBC for $500,000, but the Atlanta newspaper stood by its stories and decided to fight the matter in court in a case that is still pending. Eric Rudolph, accused of this bombing and several others at women's clinics where abortions were performed, was subsequently charged with the crime and pleaded guilty. He was sentenced to life in prison.

The case was dissected in media ethics conferences such as the one conducted by the Freedom Forum. In that conference, Rem Rieder, editor and senior vice president of *American Journalism Review*, called the media coverage "embarrassing" and a lesson for the media.

"Sometimes you need an event like this to make us re-examine the way things happen," Rieder said. "In the height of competition, the drive to get the story is very strong, and you don't want to be beaten. The thing to remember is that it's a lot better to get beaten on an individual story than to come up with something that's absolutely wrong and blows up on you. That's one of the key lessons of this case."

Rape Victims

Whether to name rape victims is another continuing ethical debate in the media. Because of the stigma associated with rape, most newspapers withhold the names of people who claim they have been raped.

Geneva Overholser, former editor of *The Des Moines* (Iowa) *Register,* wrote a column saying the stigma of rape would be reduced if it were treated like any other crime and the names of rape victims were used. As a result, Nancy Ziegenmeyer agreed to let the newspaper use her name in a story relating her ordeal as a rape victim. Reporter Jane Schorer, who won a Pulitzer Prize for the story, said she received scores of calls from rape victims who expressed gratitude that the story had been told.

The *Register* still has a policy of printing the names of alleged and confirmed rape victims only with their permission. But *The New York Times* didn't ask for permission before it decided to use the name of a woman who accused a nephew of Sen. Edward Kennedy of raping her. And the story raised a firestorm of controversy.

In addition to withholding names of alleged rape victims, the majority of newspapers, including the *Times,* usually withhold the names of suspects before they are formally charged. But newspapers throughout the country printed the name of William Kennedy Smith before he was charged with the crime, justifying their action by saying the prominence of his uncle warranted it.

The *Times* editors said they made the decision to name the woman in a profile about her because the woman had been named in a supermarket tabloid, the *Globe,* and on NBC television. Therefore, her name was already in the public domain. Media critics blasted the *Times* for weak justification. But naming rape accusers (the word *victim* implies that the suspected attacker is guilty) is gaining more favor at many newspapers.

The *Times* profile of the woman raised other objections as well. It included public records about her traffic tickets, her family history, her dating habits and the illegitimacy of her 3-year-old daughter. Were these facts relevant to a story about a crime? Would a profile about a man who was the victim of a crime include information about his traffic tickets or his dating habits? These are the kinds of questions ethical reporters should ask.

Ultimately, William Kennedy Smith was judged not guilty. After the trial, his accuser, Patricia Bowman, revealed her identity in press conferences and television interviews. Bowman said she felt the media coverage had been another assault on her.

Columbia University professor Helen Benedict says the media promote myths and stereotypes of rape in the way they portray women in sex crimes. In her book *Virgin or Vamp: How the Press Covers Sex Crimes*, she says the media characterize rape victims in one of two ways: "She is either pure and innocent, a true victim attacked by monsters—the 'virgin' . . . or she is a wanton female who provoked the assailant with her sexuality—the 'vamp.'" Benedict says one solution is to stop publishing profiles of rape victims.

Photo Subjects

Many privacy issues involve photographs. Should a photographer take a picture of a grieving mother whose son has drowned even if she doesn't want the picture taken? At what point is a photograph an invasion of privacy?

Another concern for photo editors is taste: what the reader needs to see versus what the reader wants to see. For example, should newspapers print pictures that depict gore and tragedy even if they would upset readers?

In 1987, Pennsylvania state treasurer R. Bud Dwyer convened a press conference the day before he was scheduled to be sentenced for conviction of mail fraud, perjury and racketeering. At the end of the conference, he took a gun from his briefcase, put the barrel in his mouth and pulled the trigger, killing himself instantly. Stunned photographers for television stations and newspapers shot vivid pictures of the event.

Many television stations did not air the footage of him with blood gushing from his head, and several newspapers did not publish that picture. But other newspapers published three photos, including a gory one of his head as the bullet pierced it. Readers in several locations protested loudly.

More recently, the media faced ethical decisions about publishing graphic video and photographs of Iraqi prisoners who were abused by U.S. soldiers at the Abu Ghraib prison outside Baghdad during the war in Iraq. The story, initially aired by CBS on "60 Minutes 2," and subsequently detailed in a *New Yorker* magazine article by Seymour M. Hersh, revealed torture inflicted on the prisoners by U.S. soldiers. Although *The New Yorker* did not print the photos, CBS showed some video, and *The Washington Post* later received the photos—some published in the newspaper and more photos and video published on the *Post*'s Web site. The photos, released to newspapers around the world, showed naked prisoners being taunted and humiliated by soldiers. One of the most dramatic photos shows two U.S. soldiers smiling in front of a human pyramid of naked prisoners. Another shows a soldier holding a leash around a naked man's neck.

The *Post* posted this note on its Web site with the photos: "Some of these photos may be disturbing because of their graphic or violent nature." The *Post* and other news organizations cropped or blurred photos that showed the prisoners' genitals. Both *The New York Times* and *The New York Daily News* ran a front-page photo of a naked prisoner being menaced by dogs used by the soldiers. Television news anchors also gave a warning to viewers about the graphic nature of the images they were about to see.

The public was incensed, and editors throughout the country wrestled with what they should print or air. In many cases, news organizations offered more photos on their Web pages but limited images in print. In a *New York Times* article, writer David Carr wrote that "the news media are wrestling with how many and how much of the graphic photographs they should show." Some critics accused the media of promoting an anti-war agenda. But Leonard Downie, editor of *The Washington Post,* echoed the sentiments of many other news editors when he was quoted in the article as saying "We decided that the importance of the news was the most important consideration."

The prison photographs constituted one of many ethical dilemmas that editors faced about graphic images during the war in Iraq. When Americans civilians were burned, dismembered and hanged from a bridge by Iraqis in Fallujah, editors again agonized over printing or airing photos of their charred bodies, but many newspapers printed a photo in some form on their front pages. *The Philadelphia Inquirer* received 185 complaints about showing the charred bodies. In an article for The Poynter Institute, Anne Gordon, managing editor of the *Inquirer,* said she told the paper's staff in an e-mail: "We do our job when we give readers all the news—no matter how painful or ugly. My heart bleeds for the families of these men. But personal feelings cannot dissuade us from our mission to provide the facts upon which an informed citizenry can make decisions."

Such ethical dilemmas arise daily at newspapers and television stations, although rarely involving photos as graphically disturbing as these. But how do editors make those decisions, and how can you decide what is ethical?

A Guideline for Privacy Issues

Whether it is a photo or a story, ethicist Louis Hodges suggests this guideline for privacy issues: Publish private information about public officials or public figures if it affects their public duties. But for victims of crime, publish private information only if they give their permission because these are people with special needs and vulnerability.

Ethical Reasoning

Journalists use several methods to justify their decisions. In most ethical dilemmas, editors and reporters discuss the issue and the consequences of publication before making the decision. They consider how newsworthy the

MULTIMEDIA COACH

Broadcast journalism and online journalism raise unique ethical dilemmas, but the basic principles of fairness, accuracy and minimizing harm apply to all media. For example, the use of hidden cameras and listening devices poses the issue of whether you are invading the privacy of an individual with good reason. There may be other methods to obtain the information, but they lack the "gotcha" quality of a hidden camera.

Here are the important questions to ask about hidden cameras:

- Have you discussed the use of hidden cameras with your supervisor and legal counsel?

- Are you using a hidden camera because all other investigative techniques have been exhausted?

- Are you using a hidden camera primarily for the production value of catching someone doing something wrong?

Some of the issues created by the Web spawn more questions than answers. Here are some ethical questions involving the Web:

- Should you link to hate sites, pornography and other controversial material in stories related to these topics? Opinions are divided. Some journalists believe that you should provide links and let readers decide for themselves whether the content is offensive. Others believe that linking to offensive content only furthers the message of these sites.

- Should you inform readers on your Web site that you are not responsible for content in links to related material?

- Should you review the content before you post the link? Robert M. Steele, The Poynter Institute's Scholar for Journalism Values, says it is not enough to issue a disclaimer that you aren't responsible for the material in the links. He suggests warning readers about the content in those outside sites if it could be offensive, just as broadcasters warn viewers that television content might be violent or contain sexual images.

- Should you quote messages from a public or private discussion group in a story you are writing? Legally, this may be acceptable. But ethically, even if you attribute the message to a sender or a group, it is preferable to contact the person who posted the message if you plan to publish the content.

- Should you publish online rumors or content you can't verify? The Web contains a plethora of inaccurate material. Don't use anything you can't substantiate with reliable sources.

story is and whether the public really needs this information. The process of ethical reasoning can be shown into three steps:

1 Define the dilemma. Consider all the problems the story or photograph will pose.

2 Examine all your alternatives. You can publish, not publish, wait for a while until you get more information before publishing, display the story or photo prominently or in a lesser position, or choose other options.

3 Justify your decision. Weigh the harms and the benefits of publication, or weigh such factors as relevance and importance of the story to the public.

The Poynter Institute Model

Robert M. Steele, The Poynter Institute's expert in ethical issues, suggests that journalists ask these questions before making decisions in ethical dilemmas:

- Why am I concerned about this story, photo or graphic?

- What is the news? What good would publication do?

ETHICS

The case: Your campus newspaper has received an advertisement that promotes the revisionist point of view that the Nazi Holocaust of World War II never occurred. The ad, accompanied by a $125 check, was sent by the Committee for Open Debate on the Holocaust, an organization run by Bradley R. Smith from his home in Visalia, Calif. He sent the advertisement to colleges all over the United States. In a cover letter he urges campus editors to run the ad to promote dialogue and to support the First Amendment.

You are aware that when the University of Miami campus newspaper, *The Miami Hurricane,* ran the ad, nearly 400 students demonstrated outside the newspaper. A wealthy alumnus threatened to withdraw a $2 million gift but later recanted when the school promised to offer courses on the Holocaust. Other school newspapers have refused to print the ad. You know that this ad will offend many people on your campus and in your community, but you want to uphold the First Amendment. Will you run this ad or reject it and return the check? Justify your decision.

- Is the information complete and accurate, to the best of my knowledge?
- Am I missing an important point of view?
- What does my reader need to know?
- How would I feel if the story or photo were about me or a member of my family?
- What are the likely consequences of publication? What good or harm could result?
- What are my alternatives?
- Will I be able to clearly and honestly explain my decision to anyone who challenges it?

Codes of Ethics

In addition to making decisions about what to report and write and how to present stories, journalists must consider whether their behavior is ethical as they perform their professional duties.

Many newspapers have devised codes of ethics that govern the behavior of employees. These include policies about accepting gifts or free-lance assignments, as well as guidelines about conflicts of interest.

Staff members who violate these policies at newspapers can be fired, and many have been. In some cases, reporters have been fired for entering into business relationships with a source or for using for personal gain information they get from sources. Journalism societies, such as the Radio-Television News Directors Association and the Public Relations Society of America, also have basic codes of ethics to guide members.

Principles common to all the codes include adhering to accuracy, telling the truth, minimizing harm and avoiding conflicts of interest.

For links to codes of ethics, check the Web site for this chapter at *http://communication.wadsworth.com/rich5e.*

Exercises

1 Apply ethical reasoning, using the Poynter guidelines, to the following cases (or to other cases described in this chapter):

a An anonymous source tells you that a U.S. senator for your state has voted against many gay rights issues even though he is gay. You have heard other rumors that the senator is homosexual, but the senator has denied that the rumors are true. What will you do about this story?

b Would you have pursued the story about Arthur Ashe? If you had been able to confirm the report that he had AIDS, even if he had not admitted it, would you have printed the story?

c You have heard rumors that your local nursing home is abusing its clients. However, no complaints have been filed with state regulatory agencies or with the police. You have contacted some of the clients' family members, who say they are concerned but have no proof. Will you go undercover as a volunteer aide at the nursing home (no special training required) to investigate?

2 Discuss the ethical dilemma described in the chapter about revealing the criminal record of the student government candidate who resigned before the story could be published. What would you do if you were the editor of your campus publication or broadcast station? Do you agree or disagree with the decision made by the editor of *The University Daily Kansan*?

3 You are writing a story about problems of online pornography and the groups that oppose it. The story will be published on your campus Web site. Will you link to the pornography sites that the groups find objectionable?

Featured Online Activity

Access the Chapter 14 resources at *http://communication.wadsworth.com/ rich5e* to link to "Journalism Ethics Cases Online," a database of cases that, as the site states, "raise a variety of ethical problems faced by journalists." Browse the case topics and search for cases that you find especially interesting. Then choose one case and write a brief summary, analyzing how the editor or reporter dealt with the ethical dilemma.

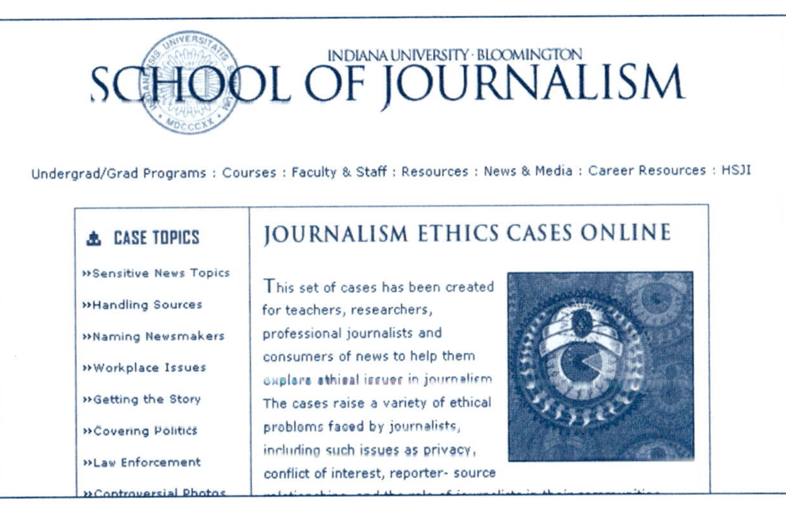

Coaching Tips

Seek sources from different racial and ethnic backgrounds for all kinds of stories, not just stories about minorities.

Ask your sources how they prefer to be addressed.

Ask yourself if you would write the same type of description for a man as for a woman, for a white source as for a person of color, for a disabled person or member of any other ethnic or special group.

CHAPTER 15

Multicultural Sensitivity

Don't call him articulate. You might be tempted to do that if you meet Tim Gallimore. A lot of people who wrote letters of recommendation for him after he got his doctorate from Indiana University called him articulate. They meant well. But Gallimore says the term is really an insult.

Gallimore is an African-American. And he says when the term *articulate* is used to compliment him, it presumes that most African-Americans can't express themselves well. So in reality it is a slur.

Gallimore, formerly a journalism professor at the University of Missouri, is a consultant working with the media and other organizations in dealing with conflict resolution and trauma victims.

In a study Gallimore conducted about the interpretation of mass media messages, he asked students to define a number of words, including *majority, ghetto* and *inner city*. He concluded that it is hard, if not impossible, to get people to agree on one meaning for a word. In fact, many African-Americans disagree with Gallimore's sensitivity about the word *articulate*. And others prefer the term *black* rather than *African-American*.

Gender, race, and geographical and ethnic background influence interpretation, Gallimore says. Consider, for example, the word *majority*. "It is remarkable that women view themselves as minorities although they are a majority of the population in every society," he says. "This can be explained only through the connotation of *majority* as possession of power—the white male-dominated majority." Other loaded terms are *ghetto* and *inner city*, which Gallimore's students tended to define as an area with drugs, poverty, crime and gangs rather than as an urban geographical location. On television, when a news anchor says "inner-city youth," the phrase is almost always followed by descriptions and visuals of young blacks killing one another for crack or high-priced athletic shoes, Gallimore says. "Language is not a neutral thing."

Tim Gallimore, consultant

The Language of Multiculturalism

Language changes, too. *African-American* is the term now preferred by many blacks, but it is not accepted at all newspapers. *Chicano* is preferred by Mexican-Americans in some parts of the country, yet it is offensive to many older members of the group.

How can a journalist know the proper term to use? Any terms that might be acceptable today could be out of vogue tomorrow. In fact, the whole concept of political correctness has become unpopular. But sensitivity to other people—regardless of gender, race or ethnic background—will always be an important tenet of journalism.

Instead of memorizing the popular term of the day, Gallimore suggests that reporters ask people of different ethnic or special interest groups how they prefer to be addressed. "The newspaper can demonstrate sensitivity with the words the person uses to define himself or herself," he says. "That gets the newspaper off the hook. If someone objects, you could say that is the person's term."

Jose D. McMurray, former executive director of the National Association of Hispanic Journalists, also stresses dealing with people as individuals, especially before using labels. "*Hispanic* is a generic term created in Washington so bureaucrats can conglomerate an ethnic group," he says. "In California, second and third generation Hispanics prefer to be called *Latinos;* some second and third generation Mexican-Americans prefer *Chicano.* It is very much an individual decision. I'm Irish Basque. I prefer to be called Latino. But I'd rather be called Jose." McMurray says it is also a misnomer to refer to Latinos as a minority in some areas of the country. "We are not a minority in El Paso, San Antonio or Los Angeles. *Ethnic* is a better term."

Minorities in the News

Gallimore recommends gathering a list of advocacy sources for different groups: by race, age, disability, gender and so on. If you choose a person from a group to check things out that might be insensitive or controversial, you have a better chance of being sensitive, he says. "We make most of our mistakes in the information gathering," Gallimore says. "No amount of expert wordsmanship can overcome faulty materials. Go to a variety of sources. Be more aware of different points of view. If the story involves some statement about a group, go to members of that group."

Mervin Aubespin, associate editor and director of staff development at *The* (Louisville, Ky.) *Courier-Journal,* says one way the media can become more sensitive to the needs of minorities is to hire more minorities. As the U.S. population becomes more diverse, the need for minority representation in the media workforce and in media coverage is only going to increase. For example, Hispanics represent 13 percent of the U.S. population, and the Census Bureau predicts that by 2050, one in every four people in this country will be Hispanic. The Asian population has also increased, to about 12.5 million people, and 51 percent of them live in the West, according to 2003 census figures.

But newspapers and broadcast media do not reflect that equation. Here are some figures of minority representation in newsrooms, based on surveys reported in 2004:

- Minorities make up 12.94 of the workforce at newspapers, much less than the 31.7 percent of minorities in the U.S. population. However, 373 newspapers have no minorities on staff, the same number as in previous years, according to surveys by the American Society of Newspaper Editors.

- Minorities make up 21.8 percent of the workforce in television and radio, an increase from the previous year, according to an annual survey in 2004 by Bob Papper, professor of telecommunications at Ball State University, who conducted the survey in conjunction with RTNDA (Radio/Television News Directors Association). In television, the minority workforce has remained steady at 20 percent for the past 10 years, but in radio it increased significantly, to 11.8 percent from 6.5 percent in 2003. More specifically, in television newsrooms the breakdown of minorities is 10.3 percent African-Americans, 8.9 percent Hispanics, 2.2 percent Asian Americans, 0.5 percent Native Americans.

- In 2004 the percentage of women in TV news remained almost the same, at 39.1 percent, but dropped in radio news from 24 to 22.4 percent. Overall, 95.8 percent of TV news stations employ women in the news staff, according to the Papper study.

Because the Hispanic population is increasing so rapidly, newspaper companies have launched several publications written in Spanish for that market. The *Dallas Morning News* created *Al Día,* which appears six days a week. In Long Island, N.Y., where the Hispanic population is increasing, *Newsday* launched a daily newspaper in Spanish called *Hoy* The major newspaper companies now publish 46 Hispanic publications, most of them weeklies. But these publications don't resolve the problems that still exist in the mainstream media.

Mervin Aubespin says hiring minorities is only the first step; editors have to encourage minority reporters to express their diversity. One of the problems is that white editors "really want black faces that write like whites," he says. A board member of the National Association of Black Journalists and recipient of numerous awards for his contributions to journalism, Aubespin says he doesn't believe there is a specific set of guidelines to give journalists sensitivity: "There is no formula, no one way to write about a minority group. The best guideline is to treat each person as an individual. We are as different as you are."

Jose McMurray is also concerned about stereotypes in coverage of Latinos. "I would like to say there is a stereotype of Latinos as hard working, family oriented, loyal people but I seldom see that," McMurray says. "Instead I get the sense there is this group of people—Lord knows where they come from—that are not trustworthy, that point guns."

Representatives of Asian groups say they are also victims of stereotypes, such as claims that Asian students are either mathematical geniuses or gang members.

Multicultural sensitivity involves not only the sources you use but also the kinds of stories you choose. Innumerable studies have been conducted to show how women and minorities are portrayed in biased or stereotypical fashion. Minorities are often featured in stories about crime but excluded as sources in general stories about lifestyles, the economy and other stories where experts are cited. Conversely, women and minorities are often portrayed as unusual if they have operated a successful business or accomplished some of the same newsworthy feats as white males.

Keith Woods, a faculty member at The Poynter Institute, says news organizations need to make different editorial decisions to overcome a history of poor and injurious coverage of minorities. "Coverage of ethnic and racial minorities still reflects too many festivals and football games and not enough family issues or finance," Woods wrote in an article for *Presstime*, a publication of the Newspaper Association of America.

Nor is the problem unique to the United States. A diversity watch group at the Ryerson University School of Journalism in Canada analyzes coverage of minorities in that country. A 2004 study by the group also reflects disproportionate hiring, with only 72 minority staffers at 37 newspapers in 10 provinces out of a total staff of 2,119. But the group also identifies stories about diversity issues.

MORDEN—One young woman's dawning awareness of racial sensitivity has sparked a firestorm in this quiet town over the high school's long-standing name of Mohawks for its school teams.

Grade 12 student Meghan Menzies was honored by native leaders at an assembly yesterday at Morden Collegiate for her quest to persuade her fellow students to drop "Mohawks."

But many students were unmoved — saying they saw nothing wrong with using the name and questioning the fuss that brought more than a dozen journalists to the packed school gym.

Nick Martin, Winnipeg Free Press

In the U.S., the Asian American Journalists Association (AAJA) goes a step further in its "Media Watch" group; it writes letters to editors or publishers when it finds stereotypical or offensive portrayal of Asian-Americans, such as this note to *The Wall Street Journal*:

I write on behalf of the Asian American Journalists Association to object to the Trend report headline of Jan. 31, "Furniture—Coping with the Asian Invasion."

"Asian invasion" implies something ominous and dangerous; it also reinforces the bigoted belief—it continues to fester in some quarters of our society—that people of Asian descent are foreigners who are to be kept out at all cost.

The editor responded, saying no bigotry was intended but also thanking the association for calling the item to his attention.

In another letter to an editor at KTNV-TV in Las Vegas, Nev., the president of AAJA applauded the station for including people of color in its newscast about a memorial to the late President Reagan but complained about a phrase:

> We want to caution you on the use of the phrase, "yellow faces," in describing Asian Americans. It is a misnomer and an outdated one at that. Asian Americans are not yellow-skinned, after all.

Even when media organizations try to include diversity, reporters tend to go to the same sources for each minority group in the community. One source does not represent the points of view of all the members of that group, so you should try to develop many minority sources in your community.

Gender Differences

Although inclusion of women on news pages and in TV broadcasts has improved, some stereotypes remain. The old stereotypes of the apron-clad housewife have given way to new ones of Superwoman moms.

"News media have long been fond of features that focus on the difficulties working mothers face when they try to 'have it all,'" writes Jennifer L. Pozner in an article on the Web site for Fairness and Accuracy in the Media. "Tales of strained Superwomen can serve to reinforce the underlying notion that unlike fatherhood, motherhood and work outside the home are naturally in conflict. . . . Media never question why fathers want careers, and rarely if ever imply that their presence in the workplace is bad for their children."

Just as women are victims of stereotypes, so are men. Women are supposed to be emotional; men are supposed to be strong. More often, the men featured in the news have no feelings at all. Women have an agenda of child support and social issues; men want to read about sports.

Nonsense, says Jack Kammer, a free-lance writer about gender issues. In an article in *Editor & Publisher,* he says it is a mistake to conclude that women have no interest in sports or business sections and that men have no interest in lifestyle sections. In fact, he says, one study showed that 84 percent of the men surveyed said family mattered most to them. Men also want a say about child care, sexual harassment and social issues.

Shifts in treatment of women and men are apparent in advertising as well. To reach the huge female buying market, advertisers have overcompensated, particularly in several television ads, by portraying men as stupid or incompetent. The use of women as sex symbols in many beer and automobile ads had declined for a while, but it appears to be returning, especially in automobile ads.

The principles for coverage of gender are the same as they are for coverage of ethnic minorities. Make an effort to include female sources as experts in general stories, not just stories geared to women. Seek diversity of opinion, but write about people as being all equal. When you write about a woman, don't include descriptive details about her appearance unless you would also include descriptive details about a man's appearance.

For example, consider the following story about Dolly Parton. The writer acknowledged that Parton (the writer didn't call her anything but Dolly) has achieved great success—a $100 million fortune—from records, movies, TV shows and her Dollywood amusement park in Tennessee. But read the selection and decide for yourself if the story, despite its tongue-in-cheek tone, is offensive:

NEW YORK—No way they're real, not *that* big.

Women would kill to have them. Men would kill to somehow get them off Dolly Parton and onto their wives. They are just so . . . so . . . what, titanic?

Ooooo, the way they sit right *up there,* so prominently, so, so, so openly.

And up close, they look different from each other. The one on the left is almost square. The other's got a kind of pear shape to it. No wonder two security guards, with guns and walkie-talkies, are right outside the fancy hotel room.

But it just seems far too crass to mention them, to come right out and ask: "Dolly, are those *real* diamond rings?"

And so you don't.

Instead, you just sit there and stare at this tiny little woman, talking and giggling, giggling and talking. . . .

You've got to hand it to her—she's no different right there on the couch than she is on the teevee, just as bubbly, just as self-deprecating. And talk about *looks.*

No lie. She is sitting there in these spike-heeled, knee-high black leather boots, jeans that must've pinched her when she was 12. And for a top, she's got on some kind of black frilly, lacy thing. Whew. It's all topped off by a silver-gray leather jacket that's got Lawrence Taylor shoulder pads and surely cost about what Lee Iacocca has made in all his years with Chrysler.

Lord have mercy, why doesn't this woman just spontaneously combust?

Of course, it's a look that Dolly Parton, now 46, has cultivated for years.

"I *l-o-v-e* all this gaud," she squeals. "It's like a kid with paints and crayons. I think it has to do with me growing up poor and wanting more. I lived in fairy tales with stories about kings and queens with their robes and diamonds. And that's what I always wanted to be."

Dolly giggles.

"I patterned myself after the trash in my home town. There was this woman, I swear." She giggles again, and leans in a bit to share a story.

"You know how every small town has a trollop or a tramp or a slut or whatever. Well, there was this woman when I was growing up. Every Saturday she'd walk the streets until somebody would pick her up. Men would be driving around, tooting the horn. She had long, blond hair that was peroxided. She wore bright red lipstick. She had long, bright-red fingernails, and tight skirts in these bright colors, and high heels.

"I thought, THAT IS HOW I WANT TO LOOK WHEN I GROW UP. I didn't know she was the town tramp. I didn't even know what that meant. So, sure enough, when I grew up, I looked like trash. But I don't feel like trash."

The giggle.

Oh, this woman is fun. Of course, she's not here just to explain her lifetime fashion philosophy. She is here because she's got a new movie out: "Straight Talk," which opened Friday.

In "ST," Dolly—sorry, but it just doesn't feel right calling her Parton—plays Shirlee Kenyon, a small-town Arkansas dance instructor, thrice divorced and stuck in a nowhere relationship.

The Philadelphia Inquirer

Most sexism is not so blatant. But the writer of the article said he had excellent rapport with Parton and she was not offended by the article. Parton does enjoy discussing her figure and her style, and she refers to herself in terms that might well be considered sexist by the politically correct.

How can you avoid sexism and gender stereotypes? Here are some tips published in *The Gannetteer,* a magazine for employees of Gannett newspapers:

- Avoid using masculine pronouns such as *he* or *his*. Instead of "Everyone should eat his own biscuit," say "Everyone should eat a biscuit." (If you must use a pronoun, use *his and her* together.)

- Avoid words that, by definition, refer to one sex or the other but not both. Instead of *governess*, use *tutor*.

- Avoid words starting or ending with *man*. Instead of *mailman*, use *mail carrier*. Instead of *fireman*, use *firefighter;* use *police officer* in place of *policeman*.

- Avoid stereotypes in illustrations and graphics. Not all quarterbacks are white. Not all basketball players are black. Not all single parents are women. Not all newspaper editors are men. Not all pro golfers are men.

- Avoid calling groups of people men, unless they are all male. A congressional group should be called lawmakers or members of Congress, not Congressmen.

- Avoid the stereotype of a mother. Don't say "chicken soup like your mother used to make." Maybe Father made the soup once in a while. Avoid such phrases as "old wives' tale," "tied to her apron strings" or "Dutch uncle."

- Avoid referring to women by their first names in stories. This is almost always patronizing, and not usually done to men.

- Avoid describing women with adjectives that dwell on sexual attributes. Ask yourself whether you would describe the walk of an IBM executive as "suggestive" if you were profiling a man, or would the walk just seem "confident"? Ditto for "feisty." When is the last time you saw a man described as "feisty"?

- Be careful with "first" stories: the first woman to pick up the garbage for a living, fly into space or run for the school board. *(However, if it is a first, it may be worth mentioning, but it does not have to be the focus of the story.)*

- Avoid phrases that carry an element of surprise such as "smart and dedicated woman." Is it unusual that someone who is smart and dedicated is a woman, too?

- Beware of approaching any story with the subconscious idea that it is more of a man's story or a woman's. Almost always we quote women in stories about child care. Why not men? A lack of child care is just as big a problem to them—or should be.

Guidelines for Writing About Special Groups

Every group has some special needs and concerns about language. A man who uses a wheelchair probably doesn't consider himself handicapped (a derogatory term). However, he may have a disability that requires him to use a wheelchair. A person who has AIDS is not a victim but rather an AIDS patient or a person living with AIDS. And not all people over age 65 are ready for the stereotypical rocking chair.

You cannot be expected to memorize dictionaries for each special interest group. However, if your beat is a specialty that frequently deals with aging, disabled people, AIDS or some other minority interest, you could call an umbrella organization and ask for guidelines. Most organizations have these printed.

However, your first source should be the people you interview. Ask them how they prefer to be addressed. Next, consult The Associated Press Stylebook, which includes guidelines under such listings as *handicapped* and *AIDS*. You'll minimize trouble by avoiding the use of adjectives to describe people.

People With Disabilities

Do not characterize someone as disabled unless that condition is crucial to the story. Avoid the word *handicapped,* unless the person uses it to describe himself or herself. If the disability is a factor, don't say "disabled people." Instead, use "people with disabilities." Avoid such terms as *crippled* and *deformed.*

Many euphemisms—such as *physically challenged, partially sighted* and *physically inconvenienced*—have come into vogue. However, disability groups object to such euphemisms because they are considered condescending. The AP Stylebook also says to avoid euphemisms such as *mentally challenged* and descriptions that connote pity, such as *afflicted with* or *suffers from* a particular disease. Just say the person has multiple sclerosis or other applicable disease.

Heather Kirkwood, a former journalism student at the University of Kansas, is legally blind but can see with the use of various aids. She doesn't like

MULTIMEDIA COACH

The Internet is a multicultural mecca for sources. More than a dozen journalism organizations devoted to racial and ethnic groups offer Web sites with sources and research. Here are some ways you can use the Web to improve your coverage of diversity:

- Read ethnic newspapers online, such as *The Amsterdam News* at *www.amsterdamnews.org* and *The Philadelphia Tribune* at *www.philatribune.com* for story ideas and sources.

- Check minority journalism organizations such as *www.nabj.org* for sources.

- Check online diversity organizations for internships, job opportunities, scholarships and guidelines to help journalists become sensitive to diversity.

- Check network and cable news stations, and analyze the coverage of people of color as well as the reporters and anchors.

- Check the Web site for this chapter for direct links to many of the sources: *http://communication.wadsworth.com/rich5e*.

being called *visually challenged* or *partially sighted*. She prefers the term *blind*. But she says organizations representing blind people disagree with her and insist that the distinction between partially and fully blind should be made.

"As far as political correctness, my own feelings are that it isn't the word, it is what the word means," Kirkwood says. "Saying 'visually impaired' instead of 'blind' doesn't really change the way the blind are viewed in society. What matters is what comes to mind when you say the word 'blind.' Progress is changing what it means to be blind, not changing the word for it."

Kirkwood acknowledges that many stories about people with disabilities have that same "gee whiz" factor as stories about successful women.

"As far as the 'amazing factor,' that must really confuse people," she says. "Many blind people truly believe they are amazing. That is because we are taught to think that from a very early age.

"While we can expect journalists to try to understand all of this, we know the general public probably won't," Kirkwood says. "We also expect journalists to understand that we are not all representative of an entire group of people, yet we know the general public won't be as fair. The biggest problem we face is not blindness, but rather the public's perception of blindness."

The Research and Training Center for Independent Living at the University of Kansas, which offers guidelines for writing about people with disabilities, says euphemisms "reinforce the idea that disabilities cannot be dealt with up front." When in doubt, ask your sources how they prefer to be addressed. Here are some more tips:

- When interviewing people with disabilities, do not speak louder unless the person has a hearing impairment. A common complaint of people who have disabilities unrelated to their hearing is that everyone treats them as though they were hearing impaired. Treat people with disabilities exactly as you would any other source.

- Avoid overcompensating by writing about people with disabilities as though they were superhuman. The hidden implication is that all people with disabilities are without talent and that your source is unusual. The same principle says to avoid calling an African-American articulate or qualified, implying that other African-Americans are not.

- Avoid writing about people with disabilities as though they don't have any faults.

- Avoid using adjectives as nouns to describe a group of people with disabilities, such as *the deaf* or *the retarded*. Say "people who are deaf " or "people with mental retardation." For people who are blind, *visually impaired* is a preferred term.

- For mental illness, avoid such terms as *crazy* and *demented*. *Psychotic* and *schizophrenic* should be used in context—and only if they are the proper medical terms. Preferred terms are *people with emotional disorders* or *people with psychiatric illness, mental problems or mental disabilities*.

- Avoid "gee whiz" stories that stress how amazing it is that this person could accomplish anything special, given his or her disability.

Stories About Aging

If there were ever a group especially prone to "gee whiz" stories, it would have to be people over age 65. Most newspaper feature stories treat people in this age group as absolutely amazing just because they walk, run, dance or accomplish anything. People over 65 are usually described as spry, sometimes feisty, but always remarkable.

Consider this feature:

> This place hops.
>
> The food's tame, the dance steps slower than they used to be, the stiffest drink comes from the water fountain.
>
> Still the Gray Crowd jams the Armory Park Senior Citizens Center. Typically, 1,200 men and women gather daily for gossip, games, and yes—even to cast some plain old-fashioned goo-goo eyes.
>
> The *(Tucson)* Arizona Daily Star

Or the story will feature a twist—surprise, surprise, they're old!

> The teams, each with two rows of participants, face one another. As the blue balloon floats through the air, the two seemingly docile teams transform into aggressive competitors.

You'd think they were teenagers. They were . . . perhaps 50 or more years ago.

Tulsa *(Okla.)* World

Make age a factor, not the focus of a person's accomplishments. Readers can decide for themselves if the person's accomplishments are surprising because of the person's age. Especially avoid the astonishment factor: Isn't it amazing this person can accomplish such and such at this age?

At this point in U.S. society, people over age 65 are often classified as older Americans entitled to certain privileges. Here are some general guidelines for dealing with people of this age:

- When writing about people over age 65, avoid such adjectives as *gray-haired* or other terms unless you would use the same type of description if the story were about a younger person with blond or brown hair.

- Avoid stereotypes. Don't introduce rocking chairs or similar stereotypical images if the people in the story aren't using them.

- Avoid *the graying population, senior citizens* and other group designations unless you are writing a trend story. And then use such a term only if it is relevant, necessary and appropriate—for example, if a group uses the term in its own name, as in Gray Power.

- Avoid saying such things as "She doesn't consider herself old," unless she says it. Even though you are meaning to extend a compliment, by writing such denials you are introducing a stereotype.

AIDS Stories

In 1989 Carolyn Warmbold was working on the final stages of her dissertation for her doctorate in English at the University of Texas, Austin.

At 1:40 that afternoon, her husband, Ted, called. He had the worst headache he had ever had. Nine days later he died, at age 45.

The doctors attributed his death to cryptococcal meningitis. The *San Antonio Light,* the newspaper of which Ted Warmbold was editor, attributed it to AIDS.

"On Sunday (a week before Ted died), when the doctors told me of his meningitis, they did not tell me of his AIDS," Carolyn Warmbold says. "The managing editor of the newspaper told me. The paper was going to mention it in his obituary. My first reaction was to get a gun and shoot both Ted and myself because he would not survive the disease, and I would not survive the stigma."

The story of how Ted Warmbold died from an AIDS-related illness got into the newspaper. This is the story that didn't. It is the story of Carolyn Warmbold, an editor at the *Atlanta Journal Constitution,* and her crusade to make journalists sensitive to the needs of people living with AIDS.

At first she worried about why the newspaper insisted on printing the cause of her husband's death from an AIDS-related disease. "How could it help the community? My privacy would be invaded," she says. "I foresaw what the disclosure would mean. People would speculate that I, too, had AIDS. The announcement would make us unpeople—unemployable, uninsurable. I swore while he was dying that I would try to keep it out of the paper. But the newspaper editors said it was likely to be rumored anyway, and if they covered it up, how could they deal with others."

The *Light* announced the cause of death only locally. The note that went to The Associated Press didn't say AIDS, but the Texas AP included the term.

For the first time Warmbold, a former reporter, was on both sides of the news. It was the last "gloriously free moment" she would experience in two years. She gave speeches and became an advocate for AIDS patients. But she suffered from the stigma.

"The doctors said I was free of the AIDS virus. But after my husband's death, the pest control man came for his regular visit and wore rubber gloves for the first time. He pointed a sprayer at me as though I were some giant cockroach. I was stuck with a scarlet letter *A* for *AIDS* on my breast."

Warmbold suggests that before publication, reporters check parts of the story with the people who are affected. You don't have to read them the story, but check the facts and tell them what you are going to say. Make sure that they are comfortable about using names. "You have to take the whole family into consideration," she says.

There is no formula for covering AIDS stories. Just be a compassionate human being, Warmbold says.

A Pulitzer-Prize AIDS story There was no formula to prepare Jacqui Banaszynski, a former reporter at the *St. Paul* (Minn.) *Pioneer Press,* for the emotional toll that AIDS can take on the patients and on the reporter who writes about them. Her stories about the life and death of a Minnesota farmer and his partner won her the 1988 Pulitzer Prize for feature writing. She spent 15 months reporting how Dick Hanson and Bert Henningson lived and died with AIDS.

She became as close to them as a family member—actually, closer than some of their family members. When Henningson was dying, his family even asked her to help decide whether they should pull the plug (she refused).

The rules change for this kind of story, Banaszynski says: "You have to be empathetic. On the other hand, you have to be honest and true to the reader who may be hostile to the subject. You walk a fine line between not blaming and not whitewashing."

Banaszynski says one of the reasons AIDS stories differ from other stories is the social stigma: "The disease is one story, the social context of the disease becomes another story. If you ignore the opportunity to deal with the societal revulsion, you miss the whole crux."

Readers don't want to read about AIDS or deal with it, she says. So she decided that the best approach was to portray these two men as two ordinary Minnesotans who had a commonality with readers: "If Joe and Suzy Reader could not relate to two gay pig farmers, they could relate to two men who plant impatiens, feed kittens and tend a vegetable garden, because that's what all Minnesotans do." In her introduction, she stresses that this is a story about people living—as well as dying—with AIDS:

Death is no stranger to the heartland. It is as natural as the seasons, as inevitable as farm machinery breaking down and farmers' bodies giving out after too many years of too much work.

But when death comes in the guise of AIDS, it is a disturbingly unfamiliar visitor, one better known in the gay districts and drug houses of the big cities, one that shows no respect for the usual order of life in the country.

The visitor has come to rural Glenwood, Minn.

Dick Hanson, a well-known liberal political activist who homesteads his family's century-old farm south of Glenwood, was diagnosed last summer with acquired immune deficiency syndrome. His partner of five years, Bert Henningson, carries the AIDS virus.

In the year that Hanson has been living—and dying—with AIDS, he has hosted some cruel companions: blinding headaches and failing vision, relentless nausea and deep fatigue, falling blood counts and worrisome coughs and sleepless, sweat-soaked nights.

He has watched as his strong body, toughened by 37 years on the farm, shrinks and stoops like that of an old man. He has weathered the family shame and community fear, the prejudice and whispered condemnations. He has read the reality in his partner's eyes, heard the death sentence from doctors and seen the hopelessness confirmed by the statistics.

But the statistics tell only half the story—the half about dying.

Statistics fail to tell much about the people they represent. About the people like Hanson—a farmer who has nourished life in the fields, a peace activist who has marched for a safer planet, an idealist and a gay activist who has campaigned for social justice, and now an AIDS patient who refuses to abandon his own future, however long it lasts.

The statistics say nothing of the joys of a carefully tended vegetable garden and new kittens under the shed, of tender teasing and magic hugs. Of flowers that bloom brighter and birds that sing sweeter and simple pleasures grown profound against the backdrop of a terminal illness. Of the powerful bond between two people who pledged for better or worse and meant it.

"Who is to judge the value of life, whether it's one day or one week or one year," Hanson said. "I find the quality of life more important than the length of life."

Much has been written about the death that comes from AIDS, but little has been said about the living. Hanson and Henningson want to change that. They have opened their homes and their hearts to tell the whole story— beginning to end.

Jacqui Banaszynski, St. Paul (Minn.) Pioneer Press

Ground rules for sensitive questions When you write about AIDS, you have to ask about dying and you have to ask about sex. How do you approach either of these sensitive questions?

"The only thing to do is to set it in context," Banaszynski says. "When I get to it, I ask as directly as I can: How many men did you sleep with? I don't warn them that this is a hard question. I set that up in the ground rules. I say, 'We're going to talk about a lot of personal things, and a lot may be embarrassing. You don't have to answer, but I'll try to get you to answer.' If you ask honestly and directly with no judgment in your voice so there is no shame involved, they will answer. If you are embarrassed, they will pick it up. I ask the question as matter-of-factly as I would about the weather."

Banaszynski is now an associate managing editor for special projects at *The Seattle Times* and also the Knight Chair in Journalism at the University of Missouri. She says people are really very eager to tell their stories. "I think you can ask anybody any question if you are nonjudgmental and a good listener. Nobody listens anymore."

She also used another interviewing technique in her many visits with Hanson and Henningson. "I did something I don't normally do," she says. "I reminded them of my mission. They got to like me so much. My job was to be responsible and remind them that I was there as a reporter. I broke rules and invented new ones. I said when the notebook was down they could talk freely. Nothing was fair game until the notebook was out. And then I would remind them again that it was now on the record."

When she wrote the stories, she also did something that is not general practice in journalism. "I called each person involved in the story and read them their quotes, and I told them the context. For example, in one case I said, 'I set you in the context of a fight with your family.' Then I told them, if you can convince me that I have erred or been insensitive, I'll consider changing it." Only one person complained. She didn't take out any of his comments, but she added a sentence that appeased him.

She also took the newspaper to Hanson and Henningson the night before it hit the morning newspaper stands so they could see it first. "They couldn't change anything, but that's just courtesy. If they allow me to invade their privacy, I owe them that courtesy."

Banaszynski says the ground rules are different when you are writing about people who are not accustomed to dealing with the media. "I do a lot of real-people stories," she says. "These people don't know the rules. I have more responsibility to tell them what I'm going to be writing, the general thrust, and what I'm trying to do."

Banaszynski predicts that it will get increasingly difficult to interest the public in AIDS stories. "The one thing you always have to remember about AIDS is that it has an overlay of homosexuality," she says. "It is a stigmatized disease that the public doesn't want to read about. You have to get past a big barrier of rejection.

"You have to focus on the common denominator. This could be your brother or neighbor or your doctor. AIDS serves as an extreme example of all the challenges in reporting more than other stories. You have got to find ways to have it connect to everyone's life."

Exercises

1   Interview members of various ethnic and racial groups in your community or on your campus about their concerns and the kinds of stories they think newspapers are not writing about them. Devise 10 story ideas based on your interviews.

2   **Sexism, ageism and racism:** Develop your own media watch group or be a member of one. Look for examples of language, description or other elements of stories that you think are sexist, racist or ageist.

3   Using highlighters of two different colors, read the news sections of your newspaper for a few days. Use one color to mark the female sources quoted and the other color for the male sources. Analyze the types of stories that feature women more than men, and vice versa. Also try to determine if multicultural sources are used in the news stories.

4   **Multicultural profile:** Interview a person on campus who is a member of a minority group — whether because of the person's race, ethnic background or sexual orientation. The focus should be this person's feelings about how the media treat

members of his or her minority. Get some background about the person. Then ask questions related to the focus. Some questions to include might be these:

- How do you prefer to be addressed? How do you think the media portray people in your minority group? Are the portrayals positive or negative? (Ask for specific examples.) Have you ever experienced insensitivity or prejudice because of your race, ethnic background, disability or special interests? (Please specify.)

- Have you ever been interviewed by the media? Was your experience good or bad? (Please specify.) What advice would you give to reporters about coverage of minorities such as yourself? (Again, ask for specifics.) Write your findings in the form of a mini-profile.

5   **Perceptions of language:** As you read the following terms, write the first descriptive words that come to your mind; then discuss whether your perceptions are stereotypes:

Texas	African-American	lesbian
ghetto	gay	truck driver
Hispanic	Asians	firefighter
Jewish	Native Americans	basketball player
Irish	Catholics	inner city

6   **Television shows:** Discuss some of your favorite television shows. Are the characters white, African-American, Asian-American or Hispanic? What races are underrepresented in television entertainment?

7   **Advertising:** Watch advertisements on television for one or two days, and analyze whether they are more inclusive of racial groups than other media. Discuss which racial groups are most represented in television advertisements. Compare those ads with print ads in your newspaper or in magazines you read. Are the ads in one medium more racially diverse than in another? Discuss how men and women are portrayed in ads, especially on television. Do the ads reflect or promote stereotypes?

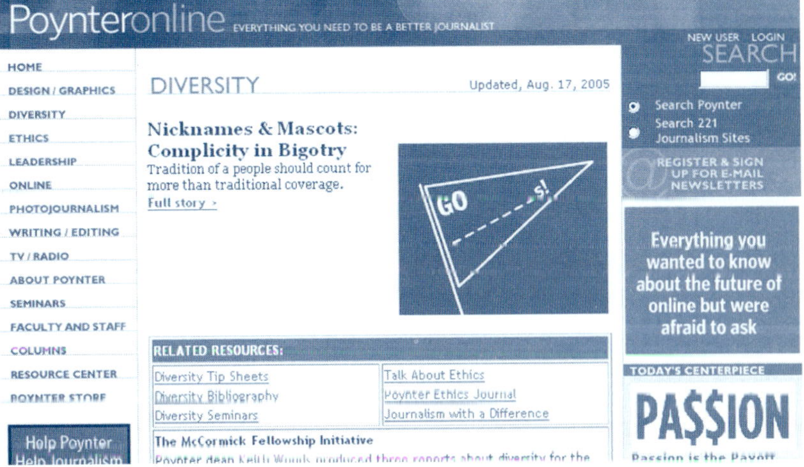

Coaching Tips

Select a particular country or region for study.

Learn a language or languages.

Study diplomacy and war.

Focus your stories on people.

Develop skills in a variety of media, including radio, television and Web reporting.

Global Journalism

Loren Jenkins, senior foreign editor,
National Public Radio

Loren Jenkins begins his day by logging on to his computer at 6 a.m. in Washington, D.C., which means it is 11 a.m. in London, 2 p.m. in Moscow and 8 p.m. in Tokyo. Jenkins, a longtime foreign correspondent for *Newsweek* and *The Washington Post,* serves as senior foreign editor of National Public Radio in Washington. In this role, he discusses stories and story ideas with correspondents in the field.

By 8 a.m. he's in the office, reading a variety of newspapers, which include *The New York Times, The Washington Post,* the *Los Angeles Times,* the *Financial Times* of London and *Le Monde* of Paris.

His first meeting of the day starts at 9:15 a.m., when he talks to his foreign staff in Washington, including editors and assignment managers. The team discusses the offerings for the four basic news programs at NPR: "Morning Edition"; "Day to Day," a noon news show; "Talk of the Nation," a talk show where correspondents are often interviewed; and "All Things Considered" in the afternoon.

At 9:30 a.m., NPR holds a general editorial meeting for the five coverage areas: national, Washington, foreign, science and culture. After that, Jenkins spends his day talking with reporters and editors about the day's events.

NPR has a relatively large, permanent international staff in China, Egypt, England, France, Germany, India, Iraq, Israel, Japan, Russia, Turkey and Vietnam. Jenkins also supervises the national security reporters, including those who cover the U.S. Department of Defense and the U.S. Department of State. In all, Jenkins supervises 22 reporters.

NPR features longer stories about news events—often running three to four minutes for a typical story and up to 12 minutes for special reports. "We like to say what we do is storytelling here. You want to cover the news as a story, which has a beginning, a middle and an end," Jenkins says. But the story needs to go beyond these basic attributes: "We find ways of covering different scenes that will form a mosaic of an overall story."

John Kifner of *The New York Times* had already established himself as one of the newspaper's best reporters. He had covered anti Vietnam war

John Kifner, foreign correspondent,
The New York Times

protests, poverty in New York and race riots in Boston. When he was summoned to the editor's desk one Friday, he got a new assignment: Iran. He had the weekend to pack for a flight on Monday.

Kifner, a history graduate from Williams College in Massachusetts, had never been outside the United States. He went to a bookstore that specialized in books on the Middle East and bought everything he could carry. He sat down with an old friend, a Muslim professor he had known for years, to learn all he could about Iran in three days and nights.

After he arrived in Iran, he heard about the killing of a religious leader. He went to the scene and employed the skills of a police reporter he had honed over the years. He spoke with witnesses. He mapped out the location. He went to the local police precinct, where a detective had found out the same information Kifner had.

Even though the detective and Kifner spoke through a translator, they were kindred spirits—a reporter and a cop trying to solve a mystery. Other reporters who did not travel to the scene of the crime wrote stories about the geopolitical implications of the events in Iran, but Kifner had a worldwide exclusive. He learned from the detective that a struggle had erupted between competing factions of the Islamic republic and that the religious leader was the victim of the deadly feud at the highest levels of government.

For the past 25 years, Kifner has combined his background in history and his skills as a street reporter to cover wars in Afghanistan, Bosnia and Iraq. He has become one of the premier foreign correspondents in the world since that day he left on his first international assignment in 1979.

"You need three things to be a good foreign reporter: languages, a serious reading program and the skills of a police reporter," Kifner says.

The Rise and Fall of International Journalism

The U.S. media have provided some of the most famous international correspondents in the history of journalism. Starting with the Spanish-American War, in which Richard Harding Davis and Stephen Crane chronicled the exploits of Teddy Roosevelt and the Rough Riders, to the World War II exploits of Ernie Pyle's infantry and John Hersey's book-length essay about the atomic bomb at Hiroshima, correspondents have written about international affairs—often to a public who may have preferred not to read or listen.

Foreign correspondents have made crucial contributions to the U.S media by writing about the horror of war in Southeast Asia and the joy of liberation from Communist rule. Moreover, during the roughly 100 years of international reporting by U.S. news organizations, many journalists have died in their efforts to bring news from throughout the world.

The international reporters have also covered diplomatic successes, artistic triumphs and intriguing stories—summed up best by the question from Charles Stanley of the *New York Herald-Tribune,* who had spent a year trying to find a famous explorer in Africa: "Dr. Livingston, I presume?"

Nevertheless, from 1989, when the Berlin Wall fell, signaling the end of the Cold War between the former Soviet Union and the United States, until Sept. 11, 2001, the U.S. news media also downplayed many significant international stories. Think back to the day before the attacks on the World Trade Center and the Pentagon. Try to answer these questions:

- Had you ever heard the name Osama Bin Laden?
- Had you ever heard about al-Qaeda?
- How much did you know about Afghanistan?
- How much did you worry about a terrorist attack of any kind *inside* the United States?

It was not your fault if you knew little or nothing about these topics because much of the mainstream media had not covered them.

The State of International News Coverage

The numbers tell the story about the changes in international coverage in the U.S. media. In 1991 the percentage of network stories about international affairs aired by ABC, CBS and NBC peaked at just over half of the stories—many of those from the first Persian Gulf War. By 1997, the share fell to 20 percent and stabilized there until Sept. 11, 2001, according to the Center for Media and Public Affairs. Airtime devoted to international and diplomatic news dropped dramatically between 1990 and 2000, according to the Tyndall Report, which monitors the networks' nightly news.

The same trend occurred at newspapers and news magazines. A 1971 Newspaper Advertising Bureau survey estimated that 10 percent of all news focused on international events. By the late 1990s, it had fallen to 2 percent, according to the American Society of Newspaper Editors. International news also vanished from the covers of the U.S. editions of the newsweeklies. In 1977 a third of the covers of *Time* and *Newsweek* featured a political or international figure. In 1997 only about 10 percent did, according to the Committee of Concerned Journalists.

After Sept. 11, 2001, the news media collectively patted themselves on the back, but it appears likely that the amount of international coverage will be reduced yet again. A recent survey of more than 200 newspaper editors, conducted for the Pew International Journalism Program, found the following:

- More than nine out of 10 editors said reader interest in foreign news increased after Sept. 11, 2001.

- Nearly eight out of 10 editors said their news hole for international news had increased.

- More than six out of 10 expected their readers to gradually lose interest in international news.

- Nearly six out of 10 expected their international news hole to shrink back to previous levels.

- Less than half of the editors thought they were doing an "excellent" or "good" job of satisfying reader interest in international news.

For example, *American Journalism Review* reported that after 2001, *no* U.S. newspaper has opened a new international bureau anywhere except in Baghdad, when the second Gulf war began. Editors and television executives apparently convinced themselves that readers and viewers were not and will not be interested in international news. But research tended to show the opposite.

In an *American Journalism Review* article, Tom Rosenstiel, director of the Washington, D.C.-based Project for Excellence in Journalism, blamed the decline in international news on financial reasons, not lack of reader interest: "My strong suspicion is that the focus is to cut costs; foreign bureaus are expensive. It's a matter of cost, not demand."

For example, the *Kansas City Star* conducted a survey and asked its readers which of 47 topics interested them the most. Before Sept. 11, 2001, international news came in ninth—eight places ahead of sports. In the post-Sept.11 period, it moved up to third, behind only local and national news.

Mark Whitaker, research and database manager for the *Star*, speculated that international news will probably fade to fifth or sixth place in subsequent surveys, but he predicts that it will remain higher than ninth for quite some time. He said his research indicates that Kansas City readership is typical of most cities.

The *Los Angeles Times* received similar survey results. The *Times* does daily tracking polls, interviewing 50 people a day, or about 250 a week. Readers are then categorized by groups. For example, more than 50 percent of frequent *Times* readers are categorized as either "cosmopolitan enthusiast" or "dedicated hard news and business." After Sept. 11, 2001, international news catapulted from around eighth or ninth to second among all readers. Sports was in 20th place before Sept. 11 and remained there. Ed Batson, research director for the *Times,* said, "Attention to national and international news is not only good journalism. It is in our enlightened self-interest."

Reporting the Story

Reporting about foreign affairs resembles almost every other type of reporting except it is done outside of the United States. As Kifner of *The New York Times* notes, the essential components of journalism need to be followed in covering international stories—good research, good reporting and good writing: "You're writing for specialists—people at the foreign policy or academic establishments that actually know a lot about the subject, and at the same time, you're writing for the commuter coming to work in the morning. So that's a challenge to try to do that at those two levels in a seamless way."

Major news outlets maintain international bureaus throughout the world, but the number of news organizations is far fewer than in the past. CNN has the most extensive array of bureaus because the network provides news for the United States and for specific regions throughout the world.

But most news organizations depend upon wire services, mainly The Associated Press and Reuters, to provide international stories. Some news outlets depend upon free-lance journalists.

The Changing Nature
of International News

After World War II, two subjects dominated international news coverage: the relationship between the Soviet Union and the United States, and the Middle East. Although wars are not the only staple of international news, the nature of life and death in war plays a significant role in the work of a foreign correspondent. That makes the job a dangerous one—one that has become even more dangerous in recent years because combatants no longer view journalists as neutral observers.

NPR's Jenkins covered the final days of Vietnam and earned a Pulitzer Prize for his coverage of the Middle East. He sees some profound differences today from when he started as a foreign correspondent in the 1970s.

"The story has shifted from a bipolar world where a lot was ordered around the Cold War stories of who's up and who's down," Jenkins says. "Was Russia gaining? Was the U.S. gaining? (It) is a much more complex and splintered world today where conflicts are all over the place and aren't necessarily related. It certainly is a more turbulent world across the spectrum. The whole thing of terror has obviously got a whole new dimension than what it used to have."

International analysts tend to look at regions when they assess the future of news coverage. At the moment, the United States stands as the lone superpower in the world, having gained that stature after the fall of the Soviet Union in early 1990s. China, a country of more than one billion people and a growing economic powerhouse despite Communist rule, is seen as the chief rival of the United States. That places Asia in the forefront of international coverage. The acquisition of nuclear weapons by North Korea creates instability in a region that has been relatively stable for the 30 years after the end of the Vietnam War.

The Middle East, although technically part of Asia, continues to occupy analysts because of its importance with respect to democratic reform, oil and terrorism. The past decade has seen changes in the rulers in a variety of countries: Algeria, Iraq, Israel, Lebanon, Jordan, Morocco, the Palestinian Authority, Saudi Arabia and Syria. Other changes will doubtless soon occur. And the success or failure of the United States in its attempts to create democratic reforms in Afghanistan and Iraq will continue to reverberate throughout the region.

Africa remains a continent to which the U.S. media pay little attention. The advance of HIV/AIDS across the continent has raised limited interest. Coverage of Central America and South America, once important regions for the U.S. media, has waned in recent years. As the threat of drugs and regional conflicts seems to have dissipated, so has the interest of U.S. media outlets.

Europe will continue to interest U.S. news outlets, primarily because of the allure of various cultures that are similar to the United States. Also, Russia and the newly independent states near it will continue to interest policymakers, although at a much reduced level from 20 years ago.

Specific subject areas often drive news coverage in these various regions. Clearly, terrorism will continue to be a focus of international reporters throughout the world. So, too, will economics.

For example, the European Union is likely to challenge the United States for supremacy in a variety of economic endeavors, including aircraft, computers and energy exploration. Leisure and travel stories lend themselves to international reporting, particularly when it is less expensive to catch an airplane to London to see excellent plays than to travel to New York to do the same.

The post-Sept. 11 events, including the invasion of Afghanistan and Iraq, have dominated international news coverage in recent years. NPR's Jenkins thinks that some coverage will remain the same while other coverage will change. He sees the emergence of China and the challenges this will create for the United States as a key story over the next decade. Moreover, he thinks that the European Union may provide an economic and political challenge to the United States. But he also believes that the Arab–Israeli conflict will continue to brew as he looks toward news in the next decade.

Reporting in the Field

It is somewhat ironic, but a large number of international stories come from Washington rather than from outside of the United States. That is because the Department of Defense, the Department of State and the intelligence agencies—the Central Intelligence Agency, the Defense Intelligence Agency, the National Security Agency and others—are located in Washington. These organizations have access to information from outside the United States and can provide news to journalists on deadline.

Many sources within these organizations take years to cultivate. Also, Chapter 4's rules about quoting sources are especially pertinent to government sources and must be followed:

- *On the record* means that a reporter can use the material without any limitation: "The secretary of defense said. . . ."
- *Background* or *not for attribution* means that a report cannot use a name as a source. The reporter and the source must determine how the source will be identified: "A reliable intelligence official said. . . ."
- *Deep background* means that the reporter can use the information but cannot mention any type of source: "The president views the treaty as a positive development."
- *Off the record* means that the information may not be reported in any way. Some sources confuse background and off the record, so the reporter should make certain to clarify the rules.

The problem of unnamed sources has grown in recent years. Unnamed sources mean that no one can be held responsible for the information other than the reporter. The reader or listener has no way to know whether the source is credible.

Diplomatic Sources

The diplomatic representatives of the United States and other countries can be useful sources. Ambassadors head embassies, but their true knowledge of a country may depend on whether they are longtime Department of State employees or political appointees. Often, large contributors to political campaigns will be rewarded with ambassadorships, so the ambassador may not be the most knowledgeable embassy official.

A U.S. embassy generally includes these sections: agriculture, commerce, consular, intelligence, military and politics. The usefulness of these sections will depend upon the type of story you are working on. Each section may have specialists in various fields, although one individual generally heads the section. In some countries, diplomats and reporters face restrictions from the host country, so the agriculture and military representatives can be particularly helpful because they often travel throughout the country. The intelligence officials frequently do not speak with reporters, but you can get some information on such matters from the ambassador or the head of the political section. The consular section generally deals with issues such as passports and visas, so it is not an area that generates much news.

Diplomats from other countries, including Canada, England and France, can be very useful, providing interesting and different perspectives. Another important way to use diplomatic contacts is to talk with the representatives of countries that border the country in which you are working. In Syria, for example, the Turkish representatives often have a good understanding of the politics of the country because the two countries border each other. Because Turkey is a country with good relations with the United States, Turkish diplomats will frequently speak with U.S. reporters.

A wide variety of governmental and nongovernmental organizations can provide useful information to a reporter, including the United Nations, independent aid groups and local journalists.

International news also depends upon building access to the powerful figures and political groups within a country. It is important to determine who holds actual power. In many countries, the president plays a largely ceremonial role, while the prime minister handles the important affairs of government. Cabinet secretaries, particularly those who handle international affairs, will be the most likely sources of information for international reporters. Representatives from opposition political groups can provide alternative viewpoints to those of the official government position—similar to the way in which reporters inside the United States seek comment from both Republicans and Democrats. Again, local groups with specific areas of expertise on issues such as business or health can provide insights into the thinking of those outside the government.

The Tools of the Trade

Language has become increasingly important in international reporting. NPR's Jenkins, who speaks French, Italian, Spanish and some Arabic, sees a growing need for the reporter who can operate without a translator. He suggests that journalists interested in covering Asia must know Chinese. Knowing Russian continues to be important in the former Soviet Union despite a growing number of people who speak English. Arabic is a must for those who want to report in the Middle East. Spanish and French remain important as

MULTIMEDIA COACH

Nearly every news organization expects its reporters to find material for the Web when working outside the United States. You should be prepared to file individual items for the Web and have a camera available to upload photographs.

If you are working for a radio or television outlet, you should plan to file for the Web as well. Broadcast outlets have almost all become 24/7 operations because of the Web. The Web story may also make it possible for your editors to know what to expect for audio and video when you are able to file for the daily broadcasts.

More news outlets encourage reporters to write personal accounts, called "Web logs" or "blogs," of their experiences. Be careful about excessive commentary, but blogging allows for a personal approach to an important story that may add context for Web users. Remember that many publications with international links exist online, such as *www.mediachannel.org*.

alternative ways of communicating throughout the world. Following are some other tips from Jenkins:

- Basic reporting skills learned at City Hall or the police department also work well in international assignments.
- Curiosity and an interest in international affairs are essential.
- International events are often unplanned and require flexibility on the part of the journalist.

If you do international reporting, remember that the local pharmacy and the audio outlet are not nearby. Make certain that you have audiotapes, backpack, bandages, batteries, comfortable boots, a chemical suit, computer, digital camera, energy bars, flak jacket, flashlight, a gas mask, helmet, medications, plastic bags, satellite telephone, sleeping bag, tape recorders, tent, trail mix, video camera, and water and water purification tablets.

Working With the Military

Knowledge of the tactics of war and the armaments of war has always been important, but it has become an increasingly important component of international reporting. The ability to understand military tactics has helped many reporters who have not served in the armed forces, particularly with the current emphasis on embedding journalists with U.S. military forces. *Jane's Defence Weekly* and other informational services at *www.janes.com* have been among top sources for defense issues for years. A wide variety of organizations offer political analysis, but the Rand Corporation (*www.rand.org*) provides information on most regional issues. An alternative list of sources and news outlets can be found at *www.mediachannel.org*, a left-leaning perspective of news and commentary. A growing number of blogs deal with international and military issues.

Embedding is a recent development in modern warfare, but it was standard operating procedure in World War II. Reporters who were "embedded" with troops in the 2003 Gulf War were considered part of the troops and traveled with them at all times, including during battles. During the 1991 Gulf War, before embedding was official, John Kifner of *The New York Times* was able to tag along with the Army's 101st Airborne Division, one of the best and most-storied groups in the U.S. military. "It was really good out there. We had a very smart general, and we bonded all very well. They broke all the rules and really took care of us," Kifner recalls.

In the 2003 Gulf War, Kifner was attached to the First Marine Division and eventually worked himself into a small squadron. "Embedding is good. It has its limitations. I mean anything that gets you more accurate information, you can't criticize," he says. "The difficulties are that you see only a small bit of things. This just depends very much on individual relationships and who you're with."

Kifner referred to his most recent experience as "the camping trip from hell." He recalls that "you could only do what your unit did. That was a disadvantage. You'd get up at four o'clock and then drive endlessly around and then eventually get to the site of the camp." But he also saw important fighting in the Sunni-held town of Fallujah.

It is important to have an understanding of the different branches of the military. The four basic branches of the military are the Air Force, Army, Navy and Marines. Technically, the Marines operate as part of the Navy, but each has a separate command. Although every military branch incorporates individuals who fight on air, land and sea, the Air Force has primary responsibility for air operations, the Army is responsible for ground operations, and the Navy has oversight of sea operations. The Marines operate on air, land and sea—as do the elite Army Rangers and Navy Seals. The Army has aircraft and sea vessels; the Navy has aircraft. Therefore, all military branches have some duplication in their missions. Table 16.1 is a breakdown of a typical Army command.

It is also important to understand the differences between the various groupings in the military and between the ranks in the various services (see the Associated Press Stylebook). If you don't understand the differences, it is

Table 16.1 Typical Military Units/Formations in an Army

Name	Number of Personnel	Number of Subordinate Units	Officer in Charge
Army group	100,000+	2+ armies	General
Army	60,000+	2+ corps	General
Corps	30,000+	2+ divisions	Lieutenant general
Division	10,000–20,000	2–4 brigades	Major general
Brigade	2,000–5,000	2+ regiments or 3–6 battalions	Colonel
Regiment	2,000–3,000	4 battalions	Colonel
Battalion	300–1,000	2–6 companies	Lieutenant colonel
Company	100–300	3–6 platoons	Captain or major
Platoon	30–40	2+ squads	First or second lieutenant
Squad	8–12	2+ fire teams	Corporal to staff sergeant
Fire team	4–5		Lance corporal to sergeant

ETHICS

You have convinced the members of a guerrilla group to let you travel with them to report about their activities. During your trip, the guerrillas find a U.S. convoy and decide to attack it.

- Should you try to warn the U.S. convoy? Why or why not?

- What is more important: the lives of the soldiers or your role as an objective observer?

- Is any attempt to warn the U.S. convoy irrelevant because you would likely fail or be silenced?

In a discussion of this topic at Columbia University, the late Peter Jennings of ABC News said he would not try to warn the convoy. Military leaders at the same session were outraged by his response. What do you think?

the same as covering the police and not knowing the difference between a detective and a patrol officer. If you don't know the ranks of the people in charge and what they command, you won't get a lot of information.

Dangers of International Reporting

Not only has the fighting made it more dangerous for journalists; reporters have also become targets. Even though reporters were kidnapped in the mid-1980s in the Middle East, the practice has become more frequent and deadlier in recent years. For example, Daniel Pearl of *The Wall Street Journal* was lured to his death in Pakistan. Few journalists carry weapons, but bodyguards often accompany reporters on routine assignments.

In a tribute to Pearl and other foreign correspondents who were killed while reporting in the Middle East, John Kifner wrote the following:

It could have been any of us.

That was the stunned reaction of experienced foreign correspondents to the news that Daniel Pearl of *The Wall Street Journal* had been killed, his throat slit by his captors. To outsiders, it might have seemed that Mr. Pearl was engaged in a dangerous—even foolhardy—endeavor, trying to interview an outlawed Islamic militant leader. Yet, quite simply, that is the kind of thing we do, day in and day out. . . .

All of us who have covered the Middle East or Central Asia have spent a considerable amount of time sitting cross-legged on the floor of one slum or another, sipping tea and listening to various forms of Islamic militancy and anti-Americanism, often late into the night.

The reason is simple: the rising tide of Islamic anger is one of the most important stories in the world today, and it is our job—our duty—to report it. To be sure, there are other elements that contribute to the experience of being a foreign correspondent: the thrill of a big story, the comradeship, the sheer joy of learning about exotic places, the adrenaline rush. But ultimately, it is the belief that trying to find out what is really happening is something intrinsically very worthwhile.

John Kifner, The New York Times

Farnaz Fassihi of *The Wall Street Journal* also described the dangers that she and her colleagues faced in covering the Middle East. She wrote the following in a diary in 2004 for the *Columbia Journalism Review:*

> The insurgents have brought the war to downtown Baghdad. For the fourth day in a row Haifa Street, a strip of old houses and Soviet-style apartment blocks, is a battleground between Americans and rebels. A few days ago, I watched Mazen, an Arab colleague with Al Arabiya news channel, get shot by an American helicopter as he was doing a live stand-up on Haifa Street. He died on television as I sipped my morning coffee. I ask Babak (a friend) if he thought we'd need therapy after we were done with this place. "Probably," he replies.

Photographers and International News

Still-camera and video photographers face some of the most significant challenges in reporting international stories. Often, the photographer's work is as close to the action as it gets. That is why photographers suffer the greatest number of casualties among journalists in international assignments.

At the same time, the photographers generally receive the greatest respect from the people involved in the coverage, particularly the military. John Kifner almost always tried to sit down at the breakfast meeting of the photographers, who mapped out where they thought the action would be that day. It is not possible to reconstruct what happened for the photographer; the photographer must be there when something happens. That means planning, to ensure the ability to get close to the action.

Writing the Story

Because many news organizations depend upon The Associated Press and Reuters for their international coverage, the summary lead remains the most frequent for foreign stories. Moreover, readers and listeners often want to know what has happened. This Associated Press story provides an example of the summary lead:

> Armed, masked thieves burst into a lightly guarded Oslo museum Sunday and snatched the Edvard Munch masterpiece "The Scream" and a second Munch painting from the walls as stunned visitors watched in shock.

The same approaches outlined in other sections of this book also apply to international reporting. Look for individuals who represent the issue you may be writing about. Readers and listeners often want stories about people rather than complicated political treatises. Joseph Geraghty, now a reporter for *The Bristol* (Tenn.) *Courier Herald,* wrote this story about a Chechen family in Russia.

Natalie Petrova was distraught all day. At around four in the afternoon tears welled up in her eyes as it appeared that her worst fears would be confirmed. The Americans would not be able to stay for dinner.

We had met her earlier in the day at her tiny apartment in Kaminsk, a small city outside of Rostov-on-Don, the capital of the southern region of the Russian Federation. This was our second trip to the town about two hours outside of Rostov and our second visit with Natalie.

I had come to Kaminsk with another American journalism student and a translator to work on a story about the plight of refugees who had fled the devastating war in Chechnya. . . .

When we entered Natalie's humble, one-room home, we realized just how important our visit was. The table, which she had to borrow from a neighbor, was set up. Her three chairs were placed around it. Bowls, plates and pots full of food covered the top of the table and it was obvious that, had we not come, she would have sadly climbed the dark stairs back to her apartment and dolefully returned the dishes to their cupboards, alone.

As it was, she dashed around the room making sure we were comfortable, then ran to the communal kitchen down the hall to heat up the food she had prepared for our visit earlier in the day.

TJ, a broadcast journalism student, asked Natalie to say something about our visit for his camera. She stood there with a look of sincere gratitude and told TJ and me that we were the first Americans she had ever met, and the first journalists ever to listen to the stories of Chechen refugees in the city. She thanked us with all her heart and told us that neither she nor anyone else we had spoken to that day would ever forget us.

This is a woman who fled Chechnya with only the clothes on her back as soldiers fought bloody battles in front of her family home. She lived alone in poverty in Kaminsk and here she was thanking us for visiting her.

And so we sat there, gorging ourselves on the food Natalie had lovingly prepared for two Americans she'd only met a week earlier, and I began to reflect on my Russian experience. I thought back to my first days in Moscow and my first impressions of Russia as a disorganized, dirty place full of depressed people all struggling to find a way out of their country.

It took a trip to a real Russian village and a visit with real Russian people to realize the truth about the country. Though Russia lags far behind the West in basic creature comforts and overall stability, the people I met there casually explained these difficulties with the catchall phrase, "It's Russia."

The difficulties of being Russian are real, though. Banks still refuse to accept American currency that looks old or tattered because their own currency, the Ruble, has been devalued and declared worthless so many times that they have learned to be cautious. Russia still has a strict internal passport system that dates back to Stalin's rule and severely restricts citizens' ability to move from one city to another. Communist monuments still litter the landscape and former Communist leaders still occupy positions of power so that real, meaningful reform that might someday lead to a stable economy remains years away.

We spoke at length with Natalie and Tanya and other Chechens about the difficulties they face in Russia. Tanya and her husband Boris were forced to flee the hills of Chechnya after Russian mortar fire destroyed their home. They left with only what they could carry. On the journey, Boris' mother was killed when a Russian jet bombed the bridge they were traveling over.

And yet the refugees we visited seemed almost universally hopeful. Not that the war would soon be over or even that their lives would drastically improve in the near future, but that their children would lead better lives than their parents had.

"I came here for my children," Tanya told us. It was a sentiment shared by all the Chechens we spoke with.

Joseph Geraghty, The *(Ithaca, N.Y.)* Ithacan

It is important to keep in mind that many or most of your readers or listeners have never been to the places about which you are reporting. Setting

NPR Web story "On the Road in China"

the scene becomes important, as NPR correspondent Rob Gifford did when he traveled 3,000 miles over 14 days to produce a seven-part report on China in 2004. The segments, each of which ran on "All Things Considered," started in Shanghai, the Pacific coast boomtown. The other stories focused on corruption, prostitution, religion, poverty, Islam and a host of other interesting tales along Highway 312, which runs from the Pacific Ocean to Kazakhstan, a newly independent country that was once part of the Soviet Union.

NPR and Gifford use many of the storytelling techniques outlined in this book. The anchor starts with a summary lead, outlining what Gifford intends to report:

ANCHOR VO (voice over)	China may well be the next world superpower in the making. It has passed Japan as Asia's economic dynamo. This vast Asian nation of 1.3 billion people has become a major manufacturing and trading nation and increasingly a competitor for world resources, but China's development still has a long way to go. To find out how far, NPR's Rob Gifford recently traveled across China from its eastern Pacific shores to its western Gobi Desert. Traveling by bus, truck and taxi, he discovered that China remains as diverse as it is populous. Today, in the first of the seven-part series "On the Road in China," Rob Gifford begins his journey in Shanghai.

Gifford turns to the hourglass approach in his opening voice over:

GIFFORD VO

> If the 21st century belongs to China, then the city that will be at the heart of it will be Shanghai. Shanghai is the boomtown of Asia, where shiny new skyscrapers seem to spring up daily like mushrooms after a spring rain. The sidewalks of this huge port city buzz with energy. Cars have displaced bicycles on the roads, and the city has become a magnet for China's growing army of yuppies. There's another army, too, the rural poor who are also swarming to Shanghai often to work in the factories that supply the world with everything.

The reporter uses sound to paint a picture of a factory and quickly turns to the focus-on-a-person storytelling method:

GIFFORD VO

> A woman, 26 years old, sits behind a sewing machine on a Shanghai factory floor. Around her, 200 other women are doing the same thing. On the floor above, the same number again. Like a scene from a Dickens novel, this is the industrial revolution come to China. Multiply this factory by thousands upon thousands, and you see the start of the transformation of a country spreading out from the coast like dye dripped upon a piece of cloth.
>
> Li Hongying is her name, and she's worked here for six years. She's traveled a thousand miles from her hometown inland, and she says she's earning five times here what she could earn at home.

Television reporting has been drastically reduced in recent years, mainly because of the cost of maintaining sizable bureaus throughout the world. That doesn't mean that TV fails to do some excellent reporting. However, what has happened is that television producers and reporters tend to work as parachute journalists—flying in to cover whatever story may happen, sometimes with limited background knowledge.

The U.S. networks—with the exception of CNN, which has expanded its international coverage—tend to concentrate their bureaus in Baghdad,

Beijing, London, Jerusalem, Paris and Tokyo. The television outlets have come to depend more and more on Associated Press Television News and Reuters Television for visuals because these operations continue to maintain news bureaus throughout the world.

Finding the Local Angle

Almost every community has a significant population of some international group. Try to find how these people contribute to your community. At times, various ethnic groups can provide insight into events outside of the United States. For example, many Muslims live in Detroit. Millions of Poles live in Chicago. Chinese and other Asian groups exist in communities throughout the United States.

Many people pay attention to particular parts of the news and may help reporters in local communities provide better coverage of these issues. Farmers watch the cost of grain in Russia and China. Aid workers react to disasters throughout the world. Rescue dog teams may go to far-off locales to help with search-and-rescue missions. Scientists follow important research in other countries. Sports interests look outside of the United States to find players for baseball, football, basketball and hockey teams. The connection between your community and other countries may be far greater than what you think.

Exercises

1   Analyze the international coverage of your local newspaper, radio station or television outlet. What are the sources of the news—staff reports or wire services?

2   Analyze the international coverage of a national newspaper, radio outlet or television network. What are the sources of the news—staff reports or wire services? What differences in content do you notice from the coverage of your local news organizations?

3   Find an international story, and see how it affects your community. Write a story about it.

4   Find a local story that has an international focus, and write about it.

5   Interview some international students about their views of U.S. media coverage of their countries.

Visit *www.mediachannel.org* to see alternative news sources on international stories. Compare the coverage of a story on this site to a story in U.S. media, such as CNN, MSNBC or a national newspaper's Web site, such as that of *The New York Times*.

October 20, 2005

A OneWorld Channel

MediaChannel.org Jobs & Internships
MediaChannel.org is looking for dedicated people to help us make our work even more relevant and impactful. We are currently looking to fill several positions. Click here to find out how you can join the MediaChannel.org family.

Support MediaChannel with a tax-deductible donation.

PayPal DONATE

MC Features   ▶ All Features

Weldon on the Warpath
Representative Curt Weldon, Republican from Pennsylvania, has declared war on his own Defense Department. Upset with the Defense Intelligence Agency over its continuing refusal to allow public scrutiny of the controversial Able Danger 'information warfare' program (which identified Mohammed Atta and three other 9/11 hijackers a year before the World Trade Center attacks,) as well as transparent DIA attempts to smear whistleblower Lt. Col. Anthony Shaffer, Weldon is calling for a full "felony investigation" of DIA's actions by the Defense Department Inspector General.

Did the Media Get It Right in the Iraq Election?
Vote figures for crucial province don't add up. Historian and Policy analyst Gareth Porter challenges the media frame in a report he's sent to Mediachannel.org.

Keeping the Light on Injustice
Step #2 of the MediaChannel campaign for media follow-up and responsibility after Hurricane Katrina.

MEDIA BLOG ROLL:

Shadowboxing While Baghdad Seethes | The 'Trial of the Century' | Are Indictments Coming? | Ted K to Join Tony S at HBO
more...

Of all the astonishments in the Judith Miller/New York

Coaching Tips

Ask one source to recommend others.

Ask people you meet what stories they would like to read in your field.

Keep a tickler file of story ideas and follow-up stories.

Contact sources regularly.

Check records on your beat.

Make stories relevant to readers.

Seek human elements in stories.

Translate jargon in technical stories or specialized fields.

Check the Internet for sources, background and records.

CHAPTER 17

Beat Reporting

> **To be a good beat reporter, you have to love what you're doing.**
>
> Sevil Hunter, reporter, *Reno* (Nev.) *Gazette-Journal*

Mark McCormick, beat reporter

When Mark McCormick began covering the religion beat for *The Courier-Journal* in Louisville, Ky., he had no sources and few story ideas. But within a few weeks he had more sources and story tips than he could cover.

"I asked each person I interviewed two things: 'If you could name five or 10 people that I would need to know to do this beat well, who would they be? If there were five stories about religion that you would like to read, what would they be?' Between those two things, I amassed a large calling list," McCormick says.

McCormick kept names of all his sources in his computer. "If five people said I needed to talk to the same people, I put a star next to that person's name," he says. "I made it a point to cultivate a relationship with those people by going to lunch with them and trying to win their confidence."

He also used the matchmaker technique, asking one source to introduce him to people who might be skeptical about dealing with him or with the media in general. "I'd say, 'Would you mind telling this person I'm not a hatchet man.' That is how I made a breakthrough in the Jewish community and the Muslim community."

In the past, religion news was relegated to a page on Saturdays to announce church services and other information. But it is becoming a significant beat because newspaper studies have shown that religion affects people's lives as much as or more than any other news in the paper.

The religion beat was a new challenge to McCormick, who had covered police and community beats in the past. "I was a little intimidated because I am not theologically trained," he says. As he soon discovered, however, the religion beat is like any other beat. The content of the news differs, but the techniques of reporting and writing do not.

A "beat" is a specific area of coverage. It can be an entire municipality or parts of the government, such as the police department, the school board or the city officials. It can be a topical beat, such as environment, business, minorities or religion.

The skills you have studied so far can be applied to all beats. Some of the following chapters will be devoted to specific beats, such as police, courts and government, but the tips from McCormick and other writers in this chapter will help you get started covering any beat.

Developing Story Ideas

Although McCormick received many tips for story ideas by asking people what they wanted to read, he also used his natural curiosity to develop ideas. One day he was covering the funeral of a 15-year-old boy who had been shot. The boy's friends showed up wearing T-shirts with the boy's picture and the words "Rest in Peace." McCormick says the shirts struck him as odd, but then he noticed similar markings on T-shirts and baseball caps after another young man died. Although it may not seem like a story for the religion beat, McCormick says this social phenomenon is, in fact, a very spiritual story.

The front of the shirts that Thomas Cooper made after the death of his friend, Tony Sullivan, read "R.I.P. T LUV" in artful script and colorful airbrushed design.

On the back was an enlarged, equally artistic design featuring "T LUV"—Sullivan's nickname.

"He's my homey; you've got to remember him," Cooper, 19, said of Sullivan, who was shot by a police officer in Lexington's Bluegrass-Aspendale housing area last month in an incident that sparked civil unrest in the city.

On Friday, Cooper was wearing a baseball cap with "T LUV" across the front. "I just got this to have something to remember him by. He was my boy."

And at Sullivan's funeral the previous week, many young people were wearing their "T LUV" T-shirts. Such shirts—with the deceased's picture or name emblazoned across them—are becoming a common sight at services for teenage victims of violence.

Some youths say wearing the shirts has nothing to do with being cool and everything to do with respecting the memory of fallen friends. Other teens and school counselors argue that many who wear the shirts don't even know the victims and are not grieving but trying to connect with a culture they see as alluring.

Mark McCormick, The *(Louisville, Ky.)* Courier-Journal

One story can lead to many others, as when McCormick wrote about a hospital chapel that was closing. "I went there and talked to people about their memories," he says. "I found a woman who had spent many hours praying in the chapel 20 years ago because her husband had cancer and was supposed to die. He is still alive today." McCormick says 135 people called him or left voice-mail messages to comment about the story, and many people told him similar touching stories about how faith had affected their lives. As a result, he had many sources for another story about the power of faith.

McCormick also checks newspaper clips, journals, newsletters, press releases and national research organizations that cover religion to keep abreast of his field: "I keep tabs of polls about young people in church, single people, why men don't go to church as much as women. I also keep everything I write in a notebook so I don't have to go to the library and look things up for follow-up stories."

Many beat reporters also check the Internet to read interactive news groups and blogs, where people express their opinions. Although this source doesn't always lead to local stories, it gives reporters an idea of what people are discussing in their field and provides sources for stories on national trends. In addition, the Internet provides a wealth of documents and resources for beat reporters. Many of these resources are listed on the Web site for this book.

But to do a good job on any beat, you still need to use the traditional reporting skills of meeting people and developing sources in person.

Cultivating and Keeping Sources

Once you find sources, you need to get them to trust you. McCormick, who has since become a columnist for *The Wichita* (Kan.) *Eagle,* says when you start any beat, it's always better to write a positive story, if you can, the first time you cover a group: "I never want my first contact to be negative."

That is especially true with groups that haven't had much coverage in the past, such as the Muslims and the African-American churches on McCormick's beat. And unlike sources on police and government beats, sources in religious organizations don't expect controversy or negative coverage in the media.

But that's what they got when McCormick covered the General Association of Baptists, an organization of more than 500 black churches. The group hadn't been covered by the newspaper in the past. At the first meeting McCormick attended, the association ousted churches that had licensed women to preach. To McCormick, the association's action was a good story. The leaders of the association didn't agree. "They still won't speak to me," he says.

McCormick says he always tries to give all sources a chance to comment or to do a follow-up story that explains the issue in depth. That approach didn't work with the General Association of Baptists. However, sources will usually be cooperative if you give them a chance to explain their views and if your story is accurate and fair, he says.

Sevil Hunter, who covered the police and courts beat for the *Reno* (Nev.) *Gazette-Journal,* recommends contacting sources regularly. She called her sources even when she had no specific story in mind. "I think you need to let them know you are taking an interest in them," she says. "When you run into them, it's important to say 'Hi, how are you.' You have to make sure they know who you are and what you look like. Meet people on the scene."

Hunter, whose *Gazette-Journal* beat is now mainly about family issues, says regular contact is particularly important on her beat because many times police, lawyers and other sources are reluctant to give information about crimes and court cases: "A lot of times people are a bit skeptical of you; they haven't sized you up yet. In my case, some of the police who read my stories were surprised when they met me because my name confused them. They said, 'We thought you were a man.'"

Sevil Hunter, reporter

ETHICS

Ethical dilemma: Should you become friends or get romantically involved with a source on your beat?

The case: You share a mutual attraction with a source on your beat, and you would really like to date this person. You know it would be a conflict of interest to date the source, but should you give up your rights to a personal life, or should you give up your beat? Can you maintain a relationship with a source without compromising your integrity and credibility? Does it make a difference if the relationship is romantic or just platonic?

Ethical values: Credibility, conflict of interest.

Ethical guidelines: The Society of Professional Journalists Code of Ethics says journalists should avoid conflicts of interest, real or perceived, and should remain free of associations and activities that may compromise integrity or damage credibility.

Because beat reporters deal with the same sources repeatedly, it is easy to become friendly with them. But Hunter says she draws the line at socializing with sources because it can cause conflicts of interest. On the other hand, if you know that a good source has a birthday or some important event in his or her life or has been ill, you can make a phone call or send a card. Many good beat reporters keep such notations about the source in their card file or in a computer source file.

Checking Records and Human Sources

Sevil Hunter didn't depend exclusively on police and attorneys for information. She says all good reporters should check records, especially on the police beat: "Check the police files, public documents in courts and go to the sources. Then do what detectives do. Knock on doors and do your homework. Ask family members and victims."

In addition to covering stories as they occur, Hunter watched for trends on her beat. For example, she noticed that the crime statistics revealed an increase in the number of young women arrested for violent crimes. She wondered what was causing this trend. Her investigation led to a package of stories, including a mainbar about why the trend was occurring and sidebars profiling women who were involved with gangs and with other criminal activity.

When the Bloods headed into Truckee Meadows from Southern California to organize a narcotics ring last year, they sought the toughest and brightest gang member to head the effort.

They found her in Reno.

When Harrah's officials and police reviewed a recent video of purse snatchings inside the downtown casino, they were surprised to see the suspect's young, female face.

When metal flashed at Sparks Middle School in March, security guards took two girls into custody on charges of carrying a concealed weapon on school grounds.

More and more young women are mirroring men, especially their rebelliousness, law-enforcement officials say. Increasingly, girls are committing violent crimes.

Now they call the shots and elicit fear from rivals.

"There's a large, solid group of females in gang activity," Reno Police Chief Jim Weston said about increases in the past two years.

Sevil Hunter, Reno *(Nev.)* Gazette-Journal

The story was accompanied by charts of statistics.

"There's a lot of mechanical work to this beat that any clerk could do. But you have to keep checking police and court files so you know the pulse and the trends," Hunter says. "And despite the blood and gore, there's always a human element. You can put compassion into any story."

Although human sources are still the most important ones on a beat, online sources and documents have become increasingly valuable to beat reporters. One of the first steps you should take when you start a beat is to check the Internet for Web pages about your community and state. Then check more general resources and documents at online sites for organizations, government agencies, businesses and journalism organizations related to your beat.

But remember that much of the information on the Internet is not reliable. For example, thousands of sites offer medical advice, but much of the information is more opinion than fact. Some sites are pure hoaxes.

Despite the accuracy and credibility problems of Web sites, the Internet is a wonderful tool for beat reporters to accumulate sources and background information. You just have to be sure that the background, documents or Web sites come from an agency, organization, business or government institution that offers credible information.

Here are some tips:

- Check whether the site offers a contact name, postal address and phone number. Call the number and verify the contact if you are using the site as a beat resource.

- Check the date of the information posted. Not all sites offer posting dates, but you should make sure that the information you use is not outdated.

- To find out who owns or manages a site, check a Whois database. You can identify owners of and contacts at nongovernmental agencies by going to *www.betterwhois.com,* but much of the information has not been updated in the past few years, so it may not be accurate. However, checking is still worth a try.

Beginning a Beat

The tips suggested by Mark McCormick and Sevil Hunter will help you get started in any beat. If you are beginning a job or internship in an area that is unfamiliar to you or if you are assigned to cover a municipality, here are some other tips for starting your beat:

Use shoe leather: Get to know your community or the agency you cover. Meet its members in person. Take a walking tour of the community. Talk to people. Eat where the politicians and the city employees eat or socialize after work. Get your hair cut by the barber or beautician who has been in town a long time. Ask people what they are interested in and what they want to read in their newspaper. Get a map. Cruise the streets. See where the rich and poor, the famous and infamous live. If you have a campus beat, introduce yourself to the officials, department heads, or leaders of a department or an organization. Tell them that you are interested in what they do and are seeking story ideas on a regular basis. In many cases, the people on your beat will want the coverage.

Check clips: The newspaper database or resource room that may have old clips is a starting place for your beat and for every story you write. When you find stories about major issues on your beat, consider an update story.

Let your fingers do the walking: Read the classified pages of your telephone book. How many churches are there of each denomination? Are massage parlors, astrologers or other unusual services advertised? Check the municipal services, sometimes listed in a separate section. Is there a poison control center or a government agency that sounds interesting? A quick scan of the classified section of your telephone book can give you some sense of your community and story ideas for a municipal beat. If you have a campus or city beat, check the directories of your school or city. Are there agencies or departments you don't know anything about? Find out what people in these jobs do, what they like and don't like about their jobs. Check campus directories for clubs and student organizations that might be worth a feature.

Study the classifieds: Check newspaper classified sections, such as the real estate section. What is for sale? What prices are the houses? This information will give you some idea of the economic climate of the community. Maybe you can write a story about why a particular area of town has many homes for sale. Sometimes you'll find a touching story in the personal ads. Check the rewards for lost dogs, cats, birds, snakes or unusual pets. And check the legal notices. They'll tell you what the city must advertise, as in notices of meetings or for items the city wants to buy. For campus beats, check classifieds and other advertisements in the college newspaper for unusual job opportunities, new organizations and other items that could be of interest to students.

Plan for the future: Read the news. Are interesting people who are worth profiles mentioned in news stories? Are briefs in the newspaper worth features? Are ideas tucked into a news story that need exploring or follow-up? Start your own idea file.

Visit the library: The local librarian is often a good source for information about the community.

Check bulletin boards: Visit the offices or agencies you cover, and read the notices on the bulletin boards. You will find notices for job openings and other interesting information that could lead to news and feature stories.

Check with your predecessor: If the person who previously covered your beat is still at the newspaper, ask for a briefing about the beat and for key sources.

Be a tourist: Visit the historical society, the chamber of commerce and other community agencies. Find the places of interest, and investigate what they were like years ago. You might develop angles for features. At the very least, you will gain some understanding of your community.

Press for news releases: Get on print and electronic mailing lists. Call the city or town clerk, and get the releases from your city and county government or from the agency you cover. Call the public relations officers of agencies and businesses in your community. Introduce yourself. Tell them you are interested in ideas for stories. It's their job to provide them. You don't have to use their handouts, but having them will give you ideas about what is happening in your community. Call agencies such as senior citizen organizations, the Red Cross, churches and social service organizations, and make sure that you are on their mailing lists for announcements, reports and news.

Find out who's in charge: Be kind to the folks who prepare the memos for officials. Get to know them, and use their names when you see them or call their offices. Talk to the janitors, the security guards and the people behind the scenes. They know what is going on, and they can be sources for tips. Meet the officials, of course, and then find out who heads the unions and professional organizations in the schools and government. The leaders of these organizations know what is going on behind the scenes. They also have stories from the workers' point of view. Use the up/down reporting principle: Go up and down the organizational ladder.

Hit records: Know how and where to find records. Start with the city or county clerk, who will direct you to municipal offices where records are available. Visit the courthouse, and familiarize yourself with the filing system there by asking the clerks for help. These are public records, and it's the clerks' job to serve the public. If your university is part of a state system, check records on campus or at the state level for fire inspection reports, police statistics or reports on environmental hazards.

Write a source book: Record names, telephone numbers and e-mail addresses for everyone you interview, call or meet on your beat. Develop a filing system and a cross-listing system. Put a memo after each name. If a source tells you something personal about a child or a family member who is ill, make a note and call in a few weeks to find out how the person is doing. Or mention the ill person the next time you talk to your source. Be thoughtful. Your source will appreciate your interest and be more receptive when dealing with you.

Join Internet discussion groups: You'll find journalism organizations related to your beat, and other resources, at *www.newslink.org/spec.html,* and many other resources at *journalismnet* (*www.journalismnet.com*), a comprehensive site created by Julian Sher, an investigative TV documentary producer and trainer of journalists around the world.

Covering Specialty Beats

You don't have to be a doctor to cover medicine or a scientist to cover the environment, but you do need to acquire knowledge of the subject in your beat. The challenge for writers of specialized subjects is to make the stories clear and to define the jargon so the average reader can understand the story.

The Education Beat

The education beat is one of the most diverse beats. It includes stories about budgets, stories about school board meetings, crime reporting, investigative reporting, statistics of test scores and enrollment, breaking news, and most of all news and features about what is happening in the schools. Stories about school life are often the most neglected because education reporters have so much to do to keep up with the school board and other administrative news.

A report commissioned a few years ago by the Education Writers Association found that readers want more education stories about substance and less about conflict. More than three-quarters of the public surveyed wanted news about academic standards, curriculum, school safety, innovative programs and quality of teachers, according to the report "Good News, Bad News: What People Really Think About the Education Press."

The Internet is providing education reporters with an opportunity to publish expanded coverage of their beats and offer some of the information that readers in the education survey wanted. Several major metropolitan newspapers offer complete Web packages about the schools in their communities. The packages feature interactive search engines that allow readers to search for test scores and other statistics for their schools.

Writing interesting stories about budgets and other technical education stories can be challenging. It requires all the skills of good writing that you have studied in other chapters, such as descriptive and expository techniques. In this award-winning story about schools in rural Alaska, called "Bush" schools and found in communities accessible only by airplane, the writers tackle a complex issue of funding and school evaluation by using a combination of descriptive and expository techniques:

Snow swirls around Bettles Field School in the Popsicle-blue light of a winter dawn.

Eight students sit at desks pushed into a circle, taking turns reading aloud from a novel. The other three classrooms are empty except for desks, chairs, cardboard boxes of books and a few computers.

All is quiet in the adjoining library, where 16-year-old Solomon Yatlin hunches in a cubicle wearing headphones and listening to the movie soundtrack "Strange Days" on a mini compact-disc player.

Solomon is the only high school student in what really should be a one-room schoolhouse.

"I'd rather go someplace bigger with a basketball team," Solomon says, looking up from his book. "It's too hard just working like this, I don't know, by yourself and all."

The Yukon Koyukuk School District is spending $19,094 this year to teach Solomon. The same is being spent on each of his eight classmates who started the school year.

Yet hundreds of millions of dollars after a landmark court settlement 20 years ago did away with mandatory boarding schools and put students like Solomon in village high schools, most graduates are ill-prepared for college and life. A diploma from a Bush school doesn't equal one from an urban campus.

The cost of Bush education is extreme and the obstacles are many. Outsiders unfamiliar with Native ways lead the classrooms. Social problems—alcoholism, child abuse, domestic violence—keep some students from learning. When students do succeed, graduating from high school or college, they find few jobs waiting in their villages.

Critics are taking note.

As the governor and Legislature wrestle with a budget shortfall, the decline in Alaska's mainstay oil industry, and education spending that outpaces inflation, Bush high schools are under more scrutiny than ever. Lawmakers wonder: Are Bush schools making the grade?

Wendy Hower and Kristan Kelly, Fairbanks *(Alaska)* Daily News-Miner

Here are some basic tips for covering the education beat:

- Check educational journals for trends and national comparisons of school performance.
- When writing about test scores or other school statistics, explain what they mean and how they affect students.
- Translate jargon.
- Make sure that you get into the schools to write stories about education.
- When you attend meetings, ask parents what they want to know about their schools.

You'll find scores of links to education resources and other stories online at the Education Writers Association Web site: *www.ewa.org.*

Health and Environmental Writing

Jonathan Bor, a medical writer for *The Sun* in Baltimore, covered crime, courts, politics and education before writing medical stories. "I learned how to convert the blather of educators, bureaucrats and cops into plain English before tackling doctor-speak," he says in an article in *Coaches' Corner,* a former publication for coaching writers. "And I learned to look first for stories about real people. I believe the hallmark of good medical writing is clear, colorful prose that takes the lay reader inside a world whose inhabitants—doctors, scientists and insurers—speak a secret language."

Good medical writing, in many ways, is simply good reporting and writing, Bor says. "It is thoroughly researched. It is written cleanly, and when possible, with a human touch. Bad medical writing, among other things, is written for insiders." Here is an excerpt from a story about a heart transplant operation that Bor wrote for his previous newspaper. He witnessed the operation and wrote the story on deadline after going without sleep for 48 hours.

MULTIMEDIA COACH

Before the Internet and electronic databases existed, newspaper stories were stored in resource rooms called "morgues." Today, with a click of a mouse, reporters can access more information on the Internet than at any time in history. The Internet should be your first stop when researching background for a story or compiling information for a beat.

- Join e-mail lists related to your beat. Request e-mail newsletters from public relations practitioners and other organizations related to your work in your community.

- Always search the Internet for background on people or topics you are covering.

- Join journalism organizations, such as the Society of Environmental Journalists, the Education Writers of America and others related to your beat.

- Create bookmarks to crucial sites, but save your bookmarks on a separate disk as well.

- Check government sites such as the U.S. Census and others for statistical and other information. Good starting places are *www.fedworld.gov* and *www.firstgov.gov.*

- Check journalism organizations and sites that compile links to resources. You'll find links to many of them in the Web sites for this book for Chapter 4 ("Sources and Online Research") and for this chapter.

He used the basic techniques of descriptive writing: show-in-action and details. Note how clearly he explains a complex procedure:

A healthy 17-year-old heart pumped the gift of life through 34-year-old Bruce Murray Friday, following a four-hour transplant operation that doctors said went without a hitch. . . .

The team—consisting of a surgeon, a physician's assistant and a nurse—removed the donor's heart at about 1:30 p.m. They placed it inside a plastic bag filled with an iced-saline solution, and they placed that bag inside three outer bags. The package was placed inside a blue beer cooler that bore the stamp "Transplant."

By the time their jet landed at Teterboro at 3 a.m., Murray was in the operating room where he was being prepped for surgery. Anesthesia put the patient into a deep sleep. A respirator breathed air into Murray's lungs via a tube inserted in his throat. Doctors cut a slit the length of Murray's chest. As many as a dozen doctors, nurses and technical assistants hovered over the patient, passing instruments, attending to heart monitors and swabbing the patient's bleeding chest.

Meanwhile, a state police escort ensured swift passage from Teterboro, over the George Washington Bridge and to the hospital for the vehicle carrying the transplant team and beer cooler. Within 10 minutes after landing, the transplant team was rushing the beer cooler through the hospital emergency room and up an elevator 18 floors.

By the time the heart arrived in the operating room, Murray's chest was wide open. Doctors had used a power saw to cut through his sternum, and a clamp-like retractor spread his chest apart. Murray's diseased heart, about half-again larger than normal, was fluttering inside the exposed chest cavity.

Surgeons swiftly turned the task of pumping blood over to the heart-lung machine. Their hands moving with quick deliberation, surgeons inserted tubes inside the heart's major blood vessels and severed the vessels from the heart.

The tangle of tubes carried the blood to a cylinder that supplied it with oxygen. From there, the blood traveled to a large console, which performs the job of the heart. Three spinning disks pumped the blood through the clear, plastic tubes back to the patient's body.

In one careful, spectacular moment, the surgical team made the exchange.

At 4:33 a.m., doctors lifted the diseased heart—milky but purple—out of Murray's chest cavity and handed it to attendants. They, in turn, placed it in the steel bowl. On a platform at the foot of the operating table, the spent heart rested for the duration. . . .

The beer cooler was opened, and the donor heart was placed inside the patient's chest. The new heart, about as large as a relaxed fist, was attached to the blood vessels.

It jerked and fluttered and became Bruce Murray's.

Jonathan Bor, The *(Syracuse, N.Y.)* Post-Standard

Bor offers these tips, which apply to all beats but are particularly useful for health and environmental stories:

- Challenge the source to speak to laymen. If that fails, allow the scientist to speak his language, but constantly challenge him with your version of the facts—"Are you saying that . . . ?"

- Never forget to ask your source the cosmic questions. What does the new treatment mean for the AIDS sufferer? Will this prolong life for days, months or more? Will the patient live longer but just as miserably, or what? Does a new medical finding represent an incremental advance or a true "breakthrough" that will change the lives of many people?

- Don't forget to give your story a sense of true proportion. If health inspectors have closed down an inner-city nursing home because of rodent infestation, it doesn't hurt to say that inspectors observed mice chewing on patients' feeding tubes and lapping the IV fluids that oozed out. If it's that bad, say it and say it vividly. Reporters need to say, however, whether the horror was an isolated finding or a condition observed throughout the nursing home.

- Anecdotes can be wonderful or tedious. At best, they bring to life the suffering of the afflicted, the benefits of new treatments or the breadth and social costs of an epidemic. At their worst, they turn a story into a tear-jerking soap opera worthy of a tacky TV-movie.

  When do anecdotes work? Perhaps they work when they vividly show the human side—the joy and suffering –of an issue. They also show the practical dimensions of a problem better than some doctor or bureaucrat spouting generalities.

- Metaphors can be nice, but they also can trivialize. I don't like stories that describe antibodies as little foot-soldiers engaged in hand-to-hand combat with disease-carrying bugs. I have seen this. Lacking something less trivial, I'd state the obvious: antibodies are substances produced by the body to fight infection.

Bor's tips apply to environmental writing as well. Stories about the environment and health have become so important that several universities are offering separate courses and programs in science writing. No single textbook chapter or portion of it can do justice to this subject. But as Bor says, these beats require the same reporting and writing techniques as any other stories.

Health writers need to be especially wary of the information offered on the Internet about diseases. Many Web sites are self-help information provided by people without medical authority, and others are offered by drug companies, which do not offer unbiased information. Check the ownership of the Web sites before you use information in a news story.

Environmental writers also have a wealth of resources available on the Internet. The Society of Environmental Journalists offers extensive links to resources and publications relating to environmental beats. You can link to it at *www.sej.org*. You can also read award-winning environmental stories linked to this site.

For four consecutive years, from 1994 to 1997, Pulitzer Prizes were awarded to environmental stories. The winners include extensive reporting and strong scientific background, but they all share good writing techniques. For example, in this excerpt from a series that won the 1997 Pulitzer Prize for public service, writer John McQuaid used a basic show-in-action descriptive lead followed by the nut graph:

Terry Shelley piloted his flat-bottomed boat through the sunlight one recent morning on his way to the oyster beds he depends on for a living. The marsh air was warming, but the wind had a sting to it and the water had taken on a wintry blue cast.

After beaching the boat, Shelley and his mate, Timmy Kirk, paused to orient themselves by the tidal eddies and southwest wind. Then they lumbered through the water, backs bent, their eyes scanning the marsh floor. Reaching down with gloved hands, they picked up oysters and tossed them into rowboats they pulled behind them.

The going was easy that morning. But it isn't always. Sometimes a fast-moving tide brings the water up to their necks. Sometimes the water recedes and they must drag the boats across desolate, wind-whipped mud flats.

Shelley can adapt to the changing mood of the marshes. It comes with the job.

But he and thousands of other fishers are helpless before man-made changes tearing across the Gulf of Mexico, leaving a swath of wrecked lives and ecological havoc in their wake.

Part of a global sea change in fishing, the forces include disappearing fish and marshlands, a flood of cheap imports and gill net bans. They threaten millions of livelihoods and the Gulf's unique fishing culture.

John McQuaid, The *(New Orleans)* Times Picayune

Business Writing

The Wall Street Journal, a newspaper devoted to business writing, is famous for its features. They just happen to be about business, financial and social trends. But the newspaper's style of writing has been emulated by newspapers all over the country for all types of stories.

In the early 1950s, *The Wall Street Journal* issued a memo to its writers about how features for the newspaper should be written. Many of the style guidelines in that memo are still applied today at this newspaper and at many others that have adopted the *Wall Street Journal* formula.

- The stories generally have one theme or point. This is usually put into a one- or two-paragraph nutshell summary high up in the story. Then the rest of the piece is made to hang together by harking back to this central theme. The story should be *clearly organized* or compartmentalized along the central thread of this theme—it should not meander around without a perceptible organization.

- We want to tell the story in terms of the *specific,* not in generalized or vague terms. One way we do this is to pack the story with lots of *detail.*

Gina Henderson, assistant business editor of *The Kansas City* (Mo.) *Star*, where the *Wall Street Journal* formula is applied to business stories as well as other types of stories

Another way we reduce the general situation to the specific is to give lots of colorful examples, anecdotes or small case histories to *illustrate* the overall situation we are describing.

We also lean heavily on illustrative *quotes*—attributable if possible though not necessarily so. The quotes need not be from government officials only; they could be from businessmen, shopkeepers, men-in-the-street, anyone who can shed some *color* on the situation or who can illustrate the general in specific, *individual terms.*

- Be sure to include all *background* the reader might need. We can assume no prior knowledge by our readers of the subject or of financial lingo. We try to spell out all situations *with super-simplicity and clarity*—from how France's inflation has been brought about over the years to the recent economic history of Australia and what led up to its present economic situation. Please explain everything in clear-cut fashion.

- We try to achieve very tight writing—short, punchy sentences and all essential information on the subject conveyed *concisely.*

- At the same time, these leaders aim at being pretty *thorough* studies of the particular subject or trend. This means the inclusion of all detail and background and interpretation mentioned above. It also means we take pains to make sure the story contains the answers to every question that the story and its statements are likely to raise in the reader's mind. We can't use a story that raises questions it does not answer, so please re-check copy for this possible pitfall—and again, be sure all points are fully and *clearly explained,* and solidly *nailed down with fact.*

Here is how that memo translates into stories currently being published by the newspaper. Notice that this business story starts with a specific example and proceeds to general nut graphs, which describe how the radio industry is trying to tackle competition from digital music players:

The Web site of radio station KCJK-FM, known as 105.1 Jack FM, features a picture of an iPod and the taunt: "Guess you won't be needing this thing anymore, huh?" After years of tight playlists and narrow music formats, KCJK in Kansas City, Mo., is trying to prove that it can give listeners the same thing an iPod does: an eclectic selection of music.

Previously, like most stations, 105.1 let computer scheduling programs pick the songs from a library of 300-400 titles, with the same 30-40 songs playing most of the time. Now the station is going against the grain of the past two decades in radio, more than tripling the number of song titles played on any given day. With more than 1,200 songs on the playlist, most songs get played only once every few days, rather than several times a day. Program director Mike O'Reilly and his assistants handpick the music and the order in which they are played.

"It's all about train wrecks," Mr. O'Reilly says, using radio terminology for two unlikely songs played back-to-back. "If you hear MC Hammer go into the Steve Miller Band, I've done my job." Indeed, the station boasts that it might play a grunge rock anthem by Nirvana alongside a disco hit by K.C. and the Sunshine Band—the kind of serendipitous combination offered by an iPod.

The station, owned by closely held Susquehanna Radio Corp., is attempting to tackle head-on a malaise that has the entire radio industry on the ropes. Radio has been an incredibly durable medium over the past seven decades, beating back challenges from new media and, as recently as five years ago, riding high on a vast consolidation that put tremendous power in the hands of a shrinking roster of large chains. Big owners sought benefits of scale through strategies like voice-tracking—having one set of deejays handle similar stations across several cities, playing the same songs at all of them.

But today, the industry is under attack from new competition that was barely on the horizon five years ago. Digital music players like Apple Computer Inc.'s iPod let listeners carry thousands of songs with them in a device the size of a pack of cigarettes. Satellite radio services like Sirius Satellite Radio Inc. and XM Satellite Radio Holdings Inc. are beginning to blossom, offering higher quality sound, a dearth of commercials and far deeper playlists than most broadcasters. Internet radio stations are siphoning off listeners by targeting small, devoted niches.

Sarah McBride, The Wall Street Journal

Sportswriting

Sportswriters have always had to rely on feature techniques of descriptive and interpretive writing, even more than other writers at a newspaper. Their readers may have seen the game, but they still want to read about it. Others who haven't seen the game want to know what happened. So sportswriters face the challenge of providing readers something more than the basic facts.

Unlike most news stories, where reporters rely on information from sources, sportswriters covering a game are witnessing the action first-hand. They have the responsibility for interpreting what they saw through interviews with coaches and players and their own analysis. They need to stress

Sports reporter Mike Lopresti filing a story from a game

angles: why and how the game was won or lost or what the strategy was. How was this game different from or similar to others?

But sports stories are not limited to game coverage. The range of topics on sports pages—profiles, trend stories and general sports features—is as broad as in any other section of the paper.

Years ago, sportswriters could rely on knowing their craft and writing primarily about games and the athletes. Today, they need to be as well-versed in court reporting and other fields as the reporters who cover the news because many stories involve athletes in legal contract disputes and court cases about drugs, violence and other criminal charges. Sportswriting also requires knowledge about games, leagues and style of sports scores. Check the Associated Press Stylebook for this information.

Some of the best writing in the newspaper—as well as some of the worst—can be found on the sports pages. Karen Brown Dunlap, president of The Poynter Institute, says all writers, especially those facing tight deadlines, could take some tips from sportswriters. She offers this advice:

- First, writers must see the same old story in different ways. . . . The characters and events in sports stories aren't necessarily more interesting than those in news stories. But in sports, more attention is paid to the people and the action. Personalities, motives and mannerisms are fleshed out to add color and meaning to stories.

- A second message from sportswriters is to keep your eyes on the story. "You can't look away when you're covering a sports story," said Merlissa Lawrence, a sportswriter for *The Pittsburgh Press*. "In that one moment something dramatic could happen."

Philip Meiring, *The University Daily Kansan*

- A third strategy is to write background information ahead of time and plan for likely eventualities. . . . It is a method commonly used by journalists covering major sports events on deadline.

- A fourth message is to give some thought to the best format for telling the story. Some games are worth only a box score. So are some meetings. Some stories require a brief; others need a long story or several textual and graphic elements.

- Finally, sportswriters write in ways that draw readers into stories. Often the readers know the score and have seen the event. The task for the writer then is to elucidate, analyze, amplify and soothe the reader with the pleasure of the words that recapture the event.

Many of the writing techniques that sportswriters use to accomplish those tasks are the same ones you have studied for other basic news, feature and specialty stories. The major difference is that sportswriters must stress interpretation, how and why, more than in basic news stories. Good sportswriters try to do that by setting a tone and developing their stories with a theme.

Here are some of the basic facts to include in game stories:

- Who played, where (stadium and city), when
- Score (placed high in the story)
- Major plays and players
- Turning points
- Injuries
- Important statistics (conference standing, records for season)
- Weather, if it had an effect on the game
- Crowd count, if relevant (fully packed stadium or sparse attendance)
- Outcome of previous games between these two teams, if relevant
- Comments from coaches and players to explain the how and why of the game

This example incorporates most of these elements:

Buffaloed!

Jayhawks' first-round loss is first since 1978

Oklahoma City—For many at the Ford Center, it was almost unimaginable.

Kansas University on Friday lost a first-round game in the NCAA Tournament—something the Jayhawks hadn't done since 1978, ending the Final Four dreams of a men's basketball team that started the season ranked No. 1 in the polls.

Third-seeded KU lost 64-63 to the Bucknell Bison, a 14th seed, after a last-second, 15-foot jump shot by Wayne Simien missed the mark.

"I don't know how many game-winning shots I made in my back yard growing up dreaming of being a Jayhawk," Simien said afterward, "and it just didn't work out this time."

A stunned pack of Jayhawk fans stood silently at the Ford Center after the game, then slowly filed out of the arena. Tears streamed down cheerleaders' faces.

"This is embarrassing," said Steve Flatt, a KU graduate from Devil Oak, Texas. "This is the biggest disappoint-

ment I've seen from KU since I started following the team in 1964."

Many of the fans leaving the game refused to discuss the loss.

"It's just disgraceful," said one who declined to give her name. "What more can you say?"

'Shock and disbelief'

Back in Lawrence late Friday night, KU fans soaked in the Jayhawks' early tournament exit with a mixture of anger, incredulity and sadness.

"Shock and disbelief," said Todd Rogers, a KU employee, as he took in the loss at Jefferson's, 743 Mass. "I've got nothing. I'm just stunned. I had no doubt going down to the wire that they were going to pull it out. I wasn't even thinking about them not advancing out of this weekend."

Some of that shock was certainly a consequence of Bucknell's status as David to KU's Goliath.

"I read something about them in the paper and I was like, 'Who is this team?'" said Kaitlin Harrell, KU senior.

But KU fans won't soon forget the Bison, the Patriot League champions from Lewisburg, Pa. Bucknell chal-

lenged the Jayhawks up and down the court, and never allowed the KU offense to settle in.

"We didn't really have an outside game tonight," said Megan Urquhart, a former KU softball player. "We tried to go inside all night long and get it to Wayne Simien. But you can't depend on just one guy."

Still, Urquhart thought the Jayhawks had a chance to win up until the clock expired.

"This whole season has been down to the wire. Almost every game has been won at the end," she said.

Second-guessing

Now, though, the season is over, leaving fans second-guessing what could have been.

"When they threw it down (to Simien), I thought he was going to hit it," said Casey Green, a KU senior. "I think he could have taken a dribble. I think he rushed it a little bit. . . ."

If fans were disappointed and angry, coach Bill Self seemed stunned.

"I don't know how I really feel," he said at a news conference after the game. "A little disappointed because we didn't have our best performance when it counted. I feel for the players because it has been such a taxing year, but give Bucknell credit. They played terrific."

The Bison advance to play Wisconsin at 3:50 p.m. Sunday in Oklahoma City. The Badgers advanced to the Round of 32 by defeating Northern Iowa 57-52 Friday evening.

The winner of Sunday's game will advance to the Sweet Sixteen in Syracuse, N.Y.

Terry Rombeck, Lawrence (Kan.) Journal-World

The article was accompanied by the following multimedia links on the newspaper's Web site:

(Video) 6Sports video: NCAA tourney ends for KU

(Audio of the coach's comments): Hear Bill: KU vs. Bucknell post-game comments

(Text) Stats: KU vs. Bucknell box score

(Text) Scorecard: Grade KU's performance against Bucknell

(Interactive) Talk about the game on our message boards

Mitch Albom, an award-winning sports columnist for the *Detroit Free Press,* says good writers need to be good readers. In an interview with The Poynter Institute after he won a distinguished writing award from the American Society of Newspaper Editors, Albom said the following:

> I read voraciously, and I don't read sports things. . . . The way you get better in your own field is by making sure you surround yourself with excellence in other fields. I've never forgotten that, and I've always tried to do that with writing. Watching good movies, reading great novels, seeing great plays all help you become a better sports writer. You just have to be open to absorb it.

Exercises

1   Using the *Wall Street Journal* formula, write a business feature about a trend in your community. For example, is business in your downtown area suffering or improving? Are stores closing or opening? Has a new business catering to students or other people opened in your community?

2   Choose a specialty subject of your choice— health, education, religion, sports, environment— and write a feature about a topic or program in this category.

3   Interview a beat reporter in the field that interests you. Write a story about the skills, tips, and reporting and writing techniques this reporter uses and recommends to other reporters in the field. Include specifics about problems the reporter faces on the job.

4   Choose a field of interest, and write a list of sources and government records available in this field on the Internet.

5   List the beats covered by your campus newspaper, and then list at least five beats that aren't covered but might be of interest to readers. Write a story from one of those beats.

6   Attend an athletic event at your college or university, and write a sports story.

Featured *News Scene* Assignment

Access *News Scene* at *http://communication.wadsworth.com/newsscene2* to view the news simulation titled "City Council Meeting," and write a news story.

Coaching Tips

Do your homework. Check clips and online sources for background about the speaker or issue at a conference or meeting.

Listen for what the speaker doesn't discuss. Then ask questions to find the answers that the readers (or viewers) will want.

Ask yourself whether the most interesting information came during a speaker's prepared comments or afterward. Then lead with that information.

Try to get as many good quotes as possible. Favor full quotes over partial ones.

Use graphics as a writing tool.

Write a highlights box—to accompany your story or to organize your story.

Speeches, News Conferences and Meetings

Mark Fagan calls himself a "converged reporter." Although he is primarily a print reporter for the *Lawrence Journal-World* in Kansas, when the newspaper's editors asked print reporters to appear on its cable TV station as well, Fagan took to it naturally. He says if you are a print or broadcast reporter, you are still applying the reporting and writing skills you already have. You're just learning a new way to use them. In the *Journal-World* newsroom, reporters from the TV station, 6 News, and the print newspaper work side by side. The multimedia desk in the center of the open atrium is the headquarters for coordinating stories for the newspaper, TV and Web sites.

When Fagan covers city government, he gets most of his news stories at meetings. But he gets most of his best quotes when the meetings end. Fagan, who has covered both government and business beats, says the most important part of a meeting story is what you cover before and after it.

One night the city commission was debating a zoning change. A business owner wanted to expand his electrical shop in a residential neighborhood. Commissioner Jo Andersen was angry. More business would bring traffic and crime to the neighborhood, she said.

Fagan headed straight for Andersen after the meeting. "Why were you so upset?" he asked.

"What I really wanted to say was that even if Jesus Christ himself wanted to expand his carpenter's shop in East Lawrence, we would respectfully request that he find another area that is more appropriate," she said.

"You can still say that," Fagan said. This is the beginning of the story he wrote the next day:

Not even divine intervention could help a proposal to expand an East Lawrence electric shop onto vacant lots next door.

During their meeting Tuesday night, Lawrence city commissioners denied a request from Patchen Electric & Industrial Supply Inc. to expand its 47-year-old business at 602 E. Ninth onto two lots zoned for apartments.

In the end, the request never had a prayer.

"If Jesus Christ himself wanted to expand his carpenter's shop in East Lawrence, we would respectfully request that he find another area that is more appropriate," Commissioner Jo Andersen said after the meeting. "It has nothing to do with a person's personality. It has everything to do with zoning."

Mark Fagan, Lawrence (Kan.) Journal-World

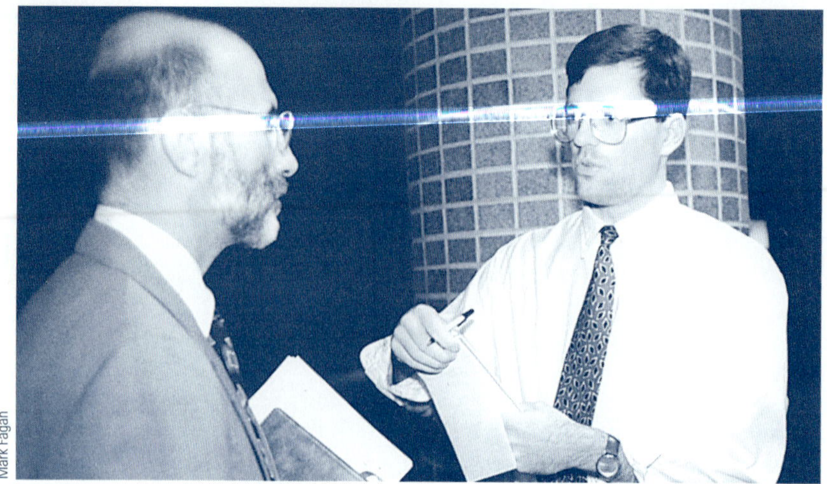

Mark Fagan (right) interviewing City
Commissioner John Nalbandian

The story continued with explanations of how zoning had changed from commercial to residential use since the business was built and why residents objected to its expansion.

"The comments officials make during a meeting are for public posturing," Fagan says. "Some of the best quotes you get are after the meeting when you ask them to explain why they did or said something."

That advice also applies to someone from the public who speaks at a meeting. "A person may speak for 30 seconds and afterward she'll tell you, 'My kid needs a safe place to walk because he was attacked two years ago,'" Fagan says. "Don't just sit in the meeting if the person leaves; follow him or her out and get those additional comments."

What you write before the meeting is even more important, Fagan says. He writes at least one story to tell readers what officials will discuss at their next meeting. If people don't know what officials plan to do, they won't get a chance to participate in government.

Although many newspapers are curtailing meeting coverage because the news is sometimes dull, Fagan thinks that's a mistake. Meetings are where officials make decisions that affect the public.

Fagan goes to at least three meetings a week: the commission's public meeting; its study meetings, where officials decide what they will discuss at public meetings; and neighborhood group meetings to learn what people are really concerned about.

"I'll write stories sometimes and no one (from the public) will show up at a meeting, and I wonder if what I do makes a difference. Then a city commissioner will say, 'I got about 20 phone calls after your article.' So I know people are reading them."

Even if people don't read his stories or attend the meetings, Fagan thinks it's important for reporters to be there as watchdogs for the public. He says the officials know he is really there for 20,000 other people: his readers.

"I put the commissioners' comments in the paper, and everyone knows where they stand," Fagan says. "That's a great power of the press."

Whenever you are covering a meeting, it's important to look beyond what officials say publicly. Fagan says reporters should ask questions before and after the public event to find out how the story affects readers.

"An item on a meeting agenda may say they are going to award bids for highway improvements on North Second Street," he says. "I look at that and say, 'What does that mean?' Are they going to widen the street? This is the only artery that connects downtown and an old neighborhood. Are they going to close the road to traffic for eight months? This is how officials plan to spend taxpayers' money. You need to find out how it affects readers."

Fagan has also covered plenty of speeches and news conferences on his beat, especially when he is writing about elections. Many of the reporting and writing principles for those events are the same as they are for meetings. Don't just write what the officials say; find out why they are making certain comments or decisions and what the impact will be for readers.

Media Manipulation

Sources who give speeches or conduct news conferences are often using the media to further their own causes. There's nothing wrong with that. It's a way of presenting news. But a responsible reporter should ask good questions after the speech or news conference and add points of view from opposing sources when possible.

For example, Operation Rescue, an anti-abortion group, waged massive demonstrations to close an abortion clinic in Wichita, Kan. The sources from that group had a definite agenda; they were clearly trying to manipulate the press, says Steven A. Smith, former managing editor of *The Wichita* (Kan.) *Eagle.* One of the leaders of Operation Rescue conducted a news conference during which he held up a fully developed fetus, which supposedly had been aborted at about seven or eight months. Smith says the situation posed a difficult ethical dilemma for the *Eagle* staff. The leader's actions were news. But there was no evidence that the fetus had been aborted at the Wichita clinic. The result: The *Eagle* published news about the protest and the leader's actions, including the statement that there was no proof the fetus came from the Wichita clinic. But the paper did not publish a picture of the fetus. Smith says he was convinced the situation was staged to manipulate the press. Television stations also refused to show the fetus.

Protesters on both sides of the abortion issue came from around the nation to converge on Wichita, and 2,600 of them were arrested for violating city laws and defying court orders prohibiting them from blocking the abortion clinic. Both sides sought to manipulate the press. Smith says the newspaper tried so hard to give balanced coverage that some of the editors

A Roman Catholic priest, leader of the pro-life group called the Lambs of Christ, being arrested after attempting to block the entrance to the Women's Health Care Center in Wichita, Kan.

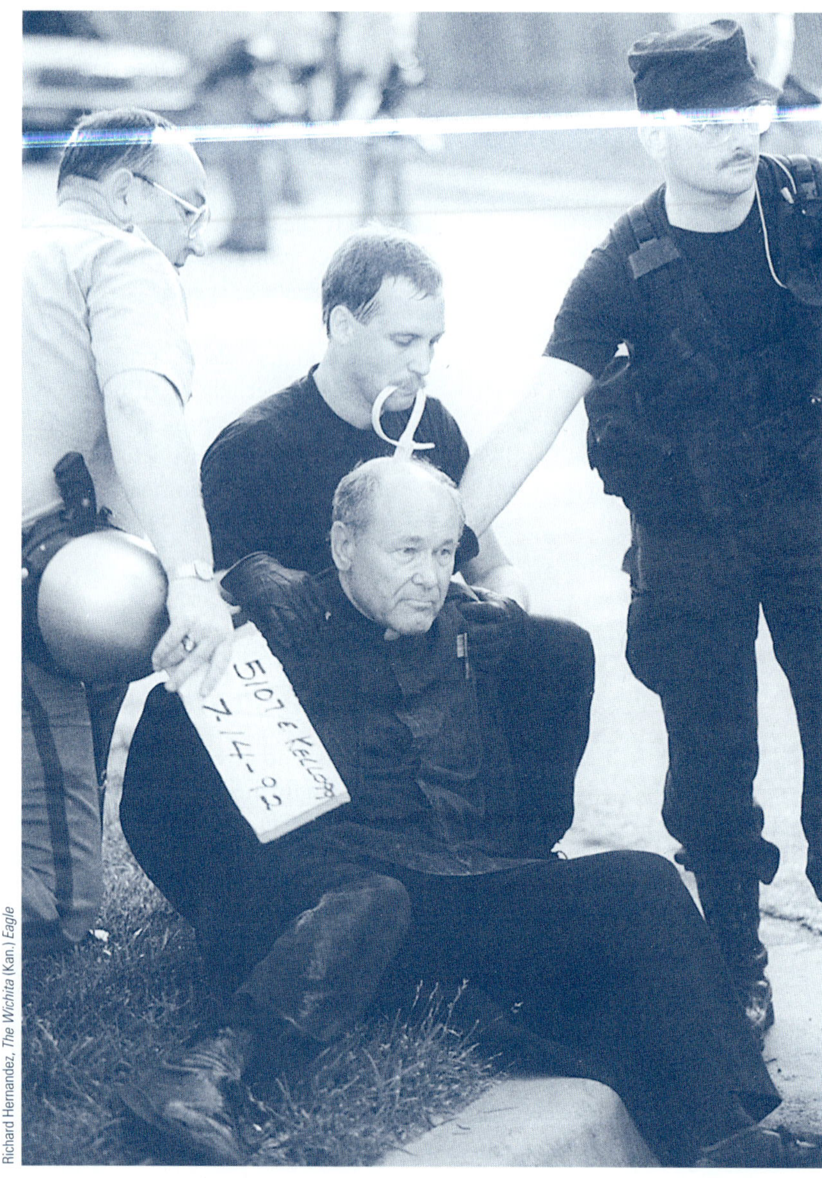

Richard Hernandez, *The Wichita (Kan.) Eagle*

actually measured the number of inches of type given to the pro-choice and anti-abortion sources to make sure that they had equal treatment.

The problems of manipulation were even greater for the three local television stations. Operation Rescue leaders staged their news conferences shortly before the 5 p.m. newscasts in hopes of receiving live coverage from television. News directors, concerned about issues of accuracy and fairness, limited the live coverage. They edited the tape to be shown at the end of the 5 p.m. newscasts or only on the 10 p.m. programs so that they could have more control and present balanced viewpoints.

ETHICS

The case: Your beat is city government for a convergod news organization, which sends you to write a story about a city council meeting for both print and broadcast, and sends with you a television camera crew to videotape the meeting. The city is going to approve an agreement with a city in Japan to become its "sister city," which will open some trade agreements and business opportunities for your city with Japan. The mayor is planning to visit the Japanese city; his trip will be funded by your city.

He is planning to take his secretary, whose trip will also be covered by city funds. Rumors have circulated for some time that the mayor, who is married, is having an affair with his secretary. He has denied that the rumors are true, but you are convinced they are. Will you print these rumors in your story about the mayor's trip? How will you write the story?

Ethical guidelines The Society of Professional Journalists Code of Ethics offers these guidelines:

- Seek the truth and report it. Journalists should be honest, fair and courageous in gathering, reporting and interpreting information.

- Test the accuracy of information from all sources and exercise care to avoid inadvertent error. Deliberate distortion is never permissible.

- Show good taste. Avoid pandering to lurid curiosity.

Preparation

Most speeches, news conferences and meetings do not pose such severe problems. Still, reporters always need to do more than listen and repeat what they hear. As Mark Fagan suggests, reporters need to ask good questions after the event as well.

To ask good questions, however, you must prepare for the event. You need to find out all you can about the speaker and the issue. Be sure to check the clips and online databases.

With a prominent speaker, you can often get the text of the speech in advance. But be careful not to rely on it. The speaker may depart from the prepared text. However, you can still use the prepared text. Just say, "The speaker said in prepared remarks" or "in a written text." Reporters sometimes have to rely on the written version, especially if their deadlines come before the speech or news conference is over.

During the speech, try to get full quotes of the important points (especially if they vary from the written text), and jot down reactions of the speaker and the audience. Note when and if the speaker shows emotion and how the audience responds. Write follow-up questions to ask the speaker after the speech or news conference.

Try to get an aisle seat. If someone asks a good question after the speech or meeting and then leaves, you should follow that person out of the room quickly so you can check the name and get more information.

Stories About Speeches

Your story should always include some basic information:

- Size of the audience
- Location of the speech
- Reason for the speech
- Highlights of the speech, including good quotes
- Reaction of the audience, especially at dramatic points during the speech

Although you need to include this basic information, don't clutter the top of your story with it—unless it is crucial to the event. Write the story just as you would any other good story.

You can lead with a hard-news approach that emphasizes a main point the speaker made or a soft-news approach that describes the person or uses an anecdote from the speech. Just don't lead with a no-news approach: Someone made a speech. Tell the reader what the speaker said.

For example, here is the kind of lead to avoid; this one appeared on a story in a campus newspaper:

> Students from Gay and Lesbian Services spoke yesterday to a psychology class about their lives and experiences.

What did they say? It's better to focus on some interesting point they made.

Speakers usually don't make their strongest points first and follow in chronological order, so your story shouldn't be written in that order. Put the most emotional or newsworthy information first. Then back it up with quotes and supporting points.

Sometimes the most interesting information isn't what happens during the speech. It can be what happens after the speech or outside the place while the person is speaking, especially if there is a protest or other major reaction to the speech.

In most cases, the audience is a minor part of a speech story. But in the next example, the people who came to protest the speech were more newsworthy than the speech itself:

> Five gay-rights activists were arrested Saturday after disrupting a speech by U.S. Rep. William Dannemeyer at a seminar on "The Preservation of the Heterosexual Ethic."
>
> While the five were handcuffed with plastic restraints after entering Power Community Church, 1026 S. East St., to disrupt the seminar, about 100 other activists picketed on the sidewalk shouting "bigot" and "hate-monger."
>
> Dannemeyer, R-Fullerton, who announced his candidacy for the U.S. Senate, shrugged off the protest, saying, "I've reached the point in my political career that if I'm not picketed, I really haven't had a good day."

Before the interruption, Dannemeyer urged an audience of about 120 people to support laws requiring doctors to notify health officials of patients who test positive for AIDS.

Scott Thomsen, The Orange County *(Calif.)* Register

You can also use storytelling techniques for speeches. In the next example, a journalism student used narrative and descriptive writing to convey the drama of a speech by a survivor of the Holocaust. Notice where the writer put the basic information: when, where and how many people attended the speech.

Zev Kedem huddled in silence with his grandparents in a pigeon coop above his family's apartment while soldiers searched for them. His grandparents were prepared to swallow vials of poison as the soldiers tried the metal door they hid behind. The door held. And the soldiers went on.

The year was 1942, and so begins Zev Kedem's story of survival that began over 50 years ago as Adolf Hitler orchestrated the Holocaust.

A "Schindler's List" survivor, Kedem spoke for over an hour as he told the story of his childhood in a Nazi concentration camp to 750 people in the Union Ballroom last night.

Gail Johnson

Here is a basic speech story that starts with a summary lead followed by a backup quote in the third paragraph. Note that the basics of location, audience size and reaction are lower in the story.

Reporter notes lower standards in journalism

Half of the reporting duo that unearthed the Watergate scandal, which led to the downfall of President Nixon, railed Saturday against what he characterized as another downfall: the media's fascination with the "loopy and lurid."

Former *Washington Post* reporter Carl Bernstein took aim at trash television, inaccurate reporting and media monopolies, primarily that of mogul Rupert Murdoch. The media are fascinated with celebrity, gossip and manufactured controversy, and pander to viewers and readers, adding to the "triumph of trash culture," he said.

"The greatest threat to the truth today may well be in our own profession," said Bernstein, who spoke for more than an hour at Budig Hall. His speech was sponsored by Kansas University's Student Union Activities.

Although every society has an "idiot subculture bubbling beneath the surface," Bernstein said a constant diet of certain television talk shows—he twice declared Jerry Springer's show to be the worst of the worst—could cause it to boil over.

The problem needs to be addressed at the root level, with reporters refusing to limit their horizons and keep digging for the "best obtainable version of the truth," he said.

"Really great reporting almost always comes from the initiative of the reporter, not the editor," said Bernstein.

Chris Koger, Lawrence *(Kan.)* Journal-World

Stories About News Conferences

News conferences are like speeches, except that the questions reporters ask after a news conference are often more important than the prepared comments the speaker makes. The answers to those questions are an important

MULTIMEDIA COACH

The Internet has made reporters' jobs easier for background research, even for meeting stories. For example, Elkton, Ky., calls itself a "slow-paced town" and has fewer than 2,000 citizens. Yet it is sophisticated enough to post all its city council agendas and minutes on the Web: *www.elktonky.com.* Here are some tips for meetings, speeches and news conferences:

- **Meeting stories:** Check to see if your community posts its agenda and previous meeting minutes on the Web. You can research background for continuing issues. Also, if the city or town has a Web site, you can check it for sources, population and other relevant information you may need before or after a meeting.

- **Speech stories:** Always check the Web for background on a speaker. If the speaker has written papers, you may find them on the Web. If the speaker is an author, check *www.amazon.com* for a summary of his or her books.

- **News conferences:** You can't anticipate some news conferences, especially if they are in response to a disaster or school shooting, for example. But you can check the Web after the conference for relevant information such as other school shootings, airplane crashes or related information that would help your readers.

part of the story—and sometimes are the story. Consider news reports after the U.S. president conducts a news conference. His prepared remarks are often less interesting than his answers to the press corps.

Stories about news conferences must include certain pieces of information:

- Person who conducted the news conference
- Reason for the news conference and background
- Highlights of the news, including responses to questions
- Location, if relevant
- Reaction from sources with similar and opposing points of view

Stories about news conferences are like most other news stories. Although reporters' questions may prompt the most interesting information, the answers are usually incorporated into the story without references such as "In response to a question" or "When asked about. . . ." The main elements for coverage of a news conference are included in this story:

CINCINNATI—The mayor declared a state of emergency and announced a citywide curfew as riots over the police shooting of an unarmed black man stretched into a fourth day today.

Only people going to and from work will be allowed on the streets between 8 p.m. and 6 a.m., Mayor Charles Luken said.

"Despite the best efforts of the good citizens of our city, the violence on our streets is uncontrolled and it runs rampant," Luken said at a news conference at City Hall.

"The time has come to deal with this seriously. The message . . . is that the violence must stop."

Officials in the city of 331,000 have considered asking the state to call out the Ohio National Guard, but no decision had been made, Luken said.

A White House news conference

The fatal shooting over the weekend of Timothy Thomas, 19, by a white officer sparked days of unrest, a federal investigation, and calls for accountability. Thomas was killed as he fled Officer Steven Roach, who was trying to arrest him for failing to appear for misdemeanor charges and traffic violations. Roach's union said he feared for his life during the encounter.

Tensions between blacks and police have heightened over the past few years Since 1995, 15 black men died at the hands of police, including four since November. . . .

Small groups of vandals roamed several neighborhoods Wednesday night and early today, breaking windows, looting stores and assaulting at least one white motorist who was dragged from her car, police said. Others in the neighborhood came to the woman's aid. . . .

At least 66 people have been arrested on such charges as disorderly conduct, criminal rioting, obstruction, felony assault, theft and breaking and entering since the violence began Monday. . . .

A man interrupted Luken at the news conference to ask whether the mayor was ready to meet with a group calling itself the New Black Panthers. He was pulled out of the room after shouting that the mayor was a "liar."

"That's the kind of incivility we've been dealing with," Luken said.

Liz Sidoti, The Associated Press

Stories About Meetings

The decisions that affect readers' daily lives—such as where they take their trash, get their water and send their children to school—are made by local government officials at meetings. Yet meeting stories are often written without explaining their real impact on the reader.

Countless surveys conducted by newspapers and news organizations reveal that local news is near or at the top of the list of the kinds of stories readers want. They just don't read them all the way to the end. Sometimes they don't read past the lead, especially when the lead is dull.

The stories don't have to be boring. They may not be as compelling as a story about a murder trial. But they can be written with flair and with an emphasis on the meeting's significance to readers.

All states have open-meeting laws requiring officials who have the authority to spend public funds to conduct their business in public. These boards may conduct executive sessions behind closed doors for certain discussions, such as personnel matters or collective bargaining, but all decisions must be made in a public meeting. Although open-meeting laws vary from state to state, most of them require public agencies to give advance notice—usually 48 hours—of their meetings and to conduct public hearings.

Understanding the System

When a board makes a decision at a meeting, you need to understand what kind of authority that board has. Suppose you are covering a zoning board meeting. The board is discussing a zoning application from a developer for a major shopping center. If the board approves a zoning change, is that the final decision? Probably not. Most zoning boards are advisory and must submit their recommendations to a city or county board of officials for final approval. When you write the story, that is essential information to include.

If you are covering meetings of your university administration, find out who can make the decisions and which boards are advisory. Who can raise the tuition—school officials or a board of regents? Is the action taken at a meeting a recommendation or a ruling? You need to explain the system as well as the next step in an action, as in this story:

The borough is trying to outlaw outhouses in neighborhoods that already have sewer and water hookups.

A measure, which doesn't apply to existing outhouses, was spurred by a neighborhood dispute and is being proposed by Fairbanks North Star Borough Assembly member Bonnie Williams.

"We should be maturing and civilizing as a community and say, 'Here are your choices, and outhouses are not on the list,'" Williams said at a meeting last week.

The ordinance says that if you've got the sewer line, either hook to the sewer or put in a septic system. No more privies.

The dispute that reportedly brought the issue to light is occurring in the Totem Park subdivision, located off College Road near University Avenue.

Jeff Bovee, a 43-year-old entrepreneur, grew up in that neighborhood. He delivered newspapers as a child to people he's known his whole life and are still his neighbors.

He lives at and runs a plumbing business from the house where he was raised. He's been buying parcels of land in the neighborhood, recycling structures and turning them into rental properties that he puts on the parcels. The neighborhood is peppered with unusual structures, such as a bus that was painted blue and turned into a dwelling.

Some of the rentals have modern plumbing, some don't, and the residents use outhouses.

Bovee's neighbors are concerned about his aesthetic judgment with the structures and about sewage from the outhouses seeping into the water table. . . .

The measure that would stop Bovee from putting up more outhouses was passed unanimously by the borough planning commission in February.

The borough assembly is accepting public comment on the issue Thursday and could vote on it.

Amanda Bohman, Fairbanks *(Alaska)* Daily News-Miner

Writing the Advance

Many times, knowing what is going to happen at a meeting is more important to readers than knowing what did happen. A story that tells readers what is being proposed can alert residents to make their concerns known before a measure is adopted by local officials. A pre-meeting story is called an "advance."

An advance is especially crucial if local officials are planning to conduct a public hearing about an issue. If the public doesn't know about it, how can the public be heard?

City and school boards usually publish an agenda in advance of their meetings. This agenda lists the items to be discussed, although new items can and usually are presented.

When you receive an agenda, look through it for items that might be of special interest to readers. Call board members and ask for comments, or ask them to pick out the items they expect to be most interesting or controversial. If the issue has previously been in the news, check clips and call other interested parties.

The point of your advance is to inform readers about items that they may want to discuss during the public comment part of a meeting or just to let readers know what their officials are proposing. If you are writing an advance for a public hearing, make sure that you give the time and location of the hearing.

Here is an example of an advance with an impact lead:

> For the first time in its 107-year history, Temple University may require all undergraduates to take a course related to race and racism.
>
> The proposal, which grew out of black students' demonstrations at Temple, is to be debated by the school's faculty senate on Friday.
>
> Among the faculty, however, the proposal has already sparked intense discussion. The debate mirrors that of other campuses—including Stanford, Wisconsin, Michigan and Berkeley—where courses related to race are required.
>
> *Huntly Collins,* The Philadelphia Inquirer

The following excerpt from an advance includes the time and location of the meeting:

> The stage is set for changing the city's human relations ordinance to include protections for homosexuals.
>
> Lawrence city commissioners agreed to set ground rules for public comment on a proposal to add the words "sexual orientation" to the city's anti-discrimination ordinance.
>
> The ground rules—such as how long people will be allowed to speak—will be determined during next week's meeting, which begins at 6:35 p.m. Tuesday at City Hall, Sixth and Massachusetts streets. A draft form of the ordinance is planned for a vote one week later on April 25.
>
> *Mark Fagan,* Lawrence (Kan.) Journal-World

Covering the Meeting

Arrive early. Find out the names of board members (usually they have nameplates), and find out who is in charge.

Ask board members, especially the head of the board, if you can talk to them after the meeting. If you know people in the audience who are leaders of a group favoring or opposing a controversial issue, greet them and tell them you would like to get comments after the meeting.

Check items on the agenda, and get any background that you need.

Check the consent agenda, a list of items on the agenda that the board will approve without discussion. They may include bids for approval or other points the board may have discussed in work sessions. A "gem" of a story may be buried in the consent agenda.

One reporter wondered why the school board had approved $30,000 in "token losses." That's a lot of money to be considered "token" losses. She discovered that it represented losses of bus tokens that the school board sold to students who had to ride public buses because there were no school buses in the city. Why $30,000 in losses? The school district had no system of monitoring the sales, and the money had been stolen at several schools. By school officials! The board didn't want to discuss this item publicly, so it was buried in the consent agenda. But the reporter wanted to discuss it. In a front-page story.

Don't remain glued to a seat at a press table. When members of the audience give public comments, get their names and more comments. Many times they will leave immediately after their testimony. Follow them out of the meeting. You can catch up with the action inside later. Or sit in the audience. Sometimes the comments of people attending the meeting are more interesting than the ones the board members make.

Stay until the end, unless your deadline prohibits staying. The most important issue could emerge at the end of a meeting when the board asks for new business or public comments. Or something dramatic could happen. The mayor could resign. Violence could erupt. You never can tell, especially if you're not there.

Writing the Story

First, how not to write it: Do not say the city council met and discussed something. Tell what they discussed or enacted. This is the kind of lead to avoid:

> The 41st Annual Environmental Engineering Conference met yesterday at the Kansas Union to discuss solutions to environmental problems.
>
> Representatives of the Kansas Department of Health and Environment, the Environmental Protection Agency and other organizations spoke to about 180 people who attended the conference.

So what did they say? This lead reveals nothing.

Some meetings are long. They can be boring. Avoid telling the reader how much you suffered listening to board members drone on and accomplish nothing in a long meeting. The reader doesn't care how much you suffer. The reader wants the news. If the length of the debate is crucial to the story, you should include it. But if the meetings are usually long and the time element is not a major factor related to the focus, don't mention it.

Here are some points to include in your story:

Type of meeting and location: But if the city council or school board meets all the time in the same building, don't mention the location.

The vote on any major issue: For instance, say "in a 4–1 vote. . . ." If the issue is particularly controversial, say who voted against it—or for it, if an affirmative vote was more controversial. If the measure was approved unanimously, say so. However, don't give the vote for every minor item.

The next step: If a major issue or ordinance cannot be adopted until a public hearing is conducted, tell readers when a hearing is scheduled or what the next step is before the action is final.

Impact on readers: Explain how the decision will affect them.

Quotes: But use only quotes that are dramatic, interesting or crucial to the story.

Background of the issues: What do readers need to know to understand what has happened?

To write the story, select one key issue for the focus. If the board approved several other measures, add them at the end: "In other business." If several important actions occurred, consider breaking another key issue into a separate story, if possible. If not, try a lead mentioning both items, or put the second key point in the second paragraph and give supporting background later, after you have developed the first point—for example, "City commissioners yesterday approved plans for the city's first shopping mall but rejected plans for a new public golf course." Then proceed with the discussion about the shopping mall.

Consider advancing the story with a second-day lead, also known as an updated lead. This kind of advance tells readers what the next step is or how the story will affect them. In most newspapers, this type of lead is becoming more popular because it makes the news more timely. However, it is optional, and a first-day lead may be acceptable. For broadcast, however, an updated lead is crucial. Viewers don't want to know what happened yesterday or last night; they want to know what is happening now. If your story will appear first on the Web, you also have to consider updating the lead for a print publication that will be published the next morning. As more news organizations become convergent, these skills of updating and providing impact for readers and viewers will become essential.

Although many meeting stories are written with summary leads, especially if the news is significant, they do not have to follow that form. If you think a softer lead is appropriate for the type of news that occurred, you can use it.

Here are some more writing tips:

- Use the tell-a-friend technique to make the story readable. This technique is especially helpful with stories about meetings

- Remember the kiss-off technique if you have three or more sources: Block comments from a single speaker in one place, and don't use the source again. However, the mayor or another well-known official may be used as a source intermittently.

A few matters of style:

- *Board* is a collective noun and therefore takes a singular verb: The board discussed the issue at *its* meeting, not *their* meeting. If this approach seems awkward in your story, say that the board *members* said *their* next meeting would be Tuesday.

- Capitalize *city council, city commission* and *school board* when they are part of a proper name—such as the Rockville City Commission—and when the reference is to a specific commission in your town—the City Commission. If you are not specifying a particular city commission, do not capitalize the term.

- Capitalize the titles of board members or other officials when they come before the name, as in *Mayor John Corrupt.* If the title follows the name—*John Corrupt, the mayor*—use lowercase letters.

- For votes, use *3–1,* not *3 to 1.*

Stories about meetings can take a hard, soft or advance-impact approach. Whichever one you use, make the story relevant to readers. Here's how:

Summary lead: what happened	LAGUNA BEACH, Calif.—Despite neighbors' objections, a North Laguna Beach couple were given permission Tuesday to adorn their home with a 17-foot-high outdoor sculpture of 30 water heaters and two house trailers.	
Vote	The City Council, after viewing a scale model of the artwork, voted 3-1 to endorse the sculpture. It will climb around a pine tree in the back courtyard of Arnold and Marie Forde's home.	
Dissenting vote	Mayor Neil Fitzpatrick dissented, saying the sculpture infringed on neighbors' views. Councilwoman Martha Collison was absent.	
Reaction	"It's a victory for the freedom of expression," said Los Angeles artist Nancy Rubins, who will craft the sculpture. "It would have been a sad day if a community that sees itself as supporting the arts struck down an artwork in a private yard."	
	The sculpture had been the focus of an intense neighborhood battle.	***Impact: so what***
	Residents who live near the Fordes have called the sculpture junk and complained that the artwork would block their view and spoil the neighborhood character.	
	David DeLo, who lives across Cliff Drive from the Fordes, said he was considering challenging the council's action in court.	***More reaction***
	"If the council wants to place a piece of junk in a residential neighborhood, that's their prerogative, but this council has been overturned before," he said.	***Next step***
	To appease neighbors, the council approved the sculpture on the condition	***Backup: conditions of council action***

that the Fordes place it as low as possible in the yard and landscape the area with another tree and a hedge. The additional plants should hide the sculpture from neighbors, officials said.

The $5,000 sculpture will take a week to build. Rubins said she did not know when it will be finished.

Harrison Fletcher, The Orange County *(Calif.)* Register

Future kicker

Exercises

1 **Speech story:** If possible, cover a speech on campus or in the community. If not, you can write a story based on this speech about political correctness by Burl Osborne, former editor of *The Dallas Morning News.* The speech is posted on this book's Web site at *http://communication.wadsworth.com/rich5e.*

2 **Online speeches:** You'll find many speeches online in text and audio form. If your computer has audio capacity, listen to one of the speeches and write a story. Links to these resources are available on the Web site for this chapter. If you have never read the spoof graduation speech by Kurt Vonnegut, access it online for this chapter and write a story based on it.

Featured *News Scene* Assignment

Access *News Scene* at *http:// communication.wadsworth.com/ newsscene2* to view the news simulation "Big Fire," and write a news story.

Coaching Tips

Write an impact, "so what" sentence on top of your story.

Try impact leads; your impact sentence could be a lead.

The more complex the information, the simpler your sentences should be.

Avoid jargon.

Write for your readers, not your sources.

Use quotes that advance the story, not the egos of the bureaucrats.

Use analogies to help readers understand numbers.

Think about graphics before you write your story. Use charts for numbers and empowerment boxes for information to help the reader.

Plan online links for your stories.

Government and Statistical Stories

Robert Zausner, reporter,
The Philadelphia Inquirer

Robert Zausner is walking through a hall in the Pennsylvania Capitol complex in Harrisburg when he sees two men changing a light bulb in a ceiling fixture. Zausner stops, observes and takes a few notes. Is this a story for a reporter who covers the legislature?

It is if you have Zausner's eye for news. It is if you want to show taxpayers how their money is spent:

How many state employees does it take to change a light bulb?

Only two.

But they also need a $9,447 machine to reach the socket, at least in part of the east wing of the Capitol complex. . . .

Although the massive building has been opened for more than two years, there was not until recently any way to reach some of the light fixtures, particularly those situated in the middle of the expansive glass ceilings and far away from any walls.

"With the new wing, there isn't anything to lean a ladder against," explained Pamela DeSalvo, press secretary for the Department of General Services.

To help shed light, the department bought a "hijacker," a device that is able to straddle obstacles on the ground—like the Senate's granite-encased fountains—and hoist a bulb changer to heights up to 40 feet.

How did the state change those bulbs before it got the machine?

It didn't.

It takes two workers to change a light bulb using the hijacker, one to screw in the bulb and the other to watch.

Robert Zausner, The Philadelphia Inquirer

Zausner, a reporter for *The Philadelphia Inquirer,* says he tries to let readers know how government works and how it affects them, especially because their money is involved. "I think you have to keep your eyes open on this kind of beat. Some of the stuff that happens around here is unbelievable.

"Every Monday I ride the elevator to the fourth floor of the Senate offices and just visit people. Usually by the time I hit the ground floor again, I've got something. I think you need to do the legwork to know what's really going on. If you write from a press release, you may have the story, but you won't have more than a surface understanding of something."

Stories about government often involve money and statistics. Although these are hard stories to write, Zausner says he tries to make his stories readable by using simple terms that people can understand. "You have to make them read it," he says. "Spit it back in simple terms that people can understand. It's safer to use the bureaucrats' terminology. It's easy. It's lazy. Someone introduces a bill, you get three quotes, and you have a story. But if you just regurgitate the stuff in the bureaucratic language, you lose everyone."

Another way of making stories readable and relevant is to focus on the people affected, as in this example from when Zausner was covering former Gov. Robert Casey:

> For the last 20 years, Mark Holmes has worked for the state. He has enjoyed his $45,000-a-year job as a telecommunications expert and the other major benefit that came with government employment—security.
>
> But now Holmes is wondering how he will support his wife and nine children, how he will keep his oldest in college. He is pondering food stamps. He thinks about the sudden predicament he finds himself in at the age of 43. And then, offering an apology, he starts to cry.
>
> Holmes is one of the 2,450 people behind the numbers. He will be out of work by month's end under a dismissal plan being put into effect to reduce a deficit approaching $1 billion. The firings, ordered by the governor, are estimated to save $154 million this fiscal year.
>
> *Robert Zausner,* The Philadelphia Inquirer

The reporter has a responsibility to interpret government for the reader, Zausner says: "If a guy announces that he's introducing a bill, but he's only trying to score some political points and you know the bill is not going anywhere, you have to say that. If you write that story and you don't say what he really wants, you are doing people a disservice. You'd be better off not to write it. I don't think it's editorializing. I think it's serving the reader."

Reporting Tips

Zausner's advice is not limited to coverage of state government. His emphasis on making government relevant to readers applies as well to stories about local government, school districts and campus administrations.

Although much government news may come from news releases and meetings, you should also try to find stories that reveal how the government operates or fails to operate in the interests of citizens. Don't just rely on officials to give you news; find it yourself.

Here are some basic tips for covering local government:

Human interest: Make government relevant to readers by finding people who are affected by the actions of government agencies.

Bulletin boards: Check them for job offerings and other announcements that could result in stories.

Memos and letters to and from city officials: Check with the city clerk or administrative assistants for access to files about any issue involving public funds. Most of these—except for personnel and labor matters—are public record.

Planning commission: Check agendas for meetings, and develop sources in planning offices. Seek information not only about future plans but also about the past. Some great stories can result from plans gone awry.

Consultants: Check who gets consulting contracts and fees, and investigate previous studies on the same subject. Sometimes, government agencies hire consultants to write studies on subjects that have already been studied frequently.

Zoning meetings: They can be full of human interest. People care about what is going up or down in their neighborhood.

Legal notices: Check them for bids and other notices. Government agencies must advertise for any major purchases. Check with disgruntled bidders for major contracts. Many good stories lurk behind these seemingly boring subjects.

Audits: Read them carefully. They can reveal misuse of public funds.

Union leaders: Cultivate heads of unions in school districts and cities as sources. They know what is going on behind the scenes.

Nonofficials: Talk to the people who do the work. In school districts, get into the schools and write about what teachers and students are doing. In cities, talk to people on the job. Spend some time learning about what they do, how they do it and whether they do it. Many good stories can result from finding out how lower-level employees work in government.

The system: Learn how it works. Are officials in your town following the laws? If you don't know how government is supposed to operate, you won't be able to find out if it is working properly.

Records: Check expense accounts, purchasing vouchers and other records pertaining to issues or officials you are covering.

Offices: Check all the offices in your government building, and find out what kind of work the people in them do. For example, do you know the function of every office in your campus administration building? You could find features or great news stories just by checking what the people in these offices do.

The Internet: Many communities, local police departments and school districts have Web pages offering a wealth of information and documents. You can find sources, news releases and even databases on their sites. In addition, Web sites for state and federal government agencies abound.

Visuals

Before you write your story, think not about what you can put in it; think about what you can pull out of it, especially when you are writing stories with statistics. Use highlights boxes, facts boxes and charts to break out key concepts of a proposal or budget. Then you don't need to clutter the story with the same information. Consider empowerment boxes, information that tells readers what the story means to them and what they can do. These boxes should contain information about where they can call for help, more information or other facts that would be useful. Once you have decided what can be displayed visually, you can present the remaining information verbally.

Here's an empowerment box from the *Reno* (Nev.) *Gazette-Journal* that accompanied a story about overdue parking tickets. The city adopted late fees that would add $30 to tickets not paid within a month.

> **To pay**
> • Pay at the city clerk's cashier office, using cash, check or Visa or Mastercard.
>
> **To protest**
> • Make an appointment. The hearing officer is setting aside time in Room 204 at City Hall. Call 334-2293.
> • Hearing times are from 5-8 p.m. on Nov. 4 and Nov. 6; 1-4 p.m. on Nov. 8; 5-8 p.m. on Nov. 13 and Nov. 14.

Writing Tips

Presuming you have found good stories, how can you make them readable?

One way is to avoid "jargon," stilted or technical words and phrases that officials use but readers don't. Writing coaches call this artificial language "journalese," long words or phrases instead of short ones that would be clearer.

ETHICS

The case: You are the news producer for a small television station in an agricultural community where dairy cattle are raised. You receive a video news release from the U.S. Department of Agriculture about a new program that will identify animals as they move from one location to another to track the point of origin of any animals that have diseases. The video is of excellent quality and features cattle in the background and two ranchers talking about the program. You don't have the staff or time to produce your own video on the subject, and the one you have seems perfect. After all, it's a news release, so you are entitled to use it without any copyright violation. Will you use the video news release? Will you identify the source as the USDA?

Guidelines: The Radio-Television News Directors Association says this in its code of ethics: "Clearly disclose the origin of information and label all material provided by outsiders." However, a *New York Times* investigative story revealed that many television stations are using video news releases from the government without identifying them as government sponsored. The problem has become such a concern that the Boston University Department of Journalism adopted a resolution condemning the practice. It states in part: "We find particularly objectionable the use of 'phony reporters' hired by one agency or another who deliver complete reports, including sign-offs, without ever mentioning their affiliation and, in some cases, misrepresenting it. We also condemn those stations that knowingly run news segments, written, shot and recorded by the government with no identification as to the source of the material. We regard these practices as unethical journalism that run the high risk of confusing or even deceiving the public."

Examples: *medication* for *medicine, restructuring* for *changing, funds* for *money.* When you need a loan from a friend, do you ask to borrow "funds"?

"Reading journalese is like having a series of small strokes," says Jack Cappon, writing coach for The Associated Press. "Unless you start writing the way your neighbors talk, you're not going to go anywhere."

Cliches are another common form of journalese in government stories. Journalists love to use words related to heat and cold: *heated debate, hotly contested, blasted, chilling effect, cooling-off period.* In this example, the reporter strained the lead by picking a holiday that had nothing to do with the story just so she could use these "heated" terms:

The Fourth of July is four months away, but insults and accusations exploded like fireworks at the tumultuous Board of Supervisors meeting yesterday.	The firecracker was Republican Supervisor John Hanson, who blasted his colleagues by calling them "crooks."

Here are some other tips:

Use short, simple sentences: The more complex the information, the simpler and shorter the sentences should be:

Complex	**Simpler**
The City Commission last night approved a resolution to authorize the city staff to apply for funding through the	The City Commission last night agreed to apply for $3.6 million from the state Department of Transportation to

systems enhancement program of the state Department of Transportation for a $3.6 million project for the expansion of U.S. Highway 77 from two to four lanes for 2.2 miles between Interstate 70 and Kansas Highway 18.

expand a portion of U.S. Highway 77 from two to four lanes.

The project would widen the highway for 2.2 miles between Interstate 70 and Kansas Highway 18.

Keep the subject and verb close together: Long clauses and phrases before the verb make it hard for the reader to remember what the subject is—who said or did what. Use subject–verb–object order.

Complex

Rather than having government inspectors sweep through businesses, finding violations and imposing fines, in Maine, officials at the federal Occupational Safety and Health Administration, in an effort to improve work conditions and save the government money, are urging employers to identify health and safety problems and then to work with the agency to correct them.

Simpler

A federal agency is urging employers in Maine to find and correct health and safety problems in their businesses instead of having government inspectors seek violations and impose fines.

The move is an attempt by the federal Occupational Safety and Health Administration to improve work conditions in businesses and save the government money.

Use vigorous verbs: Whenever possible, replace *to be* verbs and other bland verbs with words that help to paint a picture of the activity you are reporting.

A 42-year-old St. Joseph man *escaped* a blazing house without serious injuries when he *grabbed* a coffee table, *hurled* it through a picture window, and then, like a movie stunt man, *leaped* through the jagged glass to escape the heat and flames.

Terry Raffensperger, St. Joseph *(Mo.)* News-Press

Avoid starting sentences with *there:* The word *there* forces you to use a weak *to be* verb, such as *is, are, was* or *were.*

Weak

There was sadness expressed among local people gathered Thursday night to watch their team lose by two points in the NCAA finals.

Strong

Local people expressed sadness as they gathered Thursday night to watch their team lose by two points in the NCAA final.

Interpret information: Tell readers how they are affected.

> Based on the 2005 estimate, the value of real estate in the county jumped roughly $83 million in one year—an increase of about 2.7 percent. In comparison between 2003 and 2004, the value inched up 2.4 percent.
>
> What does all that mean to the average homeowner? Most likely a lower tax rate—called a mill levy—and perhaps a lower tax bill for some, Douglas County Administrator Craig Weinaug said.

Translate jargon: Explain terms in concepts or comparisons that the reader can understand.

> A spot inventory of Jeanne Johns' freezer shows the usual stuff. Ice cream. Frozen peas. TV dinners. Acid rain.
>
> Acid rain? You bet.
>
> Johns, who lives in Haslett, is one of four Michigan volunteers in the Citizen Acid Rain Monitoring Network. The network has more than 300 stations nationwide to monitor acid rain. . . .
>
> She measures the acidity on a pH scale ranging from 0 to 14, with 0 being the most acidic. The scale increases tenfold, meaning a 4.0 reading is 10 times more acidic than 5.0.
>
> Normal precipitation is usually about 5.6. A pH of 5.0 is equal to the acid content in cola. Frogs die if placed in water with a pH of 4.0. Battery acid is 1.5.
>
> *Kevin O'Hanlon,* Lansing *(Mich.)* State-Journal

Vary the pace: Avoid writing huge blocks of complicated concepts and complex sentences. Follow long sentences and long paragraphs with a short sentence as in this example:

> MAT-SU—When Mat-Su school board members voted to cut three sports and millions of dollars in jobs and services earlier this spring, they said they hoped they would be able to restore some of those cuts once the borough and state budgets were finalized.
>
> Their wish has come true.
>
> Between the Mat-Su Borough and the state, local schools will get around $3 million more next year than district officials originally anticipated.
>
> The *(Wasilla, Alaska)* Frontiersman

Focus on a person to explain impact: The way an issue affects one person makes it clear to many. That's the concept of the *Wall Street Journal* formula, and it can be used effectively in government stories. Lead with an anecdote about a person; then go from the specific to the general. It's the "one of many" technique.

Linda Green paid $42,000 in 1982 for a house on a half-acre lot in Fontana, banking on the equity that would build over the years

But if Fontana's new general plan is approved, Green is fearful her property may be worth no more than the day she bought it.

The proposed plan would change the zoning on her half-acre so no additional homes could be built on it, making the site less attractive to buyers.

Green is not alone in her fears. She was among several landowners complaining Monday that the revised general plan—a blueprint for Fontana's growth—will put their properties in less profitable zoning areas.

"I bought my land as an investment. If they zone it down, I will lose my money, and I worked hard to put my money into it," Green told the planning commission during the first public hearing on the new 20-year plan.

More than 130 people attended the hearing.

Tony Saavedra, The *(San Bernardino, Calif.)* Sun

Use an impact lead or explain impact in the story: Tell how the reader will be affected by a bureaucratic action or proposal.

A $10,000 car would cost $25 more in taxes, a $40 power saw an extra dime and a $4 six-pack of imported beer a penny extra in Rockford if Alderman Ernst Shafer, R-3rd, gets his way.

Shafer wants Rockford to join the push in Springfield for a 0.25 percent increase in the sales tax. Locally the sales tax would rise from 6.25 to 6.5 percent under the proposal.

Brian Leaf, Rockford *(Ill.)* Register Star

Avoid boring quotes: You don't have to quote an official to prove you talked to her or him. If you can express the official's point better in your own words, do so. You could say that park repairs included cutting trees, removing sand, adding soil for a seed bed and repairing a shelter. But one reporter quoted an official instead:

"The total project involved tree takedowns, removal of some of the sand and replacement with some soil that would actually provide a seed bed," he said. "We also had to make some repairs on a shelter."

Use the pull-quote test: Are your quotes strong enough to be broken out as pull quotes? That's one way of testing whether they are worth using in a story.

Use conversational style: Write the story as though you were having a conversation with a friend. Here is how one reporter used the conversational style in the lead of a government story:

How'd you like an airport for a neighbor? Or maybe a landfill or an incinerator?

Probably about as much as government officials like trying to find a site for these things.

But what if you could negotiate noise insulation for your airport-area home? Or an agreement requiring the incinerator to douse its fires if it didn't burn hot enough to eliminate most pollutants?

Those alternatives were offered Wednesday to a roomful of Twin Cities area public officials frustrated by their protracted and often doomed efforts to make people accept controversial facilities they don't want.

In an area where officials are looking for places for new landfills, a new airport, light-rail transit routes and other public works projects, the Metropolitan Council sponsored yesterday's conference in an effort to see if there's a better way.

There is, they were told by a specialist in how to make the risks of such facilities more acceptable to their neighbors.

Steve Brandt, (Minneapolis) Star Tribune

Use lists: Use them in the middle or at the end of the story, especially to explain key points of an issue. Lists are particularly helpful in stories with numbers or explanations of proposals.

Avoid the city-dump syndrome: Be selective. Use only quotes and facts that you need. Don't dump your notebook into the story.

Use the kiss-off technique: If you have more than three speakers, block the comments from each one, and then do not use the sources again unless you reintroduce them. The reader can't remember all the officials by second reference only.

Read aloud: If you read all or parts of your story aloud, you will catch the cumbersome phrases.

Statistical Stories

Jennifer LeFleur wasn't looking for a date, but she wanted to find the best places to meet single people. Using a census database, she found the information she needed—and something she didn't want. "I threw out the data for prisons," she said. "They had a high level of single men, but not men I'd want to date." Combining the statistics with some old-fashioned reporting, she discovered that the best place to meet single men was in grocery stores.

"After I did the story, an 85-year-old woman called me and said, 'I loved your story, honey, but could you do it by age?'" LeFleur said.

LeFleur, former database editor for the *San Jose* (Calif.) *Mercury News* and the *Tampa Tribune,* creates fascinating stories with computer-assisted reporting. She also trains journalists throughout the country how to use databases and the Internet. She reels off stories reported from databases—for example, what color cars get the most tickets, how many dead people voted in an election, what names are most popular for the dogs in a community. And more serious stories about bus drivers with drunken-driving records, campaign finance records and foster parents with criminal records.

Jennifer LeFleur, database editor

Jennifer LeFleur

"I'm convinced there's not a beat that you can't use database reporting for," she said. "The biggest shortage in journalism is people with computer-assisted reporting skills."

The term *computer-assisted reporting* often refers to the use of databases, but it also refers to use of the Internet to find sources, documents and information about millions of topics. You can download many government databases directly into your computer and analyze them in a spreadsheet program such as Excel or in a relational database program that allows you to find and compare data.

The information from Internet databases may be a little dated because most surveys of crime data, census data and other statistics posted on the Web are not compiled for the current year. But the data that are available can be used for comparative studies and provide excellent background information.

Every year, more government data are being posted to the Web. But much of the state or local information you might want is still not available on the Internet. You have to ask officials for it, and they may be reluctant to give it to you. Even if you have a legal right to the data, use the Freedom of Information Act as a last resort because responses to FOIA requests can be time-consuming.

LeFleur says reporters should try to find the person in a government agency who knows about computers and data. "It's usually a guy named Leon who works in the basement," she says. "I go to whatever agency I'm covering to find out how they do what they do. I also try to be overly cheery. I never first go in and demand a computer file."

Government databases may be available only in printout form. Ask if you can obtain the data on a disk. If not, find out the copying costs before you commit to getting the files. They could be expensive. Whether you get the data on a disk or on paper, you should check all the information carefully,

MULTIMEDIA COACH

Government sites with valuable statistics abound on the Web, but many of them could be outdated.

- Check the date the information was posted. Contact the agency by phone or e-mail to find out if more current information is available.

- Check your city, school district and state sites for background information on government stories.

- Check if advocacy agencies and other groups in your community have Web sites. Use these sites for sources in reaction stories and human interest.

- Follow the money: Check contributions to candidates from your state at *www.followthemoney.org* or *www.tray.com.* You may find good stories in the statistics.

especially if some of the statistics seem unusual. Data are often "dirty," meaning that they contain many mistakes.

After you get and analyze your data, don't flood your story with statistics. LeFleur bristles when people say computer-assisted stories are about numbers. They may contain only a paragraph or two of numbers, which could make the difference in the focus, but the stories still require good reporting and writing techniques.

Ken Newton, a reporter for the *St. Joseph* (Mo.) *News-Press,* wrote an interesting story about favorite names for children by using a birth records database from the Missouri Department of Health. But he didn't flood his story with statistics. A chart accompanying his story presented the numbers for the most popular names for newborn boys and girls, but the story interspersed statistics with analysis and interviews.

Will it be a Jacob or a Hannah?

Study of most popular baby names shows Northwest Missourians follow statewide trends in naming their children

Missourians love a Jacob. They added nearly 1,000 last year.

In fact, one of every 42 boys born in Northwest Missouri last year was named Jacob, which also was the most popular name statewide in 1997.

While Emily proved the most popular name for girls born in Missouri in 1997, Hannah topped the list for female newborns in this part of the state.

A computer analysis of Missouri Department of Health records for the 75,464 births in Missouri last year shows that parents in 16 Northwest Missouri counties stayed in relative tune with the rest of the state in naming newborn boys.

The top three names in the region—Jacob, Austin and Tyler—also were the top three throughout Missouri. Statewide, parents named 998 newborns Jacob; 37 of those were in this region.

In addition to those three names, four other popular male names in Northwest Missouri also made the state list: Zachary, Michael, Brandon and Andrew.

Name experts aren't surprised by this. Generally, there are fewer male names given out.

"It's been that way in the Western world for years," says Cleveland Evans, a psychology professor with a passion for onomastics, the study of names.

Diversity has set in, though. Dr. Evans, who teaches at Bellevue University in Bellevue, Neb., says that 5.5 percent of American boys were named Michael 20 years ago. Today the percentage has dropped to 2.5 percent.

"Everybody is looking more for different names for their children," he adds, noting that people seek out his lists of most popular names so they can avoid them for their newborns.

Ken Newton, St. Joseph *(Mo.)* News-Press

Whenever you are writing about numbers, you must analyze what they mean. Most reports list numbers in comparison to a previous year or time frame. Always put numbers in perspective in two ways:

- Explain change. Do the numbers show an increase or decrease from a previous period?
- State the significance. What do the numbers mean, and why are they important? Explain what is interesting or important about these statistics in a way that will make readers care.

All of the previous writing tips apply to stories with numbers. But here are a few more that are particularly important for statistical stories:

Use analogies: Whenever you are referring to large numbers, comparisons with something familiar to readers are especially helpful. This is an analogy from a story about pollution in Alabama's rivers:

Each minute, about 30 million gallons of Alabama river water, or the equivalent of what it would take to fill 60 Olympic-sized swimming pools, flush into Mobile Bay, washing over oyster beds in the northern part of the bay closed to harvesting.

Dan Morse, The *(Montgomery)* Alabama Journal

Round off numbers: In most cases it is better to round off numbers—for instance, to $3 million or $3.5 million instead of $3,499,590. Make it easy for the reader to grasp large numbers. This is especially important in broadcast stories.

Avoid bunching numbers in one paragraph: Spread numbers out over a few paragraphs rather than glutting one sentence or paragraph with them. Another good technique is to present numbers in lists.

This story is based on statistics, but the writer uses the list technique and breaks up numbers with quotes:

More fathers are going solo in raising kids.

It's a change that single fathers say shows greater acceptance by American families and courts that sometimes the best place for children is with Dad.

The 2000 census found:

- In 2.2 million households, fathers raise their children without a mother. That's about one household in 45.

- The number of single-father households rose 62 percent in 10 years.

- The portion of the country's total 105.5 million households that were headed by single fathers with children living there doubled in a decade, to 2 percent.

Single fathers say the numbers help tear down a long-standing conception that single fathers tend to abandon their kids, or at least not take as good care of them as single moms, said Vince Regan, an Internet consultant from Grand Rapids, Mich., who is raising five kids on his own.

"In time, it goes a long way to helping society think that single fathers do help their kids and want to be part of their lives," he said.

(The story continues with more quotes and these statistics:)

The percentage increase in single-father households far outpaced other living arrangements. The "Ozzie and Harriett" household, where both parents raise the children like on the old TV show, increased by 6 percent, and single-mother homes were up by 25 percent.

Father-headed households are still only a small percentage. Married couples with children make up 24 percent of all households—whether family or non-family. They were 39 percent of all homes in 1970. Single-mother homes made up 7 percent of all households in 2000, up from 5 percent over 30 years ago.

Genaro C. Armas, The Associated Press

Interpret numbers: Show the impact on readers in terms they can understand:

A 10-year analysis of enrollment patterns at Kansas University and five other state universities revealed two dating tips for college students:

- Men hoping to improve dating prospects might consider attending Emporia State University, where 60 percent of students are women.

- Women interested in more dating opportunities should look to Kansas State University, the only state university in the area with more men than women.

Tim Carpenter, Lawrence *(Kan.)* Journal-World

Use storytelling techniques: Even statistical stories can lend themselves to storytelling. In this example, the writer uses an anecdotal lead and limits the use of statistics, which were presented in a graphic accompanying the story:

James Frazier walked across the stage at Civic Arena on May 31 and picked up his diploma from Central High School. On Aug. 24, he'll head off to college.

Not bad for someone who dropped out of school in 1996.

He's one example of why the dropout rate in St. Joseph has fallen by half since 1989.

He's part of a trend that no other urban Missouri city can match. Not

Columbia. Not Springfield. Certainly not Kansas City or St. Louis.

With a dropout rate of 13.4 percent, according to figures released Thursday, the St. Joseph School District tops the list.

Figures for this year aren't in for the other school districts, but last year's dropout rate for Columbia was 31.5 percent. For Springfield it was 29.6 percent. The state average is the closest figure—22.8 percent.

Announcing the results, United Way cited its program, Profit in Education, started in 1989 to reduce the dropout rate. Barbara Sprong, coordinator for Profit in Education, credited the efforts of the entire community in lowering the dropout rate. Those efforts included innovative programs at the St. Joseph School District, such as the Learning Academy.

That program, Frazier said, made the difference for him.

"The way I was going, I would have been dead or in jail," he said. He spent a rough two years in high school, missing classes and taking drugs. Academically he was on the edge.

"The Learning Academy basically turned that all around," he said.

Dianna Borsi, St. Joseph *(Mo.)* News-Press

Use graphics: Try to get the numbers out of your story and into a separate graphic. You need to mention some of the numbers, but always consider whether a chart, graph or diagram could convey the information better.

Budget Stories

Readers want to know how the government spends money—their money. To tell them, first you need to understand the budget process of the agency you cover. Then you need to make it relevant to readers.

Budget planning starts several months before the budget is approved. Learn how to interpret the proposed budget by asking a financial officer of the city, school or agency to explain it to you before the budget is released. If he or she can't brief you on this year's proposal, use last year's budget to learn the system. In most cases, officials will be willing to cooperate because they want you to present the facts accurately.

Basically, budgets have two sections:

Revenues: The income, usually derived from taxes—primarily property taxes in municipalities. But there also are sales taxes, income taxes and fees. Look for clues about how the revenue will be raised. Will property taxes increase? If you are covering a university budget, will tuition be increased? Find out how the revenue source will affect your readers.

Expenditures: Where most of the money will be spent. Will some departments be increasing expenses more than others, such as police or fire departments? If so, why? Will salaries be increased or more people be hired?

The Kansas House of Representatives, where state budgets are hammered out

How do the expenditures for this year compare with those of the past few years?

Generally, budgets include figures from the previous year or past few years. Look for major increases and decreases in revenues and expenditures.

Before a government agency can adopt a budget, it must conduct public hearings, where the public can comment about the budget. If the budget proposal is at the hearing stage, be sure to include the dates of the hearings in your story. Taxpayers often want to attend hearings to protest cutbacks or request money for programs they support.

Budget and Tax Terms

If you want to explain budgets, you must know what these terms mean:

Assessments and property taxes: Common in municipal budgets, where taxes are based on real estate. Homeowners pay taxes based on an assessment, or estimated value, of their property. This value is determined by a city property appraiser based on a number of factors: size of the property, number of bedrooms, construction and so on. For example, suppose you decide to buy a condominium or a house selling for $160,000. That is its "market value," the price it sells for on the market. Some communities base their tax on the full market value, but most use only a percentage of the total value. The property is given an "assessed value," a value for tax purposes. If your community bases its tax on half the market value, your house would be assessed for $80,000. Your annual property taxes equal some percentage of the assessed value.

Capital budget: Money used to pay for major improvements, such as the construction of highways or new buildings. Capital is often raised by selling bonds, and people who buy the bonds receive interest. The government then uses the money and repays the bonds, plus interest, over a period of years in what is called "debt service." The process is much like buying a house: The bank lends you money; you live in the house and repay the loan plus interest on a long-term basis, often over 30 years.

Deficit: When government spends more money than it receives. Most municipalities and states require a balanced budget: The expenses must be the same as the income. The difference between the expenditures and the income is the deficit, or debt.

Fiscal year: Year in which budgeted funds will be spent. In government, the budget term often starts on July 1 and goes to June 30, instead of the calendar year. So if you use a fiscal year, give the dates: "in this fiscal year, which starts July 1." Or if you are writing about when the money will run out: "in this fiscal year, which ends June 30."

Mean: An average; the sum of all the figures divided by the number of items in the survey. If the salaries of 100 journalists total $3 million, they have a mean salary of $30,000. The salaries of the 100 journalists in the survey would be added and then divided by 100 to get the mean.

Median: An average; the value in the middle of a range. If 15 journalists in a survey earn from $20,000 to $65,000, you would list all the salaries in numerical order and find the one in the center of the list. The eighth number in the list would be the median.

Mill: Unit equal to $1 for every $1,000 that a house is assessed. Local school and city taxes are based on mills. Explain the impact of these taxes clearly. If the school tax rate is 25 mills, your story should say, "The tax rate is 25 mills, which equals $25 for every $1,000 of assessed property valuation." Or you could insert a definition: "A mill equals $1 for every $1,000 of assessed value on a property." Then give an example: "Under this tax rate, a homeowner whose property is valued at $80,000 (multiplied by 0.025) would pay $2,000 in school taxes." Try to avoid using the term *mills;* just say the tax rate will be $25 for every $1,000 of assessed property value. Follow with a specific example so residents can figure out how much their tax will be.

Operating budget: Money used to provide services (police, fire, garbage removal and so on) and to pay for the operation of government. Most of the money for this budget comes from taxes.

Other taxes: Wage tax, income tax and sales tax. Cities and states often charge these additional taxes. Check when you write your budget stories to determine whether they will be increased or decreased. If they will stay the same, say so.

Per capita: The rate per person. For example, if a community has 50 murders and a population of 175,000 people, the per capita murder rate would be determined by dividing 50 by 175,000, to yield 0.000286. However, such a small number is hard to comprehend, so it might be multiplied by 100,000 to give a number per 100,000. In this case the rate would be 28.6 murders for every 100,000 people.

Reappraisal: State or local decision to re-evaluate properties in the community, usually to increase their values. This action almost always generates good stories because it affects people dramatically. For example, Kansas had not reappraised properties for 20 years. When the state decided to do it, property values soared, and a tax revolt resulted. People who had been paying $200 in taxes on their homes were suddenly paying $1,000. A similar situation occurred in Atlanta:

A groundswell of protest over the mass reappraisal of Atlanta and Fulton County property is threatening to become a wholesale tax revolt.

Thousands of homeowners have turned out at meetings throughout the city and county to express displeasure with their new assessments, in some cases more than double last year's.

At the South Fulton County Annex, more than one thousand people gathered Monday to talk about fighting the assessments.

"My assessment went up 190 percent and I'll gladly sell my home to the county for what they think it's worth," said Mitch Skandalakis, a leader of the Task Force for Good Government, as the crowd roared.

Mark Sherman, Atlanta Constitution

Writing Techniques

Impact is crucial in budget stories. So are graphics. A chart or list of key numbers can make a story more presentable. Also get reactions from city officials, residents at public hearings or the people most affected by budget cuts. If you are writing about university budgets, get reactions from administrators, students, professors and the officials whose departments will be affected most.

Here are some key points to include in a budget story, not necessarily in this order:

- Total amount of the budget (rounded off when possible $44.6 million instead of $44,552,379). Most budgets are supposed to be balanced, so the figure applies to both revenues and expenditures.
- Amount of increase or decrease
- Tax or tuition levy, or how funds will be raised (impact on reader, comparison to current tax)
- Major expenditures (major increases and decreases in department funds)
- Consequences (impact on the government or agency—cuts in personnel, services, and so on)
- Historical comparisons (how budget compares with previous year and past few years)
- Reactions from officials and people affected by increases or decreases
- Definitions and explanations of technical terms

Here is an example of the kind of budget story you should avoid writing. It is flooded with statistics but doesn't clarify how the budget will affect the reader.

The recommended Rockville Centre city budget would require a 2.56-mill property tax increase.

City Manager Joan Weinman recommended to Rockville City Commission a budget of $55,672,309, which would require a local levy of 42.59 mills. Last year's budget of $50,322,409 required a levy of 42.03 mills.

A mill is $1 of tax for every $1,000 of assessed property valuation.

Weinman is recommending a 3 percent across-the-board salary increase for city employees. She is also recommending an addition of five police officers to the public safety department.

Here is the lead on another budget story, but this one explains the impact on homeowners:

HACKENSACK, N.J.—A $39.2 million budget that offers residents their first property-tax break in 20 years has been adopted by the City Council.

The budget, which includes $4 million in new state aid, was approved by a 4-1 vote following a public hearing Monday. No residents commented.

Despite a 6 percent increase in spending, the boost in state aid means that total property taxes for the owner of a home assessed at $180,000, the borough average, will drop $54 a year.

Tom Topousis, The *(Hackensack, N.J.)* Record

Here is another way of explaining impact in a lead that is not cluttered with statistics:

Pinellas School Superintendent Howard Hinesley has proposed a list of budget cuts for the next school year that will mean fewer textbooks, fewer teachers and fewer administrators if School Board members approve them next Wednesday.

Patty Curtin Jones, St. Petersburg *(Fla.)* Times

Don't forget that budgets affect people. So when you are writing advances and reaction stories, you can use feature techniques. Here is an example of an anecdotal–narrative approach to an advance on the city budget:

It was 8:05 on a Monday in August, Rosemary Farnon remembers, when her husband, Tony, called the police to report that their rowhouse in the Juniata Park section had been ransacked.

Amid a shambles of overturned furniture, scattered papers and food taken from the fridge, the Farnons nervously and angrily waited nearly five hours before an officer appeared. He explained apologetically that the local police district had no cops to spare.

Theirs is one story, from one neighborhood, but it typifies what is happening across Philadelphia:

Taxes are up and services are down—and residents are unhappy about it.

So Rosemary Farnon and hundreds of thousands of taxpayers will be listening closely Thursday when the mayor proposes the budget for the coming fiscal year, which begins July 1.

Dan Myers and Idris M. Diaz,
The Philadelphia Inquirer

Exercises

1   Figure your taxes using the following method:

   a   You own a home that is worth $100,000 on the market. The city appraises residential property for tax purposes at 11.5 percent of its market value. What is the assessed value of your property?

   b   Using your assessed value as calculated in **a,** figure your tax rate as follows:

      1   Write your assessed value:

      2   Divide the assessed value by 1,000 because a mill is a $1 tax on every $1,000 of assessed property value. Write that figure:

      3   The tax levy in your community is 125 mills. Multiply the amount in **b–2** times the tax levy to figure your tax bill. Write the result:

   c   Last year your taxes were $1,250. Using the answer from **b–3** for this year's taxes, figure your tax percentage increase.

   d   The city had a tax rate of 125 mills last year and is raising it to 137.5 mills this year. What is the percentage increase?

2   **Your dream home:** Envision the home you would like to own. How much will it cost? If you want a swimming pool, sauna and other amenities, make sure that you figure them into the price along with the land value in your community or wherever you want to live. When you figure the selling price, that's the market value.

   Now figure your taxes. Your community assesses property at 30 percent of its market value for tax purposes. The tax rate for city and schools combined will be 75 mills. How much will you pay in taxes?

3   You want to write a story about population growth in your state. Find the statistics in the U.S. Census database for your state. Then import the data into

Excel or other spreadsheet program, and analyze which counties in your state gained or lost the most population.

4 **Statistics:** Analyze the following information, and write a story about which sandwiches are healthiest (lowest in fat and sodium). These statistics are based on a study by the Center for Science in the Public Interest, a nonprofit consumer nutrition organization. The organization analyzed 12 sandwiches for fat, saturated fat and sodium. Daily limits of fat recommended by the Food and Drug Administration for adults are 65 grams of total fat, 20 grams of saturated fat and 2,400 milligrams of sodium.

Turkey with mustard: 6 grams fat, 2 grams saturated fat, 1,407 milligrams sodium

Roast beef with mustard: 12 grams fat, 4 grams saturated fat, 993 milligrams sodium

Chicken salad: 32 grams fat, 6 grams saturated fat, 1,136 milligrams sodium

Corned beef with mustard: 20 grams fat, 8 grams saturated fat, 1,924 milligrams sodium

Tuna salad: 43 grams fat, 8 grams saturated fat, 1,319 milligrams sodium

Ham with mustard: 27 grams fat, 10 grams saturated fat, 2,344 milligrams sodium

Egg salad: 31 grams fat, 10 grams saturated fat, 1,110 milligrams sodium

Turkey club: 34 grams fat, 10 grams saturated fat, 1,843 milligrams sodium

Bacon, lettuce and tomato: 37 grams fat, 12 grams saturated fat, 1,555 milligrams sodium

Vegetarian (cucumbers, sprouts, avocado and cheese): 40 grams fat, 14 grams saturated fat, 1,276 milligrams sodium

Grilled cheese: 33 grams fat, 17 grams saturated fat, 1,543 milligrams sodium

Reuben: 50 grams fat, 20 grams saturated fat, 3,268 milligrams sodium

Background: Interview with Jane Hurley, nutritionist for the center. She analyzed 170 sandwiches from Washington, New York, Los Angeles and Chicago delicatessens: "People tend to think of a sandwich as just a bite to eat, but many shops are giving you a dinner's worth of fat and calories. Tuna itself is fat free, but in sandwiches, it's drowning in one-third cup of mayonnaise. That's the equivalent of three McDonald's Quarter Pounders, fat-wise."

The center also did studies showing fat in Mexican, Italian and Chinese food. One of its most controversial studies showed that one bag of popcorn popped in coconut oil, as served in movie theaters, has as much saturated fat as six Big Macs.

5 Access the Web site for the crime statistics on your campus. It should be on your college or university Web site, but if you can't find it there, go to the Security on Campus Web site (*http://www.securityoncampus.org/crimestats*) and find the statistics. They may not be as recent as they should be on your university site. You might also compare the statistics for your campus with those from a neighboring or similar-size school. Look for patterns— increases and decreases. Write a news story. If possible, call your campus police department for comments.

Featured *News Scene* Assignment

Access *News Scene* at *http://communication.wadsworth.com/newsscene2* to view the news simulation titled "City Council Meeting."

Coaching Tips

Use graphic reporting skills.

Gather enough detail and specifics so you could draw a diagram or write a chronology of the crime as though you were designing a graphic.

Role-play: Ask yourself what you would want to know if you were affected by this crime.

Use the tell-a-friend technique.

Avoid the jargon of police or other legal authorities. If you don't understand a term, chances are the reader may not know it either.

Always include the background of the case, no matter how many days a police story or trial continues. Never take it for granted that the reader has read previous stories.

Be careful. Double-check your accuracy, and make sure that you don't convict someone of a crime before a judge or jury does.

Check the Internet and sex offender registries for background searches of suspects.

Crime and Punishment

The police beat, which often includes the fire department, is considered an entry-level job. Most reporters move on to other beats after a few years of covering crime stories. Edna Buchanan did not. She covered the police beat at *The Miami Herald* for more than 20 years before resigning to write books. But while she was at the *Herald,* she turned police reporting into an art form and won a Pulitzer Prize.

A soft-spoken woman, she writes with a strong punch. One Pulitzer Prize juror said, "She writes drop-dead sentences for drop-dead victims. She is never dull." Consider:

> There was music and sunlight as the paddle wheeler Dixie Bell churned north on Indian Creek Thursday. The water shimmered and the wind was brisk. And then the passengers noticed that the people in the next boat were dead.

Buchanan is most famous for the lead she wrote on a story about a man who shoved his way to the front of a line at a fried chicken restaurant. The counter clerk told the man to go to the end of the line and wait his turn. He did. But when he reached the head of the line again, the restaurant had run out of fried chicken. He battered the clerk fiercely, and he was shot fatally by a guard in the restaurant. Her lead: "Gary Robinson died hungry."

"In truth, Edna Buchanan doesn't write about cops. She writes about people," *Herald* editors wrote in the Pulitzer entry. Buchanan is the first to admit that "You learn more about people on the police beat than any other beat," she said in a speech at a convention of investigative reporters.

She said she had reported more than 5,000 violent deaths. How did she keep from getting upset by them and burned out on the job? "The thing that keeps you going is that you realize you can make things better. You may be affected like everyone else by a terrible tragedy, but you're in a position to do something about it. That's the real joy of this job. We can be catalysts for change. We can bring about justice. Sometimes we are all the victim has got. Police stories do make a difference.

"You've got to be accurate and fair and very, very careful, particularly in crime reporting. A news story mentioning somebody's name can ruin their lives or come back to haunt them 25 years later. It is there in black and white on file. It's like a police record; you never outlive it. You can do terrible damage. So you knock on one more door, ask one more question, make one last phone call. It could be the one that counts."

When Buchanan made those phone calls and someone hung up on her, she just redialed the number and said, "We were cut off." The second time, she might have gotten a relative or someone else who was willing to talk, or the first person might have changed his or her mind. But she didn't try a third time; that would be harassment, she said.

Crime Stories

Buchanan gathered her information from interviews and records. And then she wove them into stories with leads that hooked the reader. She said that crime reporters need to talk to witnesses and get color, background, ages and details—what people were wearing, doing and saying when they became crime victims or suspects. In other words, crime reporters need access.

Access

If you have the police beat, you should check the daily police log, also called the "blotter," to see the listing of all crimes recorded by police for that day. The log will list the names of the victims and the nature of the crimes. This is public record and should be available to the press and anyone else. However, the supporting documents—the actual reports filed by the officer at the scene—may not be available. Laws limiting access to these reports vary from state to state. Restrictions apply especially to records for cases under investigation, but if you develop good sources in the police department, you may gain access.

Although the incident reports contain the names of the officers who filed them, many police departments with a public information officer do not allow reporters to talk to the arresting officers. It is best to abide by the department's policies. The public information officer may give you more information about the crime than the arresting officers would. Nonetheless, if access is permitted, try to talk to the arresting officers, especially in a major crime.

For details about arrests, check the jail log, which should contain the suspect's name and address, birth date, sex, race, occupation, place of arrest, and charges.

To previous criminal records If you are a good reporter, you will want to find out if a suspect has a previous criminal record for related charges. If you are lucky, you will be able to do that. But not necessarily from the police. Again, many states restrict access to previous criminal records.

However, if someone has been convicted of a crime, that court record is usually public and should be available to you in the court jurisdiction where he or she was convicted—unless the record is sealed by order of a judge. If the person was charged with a crime and found not guilty or charges were dropped, that record is also public. You need to look up the court file (and get the case file number) under that person's name.

Depending on how the records are filed in your city, you probably will need the year of the court case, too. Filing systems vary in every municipality, so ask the court clerk for help. The court file should contain all pertinent information, including names of the lawyers involved, description of the crime and all motions filed in the case. Most important, it will tell what happened—the disposition of the case—including specific terms of the sentence or probation or dismissal.

In some cases, a person convicted of a minor crime can have his or her record erased—"expunged"—after a number of years, with permission of the court. In other cases, a judge may permit certain records to be sealed, meaning that they will be withheld from the public and available only to law enforcement officers.

The Internet has made access to some records easier:

- Sex offender registries: 32 states have Web sites listing names and offenses of people convicted of sex crimes.
- Many court records are posted online in searchable databases.
- Public records of court cases are available online in many state and federal sites. Several other Web sites, such as *www.knowx.com* and *www.casebreakers.com*, offer background research checks on individuals for a fee.

To university records In 1986 Jeanne Ann Clery, a 19-year-old student, was raped and murdered in her third-floor dormitory at Lehigh University. Her parents later learned that 38 violent crimes had been committed on the Lehigh campus in the previous three years, but the university was not required to divulge those statistics. Connie and Howard Clery wanted to make sure that their daughter's death was not in vain.

As a result of their efforts, a landmark federal law was enacted requiring all colleges and universities that have federal student financial aid programs to publish an annual report listing three years of crime statistics. The law, originally called the Campus Security Act, was amended in 1998 and renamed the Clery Act in memory of Jeanne Clery.

However, universities may withhold names on crime reports because of another federal law. The Buckley Amendment to the Family Educational Rights and Privacy Act prohibits government agencies from releasing any personal data about students and employees in institutions that receive federal funding. Universities have claimed that if they release such crime records, they could lose federal funding.

In 1991 a federal judge in Missouri ruled that Southwest Missouri State University must release names and records of crimes at that school after Traci

Bauer, editor of the campus newspaper, sued for access. That ruling did not apply to all universities. But in 1992, a new federal law exempted campus records from the restrictions of the Buckley Amendment. Universities are still not compelled to release information on crime records, but they will no longer risk losing federal funds if they do release the names.

To records of juvenile offenders All states have laws restricting the release of records that identify "juvenile offenders," people under age 18. The names are withheld by all branches of the juvenile justice system, including the social services system, but a judge can authorize their release. If a juvenile is being tried as an adult—a decision that is made by a judge—or if the juvenile's name is mentioned in open court, the name can be used. This sometimes happens when the crime is particularly heinous or the juvenile has an extensive criminal record. For example, in 1998, when juveniles were charged with shootings at schools in Jonesboro, Ark., and Springfield, Ore., with several people killed or injured, the media used the juveniles' names.

Most newspapers and broadcast stations have policies to withhold the names of juveniles, but that is more of an ethical decision than a legal one. The media may use the name if they receive it by legitimate means.

To the crime scene Police have the right to protect the crime scene and limit access to the press. If it is public property, reporters and photographers can get as close as police will allow. If the crime scene is on private property, access is at the discretion of the police or the owners of the property. Generally, police will allow some access as long as the media do not interfere with the investigation of evidence at the crime scene.

Use of Names

Many newspapers and TV news programs withhold the names of suspects in crime stories until they have been formally charged with the crime. Being arrested means only that someone has been stopped for questioning in a crime. The person becomes an official suspect after charges are filed in a court, usually at a hearing called an "arraignment." (The process will be explained in the section about courts.) In recent years, police have begun releasing the name of a suspect as a "person of interest" before actual charges are filed. This term is used most often in high-profile cases and when police have good reason to believe the suspect will soon be charged with the crime.

Some newspapers also withhold the names of crime victims to protect their privacy. A growing controversy at newspapers and television stations is whether to withhold the names of complainants in rape cases. Again, the policy varies, but most of the media do not publish the names.

When names are used in crime stories, always get the full name, including the middle initial, and double-check the spelling. Do not rely on police reports; many names on reports are spelled incorrectly. Check the names in telephone directories whenever possible. If a discrepancy exists between the name in the phone book and the one the officer gave you, call the officer again or go with the information from the police.

Using full names with initials helps reduce confusion and inaccuracies; there could be a dozen John Smiths in the community. John T. Smith is more specific, especially when followed by age and address.

Wording of Accusations

Remember that all people are innocent until they are proved guilty in court or until they plead guilty. When a suspect is arrested, the person is not officially charged with anything. A person can be arrested after an officer gets a warrant or on suspicion of a crime. But the police cannot charge anyone with a crime; a member of the district attorney's office must file the charge officially with the court (more about that later). As a result, you must be careful with wording so you don't convict a person erroneously. Most media wait until the person has been charged with the crime, except in sensational cases when the arrest is important news.

If you are writing about an arrest before the official charge, do not say, "Sallie R. Smith was arrested for robbing the bank" (that implies guilt). Do say, "Sallie R. Smith was arrested in connection with the bank robbery." If you are writing about the suspect after charges have been filed, say, "Sallie R. Smith was charged with bank robbery" or "Sallie R. Smith was arrested on a charge of bank robbery."

Also be careful before you call anyone a crime victim. If a person was killed or visibly injured during a crime, it is probably clear that the person is a crime victim. In other cases, the suspect has to be proved guilty before you can say the other person is a victim. You can say "the *alleged* victim," or, if applicable, you can call the other person the accuser—for example, "The accuser in the rape trial. . . ."

Use the official charges when possible. If they are very awkward, and they often are, don't use them in the lead. Put them in the backup to the story. For example, one man who was accused of robbing a jewelry store was also accused of carrying a gun. But police didn't charge him with possession of a gun. They charged him with possession of an instrument of crime. And there are varying degrees in the charges, such as first-degree murder, which should be cited. But don't cite the other qualifications, such as Class E felony (a category for the crime), unless you are going to explain what they mean and why the reader must know. If categories are used at all, it is for explanation of the penalties: "The crime is a Class E felony, which carries a penalty of. . . ." It is still preferable to explain the penalty without the category, which is meaningless to readers.

The word *alleged* is dangerous, so avoid it whenever possible. It means to declare or assert without proof. If you allege carelessly, you can be sued. Do not say, "Smith allegedly robbed the bank." You, the writer, are then the source of the allegation—and a good candidate for a libel suit. You can say, however, "Police accused Sallie R. Smith of robbing the bank" or "Police said Smith robbed the bank." If you must use *alleged,* say, "Police alleged that Smith robbed the bank." "Police accused Smith of allegedly robbing the bank" is redundant and awkward. Besides, police rarely allege; they accuse. An accusation is OK if it comes from police (and they are citing charges on record), not if it comes from you. Other permissible uses include "The bank was allegedly robbed" or "the alleged robbery," although such uses are not preferable.

Here's an example of the proper use of *alleged:* When basketball star Kobe Bryant was accused of rape, it would be accurate to say the "alleged rape" when referring to the incident because it was never established that the accuser was actually raped; Bryant claimed that the sex was consensual. The case was dismissed when the woman who accused Bryant of sexual assault decided not to testify. The woman also had to be considered an "alleged victim" because the charges were never proved.

Also be careful when using the word *accused.* Follow the Associated Press Stylebook guidelines: A person is accused *of,* not *with,* a crime. In addition, you should not say, "accused bank robber Sallie R. Smith" (this convicts her). Instead, say, "Sallie R. Smith, accused of the bank robbery."

Attribution

In crime stories, make sure that you attribute all accusatory information and much of the information you received secondhand (not by direct observation). Factual information does not need attribution. For example, the location of a crime is usually factual. If someone has been charged with a crime, you can state that as a fact.

To reduce the use of attribution after every sentence, you can use an overview attribution for part of your story, especially when you are recounting what happened: "Police described the incident this way."

Newspaper or TV Archives

The first thing you should do before you write your story is check newspaper clips in your library, TV file tape or online archives. They may make a big difference in your story.

A reporter for *The Hartford* (Conn.) *Courant* covered the case of a man arrested on a charge of rape. Small story for a big paper. But the reporter checked clips and discovered that the man had been previously arrested on rape charges and was free on bail when he was charged with this other rape— a much bigger story. Three months later, a different reporter was making police checks. A man had been accused of rape. The reporter checked the clips. It was the same man charged with a third rape, which occurred when he was free on bail still awaiting trial in the first rape case—a very big story. And this story led to a major front-page follow-up story on the system in Connecticut that allows rape suspects to be released on bail, no matter how many times they have been arrested and charged with that type of crime. ("Bail" is the amount of money, set by a judge, that the suspect has to deposit with the court to be released from jail pending a hearing or trial. If the suspect flees, the bail money goes to the court.)

One caution: Clips on file in your newspaper library or computer database may not be up to date. They may contain stories of someone's arrest but not the disposition of the case. Always check to see if charges were dropped or if the person is still waiting trial or was convicted.

Guidelines for Reporting Crime Stories

In any story you will seek good quotes and answers to the five W's. Here are the basic questions to ask and the basic information to include in crime stories:

Victims: Get full names, ages, addresses and occupations, if available (use if relevant).

Suspects: Get full names, ages and addresses, if available; if not, get a description. Guidelines about whether to include race or ethnic background are changing. Check your organization's style. A general rule is to avoid mentioning race or ethnicity unless it is crucial to the story or to a description of a suspect.

Cause of fatalities or injuries: Also describe the injuries, where injured people have been taken and their current condition (check with hospitals). In stories involving property, specify the causes and extent of damage.

Location of incident: Don't forget to gather specific information for a graphic.

Time of incident: Be as specific as possible.

What happened: Make sure that you understand the sequence of events; always ask about any unusual circumstances.

Arrests and charges filed: If people have been arrested, find out where they are being held, when they will be arraigned (a hearing for formal charges) or when the next court procedure will be. If they have already been arraigned, find out the amount of bail.

Eyewitness accounts: Comments from neighbors may also be relevant. Be careful about using accusations against named individuals. When in doubt, leave them out.

In addition to gathering the basic information, you may want to try some of these other reporting techniques:

Role-play: Imagine that it is your car in the accident, your home that was burglarized or burned in a fire, your friend or relative injured in a crime. What information would you want to know if you were personally affected by the story?

Play detective: What information would you want to gather to solve the crime?

Gather graphics: What information would you need to diagram the car accident, draw the crime scene or a locator map, write a highlights box or a chronology of events, or design a chart or graphic depicting how and where the crime occurred? Ask questions to gain the information you will have to convey to the artist who will draw the graphics for your story.

Use the telephone: Often you will gather information for crime stories over the telephone. Usually you will get the information from a dispatcher or public information officer who was not at the scene and is just reading a report to you. Make sure that you ask police officials to repeat any information you did not hear clearly. Also ask the police officer releasing the information to give you her or his full name and rank. Police often identify themselves only by title and last name, such as Sgt. Jones. Ask the officer to spell the names of all people involved; you can spell them back to double-check the accuracy.

Stories About Specific Types of Crimes

For the first day of a major crime story, the preferred approach is a hard-news one. For follow-up stories and sidebars, consider some of the storytelling techniques.

Motor vehicle accidents Vehicle accident stories usually are hard-news stories, unless there is an unusual angle. In addition to following the basic guidelines, make sure that you have this information:

- Speed, destination, and directions of vehicles and exact locations at the time of the accident
- Cause of accident, arrests, citations and damages
- Victims' use of required equipment, such as seat belts and bicycle or motorcycle helmets
- Weather-related information, if relevant
- Alcohol- or drug-related information, if relevant
- Rescue attempts or acts of heroism

It is customary to lead the story with fatalities and injuries. This example is very basic, structured in inverted pyramid form:

Summary lead: delayed identification, fatality and cause

A Santa Ana boy was killed when a van rear-ended the car he was riding in while it was stopped at a turn signal, police said. The van's driver was booked for vehicular manslaughter.

Identification

Robert Taylor, 10, died at UCI Medical Center in Orange.

When, where, other injured people

The 3:17 p.m. accident at First and Bristol streets in Santa Ana also critically injured the boy's mother, Griselda Taylor, 29, and his sister, Lynelle, 8. An 8-year-old boy in the car sustained minor injuries, police said. His name and relation to the Taylors were not released.

What happened and who was involved

Taylor was waiting on the eastbound side of First, in the left-turn lane, at a red light when a van driven by Don Currie Edwards, 49, struck the back of her car, police said. The impact pushed her car into the intersection, and it was then struck by a westbound car driven by Phillipe Hernandez, 18.

Taylor sustained a broken neck. She was in guarded condition at Western Medical Center in Santa Ana, hospital officials said. Lynelle sustained critical head injuries, police said.

Edwards was treated for minor injuries and arrested, police said. Hernandez was not injured.

Condition of injured people; hospital sources

The Orange County *(Calif.)* Register

Burglaries and robberies A burglary involves entry into a building with intent to commit any type of crime; robbery involves stealing with violence or a threat against people. If you are away and a person enters your home and steals your compact disc player, that's a burglary. If you are asleep upstairs and the person is downstairs stealing the player, that's still a burglary. But if the person threatens you with force, that's a robbery. A burglary always involves a place and *can* involve violence against a person; a robbery *must* involve violence or threats against a person.

For both burglaries and robberies, ask the basics: who, what, when, where, why and how. Then add the following:

- What was taken and the value of the goods
- Types of weapons used (in robberies)
- How entry was made
- Similar circumstances (frequency of crime or any odd conditions)

In burglary and robbery stories, mention in the lead any injuries or deaths. Keep the tone serious when the story involves death or serious injuries. In other cases, use your judgment and lead with any unusual angles. If there are none, stress what was taken or how the burglars entered the building, if that is the most interesting factor.

Whether you write a hard or soft lead depends on how serious the crime was, whether it is the first story on the crime and whether you have enough interesting information to warrant a soft approach.

Here's a hard-news version of a burglary story:

COUNCIL BLUFFS, Iowa (AP)—A first issue of "Iron Man" was among 44 rare comic books stolen from a Council Bluffs store.

The books, some valued at $200 to $225 each, dated back to the 1950s and '60s.

Other books stolen from Kanesville Kollectibles included a 1964 first issue of "Daredevil," 17 issues of "Spider Man," four issues of "The Incredible Hulk," "Mystery in Space," "Tales of Suspense," "Captain Marvel" and "Thor."

Police reports said rare comic books valued at $2,950, about 300 used rock 'n' roll compact discs valued at $2,200 and $50 in cash were taken from the business.

The Associated Press

In this burglary story, the tone is lighter and a soft lead is used because of the subject matter:

Someone took Burger King's "Have It Your Way" slogan too literally this week and stole a three-foot-wide Whopper hamburger display costume from a van parked in northeast Salem.

Shannon Sappingfield, a marketing representative for local Burger Kings, said the missing burger was made of sponge.

The Whopper was in a van parked at Boss Enterprise, 408-A Lancaster Drive NE. The company owns nine local Burger Kings.

When Sappingfield came to work about 6 a.m. Tuesday, she saw that the van's window had been broken. The cardboard box containing the Whopper costume was missing; two other boxes containing a milk shake costume and a french fry costume were untouched.

"I'm not convinced they realized

what they had until they were away from the site and opened the box," she said. She estimated that the costume was worth about $500. But to get another one, the company would also have to buy another milk shake and french fry costume, which cost $500 each.

(Salem, Ore.) Statesman-Journal

This is a basic hard-news robbery story with a description of the suspects:

Two armed, masked men robbed a Huntington Beach restaurant late Tuesday, escaping with $2,000 in cash.

Police Lt. John Foster said the holdup occurred shortly before 11 p.m. at Jeremiah's, 8901 Warner Ave.

He said two men armed with shotguns and wearing stockings over their heads entered through the kitchen door, forced cooks into the main area of the restaurant, then made employees and patrons lie on the floor.

The robbers took the cash from a floor safe and fled, Foster said.

The men were described as Caucasian, wearing dark clothing. One was 6-foot-1 to 6-foot-3 with a thin build and dark, curly hair. The second was 5-foot-8, about 170 pounds with a medium to stocky build.

Detectives believe the same shotgun-wielding men robbed a Pizza Hut at 17342 Beach Blvd. about 9:40 p.m. Monday. The bandits took an undisclosed amount of cash and sped away in a small blue car, possibly a Toyota or Nissan.

The Orange County *(Calif.)* Register

Here is how the hourglass form can be used to eliminate some of the attribution in a crime story. The story on the left does not use the hourglass structure, but the one on the right does. Attributions are highlighted with underlining (note the overview attribution in the right-hand story).

With hourglass structure

A robber took money from a clerk at Tom's Amoco, 3827 Topeka Blvd., early Sunday but had a change of heart, returned most of the cash and apologized before fleeing, police said.

The man showed no weapon but held what appeared to be a handgun beneath his sweater, said Detective Sgt. Greg Halford.

Halford said a 19-year-old male clerk was counting money inside the business about 4 a.m. when he saw the robber walk across Topeka Boulevard toward the service station.

The clerk told police he tried to get the money out of sight before the man came into the service station, but was unable.

Without hourglass structure

A robber took money from a clerk at Tom's Amoco, 3827 Topeka Blvd., early Sunday but had a change of heart, returned most of the cash and apologized before fleeing, police said.

The man showed no weapon but held what appeared to be a handgun beneath his sweater, said Detective Sgt. Greg Halford.

Halford described the incident as follows:

A 19-year-old male clerk was counting money inside the business about 4 a.m. when he saw the robber walk across Topeka Boulevard toward the service station.

The clerk tried to get the money out of sight before the man came into the service station, but was unable.

The robber gave the clerk five nickels and asked for a quarter, <u>Halford said</u>, then announced the robbery as the clerk was getting the quarter.	The robber gave the clerk five nickels and asked for a quarter, then announced the robbery as the clerk was getting the quarter.
The clerk asked the man if he was sure he wanted to go through with the robbery. The clerk then told him that three security guards from a nearby motel often come into the service station, <u>Halford said</u>.	The clerk asked the man if he was sure he wanted to go through with the robbery. The clerk then told him that three security guards from a nearby motel often come into the service station.
At that point, the nervous-looking robber went behind the counter and grabbed the money out of the clerk's hands, <u>the detective said</u>. Some of the money dropped onto the floor, so the robber picked it up, <u>Halford said</u>.	At that point, the nervous-looking robber went behind the counter and grabbed the money out of the clerk's hands. Some of the money dropped onto the floor, so the robber picked it up.
The robber started to leave, <u>Halford said</u>, then came back, apologized, returned almost all of the money, said he needed only a small amount of cash and left with a small amount.	The robber started to leave, then came back, apologized, returned almost all of the money, said he needed only a small amount of cash and left with a small amount.

Topeka *(Kan.)* Capital-Journal

Homicides *Homicide* is the legal term for killing. *Murder* is the term for premeditated homicide. *Manslaughter* is homicide without premeditation. A person can be arrested on charges of murder, but he or she is not a murderer until convicted of the crime. Do not call someone a murderer until then. Also, don't say someone was murdered unless authorities have established that the victim was murdered—in a premeditated act of killing—or until a court determines that. Say the person was slain or killed. Some additional information to gather:

- Weapon (specific description, such as .38-caliber revolver)
- Clues and motives (from police)
- Specific wounds
- Official cause of death (from coroner or police)
- Circumstances of suspect's arrest (result of tip or investigation, perhaps at the scene)
- Lots of details, from relatives, neighbors, friends, officials, eyewitnesses and your own observations at the crime scene

For many first-day stories about death, you may choose to use a hard-news approach. You should get the news about the death in the lead. But if there is a more compelling angle, you could put it in the second or third paragraph. Again, you must use judgment in deciding whether the story lends itself to a hard-news or a storytelling approach.

This is a hard-news approach to a homicide story:

A 32-year-old man was charged Tuesday with killing his former girlfriend when she wouldn't leave the back porch of his home.

Lester Paul Stephens of 3357 N. 2nd St. was charged with first-degree intentional homicide while armed in connection with the death of Ruby L. Hardison, 42. Hardison was shot in the head Saturday.

According to the criminal complaint, Stephens told police that he and Hardison recently had ended their relationship. But Hardison came to Stephens' home Saturday and began knocking and banging on the door and front window.

Stephens told police he got upset about the noise, and went to the back door to tell her to leave him alone. Then he went back inside and got a .32-caliber semiautomatic pistol and walked back to the porch, the complaint says.

Stephens told Hardison to get off the porch and go home, then fired one shot in the air to scare her away.

The complaint says that he then put the pistol to the right side of her head, and after they continued to argue, the gun discharged.

Stephens, who faces life plus five years in prison if convicted, was being held on $50,000 cash bail. A preliminary hearing was scheduled for April 30.

The Milwaukee Journal

Here is an excerpt from a homicide story written in a storytelling style. This story includes reporting done according to most of the guidelines: interviews with neighbors, description based on observation, information from the police report and from officials. Remember that if you can't get to the scene, you can use your cross-directory to find neighbors to contact by telephone.

Soft lead

MELBOURNE, Fla.—June Anne Sharabati had planned every aspect of her children's lives, from their tasteful clothes to their exposure to classical music.

She missed only one detail: She forgot to plan a bullet for herself.

Backup for previous statement

The woman charged in the slaying of her two children Thursday night told deputies she would have committed suicide but she ran out of ammunition.

Basic news (five W's)

When deputies were called to her home at 2410 Washington Ave., they found Stephen Faulker, 14, dead on the floor of his bedroom. The Central Junior High School student had been shot in his stomach and head with a .38-caliber revolver.

Type of weapon

Two-year-old Aisha Sharabati was in her mother's bedroom dying from similar wounds.

Sharabati, who divorced Aisha's father in 1989, told deputies that Stephen had been a discipline problem, but she gave no explanation for her daughter's death, said Brevard County sheriff's spokeswoman Joan Heller.

Possible motive (note attribution)

Stephen's father died about nine years ago. Sharabati's former husband, Mohamad, lives in Canada and is en route to Melbourne, deputies said.

The first sign of the shootings came to light shortly before midnight Thursday with Sharabati's frantic calls to police and neighbors.

Narrative based on interview with neighbor

John Marrell said he was sleeping when the phone rang.

The call was from Sharabati, his 32-year-old neighbor. He had known her for 11 years and had helped her from time to time.

Dialogue

"She said, 'Didn't you hear the shots?' and I asked, 'What shots?'" Marrell said.

"And then she said, 'You need to get over here and get these kids. They've suffered enough.'"

Marrell said he grabbed a gun and a flashlight, thinking maybe a prowler was threatening the single parent and her children.

Instead, Sharabati met him at her screen door and told him she had "killed the kids."

Marrell said he ran home and called police, not knowing they had already been called.

Information from officials

When deputies arrived at the house, Sharabati met them unarmed on the doorstep and said, "Kill me. Kill me," Heller said. Sharabati was taken into custody, and deputies went in to find the bodies.

Police report

In the investigation report, Deputy Scott Nyquist said the suspect shot her son "in a fit of rage."

Reaction from neighbors

On Friday, many neighbors in the middle class neighborhood were struggling to understand how a seemingly "ideal mother" could have committed the slayings.

Occupation of neighbor (relevant to statement)

"She was the kind of mother who would attend parent-teacher conferences," said Frances Edwards, a retired high school guidance counselor who lives across the street from Sharabati. "She often said her children were her life. I sure didn't see this coming."

Observations

Sharabati's light blue, one-story home—like most in the wooded, spacious subdivision—was well maintained. In the back yard, three lawn chairs were lined up alongside Aisha's child-sized chair.

Edwards said Sharabati wanted only the best for her children.

Backup for lead

"She bought them Mozart records to listen to and dressed them beautifully," she said. . . .

Reaction from relatives

"We are in deep shock—very, very deep shock," said Helen Faulker, Sharabati's mother.

Where suspect is, next step in court process

Sharabati is being held in the Brevard County jail, where she is scheduled to make her first court appearance at 9 a.m. today.

Laurin Sellers and Lynne Bumpus-Hooper, The Orlando (Fla.) Sentinel

Fires Although fire stories may not be crime stories, unless arson or other criminal behavior was involved, police reporters are often responsible for fire stories. Here are the important elements:

- Time fire started, time fire companies responded, time fire was brought under control
- Number of fire companies responding, number of trucks at scene
- Evacuations, if any, and where people were taken
- Injuries and fatalities (make sure that you ask if any firefighters were injured)
- Cause (ask if arson is suspected—intentional setting of fire), how and where fire started

ETHICS

Ethical dilemma: How can you balance the desire for a great story with concern about causing harm?

The case: The situation is tense. A murder suspect is holding a hostage. The suspect had been arrested for killing his lover's 4-year-old son. He was in custody in a police car when he seized an officer's gun and shot two officers who were guarding him. After stealing a truck, he led police on a 50-mile chase and killed a state highway patrolman who was pursuing him. Then he pulled into a convenience store and held the clerk as a hostage. A local radio station called the store and broadcast a live interview with him. You are a newspaper reporter in the same area. Will you call him, too?

That was what happened in Tampa. WFLA-AM called, and then a reporter for the *St. Petersburg* (Fla.) *Times* also called and conducted an interview with the suspect. *The Tampa* (Fla.) *Tribune* reporters and editors, listening to the broadcast, decided against making a similar call. Did the reporters who called, in pursuit of a great story, endanger the life of the hostage? What would you have done?

Ethical values: Thorough reporting, protection of the public.

Ethical guidelines: The Society of Professional Journalists Code of Ethics says to minimize harm.

- Who discovered the fire, extent of damage, insurance coverage
- Description of building
- Estimated cost of damages
- Presence and condition of smoke detectors or sprinkler system (especially in a public building or apartment building, if city requires them)
- Fire inspection record, fire code violations (usually for a follow-up story, especially in public buildings)

When fatalities or injuries occur in a fire, they should be mentioned in your lead, preferably a hard-news lead. If no one is injured or if heroic rescue attempts are involved, a soft lead may be appropriate. Follow-up stories and sidebars provide many opportunities for storytelling techniques.

This example follows most of the guidelines for reporting fires:

KODIAK, Alaska—A mother and infant escaped injury, but one of their two dogs perished in a house fire Sunday night.

Firefighters spent about a half hour battling the blaze, which started in the basement of the house, owned and occupied by Mario and JoAnn Alvarez.

"The cause of the fire is not known yet," said Kodiak fire chief Joe Hart.

When they arrived, firefighters saw smoke coming out of the upper parts of the house and found flames at the front door and coming out of the basement stairwell when they entered the building.

"There are char marks on the outside of the structure, and we had to break out some of the windows to ventilate," Hart said.

He estimated losses at $50,000, saying there was extensive damage from heat and smoke.

The Associated Press

Court Stories

Writing about a crime is only the first step. The next step takes place in court. To cover courts, you need a basic understanding of the process and the terminology that is used. Court procedures vary from state to state and even in counties within states. You need to find out how the system works in the area where you are working.

A complete understanding of the courts would require a three-year course called law school. But you can learn most of what you need to know as you do your reporting. Whenever you hear a term you don't understand, seek a definition. And don't use legal terms in your stories unless you explain them. In fact, avoid them as much as possible. Go by this guideline: If you don't understand something, chances are the reader won't either. It's up to you to make the story clear.

Court cases are full of drama. They are the stuff of television series and movies. Yet newspaper stories about them are often dull. Even if you use a hard-news approach to report a conviction or testimony, you can still use storytelling techniques of dialogue, description and narrative writing for portions of the story so the reader can experience the human drama that filled the courtroom.

Here are some basic guidelines for writing court stories:

- Get reactions, facial expressions and gestures of the defendant and the accusers, attorneys, relatives and other people affected by the case, especially in trial stories and verdict stories.

- Use descriptive detail and color—lively quotes, dramatic testimony and dialogue.

- Translate all jargon, and avoid legal terminology.

- State exact charges in the story.

- Give the background of the crime, no matter how many stories have been published about this case.

- Include the name of the court where the trial or hearing is being held.

- Get comments from defendants, prosecutors, defense attorneys, plaintiffs (the people who brought suit or filed charges), relatives, and jurors in all verdict stories.

- In verdict stories, include how long the jury deliberated. Also include how many jurors were on the case; not all cases have 12-member juries, the most common number. In some cases, the amount of time the jury deliberated may be a major factor—as you will see in the following example about the O.J. Simpson case. In all cases, however, the length of deliberations is part of the story.

- Write the next step—the next court appearance or, in verdict stories, plans for an appeal if the defendant is found guilty.

MULTIMEDIA COACH

An old maxim in the news business goes like this: If it bleeds, it leads. That maxim has often been applied to television more than other media, but the generalization frequently holds true. Why do journalists cover crime? Often, it is because crime is important to a community, but the event may not be representative of what is really happening in a community.

Here are some tips to add perspective to stories about crime and the legal process:

- Many states and the federal government have put crime data on the Web. Add perspective to your story by using these figures to determine how frequently the crime you are covering actually occurs. You may find the federal statistics, or the Uniform Crime Reports, at *www.fbi.gov/ucr/ucr.htm.*

- Check online court cases or other legal records that may be related to a case. Make certain that you know the difference between various crimes such as robbery, burglary and larceny.

- Check the Web for background of criminal suspects. Start with a basic search engine such as *www.google.com* and check sex offender registries — even if the person is not a suspect in a sex crime.

- Check the Web for perspective on issue stories. For example, if you are writing about a local school shooting, check online for a listing of recent school shootings or similar statistics in other crimes.

- Search newsgroups and discussion lists for messages suspects may have sent. For example, students in some of the school shooting cases had Web sites and sent messages to searchable public newsgroups: *http://groups.google.com.*

The trial of former football player O.J. Simpson captured the nation's attention for nine months, but the jury deliberated fewer than four hours before reaching a verdict of acquittal. That factor was the lead on the first Associated Press stories and was still high in later editions of the stories.

LOS ANGELES (AP)—O.J. Simpson was acquitted Tuesday of murdering his ex-wife and her friend, a suspense-filled climax to the courtroom saga that obsessed the nation. With two words, "not guilty," the jury freed the fallen sports legend to try to rebuild a life thrown into disgrace.

Simpson looked toward the jury and mouthed, "Thank you," after the panel was dismissed. He turned to his family and punched a fist into the air. He then hugged his lead defense attorney, Johnnie Cochran Jr., and his friend and attorney Robert Kardashian.

"He's going to start his life all over again," Cochran told reporters later.

"It's over from our viewpoint," District Attorney Gil Garcetti said.

After hearing nine months of testimony, the majority-black jury of 10 women and two men took fewer than four hours Monday to clear Simpson of the June 12, 1994, murders of Nicole Brown Simpson and her friend Ronald Goldman. The verdict was unsealed and read Tuesday.

The Associated Press

Criminal and Civil Cases

Court procedures fall into two categories: criminal and civil cases.

Criminal cases are violations of any laws regulating crime. If you are arrested on suspicion of drunken driving, you could be charged in a criminal case.

Civil cases involve lawsuits between two parties. If your landlord says you have not paid the rent or you have damaged your apartment, he or she can bring a civil lawsuit against you. Divorces, malpractice, libel, contract disputes and other actions not involving criminal law are civil cases.

Federal Courts and State Courts

The court system functions on two levels: a federal level and a state level. Federal courts have jurisdiction over cases involving matters related to the U.S. Constitution (such as civil rights), federal tax and antitrust matters, and any other federal laws. Federal courts also hear cases between people from different states. Here is the hierarchy of the federal court system:

U.S. District Court: This is the lowest level of the federal judicial system, where most cases involving federal issues are first heard.

U.S. Court of Appeals: There are 12 of these courts for geographical areas, plus the U.S. Court of Appeals for the D.C. (District of Columbia) Circuit. It is the intermediary court, where cases from the federal district courts are appealed.

U.S. Supreme Court: This is the highest court in the nation. Cases may be appealed to this court, but the justices do not have to rule on all the cases.

Most states also have three levels of courts: a trial court, an appeals court and a state supreme court for appeals of the last resort on the state level. Cases from the state's highest court may be appealed to the U.S. Supreme Court if there is a federal angle, such as a constitutional matter—a First Amendment issue, for example—or a civil rights violation.

The names of the state courts can be confusing. In one state a superior court may be a trial-level court, whereas in others it may be an appellate court.

There also are municipal courts, where violations of local laws, such as traffic laws or city ordinances, are heard.

In addition, within the state system there are juvenile courts (for cases involving people younger than age 18) and probate courts, where disputes involving wills and estates are heard.

When you write your court story, find out the proper name of the court—whether it is called a district court, a circuit court or a common pleas court—and write that in the story.

Criminal Court Process

Crimes are classified as misdemeanors or felonies. *Misdemeanors* are considered minor offenses that carry a potential penalty of up to a year in jail and/or a fine. *Felonies* are more serious crimes punishable by more than a year in prison. Criminal procedures differ from state to state, but there are some general processes in the court system that you should understand. The following diagram outlines court procedures for both criminal and civil cases.

Arrest The person is stopped by police for suspicion of having committed a crime and is taken to the police station for questioning or further action.

Process of criminal and civil cases

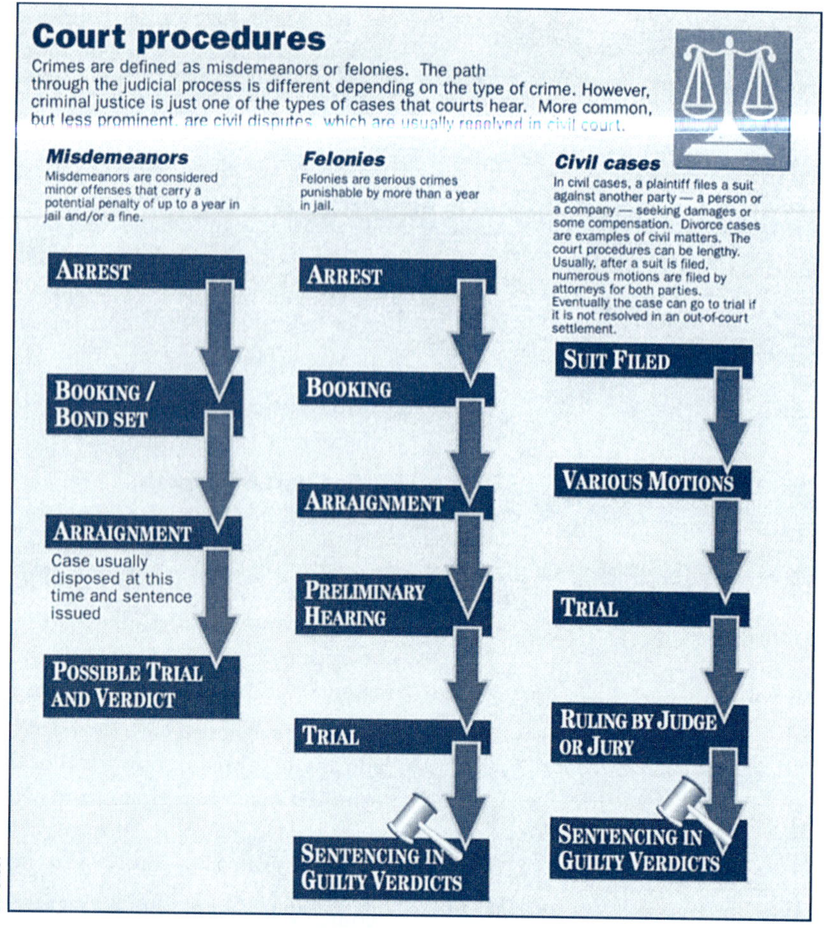

Bill Skeet

Police are required to read a person his or her rights: to remain silent (if the person does not want to discuss the issue prior to a court procedure) and to retain an attorney. These are called the Miranda warnings, based on a court case by that name.

A person can also be arrested if someone has filed a complaint with police and the police find enough probable cause to believe the complaint is true. At this point the police can notify the person of the charge that will be filed—basically, why he or she is being arrested—but the charge is not official yet.

If someone is wanted for a crime, police can also seek a warrant for that person's arrest, a legal document provided by a judge that gives police the right to make the arrest.

Booking The suspect is taken to a booking desk in the police station, where he or she is fingerprinted and photographed. Information about the person—age, address, physical description and so on—is then recorded in a police book, the log. At this point the person may be held in jail or released until formal charges are issued.

Charges The arresting police officer confers with a member of the district attorney's office, who decides if a charge against the suspect should be filed with the court. It is important for the reporter to find out if the person has been charged officially with the crime because many newspapers and broadcast stations don't publish or announce news of an arrest until charges have been filed.

Many states have standard bail fees for common or misdemeanor crimes, and the person may be able to post a bail bond at this time and be released without a hearing.

Arraignment Usually within 24 to 48 hours, a suspect will have a first hearing. At this point the charges against him or her are read in court. In some places, at this time the suspect can enter a plea of guilty, not guilty or no contest—not admitting guilt but not contesting the charge either. In some jurisdictions, the arraignment may be held just to formally read the charges; the plea comes at a later hearing.

If the suspect pleads guilty, the sentence can be issued at this point, and the matter can be settled—or the judge may delay sentencing for another hearing. Misdemeanor cases are often settled at this level.

If the person pleads not guilty, he or she has the right to a trial, and the judge can set bail at this time.

At the hearing, the judge will determine bail. If the person fails to show up for the next court appearance, the total amount of bail is forfeited to the court. When the person has no previous record, the judge may release the suspect on his own recognizance (recognition) without any bail.

Preliminary hearing In felony cases only, a judge weighs the facts presented by a prosecutor from the district attorney's office and by the defense attorney at a special hearing. Then the judge decides whether there is enough evidence (probable cause) to hold the person for trial. If not, the person is released, and charges are dropped.

In some states, the preliminary hearing is synonymous with the "first hearing" or "first appearance," and it precedes the arraignment. In other states, "arraignment" is the term for that first court appearance.

Grand jury In certain cases, particularly those involving political crimes or major drug cases and those in federal courts, a grand jury will be convened to investigate the circumstances of the case and determine if there is enough evidence—enough probable cause—that the crime has been committed.

Like a trial jury, the grand jury is a group of citizens, from 12 to 33 members, chosen to serve on the case. They listen to testimony from prosecutors and witnesses. Unlike the trial jury, however, the grand jury does not rule on guilt or innocence. It only recommends to a judge whether there is enough evidence to take the case to a trial.

If there is, the grand jury hands up (because the judge sits on a higher bench than the jury) an indictment, also called a "true bill." The defendant then enters a plea at another hearing. If the case goes to trial, another jury will be impaneled to serve at the trial.

Grand jury proceedings are secret; the jurors are sworn not to reveal deliberations to the media or anyone else (in most states). However, many reporters with good sources can find out the essence of what happened. After deliberations, if and when the grand jury issues a report, that is usually public record.

Pretrial hearings and motions Before the trial, attorneys usually file a number of motions (formal requests to the court) seeking to have the case dropped, to have the trial moved to another location (called a change of venue) or to have evidence suppressed. The judge has to rule on each motion.

Plea bargain To avoid a trial, which is time-consuming and expensive, lawyers will often negotiate a plea bargain. This is usually a deal offering the defendant a reduced sentence in return for pleading guilty to a lesser charge. The defendant could also plead "no contest," which means the person doesn't admit guilt but won't contest the court's decision.

Trial If the case goes to trial, a jury is selected and the case is heard. In some cases, particularly civil cases, a judge may decide the case without a jury.

Unanimous verdicts are required in criminal trials in most states. If the jury can't agree on a guilty or not-guilty verdict, it is called a "hung jury," and a mistrial is declared. The defendant is then technically not guilty.

If the defendant is judged guilty, you may then call him or her a murderer, rapist or whatever accusatory term fits the crime involved. But do not use accusatory terms in stories before a guilty verdict.

Sentencing After the trial, if the person is found guilty, there will be another hearing. The judge will then decide on a sentence. Sometimes the judge issues the sentence immediately after the verdict.

At any time during the criminal court process, the suspect may change his or her not-guilty plea to a guilty one and eliminate the need for a trial.

Appeal A person convicted of a crime can appeal the decision to a higher court. It is logical to ask in all court trials with convictions whether an appeal is planned. The information should be included in the story.

Civil Court Process

A civil case starts with a suit filed by a person or a company. Anyone can file a lawsuit for a fee. After filing, the lawyers for both sides file various motions with the court. If the case is not settled between the two parties at a pretrial hearing, a court hearing date is set. Civil cases may be argued in front of a judge or before a jury if one is requested. Civil suits can drag through the courts for many years. If the case goes to trial, the process is the same as for criminal trials.

Most civil cases never even get to the trial stage. At any point after motions have been filed, the judge may dismiss the case or may grant a request for a summary judgment, a ruling on the case when both parties agree to forgo a trial.

Terms Used in Court Reporting

You should become familiar with these terms so you can better understand and explain court proceedings:

Acquittal: Finding by a court or jury that a person accused of a crime is not guilty.

Adjudicate: To make a final determination or judgment by the court.

Affidavit: Sworn statement of facts.

Appeal: Plea to ask a higher court to review a judgment, verdict or order of a lower court.

Appellant: Person who files an appeal.

Arraignment: Court hearing in which a defendant in a criminal case is formally charged with the crime and given a chance to enter a plea of guilty, not guilty or no contest (nolo contendere). At this time, bail is usually set.

Bail: Amount of money set by the court that the defendant must guarantee to pay if he or she does not show up for a court trial. If the defendant can't raise the money through a bail bond company or personal sources, he or she stays in jail.

Bond: Written promise to pay bail money on the conditions stated. The bond for bail is usually 10 percent of the total amount of bail set. The term is often used interchangeably with *bail*. Very often, a person will borrow money from a bond company. Then if the person flees, the bond company loses the money.

Brief: Legal document filed with the court by a lawyer, stating the facts of the case and arguments citing how laws apply to this case.

Change of venue: Procedure to seek a change of location of the trial, usually when defense attorneys contend that the defendant can't get a fair trial in the current location because of too much pretrial publicity.

Charge: Official allegation of criminal wrongdoing.

Civil suit: Lawsuit to determine rights, duties, claims for damages, ownership or other settlements in noncriminal matters.

Complaint: Formal affidavit in which one person accuses another of violating the law.

Condemnation: Civil action to acquire ownership of property for public use. When a municipality wants to build a road or sidewalk, the government will condemn the property to gain right of way.

Contempt: Action that disregards the order or authority of the court. A lawyer who screams obscenities at the judge will probably be found in contempt of court.

Defendant: In a civil case, the person being sued. In a criminal case, the person charged with breaking the law.

Deposition: Written statement of testimony from a witness under oath.

Discovery: Pretrial examination of a person (including depositions), documents or other items to find evidence that may be used in the trial.

Dismissal: Order to drop the case.

Docket: List of cases pending before the court. A trial docket is a list of cases pending trial.

Extradition: Procedure to move a person accused of a crime from the state where he or she is residing to the state where the crime occurred and where the trial will be conducted.

Felony: Major crime punishable by a sentence of a year or more. Crimes such as robbery, homicide and kidnapping are felonies; lesser crimes such as shoplifting are misdemeanors. Legally, a felony is defined as a crime punishable by death or imprisonment in a state prison.

Grand jury: Group of citizens selected by the court to investigate whether there is enough evidence or probable cause that a crime occurred and that the person should be charged, or indicted.

Hung jury: Jury that cannot reach a unanimous verdict, a requirement in most criminal trials.

Indictment: Recommendation by the grand jury that there is enough probable cause to charge a person or group of people with the crime under investigation. The grand jury hands up an indictment to the judge (because the judge sits on a platform higher than the jury); the judge hands down rulings. It's preferable to use the word *issued*.

Injunction: Order by the court instructing a person, group or company to stop the action that was occurring, such as picketing. For example, an injunction can order a group to stop marching outside an abortion clinic.

Innocent: The term "not guilty" is preferable in court cases. The Associated Press Stylebook previously recommended using the term "innocent" in case the "not" in "not guilty" was dropped from typesetting, but that is no longer the case. AP now recommends using "not guilty."

Misdemeanor: Crime less serious than a felony; crime punishable by less than one year in jail and/or fines.

Mistrial: Trial that is set aside or declared invalid because of some mistake in proceedings or, in a criminal trial, because the jury cannot reach a unanimous verdict.

Motion: Request for the court to make a ruling or finding.

Nolo contendere: Latin for "I will not contest it" (no contest). This plea has the same effect as a guilty plea, but it is not an admission of guilt. It means the person will not fight the charge. If you agree to pay a fine for a traffic ticket but do not agree that you were speeding, you are pleading no contest. This type of plea is used as a form of bargaining to get the defendant a reduced charge in exchange for his or her agreement not to protest and to eliminate the need for a trial. Use the English term *no contest* in a story, and explain briefly that it is not an admission of guilt.

Plaintiff: Person who sues in a civil case. The defendant is the one being sued.

Plea: Defendant's response to a charge, stating that he or she is guilty, not guilty, or not willing to contest the charge.

Plea bargain: Agreement between the prosecutor and the defendant (or defense attorney) to accept a lesser charge and a lesser sentence in return for a guilty or no-contest plea. Plea bargaining is used extensively as a way to eliminate court trials. Once the defendant pleads guilty or no contest, there is no need for a trial. However, a plea bargain must be approved by the court.

Probable cause: Determination that there is enough evidence to prosecute a criminal case. Police officials also need probable cause—enough reason to believe a crime is being committed—when they seek a search warrant or any other warrant for a person's arrest.

Probation: Condition in which the person is released from serving a jail sentence if he or she meets certain terms, such as serving in the community, entering drug treatment or accepting whatever restrictions the judge decides.

Recognizance: Literally, "recognition." A person may be released from jail based on his or her own recognizance—meaning the recognition of a previously good reputation. This ruling is essentially the judge's way of saying that, because of the person's reputation, he or she is not considered a high risk for skipping the next court hearing or trial.

Subpoena: Court order commanding a person to appear in court or to release documents to the court.

Summary judgment: Procedure in a civil suit asking the court to give final judgment on the grounds that there are no further questions and no need for a trial.

Summons: Document notifying a defendant that a lawsuit or complaint has been filed against him or her.

Suspended sentence: Court order stating that the punishment of the defendant will be suspended if certain conditions are met. A person who receives probation gets a suspended sentence.

Temporary injunction: Court order to stop an action, such as a protest, for a specific amount of time until a court hearing and ruling whether the action should be enjoined, or stopped permanently.

Tort: Civil case involving damages, pain, suffering or other allegations of wrongdoing.

True bill: Indictment issued by a grand jury.

Verdict: Decision by a jury about guilt or innocence.

Warrant: Court order directing law enforcement officials to arrest a person. A search warrant gives officials authority to search a premise.

Court Story Examples

A court case is a continuing saga. From the time a person is arrested until the case is resolved, whether in a trial or a settlement, you will write many stories about it. But never assume that the reader is familiar with the case, no matter how sensational it may be. Always include the background.

Whether you take a soft or hard approach, make sure that your nut graph explains who is being accused of what, and place it high in the story.

If information is part of a court record, you may use it as fact—but it still may not be true. It's up to a judge or jury to decide whether the claims in court documents and trials are true. So you need to attribute your information, although not necessarily in the lead.

Unlike other stories, many court stories do not appear balanced. On any given day, one side in the case may present its arguments, so you won't always have a story that seems fair to both parties. The testimony will be biased; you should not be.

Some reminders:

- Explain charges and background.
- Describe defendants and witnesses.
- Specify the court where the proceeding takes place.
- Tell how long the jury deliberated in verdict stories.
- Tell a good story.

When the verdict is issued in a major trial that has garnered interest locally or nationally, a hard-news story is appropriate. A soft lead also may work, but make sure that you put the verdict very high in the story. The following story is an example of a basic hard-news approach. In this case, the judge sentenced the defendant immediately instead of at a separate hearing.

Summary lead: verdict, delayed identification	EXETER, N.H.—A high school instructor was convicted yesterday and sentenced to life in prison without parole after a sensational trial on charges that she manipulated her student-lover into murdering her husband.	The victim's mother, Judith Smart, cried out as each verdict was read, and said afterward, "She got what she deserved."
Defendant's reaction, charges, name of court	Pamela Smart, 23, stood motionless as the Superior Court jury foreman pronounced her guilty of murder-conspiracy and being an accomplice to murder.	Judith and William Smart then left the court for the cemetery where their son is buried. "We're going to tell Gregg," William Smart said. "We're going to tell him that, by God, she did do it."

Relative's reactions

Brief background

Gregg Smart, a 24-year-old insurance agent, was murdered May 1 last year, six days before his first wedding anniversary.

More reactions

Pamela Smart's parents, John and Linda Wojas were stone-faced as they left the courthouse.

Descriptive detail

"You know how I feel about that," Linda Wojas said when asked if she thought her daughter had gotten a fair trial. Wojas wore a yellow ribbon every day, symbolizing her belief that her daughter was a hostage of the judicial system.

Reaction quotes

"I feel terribly bad for the Wojas family," Judith Smart said. "I can imagine how I would feel and I feel very, very bad for them."

Jury information: time deliberated, length of trial

Other charges

The jury, which heard three weeks of testimony, deliberated 12 hours over three days before returning its verdict. Smart also was convicted of witness-tampering for encouraging her student-intern to lie to police.

Identification of court and judge, sentencing, expected appeal

Rockingham County Superior Court Judge Douglas Gray immediately announced the mandatory life sentence for the accomplice-to-murder charge. An appeal is expected.

Background and highlights of trial

Smart was the school district media coordinator when she met William Flynn, now 17, as one of his instructors in a self-awareness program at Winnacunnet High School in Hampton.

Prosecutors said the former high school cheerleader and college honor student tantalized and seduced Flynn, then 15 and a virgin, and then threatened to end their affair unless he murdered her husband. Smart testified that she broke off the affair just before the murder.

Prosecutors said Smart feared losing everything in a divorce, including her dog and furniture.

Fate of others involved (note plea bargain)

The defense called Flynn and two confessed accomplices "thrill-killers" who shot Smart on their own, then framed his widow to avoid life prison terms. In plea bargains, they face minimum sentences ranging from 18 to 28 years.

Color details

The Boston Herald, which dubbed Smart the "Ice Princess," invited readers to call in their verdicts on a 900 number. They voted guilty, 543 to 101.

More highlights of trial

The most damaging evidence against Smart was four secretly recorded conversations she had with Cecelia Pierce, 16, her student-intern and confidante. The profanity-laden tapes, made after the murder, show that Smart urged Pierce to lie to police, that she feared being jailed herself, and that she had known her husband would be murdered.

Key testimony

Flynn, sobbing as he testified on March 12, admitted pulling the trigger on a .38-cal. pistol he held to Gregg Smart's head.

He and Patrick Randall, 17, testified that they entered the Smarts' condominium through a basement door that Pamela Smart had left unlocked for them and waited for Smart to arrive home. They also said they forced him to his knees as he begged for mercy.

Shortly before the verdict, John Wojas said people were misjudging his daughter.

Reaction quote kicker

"She's not a cold little woman like they're trying to describe her," he said. "She doesn't show a lot of outright emotion. She never has."

The Associated Press

Stories about upcoming court trials lend themselves to storytelling techniques. If the story is important enough to "advance" the trial, it probably has a good story behind it. A narrative writing technique is used to advance this trial in a story that uses almost no direct attribution, except for quotes. The story is based on court records and previous admissions by the defendant. If the defendant had not admitted the crime, this story would be too accusatory.

MIAMI—He was a distraught man that day, a man who sang lullabies and wept. With one hand, he held a gun. With the other, he stroked the smooth face of his daughter, a 3-year-old existing in limbo between life and death.

An hour before, he had given her what he thought was a fatal dose of Valium. But here she was still breathing, her tiny chest rising and falling rhythmically, if ever so slightly.

She was in a crib at Miami Children's Hospital, lying on her back. She had been there for eight months, since the day she nearly suffocated. He leaned over the crib railing and looked at her eyes. They were open. They stared ahead, mirrored no emotions, saw nothing. It was the same for her other senses. The damage to her brain was total and irreversible, and because of it, she couldn't hear his weeping, and she couldn't feel his last touch goodbye before he aimed the gun at her heart.

He shot her twice. He dropped the gun. He prayed that her suffering was over. He fell into a nurse's arms, cried and said he wanted to die. He said, "Maybe I should get the electric chair to make things even. I killed my daughter. I shot her twice. But I'm glad she's gone to heaven."

On Tuesday morning in a Miami courtroom, almost five months after the death of his daughter, Joy, Charles Griffith is scheduled to go on trial for murder. The defense, says Griffith's attorney, Mark Krasnow, will be mercy. "It was an act of love," Krasnow says, "not an act of malice."

David Finkel, St. Petersburg *(Fla.)* Times

The next example is a story about a lawsuit in a civil case that has not yet come to trial. When you cover a story about a suit that has been filed, always try to contact the people involved or at least their lawyers, whose names are listed in the suit. If you wade through all the legal writing, lawsuits can be very entertaining.

What has no arms or legs and wiggles in the night?

According to Gladys Diehl and her husband, John Brehm, it's their Sealy Posturpedic mattress.

In a lawsuit filed yesterday in Bucks County Court, Diehl and Brehm contend that they endured many nights of fitful slumber because an uninvited guest shared their bed—a 26-inch snake living inside the mattress.

"There was a lot of wiggling going on," said Stephen A. Shelly, the attorney representing the Quakertown couple.

Diehl and Brehm are seeking more than $20,000 from Sealy Mattress Co., the manufacturer, and Hess's department store, which sold the mattress. They say the incident traumatized them and caused sleep disorders.

According to the suit, the couple bought a mattress on May 13 from Hess's in Richland Township, Bucks County. Soon after, they began to notice an unfamiliar movement in their bed, which they "suspected could be a living creature."

In July, they exchanged the mattress at Hess's for another Sealy, hoping for a better night's sleep. They didn't get one. The replacement mattress also slithered and shimmied, according to the couple.

After four months of suspicious bumps in the night, Diehl and Brehm took the second mattress to Laboratory Testing Inc. in Dublin for examination. Inside, workers found a dead 26-inch ribbon snake. The species is not poisonous.

The suit contends that both the manufacturer and the department store breached their warranties. . . . No date has been set for a hearing on the case.

John P. Martin, The Philadelphia Inquirer

Most court stories are serious, but some have a humorous angle. Here is a light-hearted story in a conversational style that tries to involve the reader. It is an example of how a plea bargain works—or in this case, how it didn't work out very well. This story is written in storytelling form with the clincher at the end; unfortunately, the headline gives the twist away.

Man gambles on plea, loses

He admits guilt, then is acquitted

You're the defendant. You make the call:

You're Marvin E. Johnson, 40, convicted three times of drug possession. You're facing a minimum 15 years in prison without parole if convicted of being a felon in possession of a handgun.

On Wednesday, the jury at your federal trial in Kansas City deliberates three hours without reaching a verdict. On Thursday, the jury deliberates three more hours and announces it is hopelessly deadlocked. A hung jury and a new trial loom on the horizon.

The prosecutor, Assistant U.S. Attorney Rob Larsen, offers a deal. If you plead guilty, he'll reduce the government's sentencing request to a range of 15 to 22 months.

While you ponder that deal, the jury buzzes. It has a verdict.

Do you:

A) Sign the plea agreement and serve at least 15 months in prison? Or

B) Roll the dice with the jury's verdict? If it's guilty, you get at least 15 years; if it's not guilty, you walk away.

On Thursday afternoon, Marvin E. Johnson signed the plea agreement.

Five minutes later, the jury found him not guilty.

"I'm sure glad I struck that plea agreement," Larsen said.

"I can't win for losing," said Johnson's defense lawyer, John P. O'Connor.

Tom Jackman, The Kansas City *(Mo.)* Star

Exercises

1 **Crime story:** Although the police report shown here is labeled "Standard Offense Report," it is not. Each state has its own form; however, this one is similar to many. Most of the report is self-explanatory, with some exceptions. The case number is important for reporters; if you want to follow the case through the court system, you need this number, which stays the same for all actions in the case. Time is computed as military time, from one to 24 hours. Where the stolen property is listed, codes are used to signify the type of property. A complete code sheet is usually on the back of the police report. Write a story based on the following report:

STANDARD OFFENSE REPORT
FRONT PAGE OPEN PUBLIC RECORD

On View √ Dispatched √ Citizen	Name of Agency Your town police dept.	Agency No. 0230100	Case No. 03-123456

Incident

Date offense started Use yesterday's date	Time 0700	Date offense ended Use today's date	Time ------	Date of report Today's date
Location of Offense 2339 Felony Lane	Time reported 22:36	Time arrived 22:40	Time cleared 22:55	

Offense

Description Burglary	Premise	Method of Entry • Force √ No Force	Type of Theft From building	Type of Force Unknown

Victim

Name of Victim Last First Middle Smith Jon J.	**Address** Street City State ZIP 2339 Felony Lane Your town Yours Yours	Telephone no. 555-1234

Type of victim Individual	Race W	Sex M	Age 22	Ethnicity ----	Height 6-0	Weight 195	Hair Blond	Eyes Blu	License -----	Social Security No 131-300-0123

Reporting Person

Last First Middle Doe James Brian	Address Street City State ZIP 2337 Felony Lane Your town Yours Yours	Telephone no. 555-4321

Type of victim Individual	Race W	Sex M	Age 25	Ethnicity ----	Height 5-10	Weight 170	Hair Br	Eyes Br	License -----	Social Security No 171-009-0554

Property Description - Type of Loss
1=None 2=Burned 3=Counterfeit 4=Destroyed/damaged /vandalized 5=Recovered 6= Seized 7= Stolen 8 = Unknown

Type Loss	Property Code	Description	Est. Quantity	Value	Date Recovered
7	0618	Zenith VCR	1	300	-------------
7	0618	Sharp CD player	1	350	-------------
7	1002	Cockatoo (bird)	1	1,500	-------------

Reporting Officer John Law	Badge No. 733	Date Today	Copies to Property Total 2,150	

Description of incident

At 22:56 the office was contacted by Mr. James Doe, next-door neighbor of the victim. He was watching Mr. Smith's house while Smith was away. Doe checked the door to Smith's residence at 07:00 before he went to work. When he returned home at 22:30, he again checked Smith's residence and noticed that someone had pried the deadbolt lock on the front door. I was dispatched to the residence. I searched premises but did not find any suspects. When Mr. Smith returned home, he advised that items missing were VCR, CD player and cockatoo, who answers to the name of Homer. Owner described bird as white and 10 years old. He said the bird could say his name and had limited vocabulary of "damn," "rotten" and a few curse words.

You called the police to ask more about the theft of the bird because that was unusual. The police told you that the bird was valuable and that was probably the reason it was stolen. They told you there is no rash of bird burglars, although there had been some thefts of birds several months ago. But this bird theft does not appear to be related to those because other items were taken, the police said. Police are still investigating. Use yesterday as your time frame for date of offense and today as the date reported.

2   **Fire story:** You are making a routine call to the fire department to find out if any fires occurred overnight. Fire Battalion Chief Stephen McInerny gives you this information:

A fire occurred in a ground-floor apartment in the 2700 block of Northeast 30th Place in your town at 1:12 a.m. today. Four fire engines and 16 firefighters responded at 1:15 a.m. Cause of fire: A stove was turned on, and some cookbooks and towels on the stove ignited. When firefighters arrived, they found a 2½-year-old cocker spaniel at the front door. Estimated damage: $9,000 smoke damage to apartment. Other units not affected. Apartment is uninhabitable. Dog's name is Tito. McInerny said the dog apparently started the fire by jumping on the stove, using one of the knobs for foothold. The setting on the burner was on medium high. The dog was apparently looking for food. The dog crawled to the front door. "The dog was clinically dead; it had no pulse and no respiration." McInerny said firefighter Bill Mock took the dog outside and gave it cardiopulmonary resuscitation and oxygen, and the dog came back to life. The dog was taken to the animal hospital and treated for smoke inhalation. McInerny said it is not unusual for dogs to be caught in house fires, but it is unusual for them to be revived from the dead. "That's twice in a little more than a year we've revived dogs that have been clinically dead as a result of a fire. We're getting pretty good at it."

You interview Mark Alan Leszczynski, who rented the apartment and owns the dog. He said he and a house guest went to a bar before midnight and left the dog alone. "The dog is a little mischievous. I've caught him doing this before. He has a never-ending appetite. I had just reprimanded him for going into my house guest's suitcase and stealing some candy."

3   **Court terms:** You may use your imagination for this exercise. The point of it is to see if you can use court terminology in the proper context and spell the words correctly. Use the following terms: *change of venue, affidavit, felony, misdemeanor, subpoena, mistrial, bond, arraignment, suspended sentence, plea bargain.*

Use the terms to write a story about this situation: A college student, 19, named Gold E. Locks, has been charged with a felony: breaking and entering into the home of Pa Pa Bear and his wife, Ma Ma Bear, who live at (you decide the address) with their child, Bay B. Bear.

4   **Civil court case:** Write a brief story about the following case, a petition for a name change, which was filed in the civil section of a county court (use your county court).

IN THE CIRCUIT COURT OF (YOUR COUNTY, YOUR STATE)

Joseph Weirdo, Petitioner   Case No. 99 C638

PETITION

Comes now the petitioner, Joseph Weirdo, and prays his cause of action and states as follows:

1. That he resides at 700 Louisiana St., Your City, Your State.

2. That the petitioner requests a change of name from Joseph Weirdo to Joseph Weir.

3. That the current name of the petitioner has caused him great embarrassment and suffering.

4. That petitioner is a citizen in good standing and the request for the name change is not to avoid any legal actions against said petitioner.

5. That petitioner is not seeking for redress as a means of avoiding any debts owed to any parties.

6. Wherefore, petitioner prays for favorable judgment from the court.

Joseph Weirdo
City, State, ZIP Code
On behalf of himself

You call Joseph Weirdo, and he tells you he was tired of being kidded about his name. "I didn't want to go through life being a Weirdo," he says.

You check with Circuit Court Judge Jack Musselman, who approved the petition. He says he signs hundreds of these, but most of them are name-change petitions from divorced women, foster children who want to take the name of the family they have stayed with or people with "an extremely ethnic name." "I can't recall anyone looking to play games. A lot of times people are trying to avoid creditors. There's no way of checking that out."

The court clerk tells you that more than 300 people filed to have their names changed this year. It costs $200 to file the papers.

Featured *News Scene* Assignment

Access *News Scene* at *http://communication.wadsworth.com/newsscene2* to view the three related simulations titled "Trial, Day One"; "Trial, Day Two"; and "Trial, Day Three."

Coaching Tips

Gather as much detail as possible for graphics and for your story.

Seek human-interest stories and anecdotes.

Get information to reconstruct a chronology of events.

Use descriptive and narrative techniques for sidebars.

Double-check all information; initial reports and statistics will change quickly.

Use role-playing reporting techniques: If you were a relative of someone in a tragedy, what would you want and need to know?

Plan highlights boxes and empowerment boxes when you are reporting so that you get crucial information.

Check the Internet for weather and disaster resources.

Use online sources for background perspective and consumer information.

CHAPTER 21

Disasters, Weather and Tragedies

David Handschuh

David Handschuh was buried alive. A photographer for the *New York Daily News,* Handschuh was driving to New York University to begin his first day as an adjunct professor of a photojournalism class. It was the morning of Sept. 11, 2001. He looked up and saw a mass of smoke. He turned on his police scanner and heard a voice screaming: "Send every piece of apparatus; the World Trade Center is on fire."

He called his newspaper and then called NYU to tell them to post a note that he would be "a little late this morning."

"All we knew is that it was an accident," Handschuh recalled. He said he turned his car around and crossed over the center divider of the highway to head toward the towers. As a photographer who had shot hundreds of fires, he knew many of the city's firefighters. He passed a fire truck with 11 firefighters who were waving to him. "All 11 firefighters in that truck died," Handschuh said. "They were on their way to their own funeral, and they didn't know it."

It was just one of many traumatic moments Handschuh would experience on that day and long after the terrorist attack of Sept. 11, 2001, in which 2,749 people died when two hijacked planes crashed into the World Trade Center towers in New York City. Terrorists had also hijacked two other commercial jetliners on that day and crashed one of them into the Pentagon; a fourth plane, headed toward Washington, D.C., plummeted into a field outside of Pittsburgh, Pa.

The first attack in New York was at 8:46 a.m., and Handschuh arrived at the scene at 8:48 a.m., one of the only times he remembers that day. "At that time only one plane had hit the towers," Handschuh said. "The streets of New York were eerily quiet, as though somebody had pressed a mute button." Eighteen minutes later the second plane slammed into the south tower.

Handschuh kept shooting photos. About an hour later the south tower started to collapse. "I was standing across the street," Handschuh said. "A voice in the back of my head said, 'Run.' It was like a wave at the beach. I was running one second and flying the next. The impact of the building tossed fire trucks. I wound up partially under a fire truck. I was buried alive. I never lost consciousness, I don't think. I couldn't move my legs. A fireman came and said, 'Don't worry, Brother, we'll get you out. You're hurt but you're alive.'"

The World Trade Center towers shortly after
planes crashed into them

For the next nine months he went through physical therapy. "I had to learn how to walk again," he said. His right leg had been completely crushed, and his left leg had also been "messed up." His nose and mouth had been clogged with ashes. His breathing and his lungs remain only at 50 percent capacity. But even now, several years after the 9/11 tragedy, that experience scarred him in less visible but equally significant ways. He still pauses when he hears a plane overhead.

"I never want to photograph anyone dead or dying again," Handschuh says. So these days he is a food photographer. Working with the Dart Center for Journalism & Trauma (*http://www.dartcenter.org*), Handschuh spends some of his time coaching journalists on how to deal with post-traumatic stress disorder, which can result from reporting and photographing tragedy. The center, based at the University of Washington, provides tips and tools to help journalists understand how to cover tragedies and how to cope with their own emotional stress that can result from this type of journalism. Until recently, little attention had ever been paid to the toll that disaster coverage can take on journalists who have to stifle their own emotions as they report and photograph the trauma of tragedy victims. But during these tragedies, journalists excel and suppress their own feelings to fulfill their mission to inform the public. Despite the personal toll, Handschuh stresses the crucial role of journalists by saying, "Our work became history."

Tim McGuire, editor of the *Star Tribune* in Minneapolis, explained it this way: "When you're working at top efficiency, on the biggest story of your

Cleanup at the World Trade Center disaster area in New York

life, the journalist's emotions are not like the emotions of 'real people.' You become almost ashamed of how divorced you are from the suffering. And then bam! You see something on TV, or truly absorb the impact of a story you're reading, and you drown in empathy, sympathy and dread," he wrote in an article for *The American Editor,* the magazine of the American Society of Newspaper Editors.

"Our focus had to be on doing our job out of a sense of the common good," McGuire wrote. "We were charged with delivering the news and perspective on this tragedy to our readership. If we got too close to the pain, it would have impaired our ability to do what we had to do for the greater good. . . . And what we do has felt more like a calling than it has for some time. For many of us our view of our journalistic craft has been transformed."

Images from that tragedy will be seared in people's minds and in history. "We have to take those pictures," Handschuh says, "but we don't have to publish them. These were some very tough calls."

Associated Press photographer Richard Drew captured a haunting image of a man falling headfirst from one of the twin towers of the World Trade Center. His photo became the subject of ethical discussions in newsrooms around the country as editors debated whether to use it. Many did.

Bill Marimow, former editor of *The Sun* in Baltimore, was one of them. "The horror of the event determines the use of the photos," he wrote in an article for The American Press Institute. "There are so many other things that we can adjust to minimize the sensitivity aspect, but we must not minimize the horror of the event." It was one of many ethical discussions in newsrooms throughout the country as editors struggled to document history and reporters struggled to document grief. The names and stories behind the numbers were the only way to explain the horror.

Of the 2,749 people who died in the 9/11 attacks, the remains of 1,161 victims were never identified, and efforts to analyze the DNA from remains have ended. The pain has not ended for families of the victims, and their stories explain the tragedy that lingers behind the numbers.

> The news was disheartening for many families who say they can't find closure when they don't have a body part to place in a coffin and bury in a grave.
>
> Joan Greene, 72, of Staten Island, said she knew in her heart that the chances of getting back remains of her daughter Lorraine Lee were not good, but had held out hope.
>
> "This is very hard," Greene said. "I just wish I could have something of her. It's hard to put into words but I need something to go to in the cemetery to think that part of her is there. It feels very empty."
>
> *Lindsay Farber and Carol Eisenberg,*
> New York Newsday

In 2004 a natural disaster usurped the death toll of 9/11. More than 180,000 people were believed to have died and another 100,000 were missing in more than 12 Southeast Asian countries bordering the Indian Ocean when an earthquake spawned a massive wall of water called a "tsunami" that swept entire towns and their inhabitants into the sea. It happened the day after Christmas in 2004, and months later, the search continued for victims of one of the world's worst natural disasters in 100 years. The final death toll may never be known.

But again the story was best told not by numbers but by the human toll on individuals—some searching for loved ones and others who witnessed the devastation and lived to describe it. Like this excerpt from a *Tampa* (Fla.) *Tribune* story:

> HAMBANTOTA, Sri Lanka—When T.D. Kamaldeen's toddler son asks where his Mama is, he tells him she's working abroad, making money to buy him chocolate. Or maybe a bicycle.
>
> Sometimes the 3-year-old boy with big brown eyes wants to call and talk to Mama. Kamaldeen doesn't know what to say. How do you tell a child his mother, grandmother, aunt, uncle and cousins—nine people in all—died in the ferocious water that he saw take his house?

ETHICS

You are the news editor for a newspaper or television station in your community, and the photographer has shot images of dead bodies along with several other photos of an airplane disaster scene. The photos of the bodies strewn around the crash site are the most dramatic. Until the disasters of 9/11 and subsequent images from the war in Iraq, most U.S. media did not run photos of dead bodies. However, that changed after the 9/11 terrorist attack. Will you print or air these photos? If so, how will you justify it to the victims' families?

Guidelines: As the National Press Photographers Association's code of ethics states, "Photographic and video images can reveal great truths, expose wrongdoing and neglect, inspire hope and understanding and connect people around the globe through the language of visual understanding. Photographs can also cause great harm if they are callously intrusive or are manipulated. Treat all subjects with respect and dignity. Give special consideration to vulnerable subjects and compassion to victims of crime or tragedy. Intrude on private moments of grief only when the public has an overriding and justifiable need to see."

Or this description from an Associated Press story from Indonesia, where at least 126,000 people died and 113,000 are missing:

The island of Sumatra was nearest the undersea epicenter of the magnitude 9.0 earthquake—the world's fourth largest in the past 100 years—and the mountains of water it sent rushing shoreward at jetliner speed.

Bodies were left on the streets and beaches as the waves receded. Relief workers initially laid the dead out on sidewalks for relatives to identify. But within hours, the sight and smell prompted Muslim leaders to sanction mass burials.

"Every day, we were collecting 6,000 bodies," said Eka Susila, the Indonesian Red Cross coordinator, who recalled wrapping the dead in sheets or tablecloths for lack of body bags. "We had no time to identify them. We just had to find the bodies and bury them."

Throughout the United States, news organizations sought local angles for the story by writing about disaster-relief efforts in their area and finding people personally affected by the tragedy.

Joe Hight, managing editor of *The Oklahoman* in Oklahoma City, stresses the importance of covering tragedy with sensitivity. In an article for the Dart Center for Journalism & Trauma, he reflected on the 10th anniversary of the bombing of a federal building in his city.

Alfred P. Murrah building after it was bombed

"The bombing aftermath taught me the impact of your coverage on the victims, community and journalists," he wrote. "It taught me that a tough journalist could be a sensitive journalist. And it taught me that we live in a world in which violent acts can occur anywhere at anytime, even on a nice and sunny spring day in your community."

It was in that unlikely place that journalism students at the University of Oklahoma learned how to cover a disaster that was not a class exercise.

Joy Mathis was sitting at her desk in *The Oklahoma Daily* newsroom at 9 a.m. on April 19, 1995, when someone ran in and said there had been a bomb explosion in Oklahoma City. Terrorists had bombed a nine-story federal building in Oklahoma City, 20 miles from the campus in Norman, Okla.

As managing editor of the campus newspaper, Mathis tried to find reporters to send to the scene. "No one realized what a big deal it was," she said. But within an hour after the news broke, reporters started calling Mathis and asking what they could do. Mathis didn't have a specific plan. "I was just screaming at people. I was saying, 'Get University of Oklahoma angles.' That's the kind of story I knew we could do better than anyone else."

At that time, it was the worst-known terrorist attack in the United States. Timothy McVeigh, the terrorist who bombed the building, was later convicted and executed. His accomplice, Terry Nichols, was sentenced to life in prison. The federal building was razed, and a permanent memorial and museum have been erected on the site. The memorial site includes a reflecting pool and 168 empty metal chairs, one for each of the bombing victims, each on a glass base inscribed with the name of a victim.

Omar L. Gallaga (left), Joy Mathis (middle), and Michelle Fielden working on a story about the Oklahoma City bombing

Anita Amarfio

Like the indelible inscriptions for the victims, that tragedy remains etched in the memories of the Oklahoma students, and their coverage still serves as a lesson on how to report and write about tragedy. Within hours after the bombing occurred, Mathis had at least 20 reporters and photographers gathering news on the scene in the city and around the campus. The coverage wasn't organized at this point.

By 7 p.m., most of the reporters and photographers had returned. Mathis and Tiffany Pape, editor of the newspaper, began organizing the stories and planning the pages.

"I was feeling a little panicky because we were just getting organized, and the reporters were freaking because they didn't have much time to write," Mathis says. "But by 8 p.m. we had every editor reading stories." Their 16-page newspaper included six pages of explosion news and photographs, graphics, and information boxes about where to donate blood or get more information.

Omar L. Gallaga had kept his emotions in check most of the day. Now he was tired. He returned to the newsroom and then headed for Norman Regional Hospital and the Norman Red Cross. But coverage wouldn't be easy.

"At the hospital a doctor said they had their first explosion victim," Gallaga says. "The man had been walking into an elevator when the building exploded. This was exactly what I'd been waiting and hoping for. Just when I felt it was time to approach the slightly wounded man, the (public relations) woman came in. She forbade me to speak to any patients." Everyone else was too busy to speak to him.

He headed for the Red Cross. He had better luck there. People were lined up for about two hours to give blood. He went to the waiting room. "In that waiting room I saw a poster whose content would become the lead for one of my bombing stories. It read ominously, 'A disaster can happen in any place, at any time!' WOW. I scribbled it down. I talked to some students who were getting ready to donate and left the scene. I returned to the newsroom where I would spend the rest of the day and night."

Gallaga was emotionally composed until he read Rudolf Isaza's story about a grandmother who was awaiting news about her two grandchildren, ages 5 and 3, who had been in the federal building's day-care center. The woman had told Isaza about the youngest one:

> "He liked to draw," she said. "Just the other day he showed me a drawing of a tall and short man. I asked him who it was. He said it was Shaquille O'Neal and me."
>
> Seconds later, she was rushed into the hospital with the hope that there was some news of her grandchildren. After looking through pages of hospital fatalities and treated people, there came a tragic cry.
>
> *Rudolf Isaza,* The Oklahoma Daily

"I began to cry when I read that," Gallaga says. "As the night wore on, we all pitched in to edit stories, and the stress was starting to wear us down."

It was close to deadline. Midnight came and went. By 12:30, only a half hour after deadline, the paper was ready for the printer.

The techniques of reporting and writing these stories are the same as for any other story. But there are some differences in how you gather the information.

Reporting Techniques

Before you venture out of the newsroom to report on a disaster, you should find out a few facts and take emergency precautions and supplies. Many major metropolitan newspapers have plans for covering disasters. In Fort Lauderdale, Fla., for example, *The Sun-Sentinel* has a detailed plan for coverage of disasters, particularly hurricanes. The plan spells out the responsibilities of each editor; assignments for reporters (hospitals, areas of the city, agencies); and telephone numbers of police, fire and rescue agencies, hospitals, utilities, and other places crucial to disaster coverage.

Cities also have disaster plans, and police and fire departments frequently conduct drills to test them. If you have a municipal beat, find out if the government has such a plan, and get a copy of it. If a disaster occurs, a good follow-up story is to check whether the plan was effective.

In the event of a disaster, you should follow these basic procedures before leaving your office or home:

- Check a map to see what routes lead to the scene. Are there alternative routes in case major arteries are blocked?
- Find out if temporary headquarters have been established for officials and media.
- Take plenty of change to make telephone calls to the newsroom to keep editors informed. If you have electronic equipment—a notebook computer or cellular telephone—make sure that you have the right e-mail addresses and phone numbers. Also make sure that your cell phone is fully charged. If you are calling in your story on deadline, remember that information changes frequently, and you will need to keep updating your editors.
- Take proper clothing, if necessary: boots, rain gear, a change of clothes (in cases of flood coverage) and emergency rations—food and beverage if you think you'll be stuck somewhere for an extended period, flashlight, and so on. You could be reporting for a long time in an area without utilities. It's a good idea to have this emergency kit of supplies in your car at all times.
- Make sure that you have a full tank of gas for your vehicle.
- Take plenty of notebooks, pens and even pencils, which are better than pens or electronic gear in rainy weather. Don't rely on tape recorders or notebook computers at the scene of a disaster.

When you are covering the breaking news of a plane crash or earthquake or you are in the middle of a major storm, the sources of information are disorganized and unreliable. The news changes momentarily. The death toll often changes radically within the first few hours and even weeks or months later in a major disaster. Chaos reigns. You get the best information you can from eyewitnesses and officials at the scene. And then you check back repeatedly.

How do you know what to ask? You always need to ask the basics: who, what, when, where, why and how. But another way of thinking about questions is role-playing, the "what if" technique of reporting. What if I were in this person's place? What if I were waiting to find out about a relative? What would I want to know?

For example, what if it were spring or winter break and you were expecting friends or relatives to visit you? Suddenly you hear over the radio that a plane has crashed at the international airport closest to you. What do you want to know? Make a list. Chances are that the information you want to know is the kind of information any reader would want to know. What airline, what plane, how many people died, who died, who survived, what caused the crash, how did it happen, where did it crash? Those questions will produce information for your lead and the top of your story. Then you gather details.

Think statistics. You need specifics: numbers of people killed or injured or evacuated.

Think human interest. How did people cope? How did they survive? What are their losses? What are their tragedies? Three hundred people could die in a plane crash, but the human-interest stories of a few people make that crash vivid and poignant for the reader.

Think about narrative storytelling techniques for sidebars. How would you reconstruct the incident—what was the chronology? Try to gather information about the sequence of events if the story involves such disasters as explosions, plane crashes and other events that are not acts of nature. However, even with tornadoes, earthquakes, floods and hurricanes, it helps to get the sequence of events—specific times that events occurred, the minutes involved in destruction.

Think about helpful information for empowerment boxes. Where can people get more information, donate blood, volunteer their services and so on?

Sidebars

Sidebars are not synonymous with soft news. Many sidebars are human-interest stories, but they also can be hard-news stories or informational self-help stories. A sidebar is basically a story that gives the reader some new information or more information than the mainbar can provide. The mainbar in a disaster story is comprehensive; each sidebar should be very narrowly focused on one topic. The mainbar can allude to information that is in the sidebar, such as a quote from an eyewitness, but the sidebar should not be repetitious. A mainbar without emotional quotes from people would be boring. However, an entire sidebar about the people who have been quoted extensively in the mainbar is too repetitious.

Here are some ideas for sidebars and some questions you can ask to determine whether you need them:

Helpfulness: If I were the reader, what information would I find helpful? For example, if a disaster affects utilities, as in a flood, should you have a sidebar on how to cope without electricity or fresh water? Or if it affects roads, consider a story about alternate routes. Or a story about how to get government aid.

Human interest: Is there a human-interest story that the reader might find compelling? Does someone have a story that is unusual?

Perspective: Would the reader find it interesting to know the history of other disasters of this type?

The location: Is there a color piece that is compelling about the scene or a location affected by the disaster, such as a story about the hospital scene or the shelters where evacuated people were taken?

Other angles: Is there enough information worth telling about a specific angle of the story, such as the rescue efforts, the efforts of investigators or previous problems with that type of aircraft?

Analysis: If your community has been working on a disaster plan, is there a need for an analysis piece about how rescue or government workers coordinated the disaster operations?

In most cases, especially in human-interest sidebars, you can use all the feature techniques of descriptive and narrative writing that you have studied. You should try to make the story vivid and compelling.

A sidebar still stands alone as a story, so you need to insert a reference to the main news—a brief line about the disaster or crash—especially if you have only one sidebar. If you have a huge package of several sidebars, you don't need to rehash the news statement in each one. You need to coordinate with the editor just how much of the main news needs to be in your story.

Here is an excerpt from a sidebar to the students' Oklahoma City bombing package:

Explosion prompts blood drives, donations

An ominous poster hangs in a room of the Cleveland County Red Cross. It reads, "Disaster can strike anywhere, at any time!"

As Norman residents lined up to donate blood and supplies, conversation kept going back to the explosion that ripped through downtown Oklahoma City, leaving fatalities and shock in its wake.

When the Red Cross opened its doors at 10:30 a.m., about 100 people were waiting to give blood, said Kelly Walsh, director of Red Cross donor services in Cleveland County.

Kelly said her organization will continue to accept blood of all types. "We'll need blood tomorrow, the next day and next week." Particularly, the Red Cross is looking for type O blood, which can be used universally. However, Walsh said, "We need all types because all types of blood can be used for platelets."

The Red Cross will stay open until people stop coming in and as long as the staff lasts, Walsh said. Extended hours will be kept for the remainder of the week.

Those donating blood waited an average of two hours while volunteers and about 20 staff members took donations and brought in food and supplies.

Anthony Johnson, an OU microbiology sophomore, waited to donate with a group of friends. Johnson said he was angered by the bombing. "It was a big mistake. You just don't do that. Not in this country. Not in this state."

Omar Gallaga, The Oklahoma Daily

Graphics

Almost all disaster stories are accompanied by graphics—maps, illustrations, charts—to help the reader visualize where, when and how. But only a few newspapers have graphics reporters. The job of supplying information to the graphic designer or artist falls to the news reporter.

You need to gather details. Get information about exact locations: cross streets and measurements in yards or feet of where the accident, explosion or plane crash occurred. Try to get a map from a local gas station or convenience store. Consider whether the incident lends itself to a graphic using the time of the accident. Get a chronology in minutes or hours.

In the process of gathering all the information you need to describe the scene to a person who will draw it, you will be gathering some details you can use in your story. And, of course, the observation skills you develop will help with all the descriptive writing you do to make the reader see and care.

Graphic accompanying a story
about a plane crash

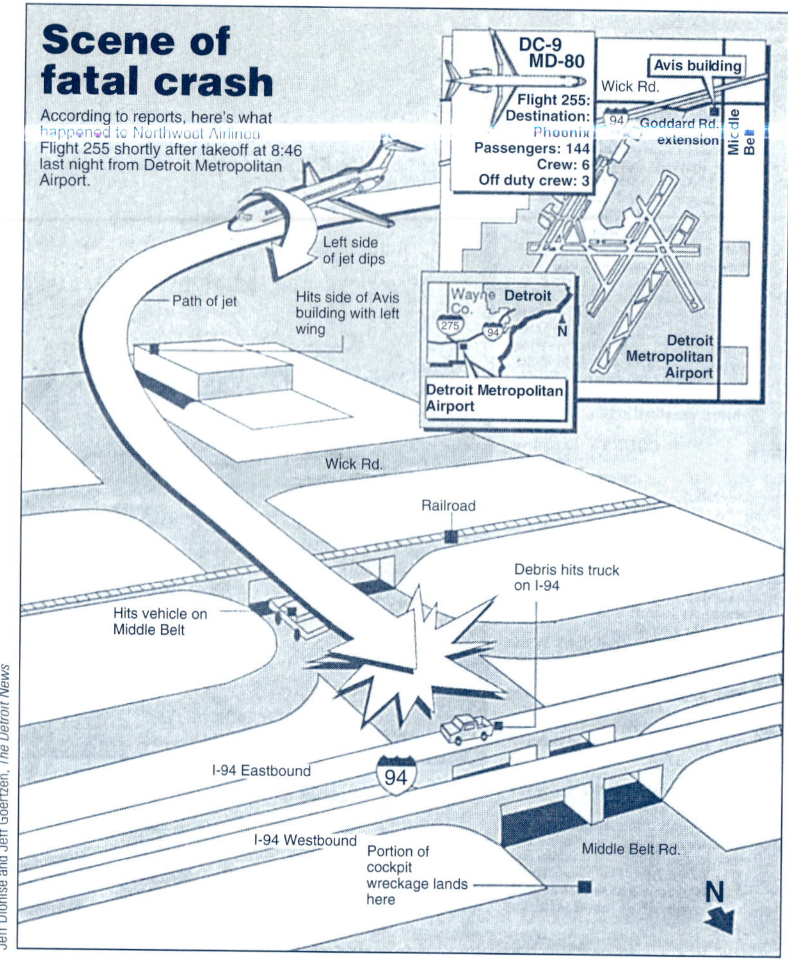

Disaster Basics

Whether you are a covering a natural disaster, such as an earthquake, or another kind, such as a plane crash or explosion, you need to gather some basic facts. With the exception of the five W's, which come first, the rest of the items are not listed in order of importance.

Who: How many people died or were injured, and how many survived? These numbers will change constantly, but "who" should be one of your first questions. In a plane crash, get the name of the airline, the flight number and type of aircraft, takeoff and destination sites, and the number of passengers and crew members on board.

What and why: In many disasters, particularly airplane crashes, the cause is not immediately known. However, you should always ask and keep asking for follow-up stories. In natural disasters, get statistics about the height of rivers in floods, the intensity of earthquakes, the velocity of winds in hurricanes and similar information.

When and where: Find out exactly what time the disaster occurred and the location. Consider graphics and a reconstruction of the event.

MULTIMEDIA COACH

Major stories involving disasters and tragedies are usually accompanied by sidebars that offer consumers helpful information and perspective on how this event compares to others of its kind. That type of information is now easy to get on the Web. As with all information from the Web, make sure that you are using a reliable source that is up to date. Here are some online tips:

- Check the Red Cross and other disaster-relief agencies for sidebars telling readers where to go for help and how to cope.

- Consider time lines or lists of other major disasters, available online from weather and government sites such as the National Hurricane Center at *http://www.nhc.noaa.gov*.

- Airlines often use the Web to provide information about disasters. The National Transportation Safety Board at *www.ntsb.gov* is the main investigating agency for aircraft, railroad and other major accidents.

- Use the Internet to obtain updated information from community government and other agencies on disaster conditions for your research. During some disasters, government and relief agencies provide faster updates online than by telephone or other media.

- Provide links to online information for consumers in Web, broadcast and printed media.

- Report information to editors as soon as you get it for posting on the publication's Web site. The Web is often users' first choice for breaking news during disasters.

- Check related resources on the Web site for this chapter at *http://communication.wadsworth.com/rich5e*.

Weather: For a weather-related disaster, get the specifics. If it is a plane crash, always find out about the weather, which could have been a factor.

Where people go: In case of evacuation—as in floods, hurricanes and earthquakes—find out where people are finding shelter.

Hospitals: Whenever people are injured, check hospitals.

Disaster scene: Gather every detail of sight, sound, emotion and other sensory feelings. You will need them for description in your stories.

Estimated cost of damages and property loss: Initially, these accounts—from insurance agents, fire departments, police officials or state offices—are often inaccurate, but they add an essential element to the story.

Eyewitness accounts: Get accounts from eyewitnesses and survivors. People make the story real and emotional. You need them for quotes in the main story and for sidebars. Ask people to reconstruct where they were and what they were doing at the time of the disaster.

Government agencies involved: In plane crashes, the Federal Aviation Administration and National Transportation Safety Board always get involved in investigations. In major disasters, find out whether the National Guard is helping and which federal, state and local agencies will provide relief.

Consumer information: Find out where to go to give blood, to get help with insurance or rebuilding, to get further information. Consumer information may be included in your story or in empowerment boxes.

Red Cross and shelters: Always check with the Red Cross and other relief agencies for their role and their needs.

Safety precautions: Check with police and fire departments and with electric, gas and water utility companies to find out about the precautions people should take. You could refer to dangerous conditions in the main story or in a separate story.

Roads: Check highway departments to find out which roads are closed or dangerous and what alternate routes people can take.

Survivors: List those who are known to be alive.

Victims: The names of people who were killed are often not released for days, but try to obtain them from officials.

Crime: Check with police to find out about looting or other post-disaster crimes or arrests in cases of human-created disasters.

Perspective: Was this the worst, second-worst or ninth-worst disaster of its kind in a certain period of time? Check online sources or an almanac to find out how this disaster ranks against previous disasters of its kind. If it is the worst of its type, that information should appear high in the story.

Background: Check the background of the airline involved in a plane crash or a business involved in a disaster. Readers will be interested in any history that may apply to this disaster.

Medical examiner: Check for information about progress in the identification of victims.

Here is how many of those basic elements worked in *The Oklahoma Daily*'s first-day story by Rudolf Isaza about the bombing in Oklahoma City. Many descriptive human-interest stories were in sidebars or some of the 14 other stories.

Bomb cripples Oklahoma City

Explosion leaves 31 dead, 300 missing

At least 31 people died and 300 were still missing Wednesday after a car bomb gouged a nine-story hole in a federal office building.

A 9:04 a.m. explosion ravaged the north side of the Alfred Murrah Federal Building at 200 NW Fifth St. in downtown Oklahoma City. Most of the more than 500 employees were in their offices.

As of midnight Wednesday, the confirmed death toll was 31 people, 12 of those children. About 300 people were missing. At least 200 people were injured, 58 critically, said Fire Chief Gary Marrs. Many more were feared trapped in the rubble.

"Firefighters are having to crawl over corpses in areas to get to people that are still alive," said Jon Hansen, assistant fire chief.

Gov. Frank Keating has called a state of emergency. Nationwide bomb experts from federal agencies have been called in to decipher the cause of the bombing. The Oklahoma National Guard was called in.

Keating said he was told by the FBI that authorities were initially looking for three people in a brown pickup truck. The Oklahoma Highway Patrol put out an all-points bulletin for three individuals, described as of Middle Eastern descent. One was described as being between the ages of 25 and 30. Another may have been between 35 and 38.

Bob Ricks, head of the Oklahoma City FBI office, said the blast left a crater 20 feet long and eight feet deep directly outside the building, meaning the source of the explosion was probably outside.

An architect said the building was stable and was not in immediate danger of falling over. Ricks said the shock was felt 50 miles away. Glass was reported shattered in businesses and homes within a 30-mile radius.

The search for people trapped in the rubble started as soon as the blast occurred, starting from the top floors down. People frantically looked for loved ones, including parents whose children were in the building's day care center. Rescuers had problems initiating the search because the elevator shaft was destroyed in the blast.

"The only way up the building is one staircase," Marrs said.

Ricks would not speculate on any suspects. "We are making no assumptions at this point," he said. "We've had hundreds, if not thousands, of leads." By midday, the government had received calls from six people saying they were from Muslim sects and asserting they were responsible for the bombing.

A police source, who requested anonymity, said FBI agents were trying to piece together a van or truck that was believed to have carried the explosives. An axle of the vehicle was found about two blocks from the scene, the source said.

General concern was that this was a direct attack on the FBI. Ricks said although the FBI did not have an office in the building, 13 brother agencies did, including the Secret Service and the Bureau of Alcohol, Tobacco and Firearms.

Also destroyed, on the second floor on the northwest side, was America's Kids, a day-care center for federal and county employees. Seventeen children had been treated as of 10 p.m. Three were treated and released, and 20 were still unaccounted for.

Oklahoma City Chief of Police Sam Gonzalez said the Oklahoma City Police Department was in charge of perimeter control and monitoring streets, and has roped off four blocks in each direction.

Oklahoma City Mayor Ron Norick requested that all people who were in the building at the time of the explosion call 297-2424 or 397-2345 to get an accurate number of people inside the building.

Rudolf Isaza, The Oklahoma Daily

Death Tolls

The day after the Oklahoma City bombing, the death toll had risen to 57. Each day thereafter, the number of dead and injured increased. The final toll was 168 people, including 19 children. The opposite situation occurred in the World Trade Center tragedy, where the death toll dropped from initial reports of more than 6,000 to about 3,000 a few months later.

In disasters, dealing with numbers of victims is difficult because they change constantly. The first day you can report the facts as Isaza did, saying "At least . . . ," or use the words "an estimated" with the specific number. The following day your lead can state that the death toll has increased, or you can just write the new death toll. You don't need to correct previous information. Readers know you haven't made an error; you are just giving the facts as they become available.

Interviews With Grief-stricken People

You have a list of people who died. Your editor wants you to call the families of victims to get biographical data and reactions. What do you do? Quit your job? Cry? Get sick? Many reporters feel like doing all three. But there are sensitive ways to cover grief. And it's difficult, if not impossible, to avoid dealing with such situations if you are going to be a newspaper or magazine reporter. So here are some suggestions about how you can cover such stories.

Jacqui Banaszynski, a senior editor for *The Seattle Times,* has covered numerous stories involving grief, so many that she claims she has the grief beat. When she is reporting about tragedy, she often tells the people she interviews that if at the end of the interview they don't like the way she has conducted herself, she will offer them her notebook and won't write anything. So far, no one has ever taken her up on her offer.

How can you ask questions about grief? Try this classroom exercise: In groups of three or four, list all the fears and anxieties you have about interviewing people who are grieving. Then discuss some reporting techniques you can use to deal with each of these concerns. After compiling your concerns and solutions, discuss them with the class as a whole.

Here are some concerns students usually express during this activity:

What if the person hangs up on me? You could try the Edna Buchanan technique of calling back and suggesting you were disconnected. Or you could just forget that interview and try calling someone else. Another suggestion is to call a neighbor and ask if he or she knows someone in the house who might talk to you. Or call the house and ask if anyone could talk to you about the situation. You don't have to ask for the person who is in the greatest pain. If you are on the scene and the person does not want to talk to you, you might give him or her your card (or a note with your name and phone number) and ask if you could talk at another time.

What questions do I ask? Don't ask, "How do you feel about your son's death?" Obviously, the person feels terrible. You might instead ask specific questions about what the person was like—in other words, biographical questions. What was the person planning, or where was he or she going when the accident happened? Then you could ask for memories about the person.

What is the first thing I should say? Introduce yourself and state your purpose. You might also express your condolences.

What if I start to cry? You can be empathetic and even a little teary. Try not to weep. But be sincere. Do not fake your emotions.

What if the person I'm interviewing starts to cry? Stop interviewing and ask if you can get the person a glass of water or a tissue, or just be quiet for a while. You might also ask if the person would prefer you to come back another time, depending on the severity of the situation.

What if I say something insensitive without knowing it? Apologize.

Why do I have to interview people in times of grief? Because these types of stories make a news event more significant and real to readers. Because people relate to other people, not to vague generalities. And remember, for some people, talking about their pain is a form of catharsis. For others, grief is a very private matter. So some people will talk to you, and others won't. Respect their needs. You won't get every story, especially if reporters from other newspapers and television stations have already talked to them. But the ones you do talk to can be wonderful.

Here is an example demonstrating how reporters interviewed friends and relatives of people who died in a plane crash. Notice from the quotes that reporters did not ask "How do you feel?" The quotes and backup information contain specific memories and details about the people who died.

Grief cuts wide swath

Relatives draw close as horror sinks in

**By Jon Pepper
and Rachel Reynolds**

The names of the dead trickled out slowly.

Among them was a professional basketball player. A weight lifter. A high school cheerleader and a successful businessman. A nursery school teacher from St. Clair Shores.

There were boyfriends and girlfriends, granddaughters and grandsons, husbands and wives.

None of the dead were positively identified by this morning. The few names that trickled out came from friends and relatives.

Kurt Dobronski, 28, vice-president of a Scottsdale, Ariz., construction firm and a former star football player at Dearborn Edsel Ford High and Central Michigan University, had come home to Dearborn for the wedding of a friend and found his 10-day visit "the best vacation he ever had," said brother Karl Dobronski.

"Things were going great for him," Karl Dobronski said. "This is a shock."

Things were also going well for Nick Vanos, a 7 foot-2 center for the Phoenix Suns basketball team. After playing only sparingly in his first two years in the National Basketball Association, Vanos was expected to start for the Suns this fall. He had come to Detroit to visit a girlfriend and boarded Flight 255 for his return to Arizona, team officials said.

"Nick Vanos was a young man who was just beginning to come into his own as a professional athlete and was about to take a giant step," said Suns general manager Jerry Coangelo. "It was very sad because he gave everything he had with his abilities. . . ."

Bill Horton of Phoenix lost his wife, Cindy, 37, who had been visiting her parents in Wisconsin. She had flown to Detroit to catch a flight to Phoenix. At midnight Sunday, he tried to calm his two stepchildren, aged 11 and 7. "They're hysterical," Horton said, sobbing. "How do you explain something like this to them?"

The Detroit News

Follow-up Stories

All major disasters require follow-up stories for many days. The second-day story should attempt to explain the cause, if that was not clear the first day. If the cause still isn't clear, you can lead with what officials are investigating. If there isn't any new information, you can describe cleanup attempts at the scene. The death toll should remain in the lead, especially if it has changed from earlier reports, or should be in the first few paragraphs. Other follow-up stories may focus on rescue efforts, human-interest elements, costs of rebuilding or any other related news.

In follow-up stories, you still need to mention what happened—when and where the plane crashed, when the earthquake occurred, and so on. In successive stories, that information can go a little bit lower. But it should still be high in the story on the second day.

Here is the second-day lead on the mainbar about the plane crash in Detroit:

Loose and broken parts caused the breakdown since mid-1985 of four jet engines like those on Northwest Flight 255, which crashed Sunday at Detroit Metropolitan Airport.

At least 154 people were killed after witnesses saw an explosion in or near the aircraft's left engine. However, the head of a National Transportation Safety Board team investigating the crash said other witnesses saw no such fire and "very preliminary" findings are that there was no failure or fire in the left engine.

Documents describing the engine failures, known to the Federal Aviation Administration (FAA) and the National Transportation Safety Board (NTSB) since April, were obtained in Washington Monday.

A U.S. Department of Transportation source claimed Monday that a serious fuel leak problem with the jet was reported by crew members less than two weeks ago. FAA officials refused to confirm such a report.

In Romulus, workers began the soul-bruising task of collecting human remains from the crash site for identification by pathologists, friends and relatives.

Ric Bohy, Fred Girard, Mike Martindale and Joel Smith, The Detroit News

Airplane Crashes

You may never have to cover a major airplane crash, but small plane crashes occur in almost every community. The principles for writing and reporting the news are the same, regardless of the size of the crash.

Almost all the disaster-related information listed earlier also applies to an airplane crash. One of your first concerns should be the number of dead or injured people. Initially, you will get only estimates, and most likely they will be wrong. But some accounting of the death and injury toll should be in the lead.

Although an actual cause may not be known for months, ask anyway because you need some idea.

You should also seek the names, ages and hometowns of victims and survivors. In major plane crashes, the list of passengers and their status is usually not released for a day or more, until the relatives have been notified. The names and status of the pilots and crew members may be available sooner.

In addition to getting accounts from eyewitnesses, reactions from relatives or people at the airport, and other human-interest stories, make sure that you get the following specifics: name of the airline and flight number of the plane; the type of plane and number of engines, especially for small planes; the origination and final destination sites.

Check for comments from the air controllers. The pilot's last words are usually not available until investigators get the plane's "black box" recording, but keep it in mind for follow-up stories.

Don't forget the perspective: how many plane crashes of this type have occurred in recent years or how this crash ranks in severity.

Here is an example of a plane crash story that illustrates most of the guidelines for disaster coverage:

20 die in La Guardia crash

The Associated Press

Lead: airline, number of people aboard, where crashed, when, death toll, destination, flight number

NEW YORK—A USAir jet carrying 51 people crashed in a snowstorm Sunday while trying to take off from La Guardia Airport and skidded part way into the frigid waters of Flushing Bay. Authorities said at least 20 people were killed.

Witnesses said USAir Flight 405, bound for Cleveland, left the ground, then fell back and exploded before sliding into the water.

Eyewitness account, color quote

"It looked like the sun coming up," witness Manny Dias told WNBC-TV. "The sky lit up. It was just about to take off. It just exploded."

Backup for lead: death toll, survivors, missing

Sgt. John Murphy of the Port Authority said 20 people were dead, 27 were known to have survived and four others were still missing.

Elaboration

Divers said they found passengers, and the plane's pilot, strapped upside down in their seats in the submerged part of the wreckage.

Status of airport, diversion of flights

The airport was closed after the accident, which occurred about 9:30 p.m. Incoming flights were diverted to nearby John F. Kennedy International Airport.

Elaboration

Twenty-one people climbed out of the plane in the water and to the Delta shuttle terminal, Port Authority police said.

Suspected cause

Neither the airline nor the Federal Aviation Administration had any immediate explanation for what caused the plane to crash during takeoff or whether the bad weather was a factor. The National Transportation Safety Board sent investigators to the scene.

Detail

Port Authority police said the plane veered left at the end of the runway and hit a snow-covered barricade just before the water.

The nose, wing and engine snapped off while the rest of the plane was in the water with its top sheared off.

Relatives, friends: secluded (no reaction possible yet)

At Cleveland's Hopkins International Airport, friends and relatives of passengers aboard the plane were in seclusion.

Airline official's comments substantiating earlier facts

USAir spokeswoman Lynn McCloud in Arlington, Va., said 51 people were on the jet, including 47 passengers, two pilots and two flight attendants. The airline said the flight originated in Jacksonville, Fla., and five passengers were booked all the way through to Cleveland.

Origination point

Weather

McCloud, the USAir spokeswoman, said the temperature was 31 degrees, wind about 15 mph, and the runway was wet with patches of snow. She said visibility was three-quarters of a mile.

The aircraft was a 6-year-old Fokker-28 4000 commuter jet, McCloud said.

Detail about plane

FAA spokesman Fred Farrar described the plane as a "relatively small two-engine jet with both engines on the rear of the fuselage."

Perspective: other crashes

It was the second time in three years a plane has skidded off a runway at La Guardia. Both were USAir flights.

Natural Disasters

All disaster stories should include the same basic information: death toll, survivors, eyewitness accounts, human-interest quotes from survivors, and details of the scene and of recovery efforts. For natural disasters, add information about the natural forces at work, such as weather conditions.

Any time you are writing about a weather-related disaster, be sure to include a weather forecast. If you are covering floods, find out how high the river crested—if that was a factor—or the height of water in feet. If winds were a cause of the destruction, get the specific miles per hour of the wind velocity. In the case of an earthquake, find out the magnitude and the location of the epicenter. Explain in simple terms how the natural phenomenon occurred. A graphic may be better than words.

Tornadoes, earthquakes, hurricanes and floods all cause extensive damage and leave people homeless. Find out where people are finding shelter and what is being done to help them. Insurance is also a big factor in natural disasters. Include consumer information, such as areas that readers should avoid and the names of impassable streets, or how people can cope. Utilities are often affected, so make sure that you check about the safety of drinking water, food supplies and electricity.

Many of these consumer elements may be in sidebars. But when you write the first-day story, the format is similar to that of a plane crash or any other disaster. Give the basic facts and a death or injury toll in the lead.

> FERNDALE, Calif.—A powerful earthquake rocked California's remote North Coast on Saturday, knocking brick facades off buildings, sparking fires that destroyed several businesses and two post offices, and sending at least 35 people to hospitals with cuts, broken bones and chest pains.
>
> Los Angeles Times

Here are excerpts from a weather disaster story that include all the basic information and human elements. Note the vivid verbs, descriptive writing, pacing of long and short sentences, and details of observation.

Napa, Sonoma hit by floods—again

Basic news lead

For the second time this winter, rain-swollen rivers flooded Napa and Sonoma county towns and vineyards Thursday, creating a colossal mess where weary residents were just getting their lives in order after fierce January storms.

Howling out of the central Pacific, the storm slammed into the state late

Weather specifics

Wednesday with steady, torrential rain and winds blasting to 60 mph. And weather forecasters expect more of the same today.

But for a few brief respites, the relentless battering continued all day Thursday.

Power problems

Torrential rains overpowered small streams and larger rivers throughout the region, triggering floods and mudslides. High winds snapped electrical power to 540,000 customers from Big Sur to Eureka, closed highways and shut down shipping in San Francisco Bay. New snow blanketed the Sierra Nevada.

Numerous rivers and streams were at or near flood stage throughout Northern California. Among communities threatened by the rising water were Susanville, Tehama and Hamilton City along the Sacramento River.

Forecast

The National Weather Service warned residents to brace for another wave of rain spinning in from a strong low-pressure system in the northeastern Pacific before dawn today.

Forecaster Brandt Maxwell at the National Weather Service's Monterey office said some areas could get as much as two inches of rain today. "Of course, any amount is going to aggravate flooding."

The rain is forecast to taper off this afternoon, with showers tonight and Saturday.

A winter storm warning was issued for the Sierra Nevada with snow levels forecast to range from 5,000 to 6,000 feet today. As much as three feet of snow could fall above the 7,000-foot elevation, according to the National Weather Service.

History/perspective

It's starting to look like January, when a disastrous series of storms caused widespread flooding and $300 million in damage, killed 11 people and displaced thousands throughout California.

For residents of Napa and Sonoma counties, still recovering from the floods of January, it was an all too-familiar story.

In St. Helena, a small town in the Napa Valley wine country, the Napa River flooded vineyards, homes, apartments and a mobile home park. Firefighters evacuated more than 1,000 people as the river rose to 19 feet—six feet above flood stage.

Several hundred others were rescued from the Vineyard Valley Mobile Home Park, which survived the January floods. On Thursday, two-thirds of the 300 mobile homes were under water.

Emergency workers in small boats evacuated people through waist-deep water that blocked access to apartment complexes. But even the rescuers had troubles. One rowboat, caught in the swift current, floated down the Napa River for five miles before another boat came to its rescue.

Human interest

Malia Barron Hendricks, about to give birth to her second child, and her husband, Charles, found the road to the hospital blocked by floodwaters. So they drove to a fire station where firefighters helped deliver a healthy baby girl. The woman and her newborn, Hope Bridget Hendricks, eventually were taken to St. Helena Hospital by an ambulance that had to negotiate flooded streets.

Shortly after the birth, the firefighters shared a bottle of expensive Napa Valley sparkling wine with the new mother and father.

By late afternoon, a sheet of water four feet deep covered much of the eastern Napa Valley, isolating flooded farmhouses in inundated vineyards.

Farther south in Napa, the river was expected to rise four feet above flood level, flooding Soscol Avenue, a main business artery. Helpless onlookers watched water creep into the street, growing deeper by the minute.

Mark Townsend, 41, owner of Soscol Antiques, hurriedly tried to waterproof his store, sealing the doors with tape and sandbags, putting his wares as high on shelves as he could, and hauling away the most valuable items in pickup trucks. He lost $10,000 worth of antiques in the flood two months ago.

"It's a little hard, but you have to remember we are going home tonight, and home will have booze and an espresso machine." Townsend said, "and there are a lot of people who don't get to go home tonight."

Frank Sweeney, Janet Rae-Dupree and Michael Dorgan, San Jose *(Calif.)* Mercury News

Weather Stories

Not all weather stories involve disaster coverage. Weather stories can be news or features about prolonged hot, cold, wet or dry spells or just a statistical roundup of rain or snow totals for the month or year. They also can be features about interesting aspects of the weather and the ways it affects people. When a major snowstorm or thunderstorm hits an area, a weather story is expected.

Weather stories also provide drama. In 2005, *Chicago Tribune* reporter Julia Keller won the Pulitzer Prize for reconstructing the terror created by a tornado that struck one block in downtown Utica, Ill., where eight people who huddled in the basement of a bar were killed. In an article about the prize, *Tribune* editor Tim Bannon said the tornado provided all the elements of a "taut drama" that would show how a brief but devastating weather event affected people. Keller was initially reluctant to do the feature story after the event because it had been so thoroughly covered by the media as breaking news. But she persevered for seven months as she pored over weather documents and conducted hundreds of interviews to write a compelling narrative account of just 10 seconds when the "wicked wind" had ripped through the town nearly a year before. The Pulitzer judges called it a "gripping, meticulously constructed account." Here is the lead on the first of three stories:

Ten seconds. Count it: One. Two. Three. Four. Five. Six. Seven. Eight. Nine. Ten. Ten seconds was roughly how long it lasted. Nobody had a stopwatch, nothing can be proven definitively, but that's the consensus. The tornado that swooped through Utica at 6:09 p.m. April 20 took some 10 seconds to do what it did. Ten seconds is barely a flicker. It's a long, deep breath. It's no time at all. It's an eternity.

If the sky could hold a grudge, it would look the way the sky looked over northern Illinois that day. Low, gray clouds stretched to the edges in a thin veneer of menace. Rain came and went, came and went, came and went. . . .

The survivors would henceforth be haunted by the oldest, most vexing question of all: whether there is a destiny that shapes our fates or whether it is simply a matter of chance, of luck, of the way the wind blows.

Here are some other ideas for features about weather stories:

- Unusual patterns in weather for your area. Include why the weather patterns are occurring.
- Effects of weather on pets, businesses, people's moods, health. For example, many people suffer from seasonal affective disorder, a depressive state usually related to a lack of light in the winter.
- Insect infestation because of weather patterns.
- People whose occupations force them to work outside during very hot or cold spells.
- Effects of snow removal on city budgets: price of salt, sand, overtime for employees and so on.
- Excessive costs of air conditioning or heating for your school or city during hot or cold spells.
- Features about upcoming seasons.
- Consumer stories or sidebars about coping with extreme heat, cold, tornadoes, hurricanes, floods or earthquakes.

Regardless of whether you are writing a feature or a breaking-news story, include these elements in all weather stories:

Forecast: Always include the forecast for the next day or for an extended period, especially when you are writing about floods, droughts, weather-related fires, or hot or cold spells.

Unusual angles: If the weather is unusual for your area or for the time of year, include explanations from weather forecasters.

Human interest: Tell how people are coping. Focus on one or a few people who have interesting stories.

Warnings: Explain how extremely hot or cold weather affects people, especially very young or old people. Tell how to cope with or prevent problems. Also include warnings about keeping animals safe. Include any road or traffic information, such as road or bridge closings and alternate routes.

Records: Explain if the weather has broken any records or come near to breaking records, especially if you are doing a roundup of statistics or a story about unusual weather. Even if no records have been broken, put the weather statistics in perspective by comparing them to other months or years or using a graphic for the statistics.

Terms: Check your Associated Press Stylebook for definitions of weather terms. If you use such a word as *blizzard* or *hurricane,* define it by explaining how high the winds must be. In any flood story, explain the flood stages of a river and how far above or below flood stage the river is or when it is expected to crest to its highest level.

Here is a basic weather feature about an excessively hot day. It includes all the basic information, such as the forecast and human-interest elements. The writer, Cheryl Wittenauer, said she checked with the guard to make sure that she wouldn't get him fired by writing that he wasn't standing at the entrance he was supposed to guard. She also said she wanted to use the "screw it" quote "because that's the way people talk," but she cleared it first with her editor.

Weather forecast blazes on

Temperatures to soar throughout weekend

At 5 o'clock, security guard Shawn Brown was halfway through his shift watching over a parking lot under construction at the downtown post office.

The Wells Fargo employee, beads of sweat popping from his brow, is supposed to take his post at the Edmond Street entrance, where the only shelter from the sun was the bill of his cap.

Nudged by the discomfort of a 102-degree heat index Wednesday, the outdoor worker deferred to his own judgment.

"Screw it," he said. "I'm staying here in the shade. . . . This is the only post without an air conditioner. It's my second day here in a row."

The day ushered in what is forecast to be a series of blazers with above-normal temperatures and wind.

"It's blast furnace-type weather," Weather Data meteorologist Jeff House said.

Today will be sunny with a high of 96. But it will only get worse. Temperatures Friday and Saturday will soar to a searing 99, with at least 50 percent humidity.

There could be slight relief Sunday and Monday if a "cold front" produces thunderstorms. Even with the cold front, highs would hover in the middle 90s.

The above-normal temperatures are the result of a strong ridge of high pressure in the upper levels of the atmosphere.

The average high for June 24 is 87 degrees. A record high of 103 was set in 1937.

Cooper, a black poodle mix, was one of seven lucky dogs that lost a winter coat Wednesday at Jeanne's Dog Grooming, 922 Alabama St.

"They come in miserable from the heat, but they're bouncing when they leave here," groomer Colleen Whitson said. "They love it. They feel so much better."

The steamy temperatures also drew people in search of quick relief to stores and social service agencies that could supply them with fans and air conditioners.

"Sales usually hit a peak when it turns hot like this," Sears salesman Bill Patrick said. "They're replacing ones that finally gave up on them."

The Economic Opportunity Corp., 817 Monterey St., has given away more than 100 air conditioners in a four-county region since June 1. The agency has fielded many additional requests from low-income clients the last few days.

AFL-CIO Community Services, 118 S. Fifth St., is seeking donations of fans and 110-volt air conditioners that plug into a standard outlet—and are in good working condition. The agency won't accept 220-volt air conditioning units because they require electrical wiring most clients' homes lack.

Cheryl Wittenauer, St. Joseph *(Mo.)* News-Press

Personal Tragedy

In the beginning, hordes of reporters descended on the tiny town of Buckner, Mo., to cover the tragedy of three brothers who died in an icy pond. It was a personal tragedy of national magnitude.

Tad Bartimus, an award-winning writer for The Associated Press, was not among the initial reporters. Bartimus called the family several weeks later and said she wanted to do a story because she didn't think the real story about the boys had ever been told. To her surprise, the family consented. But Bartimus said it was a very painful story to write.

She said her reporting style for tragedy is to treat the family as though it were her own: "I can get anyone to tell me anything. And I can empathize with people. Those are my top two strengths."

But why do the media love to do stories about personal tragedies? The media are often criticized for their coverage of grieving families. A grief counselor in Bartimus' story expresses the reason well: "The human spirit is resilient beyond belief, and that is the hope here," said Ms. Howard. "At a time like this you can get swamped by the grinding pain of it. But out of that pain comes some of the most substantial character and human elegance to be found on Earth. You learn how people can rise up and care for one another."

And that is a theme of this story. Readers want to read about how people cope with tragedy.

Bartimus didn't ask the parents insensitive questions about how they felt. When parents lose their three children, the answer is obvious. Instead, she focused on how the community reacted and the parents' memories of their children.

As a reporter, you undoubtedly will have to cover a personal tragedy at some point—probably many times—in your career. Many of those stories will focus on the community and how people cope with a tragedy that happens to their neighbors or members of their immediate family. Bartimus' story can serve as a model for questions to ask and approaches to take.

As you read Bartimus' story, note the sources she used and the way she structured the story with a circular ending that returned to the beginning of the story for concept but focused on the future. Also note the excellent details.

Band of brothers

Tad Bartimus

Associated Press

"We few, we happy few,
we band of brothers . . ."
William Shakespeare, *Henry V*

BUCKNER, Mo.—There is so little left.

A red cardboard valentine with torn paper lace, which proclaims, "I love you Mom." A carefully penned Thanksgiving essay in which the writer says he's grateful for his family "to have someone to love me." A child's "Life Story" book with extra pages left blank for future adventures.

Chad Eugene Gragg, 12, Aaron Wayne Gragg, 11, and Stephen Douglas Gragg, 8, died together at dusk on the cold afternoon of Feb. 4.

It was Aaron's 11th birthday. Despite admonishments from a teacher and a chum who rode home with him on the bus, he chose to celebrate it by sliding on the frozen surface of a farmer's pond.

The ice broke. Aaron fell into the frigid water. His big brother Chad, doing what his parents had always taught him to do, attempted to save him. He, too, fell in. Stevie, strong for his age, also tried to be his brothers' keeper. His body plunged through the thin crust.

A horrified neighbor boy ran for help. Frantic firemen pulled the brothers from the pond within 30 minutes. They weren't breathing and had no pulse. Two helicopters and an ambulance rushed them to three separate hospitals.

Thus began the agonizing pilgrimage of Charles and Mary Gragg, two ordinary people who now stagger in the footsteps of Job.

Meanwhile, word of the tragedy spread like woodsmoke over this western Missouri town of 2,800. The event would change forever Buckner's image of itself.

As doctors at St. Mary's Hospital in nearby Blue Springs told the parents their son Chad was dead, teachers and friends arrived to surround the stunned couple in a protective cocoon.

Hoping against hope, the Graggs next went to St. Luke's Hospital in Kansas City, only to be told Aaron, too, was gone.

By the time they reached Children's Mercy Hospital the Graggs were at the heart of a caravan of grief. They found Stephen on a life support system. At 10 p.m., he passed away.

In the space and time it took for the sun to set and the moon to rise, three healthy, happy, handsome little boys vanished from the lives of all who knew them.

They left behind bits of homework and smiling celluloid images, a puppy named Scooter who looks for them everywhere, empty school desks, classmates who struggle to remember their last words, teachers who wish they'd known them better.

They left behind the townspeople of Buckner, who were galvanized by the loss to dig deep within their hearts and pockets to bury the children with dignity, and continue to mourn them with honest tears.

They left behind their mother and their father, but Mary and Charles

Gragg, both 41, are no longer parents. The sounds of laughter, of life, are gone from their empty house. The only noise comes from the television set. The door to the boys' bedroom is closed.

The unbearable must now be borne.

"In our age, children aren't eligible to die because our expectations have been set up that children can survive anything," said Kathryn Howard, a grief counselor with Comprehensive Mental Health Services in nearby Independence, Mo.

"All the time we read about children who fall into freezing water and survive. Why not Aaron, or Chad, or at least Stevie? They couldn't be saved because the water wasn't deep enough or cold enough. But because of modern medical miracles, we are conditioned to believe it is outrageous that they died."

Ms. Howard, whose nonprofit agency has contracts with both the local school district and fire department, had headed grief and death counseling in Buckner since the drownings. She also helped the Graggs plan their children's funeral.

"The human spirit is resilient beyond belief, and that is the hope here," said Ms. Howard. "At a time like this you can get swamped by the grinding pain of it. But out of that pain comes some of the most substantial character and human elegance to be found on Earth. You learn how people can rise up and care for one another.

"This is now a community that speaks with one voice. That phenomena is rare—too often we are too big and fragmented a society for this to happen. But if you listen to Buckner today, what you hear is, 'We care. This matters to us. They were our children, too.'"

The Graggs had no close relatives

living nearby. Acting out of instinct and compassion, Buckner Elementary School Principal Richard Thompson stepped into the abyss.

"The school in a sense became their family," said Thompson. "Working with me, Kathryn Howard, and Jerry Brown, the funeral director, Charlie and Mary decided to have the funeral in the junior high gymnasium. The parents wanted the teachers to speak, and to be pallbearers.

"This became a chance for the community to fulfill what a community is all about. Before the accident happened you could have counted on one hand the number of people who knew Charlie and Mary Gragg. Now everyone knows them and wants to help them."

The Parent-Teacher Association mobilized to take food to the Gragg home for the next two weeks. Secretly thanking God it wasn't their own kids, mothers reached into closets and brought forth suits and ties for the boys to wear to their graves.

Funds were established to accept donations to offset medical and funeral expenses. The local bank, the savings and loan and a florist donated flower sprays for the coffins.

"It is so hard to take it in," said James B. Jones, president of the First State Bank of Missouri, where nearly $20,000 was sent in the first two weeks after the accident.

Pondering the event's anguishing mathematics, Jones wondered, "If people had only one child and lost it, isn't that just as terrible as having three and losing them all? I don't know, I simply don't know, it's just so hard to make yourself think about it."

Mortician Brown tried not to think about his own boys, aged 7 and 8, as he plotted the funeral like a general planning a battle.

"We went into this with no idea there'd be any money to pay for it. I was estimating a minimum of $2,500 each. I went to my vault manufacturer and coffin supplier and explained the situation. They were willing to share the burden, no matter what happened," said Brown, whose family has served as Buckner's only morticians for three generations.

Brown decided on three identical coffins, three identical hearses. He reserved three side-by-side plots on a gently sloping hillside in the town cemetery.

From the graves you can look out over the walnut and oak trees, past the dormant farm pastures, and down toward the creek where an angry crawdad once bit Aaron's big toe, where Chad caught a two-pound lunker of a catfish, where Stevie loved to hunt for frogs.

Those are the same hills and hollows Brown scampered over as a child. He, too, remembers sliding across frozen ponds with his buddies.

Brown steeled himself not to think about any of those memories, or the event that brought him into the Graggs' circle, "because it is so overwhelming, so awesome, that it stops you in your tracks." He'd think later. First, he had a big job to do.

When he'd finished embalming and dressing the dead children in their new clothes, he tucked each boy's favorite toy into the silk-lined caskets.

As Brown ministered to the dead, Thompson and Ms. Howard, along with every clergyman in town, local teachers and reinforcements from other schools, consoled the living.

"The day after it happened we conducted emotional triage in the halls, the library, the cafeteria, and the classrooms," said Ms. Howard. "We had kids crying with counselors in corners everywhere you looked. Part of being young is learning how to deal with your pain. The kids were shown they could support one another and that they wouldn't be alone."

Teachers read "The Taste of Blackberries" to all fourth and fifth graders. The book relates the tale of a boy who loses his best friend. Younger children heard "The 10th Good Thing About Barney," a story of a little boy whose cat dies.

Thompson sent letters home with every student, detailing the day's upheaval and warning parents their children "might have tears or depression but that is expected and is normal in the grief process. . . ." Attached were four pages of guidelines for dealing with the situation.

"That day we just put a Band-Aid on it; we flew by the seat of our pants," recalled Thompson. "We decided to leave the Gragg boys' desks empty to stress the finality of death, to show some physical remains. We talked about the details. We tried to cope with the onslaught of the media but refused to let reporters talk to teachers or students. And we braced for the funeral."

Thompson is described by faculty, city fathers, and the Graggs as the glue that held everything together through that long weekend.

Besides organizing the school's response to the tragedy, Thompson set up the junior high gymnasium for the funeral, helped teachers prepare their farewell remarks, acceded to any family wishes, and comforted students who attended the open coffin visitation and closed casket funeral.

"It was tough trying to make an appropriate setting for a funeral out of a basketball court, but we did it," said Thompson.

He had a carpenter build a wooden schoolhouse which was then covered with flowers and presented by the students of Buckner. Thompson also gave the parents a brass school bell engraved with the boys' names. The gift usually is reserved for retiring teachers.

"We consider that your boys have retired to a heavenly school," Thompson told the Graggs.

More than 600 mourners heard fourth-grade teacher Jeanne Young describe the Gragg children as "three adventuresome, energetic little boys . . . each of us has a special place in our heart, locked and guarded—it's the place just for Chad and Stephen and Aaron."

Symbols of each boy's interests rested atop the blue-gray caskets: art materials for Aaron, a soccer ball for Stephen, a basketball for Chad.

Finally, the three brothers were laid to rest in the winter's hard ground.

Mortician Brown left town for a convention in Florida, allowing himself to cry most of the way.

Mental health counselor Kathryn Howard began planning a series of forums on death and dying for the Buckner community.

Principal Thompson fielded calls from People magazine and tried to get his school back to some semblance of normalcy.

"The tragedy will long be remembered in this community," said Thompson, pausing to wipe tears from his eyes and catch his breath over the big lump in his throat. "They were rambunctious country boys who were one for all and all for one.

"Two of the boys willingly gave up their lives for the other. That is the only thing that makes it comprehensible."

Mary and Charlie Gragg's relatives have gone home and neighbors visit less now. Gragg has resumed the commute to his metal treating company in Kansas City. His wife has returned to shift work for a janitorial contractor at the nearby Lake City Army Ammunition Plant.

The Graggs believe they'll stay in the neighborhood where dogs run free and kids' boundaries are defined by a stop sign on a country road.

They speak of their sons in the present tense.

Looking at a small pile of photographs, Mary Gragg remembers each of her sons as a sturdy blue-eyed, blond-haired baby.

"They were so good. They slept through the night every night.

"Aaron is my artist, my loner, he loves his dinosaurs. Chad is his daddy made over, my helper, everybody's helper, such a good student. He loves school, he never misses, and he loves riding his bicycle. Stevie's a little slow, a shy kid. Stevie loves Alf . . ."

Charlie Gragg takes up the sentence.

"You'll never see kids that alike, that close. If one goes out the front door the other two are right behind. . . . I wasn't surprised they all died trying to pull each other out of that pond.

"I always told them, 'No matter what happens, you help your brothers.' I told them that more than once. I told

Chad he was responsible. He was in charge. He went to help Aaron, and Stevie followed."

Is there anything anyone can do for the Graggs? They say there is nothing. They are baffled that there might be an answer to such a question.

Soon it will be spring, time to go fishin' again, and frog huntin', and crawdad catchin'. That's when the children of Buckner Elementary School will plant three new trees in the memory of Aaron, Chad, and Stevie.

By then, the ice will be gone from the ponds.

Exercises

1   **Disaster coverage:** Brainstorm a package of stories about a disaster in your community. If you live in an area prone to weather disasters, such as earthquakes, tornadoes or floods, plan that type of coverage. Or you can brainstorm how you would cover a plane crash or an explosion in your community. List the stories you would do and places you should go for reporting on the type of disaster you have identified.

Featured *News Scene* Assignment

Access *News Scene* at *http://communication.wadsworth.com/newsscene2* to view the news simulation titled "Tornado."

Click on the play button to view the movie or drag the slider to scan through the movie.

Coaching Tips

For profiles: Observe descriptive details about the person, and show the source in action.

Do background research to find unusual questions the subject will enjoy discussing.

Find a unifying theme that you can weave through your story.

Write an order for your story; think about organizing it by topics or time frames (present, past, back to present and future).

For obituaries: Ask yourself, what made this person memorable?

Check the accuracy of spellings and information in profiles and obituaries.

Profiles and Obituaries

Alan Richman, magazine writer

Alan Richman enters the dark Manhattan hotel bar to await the arrival of Robert De Niro. The famous actor has agreed to meet with Richman for 15 minutes to decide whether he will grant the writer an interview for *GQ* (*Gentlemen's Quarterly*) magazine.

Richman is accustomed to writing celebrity profiles, but this time he is nervous. De Niro hates to be interviewed.

It's 6:45 p.m. The meeting is set for 7 p.m. Richman paces in the lobby. At 7:17 p.m. De Niro arrives. He startles Richman by asking him what his first five questions would be.

Richman is trying to come up with five questions the actor will like. He isn't prepared. The words don't come.

The actor says two questions will do.

Richman asks an obvious question: Why has De Niro agreed to consider an interview if he hates them so much?

De Niro says in jest that he's agreed because of the clothes he'll get by being photographed for *GQ*. Richman doesn't tell him he won't get to keep the clothes. The writer is ready to pose his second question.

He never gets the chance. De Niro says he has to go, and he leaves without agreeing to the interview.

Richman is stuck. He still has to write the profile for *GQ*. So he calls De Niro's friends and associates.

"After the interview failed, I went back and called all those people to figure how to make the story work," Richman says. "I asked them, what question could you ask that he (De Niro) would answer. Everybody told me something about De Niro you couldn't ask."

One actor who worked with De Niro said, "I don't think I'd ask him about his family or his love life. He's pretty private."

Another friend warned Richman not to talk about world politics, sports, fine wines or clothing because "he doesn't know a lot about those things."

Those and other comments about De Niro were probably more insightful than the actor would have been about himself. And that was the theme of the profile: how to interview a celebrity who doesn't like to be interviewed.

Richman had broken one of his major rules for conducting celebrity profiles. "You've got to nail them with a question they like," Richman says. "They are so bored. I always ask myself, 'What question can I ask this guy that he'll enjoy answering.' It takes thinking."

He didn't do enough thinking before he met De Niro to set up the interview. But he's had better luck with other celebrities and athletes in the 30 years that he has been a sportswriter in Philadelphia, a columnist and writing coach for *The Boston Globe,* a reporter for *The New York Times,* and a profile writer for *People* magazine.

These days, Richman has become a celebrity in his own right as the food and wine critic for *GQ,* contributing writer for several magazines, and dean of a new program in food journalism at the French Culinary Institute in New York. He has been interviewed many times and has appeared on television shows. But he has also written several celebrity profiles for magazines.

Celebrities are considered worthy of profiles because they have accomplished something more special than the average citizen. However, many profiles focus on people in the community who have done something noteworthy but do not have celebrity status.

"Everybody's got one good story to tell," Richman says. "If you talk to them long enough, you'll find it. Nobody has lived a totally uneventful life."

To find that story, Richman uses what he calls the "Columbo school of interviewing," named after the deceptively naïve TV detective. "I sort of hang around looking harmless. I try to be as unthreatening as possible. Then I use a weave-and-jab style of questioning. You can't be afraid to be a little bit rude," he says. "If the point of the interview is that they were a bigamist, I'll say: 'We all want to have two wives; tell me how you got away with it.' If it's a profile of a man growing award-winning roses, I'll say: 'I can't believe someone would spend 15 years to grow a decent rose.'"

You may have a different interviewing style, but before you even get to the interviewing stage, you should research your subject's background. If possible, try to get a résumé or an academic vitae if you are interviewing a professor. Check online as well. But don't rely on the information.

"I don't trust press releases or clips," Richman says. "I always ask the background stuff." Sometimes background questions can be boring. So Richman just puts his subjects on notice. He tells them: "'It's that time now; I've got to ask these questions.' Basically they think I have some secret that I'm going to ask them like 'Tell me about when you were 11 years old and you slept with a goat.' Then I tell them, 'I've got to go over your life.' They're relieved. I don't mess around and pretend it's going to be fun. It's more like, do me a favor. You never know what you are going to get."

Many reporters seek background from the profile subject's friends and family *before* they conduct the main interview. In De Niro's case, Richman had no choice. He had to contact the actor's friends *after* the interview failed, but he prefers that method anyway—with this caveat:

"One of my rules is never call up friends or acquaintances of stars and ask what they think of the person, because they will always lie," Richman says. "If you were doing a profile of Hitler, most journalists would call Goebbels and

Himmler and they would say, 'What a guy!' Instead, ask them for facts or anecdotes."

Terry Gross has also interviewed scores of celebrities, politicians and other people for her National Public Radio show, "Fresh Air." She is renowned for her interviewing skill. In an article for the *American Journalism Review*, Thomas Kunkel wrote: "Gross's conversational interviews are marked by intelligence, preparation and a diplomatic but firm probing of what makes people tick." She told him, "My theory of interviewing is that whatever you have, use it. If you are confused, use that. If you have raw curiosity, use that. If you have experience, use that. If you have a lot of research, use that. But figure out what it is you have and make it work for you."

After 25 years of interviewing people for her NPR show, Gross decided to write a book about the profiles she conducted. She explains her interviewing techniques in her introduction to the book, "All I Did Was Ask: Conversations With Writers, Actors, Musicians and Artists."

"I often ask my guests about what they consider to be their invisible weaknesses and shortcomings," she writes. "I do this because these are the characteristics that define us no less than our strengths. What we feel sets us apart from other people is often the thing that shapes us as individuals. . . . I also violate decorum by asking questions of my guests that you usually don't ask someone you've just met, for fear of seeming rude or intrusive. Within minutes of saying hello to a guest, I might inquire about his religious beliefs or sexual fantasies—but only if it's relevant to the subject he's come on the show to discuss. Or at some point during the interview, I might ask a question about a physical flaw, the sort that we gallantly pretend not to notice in everyday life. When I do this, my purpose isn't to embarrass my guest or to make him self-conscious. I'm trying to encourage introspection, hoping for a reply that might lead to a revelation about my guest's life that might lead, in turn, to a revelation about his art. . . . I try in my interviews to find the connections between my guests' lives and their work (the reason we care about them in the first place)."

Despite the candor Gross seeks from her sources, she also says she respects her guests' privacy. "I would never pressure anyone to reveal those thoughts and experiences he desires to keep private," she writes. "That's why before beginning an interview, I tell the guest to let me know if I'm getting too personal, in which case we'll move on to something else."

Those are the kinds of questions and tips that work well in profile interviews. They are what another editor calls "turning points."

Turning Points

Walter Dawson, a former editor at the *Monterey County Herald* in California, says regardless of the profile subject, "the heart and soul of a profile is making sure the reader understands the twists and turns and intricacies of human life." Dawson says writers should consider the following universal elements:

- Patterns: Some lives build to a climax, as for a law school student who becomes a judge.
- Decisive moments or turning points: Most lives take turns along the way. Take the law school student; perhaps she wanted to be a great defense lawyer but became a prosecutor instead. Or maybe your subject was an accountant who became head of a river-rafting company.
- Future: Every profile subject has a future, and you need to ask your subject what could lie ahead. Let the person speculate, especially about career goals. Ask the impertinent question: If this career doesn't work out, what could you do? The answers about the future could also provide an ending for the profile.

In addition to revealing the turning points, strengths and weaknesses of the source during the reporting process for your story, here are some points to consider when you write the profile.

Basic Elements of Profiles

Focus

What is the main idea of the profile? What makes this person newsworthy? Why are you writing about this person now? Those questions should be answered in the nut graph.

"I think the nut graph is even more important to the writer than the reader. You need to know what you are writing about," Richman says.

Theme

What is the difference between a nut graph and a theme? The nut graph is the reason for the story, but the theme is an angle or recurring idea that weaves throughout the story. Some general themes for profiles might be overcoming adversity, succeeding against odds, or coping with failure, illness or serious problems.

For example, this chapter features a profile of Jacklean Davis, considered the most successful homicide detective in New Orleans. That's the nut graph—why she is the subject of this profile. The theme threaded though the story is how she overcame adversity throughout her life and career.

Background

Profiles should not be written in chronological order. The subject's background should be inserted where it fits best, often in the middle of the story. But in some cases, when the background is the most interesting or crucial element, it may be the lead or in the beginning of the story, as in this example about the New Orleans detective:

Background

NEW ORLEANS—The white frame house on Barrone Street is small and gated, just as it was when Jacklean Davis was a shy, serious-eyed little girl in a world of grown-up horrors.

Here, 12 blocks from the muddy brown Mississippi River, Davis was raised by a prostitute, raped by a sailor, sexually molested by an uncle and pregnant at age 16.

By then, folks in the neighborhood were whispering that Davis was headed for the same hard life as the aunt who had reared her: selling herself to strangers. In a sense they were right—but in an entirely different way.

Nut graph

Now 34, Jackie Davis cruises the city in a police car—not just any cop but the most successful detective in New Orleans, this humid capital of good times and jazz that also happens to be one of the deadliest cities in the South, with 346 murders last year.

The GOAL Method

To discover those turning points and other qualities of your profile subject, consider using the GOAL method (goals, obstacles, achievements, logistics), discussed in Chapter 5 ("Interviewing Techniques"). Questions about obstacles the person faced can provide some of the most interesting parts of your profile. Don't stick to any order, but consider some of these questions as they arise naturally in the conversation:

- What were your original goals? What are your next goals?
- What obstacles did you face in accomplishing your goals, and what new problems loom?
- What pleasure or problems have these achievements brought?
- What background (logistics of who, what, when, where) led to your current situation?

Age and physical description: Help the reader visualize your profile subject. But use description only when it is relevant to the topic you are discussing. Make the details work for you. In this example from a profile of Willie Darden, a convicted killer who spent 15 years on Death Row in a Florida prison, the writer weaves in the age and physical description by relating them to the pressure of waiting for death:

Darden maintains a normalcy, a serenity that is surreal. His forehead is not cleaved by worry lines. His hair has not gone gray. He lifts his shackled hands and displays unbitten fingernails. "Calmness is a nice thing to have in times of stress," he says.

He gives his age as 62, but prison records say he is 52. He looks 42. It's as if the man has not only cheated the executioner, but time itself.

Or maybe time just stops when there is no future.

"Prison does tend to sustain one's youth," Darden says with an ironic grin.

"You're not doing anything that you would normally do on the outside—such as working hard every day. You've got no family problems. The wear and tear, so to speak, is on the inside."

Richard Leiby, Sunshine *(Sunday magazine, The Sun-Sentinel, Fort Lauderdale, Fla.)*

Other points of view: Seek anecdotes and comments from friends, family, colleagues and other people affected by the person at work, such as students for a profile about a professor or employees for a profile about a manager.

Visuals

Use graphics as a way to visualize your story in both the planning and writing stages. Outlining your profile by planning a facts (highlights) box can help you determine what topics to include in your story.

If the background is boring, break it out of your story. You can put key dates and such information as birthplace, education, career moves or similar items in a box. But if that information is an interesting and crucial part of your story, leave it in the body of the profile. You also can use a box to add information that doesn't fit well into your story but might be of interest, such as hobbies, favorite books, favorite saying, major goal. The major goal should also be mentioned in your story, but it works well in a facts box.

Several newspapers, magazines and Web sites use graphic devices to substitute for written profiles; others use highlights boxes to enhance profiles. For example, *The Kansas City* (Mo.) *Star* Sunday magazine profiles celebrities with blurbs following these headings:

- Vital statistics (occupation, birthday, birthplace, current home, marital status and so on)
- My fantasy is . . .
- If I could change one thing about myself, it would be . . .
- The best times of my life . . .
- Behind my back my friends say . . .
- These words best describe me . . .

Those are also good questions to ask for your profile even if you don't use the items in a visual tool. However, if you mention topics in a graphic, you don't have to repeat them in the story.

Organizing the Profile

There is no one way to organize a profile, other than having a lead, a body and an ending. Just make sure that you have a focus. Descriptive show-in-action leads, anecdotes, contrast leads and scene-setting leads work particularly well

MULTIMEDIA COACH

Check the Internet for background on your profile subject, but don't rely on the information. Make sure that you check the accuracy of anything you find in your interview with the subject. The following tips apply to profiles for print, broadcast and the Web:

- Start with a simple search for the person's name in *www.google.com* or other search engine.

- Check out any articles or books written by or about the profile subject. If the person has written books, read the book, or at least read summaries in *www.amazon.com*.

- Check for personal and academic Web sites and online résumés the person might have— especially if you are interviewing professors.

- Check athletic records in sports sites for profiles of athletes.

- Check fan sites for celebrities or athletes. These sites may contain links to articles or other information. Use them only as a guide; don't trust information from personal sites.

- For profiles about candidates, check voting records of incumbents and campaign contributions at sites such as *www.followthemoney.org* for candidates to state offices and the Federal Election Commission (*www.fec.gov*) or *www.tray.com* for candidates to federal offices.

Broadcast Profiles

- Think visually in the planning stage before you do the reporting. Background research is essential so you can ask interesting questions that will elicit good responses from your source.

- Show and tell. Write to the video, and show your subject in action.

- Read your script aloud.

- Don't introduce your sound bites by parroting what the source will say.

---

in profiles. As with any lead, make sure that you back up the lead with information that supports it later in the story.

The body of the story can be organized in many ways:

Supporting themes: Block each concept, use all relevant material, and go on to the next concept.

Time frames: Start with the present, go to the past, go back to the present, and end with the future. Or use some variation of the time frames, possibly starting with the past and then proceeding to the present.

Chronology: Look for a place in the story where chronological order might be useful, but don't write the entire profile in chronological order. A chronology might be most helpful for the background. It might also work if you are writing the profile in narrative style. In some cases, however, the story might lend itself to chronological order if a situation unfolds in that sequence. Just make sure that your nut graph tells readers why you are writing about this person now.

Point/counterpoint: If the subject lends itself to pro-and-con treatment, you might consider this method. It can be helpful in profiles of politicians.

You can include reaction quotes from other people after each controversial point is made.

Sections: Splitting the story into separate parts may work if the profile is very complex. For example, if you are doing an in-depth profile of a politician or crime victim or crime suspect, you might organize it in sections, either by time frames of the person's life, issues or different points of view.

Several types of endings work well with profiles. A quote kicker can be used to summarize a source's feelings about the subject or to summarize the subject's accomplishments. Or, with a circular ending, you can return to the lead for an idea and end on a similar note. An ending with a future theme tells what lies ahead for the person. Or try a simple factual sentence that conveys emotional impact.

Putting It All Together

Here is the entire profile of the New Orleans detective. This profile demonstrates a variety of techniques suggested in this chapter. It has a clear focus, which is the one indispensable element of a compelling profile, and a recurring theme of overcoming adversity. It includes anecdotes, the subject's turning points and several comments from other sources. Notice that the three sections feature the present, past and future, although they are not so clearly delineated.

She is the finest of New Orleans' finest

From a gritty past to the city's best detective

By Matthew Purdy

The Philadelphia Inquirer

Descriptive lead to create contrasts with past and present

NEW ORLEANS—The white frame house on Barrone Street is small and gated, just as it was when Jacklean Davis was a shy, serious-eyed little girl in a world of grown-up horrors.

Here, 12 blocks from the muddy brown Mississippi River, Davis was raised by a prostitute, raped by a sailor, sexually molested by an uncle and pregnant at age 16.

By then, folks in the neighborhood were whispering that Davis was headed for the same hard life as the aunt who had reared her: selling herself to strangers. In a sense they were right—but in an entirely different way.

Nut graph

Now 34, Jackie Davis cruises the city in a police car—not just any cop but the most successful detective in New Orleans, this humid capital of good times and jazz that also happens to be one of the deadliest cities in the South, with 346 murders last year.

Backup for nut graph (comment from colleague)

"She was the best I ever saw at solving a murder case," said David Morales, her boss during her five-year stint in the homicide unit. "There was nobody close to her in the history of the homicide division."

More backup for nut graph

Davis solved 88 of her 90 murder cases—a record better than any other detective and all the more impressive

Specifics: anecdotes

for the first black woman to join an elite corps of mostly white men who prodded her to fail.

They destroyed her case reports, told tipsters she didn't work there, placed feces in her desk drawer, pinned her mistakes on the bulletin board, and decorated her mailbox with a cartoon of a mop and bucket titled "black power."

Davis reacted by putting in longer hours. In solitary moments, exhausted, she would bow her head and sob.

"Every case that I got, I was looked at under a microscope: 'Well, what is she going to do now?'" Davis recalls matter-of-factly. "My biggest accomplishment, I consider, is not cracking under the pressure."

More backup for the "so what" factor

At a time when politicians have taken to bashing the poor for dragging on society, Davis stands out as a stunning example of someone who has succeeded precisely because of her harsh past. She is now the city's most celebrated officer—and the subject of a screenplay that has caught the eye of Whoopi Goldberg. . . .

In a life full of ironies and incongruities, Davis posed as a hooker, arresting so many men in the raucous French Quarter that 20 backup officers were assigned to her and her partner. But Davis' arrest rate so riled those in the tourist trade that her superiors had her wired to prove she wasn't entrapping men. Even so, business interest prevailed, and Davis was yanked off the street.

But not before she had nailed 300 johns.

"Having lived with a prostitute all my life, there are certain things you do, certain things you say," says Davis, chuckling over her record.

■

New section: arranged topically to reveal personal side of source

Christina Davis, 17, is a prep school senior with a B average who hopes to study engineering next year at Xavier University. It's Wednesday night in the blond-brick ranch home where she and her mother live with Gigi and Snoopy, their two dogs. Christina Davis is alone.

Her mother, like most officers in New Orleans, earns such a modest wage—$225 a week in take-home pay—that she has to work late-night security details for extra cash, stretching her workweek to 60 hours or more.

"I'm proud of her, but she had to sacrifice time with me and a lot of things we could have done together," Christina Davis says wistfully.

Transition from show-in-action present to past, including background

Losing days—and really, years—with her daughter is Jacklean Davis' greatest regret, she says one evening as she steers her unmarked Chevy through the bombed-out Desire housing project.

Her career started here 11 years ago, when she was the only woman street cop in the rough-and-ready urban squad, which worked the projects. . . .

Physical description made relevant to job

A short woman with a stocky look about her, crimped hair combed into a tight ponytail, Davis always made it a point to later return to murder scenes in street clothes. It helped, she says, that she doesn't look like a cop: being a woman, looking young, using slang.

As she rolls through the broken streets, Davis says she worries about the good people in the projects who get ground down by the force of crime and neglect.

She could have been one of them.

Davis lost her father in a car accident when she was 3. Her bereaved mother squandered the insurance and had to give her children to an aunt.

As it turned out, Davis' grand-aunt was a prostitute who bedded down with sailors. But she was a protective, strong-willed woman with a heart of gold, Davis said.

Davis' aunt was married to a merchant marine. When he was home, little Jacklean lived in stifled terror. He was sexually molesting her. Her aunt didn't know until Jacklean was 14 and her uncle was dying of cancer.

Trauma set in again when Davis was raped at 12 by a sailor who visited her aunt. By 16, she was pregnant and people in her working-class black neighborhood were whispering that she had picked up her aunt's habits.

Davis' aunt died when she was 17, about the time she was about to give birth to Christina. But she still managed to graduate from high school, faltering when it came to college. A better life seemed always out of reach, she thought as she worked clearing tables at ritzy restaurants and driving a bus.

Turning point

It all hit bottom one winter when Davis found herself homeless for a two-week stretch, huddled in her parked car with Christina, danger lurking all around.

Quote kicker to section

"I knew this was it," she says. "There was no one else. I was on my own."

■

More background to bring reader back to present and on to future

The idea to become a cop came to Jacklean Davis when she dated a rookie in the department. Problem was, when she took the exam, she flunked it—again and again and again.

It took Davis five tries to pass the test—and two to overcome her fear of guns and make it through the police academy. It was 1981 before she got her first job at the urban squad. . . .

Comment from colleague

"She puts her heart into everything," said Wayne Farve, an old partner. "I've seen her at shootings where she'll kneel down in the blood right next to them and ask them who did it and where she can get more information."

Anecdote

Back in the old neighborhood, Davis got out of her car one night, in front of her home, eight blocks from where she grew up.

"Sssssss," a man hissed, pointing a gun.

Davis froze. Here she was, holding two bags of groceries, her own gun in her handbag, in the car. She screamed, slowly stepping away, as he closed in.

Unable to reach her gun, Davis screamed louder—and the man fled.

Davis dumped her groceries, grabbed her gun and opened fire as she chased him. Then suddenly, he turned and fired back, hitting her in the leg.

Another turning point

As she recovered in a hospital, she took heart. No longer a frightened child, Jacklean Davis had fought back this time and won. A few months later, police caught the man. He had raped 14 women. Davis testified against him, helping to lock him away in Louisiana's dreaded Angola prison.

Return to present

All told, it may be the stuff of movies, Davis concedes. An agent is negotiating for her, and the latest news is that Goldberg is reading the screenplay of her life.

Quote kicker on future note

"I don't even like to think about it," she says, admitting superstition. "I don't want to put a mojo on me."

Writing Snapshot Profiles

Julie Sullivan doesn't waste words. She writes snapshot profiles that let the reader see, hear and care about the character—quickly. Her skill earned her the Best Newspaper Writing Award from the American Society of Newspaper Editors for short news writing. The award was based on profiles she wrote for *The* (Spokane, Wash.) *Spokesman-Review.* They average 8 inches, fewer than 400 words. But she reveals a lifetime in her profiles.

ETHICS

Ethical dilemmas: How much should you reveal about a person in a profile, and what is your responsibility for the consequences? Do the circumstances differ if you are writing an obituary? What should you do if you find that the deceased person was on a sex offender registry or discover that the deceased had a criminal background? Should you include items in the obituary that the family would not want?

The case: A reporter for *The News & Observer* in Raleigh, N.C., profiled a Mexican immigrant who was an illegal alien. Reporter Gigi Anders says she asked if he understood that his name and picture would be in the newspaper and if he understood the conse-

quences, according to an article in *American Journalism Review*. She recalled that he said if he got deported, that was his "destiny." However, Julio Granados, the subject of the profile, said he gave permission to use his name but not his status, according to the article. After the story ran, immigration officials apprehended Granados and five other illegal aliens, who faced deportation hearings. The Hispanic community was incensed. The newspaper editor wrote a column defending the story but said the paper should have thought more about the impact.

What would you have done? Would you have used the man's name and

identified his workplace? If you don't include both, would you mar the credibility of the story? How much responsibility do you have for the consequences of a profile if the source gives you information that could be damaging? Are the circumstances different in obituaries? Should you comply with the wishes of the family to eliminate negative material about the deceased?

Ethical guidelines: On the one hand, the Society of Professional Journalists Code of Ethics says, "Seek the truth and report it." On the other hand, the code says, "Minimize harm." Editors disagree on this subject, especially concerning obituaries. What would you do in these cases?

Her method: short sentences, few adjectives, few quotes, many details.

Now a reporter for *The Oregonian* in Portland, Ore., she began writing at a weekly newspaper in Alaska after she graduated from the University of Montana in 1985. "I started out leaning toward brevity," she said. "My first editor in Alaska would always tell me, every time you finish a story, go back over it. Figure out what words are extraneous. What can you leave out?"

That's good advice for broadcast and Web writing as well.

Sullivan takes voluminous notes but discards about half of them. "I write everything down. I don't trust my memory," she says. That includes her observations. A cracked concrete step. An automobile battery under the sink. Cockroaches scurrying across the kitchen table. A toothless smile.

How does she know which details to include in her stories? "I write what I remember without looking at my notes. What details stand out? Like Joe Peak's teeth were so significant and personal. The contrast struck me. His place was so neat that I couldn't figure out how somebody who paid so much attention to his surroundings wouldn't take the same care personally. Then I found out how he lost his teeth."

She is equally selective about the limited quotes she includes. "I really think readers glaze over quotes," she says. "I do few quotes because I think most people are pretty plain-spoken and simple. You don't need to use it just because it's in quotes."

Her tips for writing briefly: "Trust your instincts about what is important, what struck you during the interview. The rest is chaff. I generally

Julie Sullivan, reporter

bounce my lead and the most important details off my co-workers, and I can gauge from their reactions if I'm on the right track." That's the basic tell-it-to-a-friend technique.

She also stresses observation: "Pay attention to details, from the right spelling of names to finding out the date of people's birthdays."

On leads and kickers: "I tend to think readers read the beginning and the end. Never discount the lead you were throwing out. It could be a great kicker."

On structure: "You try to make a point with every paragraph."

On brevity: "Short has its place, but it won't replace more in-depth pieces; that's what a newspaper does best. I hope to continue to do both."

The profile that follows was part of a series about the problems of low-income residents in a deteriorating Spokane apartment building, the Merlin. Notice the details, and notice the strong factual kickers. As you read this profile, consider what information came from observations and what came from questions. And then decide how you could say it all in as few words.

It took twice as many words to describe Sullivan's style as she used in these stories.

Donald 'Joe' Peak

Joe Peak's smile has no teeth.

His dentures were stolen at the Norman Hotel, the last place he lived in downtown Spokane before moving to the Merlin two years ago.

Gumming food and fighting diabetes have shrunk the 54-year-old man's frame by 80 pounds. He is thin and weak and his mouth is sore.

But that doesn't stop him from frying hamburgers and onions for a friend at midnight or keeping an extra bed made up permanently in his two-room place.

"I try to make a little nest here for myself," he says.

Chock-full of furniture and cups from the 32-ounce Cokes he relishes for 53 cents apiece, Peaks' second floor apartment is almost cozy.

A good rug covers holes in the kitchen floor, clean-looking blankets cover a clean-looking bed. Dishes are stacked neatly in the kitchen sink.

But cockroaches still scurry across his kitchen table.

"I live with them," he says with a shrug. "I can't afford the insecticides, pesticides, germicides. I don't have the money."

With a $500 per month welfare check and a $175 rent payment, Peak follows a proper diet when he can afford it. He shops at nearby convenience stores where he knows prices are higher but the distance is right. He has adapted to the noisy nightlife in the hallways and sleeps when he is too exhausted to hear it.

Part Seminole Indian, Chinese and black, the Florida native moved to Spokane 20 years ago to be near relatives in Olympia. He quit school at 13 to help earn the family income and worked a string of blue-collar jobs. Along the way, someone started calling him Joe.

His voice is lyrical, his vocabulary huge, but Peak's experience with whites is long and bitter.

When conditions at the Merlin began worsening three months ago, junkies and gray mice the size of baby rats moved in next door. He hated to see it, but he isn't worried about being homeless.

He's worried about his diabetes. He's frightened by blood in his stool and sores on his gums. He wonders whether the white-staffed hospitals on the hill above him will treat a poor black man with no teeth.

Julie Sullivan, The *(Spokane, Wash.)* Spokesman-Review

Brief profiles showing a slice of life or vignettes of people are excellent formats for the Web or for a package of stories as sidebars to a main in-depth story. An idea that works well is a package of stories about diversity on campus, with profiles of international students or those from varied ethnic and racial backgrounds. A major story about an upcoming election in your town might also lend itself to mini-profiles of the candidates.

Here are some examples of vignettes written by journalism students who were following Julie Sullivan's style. The assignment was to find people behind the scenes on the campus of the University of Kansas. Students were instructed to write profiles filled with revealing details in fewer than 500 words—about one to one-and-a-half double-spaced typewritten pages. They were also told to stress show in action techniques. The frame was the university at work.

Journalism school librarian

Yvonne Martinez has carefully picked out her wardrobe.

Dressed in a navy blue skirt patterned with white boxes and a white blouse with the same pattern in blue, she had come prepared for another day of work at the School of Journalism library.

However, her outfit would not be complete without her size 6 1/2 sneakers.

The 4-foot-11 librarian does not wear them simply because they help maintain a quiet atmosphere. That is just one of the added benefits.

She wears them because she is constantly on the move.

Whether it's searching for a student's request for the last two years' worth of *Folio* magazine or sorting through the seemingly endless stack of newspapers the library receives daily, she rarely has time to sit down.

Recent cuts in the library's budget and staff have increased Martinez's work load. The sneakers are crucial.

"I'd rather be comfortable than in pain," she said.

Her duties have grown during the two years she has been working behind the counter. But now her duties include repairing the copy machine.

It is the only copy machine the library can afford on its budget, Martinez said. Overuse causes it to break down at least once a day.

As she returns to the counter, she immediately is greeted by a professor who says the machine is out of ink. She reaches under the counter and pulls out a bottle of black ink.

As she pours, the bottle slips and ink covers her hands. More students who need to be helped arrive at the counter.

Martinez stands by the machine staring at her hands as if she were auditioning for the part of Lady Macbeth. She sighs and runs off to the restroom. She quickly returns to the counter and apologizes to the students.

After all, she is the only librarian on duty.

Ranjit Arab, The University Daily Kansan

Bus driver

The sounds of a screaming Mick Jagger shake the windows of the bus.

A basket of Jolly Rancher's candies sits on the dashboard. And the driver in the blue and white Rolling Stones baseball cap is smiling.

This is Hank's bus—slap him a high five on the way off, please.

Hank Jones, who is in the middle of his fifth year as a (University of Kansas) bus driver, likes doing something extra for his passengers.

"Why shouldn't I," he says. "A little extra effort can go a long way."

One passenger remembers Hank stopping his bus on Jayhawk Boulevard last Valentine's Day just to give her a candy heart. She's been a regular ever since.

Hank began driving those green and white buses when he needed some extra money and he enjoyed it so much, he stayed with it.

The students are the best part of the job, but Hank is not without his complaints.

"They're not too quick sometimes," he says. "But they're good kids, most of them."

He tries to keep it interesting—he never plays the same tape twice in one day on his portable Sony stereo.

"I'm always partial to the Stones," he says, cracking open his pack of Marlboro cigarettes. "But I'll play requests, too."

Hank plans to keep driving for KU as long as he still enjoys it—or until he finds a wife. At 34, he hasn't found the right woman yet.

But he's in no hurry.

"Who knows?" he says. "Maybe someone will get on my bus."

Kathy Hill

Obituaries as Profiles

A feature obituary is a profile about a person who died. However, you don't write about the person's death; you write about his or her life. That's what Bill Snead did when he wrote this obituary/profile about a Kansas cowboy:

Cottonwood Falls—Frank Gaddie looked overdressed in his casket.

He was wearing a dark suit with his hands folded just so below a wide, blue and white necktie. The funeral home had done a good job making the 94-year-old horse trader look "natural," but it's doubtful Gaddie would've appreciated the powder and the makeup, or, for that matter, the suit.

No real cowboy would.

Gaddie was a cowboy from way back.

It was Monday night in the Brown-Bennett-Alexander Funeral Home in Cottonwood Falls. Gaddie's wife, Virginia, along with family members were exchanging handshakes, hugs and a few tears with old friends who dropped by to pay their respects the night before the funeral. Gaddie's open casket was at the edge of the crowd, against a wall. . . .

A couple of weeks earlier Gaddie had spent the better part of a morning talking about his life and his family, homesteaders in Bazaar in the 1870s. Bazaar is about seven miles south of Cottonwood Falls, just off Kansas Highway 177.

Bill Snead, Lawrence *(Kan.)* Journal-World

The obituary/profile continues with quotes from previous interviews and stories about Gaddie as well as quotes from his family. A broadcast or Web obituary about a person who was in the news or an entertainer would include audio and video clips of the person's quotes and accomplishments as well as comments from other people.

Jim Nicholson, a former obituary writer for the *Philadelphia Daily News,* became so famous for his obituaries that he was nicknamed "Dr. Death" by his co-workers. He called his obituaries "character portraits," filled with details of how the person lived, "warts and all," he says.

Obituaries tend to be flattering portraits. But Nicholson says they should be true portraits. He believes someone's bad habits and criminal background, if it exists, should be part of an obituary. Many editors would disagree. And families are not likely to be happy with unflattering material. Generally, news editors weigh whether a criminal background was a crucial part of the person's life and if the crime was highly publicized. If a person was arrested

Jim Nicholson ("Dr. Death"), former obituary writer for the *Philadelphia Daily News*

at one time for shoplifting or for another misdemeanor, most editors would recommend omitting such information. When you are faced with such decisions, it is wise to confer with an editor.

"Cleaning up someone's act after he or she has died does not serve the cause of the deceased or loved ones," Nicholson says. "A sanitized portrait is indistinguishable from any other. It is the irregularities that give us identity. The ultimate acclaim may be when a reader thinks, 'I wish I had known this man or woman.'"

Like the obituary for Lawrence Pompie "Mr. Buddy" Ellis, a retired maintenance man who was a leader in his church:

> He came to be known affectionately among friends as "Dial-A-Prayer" for his unceasing availability to those who wanted him to pray with them. If he couldn't meet personally with someone, he would pray with them on the telephone, said his wife, Fannie, who shared 38 years with him. . . . At 5-foot-7 and 205 pounds, Ellis loved to eat. "He loved everything about a pig," said his wife, "and if he didn't watch out, he'd catch his grunt."
>
> *Jim Nicholson,* Philadelphia Daily News

The Importance of Facts

A misspelled name or a factual error is a major problem in any story; in an obituary it is disastrous. So you should check every fact, every name, every reference. And you should check with the funeral director and the family to make sure that the person you are writing about is dead.

Someone from the *Detroit Free Press* didn't do that. And the death of Dr. Rogers Fair turned out to be greatly exaggerated, as Mark Twain would say. Fair, a Detroit physician, woke up one morning to read in the newspaper that he had died of cancer. The newspaper had received the obituary information by telephone from a woman who claimed she was Fair's aunt. And the reporter didn't call back to check with family members or a funeral home.

Fair, 40, claimed the "aunt" was a 21-year-old woman who was infatuated with him. She had wooed him with flowers and love notes, but when he rejected her and began dating another woman, he began receiving harassing telephone calls, bomb threats and vandalism to his home.

"She is obviously an obsessed person," Fair told the *Free Press*. "She has stated that if she can't have me, nobody else can."

The follow-up story was an embarrassment to the paper:

The obituary for Dr. Rogers Fair in Tuesday's Free Press took a lot of people—especially Fair—by surprise.

"My beeper was just jumping off the hook," the 40-year-old physician said Tuesday. "My secretary called me. She was in tears. . . ."

The erroneous report of Fair's demise was the second phony obituary published by the Free Press in recent years. The first prompted a revision of reporting practices, requiring all obituary information phoned in by friends and relatives to be confirmed either by a funeral home or law enforcement officials.

But Fair's obituary wasn't properly double-checked, and a woman identifying herself as Fair's aunt was able to hoodwink the Free Press with details of his death.

Detroit Free Press

Most newspapers have free or paid death notices—announcements from the family about the deceased. In addition, funeral directors and families call the newspaper to request an obituary. Almost all newspapers will publish an obituary about anyone prominent in the community.

Obituaries have become crucial to online news sites as well. In a creative twist, the Sunline Web site for the *Sun Herald* newspapers in Florida (*www.sunline.net*) offers readers a chance to write tributes to loved ones who have died.

Generally, reporters scan the paid death notices to look for interesting people, long-term residents or those active in community service. Then you make the phone calls—or double-check the validity of the ones you have received by calling a funeral home, checking the phone book, and calling the family back or calling other relatives and friends. And, as in any other story, you check newspaper clips or databases and the Internet.

Calling people about death isn't easy. But it isn't as difficult as you might expect, especially for obituaries. Most families are grateful because this is the last story—and more often the only story—printed about their loved ones. Usually, someone in the family is prepared to deal with the media.

The easiest way to start gathering information is with the funeral director, if one has been selected. The funeral director should have the basic information and should be able to tell you which family members to call and their phone numbers.

Obituary Guidelines

Obituary writing follows some basic forms, even when you are writing a special profile. All obituaries, no matter how long or short, must contain the same crucial information:

Background Research

Before you interview family members or write an obituary, you should do a background check on the Internet. Family members may have personal Web sites. The subject of your obituary could be listed online in alumni sites or sites for Rotary and other organizations.

Before you use anything from a Web site, make sure that you check it for accuracy. Was the site dated? Does it have an author? Is the site credible? Do not use anything you can't verify. If you do include something from a Web site, cite your source.

Name: Use full name, middle initial and nickname if it was commonly used. Enclose the nickname in quotation marks.

Identification: Usually, people are identified by occupation or community service. Always try to find something special to use following the name, such as "John Doe, a retired salesman" or "Jane Doe, a homemaker who was active in her church."

Age: In some cases, a family will request that you withhold the age. You should confer with an editor about honoring this request.

Date and place of death: Use the day of the week if the death occurred that week, the date if it was more than a week prior to the obituary. State the name of a hospital, if applicable, or other location where the death occurred.

Cause of death: This fact is not required at all newspapers, especially if the cause of death was suicide or AIDS-related or when the family requests that the cause be withheld. This issue has become especially controversial because of the stigma attached to AIDS-related deaths. Other news organizations require the cause of death, regardless of stigma or family wishes. So check your newspaper's policy before you gather the information. You may have to inform family members of the policy.

Address: Tell where the person lived when he or she died and previous areas of residence for any major length of time. Broadcast obituaries rarely use the specific address.

Background: Specify major accomplishments, organizations, educational background, military background and any other highlights. When people are very active in their church, mosque or synagogue, this fact should be mentioned in the obituary.

Survivors: Use the names of immediate family members (husband or wife, with her maiden name, children, brothers and sisters). Grandchildren are usually mentioned only by number: "He is survived by five grandchildren." New complications are arising these days because of changes in family relationships. Most news publications still do not list unmarried partners as survivors, or "bonded" partners (homosexual couples united in a marital ceremony), but that rule is changing. In the future, these relationships may also be a standard part of obituaries.

Services: Specify the time, date and location.

Burial: Name the place, and provide memorial information when available. When the death occurred a week or more ago, it is customary to start with information about the service or a memorial if that has not yet been conducted.

This example about the death of a local citizen follows all the basic guidelines; it also includes information about contributions:

Lucy Davis Burnett, a Dallas native and longtime civic leader, died of cancer Saturday at her home. She was 79.

A graduate of Woodrow Wilson High School in Dallas and Mary Baldwin College in Staunton, Va., Mrs. Burnett was active in numerous cultural and civic affairs.

She was past president of the Southern Methodist University Lecture Series, vice president of the Dallas Junior League and president of the Junior League Garden Club.

She was a founding member of the Dallas Slipper Club and also held memberships in the Dallas Women's Club, the Dallas Arts Museum League, the women's division of United Way of Dallas and Highland Park United Methodist.

She is survived by her husband, F.W. Burnett of Dallas; a daughter, Lucy Chambers of Vancouver, British Columbia; a son, F.W. Burnett Jr. of Dallas; and six grandchildren.

Services for Mrs. Burnett will be at 2 p.m. Tuesday at Highland Park United Methodist Church.

Memorials may be made to Children's Medical Center of Dallas, the Dallas Chapter of the American Cancer Society or a charity of the donor's choice.
The Dallas Morning News

Here are some style tips:

Names of services: Mass is celebrated, not said. The word is capitalized. Find out the exact wording you should use for the particular mass, such as Mass of Christian Burial. Likewise, ask for the proper wording of a service for other denominations.

Courtesy titles: Although many newspapers and TV news organizations have eliminated courtesy titles (*Mrs., Mr., Ms., Miss*) for news stories, several keep them for obituaries. Again, you must check your newspaper's or broadcast station's policy.

Titles for religious leaders: Check the proper title for a rabbi, minister or priest. When writing about a priest, do not use *Father* or *Pastor* for the title. Use *the Rev.* (the reverend) followed by the priest's name: "the Rev. Vince Krische." For a rabbi, use *Rabbi* before the name on first reference: "Rabbi

Jacob Katz." On second reference for clergy, including priests, use only the last name. But for second reference to high-ranking clergy, use "the cardinal," "the archbishop" and so on. Check the Associated Press Stylebook for specific religious titles.

Here is a feature obituary for Dr. Seuss that follows the guidelines. The story begins with the writer's death, some basic information about his accomplishments and then a chronology of his life. It ends with information about survivors. No information was available about services at the time, but if it had been, it would have been included at the end.

Theodor Seuss Geisel, alias Dr. Seuss, whose rhymed writing and fanciful drawings were loved worldwide and helped teach generations to read, died Tuesday night at his home in La Jolla.

Geisel's stepdaughter, Lea Dimond, told reporters the world-famous author died with his family around him. No other information was released regarding the cause of death, but Dimond said Geisel, 87, had been ill for several months.

In the 1950s and '60s, Geisel's books gave millions of children relief from the drab textbook adventures of Dick and Jane. His 48 children's books were translated into 18 languages and sold more than 100 million copies.

Geisel also drew most of the fanciful illustrations in his books, creating a menagerie of Whos, grinches, ziffs and zuffs, talking goldfish and loyal, sweet elephants. He was awarded a special Pulitzer Prize in 1984 for his contribution to children's literature.

Geisel's tales were filled with his own moral concerns, particularly for the environment and world peace. "The Lorax" warns against polluting the environment, while "The Butter Battle Book" tells of an arms race between creatures who disagree about whether it is better to eat bread with the butter side down or up.

When asked recently whether he had any final message, Geisel told a reporter from the San Diego Union: "Whenever things go a bit sour in a job I'm doing, I always tell myself, 'You can do better than this.' The best slogan I can think of to leave with the USA would be 'We can do this and we've got to do better than this.'"

Geisel was born in Springfield, Mass., on March 2, 1903. His father was a brewer and superintendent of parks, which included the zoo, where Geisel said he started drawing animals.

He graduated from Dartmouth College in 1925, having drawn cartoons for the school humor magazine. He went to England to study literature at Oxford University, but dropped out, in part, after receiving encouragement in his artistic ambitions from another American student, Helen Palmer. She became his first wife a few years later.

Geisel spent a year in Paris, where he got to know Ernest Hemingway, James Joyce and other expatriate writers. He returned to the United States in 1927, hoping to become a novelist.

He wrote humor for the magazines "Judge" and "Life," adopting his now-famous pen name, Dr. Seuss, as a spoof of scientific developments.

His first children's book was released in 1937, the same year as his first novel for adults. But the former, ". . . And to Think That I Saw It on Mulberry Street," which initially had been rejected by 27 publishers, became a smashing success. His career was off.

Among his most famous books are "The Cat in the Hat," "Green Eggs and Ham" and "Horton Hears a Who!" which was made into a popular TV special, as was "How the Grinch Stole Christmas!"

He moved to La Jolla soon after the end of World War II. During the latter part of the war he served in the Army, helping director Frank Capra make training and documentary films. Two Geisel documentaries, "Hitler Lives?" and "Design for Death," co-written with his wife, won Academy Awards for their producers in 1946 and 1947.

After the war, Geisel's work continued to be translated to movies, with his cartoon short "Gerald McBoing Boing" winning an Oscar in 1951. He turned his attention to television in the 1950s, designing and producing cartoons, including the Peabody Award-winning "How the Grinch Stole Christmas!" and "Horton Hears a Who!". . .

Geisel did not have any children of his own. His first wife died in 1967. He later married Audrey Dimond, who has two daughters from a previous marriage. He also is survived by his niece, Peggy Owens, and her son, Theodore Owens, of Los Angeles.

Laura Bleiberg, The Orange County *(Calif.)* Register

Exercises

1   Write a short profile about someone on your campus, using Julie Sullivan's style. Plan it as a vignette, considering it part of a package or a larger subject so it has a frame of reference. For example, consider a package of multicultural profiles, new professors or alumni.

2   Plan a celebrity profile of someone you would like to interview. If you enjoy sports, plan a profile of an athlete on your campus. Use Alan Richman's tips, and plan an interesting question you would use to begin the interview, as well as a preliminary theme you might pursue.

3   Coach a classmate on writing a profile. Ask your classmate some of the basic coaching questions: What's it about? What is the focus? Do you have a theme? Were there any patterns, any turning points? What anecdotes do you remember as most interesting? What is the point— why should the reader care? What order are you considering? As the writer discusses the profile, you as the coach can ask questions that occur to you.

4   **Slice-of-life snapshots:** Using the theme of "A Day in the Life" of your campus or your community, write vignettes about people and places. Each person in the class can take a different part of the campus or community.

5   **Personal profile:** Write a blog or memo about a turning point in your life or a significant experience that might make you worthy of a profile. Pairing up with a classmate, exchange your memos and interview each other for a profile. Then write your profiles and share the results with your partner.

6   **Obituary:** Gather information from news clips, magazines and online sources about a celebrity or otherwise prominent person in your community who is still alive. Write an obituary, including comments the person has made and comments about the person.

Featured *News Scene* Assignment

Access *News Scene* at *http://communication.wadsworth.com/newsscene2* to view the news simulation titled "An Extended Profile."

Coaching Tips

Call the employer and find out the person to whom you should send your application. Make sure that you have the correct name, title and gender of the person. Ask how to spell the person's first and last name.

Research the companies to which you are applying by checking the Web or library resources.

Limit your cover letter to one page.

Proofread your application carefully to eliminate spelling and typographical errors.

Make a follow-up telephone call a few weeks after you send your application.

Check online job sites and journalism organizations for internships and career opportunities.

Media Jobs and Internships

If you had one sentence or one paragraph to describe yourself to a prospective employer for a job or internship, would you use a summary lead or anecdotal approach? How would you persuade an employer that you are special and worth hiring? That is the purpose of a cover letter, which is often more difficult to write than a news story because it is hard to write about yourself without appearing egotistical. But you can use some of the same techniques that you use in a news story—a hard-news or feature lead. And most important, get to the point of your letter—the nut graph—preferably in the first, second or third graph to explain that you are applying for a job or internship at this organization.

Angelina Lopez likes to think of herself as a storyteller, so she used an anecdotal approach in her cover letter when she applied for an internship at *The Des Moines* (Iowa) *Register*:

When I was in first grade, my teacher asked me to write what I wanted to be when I grew up. I wrote down "Arthur." In confusion, my teacher called me up to her desk.

"Angelina, you want to be Arthur?"

"Yea, Arthur, you know, like one of those people who write books."

She laughed and explained that the word was "author." She wrote it out in big, black printing. I practiced spelling it again and again: AUTHOR.

I still want to be an author, but now I want to write newspaper articles instead of books. Please consider me for a reporting internship this summer. I am a junior at the University of _________, where I am majoring in journalism.

Lopez got the internship, and she was hired as a full-time reporter afterward.

Erin Rooney is a no-nonsense journalism school graduate who took a straightforward approach in her job application:

I am seeking the position of a graphic designer for the Web pages produced by Information Network of Kansas. After corresponding with you by e-mail, I realized that my skills and training fit the needs of your state agency. My background in Web design and my experience with layout of newspapers and business communications make me a qualified candidate.

She also got the job.

But a cover letter that starts "I am graduating in May from journalism school, and I am seeking an internship (or job)" will most likely land in the trash. Thousands of other applicants are also graduating from journalism schools. That lead reveals nothing special about you.

Your cover letter gives employers their first impression of you. Whether you write a cover letter with a direct or creative lead, you need to know how to present yourself. You may be a straight-A student with a fabulous personality and wonderful media skills, but if you can't sell yourself, you are just another applicant from a journalism school. And most important, avoid writing a form letter. Tailor your letter to the organization where you want to get the internship or job. Read the newspaper, watch the TV station or check the work of the public relations firm where you want to work so you can get an idea of the kind of information the organization produces; then choose the approach for your cover letter that you think is appropriate.

Technology has further complicated the job application process in the past few years. Many employers now scan applications into databases, so you need to keep your format simple and brief, preferably limited to one page each for the cover letter and the résumé. In addition, employers expect you to include an e-mail address, which makes it easier for them to contact you than by telephone. Putting a résumé on your own Web page can also enhance your chances of employment in many companies. But whether you are using traditional print or Web form, clarity, creativity and accuracy remain the most important qualities for your job application.

Dan Lovely, metro editor at *The Stuart News* in Florida, takes accuracy to another level. He says he likes to correspond with applicants by e-mail so he can see how they communicate. If their e-mails are filled with typos or poor grammar, he is not likely to hire them.

Regardless of the type of media job or internship you are seeking, the advice that follows will help you prepare your application.

Job Application Skills

For many years Paul Salsini reviewed cover letters and résumés from job applicants to the *Milwaukee Journal Sentinel,* where he was the staff development director and writing coach. He was appalled by the mistakes in these job applications. One applicant misspelled *Milwaukee* throughout her application. Another said, "I've always wanted to work at the *Minneapolis Star.*"

"Good for her," Salsini says. "Why should I care?" One of the worst mistakes applicants make is that they fail to change the text in their word processors when they are sending out multiple applications, Salsini says.

"I can't stress enough how important it is for the applicant to write a cover letter that is both clear and interesting and tells me this person is a good reporter and writer," he says. "If they're just saying they want a job, that doesn't excite me. I want that letter to entice me into their clips and résumé. The cover letter is the only original thing they send." Salsini prefers cover letters

MULTIMEDIA COACH

J.J. Harrier began looking for a job six months before he was due to graduate from the University of Alaska in Anchorage. He created a Web résumé, wrote a print résumé, and selected about 10 of his best clips from his work at the campus newspaper and from his internship at an alternative weekly newspaper.

Then he searched for newspaper reporting jobs online at *www.monster.com,* one of the largest job sites. He didn't find much. Harrier was looking in the wrong place. Few newspaper editors look for prospective employees or post their jobs listings on general job sites. Most media jobs are posted on sites for media organizations.

The American Society of Newspaper Editors posts internships for almost every state as well as links to newspaper organizations. The Public Relations Society of America also lists jobs.

- **Tips for cover letters and résumés:** One of the best online job coaches is Joe Grimm, recruiting and development editor for the *Detroit Free Press.* Grimm has created a massive Web site containing tips for writing cover letters and résumés and links to scores of media job sites at *http://www.freep.com/ jobspage/toolkit/index.htm.* Another resource with excellent tips and tools for writing cover letters, résumés and job interviews is The Journalist's Toolbox, a site affiliated with The American Press Institute at *http://www.journaliststoolbox.com/ placement/packets.html.*

- **Avoid anonymous webmasters:** Some online job sites direct you to send e-mail to an organization's webmaster, without listing the person's name. Call or find out the name of the person to whom you should send your application.

- **Create your own online résumé:** Other Web sites include résumé forms. Unless you are applying to a company that prefers you to use its online résumé form, create your own résumé so you can demonstrate your ability to express yourself— a major qualification for media jobs.

- **Identify yourself:** If you are creating your own Web résumé, make sure that you put your name and e-mail address on every page of your site. Don't use "I" or "Nancy's résumé" as an identifier.

- **White background and black type:** This is the best format for a Web résumé. Some browsers won't print white type.

- **Offer a printer-friendly résumé:** If you have a fancy Web site, offer a simple printer version.

- **Privacy:** When you list references online, check with them to see if they want their phone numbers and e-mail addresses posted. If they want their privacy respected, you can list "references available on request" in a Web site. Also be careful to protect your own privacy. Consider eliminating your phone number and address on a Web site because anyone using a map finder online can find you, including possible stalkers.

- **Job links:** Access online job sites from the Web site for this chapter at *http://communication .wadsworth.com/rich5e.*

with catchy leads that reveal something special about the applicant. Some editors prefer a hard-news lead on a cover letter. Salsini says that whether it's a direct lead or feature, it should be a good lead to a personal account of the applicant.

Salsini also stresses that applicants should attach some explanation to their clips about how they wrote the story: "If they would just write a couple of sentences to explain whether this was their story idea and why the story was important, it would help to put the clip in context. It helps an editor understand the story. That doesn't take a lot of work and it is so important."

The same principles apply to broadcast jobs. When you submit a tape, you should include an explanation of how and why you did the story.

Internships and experience on campus newspapers, radio and television stations are important. Editors want evidence of how you report and write or what you can do as a copy editor, broadcast producer or reporter. They want clips of stories you have written or edited. However, clips are edited, so they aren't always indicative of the person's writing skill, Salsini says.

If you have skills in computer-assisted reporting or online journalism technology, it's important to stress those skills in your cover letter as well as in your résumé. But the majority of editors still want evidence that you write and think clearly. You can demonstrate that you do in your cover letter.

Where to Apply

Here are some places to look for media jobs:

Online job sites Almost every major media company has a Web site listing job openings. Individual newspapers, magazines, television stations, and some public relations and advertising firms also list job and internship opportunities on their sites.

Printed directories Check a directory of publications in your field of interest for ideas about where to apply. These publications list the organization, telephone number, circulation, address and chief officers. But never rely on the publication for the names of editors or other people in charge. Journalists frequently change positions, and the directories cannot keep up with the changes. Always call and find out whom you should contact. Here are some major directories:

For newspapers: Editor & Publisher Yearbook

For newspapers and magazines: Gale's Directory of Publications

For broadcast media: Broadcasting Yearbook, Television/Cable Factbook

For magazines and public relations (in-house) publications: Gebbie House Magazine Directory, Bowkers (publications of trade organizations)

For advertising agencies: Standard Directory of Advertising Agencies

Whom to Contact

At most newspapers, you should apply to the managing editor, not the editor or publisher, unless the paper is very small and the editor or publisher is the only person in charge. For other types of organizations, check to find out who reviews the applications.

Make sure that you get the correct spelling of the person's name, the title and the gender. Some female editors and personnel directors have male-sounding names; some men's names are ambiguous, too. Remember, don't rely on directories for the names of people you should contact; call the organization to find out. Your first step as a reporter or copy editor is to check the facts. Accuracy counts. Inaccuracy in addressing your application usually means you will not be considered.

How to Apply

Here are the basic steps to take when applying for most media jobs:

Cover letter Try to limit the cover letter to one page. Always address it to a specific person, never "Dear Sir" or "Dear Madam." Write a good lead that tells something about you, but don't make it too flowery. Follow with a nut graph—your reason for writing. If you prefer a direct approach, lead with your reason for the letter. Write a few more paragraphs briefly explaining your experience, if any, and your major assets—why anyone should want to hire you—and why you want to work for this company. Then wrap it up with a brief paragraph thanking the editor for his or her attention. Your cover letter is the employer's first impression of you. Make it clear, interesting and simple.

Résumé Make sure that your résumé is free of typos and spelling errors. List two or three references, and include phone numbers and e-mail addresses where your references can be reached. Do not say "References available on request." Do everything you can to help the employer. By withholding references, you force the employer to spend more time checking on you. (However, see the "Multimedia Coach" box for some cautions about listing references in an online application.)

You may have your résumé printed on heavyweight paper and designed in an attractive way. But for most print and broadcast journalism employers, a fancy résumé is not essential. A neatly typed, simple résumé will suffice. Something fancier may be more advantageous for public relations positions because that is a promotional field. Your résumé may reflect your ability to package promotional material. However, most employers really just want the facts in an easy-to-read form.

Scannable résumés should be as simple as possible on plain white paper with black type of at least 12 points. Your headings can be in larger type, but don't mix fonts. Also eliminate borders and underlining. Web résumés also should be short and simple; they are discussed later in the chapter.

Clips or videotape Include five or six clips (or videotape for broadcast journalists, although clips or scripts help in this area as well). Choose clips with good leads. Editors rarely read past a bad lead. Try to include a variety: features and hard news, short and long. Short is better, unless you have a major project. If you have some good enterprise stories, those you developed through your own ideas, include them. The significance of the news event is not important to editors; they want to see how you wrote more than what you wrote.

Newspaper newsroom

The Gannetteer, Gannett Co., Inc.

When you copy your clips, don't reduce them in size. Cut them so they fit on standard-sized paper, even if you have to use more than one page for a story.

As Salsini suggests, attach a paragraph explaining how you got each story, why it was important or how much difficulty you might have had in getting interviews. Say something about each clip to explain why you think it is representative of your work or why you enjoyed doing it.

Follow-up phone call A week or two after you have sent your letter and résumé, call the organization to ask if they were received and if you may come for an interview. Find out when the editor you are calling is on deadline or in meetings, and try to avoid these times.

Research for the interview If you are granted an interview, make sure that you get a few copies of the publication in advance and read them thoroughly. Or check the Web site for the broadcast station and view the videotape if possible. Check the Internet or the library. Or call the circulation department of the newspaper or magazine and get it to send you a few copies. For a public relations job, try to get a media kit about the company. A little money and time invested before your interview may pay off in a paycheck.

Also do some research about the community. Find out if it has large ethnic groups. If you have special language skills that would be useful in this community, you can stress them in your letter, résumé and interview.

ETHICS

Case 1: You have an internship at a local newspaper or television station. A few weeks after you start working, your supervisor asks you out on a date. You like your supervisor and think you could get romantically involved. Should you go on a date? What are the ethical problems of dating your supervisor?

Case 2: You have been hired by the newspaper or television station where you have wanted to work for a long time. You have established some roots and really enjoy your job. You've been on the job for about a year. You are very attracted to your editor, and he or she feels the same attraction to you. Should you get romantically involved? If so, what are the ethical problems and alternatives?

Case 3: You face a similar situation as in Case 2, but this time you are attracted to a source on your beat. Can you or should you get romantically involved? Do you have to give up a romantic relationship for your job? What are the ethical issues, and what alternatives are open to you?

Interview follow-up After you have had an interview, wait a few weeks and then call to let the editor know you are aggressive and interested in the job. But don't be a pest.

Even if you are not interested in the job, send a note thanking the editor for the interview. That's just basic courtesy. And if you are interested in the job, the thank-you note lets the editor know something else about you: You're thoughtful.

Cover Letters

Make your first impression on the editor a good one. Use proper business letter form, and keep it brief—no more than one page. Editors and other employers are busy people. Double-check and triple-check your spelling. Make sure that all the names and titles are correct. A misspelled name, typo or other mechanical error can disqualify you for consideration.

Be straightforward—not cute, not boring. Start with why you are applying to this organization or something about yourself that makes you worth noticing. But get to the point quickly: why you are applying. Specify whether you are seeking an internship or full-time job.

In the middle of your letter, explain why you are eager to work for this particular organization. Even though you are including a résumé, mention its high points. Make special note of any unusual skills you may have, such as fluency in a second language or relevant experience. If someone at the organization has encouraged you to apply, mention this person's name. The adage "It's not what you know but who you know" has some validity.

Here is some additional advice from editors, excerpted from an article that Judith Clabes, president and chief executive officer of the Scripps

Howard Foundation, wrote for *Quill* magazine when she was editor of the *Kentucky Post*:

> I'm editor of a medium-sized daily, and being deluged with letters to the editor comes with the territory.
>
> Believe me, by the time I've shuffled through the "Dear Stupid" letters to the editor, the "Dear Employee" memos from corporate, and the really important "Dear Resident" mail that somehow pours into the office, I'm in no frame of mind for a job-seeker's "Dear Mr. Clabes" letter.
>
> "Dear Mr. Judith Clabes" really ticks me off.
>
> Now, this may seem quirky, but we editors are entitled to an eccentricity or two.
>
> Idiosyncrasies aside, we editors do seem to agree on the issue of introductory letters from job-seekers. We prefer:
>
> - Straightforward, one-page letters
> - Simple résumés and
> - Well-selected clips (yes, college newspaper clips are fine)
>
> In the end, the clips speak loudest. But the introductory letter may determine whether a busy editor will even bother to listen.
>
> . . . The following will automatically turn off an editor:
>
> - Grammatical errors
> - Typographical errors
> - Misspelling the name of the newspaper
> - Misspelling the name of the editor
> - Form letters
> - Incorrect titles, including courtesy titles
> - Cutesy letters
> - Bad writing, including poor sentence structure
> - Phony sales pitches
> - Lengthy, self-centered letters
>
> . . . Typos are killers. "I can't remember bothering to interview an applicant whose letter contained typos or grammatical errors," says Dee W. Bryant, former editor of *The Leaf-Chronicle* in Clarksville, Tennessee. "If a person is that careless with letters, it raises the question about carelessness as a staffer."
>
> Bryant's pet peeve, however, is the automatic—and mindless— "Mr." greeting. "If an applicant is seriously interested, he or she should have taken the time to find out. It irritates me that people make the invalid assumption that editors are men." . . .
>
> Though we editors have our own pet peeves as well as hiring strategies, we shudder over the cute stuff, the gimmicks, the overzealous attempts at creativity. . . .
>
> What will work is a simple, professional approach. Throw away fuchsia paper and the gimmicks. Invest time in investigating the newspaper. Write a simple, well-crafted (and proofread) one-page letter that demonstrates your interest in journalism generally and in that

particular newspaper specifically. Include a brief résumé and five or six well-selected clips.

Before you write your cover letter and résumé, do some research about the organization to which you are applying. If you are seeking a job at a newspaper or magazine, read the publication. You can check the Web or online databases, such as Lexis/Nexis, or get copies of the publication.

If you are applying to a corporation for a public relations or advertising position, check databases, such as Standard & Poor's Register of Corporations, and business publications to learn something about the organization. Don't just cite facts about the company; weave the information into the paragraph in your cover letter that explains why you want to work for the organization.

There is no single way to write an effective cover letter. But you should consider the lead to your cover letter as carefully as you would consider the lead to a news story. It's the attention getter. Here are some effective types of leads:

Direct approach: "Please consider me for a reporting internship (or job—and specify the type of position and the name of the organization) this summer." Follow with a line or two about who you are and why you are interested in this company. This approach does not reflect any creativity, but it is preferable to a strained lead.

Experience approach: If you had a good internship or have previous journalism-related experience, consider starting with a paragraph about what your experience was and why you are interested in or qualified for this job. If you are a graduate student or nontraditional student, you might refer to your previous experience and your reasons for studying journalism. For example, Michael Strong was a nontraditional student who was once a massage therapist. His job application began, "How many reporters do you know who have experience meeting people when they are nude? That isn't exactly traditional training for a reporter, but I'm not a traditional candidate for a reporting job."

Autobiographical approach: Start with something about your background that made you want to become a journalist (or whatever type of career position you are seeking). If you use this technique, keep it short. Don't give your life story.

Reference approach: The adage of who you know, not what you know, is still somewhat true when you are applying for a job or internship. If someone in the organization referred you to the company or if you have spoken to the recruiter, you can begin your cover letter by referring to that person or conversation.

Preferably by the second paragraph, explain the purpose of your letter—similar to a nut graph in a news story. State what type of job or internship you are seeking and why you are applying to this organization.

In the body, mention some highlights of your résumé or special skills that make you qualified or valuable for the position you seek. Elaborate briefly on any experience you've had related to this position. Try to tailor your comments to this organization rather than writing a form letter with a generic tone.

At the end, mention any enclosures, such as clips or videos. You might thank the person for attention to your application or provide any contact information that you think is necessary.

Student's home address
City, State, ZIP code
Date

Maureen Murray, Recruiter for Account Executives
Leo Burnett Company Inc.
35 W. Wacker Drive
Chicago, IL 60601

Dear Ms. Murray:

The basket of apples in your company logo indirectly led me to seek a career in advertising and to write this letter seeking a job in your agency. When I was growing up in Chicago, my grandparents told me a story about how your company used to hand out apples to people on the streets during the Depression as a good public relations gesture. I was impressed. I thought that your company would be the kind of place where I would like to work someday. Every time I see your logo, I remember that story.

Now, as a journalism student at the University of Kansas, I am even more impressed with the Leo Burnett Company, which is ranked the No. 1 advertising agency in the Midwest. Please consider me for a position as an assistant account executive in your client services division. I will graduate in December with a bachelor's degree in journalism. I have taken several advertising, public relations and news-writing courses. I would be eager to work on any of your accounts, such as Nintendo, Reebok, Hallmark Cards or Pillsbury. Any opportunity in your agency would be challenging, but a chance to assist on the Walt Disney account is my idea of the perfect job.

Although I have gained many skills from my academic training, I believe that my internships have offered me the best education. Currently I am a public relations intern for the Nelson-Atkins Museum of Art in Kansas City. I recently promoted and publicized the autobiographical exhibit of artist Andrew Wyeth. I also gained valuable experience last winter as an advertising intern for The Pioneer Press, a suburban Chicago newspaper chain. In that position, I created target account booklets, wrote reports and assisted sales representatives. When I worked in the advertising department of my college newspaper, *The University Daily Kansan,* I won an award as the best account executive.

I work well with people, and I am a good problem solver. In addition to my sales and advertising skills, I have written news stories for the university newspaper. I understand that you are seeking applicants with a broad educational background, and I believe that the media experiences I have had make me a good candidate for your firm. Although I have much to learn, I offer boundless enthusiasm and a positive work ethic.

I will call you within the next two weeks to see if you will grant me an interview. I can be reached at (913) 000-0000. I am enclosing a résumé and some examples of my work. Thank you for your consideration.

Sincerely yours,

[Signature]

Shelly Falevits
E-mail address

Sample cover letter with an autobiographical approach

Here is a more straightforward approach, mentioned at the start of the chapter, by Erin Rooney:

Student's home address
City, State, ZIP code
e-mail address
Date

Name and title of person to whom you are applying
Name of organization
Address of organization
City, State, ZIP

Dear Mr. or Ms. Name of person (don't use generic Dear Sir or Dear Madam):

I am seeking the position of a graphic designer for the Web pages produced by Information Network of Kansas. After corresponding with you by e-mail, I realized that my skills and training fit the needs of your state agency. My background in Web design and my experience with layout of newspapers and business communications make me a qualified candidate.

I can benefit your organization with my knowledge of several computer graphic design packages and programming languages. I have lived and worked in many different towns in Kansas and will use this knowledge to help develop services for the people who use your network. My internship with the Kansas Public Policy Institute also gave me an in-depth view of our state government and the politicians who represent the people.

The Information Network of Kansas is providing cutting-edge information, and I am interested in working for an agency that refuses to stagnate. I am also interested in working for an agency that provides an essential service to its community. I hope that my skills and your services will benefit both of us.

I appreciate your consideration. I can be reached by e-mail at . . . . or by phone at . . . .

Sincerely yours,

[signature]

Erin Rooney
Enc. Résumé

Résumés

Limit your résumé to one page, with a possible second page for references. Arrange your topics from most recent to previous, such as current experience followed by previous jobs. White paper is preferred. Content is more important than appearance. If you have a home page and online résumé, add the Web address to your résumé.

Organize your topics to emphasize the most important. If your experience in previous internships or jobs is more interesting than your education, put the experience category first. If you have no experience or awards, eliminate the category; don't write "none."

Online Résumés

Reading a résumé online is more difficult than reading it in print, so keep your Web résumé even shorter than your print one. Try to limit it to three screens. Don't just transfer the print résumé to an online version.

Use a different format, perhaps paragraphs or lists. Don't use the column structure you might use in print; online reading is vertical, not horizontal. If you use a one-screen design, don't offer too many links to separate categories for education, experience and so on. Endless clicking can be tedious for a potential employer. Put the basic information on one page, and link to clips or your portfolio.

Here are some other tips for Web résumés:

- Don't use a dark background with white or light type. The type may not show up if an employer wants to print your résumé. If you really prefer this type of design, offer a printable version as well, with white background and black type.

- Protect your own privacy and that of your references. Consider eliminating your address and phone number in online documents, especially if you post your photograph on your site. The same is true for your references. Although providing contact information for references is preferable in print, for online sites you may have to write "References available on request."

Templates

Microsoft Word offers several résumé templates that are attractive and acceptable for media résumés. If you choose a template, you should adapt it to your needs. Consider using "Education" as your first topic heading if you are just graduating, but if you have considerable experience, list that heading first. Interests are optional, but references are not. Make sure that you add a heading for references because one is not included in the templates. Then list your references' titles and e-mail addresses if they agree to be listed, or write "references available on request."

An example of a scannable résumé adapted from the Word professional résumé template is shown on p. 497.

Interviews

The interview is your chance to explain how much you want to work for the employer and why you would be a good choice. It is also your chance to find out more about the employer and to assess whether you would really like to work there.

Your Name
e-mail address

Permanent Address
[If it differs from school address]
Street
City, State, ZIP code

School Address
[If it differs from permanent address]
Street
City, State, ZIP code

Objective
List your career objective or position desired and date of availability:
Reporting internship; available May, Year

Education

Years	University	Location

[Give dates, from most recent to previous]
B.A., Journalism.

Years	University	Location

Years	High School	Location

Experience
List any full-time or part-time jobs, particularly any related to your field, in order starting from the most recent. Give the dates. You may add a line or two explaining your job duties.

January-May [Year]
Reporter, *The Daily Campus Newspaper;* covered university administration

July-August [Year]
Reporting internship, name of publication; covered general news for city desk and feature department

August to present
Server, Campus Bar and Grill, Location

Special Skills/Awards
Proficient in computer programs: Word, Dreamweaver, and so on.
Bilingual in Spanish and English
[Omit this section if you have no special skills.]

Activities
List only important activities and memberships, especially those that show leadership or skills related to the job you are seeking. This category may be omitted.

References
List two or three people who have given you permission to use them as references. Include their names, titles, addresses, phone numbers and e-mail addresses. References may be listed on a separate page if you don't have room on one page. Do not write "References available on request."

Sample of scannable résumé

Here are some tips:

Dress conservatively: Wear the type of clothing that employees at that organization would wear to work. Women might wear casual attire such as a skirt and blouse or more businesslike outfits such as a suit or dress, depending on the company. Men should wear a suit or sport jacket with a shirt and tie. No jeans and no sneakers!

Be prompt: Be on time for your interview. You may arrive 15 minutes early, but don't get there too early. Never be late. That's equivalent to missing a deadline. And that's equivalent to saying you are not fit for the job.

Be prepared: Be informed about the publication, organization or station. Read copies of the publication, particularly the most recently published ones, or view video on the station's Web site if possible. Public relations applicants should try to gather research about the company and the types of promotions the firm does. Memorize the names of key editors in advance.

Understand the costs: Some organizations will pay for your transportation and hotel. If not, be prepared to pay for them yourself. Small newspapers and other organizations may not have the budget for your travel costs. You have to decide if the cost is worthwhile to you. If the organization is out of state, it's fair to ask if your transportation and lodging costs will be reimbursed.

Concentrate: When you are introduced to people, try to remember their names, especially those of key editors—such as the city editor or, if you are applying for a sports job, the sports editor. Homework helps.

Be enthusiastic: Your enthusiasm is your best asset, especially if you don't have experience. Show that you're interested in the job. Smile and enjoy the interview just as if you were doing an interview for a story. If you don't really want to work for the firm, don't waste everyone's time.

Be polite: Thank the editor or key person for granting you an interview, and thank the person at the end of it as well.

Be pleasant: Even if you are frightened, smile and be responsive.

Be yourself: Do not try so hard to make a good impression that you are insincere. Be honest about what you can and cannot do and what you want to learn. Never try to give a false impression of yourself.

Ask questions: The questions you ask are as important as the ones you answer. They show your curiosity and your concern about the job—qualities of a good reporter, editor or publicist.

Editors have their favorite questions, so it is hard to prepare for the interview. However, almost all of them will ask why you want to work for their organization and why you want to be a journalist. Try to be creative but sincere. "I've always wanted to write" is such a boring answer.

Here are some other questions that are popular with newspaper editors (similar questions are often asked in other fields):

Why do you want to work for this organization? The answers are up to you: because you grew up in the area, want to remain in the area, are familiar with the community and so on. It's best to specify something you like about the paper if you are familiar with it. Or you could say you are seeking a variety of experiences, particularly if it's a small newspaper or television station, where reporters tend to do all types of stories. If it's a large organization, you could say you're attracted by the prestige of the paper or the chance to learn from very experienced journalists. If you are so eager that you will work anywhere, it's OK to say so. Just be honest.

Why did you want to become a journalist? Because it's more interesting than selling used cars, because you seek adventure, because you love the language, whatever. Here is your chance to give your real reason. It could be that someone influenced you or that you just like the type of work.

What are your goals as a journalist? You could say, "To get your job some day" or "To work here until *The New York Times* begs me to come there." A preferred answer might be because you like the work of this paper or station and you are familiar with the community (if that's true). If your goal is to be a foreign correspondent, at this point you might consider joining the Navy. Small papers don't have much use for foreign bureaus. Again, be sincere.

What books, magazines and newspapers do you read? Editors love this question. It tells them something about you.

What other interests do you have? This is another favorite question.

What can you do for this newspaper (or other organization), or why should I hire you? Don't say you can turn the paper around or make it wonderful. But do say something about the types of stories you would like to do, or say that you would be willing to do all types of stories. Don't be arrogant.

What do you think of this newspaper or TV news program? Be cautious with this one. Don't say it's terrible and you can save it. Point out something good first. Then you might point out some weakness or area that you think could be improved. Perhaps you think it could use more human approaches to stories or more hard news. If you've read it, you have a right to your opinion. Just be diplomatic.

What was your favorite story that you wrote or produced, and why did you like it? This is another question that gives insight into you as well as your professional interests.

How would you cover this issue? The editor might give you an example of a topic that is of concern in that community. You'll have to think and do the best you can to come up with some interesting approaches.

What questions do you have? This question is very important. Here's where you get your chance to ask about the company, the workload, perhaps what the editors want or expect from reporters and copy editors. You could ask about a probationary period. You could also ask about salary, benefits and other compensation; generally, however, that shouldn't be your first question.

At the end of the interview, don't forget to thank the interviewer for his or her time and interest.

Check the Web site for this chapter for links to job resources: *http://communication.wadsworth.com/rich5e.*

Exercises

1   Depending on your field of interest, interview three newspaper editors, television news directors, magazine editors or public relations employers about the qualities they seek in job candidates and the kinds of applications they want.

2   Write a few descriptive paragraphs about yourself in the third person (*she* or *he*). This exercise will give you a clue to what makes you special, and it may help you find a lead for your cover letter.

3   Write a cover letter and a résumé for a job or internship you would be interested in getting.

4   Write an online résumé.

Featured Online Activity

Access the Chapter 23 resources at *http://communication.wadsworth.com/ rich5e* to link to e-mail résumé exercises and additional guidelines. Write an e-mail résumé as directed, and rate the sample cover letters based on the information presented in the chapter.

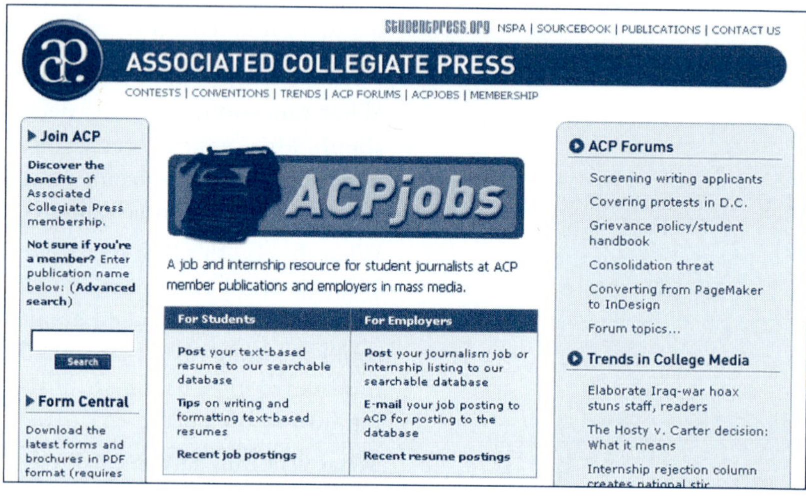

Style Guide

The Associated Press Stylebook is an essential tool for all media writers. It is filled with valuable guidelines for punctuation, spelling, word use and clear writing. Although many newspapers have their own guidelines, the Associated Press Stylebook is widely accepted. It is also used for public relations writing. However, many of the guidelines for magazines and broadcast writing differ from those for newspaper and public relations releases. This abbreviated style guide is in no way a substitute for the printed version of the Associated Press Stylebook. However, for a quick reference on common problems and uses, the following material, which is based on the Associated Press Stylebook and is used with permission, may be helpful. The AP Stylebook is also online at *www.apstylebook.com* for a registration fee. The 2005 edition includes several revisions, some of which will be mentioned here. Check the Web site for this book for interactive, online quizzes: *http://communication.wadsworth.com/rich5e.*

A

abbreviations: Avoid acronyms the reader would not easily recognize. Do not follow an organization's full name with the acronym in parentheses. If the acronym would not be clear on second reference, don't use it. See also *months, state names.*

academic degrees: Avoid abbreviations when possible. Preferred: *John Jones, who has a doctorate in psychology.* Use an apostrophe in *bachelor's degree* and *master's degree.* Use *Ph.D.* for a doctorate, and use other abbreviations, such as *M.S.* and *B.A.,* only when needed after a name. Don't use both *Ph.D* and *Dr.* to identify someone. Wrong: *Dr. Sam Jones, Ph.D.* Right: *Dr. Sam Jones, a chemist.*

academic departments: Use lowercase except for proper names such as *English* and *Spanish* but not *history department.*

academic titles: Capitalize and spell out formal titles such as *chancellor* and *chairman* when they precede a name—*Chancellor Robert Smart.* Use a lowercase letter after a name—*Robert Smart, chancellor, spoke yesterday*—and when an academic title is used elsewhere without a name. Use lowercase for *professor* and for modifiers before a name: *history professor William Oldtime.*

Don't use the title *professor* before the name on second reference; just use the last name.

addresses: Use the abbreviations *Ave., Blvd. and St.* only with a numbered address: *1600 Pennsylvania Ave.* Spell out these words when they are part of a street name without a number: *Pennsylvania Avenue.* Do not use abbreviations for *Road, Drive, Terrace* or other such words. Use figures for street numbers: *6 University Drive.* Spell out and capitalize *First* through *Ninth* when they are used as street names; use figures with two letters for 10th and above: *7 Fifth Ave., 100 21st St.*

affect, effect: *Affect* is a verb, meaning to influence. *Effect* is most commonly used as a noun, meaning the result. Consider *affect* as action and *effect* as the end result. *Effect* as a verb is less commonly used and means to cause or create, as in *He will effect changes in the department.*

ages: Always use figures: *He is 9 years old. The boy, 9, is missing.* When age is used as an adjective, as in *a 9-year-old boy,* use hyphens.

AIDS: The acronym is acceptable in all references to acquired immune deficiency syndrome, a virus that weakens the immune system. The scientific name for the virus that causes AIDS is the human immunodeficiency virus, or HIV. People who test positive for the virus, who are said to be HIV-positive, do not have AIDS; they have the AIDS virus. People do not have AIDS until they develop several serious symptoms of the disease. When writing about the deaths of people who have AIDS, say they died from AIDS-related illnesses, not from AIDS. The actual cause of death is not AIDS; it is the illnesses that result from the weakened immune system.

allege: Use this word with great care, and avoid it when possible. It does not spare you from a libel suit. Use it when you need to make it clear that the unproved action is not being treated as a fact: *the alleged rape.* Specify the exact charge and the source—police or court records—somewhere in the story. Avoid redundancy. Wrong: *Police accused her of allegedly stealing the bicycle.* Right: *Police accused her of stealing the bicycle.*

all right: two words, not *alright.* Even though *alright* is listed in the dictionary as being used in some manuscripts, it is not acceptable in journalism or modern usage.

alumnus, alumni, alumna, alumnae: *Alumnus* is one man, *alumni* is the plural for graduates, *alumna* is one woman graduate and *alumnae* is plural for women graduates. *Alumni* is the most common plural because it includes men and women.

a.m., p.m.: Use lowercase letters with periods. Avoid redundancy: *10 a.m. this morning.*

among, between: Use *between* for two items and *among* for more than two: *The money was divided between two students; the money was divided among six students.* Equally important, when using *between,* always follow it with objective pronouns such as *me, him,* or *her,* as in *between you and me,* not *between you and I.*

anybody, anyone, any one, any body: one word for indefinite reference: *Anyone can master this;* two words for singling out a person: *Any one of you can master this.*

average, mean, median, norm: The *average* is the number obtained when the totals are added and divided by the number of quantities—2, 4 and 6 equals 12, divided by 3 equals an *average* of 4. The *mean* is the figure between two extremes obtained by adding all the figures and dividing by the total number of items: The *mean* of 2, 4, 6, 8 and 10 is 6. The *median* is the middle number in a series arranged in order: The *median* grade of 60, 70 and 80 is 70. *Norm* is a standard of average performance for a group.

B

backward: not *backwards.*

bad, badly: *Bad* is an adjective but can be used with *feel* for a condition of health, meaning *I feel bad. Badly* is an adverb: *He played badly.*

because, since: *Because* denotes a cause–effect relationship; *since* is used more to denote a sense of time or when the result was related but not the direct cause: *Because you studied, you will pass the test. Since you have been in the department, the rules have changed.*

beside, besides: *Beside* means at the side of; *besides* means in addition to.

Bible: Capitalize when referring to the Old Testament or New Testament. Capitalize related terms: *Gospels, Scriptures, Holy Scriptures.* Lowercase *biblical* in all uses. Lowercase *bible* as a nonreligious term: *Her textbook was her bible.*

biweekly: every other week.

black: preferred term for people of African descent. Check with sources to see if they prefer *African-American.* Although not specified in the AP Stylebook, in some cases members of minority groups prefer the term *people of color.* You should always check with your sources for usage of appropriate terms.

blond, blonde: *blond* for males and all adjectives; *blonde* as nouns for females. *She had blond hair.*

brand names: Capitalize them: *She drank a Coke.*

brunet, brunette: Use *brunet* as a noun for males and as an adjective for both sexes. Use *brunette* as a noun for females.

burglary, larceny, robbery, theft: *Burglary* is unlawful entry of a building involving a crime, *larceny* is the legal term for taking property, *robbery* involves violence or threat in committing larceny, and *theft* is taking property without threats or violence. *Robbery* can be committed without a person present in a property, such as *his house was robbed,* but it is usually used with the threat of violence.

bus, buses: These are transportation vehicles. *Busses* means kisses.

C

cancel, canceled, canceling, cancellation

cannot: one word.

capital, capitol: *Capital* is the city where a seat of government is located. Do not capitalize. *Capitol* is the building for the seat of government in Washington or in one of the states: The legislators met in the *capitol;* the *capital* of Connecticut is Hartford; the *capitol* in Hartford looks like a white fairy-tale castle with a gold dome.

Catholic: Use *Roman Catholic Church* in the first reference. Second or more references may be the *Catholic Church* or *Catholicism*—capitalized when referring to the religion.

Centers for Disease Control and Prevention: Plural for *Centers.*

cents: Spell out the word *cents* and use lowercase. Use numerals for amounts less than a dollar: *5 cents.* Use the dollar sign and a decimal system for larger amounts: *$1.05.*

city council, city commission: Capitalize either term when it is part of a proper name: *the Hartford City Council* or the *Lawrence City Commission.* Retain the capitalization if the reference is to a specific council but the context does not require the city name: *The City Council passed an ordinance.* Use lowercase when the term is used in a generic sense, not referring to a specific body: *Every city in our state has a city council.*

city hall: Capitalize if it refers to a specific city hall, with or without the name: *Hartford City Hall.* Lowercase when used in a generic sense: *You can find records in any city hall.*

civil cases, criminal cases: Civil cases are brought by individuals or organizations seeking damages; criminal cases are filed by a government agency against people involved in a crime.

collective nouns: Nouns denoting a single unit take singular verbs and singular pronouns for agreement: The Board of Supervisors made *its* ruling; the committee *is* going to meet; the family *is* going on a picnic; the jury reached *its* verdict.

complement, compliment: *Complement* means to complete; *compliment* means to praise.

compose, comprise: *Compose* is to create or put together: The country *is composed* of 50 states. *Comprise* is to contain or include all, best used in active voice: The jury *comprises* 12 members.

composition titles: Put quotation marks around titles of books, movies, plays, poems and songs, but not the Bible or reference works, newspaper or magazine names. Even though books and other publications are italicized in manuscripts, the convention of quotes is still used in journalism because typewriters did not have italicized capabilities. Do not underline these titles as you might in a term paper bibliography.

Congress, congressional: Capitalize *U.S. Congress* and *Congress* when referring to the U.S. Senate and House of Representatives. Lowercase *congressional* unless it is part of a proper name, such as the *Congressional Record.*

Constitution, constitutional: Capitalize references to the U.S. Constitution, with or without the modifier *U.S.* Capitalize when referring to constitutions of other nations or states and using the name of the nation or state: *the Massachusetts Constitution.* Lowercase when not using the name of a state, for general references: *the state constitution, the organization's constitution.* Lowercase *constitutional* in all uses.

county, counties: Capitalize the word when it is part of a proper name: *Broward County.* Lowercase it in general references—*the county agency*—and when it is not used as a title—*the county of Broward*—and when it is part of a plural—*Broward and Westchester counties.* Capitalize *county* if it is part of a board's or agency's name: *the County Commission.*

couple: When used for two people, use a plural verb: *The couple were married.* When used as one unit, use a singular verb: *Each couple was contributing $10.*

courtesy titles: On first reference, do not use the courtesy titles *Miss, Mr., Mrs.* or *Ms.* For second references, eliminate courtesy titles in most cases unless your newspaper prefers to use them for all or for specific stories, such as obituaries. For example, use *Elma Smith* for the first reference, *Mrs. Smith* for second reference in these selected cases. When courtesy titles are used for women, ask if they prefer *Miss, Ms.* or *Mrs.* When writing about a couple with the same name, on second reference use their full names: *John and Betty Smith.*

court names: Capitalize the full proper names of courts at all levels. Retain capitalization if *U.S.* is dropped: *U.S. Supreme Court* or *Supreme Court, 2nd District Court, 8th U.S. Circuit Court of Appeals.*

D

dangling modifiers: Make sure that the modifier is followed by a noun that did the action. Wrong: *Driving at high speeds, the car crashed into a tree.* The car wasn't driving. Right: *Driving at high speeds, she crashed the car into a tree.*

data: A plural word: *The data are missing.*

database: one word.

datelines: Datelines should contain a city name all in capital letters, followed in most cases by the abbreviated name of the state in uppercase and lowercase letters: *KANSAS CITY, Mo.* Major cities that are clearly identified with their states do not need to be followed by the state name; some examples are *ATLANTA, PHILADELPHIA, NEW YORK, SAN FRANCISCO, SEATTLE, DALLAS.* For a full list, see *state names.*

days of the week: Capitalize *Monday, Tuesday* and so on. Do not abbreviate days except in tabular form.

dean's list: lowercase in all cases.

different: Use *different from,* not *different than.*

dimensions: Use figures and spell out *inches, feet, yards* and so on. Hyphenate when used as adjectives before nouns: *She is 5 feet 6 inches tall; the*

5-foot-6-inch woman; the 5-foot woman; the basketball team signed a 7-footer; the car is 17 feet long, 6 feet wide and 5 feet high.

directions and regions: Lowercase *north, south, east* and *west* when they indicate directions: Go *south* for three miles; then turn *east.* Capitalize when they indicate regions: She lived in the *South* for three years before she moved to the *Midwest.*

dollars: Use the dollar sign, *$,* with a figure in all cases except casual references, usually only for a dollar: He paid *$3* for the book; please give me *a dollar.* For amounts of $1 million or more, use the word *million* or *billion.* For amounts less than $1 million, use numerals only: *$2,000,* not *$2 thousand.*

E

effect, affect: See *affect, effect.*

either, neither: The verb agrees with the nearest subject: *Either Jane or John is going to the play; either John or the other students are going to the play.*

embarrass, embarrassment: two r's and two s's.

employee: not *employe.*

espresso

essential and nonessential clauses and phrases: An essential clause cannot be eliminated without changing the meaning of the sentence. It should not be set off by commas: *Students who do not study their stylebook should not blame professors for taking points off their papers.* The clause *who do not study their stylebook* is essential; only students who do not study their stylebook are affected. If the clause is used in a nonessential way, it should be set off by commas: *Students, who do not study their stylebook, should not blame professors for taking points off their papers.* This sentence means that all students should not blame their professors, whether they use the stylebook or not. Use *who* or *whom* to introduce a clause or phrase referring to a human being. Use *that* for all other essential clauses and phrases; use *which* for nonessential ones.

everyone, every one: *Everyone* is a pronoun that takes a singular verb: *Everyone has his or her book. Every one* means each item: *Every one of these papers is good.*

F

farther, further: *Farther* is physical distance; *further* means more time or degree. *He will walk farther to get home; she will study the matter further.*

federal: Use a capital letter when the word is part of a title: the *Federal Trade Commission.* Use lowercase when it is an adjective: *the federal court.*

felony, misdemeanor: *Felony* is a serious crime; *misdemeanor* is a minor offense. The punishments vary, but at the federal level, a misdemeanor is punishable by less than a year in jail, and a sentence for a felony is usually more than a year in prison.

fewer, less: Use *fewer* for individual items and *less* for quantity: *She had fewer than three mistakes on the test; she has less money in her bank account this month.*

fiscal year: The 12-month period used for budgets, not always starting with the calendar year. Many government organizations start their fiscal year in July.

flier, flyer: *Flier* is a handbill or notice; *flyer* is a proper name for trains and buses. If you distribute posters about an event, you are giving out *fliers*.

fractions: Spell out amounts less than one, using hyphens between the words: *two-thirds*. When using fractions with a whole number, write the whole number, a space and then the fraction: *2 1/2*.

french fries: lowercase.

G

geographic names: Do not use postal abbreviations for state names. See *state names*.

governmental bodies: Capitalize the full proper name of governmental agencies, and retain capitalization if referring to a specific body; lowercase terms used in a general sense: *the Boston City Council, the City Council* (when referring to the Boston City Council); *the city councils decide how to spend the money*.

governor: Capitalize and abbreviate in a formal title—*Gov. John Jones*.

grand jury: lowercase.

grisly, grizzly: *Grisly* is gruesome or horrible; *grizzly* is a type of bear.

H

half-mast, half-staff: On ships, flags are flown at *half-mast;* on shore, they are flown at *half-staff*.

handicapped, disabled, impaired: Do not describe people as disabled or handicapped unless the description is crucial to a story. If it is, ask the people how they prefer to be described. Avoid euphemisms such as *mentally challenged* and *afflicted with;* instead, say the woman *has multiple sclerosis,* not she *suffers from* or is *afflicted with multiple sclerosis*.

hang, hanged, hung: If someone commits suicide by hanging, he *hanged* himself. Past tense for *hanging* as in hanging a picture is *hung*.

Hanukkah: The preferred spelling for the Jewish holiday.

harass, harassment

holidays: Capitalize them: *New Year's Eve, Easter, Hanukkah, Memorial Day* and so on.

homicide, murder, manslaughter: *Homicide* is the legal term for slaying; *murder* is premeditated homicide. Do not call anyone a murderer until the person is convicted of the charge.

hopefully: Avoid it. It means in a hopeful manner and should not be used as *Hopefully, I will pass. I hope I will pass* is better.

HTML: Use this acronym for hypertext markup language. Capitalize when used alone; lowercase when used as part of an Internet address.

HTTP: Use this acronym for hypertext transfer protocol.

I

imply, infer: A speaker *implies* something; a listener *infers* something from what is said.

incorporated: Abbreviate as part of a company name, but do not set off in commas: *Dow Jones & Co. Inc.*

initials: Use periods and no space when a person uses initials instead of a first name: *I.F. Stone.*

Internet addresses: Place URLs (uniform resource locators) and other Internet addresses in a self-contained paragraph at the end of a story. Capitalize *Internet, World Wide Web* and *Web.*

it's, its: Learn the difference. *It's* is a contraction meaning "it is." *Its* is a possessive pronoun: *The dog lost its collar.*

J

Jell-O

judge: Capitalize before a name when it is part of the person's title: *U.S. District Judge Joanne Jones.* Do not use *Judge* to precede the name on second reference; use only the last name: *Jones.* Do not capitalize when used without the name: *The judge issued a ruling.*

judgment: Spell this word correctly, without an *e*—not *judgement.*

junior, senior: Abbreviate in names, but don't precede with commas: the late *John F. Kennedy Jr.*

K

kidnap, kidnapped, kidnapping: Double the *p.*

kindergarten

Kleenex: A trade name; capitalize.

Ku Klux Klan: Capitalize and also capitalize *Klan,* but *KKK* may be used on second reference when referring to this organization.

L

lay, laid, lie, lain: *Lay* means to place something, and it takes an object: *Lay the book on the table.* The past tense is *laid. Lie* means to recline or lay down. The past tense is *lay* or *had lain. She is lying down because she has a headache; she lay down for an hour because she had a headache.*

legislative titles: For congressmen and congresswomen, *U.S. Rep.* and *Rep.* are the preferred first-reference forms: *U.S. Rep. Barbara Bates.* Capitalize the titles when used before a name. On second reference, the word *congressman* or *congresswoman,* in lowercase, may be used when the name of the person is not used.

legislature: Capitalize the names of specific bodies: *the Kansas Legislature,* or *the Legislature* when referring to the specific Kansas body. Lowercase the term when used in a general sense: *The legislature of each state must approve the* amendment. Lowercase when using it as a plural: The Kansas and Missouri *legislatures* approved the amendment.

likable: not *likeable.*

like, as: *Like* should be used to compare nouns and pronouns and must be followed by an object: *He plays basketball like a professional. As* introduces clauses with verbs: *As I said, you should study your stylebook.*

***ly* words:** No hyphens between adverbs ending in *ly.*

M

magazine names: Capitalize but don't use quotation marks. Lowercase *magazine* unless it is part of the magazine's title.

majority, plurality: *Majority* is more than half; *plurality* is more than the highest number.

Mass: Mass is celebrated, not said.

master's degree: lowercase. A *master's* is acceptable on second reference.

media: The plural for news organizations such as broadcast, print and magazines is *media;* use it with a plural verb. The news *media are* upset about the ruling.

miles per hour: *mph,* no periods, is acceptable in all references.

military titles: Capitalize formal titles on first reference; use the last name only, without the title, on second reference. You may abbreviate titles: *Sgt. Maj. John Jones, Lt. Col. James Comolli.* See the Associated Press Stylebook for a complete list of such abbreviations.

million, billion: Use either word with figures: *$1 million, $13 billion, $1.3 billion, 2 million people.* In casual reference, you may use the word without figures: *I'd like to make a million dollars.*

months: Capitalize the names of months. When they are used with a specific date, abbreviate only *Jan., Feb., Aug., Sept., Oct., Nov., Dec.* For example, *Jan. 12, 2003, was the coldest day on record.* Spell out the name of a month when used without a specific date: *July 1992 was the warmest month on record.* Spell out other uses of months: *July 4 is a holiday.*

N

nationalities and races: Capitalize names of nationalities and races: *Arab, Asian, African-American, Caucasian.* Lowercase *black, white.*

newspaper names: Do not use quotation marks. Include *The* if it is part of the name.

No. 1: Use *No.* as an abbreviation before a number: *Their team is No. 1 in its league.*

none: It means no single one and takes a singular verb: *None of the council members was willing to approve the measure,* meaning not one of the members. Use a plural verb only if the sense is no two or no amount: *None of the taxes have been paid.*

numerals: Spell out numbers that start a sentence: *Twenty-one people attended the event.* Spell out the numbers one through nine; use figures for 10 and above.

O

off of: Eliminate the *of.*

OK: Use *OK,* not *okay.*

on: Do not use before days of the week unless it would be confusing otherwise: *The meeting will be held Monday.*

P

people, persons: Use *person* when speaking of an individual, *people* when referring to persons in all plural uses: *Hundreds of people attended the lecture.*

percentages: Use figures and spell out the word *percent: Taxes will increase 1 percent.* Use decimals, not fractions, for partial percentages—*3.5 percent*— and repeat *percent* after each item.

Ph.D., Ph.D.s: It's easier to say the person has a doctorate, but *Ph.D.* may be used after a name as part of a person's title. Do not use *Dr.* as a prefix for an academic title.

plead, pleaded: *Pleaded,* not *pled,* for past tense: *He pleaded guilty.*

police department: Capitalize the term when used with the formal title or when referring to a specific department: *The Los Angeles Police Department has a new chief. He will reorganize the Police Department.* Lowercase the term when it stands alone and when it's used in a general sense: *You can get the form at a police department.*

political parties: Capitalize the name of the party and the word *party* if it is part of the title: the *Republican Party, the Democratic Party.* Capitalize *Republican, Democratic, Liberal* and *Socialist* when they refer to individuals who are members of a specific political party. Lowercase these words when used to signify a way of thinking: *She is democratic in her views.*

politicians: When identifying a representative or a senator, use the party affiliation and the abbreviation for the state: *Sen. Trent Lott, R–Miss.*

possessives: For plural nouns indicating possession, add only an apostrophe: *the boys' club.* For singular possessive nouns, add an apostrophe and an *s: The boy's book was lost.*

presently: Means "in a while"; do not use for *now.*

principal, principle: *Principal* is a noun and adjective meaning someone or something in authority or first in rank: *She is the school principal and the* *principal player on the team. Principle* is a noun that means a fundamental truth or motivating force: *They fought for the principle of self-determination.*

prostate gland: not *prostrate gland.*

Q

questionnaire

quotations in news: Don't alter quotations to correct grammar or change any words; paraphrase if the quotation is not clear.

R

race: Specify only when pertinent in a story. Capitalize specific races, but lowercase *black, white,* and so on. See also *nationalities and races.*

ratios: Use figures and hyphens: *a 2–1 ratio.*

re-elect, re-election: Use a hyphen after the *re* prefix.

reference works: Do not use quotation marks around reference works, including catalogs, almanacs, dictionaries, encyclopedias and the like.

religious titles: The first reference to a clergyman or clergywoman should include a capitalized title before the person's name. In many cases, *the Rev.* is the designation that is appropriate. For example, use *the Rev.* before a priest's name, not *Father: The Rev. Vince Krishe is the priest at St. Lawrence Roman Catholic Church.* On second reference, just use the last name: *Krishe.* If a person is known only by a religious name, repeat the title on second reference: *Pope Benedict XVI.* For rabbis, use the word *Rabbi* before the name for first reference; use only the last name for second reference. For nuns, use *Sister* or *Mother* before the name in all references if the nun uses only a religious name: *Sister Agnes.*

restaurateur: not *restauranteur.*

room numbers: Capitalize *Room* with a figure: *Room 231.*

S

seasons: Don't capitalize *spring, summer, winter, fall.*

sheriff: Capitalize the word when used as a formal title before a name; use only the last name on second reference: *Sheriff Bob Jones resigned Tuesday.* Lowercase when used after the name: *Bob Jones, sheriff of Ourcounty, resigned Tuesday.*

software titles: Don't use quotation marks: *Microsoft Word.*

speeds: Use figures: *7 mph.*

state names: Spell out state names when they stand alone; abbreviate when they are used in conjunction with the name of a city, town, or village or with a dateline. Do not abbreviate the following state names: *Alaska, Hawaii, Idaho, Iowa, Maine, Ohio, Texas* and *Utah.* Use a comma after the state name if it follows the city in a sentence, as in *She is from Altoona, Pa., but now lives in Alaska.* The abbreviations for the other states are as follows (note that many differ from ZIP code abbreviations): *Ala., Ariz., Ark., Calif., Colo., Conn., Del., Fla., Ga., Ill., Ind., Kan., Ky., La., Md., Mass., Mich., Minn., Miss., Mo., Mont., Neb., Nev., N.H., N.J., N.M., N.Y., N.C., N.D., Okla., Ore., Pa., R.I., S.C., S.D., Tenn., Vt., Va., Wash., W.Va., Wis., Wyo.*

subjunctive mood: Use the subjunctive mood of a verb to convey wishes. Use the verb *were,* not *was,* to follow the singular pronoun used in a subjunctive sense: *If I were a rich woman, I would still teach. I wish it were possible to meet all the students who use this book.*

T

teenage, teenager: Do not hyphenate; this is a change in AP style, which used to require the hyphen.

temperatures: Use figures for the degrees and words for *minus* or *plus: It was minus 30 in Barrow, Alaska, today. It was 30 below zero.*

that, which, who, whom: Use *who* and *whom* when referring to people and to animals with a name. Use *that* and *which* when referring to inanimate objects and to animals without a name: *He is the man who has the book; she is the woman to whom I spoke yesterday; Fluffy is the dog who was lost; get the record that the police filed.*

their, there, they're: *Their* is possessive, *there* is a place and *they're* means "they are."

time: Use *a.m.* and *p.m.* with the specific time: *9:30 a.m., 10 p.m.*—not *10:00 p.m. Noon* and *midnight* stand alone. Use the day of the week in stories referring to any of the seven days before or after the current date, not *yesterday* or *tomorrow.*

titles: Capitalize titles when they are used before the person's name as part of the official title: *Sheriff John Jones made the arrest.* Lowercase titles when they are used to identify the person after her or his name or when used without the person's name: *John Jones, the sheriff, made the arrest. The sheriff made the arrest.*

trademarks: Capitalize brand names: *Coke, Kleenex.* Use lowercase for generic terms: *a cola drink, a tissue.*

T-shirt

U

United States: The abbreviation *U.S.* is acceptable as a noun or adjective for *United States.* This is a major change in the 2005 AP Stylebook, which used to require spelling out the words except when used as a modifier: *She came to the U.S. last year, and she is now a U.S. citizen.*

URL: Use this acronym for uniform resource locator, the computer address for a Web page.

U.S. Postal Service: Capitalize when referring to the formal title; lowercase in generic references: *The U.S. Postal Service* or the *Postal Service* operates the mail; *I went to the post office.*

U.S. Supreme Court: Capitalize and also capitalize *Supreme Court* when it is used alone.

Usenet: Use this term to refer to a particular worldwide system of discussion groups.

V

verbs: Don't split infinitives (*to* + verb): *She was ordered to leave immediately,* not *she was ordered to immediately leave.*

vice: Use two words with no hyphen: *vice chairman, vice principal, vice president.*

vote tabulations: Use figures separated by a hyphen: *The House voted 230–205.* Spell out votes below 10 in other phrases: *The City Council needed a two-thirds majority.*

W

weather: Spell out the word *degree: The temperature was 75 degrees.*

who, whom: Use *who* to refer to people and animals with names; use *that* or *which* for inanimate objects. *Who* is a subject of a sentence or clause; *whom* is an object: *Whom do you wish to see?* Turn the sentence around to find the subject when you are confused. *You* is then the subject: *You wish to see whom?*

who's, whose: *Who's* means "who is"; *whose* is possessive, "belonging to whom."

World Wide Web: Use the full term on first reference or *Web* on second reference. Capitalize these words.

Y

years: Don't use an apostrophe for plurals: *the 1990s,* not *the 1990's.*

yesterday: Use the day of the week instead of *yesterday.*

youth: The term is applicable to boys and girls from ages 13 to 17. Use *man* or *woman* for people 18 and older.

Z

ZIP code: Use all capital letters for *ZIP* but lowercase *code.*

Pain and Anger," *The Hartford* (Conn.) *Courant.* Reprinted with permission.

Chapter 7. **122:** Peanuts cartoon, April 6, 1997, reprinted by permission of United Feature Syndicate, Inc. **123:** "BBs strike stepfather after domestic violence," *St. Petersburg* (Fla.) *Times.* Reprinted with permission. **123:** "It's the water . . . ," Knight-Ridder Tribune News. Reprinted with permission. **124:** "Ordinance would outlaw reproduction of pets," *The New York Times,* Copyright © 1990 by The New York Times Company. Reprinted with permission. **124:** "Pet sterilization becomes law in San Mateo County," *Los Angeles Times.* Reprinted with permission. **125:** "Tucked above a rudder: 2 men and cocaine," *The New York Times.* Copyright © 1991 by The New York Times Company. Reprinted with permission. **126:** "Entercom programmer fired over payola revelations," Associated Press. Reprinted with permission. **127:** "2 killed, 1 injured when boat flips in rough weather," *The Orlando* (Fla.) *Sentinel.* Reprinted with permission. **127:** "Sunscreen ingredient may promote cancer," The Associated Press, March 22, 1991. Reprinted with permission. **129:** The Associated Press. **129:** "2 charged with theft of parking coins," *Minneapolis* (Minn.) *Star-Tribune.* Reprinted with permission. **129:** "Con-man sentenced," *N.Y. Newsday.* **129:** "Man who confronts gunman is shot to death," *St. Petersburg* (Fla.) *Times.* Reprinted with permission. **130:** Reprinted by permission of the *Tucson Citizen.* **130:** "Woman seeks new trial in shooting of ISU prof," *Des Moines* (Iowa) *Register.* Reprinted with permission. **131:** "Open up crime reports, judge says," *The Kansas* (Mo.) *City Star.* Reprinted with permission. **132:** "North County man, 88, killed in blaze started by smoking," *St. Louis* (Mo.) *Post-Dispatch.* Reprinted with permission. **133:** "College student arrested after making "megabomb,"" The Associated Press. Reprinted with permission. **133:** "Paroled killer held in kidnap, rape of 2 girls," *St. Paul* (Minn.) *Pioneer Press.* Reprinted with permission. **133:** "Toddler's death tied to beating," *St. Petersburg* (Fla.) *Times.* Reprinted with permission. **134:** "Penn imposes penalties on scientist," *The Philadelphia Inquirer.* Reprinted with permission. **134:** "S.J. gunman left 'little signs' before killings," *San Jose* (Calif.) *Mercury News.* Reprinted with permission. **134:** "U.S. reports sharp drop in casual drug use," *The Philadelphia Inquirer.* Reprinted with permission. **136:** "Study focuses on link between red meat and cancer," The Associated Press. **138:** "Ex-lover must pay in video case," *The Philadelphia Inquirer.* Reprinted with permission. **138:** "Neighbors squealing over pigs," *The Philadelphia Inquirer.* Reprinted with permission. **139:** "4.7 quake leaves Southcentral shaken, not stirred," *Anchorage* (Alaska) *Daily News.* Reprinted with permission. **139:** "In Santa Barbara drought, it's not easy being green," *Los Angeles Times.* Reprinted with permission. **140:** "Story about toy gun," *Fort Lauderdale* (Fla.) *Sun-Sentinel.* Reprinted with permission.

140: "Home reaches out to teen moms," *Orange County* (Calif.) *Register.* Reprinted with permission. **140–141:** "Monster loans," *The Seattle Times.* **141:** "1964 case gets fresh interest," *St. Petersburg* (Fla.) *Times.* Reprinted with permission. **141:** "Colo. poison-gas site now a wildlife haven," *The Philadelphia Inquirer.* Reprinted with permission. **141:** "Seminole man not real doctor, detectives say," *The Orlando* (Fla.) *Sentinel.* Reprinted with permission. **142:** Public library story, *The Philadelphia Inquirer.* Reprinted with permission. **142:** "Book thief gets 7 years of probation," *The Philadelphia Inquirer.* Reprinted with permission. **142:** "They know all about you," *St. Petersburg* (Fla.) *Times.* Reprinted with permission. **143:** "Lottery triangle," *Los Angeles Times.* Reprinted with permission. **143:** "Survivors tell of riding out the storm," *The Philadelphia Inquirer.* Reprinted with permission. **144:** "U.S. colleges try to confront problem of campus drinking," The Associated Press. Reprinted with permission. **144:** "L. Merion wants to ban cigarettes," *The Philadelphia Inquirer.* Reprinted with permission. **144:** "Postcards from sculptor carry messages via a piece of the rock," *Los Angeles Times.* Reprinted with permission. **144:** "True love story," *St. Paul* (Minn.) *Pioneer Press.* Reprinted with permission. **145:** "10-year-old saves choking classmate," *The Orlando* (Fla.) *Sentinel.* Reprinted with permission. **145:** "Crack: Drug tightens grip on Niagara County," *Niagara* (N.Y.) *Gazette.* **145:** "The good and bad from city hall," *N.Y. Newsday.* **146:** "It may be back to class for professors," *St. Petersburg* (Fla.) *Times.* Reprinted with permission.

Chapter 8. **156:** Dave Barry, "Childhood is a breeze compared to stress of moving," reprinted with permission of Dave Barry. **157–158:** Lansing Community College story, *Lansing* (Mich.) *State Journal.* Reprinted with permission. **158–159:** *USA Today* writing guidelines, courtesy of J. Taylor Buckley Jr., *USA Today.* **161:** "Bigamist's family stunned," *San Jose Mercury News.* Reprinted with permission. **162:** "Anatomy of a road, Part 1," *The Tampa Tribune.* **162:** "Temple racism course wins support," *The Philadelphia Inquirer.* Reprinted with permission **163:** "Doctor's AIDS death brings fear, ire," *The Philadelphia Inquirer.* Reprinted with permission. **163:** "Infected with AIDS, she longed to become a mother once again," *The Philadelphia Inquirer.* Reprinted with permission. **164:** "Deadly Meat," *The Kansas City* (Mo.) *Star,* Dec. 10, 1991. Reprinted with permission. **164:** "Double secret, double boyfriend," from series "Life at the edge of everything," *St Petersburg* (Fla.) *Times.* **165:** "For drivers, grief can be just a phone call away," *The Orlando* (Fla.) *Sentinel.* Reprinted with permission. **165:** "Judiciary panel works as the night wears on," *The Hartford* (Conn.) *Courant.* Reprinted with permission. **166:** "Alzheimer's steals fine minds," *Des Moines* (Iowa) *Register.* Reprinted with permission. **167:** "Hotmail addresses shared with site," The Associated Press, March 5, 2001. Reprinted with permission. **167:** "Rescuers work hard, but catch

Bor's guidelines, *Coaches' Corner*. Reprinted with permission. **352:** "It fluttered and became Bruce Murray's heart," *The* (Syracuse, N.Y.) *Post-Standard*. Reprinted with permission. **354:** "Are the world's fisheries doomed?" (New Orleans, La.) *The Times Picayune*. **356:** "Adjusting the dial: Hit by iPod and Satellite, radio tries new tune: Play more songs," *The Wall Street Journal*. Reprinted with permission. **357–358:** Karen F. Brown sportswriting tips, Best Newspaper Writing 1991, Poynter Institute for Media Studies, St. Petersburg, 1991, pp. 253–57. Reprinted with permission. **359–360:** "Jayhawks' first-round loss is first since 1978," *Lawrence* (Kan.) *Journal-World*. Reprinted with permission.

Chapter 18. 363: "Commission votes down expansion," *Lawrence* (Kan.) *Journal-World*. Reprinted with permission. **368–369:** "5 arrested during Dannemeyer speech," *The Orange County* (Calif.) *Register*. Reprinted with permission. **369:** "Reporter notes lower standards in journalism," *Lawrence* (Kan.) *Journal-World*. Reprinted with permission. **371:** "Cincinnati mayor imposes curfew to stop riots," The Associated Press. Reprinted with permission. **372:** "Borough weighs outhouse injunction," *Fairbanks* (Alaska) *Daily News-Miner*. Reprinted with permission. **373:** "City sets timetable for Simply Equal," *Lawrence* (Kan.) *Journal-World*. Reprinted with permission. **373:** "Temple idea: All to take race class," *The Philadelphia Inquirer*. Reprinted with permission. **374:** "Meeting addresses solutions to environmental problems," *The University Daily Kansan*. Reprinted with permission. **376–377:** "Water heater sculpture approved," *Orange County* (Calif.) *Register*. Reprinted with permission.

Chapter 19. 379: "In Capitol, a bulb change carries a high price indeed," *The Philadelphia Inquirer*. Reprinted with permission. **380:** "20 years' service, nine children and no job," *The Philadelphia Inquirer*. Reprinted with permission. **385:** Reprinted by permission of the *Lansing-State Journal*. **385:** "School board's wish granted," *Frontiersman* (Wasilla, Alaska). **386:** Rockford sales tax story, *Rockford* (Ill.) *Register-Star*. **386:** "Fontana landowners fear new general plan will trim values," *The* (San Bernardino) *Sun*. Reprinted with permission. **387:** "City officials get guidelines on handling controversies," *Minneapolis Star Tribune*. Reprinted with permission. **389–390:** "Will it be a Jacob or a Hananah," *St. Joseph* (Mo.) *News-Press*. Reprinted with permission. **390:** "Alabama's Rivers: Endangered Resource," *The Alabama Journal*. **391:** "Single-father homes on the rise," The Associated Press. Reprinted with permission. **391:** "Universities gender makeup changing," *Lawrence* (Kan.) *Journal-World*. Reprinted with permission. **392:** "City touts lowest rate of dropouts," *St. Joseph* (Mo.) *News-Press*. Reprinted with permission. **395:** "Storm brews over reappraisal," *Atlanta Constitution*. Reprinted with permission. **396:** Reprinted by permission of the *St. Petersburg Times*. **396:** "Homeowners getting 1st break in 20 years," *The* (Hackensack, N.J.) *Record*. **397:** Philadelphia city budget advance, *The Philadelphia Inquirer*. Reprinted with permission.

Chapter 20. 408: "Boy dies in car crash," *Orange County* (Calif.) *Register*. Reprinted with permission. **409:** "Rare comic books stolen from Council Bluffs store," The Associated Press. Reprinted with permission. **409–410:** "Burger burglar makes off with a Whopper of a haul," *The* (Salem, Ore.) *Statesman-Journal*. Reprinted with permission. **410:** "Robber does flipflop," *Topeka* (Kan.) *Capital-Journal*. **410:** "Robbers sought," *The Orange County* (Calif.) *Register*. Reprinted with permission. **412:** "Man charged in woman's death," *The Milwaukee Journal*. Reprinted with permission. **413:** "Shattered dreams; 'Perfect' kids shot, mom jailed," *The Orlando* (Fla.) *Sentinel*. Reprinted with permission. **414:** "Mom, infant escape Kodiak fire," The Associated Press. Reprinted with permission. **416:** "Simpson acquitted of murders," The Associated Press. Reprinted with permission. **424–425:** "N.H. Prosecutors get Smart," The Associated Press. Reprinted with permission. **426:** "A snake in a mattress twists its way into court," *The Philadelphia Inquirer*. Reprinted with permission. **426:** "Joy Griffiths' killing: Act of love or murder?" *St. Petersburg* (Fla.) *Times*. Reprinted with permission. **427:** "Man gambles on plea, loses," *The Kansas City* (Mo.) *Star*. Reprinted with permission.

Chapter 21. 436: "Remains of 1,161 WTC victims will go unnamed," *New York Newsday*. **436:** "Tsunami survivors, families in camps give anguishing accounts," *The Tampa* (Fla.) *Tribune*. **437:** "Accuracy of Tsunami death toll questioned," The Associated Press. **440, 446–447:** Excerpts from stories in *The Oklahoma Daily*, plus photographs and excerpts from the diaries of Omar Gallaga. Reprinted with permission. **443:** "Explosion prompts blood drives, donations," *The Oklahoma Daily*. Reprinted with permission. **444:** *The Detroit News*, graphic and excerpts from "The crash of flight 255." Reprinted with permission. **449:** Reprinted by permission of *The Detroit News*. **449:** "Grief cuts wide swath," *The Detroit News*, special report. Reprinted with permission. **451:** "20 die in La Guardia crash," The Associated Press. Reprinted with permission. **452–454:** "Napa, Sonoma hit by floods again," *San Jose* (Calif.) *Mercury News*. Reprinted with permission. **454–455:** "A wicked wind takes aim," *Chicago Tribune*. **456:** "Weather forecast blazes on," *St. Joseph* (Mo.) *News-Press*. Reprinted with permission. **457–460:** "Band of brothers," The Associated Press. Reprinted with permission.

Chapter 22. 465: Excerpt from book, All I did was ask, by Terry Gross. **467–468:** "A time to die," *Sunshine* magazine, (Fort Lauderdale, Fla.) *Sun-Sentinel*. Reprinted with permission. **470–472:** "She is the finest of New Orleans' finest," *The*

Photo Credits